" . . . Probably the best textbook I have ever had, not to mention one of the least expensive. . . . Easier to pay attention to, and is actually kind of enjoyable to read. I really like it a lot."
– *Chantel Harwood, student at Utah State University, UT*

GOVT... for the way students learn

"The ***Chapter-in-Review* cards** at the back of the book would be **a perfect guide for a study group."**
– *A student at Moorpark College, CA*

"I like the way that the back of the book has all the key parts of each chapter available for you to remove so you don't have to take the book anywhere you need to go."
– *A student at Raritan Valley Community College, NJ*

"After reading through GOVT, I realize it is possible to enjoy what I'm reading. The layout is perfect."
– *Shelby Springer, student at Truckee Meadow Community College, NV*

"I love the book, and the online resources help a lot. The design makes reading much easier and everything is more inviting than a regular textbook. Thanks a lot!"
– *Austin Jensen, student at Western Illinois University, IL*

GOVT 2nd Edition

Edward Sidlow and Beth Henschen
Eastern Michigan University

Publisher: Suzanne Jeans
Executive Editor: Carolyn Merrill
Acquiring Sponsoring Editor: Edwin Hill
Development Editor: Rebecca Green
Assistant Editor: Kate MacLean
Editorial Assistant: Matthew DiGangi
Associate Media Editor: Caitlin Holroyd
Senior Marketing Manager: Amy Whitaker
Marketing Communications Manager: Heather Baxley
Marektking Coordinator: Josh Hendrick
Senior Content Production Manager: Ann Borman
Print Buyer: Rebecca Cross
Photo Research: Ann Hoffman
Copy Editor: Beverly Peavler
Proofreaders: Judy Kiviat, Cyndi Mathews
Indexer: Terry Casey
Art Director: Linda Helcher
Interior Design: Ke Design
Cover Design: Lisa Kuhn
Cover image credits: Fancy Photography/©Veer
Compositor: Parkwood Composition Service

Library of Congress Control Number: 2009939804

Student Edition ISBN-13: 978-1-4390-8218-8
Student Edition ISBN-10: 1-4390-8218-9

Instructor's Edition ISBN-13: 978-1-4390-8223-2
Instructor's Edition ISBN-10: 1-4390-8223-5

Wadsworth Political Science
20 Channel Center
Boston, MA 02210
USA

Cengage Learning products are represented in Canada by Nelson Education, Ltd.

For your course and learning solutions, visit **academic.cengage.com**
Purchase any of our products at your local college store or at our preferred online store **www.ichapters.com**

Chapter Opener photo credits: Ch 1: AP Photo/Paul Sakuma; Ch 2: Shutterstock.com; Ch 3: Richard Schultz/Corbis; Ch 4: Peter Maiden/Sygma/Corbis; Ch 5: AP Photo/Charles Tasnadi; Ch 6: Mark Lyons/Getty Images; Ch 7: Damon Winter/*The New York Times*/Redux; Ch 8: Don Emmert/AFP/Getty Images; Ch 9: AP Photo/Alex Brandon; Ch 10: Chip Somodevilla/Getty Images; Ch 11: Doug Mills/*The New Yorker*/Redux; Ch 12: Stephen Crowley/*The New York Times*/Redux; Ch 13: Paul J. Richards/AFP/Getty Images; Ch 14: AP Photo/Ross William Hamilton, Pool; Ch 15: Luke Sharrett/*The New York Times*/Redux; Ch 16: AP Photo/Farah Abdi Warsameh

Printed in the United States of America
2 3 4 5 6 7 13 12 11 10

EDWARD SIDLOW & BETH HENSCHEN

GOVT

Brief Contents

EDWARD SIDLOW & BETH HENSCHEN

GOVT

Contents

1 The Foundations of Our American System 1

Chapter 1
The Contours of American Democracy 1

Chapter 2
The Constitution 22

Chapter 3
Federalism 49

2 Our Liberties and Rights 74

Chapter 4
Civil Liberties 74

Chapter 5
Civil Rights 101

3 The Politics of Democracy 129

Chapter 6
Interest Groups 129

Chapter 7
Political Parties 151

Chapter 8
Public Opinion and Voting 174

Chapter 9
Campaigns and Elections 199

Chapter 10
Politics and the Media 223

4 Institutions 245

Chapter 11
Congress 245

Chapter 12
The Presidency 269

Chapter 13
The Bureaucracy 295

Chapter 14
The Judiciary 319

5 *Public Policy 343*

Chapter 15
Domestic Policy 343

Preface

The United States is currently suffering through a relatively short (we hope) period of great economic and political stress. Officially starting in December 2007, but really picking up steam by the fall of 2008, our economy entered what is now called the Great Recession. President Barack Obama was not allowed very long to bask in the glow of being the first African American elected as head of this country. He and his administration went into action almost immediately to prevent the Great Recession from becoming the second Great Depression. In the process, the federal government deficit ballooned to over $1.4 trillion, while the unemployment rate rose to almost 10 percent. During 2009, the infighting in Congress continued.

Our Government's Response to the Economic Crisis

We felt that we should add a special new feature to this edition of GOVT. We call it *Our Government's Response to the Economic Crisis.* Almost every chapter in this new edition has this feature. Here are some examples:

- Making and Fixing an Economic Mess (Chapter 1)
- Obama's Huge Stimulus Bill (Chapter 3)
- Do We Lose Liberties When the Government Changes the Rules? (Chapter 4)
- Bailing Out the Banks—Big Time (Chapter 11)
- Red Ink as Far as the Eye Can See (Chapter 15)

New Join the Debate *Features, Too*

In keeping with our goal of currency, we have redone almost all of the *Join the Debate* features. Your students and you will now be able to debate:

- Should the Federal Government Guarantee State and Local Debt? (Chapter 3)
- Should We Punish Countries That Don't Limit Carbon Emissions? (Chapter 6)
- Should D.C. Residents Have a Representative? (Chapter 9)
- Should the Attorney General Be Independent of the President? (Chapter 13)
- Can We Tolerate a Nuclear Iran? (Chapter 16)

New America at Odds *Chapter-Opening Feature*

Most of the chapter-opening *America at Odds* features are new to this edition. They include:

- Should Government Entities Enjoy Freedom of Speech? (Chapter 4)
- Is the 1965 Voting Rights Act Obsolete? (Chapter 8)
- Are Early Primaries Really Such a Bad Thing? (Chapter 9)
- Can We Do Without Newspapers? (Chapter 10)
- Just How Liberal Is President Obama? (Chapter 12)
- Are There Prisoners We Must Detain without Trial? (Chapter 14)

New Perception versus Reality *Features*

Many of the *Perception versus Reality* features are completely new to this edition. They include:

- Did the Civil War Destroy the Economy of the South? (Chapter 3)
- Obama's Antiterrorism Stance Compared With Bush's (Chapter 4)
- The Youth Vote Elected Obama (Chapter 7)

- Twitter and Tweets—Much Ado about Nothing (Chapter 10)
- Obama and Open Government (Chapter 12)

New The Rest of the World *Features*

Finally, many of *The Rest of the World* features are also new to this edition. They include:

- Should We Ever Impose Values on Other Countries? (Chapter 1)
- An Improved Image of the U.S. Abroad? (Chapter 8)
- China's Mastery of Internet Censorship (Chapter 10)
- Mexico's Security Problem—The Drug Wars (Chapter 13)

A Groundbreaking Format

GOVT's daring format has been designed to engage even the most apathetic American government student with its glossy, magazine-style look and dynamic visual appeal. Streamlined, portable, and complete with study resources, this text does more than ever before to accommodate the way students actually use their textbooks. At the same time, our "debate-the-issues" approach effectively involves them in discussing and debating concepts of American government. **Chapter Review tear-out cards** at the end of the book provide learning objectives with summaries of key concepts, visuals, and key terms for each chapter—making it easier for students to prepare for class and for exams. And because today's students are technologically savvy, we provide **portable study resources in multiple formats** via this text's companion Web site at **www.4ltrpress.cengage.com/govt.** Resources there include flashcards, podcasts, chapter reviews, quizzes, and more that students can download whichever way they prefer (cell phone, computer, MP3 files, and so on) in order to study more efficiently. Access to the site is available at no additional cost when packaged with each student text.

Features That Teach

As exciting as the innovative new GOVT format may be, we have not lost sight of the essential goals and challenges of teaching American government. Any American government text must present the basics of the American political process and its institutions, and it must excite and draw the student into the *subject.*

Additionally, we present many of today's controversial political issues in special features. Each of the more than one hundred features contained in the text covers a topic of high interest to students. GOVT includes the following different types of features, in addition to the features outlined earlier:

- ***Learning Objectives***—Every chapter-opening page includes a list of three or more Learning Objectives that lets students know what concepts will be covered in the chapter. Each Learning Objective has an identifying number (such as LO1 or LO2). The same number also precedes the major heading of the chapter section in which that topic is presented. This allows students to quickly locate where in the chapter a particular topic is discussed.
- **Chapter-ending *America at Odds* feature**—This feature often opens with a general discussion of the historical evolution of the aspect of government addressed in the chapter. When relevant, the founders' views and expectations relating to the topic are set forth and then compared to the actual workings of our political system in that area today. This part of the feature is designed to indicate how American politics and government currently measure up to the expectations of the founders or to those of today's Americans. Following this discussion, we present two questions for debate and discussion. Each question briefly outlines two sides of a current political controversy and then asks the student to identify her or his position on the issue. The feature closes with a "Take Action" section that offers tips to students on what they can do to make a difference in an area of interest to them.
- ***Politics on the Web***—This section gives selected Web sites that students can access for more information on issues discussed in the chapter.
- ***Online Resources for This Chapter***—This section directs students to the text's companion Web site, where they can find additional resources for the chapter.

The Supplements

Both instructors and students today expect, and indeed require, a variety of accompanying supplements to teach and learn about American government. GOVT takes the lead in providing the most comprehensive and user-friendly supplements package on the market today. These supplements include those listed and described below.

Supplements for Instructors

- **A PowerLecture DVD with JoinIn™ and ExamView®**, ISBN: 1-439-08225-1, is available to instructors who adopt the text.
  - The interactive **PowerPoint® lectures** bring together outlines specific to every chapter of GOVT; audio and video clips depicting historic and current events; NEW animated learning modules illustrating key concepts; tables, statistical charts, and graphs; and photos from the book as well as outside sources.
  - *Written by author Beth Henschen!* A **test bank** in Microsoft® Word and ExamView computerized testing offers a large array of multiple-choice and essay questions, along with answers and page references. Professor Henschen has added at least five new questions per chapter.
  - *Written by author Beth Henschen!* An **Instructor's Manual** includes learning objectives, chapter outlines, discussion questions, suggestions for stimulating class activities and projects, suggested Web resources, step-by-step instructions on how to create your own podcasts, and a section designed to help teaching assistants and adjunct instructors.
  - **JoinIn** offers book-specific "clicker" questions that test and track student comprehension of key concepts. Save the data from students' responses all semester—track their progress and show them how political science works by incorporating this exciting new tool into your classroom. It is available for college and university adopters only.
  - The **Resource Integration Guide** outlines the rich collection of resources available to instructors and students within the chapter-by-chapter framework of the book.
- **Instructor Premium Website**
  - The Instructor's Manual, PowerPoint Lecture Outlines, JoinIn Clickers, and Word Test Bank files will also be available on the book's premium website at **www.4ltrpress.cengage.com/govt/**.
  - New! **NewsNow PowerPoint®** slides NewsNow brings news to the classroom through a combination of Associated Press news stories, videos, and images. These multimedia-rich PowerPoint slides are posted each week to the password-protected area of the text's companion site. And because this all-in-one presentation tool includes the text of the original newsfeed, along with videos, photos, and discussion questions, no Internet connection is required!
- **WebTutor™ on WebCT®, Blackboard®, or Angel**
  For instructors, this Web-based teaching and learning tool includes course management, study/mastery, and communication tools. Use WebTutor to provide virtual office hours, post your syllabus, and track student progress with WebTutor's quizzing material. For students, WebTutor offers real-time access to interactive online tutorials and simulations, practice quizzes, and Web links—all correlated to GOVT.
- **The Obama Presidency—Year One**
  ISBN 0-495-90837-1
  Much happens in the first year of a presidency, especially an historic one like that of Barack Obama. Students can learn more by reading the full-color sixteen-page supplement The Obama Presidency—Year One, by Kenneth Janda, Jeffrey M. Berry, and Jerry Goldman. The authors analyze such issues as healthcare, the economy and the stimulus package, changes in the U.S. Supreme Court, and the effect Obama policy has had on global affairs.
- **Political Theatre 2.0**
  ISBN 0-495-79360-4
  Bring politics home to students with Political Theatre 2.0, up-to-date through the 2008 election season. This is the second edition of this three-DVD series and includes real video clips that show American political thought throughout the public sector. Clips include both classic and contemporary political advertisements, speeches, interviews and more. Available to adopters of Cengage textbooks, version 2.0 provides added functionality with this updated edition.
- **JoinIn on Turning Point® for Political Theatre 2.0.**
  ISBN 0-495-09550-8
  For even more interaction, combine Political Theatre with the innovative teaching tool of a classroom response system. Poll your students with questions provided, or create your own questions. Built within the Microsoft PowerPoint software, JoinIn is easy to integrate into current lectures in conjunction with the "clicker" hardware of your choice.
- **Wadsworth Video: Speeches by President Barack Obama**
  ISBN 1-439-08247-2
  This DVD of nine famous speeches by President Barack Obama, from 2004 to present day, includes his speech at the 2004 Democratic National Convention; his 2008 speech on race, "A More Perfect

Union"; and his 2009 inaugural address. Speeches are divided into short video segments for easy, time-efficient viewing. This instructor supplement also features critical-thinking questions and answers for each speech, designed to spark classroom discussion.

- **The Wadsworth News Videos for American Government 2011 DVD**
  ISBN 0-495-90488-0
  This collection of two- to six-minute video clips on relevant political issues serves as a great lecture or discussion launcher.
- **California Edition of GOVT**
  If you live in California and cover California Politics as part of your American Government course, consider this alternate version of the text which includes additional content by Larry Gerston and Terry Christianson.

Consider for Students—Available Packaged with the Book

- **Premium Website** The premium website offers a variety of rich online learning resources designed to enhance the student experience. These resources include audio summaries, critical-thinking activities, simulations, animated learning modules, timelines, flashcards, and videos. Chapter resources are correlated with key chapter learning concepts, and users can browse or search for content in a variety of ways.
- **NewsNow** brings news to the classroom through a combination of Associated Press news stories, videos, and images that bring current events to life. For students, a collection of news stories and accompanying videos are served up each week via the premium website that accompanies their American Government text.
- **Multimedia E-Book** We provide separate options for the delivery of an interactive, multimedia eBook that contains links to simulations, flashcards, and other interactive activities.

Acknowledgments

A number of political scientists have reviewed GOVT, and we are indebted to them for their thoughtful suggestions on how to create a text that best suits the needs of today's students and faculty.

Anita Anderson
University of Alabama

Yan Bai
Grand Rapids Community College

Janet Barton
Mineral Area College

J. St. Lawrence Brown
Spokane Community College

Michael Ceriello
Clark College

Andrew Civettini
Knox College

Frank DeCaria
West Virginia Northern Community College

Robert De Luna
St. Philip's College

Shawn Fonville
Western Texas College

Barry D. Friedman
North Georgia College & State University

Arie Halachmi
Tennessee State University

David M. Head
John Tyler Community College

Steve Hoggard
Chowan University

Jose Luis Irizarry
St. Francis College

Jean Gabriel Jolivet
Southwestern College

Michael Kanner
University of Colorado

David R. Katz III
Mohawk Valley Community College

Christine Kelleher
University of Michigan

John Kerr
University of Arkansas

Jeffrey Kraus
Wagner College

Kevin Lasher
Francis Marion University

William Lester
Jacksonville State University

William D. Madlock
University of Memphis

Khalil Marrar
DePaul University and The University of Chicago

Matthew McNiece
Howard Payne University

Gay Michele
El Centro College

Amy Miller
Western Kentucky University

Eric Miller
Blinn College-Bryan

Kathleen Murnan
Ozarks Technical Community College

Leah A. Murray
Weber State University

Jalal Nejad
Northwest Vista College

Joseph L. Overton
Kapiolani Community College

James Peterson
Valdosta State University

Daniel Ponder
Drury University

Brett Ramsey
Austin Peay State University

Rob Robinson
University of Alabama-Birmingham

Cy Rosenblatt
University of Mississippi

Robert Sahr
Oregon State University

John Shively
Longview Community College

Susan Siemens
Ozarks Technical Community College

Frank Signorile
Campbell University

Chris Sixta-Rinehart
Francis Marion University

Robert Sullivan
Dallas Baptist University

Gerald Watkins
West Kentucky Community and Technical College

Stephen Wiener
UC Santa Barbara

Donald C. Williams
Western New England College

Bruce M. Wilson
University of Central Florida

Robert S. Wood
University of North Dakota

Mary Young
Southwestern Michigan College

Maryann Zihala
Ozarks Technical Community College

Our styles of teaching and mentoring students were shaped in important ways by our graduate faculty at Ohio State University. We thank Lawrence Baum, Herbert Asher, Elliot Slotnick, and Randall Ripley for lessons well taught. The students we have had the privilege of working with at many fine universities during our careers have also taught us a great deal. We trust that some of what appears on these pages reflects their insights, and we hope that what we have written will capture the interest of current and future students. Of course, we owe an immeasurable debt to our families, whose divergent views on political issues reflect an America at odds.

We thank Sean Wakely, president of Wadsworth Publishing Company, for all of his encouragement and support throughout our work on this project. We were also fortunate to have the editorial advice of Edwin Hill, acquiring sponsoring editor, and Carolyn Merrill, executive editor. We are grateful for the assistance of Rebecca Green, our developmental editor, who supervised all aspects of the text and carefully read the page proofs. We thank Kate MacLean, assistant editor, for her coordination of the supplements and related items, Caitlin Holroyd for her work on the Premium Website, and Matthew DiGangi for his editorial assistance. We thank Gregory Scott for his tremendous help in researching the project and for his copyediting and proofreading assistance. We also thank Roxie Lee for her project management and other assistance that ensured a timely and accurate text. The copyediting services of Beverly Peavler and the proofreading by Judy Kiviat and Cyndi Mathews will not go unnoticed. We are also grateful to Sue Jasin of K&M Consulting.

We are especially indebted to the staff at Parkwood Composition. Their ability to generate the pages for this text quickly and accurately made it possible for us to meet our ambitious schedule. Ann Borman and Ann Hoffman, our cheerful content project managers at Cengage Learning, made sure that all the pieces came together accurately, attractively, and on time. We appreciate the enthusiasm of Amy Whitaker, Heather Baxley, and Josh Hendrick, our hardworking marketing and communications managers and marketing coordinator. We would also like to acknowledge Linda Helcher, art director, for her part in producing the most attractive and user-friendly American government text on the market today.

If you or your students have ideas or suggestions, we would like to hear from you. You can e-mail our marketing manager, Amy, at amy.Whitaker@cengage.com, or send us information through Wadsworth, a part of Cengage Learning. Our Web site is **www.cengage.com/political science.**

E.I.S.
B.M.H.

The Contours of American Democracy

GOVT 1

LEARNING OBJECTIVES

LO1 Explain what is meant by the terms *politics* and *government*.

LO2 Identify the various types of government systems.

LO3 Summarize some of the basic principles of American democracy and the basic American political values.

LO4 Describe how the various topics discussed in this text relate to the "big picture" of American politics and government.

AMERICA AT ODDS

Do We Really Have a Representative Democracy?

Some people sarcastically say that we have the best democracy that money can buy. Others like our democracy just the way it is—the system has worked for more than two hundred years, so what is the problem? Perhaps the real debate is over whether we still have a *representative democracy*. As you will find out later in this chapter, in this type of political system the public elects representatives, who then carry out the public's will by passing legislation. In a nation of more than 300 million people, though, even the most astute elected representative finds it impossible to determine "the public's will." This is because members of the public often have conflicting opinions on any given issue. Therefore, even under the best of circumstances, our representative democracy will not create a nation in which everyone is happy with what the government does.

A Representative Democracy? Nothing Could Be Further from the Truth

We elect members of Congress. They are supposed to serve their *constituents* (the people who live in their state if the members are senators and those who live in their district if they are representatives). Members of Congress who don't serve the interests of their constituents should at least act in the best interests of the nation. The reality, though, is something else entirely.

Congress has been sold to the highest bidder. The main job of a member of Congress is to be reelected. The best way to be reelected is to amass bigger and bigger reelection campaign war chests. Members do this by giving in to the pressures brought by certain industries or groups, which in turn help fund reelection campaigns. Consider just one example: Leaving aside lobbying on tobacco (an issue all to itself), agribusiness lobbyists spent $83 million in 2007, mostly to influence Congress. One result was the 2008 farm bill, which, in addition to antipoverty measures, contained $300 billion in farm subsidies to be paid out over a five-year period. Most of these payments go to the nation's most successful farmers, who are typically millionaires. Such "congressional vote buying" goes on all the time.

Moreover, how representative of the people's will is the presidency? Americans opposed bailing out Chrysler and General Motors by margins ranging from 59 to 72 percent. Did these attitudes change the policies of the Obama administration? Not at all.

We Are the Envy of the World, So What Is the Problem?

Those who claim that we do not really have a representative democracy also point to the relatively low voter turnout in local, state, and federal elections. Others, however, assert that low voter turnout may actually be a good sign. It means that most people are satisfied with how America is being governed. When Americans become dissatisfied with their government, voter turnout increases, as it did in 2008.

After all, when the government ignores the wishes of the electorate for too long, citizens do have recourse: they can simply refuse to reelect their representatives in the next congressional elections.

When Americans became increasingly dissatisfied with President George W. Bush's policies, particularly his insistence on continuing the war in Iraq, they punished him. In the 2006 midterm elections, the voters gave the Democrats control over both chambers of Congress. Was the new Congress unable to make President Bush respect public opinion? The answer of the voters was to elect a Democratic president in 2008 and to increase the Democrats' margins in Congress. It may take a while, but the desires of the people will eventually prevail.

WHERE DO YOU STAND?

1. **How important do you think it is for elected government officials to represent their constituents' interests? What if the national interest is different?**
2. **Do you think that low voter turnout means that people are satisfied with our government or that they are simply "turned off" by government? Why?**

EXPLORE THIS ISSUE ONLINE

- **Students interested in curbing the impact of wealthy special interests on politics can visit Democracy Matters at www.democracymatters.org. NBA basketball star Adonal Foyle founded this activist group.**
- **For a series of arguments on why campaign finance reform is dangerous, check out the writings of the Cato Institute, a conservative/libertarian think tank, at www.cato.org/research/crg/finance.html.**

Introduction

Regardless of how Americans feel about government, one thing is certain: they can't live without it. James Madison (1751–1836) once said, "If men were angels, no government would be necessary." Today, his statement still holds true. People are not perfect. People need an organized form of government and a set of rules by which to live.

Note, though, that even if people were perfect, they would still need to establish rules to guide their behavior. They would somehow have to agree on how to divide up a society's resources, such as its land, among themselves and how to balance individual needs and wants against those of society generally. These perfect people would also have to decide *how* to make these decisions. They would need to create a process for making rules and a form of government to enforce those rules. It is thus not difficult to understand why government is one of humanity's oldest and most universal **institutions**. No society has existed without some form of government. The need for authority and organization will never disappear.

> **"THE ULTIMATE RULERS** of our democracy are . . . the voters of this country."
>
> ~ FRANKLIN D. ROOSEVELT ~ THIRTY-SECOND PRESIDENT OF THE UNITED STATES 1933–1945

As you will read in this chapter, a number of different systems of government exist in the world today. In the United States, we have a democracy in which decisions about pressing issues ultimately are made by the people's representatives in government. Because people rarely have identical thoughts and feelings about issues, it is not surprising that in any democracy citizens are often at odds over many political and social issues, including the issue discussed in the chapter-opening feature. Throughout this book, you will read about contemporary issues that have brought various groups of Americans into conflict with one another.

Differences in opinion are part and parcel of a democratic government. Ultimately, these differences are resolved, one way or another, through the American political process and our government institutions.

With more than 300 million people living in the United States, there are bound to be conflicts. Here, Americans demonstrate in front of the United States Supreme Court building in Washington, D.C. Is such conflict necessarily bad for America?

dbking/Creative Commons

LO1 What Are Politics and Government?

Politics means many things to many people. To some, politics is an expensive and extravagant game played in Washington, D.C., in state capitols, and in city halls, particularly during election time. To others, politics involves all of the tactics and maneuvers carried out by the president and Congress. Most formal definitions of politics, however, begin with the assumption that **social conflict**—disagreements among people in a society over what the society's priorities should be—is inevitable. Conflicts will naturally arise over

institution An ongoing organization that performs certain functions for society.

social conflict Disagreements among people in a society over what the society's priorities should be when distributing scarce resources.

politics The process of resolving conflicts over how society should use its scarce resources and who should receive various benefits, such as public health care and public higher education. According to Harold Lasswell, politics is the process of determining "who gets what, when, and how" in a society.

government The individuals and institutions that make society's rules and that also possess the power and authority to enforce those rules.

power The ability to influence the behavior of others, usually through the use of force, persuasion, or rewards.

authority The ability to legitimately exercise power, such as the power to make and enforce laws.

public services Essential services that individuals cannot provide for themselves, such as building and maintaining roads, providing welfare programs, operating public schools, and preserving national parks.

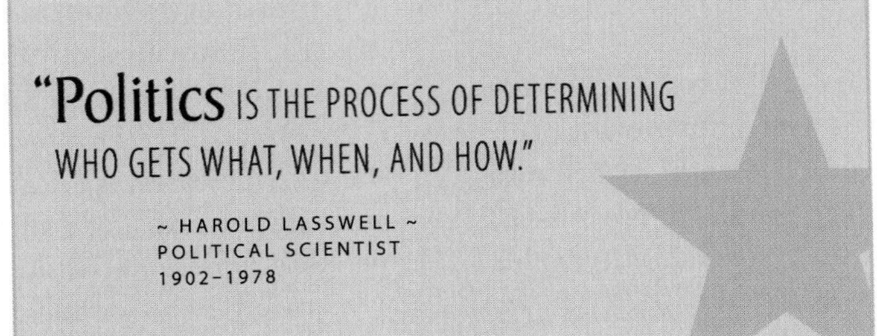

how the society should use its scarce resources and who should receive various benefits, such as wealth, status, health care, and higher education. Resolving such conflicts is the essence of **politics.** Political scientist Harold Lasswell perhaps said it best when he defined politics as the process of determining "who gets what, when, and how" in a society.[1]

There are also many different notions about the meaning of government. From the perspective of political science, though, **government** can best be defined as the individuals and institutions that make society's rules and that also possess the *power* and *authority* to enforce those rules. Although this definition of government sounds remote and abstract, what the government does is very real indeed. As one scholar put it, "Make no mistake. What Congress does directly and powerfully affects our daily lives."[2] The same can be said for decisions made by state legislators and local government officials, as well as for decisions rendered by the courts—the judicial branch of government. Of course, a key question remains: How do specific individuals obtain the power and authority to govern? As you will read shortly, the answer to this question varies from one type of political system to another.

To understand what government is, you need to understand what it actually does for people and society. Generally, in any country government serves at least three essential purposes: (1) it resolves conflicts, (2) it provides public services, and (3) it defends the nation and its culture against attacks by other nations.

Resolving Conflicts

Even though people have lived together in groups since the beginning of time, none of these groups has been free of social conflict. As mentioned, disputes over how to distribute a society's resources inevitably arise because valued resources, such as property, are limited, while people's wants are unlimited. To resolve such disputes, people need ways to determine who wins and who loses, and how to get the losers to accept those decisions. Who has the legitimate power—the authority—to make such decisions? This is where government steps in.

Governments decide how conflicts will be resolved so that public order can be maintained. Governments have **power**—the ability to influence the behavior of others. Power is getting someone to do something that he or she would not otherwise do. Power may involve the use of force (often called coercion), persuasion, or rewards. Governments typically also have **authority,** which they can exercise only if their power is legitimate. As used here, the term *authority* means power that is collectively recognized and accepted by society as legally and morally correct. Power and authority are central to a government's ability to resolve conflicts by making and enforcing laws, placing limits on what people can do, and developing court systems to make final decisions.

For example, the judicial branch of government—specifically, the United States Supreme Court—resolved the conflict over whether the votes in certain Florida counties should be recounted after the disputed 2000 presidential elections. Because of the Court's stature and authority as a government body, there was little resistance to its decision *not* to allow the recounting—although the decision was strongly criticized by many because it virtually handed the presidency to George W. Bush.

Providing Public Services

Another important purpose of government is to provide **public services**—essential services that many individuals cannot provide for themselves. Governments undertake projects that individuals usually would not or could not carry out on their own, such as building and maintaining roads, providing welfare programs, operating public schools, and preserving national parks. Governments also provide such services as law enforcement, fire protection, and public health and safety programs. As Abraham Lincoln once stated:

> The legitimate object of government is to do for a community of people, whatever they need to have done, but cannot do, *at all,* or cannot, *so well* do, for themselves—in their separate, individual capacities. In all that the people can individually do as well for themselves, government ought not to interfere.[3]

"In all that the people can individually do as well for themselves, **GOVERNMENT OUGHT NOT TO INTERFERE."**

~ ABRAHAM LINCOLN ~
SIXTEENTH PRESIDENT OF THE UNITED STATES
1861–1865

Some public services are provided equally to all citizens of the United States. For example, government services such as national defense and domestic law enforcement allow all citizens, at least in theory, to feel that their lives and property are safe. Laws governing clean air and safe drinking water benefit all Americans. Other services are provided only to citizens who are in need at a particular time, even though they are paid for by all citizens through taxes. Examples of such services include health and welfare benefits, as well as public housing. Laws such as the Americans with Disabilities Act explicitly protect the rights of people with disabilities, although all Americans pay for such protections whether they have disabilities or not.

One of the most crucial public services that the government is expected to provide is protection from hardship caused by economic recessions or depressions. In recent years, this governmental objective has become more important than almost any other, due to the severity of the recession that began in December 2007. We introduce some of the steps the federal government has taken to combat the recession in this chapter's *Our Government's Response to the Economic Crisis* feature on the next page. Additional features throughout the book will supply greater detail.

Defending the Nation and Its Culture

Historically, matters of national security and defense have been given high priority by governments and have demanded considerable time, effort, and expense. The U.S. government provides for the common defense and national security with its Army, Navy, Marines, Air Force, and Coast Guard. The departments of State, Defense, and Homeland Security, plus the Central Intelligence Agency, National Security Agency, and other agencies, also contribute to this defense network. As part of an ongoing policy of national security, many departments and agencies in the federal government are constantly dealing with other nations. The Constitution gives our national government exclusive power over relations with foreign nations. No individual state can negotiate a treaty with a foreign nation.

Of course, in defending the nation against attacks by other nations, a government helps to preserve the nation's culture, as well as its integrity as an independent unit. Failure to defend successfully against foreign attacks may have significant consequences for a nation's culture. For example, consider what happened in Tibet in the 1950s. When that country was taken over by the People's Republic of China, the conquering Chinese set out on a systematic program, the effective result of which was to destroy Tibet's culture.

Since the terrorist attacks on the World Trade Center and the Pentagon in 2001, defending the homeland against future terrorist attacks has become a priority of our government.

AP Photo/Abd Raouf

This is a photo of Sudanese president Omar al-Baschir in the spring of 2009. An international court issued an arrest warrant for him on charges of war crimes and crimes against humanity. He retorted that this warrant was simply an attempt to destabilize his country. Do you think a U.S. court could issue such an arrest warrant against him?

Our Government's Response to the Economic Crisis

Making and Fixing an Economic Mess

In recent years, we have witnessed what has been called the Great Recession—so named because it was worse than any other economic downturn since the Great Depression of the 1930s. One of the goals of government, as stated in the preamble to the U.S. Constitution, is "to promote the general Welfare." Maintaining economic prosperity is about as close as you can get to a definition of promoting the general welfare.

Unless You Are in Your Nineties, You Don't Know How Bad It Can Get

If any of your great-grandparents are still alive, they might remember the years of the Great Depression, which began in 1929. By 1933, the rate of unemployment had hit 25 percent. Economic output had dropped by over a third. More than four thousand banks failed in 1933 alone.

Republican Herbert Hoover, president until March 4, 1933, was voted out of office because the public considered his response to the economic crisis to be inadequate. The new Democratic Congress and president—Franklin D. Roosevelt—undertook an astonishingly large number of initiatives, collectively known as the "New Deal." Some of these measures helped relieve the suffering of the unemployed and the poor, but the New Deal did not succeed in pulling us out of the Great Depression. That happened later.

Fast Forward to the Great Recession

In the years from 2002 to 2007, the United States experienced boom times. Credit was easy, production increased, and billionaires were made weekly. Rising prosperity seemed like a birthright. Americans with low incomes were able to buy houses with borrowed money at low initial interest rates. But what goes up can come down.

The first danger signs appeared in 2006, when housing prices, which had been rising fast, began to fall. By 2007, many people were unable to make payments on their mortgages, in some instances because their adjustable-rate loans had reset at a higher interest rate. Many investments based on mortgages lost value. By 2008, major investment firms were failing. On September 15, 2008, Lehman Brothers, a prominent investment bank, failed. Panic ensued. Banks refused to lend to each other, for fear that they would not get their money back. As the financial markets froze up, our government decided that it had to step in.

Our Modern Government Responds to an Economic Crisis

The government reacted to the crisis more quickly than in the 1930s, and its reaction was much more sweeping. The George W. Bush administration was in its final months, but it swung into action. Treasury secretary Hank Paulson obtained $700 billion from Congress to buy up mortgage-backed securities held by banks—the so-called toxic assets. The goal was to inject funds into banks so that they would start lending again. Within weeks, Paulson changed course and invested these Troubled Asset Relief Program (TARP) dollars directly into leading banks.

After Barack Obama became president in January 2009, he obtained from Congress a $787 billion stimulus package made up of spending increases and tax cuts. Ben Bernanke, the head of our central bank—the Federal Reserve, or Fed—did his part. Bernanke knew that one of the chief causes of the Great Depression was that the Fed had permitted a collapse of the nation's money supply. This shortage of money choked the life out of the economy. Bernanke once said that he would do whatever it took to prevent another depression, even if it meant shoveling money out of helicopters. This earned him the nickname "Helicopter Ben." After September 2008, Helicopter Ben was true to his word. The Fed loaned out over a trillion dollars in freshly created money through more than a dozen new programs.

Were These Responses the Right Way to Go?

The responses were huge—but were they the correct policy? In time, the Great Recession would come to an end. What about the legacy of the government's actions? The difference between the federal government's revenues and its income—the deficit—jumped by a trillion dollars in one year. If federal budget deficits continue, we won't be able to avoid substantial tax increases.

Also, there is the issue of inflation. In 2008, Bernanke could easily create truckloads of new money because prices were falling. But all that new money might eventually cause prices to rise. How might Americans react to rising prices—that is, inflation?

For Critical Analysis *When economic times are tough, how do you react? Does the federal government react differently? Why or why not?*

Primarily, the government's focus has been on physical terrorism (attacks using bombs and other explosive devices). Yet terrorism can also take place in cyberspace. For example, in 2007 and 2008, Estonia and Georgia experienced a series of crippling cyberattacks launched from Russia.

LO2 *Different Systems of Government*

Through the centuries, the functions of government just discussed have been performed by many different types of government structures. A government's structure is influenced by a number of factors, such as history, customs, values, geography, resources, and human experiences and needs. No two nations have exactly the same form of government. Over time, however, political analysts have developed ways to classify different systems of government. One of the most meaningful ways is according to *who* governs. Who has the power to make the rules and laws that all must obey?

Rule by One: Autocracy

In an **autocracy,** the power and authority of the government are in the hands of a single person. At one time, autocracy was a common form of government, and it still exists in some parts of the world. Autocrats usually obtain their power either by inheriting it or by force.

MONARCHY One form of autocracy, known as a **monarchy,** is government by a king, queen, emperor, empress, tsar, or tsarina. In a monarchy, the monarch, who usually acquires power through inheritance, is the highest authority in the government.

Historically, many monarchies were *absolute monarchies,* in which the ruler held complete and unlimited power. Until the eighteenth century, the theory of divine right was widely accepted in Europe. The **divine right theory,** variations of which had existed since ancient times, held that God gave those of royal birth the unlimited right to govern other men and women. In other words, those of royal birth had a "divine right" to rule, and only God could judge them. Thus, all citizens were bound to obey their monarchs, no matter how unfair or unjust they seemed to be. Challenging this power was regarded not only as treason against the government but also as a sin against God.

Most modern monarchies, however, are *constitutional monarchies,* in which the monarch shares governmental power with elected lawmakers. Over time, the monarch's power has come to be limited, or checked, by other government leaders and perhaps by a constitution or a bill of rights. Most constitutional monarchs today serve merely as *ceremonial* leaders of their nations, as in Spain, Sweden, and the United Kingdom (Britain).

DICTATORSHIP Another form of autocracy is a **dictatorship,** in which a single leader rules, although not typically through inheritance. Dictators often gain supreme power by using force, often by overthrowing another dictator or leader. Dictators hold absolute power and are not accountable to anyone else.

A dictatorship can also be *totalitarian,* which means that a leader (or group of leaders) seeks to control almost all aspects of social and economic life. The needs of the nation come before the needs of individuals, and all citizens must work for the common goals established by the government. Examples of this form of government include Adolf Hitler's Nazi regime in Germany from 1933 to 1945, Benito Mussolini's rule in Italy from 1923 to 1943, and Joseph Stalin's dictatorship in the Soviet Union from 1929 to 1953. More contemporary examples of totalitarian dictators include Fidel Castro in Cuba, Kim Jong Il in North Korea, and, until his government was dismantled in 2003, Saddam Hussein in Iraq.

Rule by Many: Democracy

The most familiar form of government to Americans is **democracy,** in which the supreme political authority rests with the people. The word *democracy* comes from the Greek *demos,* meaning "the people," and *kratia,* meaning "rule." The main idea of democracy is that government exists only by the consent of the people and reflects the will of the majority.

autocracy A form of government in which the power and authority of the government are in the hands of a single person.

monarchy A form of autocracy in which a king, queen, emperor, empress, tsar, or tsarina is the highest authority in the government; monarchs usually obtain their power through inheritance.

divine right theory The theory that a monarch's right to rule was derived directly from God rather than from the consent of the people.

dictatorship A form of government in which absolute power is exercised by a single person who usually has obtained his or her power by the use of force.

democracy A system of government in which the people have ultimate political authority. The word is derived from the Greek *demos* ("the people") and *kratia* ("rule").

AP Photo/Toby Talbot

These voters are listening to a debate at a town hall meeting in Plainfield, Vermont. Some New England towns use such meetings to engage in a form of direct democracy. Why doesn't the U.S. as a nation have direct democracy?

THE ATHENIAN MODEL OF DIRECT DEMOCRACY

direct democracy A system of government in which political decisions are made by the people themselves rather than by elected representatives. This form of government was practiced in some areas of ancient Greece.

representative democracy A form of democracy in which the will of the majority is expressed through smaller groups of individuals elected by the people to act as their representatives.

republic Essentially, a representative democracy in which there is no king or queen and the people are sovereign.

Democracy as a form of government began long ago. **Direct democracy** exists when the people participate directly in government decision making. In its purest form, direct democracy was practiced in Athens and other ancient Greek city-states about 2,500 years ago. Every Athenian citizen participated in the governing assembly and voted on all major issues. Although some consider the Athenian form of direct democracy ideal because it demanded a high degree of citizen participation, others point out that most residents in the Athenian city-state (women, foreigners, and slaves) were not deemed to be citizens and thus were not allowed to participate in government.

Clearly, direct democracy is possible only in small communities in which citizens can meet in a chosen place and decide key issues and policies. Nowhere in the world does pure direct democracy exist today. Some New England towns, though, and a few of the smaller political subunits, or cantons, of Switzerland still use a modified form of direct democracy.

REPRESENTATIVE DEMOCRACY Although the founders of the United States were aware of the Athenian model and agreed that government should be based on the consent of the governed, they believed that direct democracy would deteriorate into mob rule. They thought that large groups of people meeting together would ignore the rights and opinions of people in the minority and would make decisions without careful thought. They believed that representative assemblies were superior because they would enable public decisions to be made in a calmer and more deliberate manner.

In a **representative democracy,** the will of the majority is expressed through smaller groups of individuals elected by the people to act as their representatives. These representatives are responsible to the people for their conduct and can be voted out of office. Our founders preferred to use the term **republic,** which means essentially a representative democracy—with one qualification. A republic, by definition, has no king or queen; rather, the people are sovereign. In contrast, a representative democracy may be headed by a monarch. For example, as Britain evolved into a representative democracy, it retained its monarch as the head of state (but with no real power).

In the modern world, there are basically two forms of representative democracy: presidential and parliamentary. In a *presidential democracy,* the lawmaking and law-enforcing branches of government are separate but equal. For example, in the United States, Congress is charged with the power to make laws, and the president is charged with the power to carry them out. In a *parliamentary democracy,* the lawmaking and law-enforcing branches of government overlap. In Britain, for example, the prime minister and the cabinet are members of the legislature, called Parliament, and are responsible to that body. Parliament thus both enacts the laws and carries them out.

Other Forms of Government

Autocracy and democracy are but two of many forms of government. Traditionally, other types of government have included governments that are ruled "by the few." For example, an aristocracy (from the Greek word *aristos,* or "best") is a government in which a small privileged class rules. A *plutocracy* is a government in which the wealthy (*ploutos* in Greek means "wealth") exercise ruling power. A *meritocracy* is a government in which the rulers have earned, or merited, the right to govern because of their special skills or talents.

A difficult form of government for Americans to understand is *theocracy*—a term derived from the Greek words meaning "rule by the deity" or "rule by God." In a theocracy, there is no separation of church and state. Rather, the government rules according to religious precepts. In most Muslim countries, government and the Islamic religion are intertwined to a degree that is quite startling to both Europeans and Americans. In Iran, for example, the Holy Koran (or Qur'an), not the national constitution, serves as the basis for the law. The Koran consists of sacred writings that Muslims believe were revealed to the prophet Muhammad by God. In Iran, the Council of Guardians, an unelected group of religious leaders, ensures that laws and lawmakers conform to their intepretation of the teachings of Islam.

LO3 *American Democracy*

> This country, with all its institutions, belongs to the people who inhabit it. Whenever they shall grow weary of the existing government, they can exercise their constitutional right to amend it, or their revolutionary right to dismember or overthrow it.[4]

With these words, Abraham Lincoln underscored the most fundamental concept of American government: that the people, not the government, are ultimately in control.

The British Legacy

In writing the U.S. Constitution, the framers incorporated two basic principles of government that had evolved in England: *limited government* and *representative government.* In a sense, then, the beginnings of our form of government are linked to events that occurred centuries earlier in England. They are also linked to the writings of European philosophers, particularly the English political philosopher John Locke. From these writings, the founders of our nation derived ideas to justify their rebellion against Britain and the establishment of a "government by the people."

"PEOPLE OFTEN SAY THAT, IN A DEMOCRACY, DECISIONS ARE MADE BY A MAJORITY OF THE PEOPLE. OF COURSE, THAT IS NOT TRUE. **Decisions are made by a majority of . . . the people who vote** —A VERY DIFFERENT THING."

~ WALTER H. JUDD ~
U.S. REPRESENTATIVE FROM MINNESOTA
1943–1963

LIMITED GOVERNMENT At one time, the English monarch claimed to have virtually unrestricted powers. This changed in 1215, when King John was forced by his nobles to accept the Magna Carta, or Great Charter. This monumental document provided for a trial by a jury of one's peers (equals). It prohibited the taking of a free man's life, liberty, or property except through due process of law. The Magna Carta also forced the king to obtain the nobles' approval of any taxes he imposed on his subjects. Government thus became a contract between the king and his subjects.

The importance of the Magna Carta to England cannot be overemphasized, because it clearly established the principle of **limited government**—a government on which strict limits are placed, usually by a constitution. Hence, the Magna Carta signaled the end of the monarch's absolute power. Although many of the rights provided under the original Magna Carta applied only to the nobility, the document formed the basis of the future constitutional government for England and eventually the United States.

limited government
A form of government based on the principle that the powers of government should be clearly limited either through a written document or through wide public understanding; characterized by institutional checks to ensure that government serves public rather than private interests.

The principle of limited government was expanded four hundred years later, in 1628, when King Charles I signed the Petition of Rights. Among other things, this petition prohibited the monarch from imprisoning political critics without a jury trial. Perhaps more important, the petition declared that even the king or queen had to obey the law of the land.

In 1689, the English Parliament (described shortly) passed the English Bill of Rights, which further extended the concept of limited government. This document included several important ideas:

National Archives

The Magna Carta.

- The king or queen could not interfere with parliamentary elections.
- The king or queen had to have Parliament's approval to levy (collect) taxes or to maintain an army.
- The king or queen had to rule with the consent of the people's representatives in Parliament.
- The people could not be subjected to cruel or unusual punishment or to excessive fines.

The English colonists in North America were also English citizens, and thus the English Bill of Rights of 1689 applied to them as well. As a result, virtually all of the major concepts in the English Bill of Rights became part of the American system of government.

parliament The name of the national legislative body in countries governed by a parliamentary system, such as Britain and Canada.

bicameral legislature A legislature made up of two chambers, or parts. The United States has a bicameral legislature, composed of the House of Representatives and the Senate.

social contract A voluntary agreement among individuals to create a government and to give that government adequate power to secure the mutual protection and welfare of all individuals.

natural rights Rights that are not bestowed by governments but are inherent within every man, woman, and child by virtue of the fact that he or she is a human being.

REPRESENTATIVE GOVERNMENT In a representative government, the people, by whatever means, elect individuals to make governmental decisions for all of the citizens. Usually, these representatives of the people are elected to their offices for specific periods of time. This group of representatives is often referred to as a **parliament,** which is frequently a **bicameral** (two-house) **legislature.** The English Parliament consists of the House of Lords (upper chamber) and the House of Commons (lower chamber). The English form of government provided a model for Americans to follow. Many of the American colonies had bicameral legislatures—as did, eventually, the U.S. Congress that was established by the Constitution.

POLITICAL PHILOSOPHY—SOCIAL CONTRACTS AND NATURAL RIGHTS Our democracy resulted from what can be viewed as a type of **social contract** among early Americans to create and abide by a set of governing rules. Social-contract theory was developed in the seventeenth and eighteenth centuries by such philosophers as John Locke (1632–1704) and Thomas Hobbes (1588–1679) in England and Jean-Jacques Rousseau (1712–1778) in France. According to this theory, individuals voluntarily agree with one another, in a "social contract," to give up some of their freedoms to obtain the benefits of orderly government. The government is given adequate power to secure the mutual protection and welfare of all individuals. Generally, social-contract theory, in one form or another, provides the theoretical underpinnings of most modern democracies, including that of the United States.

Although Hobbes and Rousseau also posited social contracts as the bases of governments, neither theorist was as influential in America as John Locke was. Locke argued that people are born with **natural rights** to life, liberty, and property. He theorized that the purpose of government was to protect those rights; if it did not, it would lose its legitimacy and need not be obeyed. Locke's assumption that people, by nature, are rational and are endowed with certain rights is an essential component of his theory that people can govern themselves. As you will read in Chapter 2, when the American colonists rebelled against British rule, such concepts as "natural rights" and a government based on a "social contract" became important theoretical tools in justifying the rebellion.

Principles of American Democracy

We can say that American democracy is based on five fundamental principles:

- *Equality in voting.* Citizens need equal opportunities to express their preferences about policies or leaders.
- *Individual freedom.* All individuals must have the greatest amount of freedom possible without interfering with the rights of others.
- *Equal protection of the law.* The law must entitle all persons to equal protection.
- *Majority rule and minority rights.* The majority should rule, while guaranteeing the rights of minorities.
- *Voluntary consent to be governed.* The people who make up a democracy must collectively agree to be governed by the rules laid down by their representatives.

These principles frame many of the political issues that you will read about in this book. They also frequently lie at the heart of America's political conflicts. Does the principle of minority rights mean that minorities should receive preferential treatment in hiring and firing decisions? Does the principle of individual freedom mean that individuals can express whatever they want on the Internet, including hateful, racist comments? Such conflicts over individual rights and freedoms and over society's priorities are natural and inevitable. Resolving these conflicts is what politics is all about. What is important is that Americans are able to reach acceptable compromises because of their common political heritage.

American Political Values

Historically, as the nations of the world emerged, the boundaries of each nation normally coincided with the boundaries of a population that shared a common ethnic heritage, language, and culture. From its beginnings as a nation, however, America has been defined less by the culture shared by its diverse population than by a set of ideas, or its political culture.

Digital Vision/Getty Images

A **political culture** can be defined as a patterned set of ideas, values, and ways of thinking about government and politics.

The ideals and standards that constitute American political culture are embodied in the Declaration of Independence, one of the founding documents of this nation, which will be discussed further in Chapter 2 and presented in its entirety in Appendix A. The political values outlined in the Declaration of Independence include natural rights (to life, liberty, and the pursuit of happiness), equality under the law, government by the consent of the governed, and limited government powers. In some ways, the Declaration of Independence defines Americans' sense of right and wrong. It presents a challenge to anyone who might wish to overthrow our democratic processes or deny our citizens their natural rights.

Fundamental political values shared by most Americans include the rights to liberty, equality, and property. These values provide a basic framework for American political discourse and debate because they are shared by most Americans, yet individual Americans often interpret their meanings quite differently. Many of our values are shared by other countries, but in some nations they are rejected. Do circumstances ever exist in which we should impose our values on foreign countries? We look at that issue in this chapter's *The Rest of the World* feature on the next page.

LIBERTY The term **liberty** refers to a state of being free from external controls or restrictions. In the United States, the Constitution sets forth our *civil liberties* (see Chapter 4), including the freedom to practice whatever religion we choose and to be free from any state-imposed religion. Our liberties also include the freedom to speak freely on any topics and issues. Because people cannot govern themselves unless they are free to voice their

political culture The set of ideas, values, and attitudes about government and the political process held by a community or a nation.

liberty The freedom of individuals to believe, act, and express themselves as they choose so long as doing so does not infringe on the rights of other individuals in the society.

Should We Ever Impose Our Values on Other Countries?

The United States shares a common set of values with Britain, France, and most other Western countries. We believe in freedom of speech, freedom of religion, the equality of men and women, and a spirit of tolerance toward others. But does support for tolerance mean we should never impose our values on other countries?

In the old days, Western powers certainly had no compunctions about forcing their version of civilized behavior on other peoples. Consider what the nineteenth-century British commander in chief in India, Sir Charles James Napier, said to a delegation of men who defended the practice of *sati*—in which widows were burned alive on their husbands' funeral pyres:

> You say that it is your custom to burn widows. Very well. We also have a custom: when men burn a woman alive, we tie a rope around their necks and hang them. Build your funeral pyre; beside it, my carpenters will build a gallows. You may follow your custom. And then we will follow ours.

AP Photo/Emilio Morenatti

Most Afghan women have few rights and are essentially kept out of civil life. Should the U.S. impose our values on that country to change this situation?

We Shouldn't Impose Our Values on Other Countries, but . . .

In 2009, Barack Obama observed: "The danger I think is when the United States or any country thinks that we can simply impose these values on another country with a different history and a different culture." Yet he went on to say: "Democracy, rule of law, freedom of speech, freedom of religion—those are not simply principles of the West to be foisted on these countries, but rather what I believe to be universal principles." On the one hand, then, we should not impose our values on other countries. But on the other hand, certain values are universal, and all countries should observe them.

An Afghan Problem—Women's Rights

We are fighting a war in Afghanistan. Whether we should impose our values on another country is therefore a serious policy issue there. The role of women in Afghanistan is a particularly contentious issue. To this day, Afghan women are kept behind walls, kept out of schools, and kept out of civil life. Women have been killed for actions that would be unremarkable in the United States. Afghanistan is the only country in the world where the suicide rate is higher for women than for men.

Some would say that the men of Afghanistan are the brothers, fathers, sons, and cousins of the same women that the West wants to save. Will painting these men as monsters actually help Afghan women? Helping should not be based on the assumption that there is something wrong with the people being helped.

Others argue that tolerance ends where harm begins. Afghanistan is a signatory of the United Nations' Universal Declaration of Human Rights, which forbids sex discrimination. Yet a proposed law would have forbidden wives in the Shiite Muslim community from leaving the house without their husbands' consent and would have condoned marital rape. Tolerance is only appropriate in areas where no one is hurt, such as diet, dress, music, and matters of religious ceremony. America is not powerless to influence Afghanistan—we are deeply engaged there and have some leverage.

Another Afghan Problem—Opium Poppies

In Afghanistan, opium poppies have been a crop for decades. Opium, however, is the base from which heroin is made. Heroin consumption violates our values, harms our citizens, and is illegal everywhere. Opium even helps fund the Taliban—the group that we are fighting against. The U.S. military has set aside $250 million for agricultural projects to help Afghan farmers find alternative crops, but there are no other crops as profitable as poppies. Not surprisingly, when U.S. soldiers show up in the middle of a poppy field, they are attacked from all sides. Pulling up poppies presents a huge problem if we are trying to "win hearts and minds." We face a contradiction between our values and the realism needed to fight a guerilla war.

For Critical Analysis *Critics of the West claim that we are intolerant liberals who don't understand other cultures and ways of life. Consequently, we should never attempt to impose our values elsewhere. Do you agree? Explain.*

AP Photo/Haraz N. Ghanbari

Did the election of President Barack Obama indicate that we are now the "land of opportunity" and equality?

opinions, freedom of speech is a basic requirement in a true democracy.

Clearly, though, if we are to live together with others, there have to be some restrictions on individual liberties. If people were allowed to do whatever they wished, without regard for the rights or liberties of others, pandemonium would result. Hence, a more accurate definition of liberty would be as follows: *liberty is the freedom of individuals to believe, act, and express themselves as they choose so long as doing so does not infringe on the rights of other individuals in the society.*

EQUALITY The goal of **equality** has always been a central part of American political culture. Many of the first settlers came to this country to be free of unequal treatment and persecution. They sought the freedom to live and worship as they wanted. They believed that anyone who worked hard could succeed, and America became known as the "land of opportunity." The Declaration of Independence confirmed the importance of equality to early Americans by stating, "We hold these Truths to be self-evident, that all Men are created equal." Because of the goal of equality, the Constitution prohibited the government from granting titles of nobility. Article I, Section 9, of the Constitution states, "No Title of Nobility shall be granted by the United States." (The Constitution did not prohibit slavery, however—see Chapter 2.)

But what, exactly, does equality mean? Does it mean simply political equality—the right to vote and run for political office? Does it mean that individuals should have equal opportunities to develop their talents and skills? What about those who are poor, suffer from disabilities, or are otherwise at a competitive disadvantage? Should it be the government's responsibility to ensure that such individuals also have equal opportunities? Although most Americans believe that all persons should have the opportunity to fulfill their potential, few contend that it is the government's responsibility to totally eliminate the economic and social differences that lead to unequal opportunities. Indeed, some contend that efforts to achieve equality, in the sense of equal treatment for all, are misguided attempts to create an ideal society that can never exist.

PROPERTY As noted earlier, the English philosopher John Locke asserted that people are born with "natural" rights and that among these rights are life, liberty, and *property.* The Declaration of Independence makes a similar assertion: people are born with certain "unalienable" rights, including the right to life, liberty, and the pursuit of happiness. For Americans, property and the *pursuit of happiness* are closely related. Americans place a great value on land ownership, on material possessions, and on their businesses. Property gives its owners political power and the liberty to do whatever they want—within limits.

Private property in America is not limited to personal possessions such as automobiles and houses. Property also consists of assets that can be used to create and sell goods and services, such as factories, farms, and shops. Private ownership of wealth-producing property is at the heart of our capitalist economic system. **Capitalism** enjoys such widespread support in the United States that we can reasonably call it one of the nation's fundamental political values. In addition to the private ownership of productive property, capitalism is based on *free markets*—markets in which people can freely buy and sell goods, services, and financial investments without undue constraint by the government. Freedom to make binding contracts

equality A concept that holds, at a minimum, that all people are entitled to equal protection under the law.

capitalism An economic system based on the private ownership of wealth-producing property, free markets, and freedom of contract. The privately owned corporation is the preeminent capitalist institution.

ideology Generally, a system of political ideas that are rooted in religious or philosophical beliefs concerning human nature, society, and government.

is another element of the capitalist system.

The preeminent capitalist institution is the privately owned corporation. Do such companies have responsibilities to the rest of society, over and above the responsibility to make a profit while obeying the law? We examine that question in this chapter's *Join the Debate* feature.

Political Values in a Multicultural Society

From the earliest English and European settlers to the many cultural groups that today call America their home, American society has always been a multicultural society. Until recently, most Americans viewed the United States as the world's melting pot. They accepted that American society included numerous ethnic and cultural groups, but they expected that the members of these groups would abandon their cultural distinctions and assimilate the language and customs of earlier Americans. One of the outgrowths of the civil rights movement of the 1960s, however, was an emphasis on *multiculturalism*, the belief that the many cultures that make up American society should remain distinct and be protected—and even encouraged—by our laws.

The ethnic makeup of the United States has changed dramatically in the last two decades and will continue to change (see Figure 1–1). Already, non-Hispanic whites are a minority in California. For the nation as a whole, non-Hispanic whites will be in the minority by the year 2050. Some Americans fear that rising numbers of immigrants will threaten traditional American political values and culture.

"THE THING ABOUT DEMOCRACY, beloveds, is that it is not neat, orderly or quiet. It requires a certain relish for confusion."

~ MOLLY IVINS ~
AMERICAN JOURNALIST
1944–2007

American Political Ideology

In a general sense, **ideology** refers to a system of political ideas. These ideas typically are rooted in religious or philosophical beliefs about human nature, society, and government. Generally, assumptions as to what the government's role should be in promoting basic values, such as liberty and equality, are important determinants of political ideology.

When it comes to political ideology, Americans tend to fall into two broad political camps: liberals

Figure 1–1

Distribution of the U.S. Population by Race and Hispanic Origin, 2000 to 2050

Even before 2050, minorities will constitute a majority of the U.S. population.

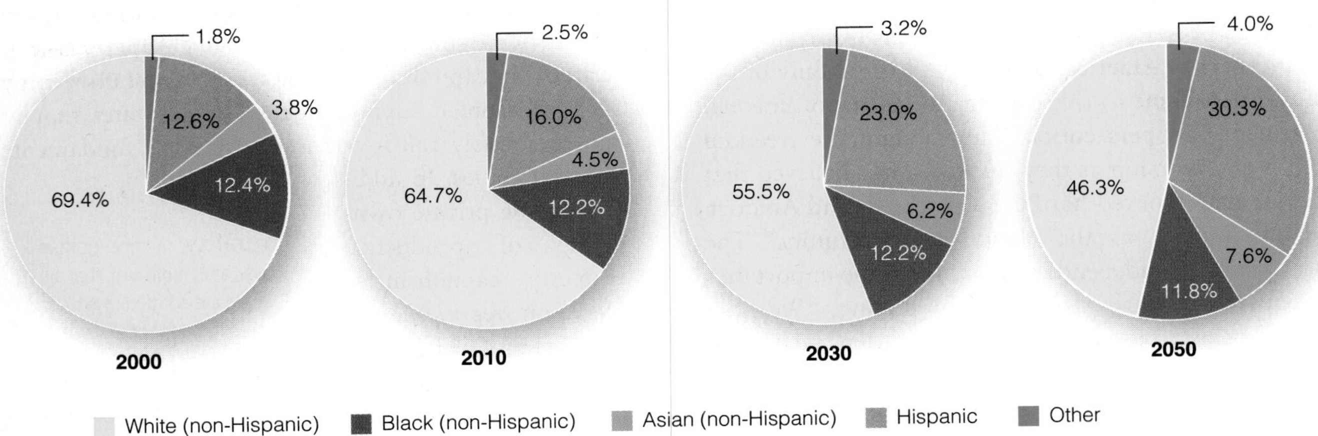

Data for 2010, 2030, and 2050 are projections.

Figures do not necessarily sum to 100%, because of rounding. Hispanics may be of any race. The chart categories "White," "Black," "Asian," and "Other" are limited to non-Hispanics. "Other" consists of the following non-Hispanic groups: "American Indian," "Alaska Native," "Native Hawaiian," "Other Pacific Islander," and "Two or More Races."
Sources: U.S. Bureau of the Census and authors' calculations.

JOIN THE DEBATE

Should Wal-Mart Address Social Issues?

Wal-Mart Stores, Inc., is big, with more than $400 billion in revenues per year, more than $170 billion in assets, and more than 2 million employees. Indeed, Wal-Mart is the largest private employer in the United States. It is also the largest grocery retailer. Because Wal-Mart's sales are as big as the total national income of certain countries, some have argued that it should govern itself better than it does.

What does "better" mean? Ethical behavior is one answer. After all, good government at the federal, state, and local levels should be ethical. Shouldn't owners and managers of large corporations also act ethically? Protecting the environment seems an obvious issue, too. Offering products that have smaller carbon footprints and are produced with less pollution should be a goal. Workplace diversity should be another goal. Is the world's largest retailer doing enough? Not according to Wal-Mart's critics.

Don't Be Fooled—Wal-Mart Is Just as Bad as They Say

For years, Wal-Mart has been blamed for paying low wages, discriminating against women in its workforce, opposing unions, and sourcing its products in countries that exploit workers and pollute the environment. Clearly, these criticisms bother the company's executives. Indeed, if you go to Wal-Mart's Web site, you'll get the impression that the company cares as much about environmental sustainability and ethical workplaces as it does about profits.

The reality, of course, is different. Wal-Mart employees are some of the lowest paid in the country. In the not-too-distant past, Wal-Mart discriminated against female employees by paying them less than their male counterparts. While Wal-Mart claims to be socially responsible, it still purchases most of its products in countries that pollute and violate child labor laws, such as China. Wal-Mart accounts for a staggering 10 percent of all imports from China in any one year. Wal-Mart continues to fight unionization. In the last election cycle, Wal-Mart not so subtly warned managers and department heads about the perils of an Obama presidency. Wal-Mart's executives feared that Obama would be too friendly to unions.

AP Photo/Lisa Poole

Wal-Mart Isn't Perfect, but It Is Getting Better

Much of the bad press that Wal-Mart receives is based on outdated information. Just take diversity. Today, more than 60 percent of Wal-Mart employees are female, almost 18 percent are African American, and 11.5 percent are Hispanic. Wal-Mart cares about civic participation, too. Beginning with the midterm elections in 2006, Wal-Mart has consistently campaigned to register all of its employees to vote. Given the makeup of its labor force, a very large share of these voters have to be Democrats.

On the environmental front, Wal-Mart instituted a fuel efficiency program that will reduce gasoline use in its trucks by 50 percent by 2014. It is striving to reduce greenhouse gases and to reduce solid waste generated by its U.S. stores. It seeks ultimately to use only renewable energy sources and produce zero waste. It has experimental stores in Colorado, Nevada, and Texas that are powered by wind turbines, solar panels, and boilers capable of burning biofuel. Wal-Mart seeks to eliminate excess packaging in order to save trees and oil.

Finally, some argue that Wal-Mart should just continue doing what it does best—offer lots of products to lots of people at the lowest prices possible. By doing so, Wal-Mart generates profits, and that is a good thing. Corporations are profitable only when they offer goods and services that society desires. Profitability is good for those who invest in Wal-Mart, too, and many investors are people who are saving for their retirement years.

For Critical Analysis *Because Wal-Mart is so large, should its governance policies be similar to those of a state government? Why or why not?*

and conservatives. The term *liberal* has been used to refer to someone who advocates change, new philosophies, and new ideas. The term *conservative* has described a person who values past customs and traditions that have proved their value over time. In today's American political arena, however, the terms *liberalism* and *conservatism* have both taken on additional meanings.

LIBERALISM Modern **liberalism** in the United States traces its roots to the administration of Franklin D. Roosevelt (1933–1945). Roosevelt's New Deal programs, launched to counter the effects of the Great Depression, involved the government in the American economic sphere to an extent hitherto unknown. From that time on, the word *liberalism* became associated with the concept of "big government"—that is, with government intervention to aid economically disadvantaged groups and to promote equality.

Today's liberals continue to believe that the government has a responsibility to undertake social-welfare programs, at the taxpayers' expense, to assist the poor and the disadvantaged. Further, today's liberals believe that the national government should take steps to ensure that our civil rights and liberties are protected and that the government must look out for the interests of the individual against the majority. Liberals typically believe in the separation of church and state, and generally think that the government should not involve itself in the moral or religious life of the nation. In this area, at least, liberals do not stand for big government, but rather the reverse.

CONSERVATISM Modern **conservatism** in this country can also trace its roots to the Roosevelt administration. Roosevelt gave conservatives a common cause: opposition to the New Deal and to big government. As one author noted, "No factor did more to stimulate the growth of modern conservatism than the election of Franklin Roosevelt. . . . He is the man conservatives most dislike, for he embodies the big-government ideology they most fear."[5]

As conservative ideology evolved in the latter half of the twentieth century, it incorporated a number of other elements in addition to the emphasis on free enterprise and antipathy toward big government. By the time of Ronald Reagan (1981–1989), conservatives placed a high value on the principles of community, law and order, states' rights, family values, and individual initiative. Today's conservatives tend to fall into two basic categories: *economic conservatives* (those who seek to minimize government spending and intervention in the economy) and *social conservatives* (those, such as Christian evangelicals, who seek to incorporate religious and family values into politics and government).

LIBERALS AND PROGRESSIVES Not all political labels are equally popular, and the term *liberal* has taken a particular beating in the political wars of the last several decades. One result is that most politicians

President Franklin D. Roosevelt signs legislation to expand federal government activities. The Roosevelt administration embodied modern liberalism and served as an example of what conservatives do not want—big government.

Library of Congress

liberalism A set of political beliefs that include the advocacy of active government, including government intervention to improve the welfare of individuals and to protect civil rights.

conservatism A set of beliefs that include a limited role for the national government in helping individuals and in the economic affairs of the nation, support for traditional values and lifestyles, and a cautious response to change.

who might have called themselves liberals in the past have abandoned the term and have labeled their philosophy **progressivism** instead. The benefits of the new label are clear. In public opinion polls, voters strongly prefer the term *conservative* to the term *liberal.* In 2009, however, a survey asked Americans to report whether they considered themselves liberal, progressive, conservative, or libertarian. Counting "leaners," the liberals and progressives together were almost as numerous as the conservative/libertarian block.[6]

The term *progressive* dates back to the first years of the twentieth century, when a reforming spirit arose in both major political parties. These "progressives" believed that stronger government was necessary to counterbalance the growing power of large corporations. In the presidential elections of 1912, the two strongest candidates, Theodore Roosevelt and Woodrow Wilson, called themselves progressives, although they disagreed on many issues. Thereafter, the progressive label dropped from sight until it was resurrected in recent years.

The Traditional Political Spectrum

Traditionally, liberalism and conservatism have been regarded as falling within a political spectrum that ranges from the far left to the far right. As Figure 1–2 illustrates, there is a close relationship between those holding conservative views and those identifying themselves politically as Republicans. Similarly, in terms of party affiliation and voting, liberals—or progressives—identify with the Democratic Party.

MODERATES People whose views fall in the middle of the traditional political spectrum are generally called **moderates.** Moderates rarely classify themselves as either liberal or conservative, and they may vote for either Republicans or Democrats. Many moderates do not belong to either major political party and often describe themselves as *independent* (see Chapter 7).

THE EXTREME LEFT AND RIGHT On both ends of the spectrum are those who espouse radical views. The **radical left** consists of those who would like significant changes in the political order, usually to promote egalitarianism (human equality). Socialists, who have a significant presence in Europe and elsewhere, generally support democracy and work within established political systems to realize their ideals. Communists, in contrast, have sought to reach their goals through revolutionary violence and totalitarian dictatorships. The political philosopher Karl Marx (1818–1883) is widely considered to be the most important founder of the radical left as it developed in the nineteenth and twentieth centuries.

The **radical right** includes reactionaries, those who wish to turn the clock back to some previous era when, for example, there weren't so many civil rights for the nation's minorities and women. Reactionaries strongly oppose liberal and progressive politics and resist political and social change. Like those on the radical left, members of the radical right may even advocate the use of violence to achieve their goals. This is especially true of fascist movements such as Hitler's Nazi Party. When in power, fascists have created totalitarian systems based on philosophies of racism or extreme nationalism.

Ideology and Today's Electorate

Those who hold strongly to political ideologies that are well thought out and internally coherent and consistent are called **ideologues.** Ideologues usually fit easily on one side or the other of the political spectrum. Many Americans, though, do

progressivism An alternative, more popular term for the set of political beliefs also known as liberalism.

moderate A person whose views fall in the middle of the political spectrum.

radical left Persons on the extreme left side of the political spectrum, who would like to significantly change the political order, usually to promote egalitarianism (human equality).

radical right Persons on the extreme right side of the political spectrum. The radical right includes reactionaries (who would like to return to the values and social systems of some previous era) and libertarians (who believe in no regulation of the economy or individual behavior).

ideologue An individual who holds very strong political opinions.

Figure 1–2

The Traditional Political Spectrum

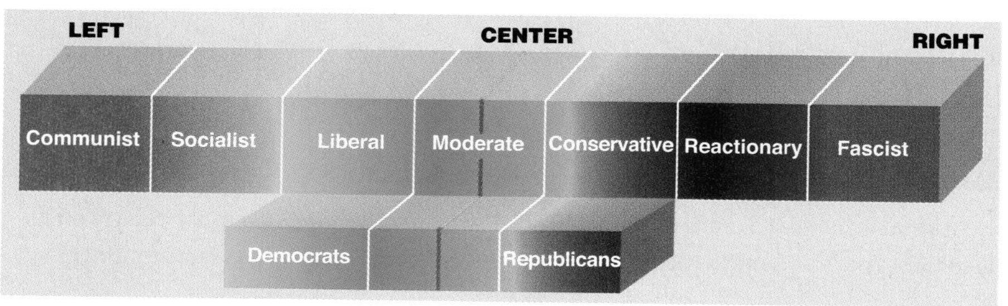

not adhere firmly to a particular political ideology. They may not be interested in all political issues and may have a mixed set of opinions that do not neatly fit under a liberal or conservative label.

One complication is that many Americans are conservative on economic issues, such as the degree of government intervention in the economy, and at the same time are liberal on social issues, such as abortion. Indeed, the ideology of *libertarianism* favors just this combination. Libertarians oppose government action to regulate the economy, just as they oppose government involvement in issues of private morality. Like the word *liberal,* the term *libertarian* is not particularly popular, and many people who clearly have libertarian beliefs are unwilling to adopt the label. As you will learn later in this book, however, wealthy Americans often have libertarian attitudes.

Many other voters are liberal on economic issues even as they favor conservative positions on social matters. These people favor government intervention to promote both economic "fairness" *and* moral values. Low-income people frequently are social conservatives and economic progressives. A large number of African Americans and Hispanics fall into this camp. While it is widespread within the electorate, this "anti-libertarian" point of view has no agreed-upon name.

Figure 1–3

A Two-Dimensional Political Classification

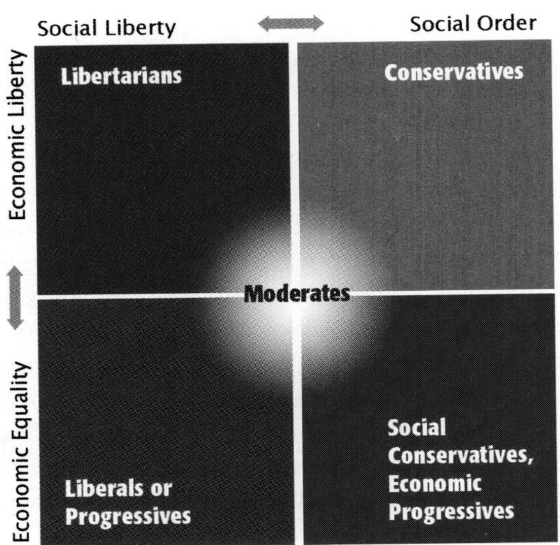

In sum, millions of Americans do not fit neatly into the traditional liberal-conservative spectrum. We illustrate an alternative, two-dimensional political classification in Figure 1–3 above.

Wally McNamee/Corbis

One political institution created by the Constitution was the U.S. Senate, shown here. Today, one hundred senators debate on a regular basis in this room. Do you think any members of the Senate can be labeled as part of the radical left or radical right?

LO4 American Democracy at Work

Even the most divisive issues can be and are resolved through the political process. How does this process work? Who are the key players? These questions will be answered in the remaining chapters of this book. In the meantime, though, it is helpful to have some kind of a "road map" to guide you through these chapters so that you can see how each topic covered in the text relates to the big picture.

The Big Picture

The U.S. Constitution is the supreme law of the land. It sets forth basic governing rules by which Americans, when they ratified the Constitution, agreed to abide. It is appropriate, then, that we begin this text, following this introductory chapter, with a discussion of how and why the Constitution was created, the type of governing structure it established, and the rights and liberties it guarantees for all Americans. These topics, covered in Chapters 2 through 5, are necessarily the point of departure for any discussion of our system of government. As you will see, some of the most significant political controversies today have to do with how various provisions in this founding document should be applied, more than two hundred years later, to modern-day events and issues.

Who Governs?

Who acquires the power and authority to govern, and how do they obtain that power and authority? Generally, of course, the "winners" in our political system are the successful candidates in elections. But the electoral process is influenced by more than just the issue positions taken by the candidates. As you read Chapters 6 through 10, keep the following questions in mind: How do interest groups influence elections? How essential are political parties to the electoral process? To what extent do public opinion and voting behavior play a role in determining who the winners and losers will be? Why are political campaigns so expensive, and what are the implications of high campaign costs for our democracy? Finally, what role do the media, including the Internet, play in fashioning the outcomes of campaigns?

Once a winning candidate assumes a political office, that candidate becomes a part of one of the institutions of government. In Chapter 11 and the remaining chapters of this text, we examine these institutions and the process of government decision making. You will learn how those who govern the nation make laws and policies to decide "who gets what, when, and how" in our society. Of course, the topics treated in these chapters are not isolated from the materials covered earlier in the text. For example, when formulating and implementing federal policies, as well as state and local policies, policymakers cannot ignore the wishes of interest groups, particularly those of wealthy groups that can help to fund the policymakers' reelections. And public opinion and the media not only affect election outcomes but also influence which issues will be included on the policymaking agenda.

The political system established by the founders of this nation has endured for more than two hundred years. The challenge facing Americans now is how to make sure that it will continue to endure.

PhotoDisc

AMERICA AT ODDS *The Contours of American Democracy*

As you learned in this chapter, American citizens do not participate directly in making government decisions, as in a direct democracy. Rather, the people elect representatives to make such decisions. In Chapter 2, you will read about the founders' distaste for direct democracy. They feared that if "the masses" were directly involved in government decision making, the result would be instability, if not chaos. Indeed, the Constitution as originally written allowed citizens to vote only for members of the House of Representatives, not for members of the Senate. Senators were initially elected by their respective state legislatures. (The Seventeenth Amendment to the Constitution, which was adopted in 1913, changed this procedure, and Americans now vote directly for members of the Senate as well.) Even today, the president is not elected directly by the people but by the electoral college, as will be explained in Chapter 9.

It is useful to compare the founders' intentions with today's practices because doing so helps us to assess whether and in what ways we have strayed from the founders' intentions. The final feature in each chapter of this text—the feature you are reading now—will look at the chapter topic in this light to provide a better understanding of the current status of our democracy. In this first chapter-ending feature, we return to the important question raised in the opening *America at Odds* feature: Do we really have a representative democracy? Certainly, the founders could not have envisioned a Congress so strongly influenced by monied interests and party politics. Nor, in all likelihood, could they have foreseen the failure of so many of today's Americans to participate in our democracy. On average, only about half of the voting-age population actually turns out to vote. The conclusion is obvious: if Americans truly want a representative democracy, their participation in the political process is crucial. Our elected leaders cannot represent the people if the people do not let their opinions be known.

As you read through the pages of this book, you will see that Americans are at odds over many issues that affect this country's performance and leadership, including the issues for debate and discussion presented next. You will also learn about how you can take part in political debate and action, and let your voice be heard. As President Dwight D. Eisenhower (1953–1961) once said, "Politics ought to be the part-time profession of every citizen who would protect the rights and privileges of free people and who would preserve what is good and fruitful in our national heritage."

ISSUES FOR DEBATE & DISCUSSION

1. **Young Americans have the lowest voter-turnout rate in the country. Some maintain that this is because it is too difficult to vote—you have to register, get to the polling place, and then try to decipher the ballot. In contrast, to vote for the next American Idol, all you have to do is pick up the phone and dial a number. Some believe that if voting were made simpler, young Americans would turn out in greater numbers. Others believe that America's youth stay away from the polls because they are not interested in politics, if not alienated by the political system. What is your position on this issue?**
2. **Suppose that you are a representative in Congress. Public opinion polls show that nearly 70 percent of the voters in your district support strong barriers to goods imported from other countries. You believe that such restrictions would be disastrous for the United States. In this situation, some would claim that because you were elected to represent your constituents' interests, you should vote to bar foreign goods. Others would argue that you should vote as your conscience dictates, even if that is contrary to the wishes of your constituents or the majority of Americans—and even if it means that you will not be reelected to Congress. What position do you take on this issue?**

TAKE ACTION

From the time you are born until you die, government affects your everyday life. It affects your ability to express yourself freely, to join others to share like interests or to advocate a position on an issue that is important to you, to practice the religion of your choice (or not to practice any religion), and to exercise important rights if you are accused of a crime. Government decision making also affects the health and safety of our population, as well as the health of our environment.

Because our democracy is now more than two hundred years old, it is easy to assume that it will last forever. It is also easy to forget that the reason we still enjoy these rights and benefits is that whenever they have been threatened in the past, people have spoken out—they have taken action to remove the threat. Americans can take advantage of numerous methods to influence their society and their government. In the remaining chapters of this book, this *Take Action* section will give examples of how you can take action to make a difference when you are at odds with government policymakers on important issues.

POLITICS ON THE WEB

Each chapter of *GOVT* concludes with a list of Internet resources and addresses. Once you are on the Internet, you can use the addresses, or uniform resource locators (URLs), listed in the *Politics on the Web* sections in this book to access the ever-growing number of resources available on the Internet relating to American politics and government.

Internet sites tend to come and go, and there is no guarantee that a site included in a *Politics on the Web* feature will be there by the time this book is in print. We have tried, though, to include sites that have so far proved to be fairly stable. If you do have difficulty reaching a site, do not immediately assume that the site does not exist. First, recheck the URL shown in your browser. Remember, you have to type the URL exactly as written: uppercase and lowercase are sometimes important. If the URL appears to be keyed in correctly, then try the following technique: delete all of the information after the forward slash mark that is farthest to the right in the address, and press "enter." This may allow you to reach a home page, from which you can link to the topic at issue.

A seemingly infinite number of sites on the Web offer information on American government and politics. A list of even the best sites would fill pages. For reasons of space, in this chapter and in those that follow, the *Politics on the Web* sections will include references to only a few selected sites. Following the links provided by these sites will take you to a host of others. The Web sites listed in the next column all provide excellent points of departure for those who wish to learn more about American government and politics today.

- The U.S. government's "official" Web site offers extensive information on the national government and the services it provides for citizens. To access this site, go to **www.usa.gov**
- This Nation is a nonpartisan site dealing with current political questions. To access this site, go to **www.thisnation.com**
- To find news on the Web, you can go to the site of any major news organization or even your local newspaper. Links to online newspapers, both within the United States and in other countries, are available at **www.newspapers.com**
- Additionally, CNN's Politics Web site offers a wealth of news, news analysis, polling data, and news articles dating back to 1996. Go to **www.cnn.com/POLITICS**
- To learn how new computer and communications technologies are affecting the constitutional rights and liberties of Americans, go to the Web site of the Center for Democracy and Technology at **www.cdt.org**
- The Pew Research Center for the People and the Press offers survey data online on a number of topics relating to American politics and government. The URL for the center's site is **people-press.org**
- Yale University Library, one of the great research institutions, has an excellent collection of sources relating to American politics and government. Go to **www.library.yale.edu/socsci**

Online resources for this chapter

This text's Companion Web site, at **www.4ltrpress.cengage.com/govt**, offers links to numerous resources that you can use to learn more about the topics covered in this chapter.

Andersen Ross/Photodisc/Getty Images

GOVT 2 The Constitution

LEARNING OBJECTIVES

LO1 Point out some of the influences on the American political tradition in the colonial years.

LO2 Explain why the American colonies rebelled against Britain.

LO3 Describe the structure of government established by the Articles of Confederation and some of the strengths and weaknesses of the Articles.

LO4 List some of the major compromises made by the delegates at the Constitutional Convention, and discuss the Federalist and Anti-Federalist positions on ratifying the Constitution.

LO5 Summarize the Constitution's major principles of government, and describe how the Constitution can be amended.

AMERICA AT ODDS

Should Individuals Have the Right to Bear Arms?

The Second Amendment to the Constitution of the United States says, "A well regulated Militia, being necessary to the security of a free State, the right of the people to keep and bear Arms, shall not be infringed." It seems clear, doesn't it? Actually, it is not clear. Does this amendment allow any individual in the United States to own a gun? Or does it guarantee the right to bear arms only to those who serve in a militia, such as the National Guard?

For decades, those who oppose gun control have argued that the first statement is correct. Gun control advocates have argued that the second statement is what the founders meant. In 2008, the United States Supreme Court ruled on a challenge to a strict gun control law in the District of Columbia. Five of the nine justices agreed that the right to bear arms is indeed an individual right.[1] Just because the Supreme Court made this ruling 217 years after the Second Amendment was ratified as part of the Bill of Rights, however, does not mean that Americans are finally in agreement about firearms. Far from it. The Supreme Court's decision still allows substantial regulation of gun ownership and possession. The District of Columbia, the subject of the Court's ruling, is not a state—rather, it is under direct federal control. State and local governments may still prohibit the carrying of concealed weapons. They may also bar "dangerous and unusual weapons," such as submachine guns.

The Supreme Court's Ruling Has Finally Clarified the Issue

Those who oppose gun control legislation strongly approve of the way the Supreme Court has interpreted the Second Amendment. They argue that the "militia" phrase in the Second Amendment is merely a preamble. James Madison, who drafted it, was providing an explanation of why the amendment was desirable, and not placing a limit on its applicability. The federal government cannot prevent individuals from owning guns, and under the Fourteenth Amendment, the states should not have that right either. Sixty million Americans own guns. Barely one-third of Americans believe that the way to combat gun violence is through stricter gun laws.

"If guns are made criminal, only criminals will have guns." Studies conducted in cities where concealed weapons are allowed show that there are fewer robberies and murders than in jurisdictions where concealed weapons are *not* allowed. Washington, D.C., had a total ban on guns, and yet it has one of the nation's highest rates of murder, 80 percent of which are committed with firearms.

Without Gun Control, More Americans Will Die Senselessly

When drafted, the Second Amendment was an accommodation to the Anti-Federalists of the time, who believed that "the people in arms" could serve as an effective fighting force. This notion had already been proved wrong in the Revolutionary War. The current Supreme Court ruling on gun control laws can only have a negative effect on the well-being of Americans. Gun rights advocates will use this decision as a legal tool to strike down effective gun control laws nationwide. More than thirty thousand Americans are killed by guns every year. A third of these deaths are instances of murder; the rest are suicides or accidents.

Those in favor of gun control laws will continue to fight for them. They can do so because the Supreme Court decision did allow for certain types of gun restrictions, particularly bans on gun possession by felons and mentally ill individuals. We know that European nations that have banned almost all gun ownership have much lower homicide rates than we do in the United States. Isn't that enough evidence?

WHERE DO YOU STAND?

1. **As you will learn in Chapter 4, the Supreme Court has incorporated various rights and liberties protected by the Bill of Rights into the liberties protected under the Fourteenth Amendment, which specifically limits the power of the states. In this way, the states are banned from violating such rights as freedom of speech. In the District of Columbia case, the Court did not rule on whether the Second Amendment applies to state governments. Should it? Why or why not?**
2. **Why do you think so many Americans own firearms?**

EXPLORE THIS ISSUE ONLINE

Given the heat of the gun control controversy and the number of people who have taken positions on the issue, it's no surprise that you can find many Web sites on either side.

- **Web sites that advocate the regulation of firearms are maintained by the Brady Campaign to Prevent Gun Violence at www.bradycampaign.org, the Violence Policy Center at www.vpc.org, and the Legal Community Against Violence at www.lcav.org.**
- **Gun rights sites are maintained by the Gun Owners of America at www.gunowners.org, the National Rifle Association at www.nra.org, and the Second Amendment Foundation at www.saf.org.**

AP Photo/Jose Luis Magana

This pro-gun rights supporter holds a banner outside the Supreme Court building in Washington, D.C. The Court had just ruled that Americans have a constitutional right to keep guns in their homes for self-defense. Do you think the Supreme Court has ruled often on the issue of gun control?

Introduction

Whether Americans as individuals have a constitutional right to own firearms is just one of many debates concerning the government established by the U.S. Constitution. The Constitution, which was written more than two hundred years ago, continues to be the supreme law of the land. Time and again, its provisions have been adapted to the changing needs and conditions of society. The challenge before today's citizens and political leaders is to find a way to apply those provisions to a society and an economy that could not possibly have been anticipated by the founders. Will the Constitution survive this challenge? Most Americans assume that it will—and with good reason: no other written constitution in the world today is as old as the U.S. Constitution. To understand the principles of government set forth in the Constitution, you have to go back to the beginnings of our nation's history.

LO1 *The Beginnings of American Government*

When the framers of the Constitution met in Philadelphia in 1787, they brought with them some valuable political assets. One asset was their English political heritage (see Chapter 1). Another was the hands-on political experience they had acquired during the colonial era. Their political knowledge and experience enabled them to establish a constitution that could meet not only the needs of their own time but also the needs of generations to come.

The American colonies were settled by individuals from many nations, including England, France, the Netherlands, Norway, Spain, and Sweden. The majority of the colonists, though, came from England and Scotland. The British colonies in North America were established by private individuals and private trading companies and were under the rule of the British Crown. The colonies, which were located along the Atlantic seaboard of today's United States, eventually numbered thirteen.

Although American politics owes much to the English political tradition, the colonists actually derived most of their understanding of social compacts, the rights of the people, limited government, and representative government from their own experiences. Years before Parliament adopted the English Bill of Rights or John Locke wrote his *Two Treatises on Government* (1690), the American colonists were putting the ideas expressed in those documents into practice.

John Locke (1632–1704), an English philosopher. Locke argued that human beings were equal and endowed by nature with certain rights, such as the right to life, liberty, and property. The purpose of government, according to Locke, was to protect those rights. Locke's theory of natural rights and his contention that government stemmed from a social contract among society's members were an important part of the political heritage brought to this country by the English colonists.

The Granger Collection

The First English Settlements

The first permanent English settlement in North America was Jamestown, in what is now Virginia.[2] Jamestown was established in 1607 as a trading post of the Virginia Company of London.[3]

The first New England colony was founded by the Plymouth Company in 1620 at Plymouth, Massachusetts. Most of the settlers at Plymouth were Pilgrims, were a group of English Protestants who came to the New World on the ship *Mayflower.* Even before the Pilgrims went ashore, they drew up the **Mayflower Compact**, in which they set up a government and promised to obey its laws. The reason for the compact was that the group was outside the jurisdiction of the Virginia Company, which had arranged for them to settle in Virginia, not Massachusetts. Fearing that some of the passengers might decide that they were no longer subject to any rules of civil order, the leaders on board the *Mayflower* agreed that some form of governmental authority was necessary. The Mayflower Compact, which was essentially a social contract, has historical significance because it was the first of a series of similar contracts among the colonists to establish fundamental rules of government.[4]

The Massachusetts Bay Colony was established as another trading outpost in New England in 1630. In 1639, some of the Pilgrims at Plymouth, who felt that they were being persecuted by the Massachusetts Bay Colony, left Plymouth and settled in what is now Connecticut. They developed America's first written constitution, which was called the Fundamental Orders of Connecticut. This document called for the laws to be made by an assembly of elected representatives from each town. The document also provided for the popular election of a governor and judges. Other colonies, in turn, established fundamental governing rules. The Massachusetts Body of Liberties protected individual rights. The Pennsylvania Frame of Government, passed in 1682, and the Pennsylvania Charter of Privileges of 1701 established principles that were later expressed in the U.S. Constitution and **Bill of Rights** (the first ten amendments to the Constitution). By 1732, all thirteen colonies had been established, each with its own political documents and constitution (see Figure 2–1).

Figure 2–1

The Thirteen Colonies

The thirteen colonies before the American Revolution. The western boundary of the colonies was set by the Proclamation Line of 1763, which banned European settlement in western territories that were reserved for Native Americans.

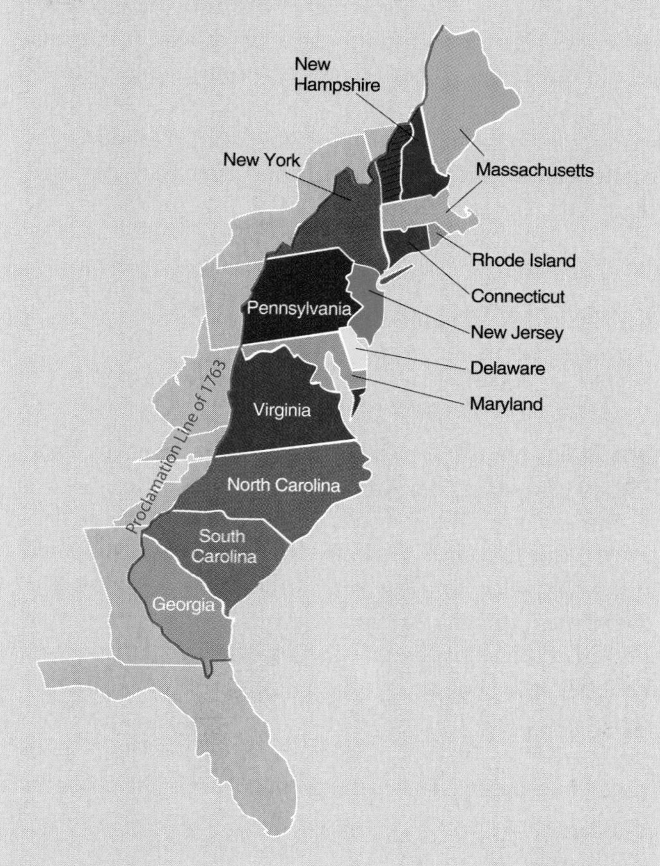

Colonial Legislatures

As mentioned, the British colonies in America were all under the rule of the British monarchy. Britain, however, was thousands of miles away—it took two months to sail across the Atlantic. Thus, to a significant extent, colonial legislatures carried on the "nuts and bolts" of colonial government. These legislatures, or *representative assemblies,* consisted of representatives elected by the colonists. The earliest colonial legislature was the Virginia House of Burgesses, established in 1619. By the time of the American Revolution, all of the colonies had representative assemblies, many of which had been in existence for more than a hundred years.

Through their participation in colonial governments, the colonists

Mayflower Compact A document drawn up by Pilgrim leaders in 1620 on the ship *Mayflower.* The document stated that laws were to be made for the general good of the people.

Bill of Rights The first ten amendments to the U.S. Constitution. They list the freedoms—such as the freedoms of speech, press, and religion—that a citizen enjoys and that cannot be infringed on by the government.

gained crucial political experience. Colonial leaders became familiar with the practical problems of governing. They learned how to build coalitions among groups with diverse interests and how to make compromises. Indeed, according to Yale University professor Jon Butler, by the time of the American Revolution in 1776, Americans had formed a complex, sophisticated political system. They had also created a wholly new type of society characterized by, among other things, ethnic and religious diversity.[5] Because of their political experiences, the colonists were quickly able to set up their own constitutions and state systems of government—and eventually a new national government—after they declared their independence from Britain in 1776.

LO2 *The Rebellion of the Colonists*

Scholars of the American Revolution point out that, by and large, the American colonists did not want to become independent of Britain. For the majority of the colonists, Britain was the homeland, and ties of loyalty to the British monarch were strong. Why, then, did the colonists revolt against Britain and declare their independence? What happened to sever the political, economic, and emotional bonds that tied the colonists to Britain? The answers to these questions lie in a series of events in the mid-1700s that culminated in a change in British policy toward the colonies. Table 2–1 shows the chronology of the major political events in early U.S. political history.

One of these events was the Seven Years' War (1756–1763) between Britain and France, which Americans often refer to as the French and Indian War. The British victory in the Seven Years' War permanently altered the relationship between Britain and its American colonies. After successfully ousting the French from North America, the British expanded their authority over the colonies. To pay its war debts and to finance the defense of its expanded North American empire, Britain needed revenues. The British government decided to obtain some of these revenues by imposing taxes on the American colonists and exercising more direct control over colonial trade. At the same time, Americans were beginning to distrust the expanding British presence in the colonies. Having fought alongside British forces, Americans thought that they deserved more credit for the victory. The British, however, attributed the victory solely to their own war effort.

Table 2–1

Significant Events in Early U.S. Political History

1607	Jamestown established; Virginia Company lands settlers.
1620	Mayflower Compact signed.
1630	Massachusetts Bay Colony set up.
1639	Fundamental Orders of Connecticut adopted.
1641	Massachusetts Body of Liberties adopted.
1682	Pennsylvania Frame of Government passed.
1701	Pennsylvania Charter of Privileges written.
1732	Last of thirteen colonies established (Georgia).
1756	French and Indian War declared.
1765	Stamp Act; Stamp Act Congress meets.
1773	Boston Tea Party.
1774	First Continental Congress.
1775	Second Continental Congress; Revolutionary War begins.
1776	Declaration of Independence signed.
1777	Articles of Confederation drafted.
1781	Last state signs Articles of Confederation.
1783	"Critical period" in U.S. history begins; weak national government until 1789.
1786	Shays' Rebellion.
1787	Constitutional Convention.
1788	Ratification of Constitution.
1791	Ratification of Bill of Rights.

"Every generation NEEDS A NEW REVOLUTION."

~ THOMAS JEFFERSON ~
THIRD PRESIDENT OF THE UNITED STATES
1801–1817

Furthermore, the colonists began to develop a sense of identity separate from the British. Americans were shocked at the behavior of some of the British soldiers and the cruel punishments meted out to enforce discipline among the British troops. The British, in turn, had little good to say about the colonists alongside whom they had fought. They considered them brutish, uncivilized, and undisciplined. It was during this time that the colonists began to use the word *American* to describe themselves.

"Taxation without Representation"

In 1764, in an effort to obtain needed revenues, the British Parliament passed the Sugar Act, which imposed a tax on all sugar imported into the American colonies. Some colonists, particularly in Massachusetts, vigorously opposed this tax and proposed a boycott of certain British imports. This boycott developed into a "nonimportation" movement that soon spread to other colonies.

THE STAMP ACT OF 1765 The following year, in 1765, Parliament passed the Stamp Act, which imposed the first direct tax on the colonists. Under the act, all legal documents and newspapers, as well as certain other items, including playing cards and dice, had to use specially embossed (stamped) paper that was purchased from the government.

The Stamp Act generated even stronger resentment among the colonists than the Sugar Act had aroused. James Otis, Jr., a Massachusetts attorney, declared that there could be "no taxation without representation." The American colonists could not vote in British elections and therefore were not represented in the British Parliament. They viewed Parliament's attempts to tax them as contrary to the principle of representative government. The British saw the matter differently. From the British perspective, it was only fair that the colonists pay taxes to help support the costs incurred by the British government in defending its American territories and maintaining the troops that were permanently stationed in the colonies following the Seven Years' War.

In October 1765, nine of the thirteen colonies sent delegates to the Stamp Act Congress in New York City. The delegates prepared a declaration of rights and grievances, which they sent to King George III. This action marked the first time that a majority of the colonies had joined together to oppose British rule. The British Parliament repealed the Stamp Act.

During the so-called Boston Tea Party in 1773, the colonists dumped chests of British tea into Boston Harbor as a gesture of tax protest.

Time Life Pictures/Mansell/Getty Images

FURTHER TAXES AND THE COERCIVE ACTS Soon, however, Parliament passed new laws designed to bind the colonies more tightly to the central government in London. Laws that imposed taxes on glass, paint, lead, and many other items were passed in 1767. The colonists protested by boycotting all British goods. In 1773, anger over taxation reached a powerful climax at the Boston Tea Party, in which colonists dressed as Mohawk Indians dumped almost 350 chests of British tea into Boston Harbor as a gesture of tax protest.[6]

The British Parliament was quick to respond to the Tea Party. In 1774, Parliament passed the Coercive Acts (sometimes called the "Intolerable Acts"), which closed Boston Harbor and placed the government of Massachusetts under direct British control.

The Continental Congresses

In response to the "Intolerable Acts," New York, Pennsylvania, and Rhode Island proposed a colonial congress. The Massachusetts House of Representatives requested that all colonies select delegates to send to Philadelphia for such a congress.

THE FIRST CONTINENTAL CONGRESS The **First Continental Congress** met on September 5, 1774, at Carpenter's Hall in Philadelphia. Of the thirteen colonies, only Georgia did not participate. The congress decided that the colonies should send a petition to King George III to explain their grievances, which they did. The congress also passed other

First Continental Congress A gathering of delegates from twelve of the thirteen colonies, held in 1774 to protest the Coercive Acts.

Library of Congress

Patrick Henry addressing the Virginia Assembly in the spring of 1775. His passionate speech in favor of independence concluded with the words, "Give me liberty or give me death!"—which became a battle cry of the Revolution.

resolutions calling for a continued boycott of British goods and requiring each colony to establish an army.

To enforce the boycott and other acts of resistance against Britain, the delegates to the First Continental Congress urged that "a committee be chosen in every county, city and town, by those who are qualified to vote for representatives in the legislature, whose business it shall be attentively to observe the conduct of all persons." Over the next several months, all colonial legislators supported this action. The committees of "safety" or "observation," as they were called, organized militias, held special courts, and suppressed the opinions of those who remained loyal to the British Crown. Committee members spied on neighbors' activities and reported to the press the names of those who violated the boycott against Britain. The names were then printed in the local papers, and the transgressors were harassed and ridiculed in their communities.

> **"THE CONSTITUTION**
> ...is an instrument for the people to restrain the government—lest it come to dominate our lives and interests."
>
> ~ PATRICK HENRY ~
> AMERICAN STATESMAN AND SIGNER OF THE CONSTITUTION
> 1736–1799

Second Continental Congress The congress of the colonies that met in 1775 to assume the powers of a central government and to establish an army.

THE SECOND CONTINENTAL CONGRESS

Almost immediately after receiving the petition, the British government condemned the actions of the First Continental Congress as open acts of rebellion. Britain responded with even stricter and more repressive measures. On April 19, 1775, British soldiers (Redcoats) fought with colonial citizen soldiers (Minutemen) in the towns of Lexington and Concord in Massachusetts, the first battles of the American Revolution.

Less than a month later, delegates from all thirteen colonies gathered in Pennsylvania for the **Second Continental Congress**, which immediately assumed the powers of a central government. The Second Continental Congress declared that the militiamen who had gathered around Boston were now a full army. It also named George Washington, a delegate to the Second Continental Congress who had some military experience, as its commander in chief.

The delegates to the Second Continental Congress still intended to reach a peaceful settlement with the British Parliament. One declaration stated specifically that "we [the congress] have not raised armies with ambitious designs of separating from Britain, and establishing independent States." The continued attempts to effect a reconciliation with Britain, even after the outbreak of fighting, underscore the colonists' reluctance to sever their relationship with the home country. As one scholar put it, "Of all the world's colonial peoples, none became rebels more reluctantly than did Anglo-Americans in 1776."[7]

Breaking the Ties: Independence

Public debate about the problems with Britain continued to rage, but the stage had been set for declaring independence. One of the most rousing arguments in favor of independence was presented by Thomas Paine, a former English schoolmaster and corset maker, who wrote a pamphlet called *Common Sense*. In that pamphlet, which was published in Philadelphia in January 1776, Paine addressed the crisis using "simple fact, plain argument, and common sense." He mocked

Thomas Paine (1737–1809). In addition to his successful pamphlet *Common Sense,* Paine also wrote a series of sixteen pamphlets, under the title *The Crisis,* during the American Revolution. He returned to England and, in 1791 and 1792, wrote *The Rights of Man,* in which he defended the French Revolution. Paine returned to the United States in 1802.

Time Life Pictures/Mansell/Getty Images

King George III and attacked every argument that favored loyalty to the king. He called the king a "royal brute" and a "hardened, sullen-tempered Pharaoh [Egyptian king in ancient times]."[8]

Paine's writing went beyond a personal attack on the king. He contended that America could survive economically on its own and no longer needed its British connection. He wanted the developing colonies to become a model republic in a world in which other nations were oppressed by strong central governments.

None of Paine's arguments was new; in fact, most of them were commonly heard in tavern debates throughout the land. Instead, it was the pungency and eloquence of Paine's words that made *Common Sense* so effective:

> A government of our own is our natural right: and when a man seriously reflects on the precariousness of human affairs, he will become convinced, that it is infinitely wiser and safer, to form a constitution of our own in a cool and deliberate manner, while we have it in our power, than to trust such an interesting event to time and chance.[9]

Many historians regard Paine's *Common Sense* as the single most important publication of the American Revolution. The pamphlet became a best seller; more than 100,000 copies were sold within a few months after its publication.[10] It put independence squarely on the agenda. Above all, *Common Sense* helped sever the remaining ties of loyalty to the British monarch, thus removing the final psychological barrier to independence. Indeed, later John Adams would ask,

> What do we mean by the Revolution? The War? That was no part of the Revolution. It was only an effect and consequence of it. The Revolution was in the minds of the people, and this was effected, from 1760 to 1775, in the course of fifteen years before a drop of blood was drawn at Lexington.[11]

INDEPENDENCE FROM BRITAIN—THE FIRST STEP By June 1776, the Second Continental Congress had voted for free trade at all American ports with all countries except Britain. The congress had also suggested that all colonies establish state governments separate from Britain. The colonists realized that a formal separation from Britain was necessary if the new nation was to obtain supplies for its armies and commitments of military aid from foreign governments. On June 7, 1776, the first formal step toward independence was taken when Richard Henry Lee of Virginia placed the following resolution before the congress:

> RESOLVED, That these United Colonies are, and of right ought to be, free and independent States, that they are absolved from allegiance to the British Crown, and that all political connection between them and the state of Great Britain is, and ought to be, totally dissolved.

The congress postponed consideration of Lee's resolution until a formal statement of independence could be drafted. On June 11, a "Committee of Five" was appointed to draft a declaration that would present to the world the colonies' case for independence.

THE SIGNIFICANCE OF THE DECLARATION OF INDEPENDENCE The Declaration of Independence is one of the world's most famous documents. Like Paine, Thomas Jefferson, who wrote most of the document, elevated the dispute between Britain and the

The committee chosen to draft a declaration of independence is shown at work in this nineteenth-century engraving. They are, from the left, Benjamin Franklin, Thomas Jefferson, John Adams, Philip Livingston, and Roger Sherman.

Library of Congress

American colonies to a universal level. Jefferson opened the second paragraph of the declaration with the following words, which have since been memorized by countless American schoolchildren and admired the world over:

> We hold these Truths to be self-evident, that all Men are created equal, that they are endowed by their Creator with certain unalienable Rights, that among these are Life, Liberty, and the Pursuit of Happiness—That to secure these Rights, Governments are instituted among Men, deriving their just Powers from the Consent of the Governed, that whenever any Form of Government becomes destructive of these Ends, it is the Right of the People to alter or to abolish it, and to institute new Government.

The concepts expressed in the Declaration of Independence clearly reflect Jefferson's familiarity with European political philosophy, particularly the works of John Locke.[12] Locke's philosophy, though it did not cause the American Revolution, provided philosophical underpinnings by which it could be justified.

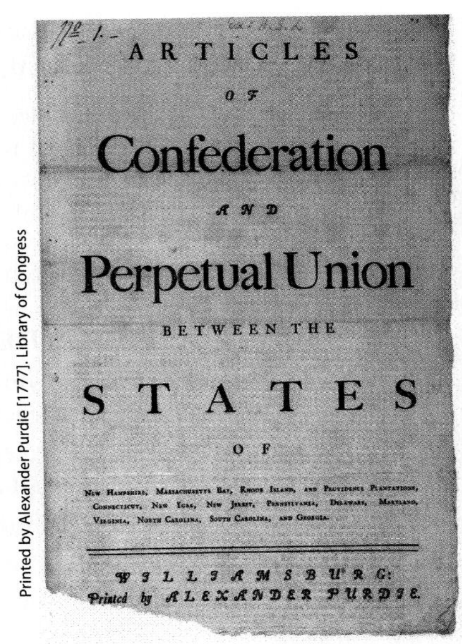
ARTICLES
OF
Confederation
AND
Perpetual Union
BETWEEN THE
STATES
OF
New Hampshire, Massachusetts Bay, Rhode Island, and Providence Plantations, Connecticut, New York, New Jersey, Pennsylvania, Delaware, Maryland, Virginia, North Carolina, South Carolina, and Georgia.

WILLIAMSBURG:
Printed by ALEXANDER PURDIE.

Printed by Alexander Purdie [1777]. Library of Congress

The Articles of Confederation, signed by all thirteen colonies on March 1, 1781, was America's first national constitution.

FROM COLONIES TO STATES Even before the Declaration of Independence, some of the colonies had transformed themselves into sovereign states with their own permanent governments. In May 1776, the Second Continental Congress had directed each of the colonies to form "such government as shall . . . best be conducive to the happiness and safety of their constituents [those represented by the government]." Before long, all thirteen colonies had created constitutions. Eleven of the colonies had completely new constitutions; the other two colonies, Rhode Island and Connecticut, made minor modifications to old royal charters. Seven of the new constitutions contained bills of rights that defined the personal liberties of all state citizens. All constitutions called for limited governments.

REPUBLICANISM Many citizens were fearful of a strong central government because of their recent experiences under the British Crown. They opposed any form of government that resembled monarchy in any way. Consequently, wherever such antiroyalist sentiment was strong, the legislature—composed of elected representatives—became all-powerful. In Pennsylvania and Georgia, for example, **unicameral** (one-chamber) **legislatures** were unchecked by any executive authority. Indeed, this antiroyalist—or *republican*—sentiment was so strong that the executive branch was extremely weak in all thirteen states.

The republican spirit was strong enough to seriously interfere with the ability of the new nation to win the Revolutionary War, for example by failing to adequately supply General Washington's army. Republicans of the Revolutionary Era (not to be confused with supporters of the later Republican Party) were suspicious not only of executive authority in their own states but also of national authority as represented by the Continental Congress. This antiauthoritarian, localist impulse contrasted with the *nationalist* sentiments of many of the nation's founders, especially such leaders as George Washington and Alexander Hamilton. Nationalists favored an effective central authority. Of course, many founders, such as Thomas Jefferson, harbored both republican and nationalist impulses.

Who were the republicans? As with all political movements of the time, the republicans were led by men of "property and standing." Leaders who were strongly republican, however, tended to be less prominent than their nationalist or moderate counterparts. Small farmers may have been the one group that was disproportionately republican. Small farmers, however, were a majority of the voters in every state.

LO3 *The Confederation of States*

Republican sentiments influenced the thinking of the delegates to the Second Continental Congress, who formed a committee to draft a plan of confederation. A **confederation** is a voluntary association of

unicameral legislature A legislature with only one chamber.

confederation A league of independent states that are united only for the purpose of achieving common goals.

Figure 2–2

American Government under the Articles of Confederation

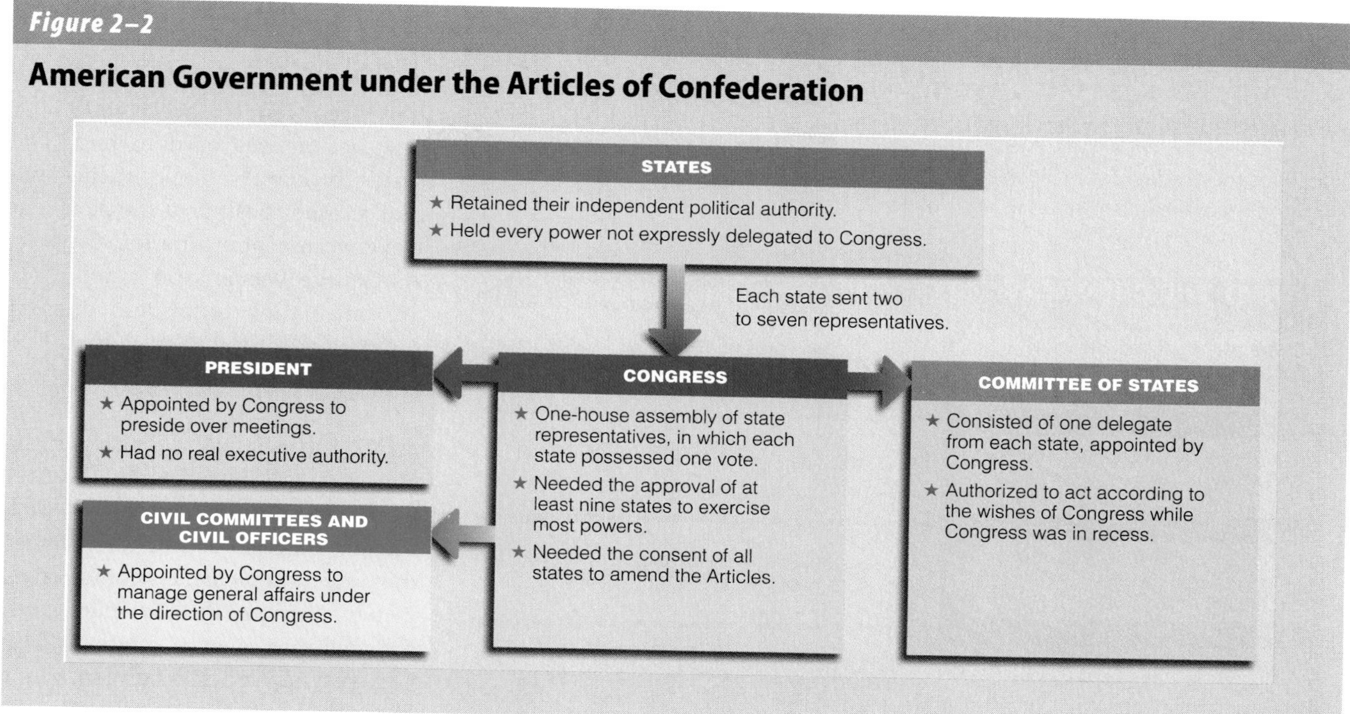

independent states (see Chapter 3). The member states agree to let the central government undertake a limited number of activities, such as forming an army, but do not allow the central government to place many restrictions on the states' own actions. The member states typically can still govern most state affairs as they see fit.

On November 15, 1777, the Second Continental Congress agreed on a draft of the plan, which was finally signed by all thirteen colonies on March 1, 1781. The **Articles of Confederation**, the result of this plan, served as this nation's first national constitution and represented an important step in the creation of our governmental system.[13]

The Articles of Confederation established the Congress of the Confederation as the central governing body. This congress was a unicameral assembly of representatives, or ambassadors, as they were called, from the various states. Although each state could send from two to seven representatives to the congress, each state, no matter what its size, had only one vote. The issue of sovereignty was an important part of the Articles of Confederation:

> Each State retains its sovereignty, freedom, and independence, and every power, jurisdiction, and right, which is not by this Confederation expressly delegated to the United States in Congress assembled.

The structure of government under the Articles of Confederation is shown in Figure 2–2 above.

Powers of the Government of the Confederation

Congress had several powers under the Articles of Confederation, and these enabled the new nation to achieve a number of accomplishments (see Figure 2–3 on page 32). The Northwest Ordinance settled states' claims to many of the western lands and established a basic pattern for the government of new territories. Also, the 1783 peace treaty negotiated with Britain granted to the United States all of the territory from the Atlantic Ocean to the Mississippi River and from the Great Lakes and Canada to what is now northern Florida.

In spite of these accomplishments, the central government created by the Articles of Confederation was quite weak. The Congress of the Confederation had no power to raise revenues for the militia or to force the states to meet military quotas. Essentially, this meant that the new government did not have the power to enforce its laws. Even passing laws was difficult because the Articles of Confederation provided that nine states had to approve any law before it was enacted. Figure 2–4 on page 33 lists these and

Articles of Confederation The nation's first national constitution, which established a national form of government following the American Revolution. The Articles provided for a confederal form of government in which the central government had few powers.

Figure 2–3

Powers of the Central Government under the Articles of Confederation

Although the Articles of Confederation were later scrapped, they did allow the early government of the United States to achieve several important goals, including winning the Revolutionary War.

WHAT THE CONGRESS COULD DO	ACCOMPLISHMENT
Congress could establish and control the armed forces, declare war, and make peace.	The United States won the Revolutionary War.
Congress could enter into treaties and alliances.	Congress negotiated a peace treaty with Britain.
Congress could settle disputes among the states under certain circumstances.	Congress passed the Northwest Ordinance, which settled certain states' land claims.
Congress could regulate coinage (but not paper money) and set standards for weights and measures.	Congress carried out these functions, but the inability to regulate paper money proved a major weakness.
Congress could borrow money from the people.	Congress did borrow money, but without the power to tax, it had trouble repaying the loans or obtaining new ones.
Congress could create a postal system, courts to address issues related to ships at sea, and government departments.	Congress created a postal system and departments of foreign affairs, finance, and war.

other powers that the central government lacked under the Articles of Confederation.

Nonetheless, the Articles of Confederation proved to be a good "first draft" for the Constitution, and at least half of the text of the Articles would later appear in the Constitution. The Articles were an unplanned experiment that tested some of the principles of government that had been set forth earlier in the Declaration of Independence. Some argue that without the experience of government under the Articles of Confederation, it would have been difficult, if not impossible, to arrive at the compromises that were necessary to create the Constitution several years later.

Shays' Rebellion A rebellion of angry farmers in western Massachusetts in 1786, led by former Revolutionary War captain Daniel Shays. This rebellion and other similar uprisings in the New England states emphasized the need for a true national government.

A Time of Crisis—The 1780s

The Revolutionary War ended on October 18, 1781. The Treaty of Paris, which confirmed the colonies' independence from Britain, was signed in 1783. Peace with the British may have been won, but peace within the new nation was hard to find. The states bickered among themselves and refused to support the new central government in almost every way. As George Washington stated, "We are one nation today and thirteen tomorrow. Who will treat [with] us on such terms?"

Indeed, the national government, such as it was, did not have the ability to prevent the various states from entering into agreements with foreign powers, despite the danger that such agreements could completely disrupt the confederation, pitting state against state. When Congress proved reluctant to admit Vermont into the Union, Britain began negotiations with influential Vermonters with the aim of annexing the district to Canada. Likewise, the Spanish governor of Louisiana energetically sought to detach Tennessee and the lands south of it from the United States. Several prominent individuals—including Daniel Boone—accepted Spanish gold.

The states also increasingly taxed each other's imports and at times even prevented trade altogether. By 1784, the new nation was suffering from a serious economic depression. States started printing their own money at dizzying rates, which led to inflation. Banks were calling in old loans and refusing to issue new ones. Individuals who could not pay their debts were often thrown into prison.

SHAYS' REBELLION The tempers of angry farmers in western Massachusetts reached the boiling point in August 1786. Former Revolutionary War captain Daniel Shays, along with approximately two thousand armed farmers, seized county courthouses and disrupted the debtors' trials. Shays and his men then launched an attack on the national government's arsenal in Springfield. **Shays' Rebellion** continued to grow in intensity and lasted into the winter, when it was finally stopped by the Massachusetts volunteer army, paid by private funds.[14]

Similar disruptions occurred throughout most of the New England states and in some other areas as well.

Figure 2–4

Powers That the Central Government Lacked under the Articles of Confederation

The government's lack of certain powers under the Articles of Confederation taught the framers of the Constitution several important lessons, which helped them create a more effective government under that new document.

WHAT THE CONGRESS COULD NOT DO	RESULT
Congress could not force the states to meet military quotas.	The central government could not draft soldiers to form a standing army.
Congress could not regulate commerce between the states or with other nations.	Each state was free to set up its own system of taxes on goods imported from other states. Economic quarrels among the states broke out. There was difficulty in trading with other nations.
Congress could enter into treaties but could not enforce its power or control foreign relations.	The states were not forced to respect treaties. Many states entered into treaties independent of Congress.
Congress could not directly tax the people.	The central government had to rely on the states to collect and forward taxes, which the states were reluctant to do. The central government was always short of money.
Congress had no power to enforce its laws.	The central government depended on the states to enforce its laws, which they rarely did.
Nine states had to approve any law before it was enacted.	Most laws were difficult, if not impossible, to enact.
Any amendment to the Articles required all thirteen states to consent.	In practice, the powers of the central government could not be changed.
There was no national judicial system.	Most disputes among the states could not be settled by the central government.
There was no executive branch.	Coordinating the work of the central government was almost impossible.

Constitutional Convention The convention (meeting) of delegates from the states that was held in Philadelphia in 1787 for the purpose of amending the Articles of Confederation. In fact, the delegates wrote a new constitution (the U.S. Constitution) that established a federal form of government to replace the governmental system that had been created by the Articles of Confederation.

The upheavals, and particularly Shays' Rebellion, were an important catalyst for change. The revolts scared American political and business leaders and caused more and more Americans to realize that a *true* national government had to be created.

THE ANNAPOLIS MEETING The Virginia legislature called for a meeting of representatives from all of the states at Annapolis, Maryland, on September 11, 1786, to consider extending national authority to issues of commerce. Five of the thirteen states sent delegates, two of whom were Alexander Hamilton of New York and James Madison of Virginia. Both of these men favored a strong central government.[15] They persuaded the other delegates to issue a report calling on the states to hold a convention in Philadelphia in May of the following year.

The Congress of the Confederation at first was reluctant to give its approval to the Philadelphia convention. By mid-February 1787, however, seven of the states had named delegates to the Philadelphia meeting. Finally, on February 21, the congress called on the states to send delegates to Philadelphia "for the sole and express purpose of revising the Articles of Confederation." That Philadelphia meeting became the **Constitutional Convention**.

LO4 *Drafting and Ratifying the Constitution*

Although the convention was supposed to start on May 14, 1787, few of the delegates had actually arrived in Philadelphia on that date. The convention formally opened in the East Room of the Pennsylvania State House

Library of Congress

The delegates to the Constitutional Convention discuss the fine points of the new Constitution in 1787.

business owners, and twenty-one had fought in the Revolutionary War. In other words, the delegates to the convention constituted an elite assembly. No ordinary farmers or merchants were present. Indeed, in his classic work on the Constitution, Charles Beard maintained that the Constitution was produced primarily by wealthy bondholders who had made loans to the government under the Articles and wanted a strong central government that could prevent state governments from repudiating debts.[17] Later historians, however, rejected Beard's thesis, concluding that bondholders played no special role in writing the Constitution.

on May 25, after fifty-five of the seventy-four delegates had arrived.[16] Only Rhode Island, where feelings were strong against creating a more powerful central government, did not send any delegates.

Who Were the Delegates?

Among the delegates to the Constitutional Convention were some of the nation's best-known leaders. George Washington was present, as were Alexander Hamilton, James Madison, George Mason, Robert Morris, and Benjamin Franklin (then eighty-one years old), who had to be carried to the convention on a portable chair. Some notable leaders were absent, including Thomas Jefferson and John Adams, who were serving as ambassadors in Europe, and Patrick Henry, who did not attend because he "smelt a rat." (Henry was one of Virginia's most strongly republican leaders.)

For the most part, the delegates were from the best-educated and wealthiest classes. Thirty-three delegates were lawyers, nearly half of the delegates were college graduates, three were physicians, seven were former chief executives of their respective states, six owned large plantations, at least nineteen owned slaves, eight were important

"THE CONSTITUTION only gives people the right to pursue happiness. You have to catch it yourself."

~ BENJAMIN FRANKLIN ~
AMERICAN STATESMAN AND SIGNER OF THE CONSTITUTION
1706–1790

The Virginia Plan

James Madison had spent months reviewing European political theory before he went to the Philadelphia convention. His Virginia delegation arrived before anybody else, and he immediately put its members to work. On the first day of the convention, Governor Edmund Randolph of Virginia was able to present fifteen resolutions outlining what was to become known as the *Virginia Plan.* This was a masterful political stroke on the part of the Virginia delegation. Its proposals immediately set the agenda for the remainder of the convention.

The fifteen resolutions contained in the Virginia Plan proposed an entirely new national government under a constitution. The plan, which favored large states such as Virginia, called for the following:

- A bicameral legislature. The lower house was to be chosen by the people. The smaller upper house was to be chosen by the elected members of the lower house. The number of representatives would be in proportion to each state's population (the larger states would have more representatives). The legislature could void any state laws.
- A national executive branch, elected by the legislature.

The Bridgeman Art Library/Getty Images

The international trade in slaves continued until 1808.

- A national court system, created by the legislature.

The smaller states immediately complained because they would have fewer representatives in the legislature. After two weeks of debate, they offered their own plan—the *New Jersey Plan.*

The New Jersey Plan

William Paterson of New Jersey presented an alternative plan favorable to the smaller states. He argued that because each state had an equal vote under the Articles of Confederation, the convention had no power to change this arrangement. The New Jersey Plan proposed the following:

- Congress would be able to regulate trade and impose taxes.
- Each state would have only one vote.
- Acts of Congress would be the supreme law of the land.
- An executive office of more than one person would be elected by Congress.
- The executive office would appoint a national supreme court.

The Compromises

Most delegates were unwilling to consider the New Jersey Plan. When the Virginia Plan was brought up again, however, delegates from the smaller states threatened to leave, and the convention was in danger of dissolving. On July 16, Roger Sherman of Connecticut broke the deadlock by proposing a compromise plan. Compromises on other disputed issues followed.

THE GREAT COMPROMISE Roger Sherman's plan, which has become known as the **Great Compromise** (or the Connecticut Compromise), called for a legislature with two houses:

- A lower house (the House of Representatives), in which the number of representatives from each state would be determined by the number of people in that state.
- An upper house (the Senate), which would have two members from each state; the members would be elected by the state legislatures.

The Great Compromise gave something to both sides: the large states would have more representatives in the House of Representatives than the small states, yet each state would be granted equality in the Senate—because each state, regardless of size, would have two senators. The Great Compromise thus resolved the small-state/large-state controversy.

THE THREE-FIFTHS COMPROMISE A second compromise had to do with how many representatives each state would have in the House of Representatives. Although slavery was legal in parts of the North, most slaves and slave owners lived in the South. Indeed, in the southern states, slaves constituted about 40 percent of the population. Counting the slaves as part of the population would thus greatly increase the number of southern representatives in the House. The delegates from the southern states wanted the slaves to be counted as persons; the delegates from the northern states disagreed. Eventually, the **three-fifths compromise** settled this deadlock: each slave would count as three-fifths of a person in determining representation in Congress. (The three-fifths compromise was eventually overturned in 1868 by the Fourteenth Amendment.)

Great Compromise A plan for a bicameral legislature in which one chamber would be based on population and the other chamber would represent each state equally. The plan, also known as the Connecticut Compromise, resolved the small-state/large-state controversy.

three-fifths compromise A compromise reached during the Constitutional Convention by which three-fifths of all slaves were to be counted for purposes of representation in the House of Representatives.

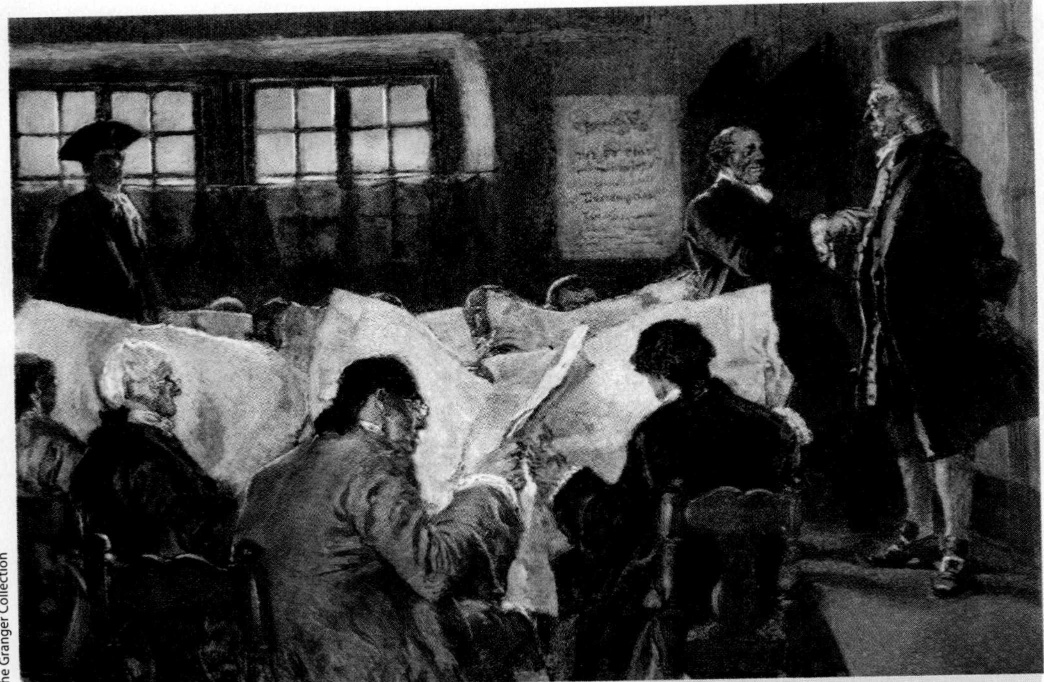
The Granger Collection

The fate of the proposed Constitution was decided in the state ratifying conventions (nine states had to ratify for the Constitution to take effect), but it was the subject of intense debates everywhere—in homes, taverns, coffeehouses, and newspapers. By the time New Hampshire became the ninth state to ratify the Constitution in June 1788, it had become clear that the people of the United States demanded a bill of rights.

SLAVE IMPORTATION The three-fifths compromise did not satisfy everyone at the Constitutional Convention. Many delegates wanted slavery to be banned completely in the United States. The delegates compromised on this question by agreeing that Congress could prohibit the importation of slaves into the country beginning in 1808. The issue of slavery itself, however, was never really addressed by the delegates to the Constitutional Convention. As a result, the South won twenty years of unrestricted slave trade and a requirement that escaped slaves who had fled to the northern states be returned to their owners. Domestic slave trading was untouched.

BANNING EXPORT TAXES The South's economic health depended in large part on its exports of agricultural products. The South feared that the northern majority in Congress might pass taxes on these exports. This fear led to yet another compromise: the South agreed to let Congress have the power to regulate **interstate commerce** as well as commerce with other nations; in exchange, the Constitution guaranteed that no export taxes would ever be imposed on products exported by the states. Today, the United States is one of the few countries that does not tax its exports.

interstate commerce
Trade that involves more than one state.

The Final Draft Is Approved

The Great Compromise was reached by mid-July. Still to be determined was the makeup of the executive branch and the judiciary. A five-man Committee of Detail undertook the remainder of this work and on August 6 presented a rough draft to the convention. On September 8, a committee was named to "revise the stile [style] of, and arrange the Articles which had been agreed to" by the convention. The Committee of Style was headed by Gouverneur Morris of Pennsylvania.[18] On September 17, 1787, the final draft of the Constitution was approved by thirty-nine of the remaining forty-two delegates (some delegates left early).

Looking back on the drafting of the Constitution, an obvious question emerges: Why didn't the founders ban slavery outright? Certainly, as already mentioned, many of the delegates thought that slavery was morally wrong and that the Constitution should ban it entirely. Many Americans have since regarded the framers' failure to deal with the slavery issue as a betrayal of the Declaration of Independence, which proclaimed that "all Men are created equal." Others have pointed out how contradictory it was that the framers of the Constitution complained about being "enslaved" by the British yet ignored the problem of slavery in this country.

A common argument supporting the framers' action (or lack of it) with respect to slavery is that they had no alternative but to ignore the issue. If they had taken a stand on slavery, the Constitution certainly would not have been ratified. Indeed, if the antislavery delegates had

PERCEPTION VERSUS
REALITY
The Slavery Issue

In the Declaration of Independence, Thomas Jefferson, a Virginia slave owner, pronounced, "all Men are created equal." Jefferson considered slavery a "hideous blot" on America. George Washington, also a southern slave owner, regarded the institution of slavery as "repugnant." Patrick Henry, another southerner, also publicly deplored slavery. Given such views among the leading figures of the era, why didn't the founders stay true to the Declaration of Independence and free the slaves?

The Perception

Most Americans assume that southern economic interests and racism alone led the founders to abandon the principles of equality expressed in the Declaration of Independence. African slaves were the backbone of American agriculture, particularly for tobacco, the most profitable export. Without their slaves, southern plantation owners would not have been able to earn such high profits. Presumably, southerners would not have ratified the Constitution unless it protected the institution of slavery.

The Reality

The third chief justice of the United States Supreme Court, Oliver Ellsworth, declared that "as population increases, poor laborers will be so plenty as to render slaves useless. Slavery in time will not be a speck in our country."[19] He was wrong, of course. But according to Pulitzer Prize–winning historian Gordon S. Wood, Ellsworth's sentiments mirrored those of most prominent leaders in the United States in the years leading up to the creation of our Constitution. Indeed, great thinkers of the time firmly believed that the liberal principles of the Revolution would destroy the institution of slavery.

At the time of the Constitutional Convention, slavery was disappearing in the northern states (it would be eliminated there by 1804). Many founders thought the same thing would happen in the southern states. After all, there were more antislavery societies in the South than in the North. The founders also thought that the ending of the international slave trade in 1808 would eventually end slavery in the United States. Consequently, the issue of slavery was taken off the table when the Constitution was created simply because the founders had a mistaken belief about the longevity of the institution. They could not have predicted at the time that the slave states, particularly Virginia, could produce slaves for the expanding areas of the Deep South and the Southwest.[20]

Blog On *Slavery and the Constitution is just one of many subjects that you can read about in the Legal History Blog at* **legalhistoryblog.blogspot.com.** *If you type "slavery" into the Search Blog box and hit Enter, you will see the full list of postings on this topic.*

insisted on banning slavery, the delegates from the southern states might have walked out of the convention—and there would have been no Constitution to ratify. For another look at this issue, however, see this chapter's *Perception versus Reality* feature above.

The Debate over Ratification

The ratification of the Constitution set off a national debate of unprecedented proportions. The battle was fought chiefly by two opposing groups—the **Federalists** (those who favored a strong central government and the new Constitution) and the **Anti-Federalists** (those who opposed a strong central government and the new Constitution).

In the debate over ratification, the Federalists had several advantages. They assumed a positive name, leaving their opposition with a negative label. (Indeed, the Anti-Federalists could well have called themselves republicans and their opponents nationalists.) The Federalists also had attended the Constitutional Convention and thus were familiar with the arguments both in favor of and against various

Federalists A political group, led by Alexander Hamilton and John Adams, that supported the adoption of the Constitution and the creation of a federal form of government.

Anti-Federalists A political group that opposed the adoption of the Constitution because of the document's centralist tendencies and because it did not include a bill of rights.

constitutional provisions. The Anti-Federalists, in contrast, had no actual knowledge of those discussions because they had not attended the convention. The Federalists also had time, money, and prestige on their side. Their impressive list of political thinkers and writers included Alexander Hamilton, John Jay, and James Madison. The Federalists could communicate with one another more readily because many of them were bankers, lawyers, and merchants who lived in urban areas, where communication was easier. The Federalists organized a quick and effective ratification campaign to elect themselves as delegates to each state's ratifying convention.

THE FEDERALISTS ARGUE FOR RATIFICATION

Alexander Hamilton, a leading Federalist, began to answer the Constitution's critics in New York by writing newspaper columns under the pseudonym "Caesar." The Caesar letters appeared to have little effect, so Hamilton switched his pseudonym to "Publius" and enlisted John Jay and James Madison to help him write the papers. In a period of less than a year, these three men wrote a series of eighty-five essays in defense of the Constitution. These essays, which were printed not only in New York newspapers but also in other papers throughout the states, are collectively known as the *Federalist Papers*.

Generally, the papers attempted to allay the fears expressed by the Constitution's critics. One fear was that the rights of minority groups would not be protected. Another was that a minority might block the passage of measures that the majority felt were in the national interest. Many critics also feared that a republican form of government would not work in a nation the size of the United States. Various groups, or **factions**, would struggle for power, and chaos would result. Madison responded to the latter argument in *Federalist Paper* No. 10 (see Appendix F), which is considered a classic in political theory. Among other things, Madison argued that the nation's size was actually an advantage in controlling factions: in a large nation, there would be so many diverse interests and factions that no one faction would be able to gain control of the government.[21]

THE ANTI-FEDERALISTS' RESPONSE Perhaps the greatest advantage of the Anti-Federalists was that they stood for the status quo. Usually, it is more difficult to institute changes than it is to keep what is already known and understood. Among the Anti-Federalists were such patriots as Patrick Henry and Samuel Adams. Patrick Henry said of the proposed Constitution: "I look upon that paper as the most fatal plan that could possibly be conceived to enslave a free people."

faction A group of persons forming a cohesive minority.

tyranny The arbitrary or unrestrained exercise of power by an oppressive individual or government.

In response to the *Federalist Papers,* the Anti-Federalists published their own essays, using such pseudonyms as "Montezuma" and "Philadelphiensis." They also wrote brilliantly, attacking nearly every clause of the new document. Many Anti-Federalists contended that the Constitution had been written by aristocrats and would lead the nation to aristocratic **tyranny** (the exercise of absolute, unlimited power). Other Anti-Federalists feared that the Constitution would lead to an overly powerful central government that would limit personal freedom.[22]

The Anti-Federalists strongly argued that the Constitution needed a bill of rights. They warned that without a bill of rights, a strong national government might take away the political rights won during the American Revolution. They demanded that the new Constitution clearly guarantee personal freedoms. The Federalists generally did not think that a bill of rights was all that important. Nevertheless, to gain the necessary support, the Federalists finally promised to add a bill of rights to the Constitution as the first order of business under the new government. This promise turned the tide in favor of the Constitution.

Ratification

The contest for ratification was close in several states, but the Federalists finally won in all of the state conventions. In 1787, Delaware, Pennsylvania, and New Jersey voted to ratify the Constitution, followed by Georgia and Connecticut early in the following year. Even though the Anti-Federalists were perhaps the majority in Massachusetts, a successful political campaign by the Federalists led to ratification by that state on February 6, 1788.

Following Maryland and South Carolina, New Hampshire became the ninth state to ratify the Constitution on June 21, 1788, thus formally putting the Constitution into effect. New York and Virginia had not yet ratified, however, and without them the Constitution would have no true power. That worry was dispelled in the summer of 1788, when both Virginia and New York ratified the new Constitution. North Carolina waited until November 21 of the following year to ratify the Constitution, and Rhode Island did not ratify until May 29, 1790.

LO5 *The Constitution's Major Principles of Government*

The framers of the Constitution were fearful of the powerful British monarchy, against which they had so recently rebelled. At the same time, they wanted a central government strong enough to prevent the kinds of crises that had occurred under the weak central authority of the Articles of Confederation. The principles of government expressed in the Constitution reflect both of these concerns.

Limited Government and Popular Sovereignty

The Constitution incorporated the principle of limited government, which means that government can do only what the people allow it to do through the exercise of a duly developed system of laws. This principle can be found in many parts of the Constitution. For example, while Articles I, II, and III indicate exactly what the national government *can* do, the first nine amendments to the Constitution list the ways in which the government *cannot* limit certain individual freedoms.

Implicitly, the principle of limited government rests on the concept of popular sovereignty. Remember the phrases that frame the Preamble to the Constitution: "We the People of the United States . . . do ordain and establish this Constitution for the United States of America." In other words, it is the people who form the government and decide on the powers that the government can exercise. If the government exercises powers beyond those granted to it by the Constitution, it is acting illegally. The idea that no one, including government officers, is above the law is often called the **rule of law.**

Ultimately, the viability of a democracy rests on the willingness of the people and their leaders to adhere to the rule of law. A nation's written constitution, such as that of Iraq under the dictator Saddam Hussein, may guarantee numerous rights and liberties for its citizens. Yet, unless the government of that nation enforces those rights and liberties, the law does not rule the nation. Rather, the government decides what the rules will be. Consider the situation in Russia today. After the collapse of the Soviet Union, Russia established a federal republic. By all appearances, though, Vladimir Putin, Russia's leader, is not constrained by the principles set forth in Russia's constitution—see this chapter's *The Rest of the World* feature on the next page for details.

"The liberties of a people NEVER WERE NOR EVER WILL BE SECURE WHEN THE TRANSACTIONS OF THEIR RULERS MAY BE CONCEALED FROM THEM."

~ PATRICK HENRY ~
AMERICAN STATESMAN AND SIGNER OF THE CONSTITUTION
1736–1799

The Principle of Federalism

The Constitution also incorporated the principle of federalism. In a **federal system** of government, the central (national) government shares sovereign powers with the various state governments. Federalism was the solution to the debate over whether the national government or the states should have ultimate sovereignty.

The Constitution gave the national government significant powers—powers that it had not had under the Articles of Confederation. For example, the Constitution expressly states that the president is the nation's chief executive as well as the commander in chief of the armed forces. The Constitution also declares that the Constitution and the laws created by the national government are supreme—that is, they take precedence over conflicting state laws. Other powers given to the national government include the power to coin money, to levy and collect taxes, and to regulate interstate commerce, a power granted by the **commerce clause.** Finally, the national government was authorized to undertake all laws that are "necessary and proper" to carrying out its expressly delegated powers.

The founders granted the federal government exclusive rights over creating money because in previous years, several states had printed excessive quantities of paper money, thus devaluing the currency. How might the founders react to the way in which today's federal government manages the money supply? Consider that question as you read this chapter's *Our Government's Response to the Economic Crisis* feature on page 41.

rule of law A basic principle of government that requires those who govern to act in accordance with established law.

federal system A form of government that provides for a division of powers between a central government and several regional governments. In the United States, the division of powers between the national government and the states is established by the Constitution.

commerce clause The clause in Article I, Section 8, of the Constitution that gives Congress the power to regulate interstate commerce (commerce involving more than one state).

THE REST OF THE WORLD

Russia's Short-Lived Flirtation with Democracy

From the Russian Revolution in 1917 to the end of the Soviet Union in 1991, Russians lived under a Communist dictatorship. For centuries prior to 1917, they had lived under an autocracy headed by a tsar. In short, Russians had no experience with democracy before the fall of the Soviet Union.

A Democracy at Last . . .

On December 25, 1993, the Russian Federation (its formal name) saw its first independent constitution. If you read a translation of that constitution, you would conclude that modern Russia is now a democracy. That conclusion seemed to be true for a number of years because Russians freely voted for members of the Duma (the Russian counterpart of our Congress). They voted overwhelmingly in favor of President Vladimir Putin in 2000, too. Western commentators expressed some concern when Putin was formerly the head of the Soviet Union's brutal secret service. Nevertheless, after meeting Putin, President George W. Bush said, "I looked him in the eyes, and I know I can work with this man."

. . . or Not

Perhaps Putin showed his true colors when he referred to the collapse of the Soviet Union as "the greatest geopolitical catastrophe of the twentieth century." Under Putin, freedom of the press all but disappeared—the state simultaneously shut down independent sources of information and expanded government ownership of the media. A formerly promising independent court system all but vanished. In 2005, the election of regional governors was abolished. Governors are now appointed by the president. Beginning in 2006, Putin's administration instituted electoral reforms so that his political party, United Russia, was guaranteed control of the Duma and the presidency. The government won the right to exclude candidates from party slates and to bar parties from running altogether.

Increasingly, Russian authorities arrested and detained public activists. In the economy, the Russian government gradually took control of all oil, natural gas, and other natural resources. Anyone who did not go along with Putin ended up in prison.

The Russian Public's Reaction

Are Russian citizens worried about this reversion to an undemocratic state? Apparently not, for public opinion polls in Russia have shown that more than 80 percent of the Russian people approve of Putin's "strong leadership."

In March 2008, Putin's second term as president came to an end, and under the constitution he could not immediately run again. Instead, he sponsored the election of Dmitry Medvedev, a supporter, as president. Medvedev named Putin as Russia's prime minister, and events soon proved that Putin still held the real power in the government. Putin recently hinted that he may return as president in 2012. Given that in that year the presidential term will expand from four years to six, Putin could remain in power until 2024.

For Critical Analysis *Why do you think so many Russians are unconcerned about the erosion of democracy in their country?*

Because the states feared too much centralized control, the Constitution also allowed for many states' rights. These rights include the power to regulate commerce within state borders and generally the authority to exercise any powers that are not delegated by the Constitution to the central government. (See Chapter 3 for a detailed discussion of federalism.)

Madisonian Model The model of government devised by James Madison, in which the powers of the government are separated into three branches: executive, legislative, and judicial.

separation of powers The principle of dividing governmental powers among the executive, the legislative, and the judicial branches of government.

checks and balances A major principle of American government in which each of the three branches is given the means to check (to restrain or balance) the actions of the others.

Separation of Powers

As James Madison once said, after you have given the government the ability to control its citizens, you have to "oblige it to control itself." To force the government to "control itself" and to prevent the rise of tyranny, Madison devised a scheme, the **Madisonian Model**, in which the powers of the national government were separated into different branches: legislative, executive, and judicial.[23] The legislative branch (Congress) passes laws; the executive branch (the president) administers and enforces the laws; and the judicial branch (the courts) interprets the laws. By separating the powers of government, the framers ensured that no one branch would have enough power to dominate the others. This principle of **separation of powers** is laid out in Articles I, II, and III of the Constitution.

Checks and Balances

A system of **checks and balances** was also devised to ensure that no one group or branch of government can exercise exclusive control. Even though each branch of government is independent of the others, it can also

Our Government's Response to the Economic Crisis

Keep Printing Money!

AP Photo/Doug Mills

The U.S. Constitution in Article I, Section 8, gave Congress the power "To borrow Money on the credit of the United States" and "To coin Money [and] regulate the value thereof." Today, the framers of the Constitution are probably turning over in their graves at what the federal government has done with the supply of money in circulation in this country.

What Is Monetary Policy?

Monetary policy involves changing the amount of money in circulation to affect interest rates, credit markets, the rate of inflation, the rate of economic growth, and the rate of unemployment. Monetary policy is not under the direct control of Congress and the president. Instead, it is determined by the Federal Reserve System (the Fed), an independent agency. The Fed was established by Congress as the nation's central bank in 1913. It is controlled by a board of seven governors, including the very powerful chairperson, currently Ben Bernanke. The president appoints the members of the board of governors, and the Senate must approve the nominations. Although the Fed's board of governors acts independently, the Fed has, on occasion, yielded to presidential pressure.

Before we analyze the current monetary policy in the face of the Great Recession that began in 2007, consider what happened during the Great Depression of the 1930s.

The Fed's Response to the Great Depression

The Fed was created to be the "lender of last resort" for the banking system, a bank that could lend to other banks when no one else would. It turns out that as the Great Depression took hold, the Fed acted in the opposite manner. Indeed, many scholars argue that the Fed was responsible for the severity of the Great Depression. Through a series of badly conceived actions, the Fed allowed the money supply in circulation to fall by fully one-third by 1933. The result was a severe contraction in economic activity. If we were grading the federal government's response to the Great Depression, we would have to say that when it comes to monetary policy, the government should receive an F.

Monetary Policy during the Current Economic Crisis

An examination of the Fed's monetary policy in the first decade of the twenty-first century results in a grade higher than F but certainly lower than A. The Fed overreacted to a short recession in 2001 with a radically lax monetary policy. It lowered interest rates on a regular basis, and so the money supply grew much more quickly than its historical average. (This was the equivalent of printing more money.) The result was a boom in housing and commodity prices that lasted for several years.

When the Great Recession began in December 2007, the Fed appeared not quite sure what to do. When the crisis became acute in September 2008, the Fed went along with the Bush administration's request to Congress to provide a fund of $700 billion to buy banking institutions' bad assets (many of which were mortgages that had gone sour). Bernanke worked closely with Treasury secretary Hank Paulson, and the Fed's traditional independence from the rest of the government disappeared.

To keep the crisis from getting worse, the Fed pushed the interest rate on short-term government debt down almost to zero. While this appeared to be a textbook example of the correct response to a recession, the Fed also began doing something it had never done before. It started buying huge quantities of debt directly from the private sector—bonds backed up by mortgages, credit-card debt, and student loans. This practice has been named "quantitative easing." These purchases have the effect of creating new money and expanding the money supply.

What the Future Holds

Many economists fear that by creating money in this way, the Fed has guaranteed that inflation will be a serious problem when the recession comes to an end. True, for the moment, the newly created money simply replaces funds that are "parked by the curb"—that is, pulled out of action by institutions and investors that are afraid to lend. Sooner or later, though, that sidelined money will be put to work again, and that's when inflation becomes a danger. Will the Fed be able to react quickly enough to prevent a big rise in prices? The historical record is not encouraging.

For Critical Analysis *Why do you think Congress gave control over monetary policy to an independent body?*

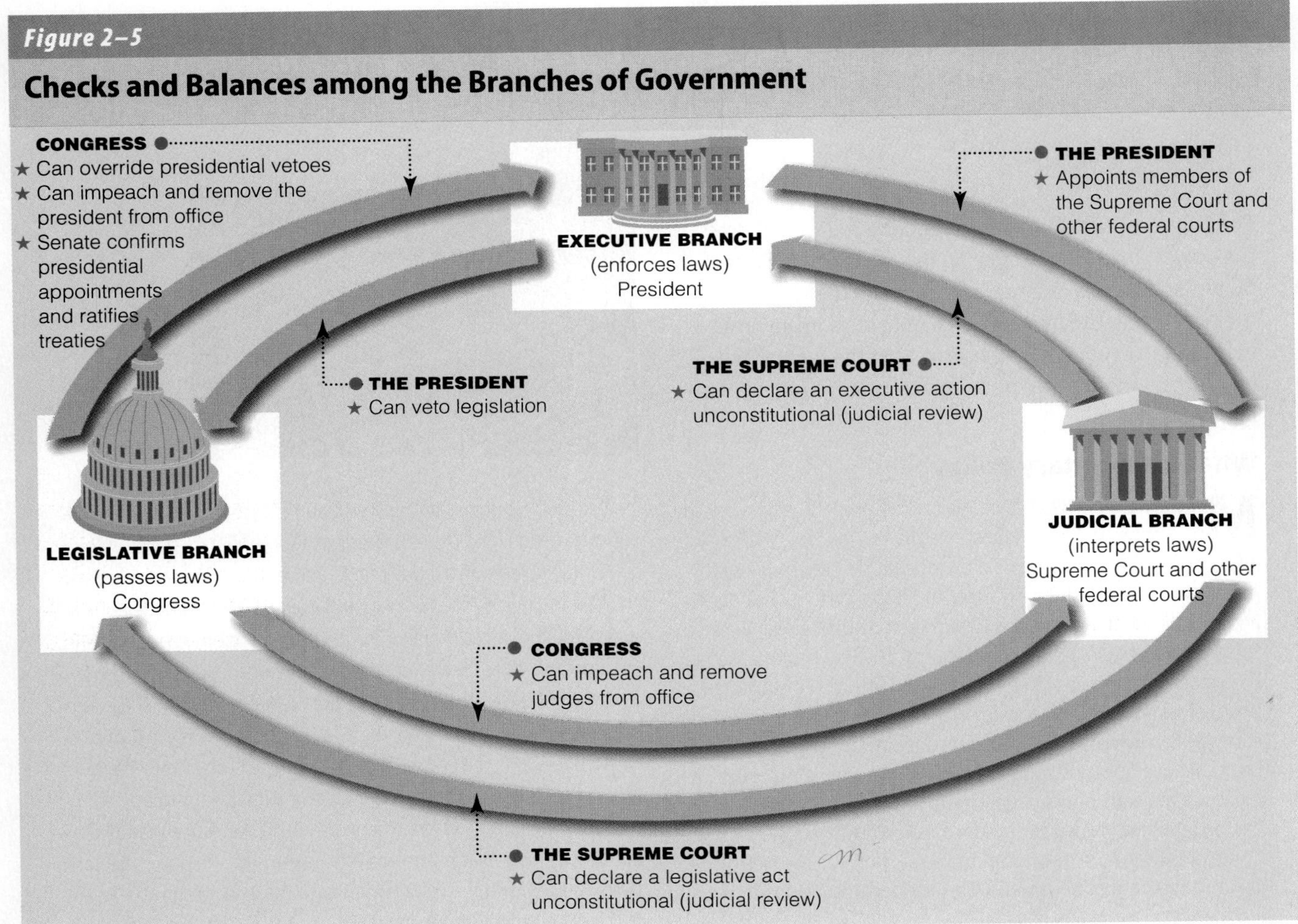

Figure 2–5

Checks and Balances among the Branches of Government

check the actions of the others. Look at Figure 2–5 above, and you can see how this is done. As the figure shows, the president checks Congress by holding a **veto power**, which is the ability to return bills to Congress for reconsideration. Congress, in turn, controls taxes and spending, and the Senate must approve presidential appointments. The judicial branch of government can also check the other branches of government through *judicial review*—the power to rule congressional or presidential actions unconstitutional.[24] In turn, the president and the Senate exercise some control over the judiciary through the president's power to appoint federal judges and the Senate's role in confirming presidential appointments.

veto power A constitutional power that enables the chief executive (president or governor) to reject legislation and return it to the legislature with reasons for the rejection. This prevents or at least delays the bill from becoming law.

Among the other checks and balances built into the American system of government are staggered terms of office. Members of the House of Representatives serve for two years, members of the Senate for six, and the president for four. Federal court judges are appointed for life but may be impeached and removed from office by Congress for misconduct. Staggered terms and changing government personnel make it difficult for individuals within the government to form controlling factions. The American system of government also includes numerous other checks and balances, many of which you will read about in later chapters of this book. We look next at another obvious check on the powers of government: the Bill of Rights.

The Bill of Rights

To secure the ratification of the Constitution in several important states, the Federalists had to provide assurances that amendments would be passed to protect individual liberties against violations by the national government. At the state ratifying conventions, delegates set forth specific rights that should be protected.

James Madison considered these recommendations as he labored to draft what became the Bill of Rights.

After sorting through more than two hundred state recommendations, Madison came up with sixteen amendments. Congress tightened the language somewhat and eliminated four of the amendments. Of the remaining twelve, two—one dealing with the apportionment of representatives and the other with the compensation of the members of Congress—were not ratified by the states during the ratification process.[25] By 1791, all of the states had ratified the ten amendments that now constitute our Bill of Rights. Table 2–2 on the following page presents the text of the first ten amendments to the Constitution, along with explanatory comments. Note that many phrases in the Bill of Rights are imprecise and call for further judicial interpretation. For example, what exactly did the founders mean by "cruel and unusual punishments" (Eighth Amendment)? We consider that issue in this chapter's *Join the Debate* feature on page 45.

The Constitution Compared with the Articles of Confederation

As mentioned earlier, the nation's experiences under the government of the Confederation, particularly the weakness of the central government, strongly influenced the writing of the U.S. Constitution. As a result, the Constitution shifted many powers from the states to the central government.

James Madison (1751–1836). Madison's contributions at the Constitutional Convention in 1787 earned him the title "Master Builder of the Constitution." As a member of Congress from Virginia, he advocated the Bill of Rights. He was secretary of state under Thomas Jefferson (1801–1809) and became our fourth president in 1809.

Library of Congress

One of the weaknesses of the Confederation had been the lack of an independent executive authority. The Constitution remedied this problem by creating an independent executive—the president—and by making the president commander in chief of the army and navy and of the state militias when called into national service. The president was also given extensive appointment powers, although Senate approval was required for certain appointments.

Another problem under the Confederation was the lack of a judiciary that was independent of the state courts. The Constitution established the United States Supreme Court and authorized Congress to establish other "inferior" federal courts.

To protect against possible wrongdoing, the Constitution also provided for a way to remove federal officials from office—through the impeachment process. The Constitution provides that a federal official who commits "Treason, Bribery, or other high Crimes and Misdemeanors" may be impeached (accused, or charged with wrongdoing) by the House of Representatives and tried by the Senate. If found guilty of the charges by a two-thirds vote in the Senate, the official can be removed from office and prevented from ever assuming another federal government post. The official may also face judicial proceedings for the alleged wrongdoing after removal from office.

Under the Articles of Confederation, amendments to the Articles required the unanimous consent of the states. As a result, it was virtually impossible to amend the Articles. As you will read shortly, the framers of the Constitution provided for an amendment process that requires the approval of three-fourths of the states. Although the process is still extraordinarily cumbersome, it is easier to amend the Constitution than it was to change the Articles of Confederation.

Amending the Constitution

Since the Constitution was written, more than eleven thousand amendments have been introduced in Congress. Nonetheless, in the years since the ratification of the Bill of Rights, the first ten amendments to the Constitution, only seventeen proposed amendments have actually survived the amendment process and become a part of our Constitution. It is often contended that members of Congress use the amendment process simply as a political ploy. By proposing an amendment, a member of Congress can show her or his position on an issue, knowing that the odds *against* the amendment's being adopted are high.

Table 2–2

The Bill of Rights

Amendment I.
Religion, Speech, Press, Assembly, and Petition

Congress shall make no law respecting an establishment of religion, or prohibiting the free exercise thereof; or abridging the freedom of speech, or of the press; or the right of the people peaceably to assemble, and to petition the Government for a redress of grievances.

Congress may not create an official church or enact laws limiting the freedom of religion, speech, the press, assembly, and petition. These guarantees, like the others in the Bill of Rights (the first ten amendments), are not absolute—each may be exercised only with regard to the rights of other persons.

Amendment II.
Militia and the Right to Bear Arms

A well regulated Militia, being necessary to the security of a free State, the right of the people to keep and bear Arms, shall not be infringed.

Each state has the right to maintain a volunteer armed force. Although individuals have the right to bear arms, states and the federal government may regulate the possession and use of firearms by individuals.

Amendment III.
The Quartering of Soldiers

No Soldier shall, in time of peace be quartered in any house, without the consent of the Owner, nor in time of war, but in a manner to be prescribed by law.

Before the Revolutionary War, it had been common British practice to quarter soldiers in colonists' homes. Military troops do not have the power to take over private houses during peacetime.

Amendment IV.
Searches and Seizures

The right of the people to be secure in their persons, houses, papers, and effects, against unreasonable searches and seizures, shall not be violated, and no Warrants shall issue, but upon probable cause, supported by Oath or affirmation, and particularly describing the place to be searched, and the persons or things to be seized.

Here, the word warrant *refers to a document issued by a magistrate or judge indicating the name, address, and possible offense committed. Anyone asking for the warrant, such as a police officer, must be able to convince the magistrate or judge that an offense probably has been committed.*

Amendment V.
Grand Juries, Self-Incrimination, Double Jeopardy, Due Process, and Eminent Domain

No person shall be held to answer for a capital, or otherwise infamous crime, unless on a presentment or indictment of a Grand Jury, except in cases arising in the land or naval forces, or in the Militia, when in actual service in time of War or public danger; nor shall any person be subject for the same offense to be twice put in jeopardy of life or limb; nor shall be compelled in any criminal case to be a witness against himself, nor be deprived of life, liberty, or property, without due process of law; nor shall private property be taken for public use, without just compensation.

There are two types of juries. A grand jury considers physical evidence and the testimony of witnesses and decides whether there is sufficient reason to bring a case to trial. A petit jury hears the case at trial and decides it. "For the same offense to be twice put in jeopardy of life or limb" means to be tried twice for the same crime. A person may not be tried for the same crime twice or forced to give evidence against herself or himself. No person's right to life, liberty, or property may be taken away except by lawful means, called the due process of law. Private property taken for public purposes must be paid for by the government.

Amendment VI.
Criminal Court Procedures

In all criminal prosecutions, the accused shall enjoy the right to a speedy and public trial, by an impartial jury of the State and district wherein the crime shall have been committed, which district shall have been previously ascertained by law, and to be informed of the nature and cause of the accusation; to be confronted with the witnesses against him; to have compulsory process for obtaining witnesses in his favor, and to have the Assistance of Counsel for his defence.

Any person accused of a crime has the right to a fair and public trial by a jury in the state in which the crime took place. The charges against that person must be so indicated. Any accused person has the right to a lawyer to defend him or her and to question those who testify against him or her, as well as the right to call people to speak in his or her favor at trial.

Amendment VII.
Trial by Jury in Civil Cases

In Suits at common law, where the value in controversy shall exceed twenty dollars, the right of trial by jury shall be preserved, and no fact tried by a jury, shall be otherwise re-examined in any Court of the United States, than according to the rules of the common law.

A jury trial may be requested by either party in a dispute in any case involving more than $20. If both parties agree to a trial by a judge without a jury, the right to a jury trial may be put aside.

Amendment VIII.
Bail, Cruel and Unusual Punishment

Excessive bail shall not be required, nor excessive fines imposed, nor cruel and unusual punishments inflicted.

Bail is that amount of money that a person accused of a crime may be required to deposit with the court as a guarantee that she or he will appear in court when requested. The amount of bail required or the fine imposed as punishment for a crime must be reasonable compared with the seriousness of the crime involved. Any punishment judged to be too harsh or too severe for a crime shall be prohibited.

Amendment IX.
The Rights Retained by the People

The enumeration in the Constitution, of certain rights, shall not be construed to deny or disparage others retained by the people.

Many civil rights that are not explicitly enumerated in the Constitution are still held by the people.

Amendment X.
Reserved Powers of the States

The powers not delegated to the United States by the Constitution, nor prohibited by it to the States, are reserved to the States respectively, or to the people.

Those powers not delegated by the Constitution to the federal government or expressly denied to the states belong to the states and to the people. This clause in essence allows the states to pass laws under their "police powers."

JOIN THE DEBATE

Is the Death Penalty a Cruel and Unusual Punishment?

The Bill of Rights is a series of amendments added to the U.S. Constitution in 1791. The Eighth Amendment explicitly states that the government cannot inflict "cruel and unusual punishments." Throwing a prisoner into a lake in Minnesota in the middle of winter and allowing him to die would certainly be considered a violation of the Eighth Amendment. Still, less painful methods of executing criminals have played a role in sentencing since the earliest days of the republic.

Even before there were prisons in America, we had the death penalty, also called "capital punishment." In 1608, a man named George Kendall was executed by a firing squad in Virginia on charges of spying for Spain. Since Kendall's time, more than 18,000 Americans have been executed as punishment for their crimes. In addition to murder, a variety of other crimes have been punished by death in this country. During the 1600s, colonists could be executed for murder (of course), but also for witchcraft, blasphemy, sodomy, and adultery. In the 1700s, citizens were executed for robbery, forgery, and illegally cutting down trees.

No state executes people for such crimes today. In our modern world, though, is the death penalty itself cruel and unusual, and therefore a violation of the Eighth Amendment?

An Eye for an Eye Makes the Whole World Blind

Some argue that the death penalty is inappropriate even for someone who has committed murder. Violence and death may always be with us, but the law should not encourage violent sentiments. When a government ceremoniously carries out the execution of a prisoner, that government is lending support to the destructive side of our nature. Already in 1764, the Italian jurist Cesare Beccaria asserted that "the death penalty cannot be useful, because of the example of barbarity it gives men."

As U.S. Supreme Court Justice Arthur J. Goldberg once wrote, "The deliberate institutionalized taking of human life by the state is the greatest conceivable degradation of the dignity of a human personality." Face it—capital punishment is barbaric whether it is carried out by a firing squad, an electric chair, a gas chamber, lethal injection, or hanging. Nations other than the United States that permit capital punishment are not ones that we would seek to emulate: they include China, Iran, North Korea, and Saudi Arabia. Almost all of our allies have abolished the practice. Even in the United States, the Supreme Court has ruled that the execution of persons who are mentally retarded or who committed their crimes while minors is cruel and unusual and therefore unconstitutional.

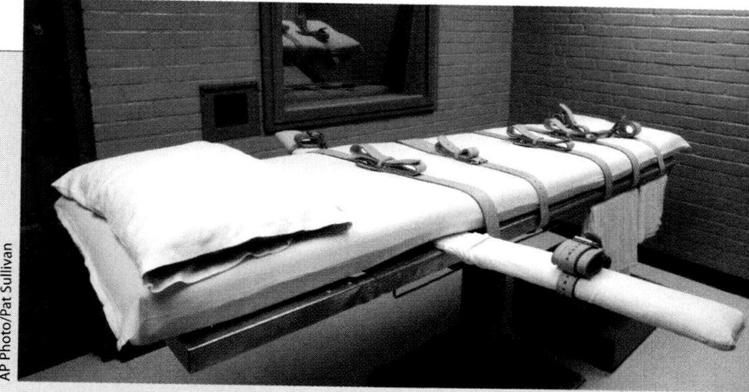
AP Photo/Pat Sullivan

There Is Nothing Cruel and Unusual about Executing a Murderer

In 1890, the Supreme Court stated that "punishments are cruel when they involve torture or a lingering death; but the punishment of death is not cruel, within the meaning of that word as used in the Constitution. [Cruel] implies . . . something inhuman and barbarous, something more than the mere extinguishment of life."

Strangely enough, some who are against capital punishment have argued that life in prison without parole is even crueler than death. Prisoners are confined in an environment of violence where they are treated like animals, and the suffering goes on for decades. If you think about it, this is an argument that the death sentence can be merciful. In any event, capital punishment is not cruel and unusual as meant by the Eighth Amendment. Indeed, the current method of execution used in most states—lethal injection—appears quite civilized compared with methods of execution used in England back in the 1700s, which included drawing and quartering and burning at the stake.

For Critical Analysis *Can there be a humane method of extinguishing someone's life? Why or why not?*

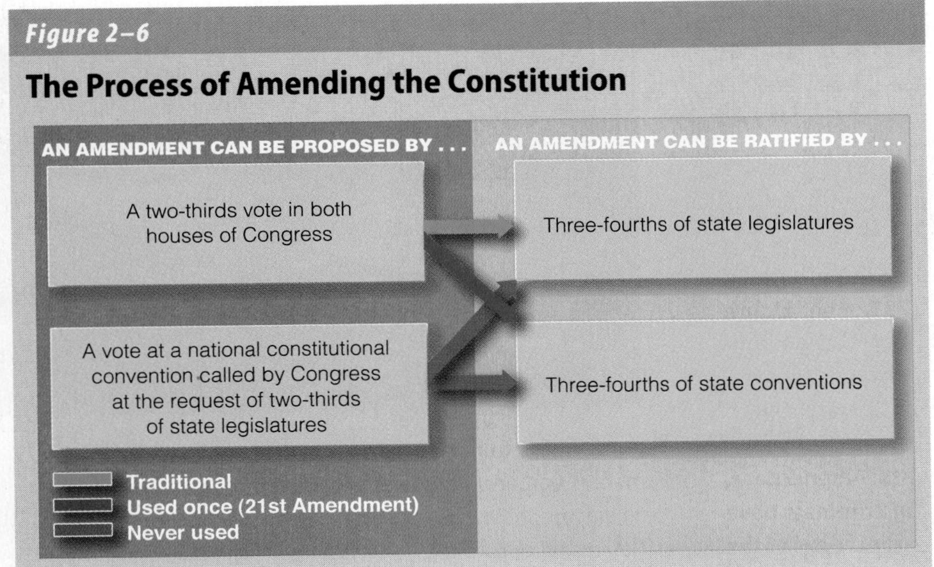

Figure 2–6

The Process of Amending the Constitution

One of the reasons there are so few amendments is that the framers, in Article V, made the formal amendment process difficult (although it was easier than it had been under the Articles of Confederation, as just discussed). There are two ways to propose an amendment and two ways to ratify one. As a result, there are four possible ways for an amendment to be added to the Constitution.

"The truth is that all men having power OUGHT TO BE MISTRUSTED."

~ JAMES MADISON ~
FOURTH PRESIDENT OF THE UNITED STATES
1809–1817

METHODS OF PROPOSING AN AMENDMENT The two methods of proposing an amendment are as follows:

1. A two-thirds vote in the Senate and in the House of Representatives is required. All of the twenty-seven existing amendments have been proposed in this way.
2. If two-thirds of the state legislatures request that Congress call a national amendment convention, then Congress must call one. The convention may propose amendments to the states for ratification. There has yet to be a successful amendment proposal using this method.

The notion of a national amendment convention is exciting to many people. Many national political and judicial leaders, however, are very uneasy about the prospect of convening a body that conceivably could do what the Constitutional Convention did—create a new form of government.

In two separate instances, the call for a national amendment convention almost became reality. Between 1963 and 1969, thirty-three state legislatures (out of the necessary thirty-four) attempted to call a convention to amend the Constitution to overturn the Supreme Court's "one person, one vote" decisions (see Chapter 11). Since 1975, thirty-two states have asked for a national convention to propose an amendment requiring that the federal government balance its budget. Generally, the major national convention campaigns have reflected dissatisfaction on the part of conservative and rural groups with the national government's social and economic policies.

METHODS OF RATIFYING AN AMENDMENT There are two methods of ratifying a proposed amendment:

1. Three-fourths of the state legislatures can vote in favor of the proposed amendment. This method is considered the "traditional" ratification method and has been used twenty-six times.
2. The states can call special conventions to ratify the proposed amendment. If three-fourths of the states approve, the amendment is ratified. This method has been used only once—to ratify the Twenty-first Amendment.[26]

You can see the four methods for proposing and ratifying amendments in Figure 2–6 above. As you can imagine, to meet the requirements for proposal and ratification, any amendment must have wide popular support in all regions of the country.

Independence Hall in Philadelphia.

AMERICA AT ODDS *The Constitution*

At the time the Constitution was created, there was a great deal of doubt about whether the arrangement would actually work. James Madison, among others, hoped that the framers had created a government "for the ages." Indeed, Madison's vision has been realized, in large part because of the division of governmental powers and the various checks and balances that were incorporated into the Constitution. These constitutional provisions have safeguarded the nation against tyranny—one of the greatest fears of the founders.

Yet, when drafting the Constitution, the framers left many issues unresolved. For example, Americans fighting the Revolutionary War agreed that they were fighting for liberty and equality. Once the war was over, however, there was little consensus on the meaning of these terms, and Americans have been at odds over how they should be interpreted for more than two hundred years. Additionally, as you read in this chapter, the founders left the issue of slavery to be debated by future generations—leading ultimately to the bloodbath of the Civil War and to problems that continue to challenge Americans even today. The fundamental disagreement between the Federalists and Anti-Federalists over how powerful the central government should be relative to the states is another conflict that has surfaced again and again. One of the most heated recent debates concerning the Constitution was whether President George W. Bush's expansion of presidential powers relative to those of Congress and the judiciary destroyed the balance of powers envisioned by the framers.

ISSUES FOR DEBATE & DISCUSSION

Some Americans believe that too many significant issues involving our constitutional rights and liberties are ultimately decided not by our elected representatives, but by the nine unelected justices on the Supreme Court. These Americans would like to see the constitutional amendment process be made simpler so that when disputes arise over the meaning of certain constitutional terms or concepts, such as whether the right to privacy includes the right to have an abortion, the Constitution could be amended to resolve the issue. Others believe that the framers made the amendment process difficult precisely so that the Constitution wouldn't be amended every time opinions on a certain issue changed. What is your position on this?

TAKE ACTION

As you have read, the founders envisioned that the Constitution, to remain relevant, would need to be changed over time. It has been amended twenty-seven times, but many more amendments have been proposed. You can take action in a debate over the Constitution by supporting or opposing a proposed amendment, such as the flag-burning amendment. In 1989, the Supreme Court ruled that state laws prohibiting the burning of the American flag as part of a peaceful protest violate the freedom of expression protected by the First Amendment. Until the Constitution is amended to allow flag-burning to be prohibited, the Supreme Court's ruling remains the law of the land. Congress has introduced resolutions on several occasions in the past, and again in January 2007, Congress introduced a resolution to propose a constitutional amendment giving Congress the power "to prohibit the physical desecration of the flag of the United States." If you strongly support or oppose this amendment, you can take action by writing your representatives and senators in Congress or by forming organizations to voice your concerns.

Samuel Peebles/*El Dorado News-Times*/AP

Amendments that would prohibit the burning of the American flag have been proposed in the past, but none has ever been ratified and become a part of the U.S. Constitution.

- A World Wide Web version of the Constitution provides hypertext links to amendments and other changes. Go to **www.law.cornell.edu/constitution/constitution.overview.html**
- The National Constitution Center in Philadelphia has a Web page at **www.constitutioncenter.org**. The site offers basic facts about the Constitution and Constitution puzzles.
- James Madison's notes are one of our most important sources for the debates and exchanges that took place during the Constitutional Convention. These notes are now online at **www.thisnation.com/library/madison/index.html**
- An online version of the Anti-Federalist Papers is available at the Web site of the West El Paso Information Network (WEPIN). Go to **wepin.com/articles/afp/index.htm**
- For information on the effect of new computer and communications technologies on the constitutional rights and liberties of Americans, go to the Center for Democracy and Technology at **www.cdt.org**
- The constitutions of almost all of the states are online. You can find them at **www.findlaw.com/11stategov**
- To find historical documents from the founding period, including a charter issued to Sir Walter Raleigh in 1584, the Royal Proclamation of 1763, and writings by Thomas Paine, go to **www.law.yale.edu/library**
- You can find constitutions of other countries at **www.servat.unibe.ch/law/icl/index.html**

YOUR VOTE COUNTS

Online resources for this chapter

This text's Companion Web site, at **www.4ltrpress.cengage.com/govt**, offers links to numerous resources that you can use to learn more about the topics covered in this chapter.

Federalism

GOVT

3

LEARNING OBJECTIVES

LO1 Explain what federalism means, how federalism differs from other systems of government, and why it exists in the United States.

LO2 Indicate how the Constitution divides governing powers in our federal system.

LO3 Summarize the evolution of federal-state relationships in the United States over time.

LO4 Describe developments in federalism in recent years.

LO5 Explain what is meant by the term *fiscal federalism.*

AMERICA AT ODDS

Should the States Lower the Drinking Age?

Our political system is a federal one in which power is shared between the states and the federal government. The Tenth Amendment to the U.S. Constitution reserves all powers not delegated to the national government to the states and to the people. Nonetheless, the federal government has been able to exercise control over matters that traditionally have been under the control of state governments, such as the minimum age for drinking alcoholic beverages. The federal government has been able to do so by its power to give or withhold federal grants. The provision of grants to the states by the federal government is known as *fiscal federalism,* and these grants give the federal government considerable influence over state policies.

In the 1980s, for example, the national government wanted the states to raise the minimum drinking age to twenty-one years. States that refused to do so were threatened with the loss of federal highway construction funds. The threat worked—it was not long before all of the states had changed their minimum-drinking-age laws accordingly. In the 1990s, Congress used the same threat to encourage the states to lower their blood-alcohol limits for drunk driving to 0.08 percent by 2004. Again, states that failed to comply faced reductions in federal highway funds.

It's Time to End This Charade—College Students Still Drink

Underage drinking did not disappear when the minimum-drinking-age requirement was raised to twenty-one years. Indeed, the problem got worse. Millions of young people today are, in effect, criminals, because they are breaking the law by drinking. Moreover, the law encourages young people to binge in secret in order to avoid apprehension and prosecution by the local police. The minimum drinking age of twenty-one years has not reduced drunk driving among teenagers, because it is largely unenforceable. Additionally, it has bred contempt for the law in general among teenagers. That is why in July 2008, a group of 134 U.S. college presidents and chancellors endorsed the Amethyst Initiative, a movement calling for the reconsideration of U.S. drinking-age laws. Prohibition did not work in the 1920s, and prohibiting those under twenty-one from drinking will not work in the 2000s. Almost no other country has such a high minimum drinking age. It is time to lower the drinking age everywhere in the United States. Responsible drinking can be taught through role modeling by parents and through educational programs.

Keep the Age-Twenty-One Requirement Because It's Working

Mothers Against Drunk Driving (MADD) leads the opposition to lowering the drinking age. That group contends that the current drinking-age laws have saved more than twenty thousand lives. The National Transportation Safety Board, the American Medical Association, and the Insurance Institute for Highway Safety all agree. After all, young persons' brains are not fully developed, so they are more susceptible to alcohol. When the drinking age limit is twenty-one, it helps to protect young people from being pressured to drink. Teenagers who drink are a danger not only to themselves but also to others—particularly when driving. Young people away at college must deal with enough new responsibilities. They don't need drinking as yet another problem. Fatalities involving eighteen- to twenty-year-old drivers have decreased since the laws establishing the minimum drinking age of twenty-one were enacted. These laws are working as planned—so we should keep them.

WHERE DO YOU STAND?

1. **Is it appropriate to compare what happened during the era of Prohibition, when *all* drinking was illegal, to what is happening to teenagers today, when the minimum drinking age is twenty-one? Why or why not?**
2. **"One can join the military at the age of eighteen and die for this country, so it is absurd not to allow those between the ages of eighteen and twenty-one to drink." Analyze this statement.**

EXPLORE THIS ISSUE ONLINE

- **Professor David Hanson, of the State University of New York at Potsdam, maintains a Web site that explores alcohol-related issues, including the minimum-drinking-age controversy. You can find it at www2.potsdam.edu/hansondj.**
- **You can find an academic study of college-age drinking by researchers at the Harvard School of Public Health at www.hsph.harvard.edu/cas/Documents/underminimum/DrinkingBehavior.pdf.**
- **The Mothers Against Drunk Driving (MADD) site is at www.madd.org. You can find a related organization, Students Against Destructive Decisions (SADD), at www.sadd.org.**

Introduction

The controversy over the drinking age is just one example of how different levels of government in our federal system can be at odds with one another. Let's face it—those who work for the national government based in Washington, D.C., would like the states to fully cooperate with the national government in the implementation of national policies. At the same time, those who work in state government don't like to be told what to do by the national government, especially when the implementation of a national policy is costly for the states. Finally, those who work in local governments would like to run their affairs with the least amount of interference from both their state governments and the national government.

Such conflicts arise because our government is based on the principle of **federalism**, which means that government powers are shared by the national government and the states. When the founders of this nation opted for federalism, they created a practical and flexible form of government capable of enduring for centuries. At the same time, however, they planted the seeds for future conflict between the states and the national government over how government powers should be shared. As you will read in this chapter—and throughout this book—many of today's most pressing issues have to do with which level of government should exercise certain powers. Sometimes two levels of government collaborate. For example, California and the federal government jointly manage the Redwood National Park.

The relationship between the national government and the governments at the state and local levels has never been free of conflict. Indeed, even before the Constitution was adopted, the Federalists and Anti-Federalists engaged in a heated debate over the issue of national versus state powers. As you learned in Chapter 2, the Federalists won the day by convincing Americans to adopt the Constitution. The Anti-Federalists' concern for states' rights, however, has surfaced again and again in the course of our history.

Why does lowering the drinking age remain controversial?

Scott Houston/Sygma/Corbis

LO1 Federalism and Its Alternatives

There are various ways of ordering relations between central governments and local units. Federalism is one of these ways. Learning about federalism and how it differs from other forms of government is important to understanding the American political system.

What Is Federalism?

Nowhere in the Constitution does the word *federalism* appear. This is understandable, given that the concept of federalism was an invention of the founders. Since the Federalists and the Anti-Federalists argued more than two hundred years ago about what form of government we should have, hundreds of definitions of federalism have been offered. Basically, though, as mentioned in Chapter 2, in a *federal system,* government powers are divided between a central government and regional, or subdivisional, governments.

Although this definition seems straightforward, its application certainly is not. After all, virtually all nations—even the most repressive totalitarian regimes—have some kind of subnational governmental units. Thus, the existence of national and subnational governmental units by itself does not make a system federal. *For a system to be truly federal, the powers of both the national units and the subnational units must be specified and limited.* Under true federalism, individuals are governed by two separate governmental authorities (national and state authorities) whose expressly designated powers cannot be altered without changing the fundamental nature of the system—for example, by amending

federalism A system of shared sovereignty between two levels of government—one national and one subnational—occupying the same geographic region.

a written constitution. Table 3–1 lists some of the countries that the Central Intelligence Agency has classified as having a federal system of government.[1]

Federalism in theory is one thing; federalism in practice is another. As you will read shortly, the Constitution sets forth specific powers that can be exercised by the national government and provides that the national government has the implied power to undertake actions necessary to carry out its expressly designated powers. All other powers are "reserved" to the states. The broad language of the Constitution, though, has left much room for debate over the specific nature and scope of certain powers, such as the national government's implied powers and the powers reserved to the states. Thus, the actual workings of our federal form of government have depended, to a great extent, on the historical application of the broad principles outlined in the Constitution.

To further complicate matters, the term *federal government,* as it is used today, refers to the national, or central, government. When individuals talk of the federal government, they mean the national government based in Washington, D.C., they are *not* referring to the federal *system* of government, which is made up of both the national government and the state governments.

Table 3–1

Countries That Have a Federal System Today

Country	Population (in Millions)
Argentina	40.9
Australia	21.3
Austria	8.2
Brazil	198.7
Canada	33.5
Ethiopia	85.2
Germany	82.3
India	1,166.1
Malaysia	25.7
Mexico	111.2
Nigeria	149.2
Pakistan	176.2
Switzerland	7.6
United States	307.2
Venezuela	26.8

Source: Central Intelligence Agency, *The World Fact Book,* 2009 (Washington, D.C.: U.S. Government Printing Office, 2009).

Alternatives to Federalism

Perhaps an easier way to define federalism is to discuss what it is *not.* Most of the nations in the world today have a **unitary system** of government. In such a system, the constitution vests all powers in the national government. If the national government so chooses, it can delegate certain activities to subnational units. The reverse is also true: the national government can take away, at will, powers delegated to subnational governmental units. In a unitary system, any subnational government is a "creature of the national government." The governments of Britain, France, Israel, Japan, and the Philippines are examples of unitary systems. In the United States, because the Constitution does not mention local governments (cities and counties), we say that city and county governmental units are "creatures of state government." That means that state governments can—and do—both give powers to and take powers from local governments.

unitary system A centralized governmental system in which local or subdivisional governments exercise only those powers given to them by the central government.

confederal system A league of independent sovereign states, joined together by a central government that has only limited powers over them.

The Articles of Confederation created a confederal system (see Chapter 2). In a **confederal system,** the national government exists and operates only at the direction of the subnational governments. Few true confederal systems are in existence today, although some people contend that the European Union—a group of European nations that has established many common institutions—qualifies as such a system.

Federalism—An Optimal Choice for the United States?

The Articles of Confederation failed because they did not allow for a sufficiently strong central government. The framers of the Constitution, however, were fearful of tyranny and a too-powerful central government. The natural outcome had to be a compromise—a federal system.

The appeal of federalism was that it retained state powers and local traditions while establishing a strong national government capable of handling common problems, such as national defense. A federal form of government also furthered the goal of creating a division of powers (to be discussed shortly). There are other reasons why the founders opted for a federal system, and a federal structure of government continues to offer many advantages (as well as some disadvantages) for U.S. citizens.

ADVANTAGES OF FEDERALISM One of the reasons a federal form of government is well suited to the United States is its large size. Even in the days when the United States consisted of only thirteen states, its geographic area was larger than that of England or France. In those days, travel was slow and communication was difficult, so people in outlying areas were isolated. The

Figure 3–1

Governmental Units in the United States Today

The most common type of governmental unit in the United States is the special district, which is generally concerned with a specific issue such as solid waste disposal, mass transportation, or fire protection. Often, the jurisdiction of special districts crosses the boundaries of other governmental units, such as cities or counties. Special districts also tend to have fewer restrictions than other local governments as to how much debt they can incur and so are created to finance large building projects.

THE NUMBER OF GOVERNMENTS IN THE UNITED STATES TODAY

Government	Number
Federal government	1
State governments	50
Local governments	
Counties	3,034
Municipalities (mainly cities or towns)	19,429
Townships (less extensive powers)	16,504
Special districts (water, sewer, and so on)	36,052
School districts	13,506
Subtotal local governments	88,525
Total	**88,576**

PERCENTAGE OF ALL GOVERNMENTS IN THE UNITED STATES TODAY

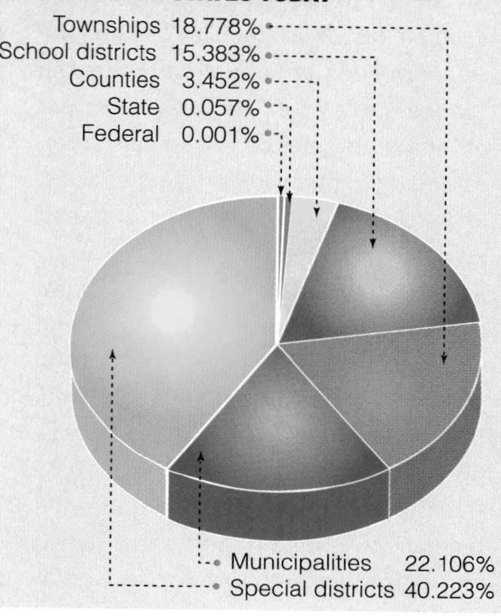

Source: U.S. Census Bureau.

news of any particular political decision could take several weeks to reach everyone. Therefore, even if the framers of the Constitution had wanted a more centralized system (which most of them did not), such a system would have been unworkable.

Look at Figure 3–1 above. As you can see, to a great extent the practical business of governing this country takes place in state and local governmental units. Federalism, by providing a multitude of arenas for decision making, keeps government closer to the people and helps make democracy possible.

The existence of numerous government subunits in the United States also makes it possible to experiment with innovative policies and programs at the state or local level. Many observers, including Supreme Court justice Louis Brandeis (1856–1941), have emphasized that in a federal system, state governments can act as "laboratories" for public-policy experimentation. For example, many states have adopted minimum wage laws that go well beyond the minimum wage set by national (national) legislation. Several states, including Hawaii and Massachusetts, are experimenting with health-care programs that extend coverage to most or all of the states' citizens. Depending on the outcome of a specific experiment, other states may (or may not) implement similar programs. State innovations can also serve as models for federal programs. For instance, California was a pioneer in air-pollution control. Many of that state's regulations were later adapted by other states and eventually by the federal government.

We have always been a nation of different political subcultures. The Pilgrims who founded New England were different from the settlers who established the agricultural society of the South. Both of these groups were different from those who populated the Middle Atlantic states. The groups that founded New England had a religious focus, while those who populated the Middle Atlantic states were more business oriented. Those who settled in the South were more individualistic than the other groups; that is, they were less inclined to act as a collective and more inclined to act independently of each other. A federal system of government allows the political and cultural interests of regional groups to be reflected in the laws governing those groups.

As we noted earlier, nations other than the United States have benefited from the principle of federalism. One of them is Canada, our neighbor to the north. Because federalism permits the expression of varying regional cultures, Canadian federalism naturally differs from the American version, as you will discover in this chapter's *The Rest of the World* feature on page 54.

SOME DRAWBACKS TO FEDERALISM Federalism offers many advantages, but it also has some drawbacks. Consider that although federalism in many ways promotes greater self-rule, or democracy, some scholars point out that local self-rule may not always be in society's best interests. These observers argue that the smaller the political unit, the higher the probability that it will be dominated by a single political group, which

Canadian versus American Federalism

American comedian Robin Williams once compared Canada to a large group of people on a balcony looking down at a great party but unable to join it. Certainly, Canadians aren't quite like Americans. Interestingly, though, Canada has a federal system similar in many ways to that of the United States. It's similar, that is, with some serious differences. The 1867 Constitution Act (formerly known as the British North America Act) established Canada's initial constitution. When the constitution was drafted, the United States was in the midst of the Civil War. Canada's founders viewed this war as being due to the weakness of the U.S. central government. Therefore, the Canadian constitution gave far more power to the central government than did the U.S. Constitution.

The Powers of Lower-Level Governments

Our lower levels of government are called states, whereas in Canada they are called provinces. Right there, the powers of the center are emphasized. The word *state* implies sovereignty, if not actual independence. A *province,* however, is never sovereign and is typically set up solely for the convenience of the central government. The U.S. Constitution limits the powers of the national government to the list given under Article I, Section 8. In the Canadian constitution, in contrast, the powers of the provinces are defined and limited by a list. The Tenth Amendment to the U.S. Constitution reserves residual powers to the states or to the people. In Canada, residual powers are granted to the national government. Under the Canadian constitution, the central government can veto any and all provincial legislation. No such clause appears anywhere in the U.S. Constitution.

Changes over Time

By land area, Canada is the second-largest country in the world. Its east-to-west extent is vast. Most people live along the southern edge of the nation, where the climate is tolerable. The populated areas of Canada, therefore, are like a thin ribbon extending from the Atlantic to the Pacific. Physically, the country seems designed for a federal system of government.

Later in this chapter, we describe how, over time, the powers of the U.S. federal government grew at the expense of the states. The opposite happened in Canada. In almost every decade, the provinces grew more powerful and self-reliant. By the end of the nineteenth century, the federal government had abandoned the power to veto provincial legislation. The national government regained many powers during World War I and World War II, but authority slipped back to the provinces in times of peace. The difference between the Canadian and American experiences is well illustrated by the effect of the Great Depression on the federal system. In the United States, the Depression strengthened the federal government. In Canada, it strengthened the provinces.

Two Languages

Another striking difference between Canada and the United States is that Canada has two national languages. Most provinces are English-speaking, but the overwhelming majority of the population of Québec speak French. At the beginning of the 1960s, Québec experienced a "quiet revolution" that resulted in a great strengthening of the province's special identity. The Parti Québécois, which supports making Québec a separate country, has gained power in that province twice. Both times, it held referenda on whether Québec should demand the status of "sovereignty-association," a euphemism for independence. In 1995, the Parti Québécois almost obtained a majority vote for its position. The party has promised to hold another referendum if it returns to power. The possibility exists, therefore, that our neighbor to the north could actually break apart.

http://www.lesindependants.qc.ca/Actualites-Grande-marche-vers-l-independance-du-Quebec

This poster was seen everywhere when Québec sought to become independent.

For Critical Analysis *The Canadian constitution is based on the principles of "peace, order, and good government." Contrast that phrase with the preamble to the U.S. Constitution. How do the two statements differ?*

may or may not be concerned with the welfare of many of the local unit's citizens. For example, entrenched segregationist politicians in southern states denied African Americans their civil rights and voting rights for decades, as we discuss further in Chapter 5.

Powerful state and local interests can block progress and impede national plans. State and local interests often diverge from those of the national government. For example, several of the states have recently been at odds with the national government over how to address the problem of global warming. Finding acceptable solutions to such conflicts has not always been easy. Indeed, as will be discussed shortly, in the 1860s, war—not politics—decided the outcome of a struggle over states' rights.

Federalism has other drawbacks as well. One of them is the lack of uniformity of state laws, which can complicate business transactions that cross state borders. Another problem is the difficulty of coordinating government policies at the national, state, and local levels. Additionally, the simultaneous regulation of business by all levels of government creates red tape that imposes substantial costs on the business community.

Finally, in a federal system, there is always the danger that national power will be expanded at the expense of the states. President Ronald Reagan (1981–1989) once said, "The Founding Fathers saw the federalist system as constructed something like a masonry wall. The States are the bricks, the national government is the mortar. . . . Unfortunately, over the years, many people have increasingly come to believe that Washington is the whole wall."[2]

LO2 *The Constitutional Division of Powers*

The founders created a federal form of government by dividing sovereign powers into powers that could be exercised by the national government and powers that were to be reserved to the states. Although there is no systematic explanation of this **division of powers** between the national and state governments, the original Constitution, along with its amendments, provides statements on what the national and state governments can (and cannot) do.

The Powers of the National Government

The Constitution delegates certain powers to the national government. It also prohibits the national government from exercising certain powers.

POWERS DELEGATED TO THE NATIONAL GOVERNMENT The national government possesses three types of powers: expressed powers, implied powers, and inherent powers. Article I, Section 8, of the Constitution expressly enumerates twenty-seven powers that Congress may exercise. Two of these **expressed powers** are the power to coin money and the power to regulate interstate commerce. Constitutional amendments have provided for other expressed powers. For example, the Sixteenth Amendment, added in 1913, gives Congress the power to impose a federal income tax. Article II, Section 2, of the Constitution expressly delegates certain powers to the president. These powers include making treaties and appointing certain federal officeholders. Laws enacted by Congress can also create expressed powers.

The constitutional basis for the **implied powers** of the national government is found in Article I, Section 8, Clause 18, often called the **necessary and proper clause.** This clause states that Congress has the power to make "all Laws which shall be necessary and proper for carrying into Execution the foregoing [expressed] Powers, and all other Powers vested by this Constitution in the Government of the United States, or in any Department or Officer thereof." The necessary and proper clause is often referred to as the *elastic clause,* because it gives elasticity to our constitutional system.

The national government also enjoys certain **inherent powers**—powers that governments must have simply to ensure the nation's integrity and survival as a political unit. For example, any national government must have the inherent ability to make treaties, regulate

division of powers A basic principle of federalism established by the U.S. Constitution, by which powers are divided between the federal and state governments.

expressed powers Constitutional or statutory powers that are expressly provided for by the U.S. Constitution or by congressional laws.

implied powers The powers of the federal government that are implied by the expressed powers in the Constitution, particularly in Article I, Section 8.

necessary and proper clause Article I, Section 8, Clause 18, of the Constitution, which gives Congress the power to make all laws "necessary and proper" for the federal government to carry out its responsibilities; also called the *elastic clause.*

inherent powers The powers of the national government that, although not always expressly granted by the Constitution, are necessary to ensure the nation's integrity and survival as a political unit. Inherent powers include the power to make treaties and the power to wage war or make peace.

> "The great difficulty lies in this:
> YOU MUST FIRST ENABLE THE GOVERNMENT TO CONTROL THE GOVERNED; AND IN THE NEXT PLACE, OBLIGE IT TO CONTROL ITSELF."
>
> ~ JAMES MADISON ~
> FOURTH PRESIDENT OF THE UNITED STATES 1809–1817

immigration, acquire territory, wage war, and make peace. Although the national government's inherent powers are few, they are important.

POWERS PROHIBITED TO THE NATIONAL GOVERNMENT The Constitution expressly prohibits the national government from undertaking certain actions, such as imposing taxes on exports, and from passing laws restraining certain liberties, such as the freedom of speech or religion. Most of these prohibited powers are listed in Article I, Section 9, and in the first eight amendments to the Constitution. Additionally, the national government is prohibited from exercising powers, including the power to create a national public school system, that are not included among its expressed and implied powers.

The Powers of the States

The Tenth Amendment to the Constitution states that powers that are not delegated to the national government by the Constitution, nor prohibited to the states, "are reserved to the States respectively, or to the people."

POLICE POWERS The Tenth Amendment thus gives numerous powers to the states, including the power to regulate commerce within their borders and the power to maintain a state militia. In principle, each state has the ability to regulate its internal affairs and to enact whatever laws are necessary to protect the health, morals, safety, and welfare of its people. These powers of the states are called **police powers.**

police powers The powers of a government body that enable it to create laws for the protection of the health, morals, safety, and welfare of the people. In the United States, most police powers are reserved to the states.

The establishment of public schools and the regulation of marriage and divorce are uniquely within the purview of state and local governments.

Because the Tenth Amendment does not specify what powers are reserved to the states, these powers have been defined differently at different times in our history. In periods of widespread support for increased regulation by the national government, the Tenth Amendment tends to recede into the background of political discourse. When the tide turns the other way, the Tenth Amendment is resurrected to justify arguments supporting increased states' rights (see, for example, the discussion of the new federalism later in this chapter). Because the United States Supreme Court is the ultimate arbiter of the Constitution, the outcome of disputes over the extent of state powers often rests with the Court.

POWERS PROHIBITED TO THE STATES Article I, Section 10, denies certain powers to state governments, such as the power to tax goods that are transported across state lines. States are also prohibited from entering into treaties with other countries. In addition, the Thirteenth, Fourteenth, Fifteenth, Nineteenth, Twenty-fourth, and Twenty-sixth Amendments prohibit certain state actions. (The complete text of these amendments is included in Appendix B.)

Interstate Relations

The Constitution also contains provisions relating to interstate relations. The states have constant commercial and social interactions among themselves, and these interactions often do not directly involve the national government. The relationships among the states in our federal system of government are sometimes referred to as *horizontal federalism.*

The Constitution outlines a number of rules for interstate relations. For example, the Constitution's full faith

States have the power to protect the health, morals, safety, and welfare of their citizens.

Myrleen Ferguson Cate/PhotoEdit

AP Photo/Marcio Jose Sanchez

Each state can decide its own laws with respect to marriage. These supporters of same-sex marriages protest California's Proposition 8 that outlawed such marriages.

and credit clause requires each state to honor every other state's public acts, records, and judicial proceedings. The issue of gay marriage, however, has made this constitutional mandate difficult to follow. If a gay couple legally married in Massachusetts moves to a state that bans same-sex marriage, which state's law takes priority? The federal government attempted to answer that question through the 1996 Defense of Marriage Act, which provided that no state is *required* to treat a relationship between persons of the same sex as a marriage, even if the relationship is considered a marriage in another state. Ultimately, however, the United States Supreme Court may have to decide this issue.

Horizontal federalism also includes agreements, known as *interstate compacts,* among two or more states to regulate the use or protection of certain resources, such as water or oil and gas. California and Nevada, for example, have formed an interstate compact to regulate the use and protection of Lake Tahoe, which lies on the border between those states.

Concurrent Powers

Concurrent powers can be exercised by both the state governments and the federal government. Generally, a state's concurrent powers apply only within the geographic area of the state and do not include functions that the Constitution delegates exclusively to the national government, such as the coinage of money and the negotiation of treaties. An example of a concurrent power is the power to tax. Both the states and the national government have the power to impose income taxes—and a variety of other taxes. States, however, are prohibited from imposing tariffs (taxes on imported goods), and the federal government may not tax articles exported by any state. Figure 3–2 on the next page, which summarizes the powers granted and denied by the Constitution, lists other concurrent powers.

The Supremacy Clause

The Constitution makes it clear that the federal government holds ultimate power. Article VI, Clause 2, known as the **supremacy clause,** states that the U.S. Constitution and the laws of the federal government "shall be the supreme Law of the Land." In other words, states cannot use their reserved or concurrent powers to counter national policies. Whenever state or local officers, such as judges or sheriffs, take office, they become bound by an oath to support the U.S. Constitution. National government power always takes precedence over any conflicting state action.[3]

LO3 *The Struggle for Supremacy*

Much of the political and legal history of the United States has involved conflicts between the supremacy of the national government and the desire of the states to remain independent. The most extreme example of this conflict was the Civil War in the 1860s. Through the years, because of the Civil War and several key Supreme Court decisions, the national government has increased its power.

Early U.S. Supreme Court Decisions

Two Supreme Court cases, both of which were decided in the early 1800s, played a key role in establishing the constitutional foundations for

concurrent powers Powers held by both the federal and the state governments in a federal system.

supremacy clause Article VI, Clause 2, of the Constitution, which makes the Constitution and federal laws superior to all conflicting state and local laws.

Figure 3–2

The Constitutional Division of Powers

The Constitution grants certain powers to the national government and certain powers to the state governments, while denying them other powers. Some powers, called *concurrent powers,* can be exercised at either the national or the state level, but generally the states can exercise these powers only within their own borders.

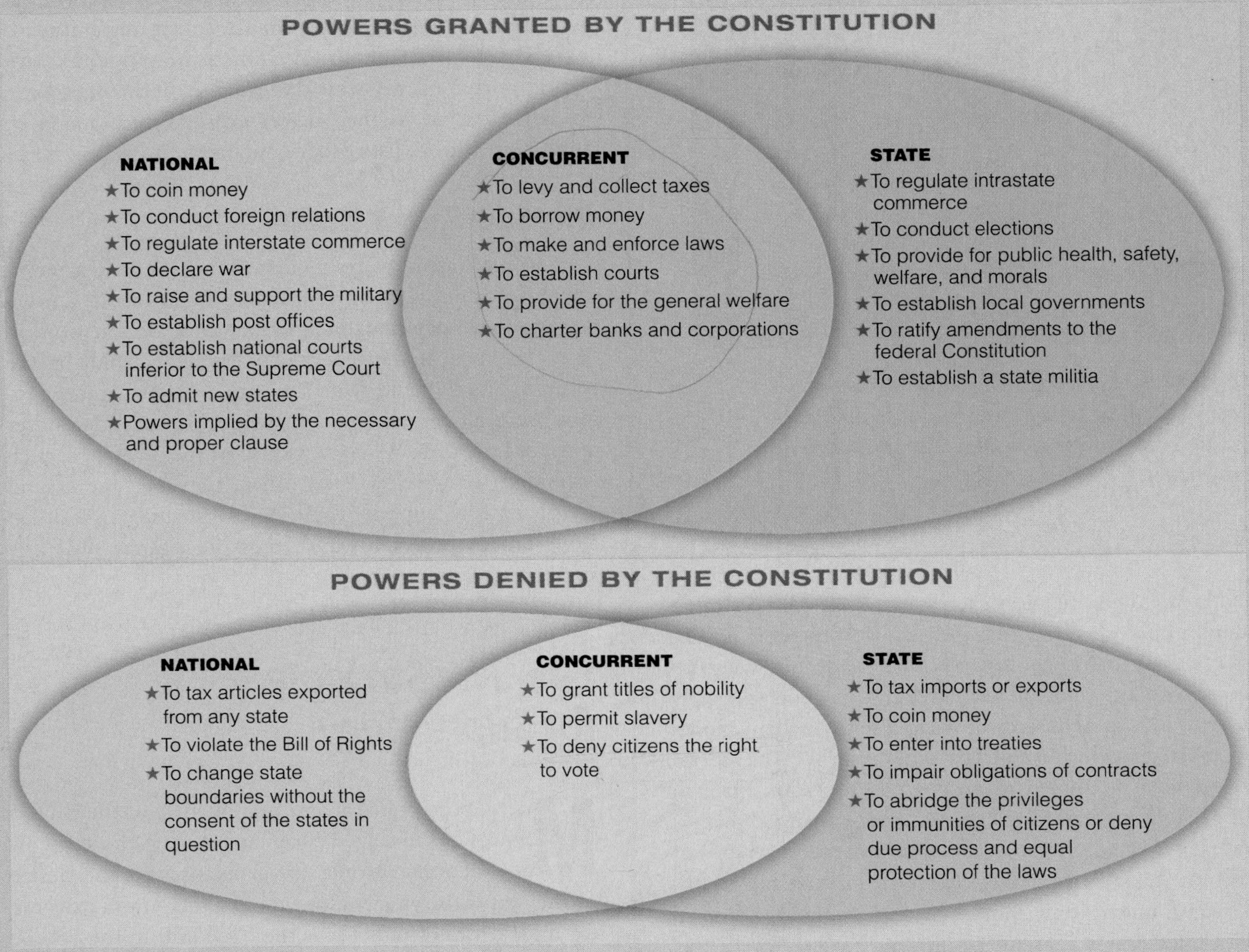

POWERS GRANTED BY THE CONSTITUTION

NATIONAL
- ★To coin money
- ★To conduct foreign relations
- ★To regulate interstate commerce
- ★To declare war
- ★To raise and support the military
- ★To establish post offices
- ★To establish national courts inferior to the Supreme Court
- ★To admit new states
- ★Powers implied by the necessary and proper clause

CONCURRENT
- ★To levy and collect taxes
- ★To borrow money
- ★To make and enforce laws
- ★To establish courts
- ★To provide for the general welfare
- ★To charter banks and corporations

STATE
- ★To regulate intrastate commerce
- ★To conduct elections
- ★To provide for public health, safety, welfare, and morals
- ★To establish local governments
- ★To ratify amendments to the federal Constitution
- ★To establish a state militia

POWERS DENIED BY THE CONSTITUTION

NATIONAL
- ★To tax articles exported from any state
- ★To violate the Bill of Rights
- ★To change state boundaries without the consent of the states in question

CONCURRENT
- ★To grant titles of nobility
- ★To permit slavery
- ★To deny citizens the right to vote

STATE
- ★To tax imports or exports
- ★To coin money
- ★To enter into treaties
- ★To impair obligations of contracts
- ★To abridge the privileges or immunities of citizens or deny due process and equal protection of the laws

the supremacy of the national government. Both decisions were issued while John Marshall was chief justice of the Supreme Court. In his thirty-four years as chief justice (1801–1835), Marshall did much to establish the prestige and the independence of the Court. In *Marbury v. Madison,*[4] he clearly enunciated the principle of judicial review, which has since become an important part of the checks and balances in the American system of government. Under his leadership, the Supreme Court also established, through the following cases, the superiority of federal authority under the Constitution.

***McCULLOCH V. MARYLAND* (1819)** The issue in *McCulloch v. Maryland,*[5] a case decided in 1819, involved both the necessary and proper clause and the supremacy clause. When the state of Maryland imposed a tax on the Baltimore branch of the Second Bank of the United States, the branch's chief cashier, James McCulloch, declined to pay the tax. The state court ruled that McCulloch had to pay it, and the national government appealed to the United States Supreme Court. The case involved much more than a question of taxes. At issue was whether Congress had the authority under the Constitution's necessary and proper clause to charter and contribute capital to the Second Bank of the United States. A second constitutional issue was also involved: If the bank was constitutional, could a state tax it? In other words, was a state action that conflicted with a national government action invalid under the supremacy clause?

Chief Justice Marshall pointed out that no provision in the Constitution grants the national government the *expressed* power to form a national bank. Nevertheless, if establishing such a bank helps the national government exercise its expressed powers, then the authority to do so could be implied. Marshall also said that the necessary and proper clause included "all means that are appropriate" to carry out "the legitimate ends" of the Constitution.

"A LEGISLATIVE ACT contrary to the Constitution is not law."

~ JOHN MARSHALL ~
CHIEF JUSTICE OF THE UNITED STATES SUPREME COURT
1801–1835

Having established this doctrine of implied powers, Marshall then answered the other important constitutional question before the Court and established the doctrine of national supremacy. Marshall declared that no state could use its taxing power to tax an arm of the national government. If it could, the Constitution's declaration that the Constitution "shall be the supreme Law of the Land" would be empty rhetoric without meaning. From that day on, Marshall's decision became the basis for strengthening the national government's power.

John Marshall, chief justice of the United States Supreme Court from 1801 to 1835, was instrumental in establishing the supremacy of the national government.

The Granger Collection

***GIBBONS V. OGDEN* (1824)** As Chapter 2 explained, Article I, Section 8, gives Congress the power to regulate commerce "among the several States." But the framers of the Constitution did not define the word *commerce*. At issue in *Gibbons v. Ogden*[6] was how the *commerce clause* should be defined and whether the national government had the exclusive power to regulate commerce involving more than one state. The New York legislature had given Robert Livingston and Robert Fulton the exclusive right to operate steamboats in New York waters, and Livingston and Fulton licensed Aaron Ogden to operate a ferry between New York and New Jersey. Thomas Gibbons, who had a license from the U.S. government to operate boats in interstate waters, decided to compete with Ogden, but he did so without New York's permission. Ogden sued Gibbons in the New York state courts and won. Gibbons appealed.

Chief Justice Marshall defined *commerce* as including all business dealings, including steamboat travel. Marshall also stated that the power to regulate interstate commerce was an *exclusive* national power and had no limitations other than those specifically found in the Constitution. Since this 1824 decision, the national government has used the commerce clause numerous times to justify its regulation of virtually all areas of economic activity.

The Civil War—The Ultimate Supremacy Battle

The great issue that provoked the Civil War (1861–1865) was the future of slavery. Because people in different sections of the country had radically different beliefs about slavery, the slavery issue took the form of a dispute over states' rights versus national supremacy. The war brought to a bloody climax the ideological debate that had been outlined by the Federalist and Anti-Federalist factions even before the Constitution was ratified.

As just discussed, the Supreme Court headed by John Marshall interpreted the commerce clause in such a way as to increase the power of the national government at the expense of state powers. By the late 1820s, however, a shift back to states' rights had begun, and the question of the regulation of commerce became one of the major issues in federal-state relations. When the national government, in 1828 and 1832, passed laws imposing tariffs (taxes) on goods imported into the United States, southern states objected, believing that such taxes were against their interests.

One southern state, South Carolina, attempted to *nullify* the tariffs, or to make them void. South Carolina claimed that in conflicts between state governments and the national government, the states should have the ultimate authority to determine the welfare of their citizens. President Andrew Jackson was prepared to use force to uphold national law, but Congress reduced the tariffs. The crisis passed.

"We here highly resolve that . . . **THIS NATION . . . SHALL HAVE A NEW BIRTH OF FREEDOM;** and that government of the people, by the people, for the people, shall not perish from the earth."

~ ABRAHAM LINCOLN ~
GETTYSBURG ADDRESS
1863

Additionally, some southerners believed that democratic decisions could be made only when all the segments of society affected by those decisions were in agreement. Without such agreement, a decision should not be binding on those whose interests it violates. This view was used to justify the **secession**—withdrawal—of the southern states from the Union in 1860 and 1861.

The defense of slavery and the promotion of states' rights were both important elements in the South's decision to secede, and the two concepts were commingled in the minds of Southerners of that era. Which of these two was the more important remains a matter of controversy even today. Modern defenders of states' rights and those who distrust governmental authority often present southern secession as entirely a matter of states' rights. Liberals and those who champion the rights of African Americans see slavery as the sole cause of the crisis. Economic historians can provide helpful insights into the background to secession, as you will learn in this chapter's *Perception versus Reality* feature on the facing page.

When the South was defeated in the war, the idea that a state has a right to secede from the Union was defeated also. Although the Civil War occurred because of the South's desire for increased states' rights, the result was just the opposite—an increase in the political power of the national government.

Dual Federalism—From the Civil War to the 1930s

Scholars have devised various models to describe the relationship between the states and the national government at different times in our history. These models are useful in describing the evolution of federalism after the Civil War.

The model of **dual federalism** assumes that the states and the national government are more or less equals, with each level of government having separate and distinct functions and responsibilities. The states exercise sovereign powers over certain matters, and the national government exercises sovereign powers over others.

For much of our nation's history, this model of federalism prevailed. Certainly, after the Civil War the

The Civil War is known in the South as the War between the States, but the official Union designation was the War of the Rebellion. The first shot of the Civil War was fired on April 12, 1861, at Fort Sumter, South Carolina.

Library of Congress

secession The act of formally withdrawing from membership in an alliance; the withdrawal of a state from the federal Union.

dual federalism A system of government in which the federal and the state governments maintain diverse but sovereign powers.

PERCEPTION VERSUS REALITY

Did the Civil War Destroy the Economy of the South?

The American Civil War imposed great destruction on the South. Much has been written about the Union Army's burning of Atlanta, not to mention Columbia and Richmond. General William T. Sherman wreaked havoc on Georgia during his march to the sea, and General Philip Sheridan's cavalry famously destroyed the farms and railroads of Virginia's Shenandoah Valley. In addition to the loss of life, the South lost work animals and other livestock, houses, barns, railroads, bridges, and fences. In the cities, Union forces destroyed factories, warehouses, and transportation equipment.

The Bridgeman Art Library/Getty Images

Mississippi in wartime, circa 1865, by Currier and Ives.

The Perception

The common perception of the South's condition after the Civil War has been much shaped by the suffering depicted in *Gone with the Wind* and other popular works. According to James L. Sellers, a noted historian, "the census of 1900 showed that after the lapse of a full generation, the South had hardly recovered the economic development of 1860."[7] Many Americans from both the South and the North have long believed that the destruction of southern wealth by the war made economic recovery impossible. Union generals and soldiers were responsible for this devastation and therefore were to blame for the painfully long and slow economic recovery of the South after the war. A further point: Although it was inevitable and proper that the slaves were freed, the North did not compensate the former slave owners for the loss. This immediately destroyed several billion dollars' worth of southern capital, at a time when a billion dollars was real money.

The Reality

The industrial parts of the South actually recovered quite rapidly. For example, southern railroads were quickly restored to full operation. As one example, by 1867, the railroads between Washington, D.C., and Charleston, South Carolina, were as good as they had been before the war. Manufacturing activity resumed quickly, too. By 1869, total manufacturing output and investment exceeded their pre-war levels.

The South's problem lay in its cotton-based agriculture. You have heard about the huge bubble in housing prices that helped cause the Great Recession of 2008 and 2009. There have been many bubbles in the past. In the 1850s, the world experienced a cotton bubble. High prices for cotton led to a bubble in the price of slaves. The high prices also led to a dangerous degree of overconfidence in the South. Slave owners believed that even if Lincoln swore not to interfere with slavery in the states, his presidency still threatened the price of slaves. Secession would serve as a protection. The North could not possibly risk a war on cotton, and if it did, cotton-dependent Britain would intervene on the side of the South. As a southern lady wrote to her daughters, "Civil War was *foreign to the original plan*."[8]

In fact, just before the beginning of the war, the price of cotton started to fall because the production of cotton textiles began to exhaust their market potential. British per-capita consumption of cotton goods did not exceed 1860 levels until after World War I. In short, the cotton industry was about to experience a major crisis of overproduction.

After the Civil War, cotton prices rose a little and then continued a downward trend until almost the end of the century. The Civil War masked the fact that the cotton bubble had burst. Ultra-low cotton prices—with no good economic alternatives for southern farmers—were the true source of the post–Civil War economic distress, and not the devastation caused by the Union Army.

Blog On *Dick "Shotgun" Weeks administers a gateway to the Web's vast collection of Civil War materials—see Shotgun's Home of the American Civil War at* **www.civilwarhome.com**. *For information on economic history, try* **eh.net**, *a Web site supported by the Economic History Association and other bodies. One of the site's most popular services lets you convert modern prices into those of any past year, or vice-versa.*

In a 1938 radio broadcast, President Franklin D. Roosevelt called upon the nation's voters to elect New Deal candidates. The Roosevelt administration's New Deal programs were an attempt to mitigate the effects of the Great Depression.

Cooperative federalism grew out of the need to solve the pressing national problems caused by the Great Depression, which began in 1929. In 1933, to help bring the United States out of the depression, President Franklin D. Roosevelt (1933–1945) launched his **New Deal,** which involved many government-spending and public-assistance programs. Roosevelt's New Deal legislation not only ushered in an era of cooperative federalism, which has more or less continued until the present day, but also marked the real beginning of an era of national supremacy.

courts tended to support the states' rights to exercise their police powers and tended to strictly limit the powers of the federal government under the commerce clause. In 1918, for example, the Supreme Court ruled unconstitutional a 1916 federal law excluding from interstate commerce the products created through the use of child labor. The law was held unconstitutional because it attempted to regulate a local problem.[9] The era of dual federalism came to an end in the 1930s, when the United States was in the depths of the greatest economic depression it had ever experienced.

Cooperative Federalism and the Growth of the National Government

The model of **cooperative federalism,** as the term implies, involves cooperation by all branches of government. This model views the national and state governments as complementary parts of a single governmental mechanism, the purpose of which is to solve the problems facing the entire United States. For example, federal law enforcement agencies, such as the Federal Bureau of Investigation, lend technical expertise to solve local crimes, and local officials cooperate with federal agencies.

cooperative federalism The theory that the states and the federal government should cooperate in solving problems.

New Deal A program ushered in by the Roosevelt administration in 1933 in an attempt to bring the United States out of the Great Depression. The New Deal included many government-spending and public-assistance programs, in addition to thousands of regulations governing economic activity.

Before the period of cooperative federalism could be truly established, it was necessary to obtain the concurrence of the United States Supreme Court. As mentioned, in the early part of the twentieth century, the Court held a very restrictive view of what the federal government could do under the commerce clause. In the 1930s, the Court ruled again and again that various economic measures were unconstitutional. In 1937, Roosevelt threatened to "pack" the court with up to six new members who presumably would be more favorable to federal action. This move was widely considered to be an assault on the Constitution, and Congress refused to support it. Clearly, however, the Court got the message: after 1937, it ceased its attempts to limit the scope of the commerce clause.

COOPERATIVE FEDERALISM AND THE WELFARE STATE The 1960s and 1970s saw an even greater expansion of the national government's role in domestic policy. The Great Society legislation of President Lyndon Johnson's administration (1963–1969) created Medicaid, Medicare, the Job Corps, Operation Head Start, and other programs. The Civil Rights Act of 1964 prohibited discrimination in public accommodations, employment, and other areas on the basis of race, color, national origin, religion, or gender. In the 1970s, national laws protecting consumers, employees, and the environment imposed further regulations on the economy. Today, few activities are beyond the reach of the regulatory arm of the national government.

Nonetheless, the massive social programs undertaken in the 1960s and 1970s also precipitated greater involvement by state and local governments. The

AP Photo/Greg Wahl-Stephens

During the 1960s and 1970s, the federal government created numerous nationwide programs, such as Head Start, which promotes school readiness for low-income children. State and local governments were called upon to organize and administer these programs, as well as to contribute additional funding. Here, a teacher in a Head Start program in Hillsboro, Oregon, works with preschoolers on an outdoor art project.

national government simply could not implement those programs alone. For example, Head Start, a program that provides preschool services to children of low-income families, is administered by local nonprofit organizations and school systems, although it is funded by federal grants. The model in which every level of government is involved in implementing a policy is sometimes referred to as **picket-fence federalism.** In this model, the policy area is the vertical picket on the fence, while the levels of government are the horizontal support boards. America's welfare system has relied on this model of federalism, although, as you will read, relatively recent reforms have attempted to give more power to state and local governments.

UNITED STATES SUPREME COURT DECISIONS AND COOPERATIVE FEDERALISM The two United States Supreme Court decisions discussed earlier, *McCulloch v. Maryland* and *Gibbons v. Ogden,* became the constitutional cornerstone of the regulatory powers that the national government enjoys today. From 1937 on, the Supreme Court consistently upheld Congress's power to regulate domestic policy under the commerce clause. Even activities that occur entirely within a state were rarely considered to be outside the regulatory power of the national government. For example, in 1942 the Supreme Court held that wheat production by an individual farmer intended wholly for consumption on his own farm was subject to federal regulation because the home consumption of wheat reduced the demand for wheat and thus could have an effect on interstate commerce.[10]

In 1980, the Supreme Court acknowledged that the commerce clause had "long been interpreted to extend beyond activities actually in interstate commerce to reach other activities that, while wholly local in nature, nevertheless substantially affect interstate commerce."[11] Today, Congress can regulate almost any kind of economic activity, no matter where it occurs. In recent years, though, the Supreme Court has, for the first time since the 1930s, occasionally curbed Congress's regulatory powers under the commerce clause. You will read more about this development shortly.

John Marshall's validation of the supremacy clause of the Constitution has also had significant consequences for federalism. One important effect of the supremacy clause today is that the clause allows for federal **preemption** of certain areas in which the national government and the states have concurrent powers. When Congress chooses to act exclusively in an area in which the states and the national government have concurrent powers, Congress is said to have *preempted* the area. In such cases, the courts have held that a valid federal law or regulation takes precedence over a conflicting state or local law or regulation covering the same general activity.

LO4 *Federalism Today*

By the 1970s, some Americans had begun to question whether the national government had acquired too many powers. Had the national government gotten too big? Had it become, in fact, a threat to the power of the states and the liberties of the people? Should steps be taken to reduce the regulatory power and scope of the national government? Since that time, the model of federalism has evolved in ways that reflect these and other concerns.

picket-fence federalism A model of federalism in which specific policies and programs are administered by all levels of government—national, state, and local.

preemption A doctrine rooted in the supremacy clause of the Constitution that provides that national laws or regulations governing a certain area take precedence over conflicting state laws or regulations governing that same area.

The New Federalism—More Power to the States

Starting in the 1970s, several administrations attempted to revitalize the doctrine of dual federalism, which they renamed the "new federalism." The **new federalism** involved a shift from *nation-centered* federalism to *state-centered* federalism. One of the major goals of the new federalism was to return to the states certain powers that had been exercised by the national government since the 1930s. The term **devolution**—the transfer of powers to political subunits—is often used to describe this process. Although a product of conservative thought and initiated by Republicans, the devolutionary goals of the new federalism were also espoused by the Clinton administration (1993–2001). An example of the new federalism is the welfare reform legislation passed by Congress in 1996, which gave the states more authority over welfare programs.

Seth Joel/Getty Images

Under our federal system, truck emissions can be regulated in Washington, D.C., no matter through which states trucks travel.

The Supreme Court and the New Federalism

During and since the 1990s, the Supreme Court has played a significant role in furthering the cause of states' rights. In a landmark 1995 decision, *United States v. Lopez,*[12] the Supreme Court held, for the first time in sixty years, that Congress had exceeded its constitutional authority under the commerce clause. The Court concluded that the Gun-Free School Zones Act of 1990, which banned the possession of guns within one thousand feet of any school, was unconstitutional because it attempted to regulate an area that had "nothing to do with commerce." In a significant 1997 decision, the Court struck down portions of the Brady Handgun Violence Prevention Act of 1993, which obligated state and local law enforcement officers to do background checks on prospective handgun buyers until a national instant check system could be implemented. The Court stated that Congress lacked the power to "dragoon" state employees into federal service through an unfunded **federal mandate** of this kind.[13]

new federalism A plan to limit the federal government's role in regulating state governments and to give the states increased power to decide how they should spend government revenues.

devolution The surrender or transfer of powers to local authorities by a central government.

federal mandate A requirement in federal legislation that forces states and municipalities to comply with certain rules. If the federal government does not provide funds to the states to cover the costs of compliance, the mandate is referred to as an *unfunded* mandate.

Since then, the Court has continued to limit the national government's regulatory powers. In 2000, for example, the Court invalidated a key provision of the federal Violence Against Women Act of 1994, which allowed women to sue in federal court when they were victims of gender-motivated violence, such as rape. The Court upheld a federal appellate court's ruling that the commerce clause did not justify national regulation of noneconomic, criminal conduct.[14]

In the twenty-first century, the U.S. Supreme Court has been less noticeably guided by an ideology of states' rights, but some of its decisions have had the effect of enhancing the power of the states. For example, in one case, *Massachusetts v. Environmental Protection Agency,*[15] Massachusetts and several other states sued the Environmental Protection Agency (EPA) for failing to regulate greenhouse-gas emissions. The states asserted that the agency was required to do so by the Clean Air Act of 1990. The EPA argued that it lacked the authority under the Clean Air Act to regulate greenhouse-gas emissions alleged to promote global warming. The Court ruled for the states, holding that the EPA did have the authority to regulate such emissions and should take steps to do so.

Tim Sloan/AFP/Getty Images

Former president George W. Bush waves from the stage during a bill signing ceremony for the 'No Child Left Behind' Act, an education reform bill passed in 2001.

The Shifting Boundary between Federal and State Authority

Clearly, the boundary between federal and state authority has been shifting. Notably, issues relating to the federal structure of our government, which at one time were not at the forefront of the political arena, have in recent years been the subject of heated debate among Americans and their leaders. The federal government and the states seem to be in a constant tug-of-war over federal regulation, federal programs, and federal demands on the states.

THE POLITICS OF FEDERALISM The Republican Party is often viewed as the champion of states' rights. Certainly, the party has claimed such a role. For example, when the Republicans took control of both chambers of Congress in 1995, they promised devolution—which, as already noted, refers to a shifting of power from the national level to the individual states. Smaller central government and a state-centered federalism have long been regarded as the twin pillars of Republican ideology. In contrast, Democrats usually have sought greater centralization of power in Washington, D.C.

Since the Clinton administration, however, the party tables seem to have turned. As mentioned earlier, it was under Clinton that welfare reform legislation giving more responsibility to the states—a goal that had been endorsed by the Republicans for some time—became a reality. Conversely, the No Child Left Behind Act of 2001, passed at the request of Republican president George W. Bush, gave the federal government a much greater role in education and educational funding than ever before. Many Republicans also supported a constitutional amendment that would ban same-sex marriages nationwide. Liberals, recognizing that it was possible to win support for same-sex marriages only in a limited number of states, took a states' rights position on this issue. Finally, consider that Bush's first attorney general, John Ashcroft, made repeated attempts to block California's medical-marijuana initiative and Oregon's physician-assisted suicide law.

FEDERALISM AND THE "WAR ON TERRORISM" In modern times, terrorism—the use of violence to intimidate or coerce—has become so large-scale and has claimed so many victims that it is hard to consider it an ordinary crime. Terrorism has many of the characteristics of war, not just of crime—hence the term *war on terrorism*. Unlike war, however, terrorism involves nongovernmental actors. Some authorities suggest thinking of terrorism as a "supercrime."[16]

The U.S. Constitution gives Congress the power and authority to provide for the common defense. Nevertheless, most of the burden of homeland defense falls on state and local governments. These governments are the "first responders" to crises, including terrorist attacks. Additionally, state and local governments are responsible for detecting, preparing for, preventing, and recovering from terrorist attacks.

After the terrorist attacks of September 11, 2001, the Bush administration increased demands on state and local governments to participate in homeland security. As with the implementation of any national policy, the requirements imposed on the states to support homeland security were costly. Firefighting departments needed more equipment and training. Emergency communications equipment had to be purchased. State and local governments were required to secure ports, ensure water safety and airport security, install new bomb-detecting equipment, and take a multitude of other steps. Since 9/11, almost every state law enforcement agency and about a quarter of local agencies (most of them in larger cities) have formed specialized antiterrorism units. Although the federal government has provided funds to the states to cover some of these expenses, much of the cost of homeland security is borne by the states.

The war in Iraq also depleted the ranks of state and local police, firefighters, and other emergency personnel. Many individuals working in these areas were also in the National Guard and were called up to active duty.

FEDERALISM AND THE ECONOMIC CRISIS Unlike the federal government, state governments are

AP Photo/Timothy A. Clary, Pool

Presidential candidates John McCain and Barack Obama toss flowers into the reflecting pool at Ground Zero in New York City. They were commemorating the seventh anniversary of the September 11 terrorist attacks on the World Trade Center towers. Both candidates temporarily pushed aside their differences during this emotional moment.

required to balance their budgets. This requirement is written into the constitution of every state except Vermont. Such requirements do not, of course, prevent the states from borrowing money, but typically when a state borrows it must follow a strict series of rules laid down in its constitution. Frequently, a vote of the people is required before a state or local government can go into debt by issuing bonds. In contrast, when the federal government runs a budget deficit, the borrowing that results takes place almost automatically—the U.S. Treasury continually issues new Treasury bonds.

A practical result is that when a major recession occurs, the states are faced with severe budget problems. Because state citizens are earning and spending less, state income and sales taxes fall. At the same time, people who have lost their jobs require more state services. The costs of welfare, unemployment compensation, and Medicaid (health care for low-income persons) all rise. During a recession, state governments may be forced either to reduce spending and lay off staff—or raise taxes. Either choice helps make the recession worse. State spending patterns tend to make economic booms more energetic and busts more painful—in a word, they are *procyclical.*

Unlike the states, the federal government has no difficulty in spending more on welfare, unemployment compensation, and Medicaid during a recession. Even though revenue raised through the federal income tax may fall, the federal government often cuts taxes in a recession to spur the economy. It makes up the difference by going further into debt, an option not available to the states. The federal government even has the power to reduce its debt by issuing new money, with inflationary results. (This technique is generally considered to be irresponsible, however.) In a recession, the actions of the federal government are normally *anticyclical.*

One method of dealing with the procyclical nature of state spending is to increase federal grants to the states during a recession. For more details on how that can work, see this chapter's *Our Government's Response to the Economic Crisis* feature.

LO5 *The Fiscal Side of Federalism*

Since the advent of cooperative federalism in the 1930s, the national government and the states have worked hand in hand to implement programs mandated by the national government. Whenever Congress passes a law that preempts a certain area, the states are, of course, obligated to comply with the requirements of that law. As already noted, a requirement that a state provide a service or undertake some activity to meet standards specified by a federal law is called a *federal mandate.* Many federal mandates concern civil rights or environmental protection. Recent federal mandates require the states to provide persons with disabilities

Our Government's Response to the Economic Crisis

Obama's Huge Stimulus Bill

In an attempt to prevent the Great Recession from turning into another Great Depression, President Barack Obama called for massive stimulus legislation—at a cost of hundreds of billions of dollars. He and his top advisers believed (and still do) that fiscal policy can have profound effects on the nation's economy, particularly during a time of economic crisis. *Fiscal policy* refers to the government's spending and taxation programs.

The logic behind fiscal policy seems straightforward. When unemployment is rising and the economy is in a recession, fiscal policy should stimulate economic activity by increasing government spending, decreasing taxes, or both. When unemployment is decreasing and prices are rising (in other words, when there is inflation), fiscal policy should curb excessive economic activity by reducing government spending, increasing taxes, or both.

This particular view of fiscal policy is an outgrowth of the economic theories of the British economist John Maynard Keynes (1883–1946). Keynes's theories were the result of his study of the Great Depression of the 1930s. According to Keynes, at the beginning of the Great Depression, the government should have filled the gap that was created when businesses and consumers stopped borrowing and spending. The government could have done so by increasing its own borrowing and spending. (It's worth noting, by the way, that not all economists agree with Keynes's theories.)

How to Put Fiscal Policy into Action, Fast

Past criticisms of fiscal policy have focused on timing problems. It can take time for the government to realize that a recession has begun. It takes more time for a bill authorizing a tax cut or spending increase to work its way through Congress. It takes still more time for the change in taxation or spending to take effect. By the time fiscal policy is actually stimulating the economy, the recession may be over, and the government's policy may be the reverse of what is now desirable. Obama moved quickly, however. He essentially gave the Democrats in Congress carte blanche—that is, total freedom—to come up with a bill, as long as they did it fast. Indeed, Congress came up with a massive stimulus bill, nominally valued at $787 billion, in record time. How could Congress write a bill so quickly?

AP Photo/Bill Waugh

Relying on "Pent-Up Demand" for Government Projects

Members of the House and the Senate already had a long list of requests for federal grants to the states. After all, state and local governments make grant proposals on a continuing basis, and the federal government makes grants to the states on a continuing basis.

Thousands of such proposals from state and local governments were ready to be submitted to Congress as part of the proposed stimulus legislation. Obama therefore promised the American people that the stimulus bill would concentrate on "shovel-ready" projects. In other words, the government would pick and choose from proposed state and local projects that were ready to be started immediately upon the receipt of federal funds.

What the Stimulus Really Funded

Given that America has thousands of bridges that need repair, highways that need resurfacing, and other serious infrastructure problems, supporters of stimulus spending thought that there was hope for improving existing infrastructure. In fact, infrastructure turned out to be a small part of the total. Of the $787 billion, $264 billion was devoted to tax cuts (mostly for individuals), and the rest to spending. Infrastructure for transportation, the environment, and other categories received less than $100 billion of this spending. Benefits to individuals through unemployment compensation, food stamps, and other programs totaled more than $100 billion. Health care received approximately $150 billion, and education roughly another $100 billion. Critics of the stimulus bill believed that the only employment that would be created by such projects would be in high-paying jobs for skilled individuals.

In spite of the talk about "shovel-ready" projects, much of the infrastructure spending provided for in the stimulus legislation was slow to get off the ground. The larger the project, of course, the longer it takes to start it. Moreover, the federal government did not immediately have the staff to oversee so much increased federal spending. In any event, some of the infrastructure spending will drag on as late as 2014.

For Critical Analysis ***The other part of the fiscal policy equation involves a reduction in tax rates. Business tax reductions in the stimulus bill, however, amounted to only $32 billion. Why do you think Obama was reluctant to cut tax rates further?***

> **"GIVING MONEY AND POWER TO GOVERNMENT** is like giving whiskey and car keys to teenage boys"
>
> ~ P.J. O'ROURKE ~
> AMERICAN HUMORIST
> 1947–PRESENT

with access to public buildings, sidewalks, and other areas; to establish minimum water-purity and air-purity standards for specific localities; and to extend Medicaid coverage to all poor children.

To help the states pay for some of the costs associated with implementing national policies, the national government gives back some of the tax dollars it collects to the states—in the form of grants. As you will see, the states have come to depend on grants as an important source of revenue. When taxes are collected by one level of government (typically the national government) and spent by another level (typically state or local governments), we call the process **fiscal federalism.**

Federal Grants

Even before the Constitution was adopted, the national government granted lands to the states to finance education. Using the proceeds from the sale of these lands, the states were able to establish elementary schools and, later, *land-grant colleges*. Cash grants started in 1808, when Congress gave money to the states to pay for the state militias. Federal grants were also made available for other purposes, such as building roads and railroads.

Only in the twentieth century, though, did federal grants become an important source of funds to the states. The major growth began in the 1960s, when the dollar amount of grants quadrupled to help pay for the Great Society programs of the Johnson administration. Grants became available for education, pollution control, conservation, recreation, highway construction and maintenance, and other purposes.

There are two basic types of federal grants: categorical grants and block grants. A **categorical grant** is targeted for a specific purpose as defined by federal law—the federal government defines hundreds of categories of state and local spending. Categorical grants give the national government control over how states use the money by imposing certain conditions. For example, a categorical grant may require that the funds not be used for purposes that discriminate against any group or for construction projects that pay below the local prevailing wage. Depending on the project, the government might require that an environmental impact statement be prepared.

In contrast, a **block grant** is given for a broad area, such as criminal justice or mental-health programs. First issued in 1966, block grants now constitute a growing percentage of all federal aid programs. A block grant gives the states more discretion over how the funds will be spent. Nonetheless, the federal government can exercise control over state decision making through these grants by using *cross-cutting requirements,* or requirements that apply to all federal grants. Title VI of the 1964 Civil Rights Act, for example, bars

fiscal federalism The allocation of taxes collected by one level of government (typically the national government) to another level (typically state or local governments).

categorical grant A federal grant targeted for a specific purpose as defined by federal law.

block grant A federal grant given to a state for a broad area, such as criminal justice or mental-health programs.

AP Photo/*Alamogordo Daily News*, Ellis Neel

By using funds from a federal grant, this police officer was able to purchase crash dummies to demonstrate the effect of drunk driving in front of a New Mexico high school.

Gary Tramontina/Bloomberg News/Landov

Competitive federalism includes state tax-reduction incentives, through which states offer lower taxes to manufacturing firms that agree to locate in their states. Such an incentive was one reason Toyota opened a plant in Huntsville, Alabama.

discrimination in the use of all federal funds, regardless of their sources.

Using Federal Grants to Control the States

Grants of funds to the states from the national government are one way that the Tenth Amendment to the U.S. Constitution can be bridged. Remember that the Tenth Amendment reserves all powers not delegated to the national government to the states and to the people. You might well wonder, then, how the federal government has been able to exercise control over matters that traditionally have been under the control of state governments, such as the minimum drinking age. The answer involves the giving or withholding of federal grant dollars.

For example, as noted in the *America at Odds* feature at the beginning of this chapter, the national government forced the states to raise the minimum drinking age to twenty-one by threatening to withhold federal highway funds from states that did not comply. The education reforms embodied in the No Child Left Behind (NCLB) Act also rely on federal funding for their implementation. The states receive block grants for educational purposes and, in return, must meet federally imposed standards for testing and accountability. A common complaint, however, is that the existing NCLB Act is an underfunded federal mandate. Critics argue that the national government does not provide sufficient funds to implement it.

The Cost of Federal Mandates

As mentioned, when the national government passes a law preempting an area in which the states and the national government have concurrent powers, the states must comply with that law in accordance with the supremacy clause of the Constitution. Thus, when such laws require the states to implement certain programs, the states must comply—but compliance with federal mandates can be costly. The estimated total cost of complying with federal mandates to the states in the 2000s has been calculated as $29 billion annually. Although Congress passed legislation in 1995 to curb the use of unfunded federal mandates, that legislation was more rhetoric than reality. Considering the cost of the programs that the federal government imposes on the states, should the federal government consider guaranteeing state debts in an attempt to lower the interest rates that the states are required to pay? We consider that issue in this chapter's *Join the Debate* feature on page 70.

Competitive Federalism

The debate over federalism is sometimes reduced to a debate over taxes. Which level of government will raise taxes to pay for government programs, and which will cut services to avoid raising taxes?

How states answer that question gives citizens an option: they can move to a state with fewer services and lower taxes, or to a state with more services but higher taxes. Political scientist Thomas R. Dye calls this model of federalism **competitive federalism.** State and local governments compete for businesses and citizens. If the state of Ohio offers tax advantages for locating a factory there, for example, a business may be more likely to build its factory in Ohio, providing more jobs for Ohio residents. If Ohio has very strict

competitive federalism
A model of federalism devised by Thomas R. Dye in which state and local governments compete for businesses and citizens, who in effect "vote with their feet" by moving to jurisdictions that offer a competitive advantage.

JOIN THE DEBATE

AP Photo/Tony Avelar, California School Employees Association

Should the Federal Government Guarantee State Debts?

Because of our federal system, state governments are separate from the national government. The states determine how much they spend, how much they tax, and how much they borrow. As a result of the economic crisis, however, state governments in 2009 faced a projected revenue shortfall of $230 billion through 2011. California alone was looking at a $43 billion shortfall. Borrowing, by selling state bonds, was becoming more and more expensive. Investors were leery about the risks involved in these bonds and were demanding higher interest rates in compensation. At the local government level, the municipal bond market consists of almost $3 trillion in debt issued by fifty thousand public entities. That debt market was in trouble, too, because of perceived risk. Now we are talking serious money.

State and local politicians, as well as their allies in Washington, D.C., have asked the federal government to guarantee state and local debt. Is this a good idea? Is it appropriate in a federal system?

State Governments Can't Be Allowed to Melt Down

The economic downturn eroded state and local government tax bases in ways that these governments could never have anticipated. By the summer of 2009, it looked as if the economy was finally starting to pull itself out of the recession. The last thing we needed was state and local governments slashing their payrolls because they could not borrow funds to cover their deficits.

And what would happen if states began to default on, or fail to pay, their debts? To take just one example, if California defaulted on its debt, the effects would be felt all across the United States. California's economy is larger than Brazil's or Canada's.

To prevent such an occurrence, the federal government wouldn't need to bail out California, or any other state or local government, directly. All it would have to do is to guarantee the debt issued by state and local governments. That's like having your parents cosign a college loan. And there is precedent. Years ago, when New York City faced a crisis, the federal government guaranteed its debt. The government charged for this service and actually made money on the deal.

Lending the full faith and credit of the federal government to the borrowing of state and local governments would lower their interest costs and allow them to restore their finances more quickly. Only in a dire situation in which a government repudiated its debts would American taxpayers lose anything. Federal guarantees are the way to go.

The States Created Their Own Mess, So Let Them Solve It Themselves

How did state and local governments get into this problem in the first place? Clearly, they let their budgets get out of hand during boom times. If the federal government has no say on the level of state and local spending or the rate at which that spending grows, why should it be required to come to the state and local governments' rescue? After all, in a federal system, the central government and state governments are independent of each other.

Representative John Campbell (R., Cal.), a member of the House Financial Services Committee, has pointed out that any federal intervention would interfere with states' efforts to come to terms with their bloated budgets. Indeed, such intervention could create incentives to spend even more.

There is also a serious question of equity. Many states spent within their means before the Great Recession. When the recession hit, they did not experience serious financial trouble. Why should residents of those states see their taxes used to guarantee the debts of less prudent state and local governments? Don't kid yourself into believing that the cost to federal taxpayers will be zero. If there were no costs in insuring state and local government debt, then these governments would not be asking for guarantees.

For Critical Analysis *What happens to a city when the local government is unable to raise cash by selling municipal bonds?*

> "Taxes, AFTER ALL, ARE THE DUES THAT WE PAY FOR THE PRIVILEGES OF MEMBERSHIP IN AN organized society."
>
> ~ FRANKLIN D. ROOSEVELT ~
> THIRTY-SECOND PRESIDENT OF THE UNITED STATES
> 1933–1945

environmental regulations, however, that same business may choose not to build there, no matter how beneficial the tax advantages, because complying with the regulations would be costly. Although Ohio citizens lose the opportunity for more jobs, they may enjoy better air and water quality than citizens of the state where the new factory is ultimately built.

Some observers consider such competition an advantage: Americans have several variables to consider when they choose a state in which to live. Others consider it a disadvantage: a state that offers more social services or lower taxes may experience an increase in population as people "vote with their feet" to take advantage of that state's laws. This population increase can overwhelm the state's resources and force it to cut social services or raise taxes.

It appears likely, then, that the debate over how our federal system functions, as well as the battle for control between the states and the federal government, will continue. The Supreme Court, which has played umpire in this battle, will also likely continue to issue rulings that influence the balance of power.

Mark Peterson/Redux

No matter what the concern, Americans will hold contrasting views on how to resolve it. These demonstrators express their dislike at a proposed health-care reform initiative. Others are in favor of it. Why do you think that the president and Congress became involved in health care, rather than leaving this issue to the states?

AMERICA AT ODDS *Federalism*

The federal form of government established by our nation's founders was, in essence, an experiment—a governmental system that was new to the annals of history. Indeed, federalism has been an ongoing experiment throughout our nation's life. More than once in our history, the line dividing state and national powers has shifted, sometimes giving the states more prominence and at other times giving the national government a more dominant role. Today, more than two hundred years after our national experiment began, we can say that the framers' choice of a federal form of government was a wise one. On the whole, with the one exception of the Civil War in the 1860s, the federal structure has allowed this country to thrive and prosper—and to offer a variety of living environments for its citizens.

The fact that we have a federal form of government allows the fifty states to have significant influence over such matters as the level of taxation, the regulation of business, and the creation and enforcement of criminal laws. For example, in Nevada you can purchase alcoholic beverages 24 hours a day, 365 days a year. In the neighboring state of Utah, the purchase of alcoholic beverages is severely restricted. Whether you can legally carry a concealed gun is a function of the state where you live. In some states, concealed firearms are allowed; in others, they are strictly forbidden. The funding and quality of education also vary from state to state. In sum, our federal arrangement gives you a choice that you would not have in a country with a unitary system of government, such as France. In the United States, you can pick up and move to another state in search of a business, job, or moral and social environment more appealing than the one offered by your state.

ISSUES FOR DEBATE & DISCUSSION

1. **Several years ago, decisions in the state courts of Florida allowed the husband of Terri Schiavo, a woman who had been in a persistent vegetative state for many years, to have her feeding tube removed. Members of the right-to-life movement strongly opposed this decision. Claiming that they were promoting "a culture of life," members of Congress enacted a law, which President George W. Bush supported, allowing Schiavo's case to be heard by a federal court. Bush's collaboration with Congress in the Schiavo matter won strong approval from many Christians on the evangelical right, who applauded his moral leadership. Others claimed that the federal government's involvement in the Schiavo matter blatantly violated the constitutionally established division of powers in our federal system. What is your position on this issue?**
2. **The Clean Air Act of 1990 gave California the right to establish its own environmental standards if the state first obtained a waiver from the federal Environmental Protection Agency (EPA). (This exception was made because California faces unique problems, including a high concentration of emissions due to the geography of the Los Angeles basin.) In an attempt to curb global warming, California later passed a law calling for strict emissions standards for automobiles, trucks, and sport utility vehicles. Following California, a number of other states passed similar laws. Only after the 2008 elections did the ERA provide the waiver that would allow California and the other states to implement this legislation. Some contend that the states should have more authority to regulate environmental pollutants and greenhouse gases. Others argue that air pollution is a national problem and thus should be regulated by the national government, not by the individual states. What is your position on this issue? What arguments can you think of to support either side of this debate?**

TAKE ACTION

Individuals who want to take action to improve our society and government sometimes think that improvements must be made at the national level. If we are to reduce poverty or homelessness, improve health care, protect the environment, or create a safer and healthier world for children, the national government will have to take the lead. In fact, though, because of our federal structure, if you want to make a difference in these or other areas, you can do so by "thinking locally." By volunteering your services to a cause that concerns you, such as improving the environment or helping the poor, you can make a big difference in the lives that you touch.

Arthur Blaustein, who teaches community development at the University of California at Berkeley, has volunteered his services to a variety of causes over the past thirty years. For Blaustein, community service is both personally gratifying and energizing. It involves more than just giving; it is also about receiving and is "very much a two-way street." He suggests that if you want to volunteer, you will be more likely to stick with your decision if you choose an activity that suits your individual talents and interests. It is also important to make a definite time commitment, whether it be a few hours each week or even just a few hours each month. To find information on volunteering, you can use VolunteerMatch. Enter your ZIP code on its Web site (**www.volunteermatch.org**) to find volunteer opportunities in your community. Other organizations that work to meet critical needs in education, health, and the environment include AmeriCorps (**www.americorps.org**) and the Corporation for National and Community Service (**www.nationalservice.gov**).

POLITICS ON THE WEB

- You can access the *Federalist Papers*, as well as state constitutions, information on the role of the courts in resolving issues relating to federalism, and information on international federations, at the following site: **www.constitution.org/cs_feder.htm**
- You can find information on state governments, state laws and pending legislation, and state issues and initiatives at **www.statescape.com**
- Supreme Court opinions, including those discussed in this chapter, can be found at the Court's official Web site. Go to **www.supremecourtus.gov**
- A good source of information on state governments and issues concerning federalism is the Web site of the Council of State Governments. Go to **www.csg.org**
- The Brookings Institution, the nation's oldest think tank, is a good source for information on emerging policy challenges, including federal-state issues, and for practical recommendations for dealing with those challenges. To access the institution's home page, go to **www.brookings.edu**
- If you are interested in a libertarian perspective on issues such as federalism, you can visit the Cato Institute's Web site at **www.cato.org**
- The Web site of the National Governors Association offers information on many issues affecting the nation, ranging from health-care reform, to education, to new and innovative state programs. You can access information on these issues, as well as many key issues relating to federalism, at **www.nga.org**
- *Governing* magazine, an excellent source of state and local news, can be found online at **www.governing.com**

Online resources for this chapter

This text's Companion Web site, at **www.4ltrpress.cengage.com/govt**, offers links to numerous resources that you can use to learn more about the topics covered in this chapter.

Thomas Barwick/Digital Vision/Getty Images

GOVT

4 Civil Liberties

LEARNING OBJECTIVES

LO1 Define the term *civil liberties,* explain how civil liberties differ from civil rights, and state the constitutional basis for our civil liberties.

LO2 List and describe the freedoms guaranteed by the First Amendment and explain how the courts have interpreted and applied these freedoms.

LO3 Discuss why Americans are increasingly concerned about privacy rights.

LO4 Summarize how the Constitution and the Bill of Rights protect the rights of accused persons.

AMERICA AT ODDS

Should Government Entities Enjoy Freedom of Speech?

We all know that the First Amendment to the U.S. Constitution states that Congress shall make no law "abridging the freedom of speech." Indeed, citizens of the United States may enjoy greater freedom of speech than the citizens of any other country. But what about government entities? Do they, too, enjoy freedom of speech? Can government bodies decide without constraint the messages they wish to communicate to the public?

This question becomes important when we consider whether religious displays can be allowed on government property. Until recently, the legal battles over such displays have centered on another part of the First Amendment—the establishment clause, which states: "Congress shall make no law respecting an establishment of religion." On several occasions, the Supreme Court has been asked to decide whether Christmas nativity scenes on public property violate the establishment clause. The Court has found that they do, unless equal space is provided for secular displays or the symbols of other religions.

Recently, the Supreme Court grappled with a case in which a small religious group, Summum, wanted to force Pleasant Grove, Utah, to accept a granite monument containing "the Seven Aphorisms of Summum" and place it in a public park. The city had earlier accepted a monument containing the Ten Commandments as one of several dozen displays in the park. Summum claimed that the city had violated the group's free speech rights by refusing to accept its donation. The Court backed the arguments of the city, however, and ruled that "the placement of a permanent monument in a public park is best viewed as a form of government speech and is therefore not subject to scrutiny under the Free Speech Clause." Because it was the city speaking, and not the groups that donated the monuments, none of the organizations could make a free speech claim. In short, government bodies enjoy their own rights to free speech. Is this appropriate?

Obviously, the Government Has a Right to Free Speech

The free speech clause involves government regulation of private speech; it does not regulate government speech. A government entity has the right to "speak for itself" and is entitled to say what it wishes. How could any government body function if it lacked this basic freedom? If citizens had the right to insist that no official paid with public funds could express a view with which that citizen disagreed, debate over issues of public concern would be severely limited. The process of government would be radically transformed. To govern, governments have to say something.

Governments own public land, including parks. Government officials have to decide what expressions of speech should be affixed permanently to public land. If the government did not have the right to decide, every single religious body and special interest group could demand that their monuments be placed on public land. Alongside the Statue of Liberty, New York might be required to erect a "statue of autocracy." In the end, governments would be forced to ban monuments or statues of any description. We cannot take away government bodies' rights to decide in such instances.

It's the Edge of the Wedge

To apply the concept of freedom of speech to governments is asking for trouble. It may be that by accepting a privately financed and donated monument, a government body has exercised a kind of government speech and has implicitly accepted the ideas represented by such monuments. Such thinking raises serious establishment clause issues. If the privately donated monuments are religious in nature, as was true in the Pleasant Grove case, the government is implicitly violating the establishment clause of the First Amendment.

We must make sure that government bodies understand that they cannot even hint at preferring one religion over another. If a government does accept one religious monument, then it had better accept a variety of others. The "government speech doctrine," newly developed by the Supreme Court, must not allow government bodies to escape the establishment clause's ban on discriminating among religious sects or groups. Several Supreme Court justices in the Pleasant Grove case argued that the Court could have ruled for the city without reference to any theory of free speech for governments. The Court's majority should have taken their advice.

WHERE DO YOU STAND?

1. **How can voters hold governments accountable for their decisions about which monuments to display and which not to display?**
2. **Several courts have held that any opinions communicated by specialty license plates are those of the driver, not the state. Why are license plates different from monuments in parks?**

EXPLORE THIS ISSUE ONLINE

- **The Findlaw Web site lets you browse through recent decisions by the Supreme Court on a wide variety of topics. Civil liberties issues are grouped together with civil rights. To locate cases, use the search box at www.findlaw.com/casecode.**
- **Adam Liptak, the Supreme Court correspondent of the *New York Times,* writes a regular column called "Sidebar." To see Liptak's perceptive columns, go to www.nytimes.com and type "sidebar" into the search box.**

CIVIL LIBERTIES are legal and constitutional rights that protect citizens from government actions.

Introduction

The debate over government free speech discussed in the chapter-opening *America at Odds* feature is but one of many controversies concerning our civil liberties. **Civil liberties** are legal and constitutional rights that protect citizens from government actions. For example, the First Amendment to the U.S. Constitution prohibits Congress from making any law that abridges the right to free speech. The First Amendment also guarantees freedom of religion, freedom of the press, and freedom to assemble (to gather together for a common purpose, such as to launch a protest against a government policy or action). These and other freedoms and guarantees set forth in the Constitution and the Bill of Rights are essentially *limits* on government action.

Perhaps the best way to understand what civil liberties are and why they are important to Americans is to look at what might happen if we did not have them. If you were a student in China, for example, you would have to exercise some care in what you said and did. That country prohibits a variety of kinds of speech, notably any criticism of the leading role of the Communist Party. If you criticized the government in e-mail messages to your friends or on your Web site, you could end up in court on charges that you had violated the law—and perhaps even go to prison.

civil liberties Individual rights protected by the Constitution against the powers of the government.

writ of *habeas corpus* An order that requires an official to bring a specified prisoner into court and explain to the judge why the person is being held in prison.

bill of attainder A legislative act that inflicts punishment on particular persons or groups without granting them the right to a trial.

***ex post facto* law** A criminal law that punishes individuals for committing an act that was legal when the act was committed.

Note that some Americans confuse *civil liberties* (discussed in this chapter) with *civil rights* (discussed in the next chapter) and use the terms interchangeably. Nonetheless, scholars make a distinction between the two. They point out that whereas civil liberties are limitations on government action, setting forth what the government *cannot do,* civil rights specify what the government *must* do—to ensure equal protection under the law for all Americans, for example.

LO1 *The Constitutional Basis for Our Civil Liberties*

The founders believed that the constitutions of the individual states contained ample provisions to protect citizens from government actions. Therefore, the founders did not include many references to individual civil liberties in the original version of the Constitution. These references were added by the Bill of Rights, ratified in 1791. Nonetheless, the original Constitution did include some safeguards to protect citizens against an overly powerful government.

Safeguards in the Original Constitution

Article I, Section 9, of the Constitution provides that the writ of *habeas corpus* (a Latin phrase that roughly means "produce the body") will be available to all citizens except in times of rebellion or national invasion. A **writ of *habeas corpus*** is an order requiring that an official bring a specified prisoner into court and show the judge why the prisoner is being kept in jail. If the court finds that the imprisonment is unlawful, it orders the prisoner to be released. If our country did not have such a constitutional provision, political leaders could jail their opponents without giving them the opportunity to plead their cases before a judge. Without this opportunity, many opponents might conveniently disappear or be left to rot away in prison.

The Constitution also prohibits Congress and the state legislatures from passing bills of attainder. A **bill of attainder** is a legislative act that directly punishes a specifically named individual (or a group or class of individuals) without a trial. For example, no legislature can pass a law that punishes a named Hollywood celebrity for unpatriotic statements.

Finally, the Constitution also prohibits Congress from passing *ex post facto* laws. The Latin term *ex post facto* roughly means "after the fact." An ***ex post facto* law** punishes individuals for committing an act that was legal when it was committed.

The Bill of Rights

As you read in Chapter 2, one of the contentious issues in the debate over ratification of the Constitution was the lack of protections for citizens from government actions. Although many state constitutions provided such protections, the Anti-Federalists wanted more. The promise of the addition of a bill of rights to the Constitution ensured its ratification.

The Bill of Rights was ratified by the states and became part of the Constitution on December 15, 1791. Look at the text of the Bill of Rights on page 45 in Chapter 2. As you can see, the first eight amendments grant the people specific rights and liberties. The remaining two amendments reserve certain rights and powers to the people and to the states.

Basically, in a democracy, government policy tends to reflect the view of the majority. A key function of the Bill of Rights, therefore, is to protect the rights of those in the minority against the will of the majority. When there is disagreement over how to interpret the Bill of Rights, the courts step in. The United States Supreme Court, as our nation's highest court, has the final say on how the Constitution, including the Bill of Rights, should be interpreted. The civil liberties that you will read about in this chapter have all been shaped over time by Supreme Court decisions. For example, it is the Supreme Court that determines where freedom of speech ends and the right of society to be protected from certain forms of speech begins.

Ultimately, the responsibility for protecting minority rights lies with the American people. Each generation has to learn anew how it can uphold its rights by voting, expressing opinions to elected representatives, and bringing cases to the attention of the courts when constitutional rights are threatened.

The Supreme Court building in Washington, D.C., was completed in 1935. Before then, the justices met in a small basement room of the Capitol building. Why is the Court so important today?

Chris Mueller/Redux

The Incorporation Issue

For many years, the courts assumed that the Bill of Rights limited only the actions of the national government, not the actions of state or local governments. In other words, if a state or local law was contrary to a basic freedom, such as the freedom of speech or the right to due process of law, the federal Bill of Rights did not come into play. The founders believed that the states, being closer to the people, would be less likely to violate their own citizens' liberties. Moreover, state constitutions, most of which contain bills of rights, protect citizens against state government actions. The United States Supreme Court upheld this view when it decided, in *Barron v. Baltimore* (1833), that the Bill of Rights did not apply to state laws.[1]

Eventually, however, the courts—and notably, the Supreme Court—began to take a different view. Because the Fourteenth Amendment played a key role in this development, we look next at the provisions of that amendment.

THE RIGHT TO DUE PROCESS In 1868, three years after the end of the Civil War, the Fourteenth Amendment was added to the Constitution. The **due process clause** of this amendment ensures that state governments will protect their citizens' rights. The due process clause reads, in part, as follows:

> No State shall . . . deprive any person of life, liberty, or property, without due process of law.

The right to **due process of law** is simply the right to be treated fairly under the legal system. That system and its officers must follow "rules of fair play" in making decisions, in determining guilt or innocence, and in punishing those who have been found guilty.

due process clause The constitutional guarantee, set out in the Fifth and Fourteenth Amendments, that the government will not illegally or arbitrarily deprive a person of life, liberty, or property.

due process of law The requirement that the government use fair, reasonable, and standard procedures whenever it takes any legal action against an individual; required by the Fifth and Fourteenth Amendments.

PROCEDURAL DUE PROCESS. *Procedural* due process requires that any governmental decision to take life, liberty, or property be made equitably. For example, the government must use fair procedures in determining whether a person will be subjected to punishment or have some burden imposed on him or her. Fair procedure has been interpreted as requiring that the person have at least an opportunity to object to a proposed action before an impartial, neutral decision maker (which need not be a judge).

Table 4–1

Incorporating the Bill of Rights into the 14th Amendment

Year	Issue	Amendment Involved	Court Case
1925	Freedom of speech	I	*Gitlow v. New York,* 268 U.S. 652.
1931	Freedom of the press	I	*Near v. Minnesota,* 283 U.S. 697.
1932	Right to a lawyer in capital punishment cases	VI	*Powell v. Alabama,* 287 U.S. 45.
1937	Freedom of assembly and right to petition	I	*De Jonge v. Oregon,* 299 U.S. 353.
1940	Freedom of religion	I	*Cantwell v. Connecticut,* 310 U.S. 296.
1947	Separation of church and state	I	*Everson v. Board of Education,* 330 U.S. 1.
1948	Right to a public trial	VI	*In re Oliver,* 333 U.S. 257.
1949	No unreasonable searches and seizures	IV	*Wolf v. Colorado,* 338 U.S. 25.
1961	Exclusionary rule	IV	*Mapp v. Ohio,* 367 U.S. 643.
1962	No cruel and unusual punishments	VIII	*Robinson v. California,* 370 U.S. 660.
1963	Right to a lawyer in all criminal felony cases	VI	*Gideon v. Wainwright,* 372 U.S. 335.
1964	No compulsory self-incrimination	V	*Malloy v. Hogan,* 378 U.S. 1.
1965	Right to privacy	Various	*Griswold v. Connecticut,* 381 U.S. 479.
1966	Right to an impartial jury	VI	*Parker v. Gladden,* 385 U.S. 363.
1967	Right to a speedy trial	VI	*Klopfer v. North Carolina,* 386 U.S. 213.
1969	No double jeopardy	V	*Benton v. Maryland,* 395 U.S. 784.

SUBSTANTIVE DUE PROCESS. *Substantive* due process focuses on the content, or substance, of legislation. If a law or other governmental action limits a *fundamental right,* it will be held to violate substantive due process, unless it promotes a *compelling* or *overriding state interest.* All First Amendment rights plus the rights to interstate travel, privacy, and voting are considered fundamental. Compelling state interests could include, for example, the public's safety.

OTHER LIBERTIES INCORPORATED The Fourteenth Amendment also states that no state "shall make or enforce any law which shall abridge the privileges or immunities of citizens of the United States." For some time, the Supreme Court considered the "privileges and immunities" referred to in the amendment to be those conferred by state laws or constitutions, not the federal Bill of Rights.

Starting in 1925, however, the Supreme Court gradually began using the due process clause to say that states could not abridge a civil liberty that the national government could not abridge. In other words, the Court *incorporated* the protections guaranteed by the national Bill of Rights into the liberties protected under the Fourteenth Amendment. As you can see in Table 4–1 above, the Supreme Court was particularly active during the 1960s in broadening its interpretation of the due process clause to ensure that states and localities could not infringe on civil liberties protected by the Bill of Rights. Today, the liberties still not incorporated include the right to refuse to quarter soldiers and the right to a grand jury hearing. Whether the right to bear arms described in the Second Amendment will be incorporated is currently an open question. The Supreme Court has announced that it intends to rule on this issue during the 2009–2010 term.

The civil liberties outlined in the Bill of Rights and contained in the original body of the Constitution provide broad protections to individual citizens in their relationships with the government. We can, however, conceive of other classes of liberties as well. Under our capitalist system, we normally enjoy broad liberties to buy and sell, to enter into contracts, and to own wealth-producing assets. These "economic liberties" are not listed in the Constitution. Under the commerce clause and other provisions of the Constitution, the federal government has the power to regulate economic matters and limit economic liberties in ways that would be out of the question for civil liberties. Is this a problem? We examine that issue in this chapter's *Our Government's Response to the Economic Crisis.*

Do We Lose Liberties When the Government Changes the Rules?

The federal government has intervened in the economy extensively since the Great Recession entered its crisis stage. Government regulation of economic matters has been around for decades, of course, and Americans have become used to the federal (and state and local) bureaucracy meddling in their affairs. We accept that the Consumer Product Safety Commission may prevent certain products from entering the stream of commerce if they are deemed unsafe—we don't have the liberty to buy just anything. We accept that we cannot buy medical services from unlicensed individuals, legal services from unlicensed practitioners, and even plumbing services from an unlicensed tradesperson. In late 2008 and in 2009, however, the federal government intervened in the economy in ways that many did not quite expect. Take the automobile industry.

Forget Contracts, This Is an Emergency

The Constitution (Article I, Section 10) provides that "No State shall . . . pass any . . . Law impairing the Obligation of Contracts. . . ." This clause does not apply to the federal government, but any substantial contract impairment would be forbidden by the due process clause of the Fifth Amendment. Yet some claim that contract impairments are exactly what the federal government perpetrated when it intertwined itself in the bankruptcy reorganization of Chrysler and General Motors.

Some institutions, investment firms, and pension plans loaned money to Chrysler Corporation by purchasing the company's bonds. They received contractual guarantees that they would obtain repayment before anyone else if the company failed. They were "senior creditors." Nevertheless, the Obama administration forced these bondholders to give up their place in line in favor of other creditors. The bondholders received only about 25 cents on the dollar. In contrast, parts suppliers and customers with warranties were paid in full, even though they lacked senior status. The United Auto Workers pension fund was also privileged over the bondholders. Those who owned bonds issued by General Motors suffered a similar fate, though their contractual protections were not as great as those of the Chrysler bondholders. (General Motors is now owned 60 percent by U.S. taxpayers and 12.2 percent by Canadian taxpayers.)

Our government's response to the economic crisis has involved other economic interventions as well. Many have been very popular, but constitutionally dubious. They include the attempt to limit bonuses provided to executives of leading financial institutions that received Troubled Asset Relief Program (TARP) money from the government. What makes the pay limits questionable is that the nation's top banks did not really have the option of turning down the TARP funds. As columnist Charles Krauthammer put it, "The last Treasury secretary brought the nine largest banks into his office and informed them that henceforth he was their partner."

Going After Smokers

In 2009, President Obama (himself a former smoker who has been known to "fall off the wagon") signed a landmark antismoking bill. The new law lets the Food and Drug Administration regulate the contents of tobacco products, publicize their ingredients, and—notably—prohibit specified marketing campaigns. While advertising does not receive full First Amendment protection, some are troubled when the government effectively prohibits truthful communication about a legal product.

Conceived as part of the administration's sweeping health-care reforms, this measure is only the most recent in a long series of federal laws directed against tobacco consumption. Smoking opponents claim that heavy taxes on tobacco are necessary because of the health-care expenses incurred by smokers. Pension plan executives, however, know full well that premature deaths of smokers actually save society billions of dollars in pension benefits. In any event, current laws penalize even those who smoke in private, bothering no one else. Some would claim that laws against marijuana have a similar effect.

© JoLin Shutterstock

For Critical Analysis *Is it legitimate to argue that people who do not receive an appropriate education or adequate health care have lost liberty, because they have lost the ability to live up to their potential? When the government collects taxes, does the resulting loss of wealth or income constitute a loss of liberty? Do government actions to fight a recession involve liberty trade-offs? In each example, why or why not?*

LO2 *Protections under the First Amendment*

As mentioned earlier, the First Amendment sets forth some of our most important civil liberties. Specifically, the First Amendment guarantees the freedoms of religion, speech, the press, and assembly, as well as the right to petition the government. In the pages that follow, we look closely at each of these freedoms and discuss how, over time, Supreme Court decisions have defined their meaning and determined their limits.

AP Photo/*Salt Lake Tribune*/Al Hartmann

The right to bear arms is included in the Second Amendment to the U.S. Constitution. In 2008, the Supreme Court ruled for the first time that this right applies to individuals, not just state militias. So far, however, the Court's ruling applies only to the federal government.

Freedom of Religion

The First Amendment prohibits Congress from passing laws "respecting an establishment of religion, or prohibiting the free exercise thereof." The first part of this amendment is known as the **establishment clause.** The second part is called the **free exercise clause.**

That the freedom of religion was the first freedom mentioned in the Bill of Rights is not surprising. After all, many colonists came to America to escape religious persecution. Nonetheless, these same colonists showed little tolerance for religious freedom within the communities they established. For example, in 1610 the Jamestown colony enacted a law requiring attendance at religious services on Sunday "both in the morning and the afternoon." Repeat offenders were subjected to particularly harsh punishments. For those who twice violated the law, for example, the punishment was a public whipping. For third-time offenders, the punishment was death. The Maryland Toleration Act of 1649 declared that anyone who cursed God or denied that Jesus Christ was the son of God was to be punished by death. In all, nine of the thirteen colonies had established official religions by the time of the American Revolution.

establishment clause The section of the First Amendment that prohibits Congress from passing laws "respecting an establishment of religion." Issues concerning the establishment clause often center on prayer in public schools, the teaching of fundamentalist theories of creation, and government aid to parochial schools.

free exercise clause The provision of the First Amendment stating that the government cannot pass laws "prohibiting the free exercise" of religion. Free exercise issues often concern religious practices that conflict with established laws.

This context is helpful in understanding why, in 1802, President Thomas Jefferson, a great proponent of religious freedom and tolerance, wanted the establishment clause to be "a wall of separation between church and state." The context also helps to explain why even state leaders who supported state religions might have favored the establishment clause—to keep the national government from interfering in such state matters. After all, the First Amendment says only that *Congress* can make no law respecting an establishment of religion; it says nothing about whether the *states* could make such laws. And, as noted earlier, the protections in the Bill of Rights initially applied only to actions taken by the national government, not the state governments.

THE ESTABLISHMENT CLAUSE The establishment clause forbids the government to establish an official religion. This makes the United States different from countries that are ruled by religious governments, such as the Islamic government of Iran. It also makes us different from nations that have in the past strongly discouraged the practice of any religion at all, such as the People's Republic of China.

What does this separation of church and state mean in practice? For one thing, religion and government, though constitutionally separated in the United States, have never been enemies or strangers. The establishment clause does not prohibit government from supporting religion in *general;* it remains a part of public life. Most government officials take an oath of office in the name of God, and our coins and paper currency carry the motto "In God We Trust." Clergy of different religions serve in each branch of the armed forces. Public meetings and even sessions of Congress open with prayers. Indeed, the establishment clause often masks the fact that Americans are, by and large, religious and would like their political leaders to be people of faith.

The First Amendment TO THE CONSTITUTION MANDATES SEPARATION OF CHURCH AND STATE. NONETHELESS, REFERENCES TO GOD ARE COMMON IN PUBLIC LIFE, AS THE PHRASE, "IN GOD WE TRUST" ON THIS COIN DEMONSTRATES.

The "wall of separation" that Thomas Jefferson referred to, however, does exist and has been upheld by the Supreme Court on many occasions. An important ruling by the Supreme Court on the establishment clause came in 1947 in *Everson v. Board of Education.*[2] The case involved a New Jersey law that allowed the state to pay for bus transportation of students who attended parochial schools (schools run by churches or other religious groups). The Court stated as follows: "No tax in any amount, large or small, can be levied to support any religious activities or institutions." The Court upheld the New Jersey law, however, because it did not aid the church *directly* but provided for the safety and benefit of the students. The ruling both affirmed the importance of separating church and state and set the precedent that not *all* forms of state and federal aid to church-related schools are forbidden under the Constitution.

A full discussion of the various church-state issues that have arisen in American politics would fill volumes. Here we examine three of these issues: prayer in the schools, evolution versus creationism, and government aid to parochial schools.

PRAYER IN THE SCHOOLS. On occasion, some public schools have promoted a general sense of religion without proclaiming allegiance to any particular church or sect. Whether the states have a right to allow this was the main question presented in 1962 in *Engel v. Vitale,*[3] also known as the "Regents' Prayer case." The State Board of Regents in New York had composed a nondenominational prayer (a prayer not associated with any particular church) and urged school districts to use it in classrooms at the start of each day. The prayer read as follows:

> Almighty God, we acknowledge our dependence upon Thee, and we beg Thy blessings upon us, our parents, our teachers, and our Country.

Some parents objected to the prayer, contending that it violated the establishment clause. The Supreme Court agreed and ruled that the Regents' Prayer was unconstitutional. Speaking for the majority, Justice Hugo Black wrote that the First Amendment must at least mean "that in this country it is no part of the business of government to compose official prayers for any group of the American people to recite as a part of a religious program carried on by government."

These students at Trey Whitfield School, in Brooklyn, New York—a private school—are engaged in prayers. Why is it constitutional to allow prayers in private schools but not in public schools?

Marilynn K. Yee/New York Times/Redux

PRAYER IN THE SCHOOLS—THE DEBATE CONTINUES. Since the *Engel v. Vitale* ruling, the Supreme Court has continued to shore up the wall of separation between church and state in a number of decisions. Generally, the Court has had to walk a fine line between the wishes of those who believe that religion should have a more prominent place in our public institutions and those who do not. For example, in a 1980 case, *Stone v. Graham,*[4] the Supreme Court ruled that a Kentucky law requiring that the Ten Commandments be posted in all public schools violated the establishment clause. Many groups around the country opposed this ruling. Currently, a number of states have passed or proposed laws permitting (but not *requiring,* as the Kentucky law did) the display of the Ten Commandments on public property, including public schools. Supporters of such displays contend that they will help reinforce the fundamental religious values that are a part of the American heritage. Opponents claim that the displays blatantly violate the establishment clause.

Another controversial issue is whether "moments of silence" in the schools are constitutional. In 1985, the Supreme Court ruled that an Alabama law authorizing a daily one-minute period of silence for meditation and voluntary prayer was unconstitutional. Because the law specifically endorsed prayer, it appeared to support religion.[5] Since then, the lower courts have generally held that a school may require a moment of silence, but only if it serves a clearly secular purpose (such as to meditate on the day's activities).[6] Yet another issue concerns prayers said before public school sporting events, such as football games. In 2000, the Supreme Court held that student-led pregame prayer using the school's public-address system was unconstitutional.[7]

In sum, the Supreme Court has ruled that the public schools, which are agencies of government, cannot sponsor religious activities. It has *not,* however, held that individuals cannot pray, when and as they choose, in schools or in any other place. Nor has it held that the schools are barred from teaching *about* religion, as opposed to engaging in religious practices.

EVOLUTION VERSUS CREATIONISM. Certain religious groups have long opposed the teaching of evolution in the schools. These groups contend that evolutionary theory, a theory with overwhelming scientific support, directly counters their religious belief that human beings did not evolve but were created fully formed, as described in the biblical story of the creation. In fact, surveys have repeatedly shown that a majority of Americans believe that humans were directly created by God rather than having evolved from other species. The Supreme Court, however, has held that state laws forbidding the teaching of evolution in the schools are unconstitutional.

For example, in *Epperson v. Arkansas,*[8] a case decided in 1968, the Supreme Court held that an Arkansas law prohibiting the teaching of evolution violated the establishment clause because it imposed religious beliefs on students. In 1987, the Supreme Court also held unconstitutional a Louisiana law requiring that the biblical story of the creation be taught along with evolution. The Court deemed the law unconstitutional in part because it had as its primary purpose the promotion of a particular religious belief.[9]

Nevertheless, some state and local groups continue their efforts against the teaching of evolution. Recently, for example, Alabama approved a disclaimer to be inserted in biology textbooks, stating that evolution is "a controversial theory some scientists present as a scientific explanation for the origin of living things." Laws and policies that discourage the teaching of evolution are also being challenged on constitutional grounds. For example, in Cobb County, Georgia, stickers were inserted into science textbooks stating that "evolution is a theory, not a fact" and that "the theory should be approached with an open mind, studied carefully, and critically considered." When Cobb County's actions were challenged in court as unconstitutional, a federal judge

When an Oklahoma school attempted to bar a young Muslim girl from wearing a head scarf to school, the federal government intervened. Why would the U.S. government protect the right to wear religious symbols in public schools? What other civil liberties ensured by the U.S. Constitution might protect the right to wear religious dress in public schools?

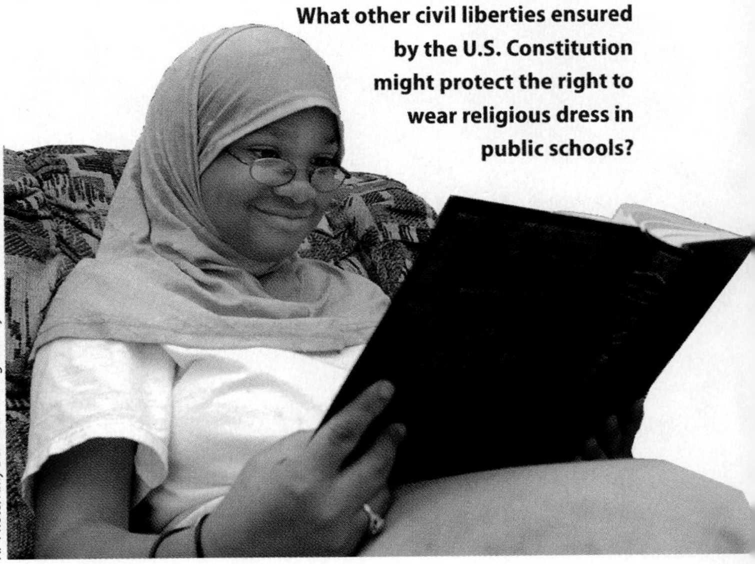

AP Photo/Amy DeMoss/*Muskogee Daily Phoenix*

AP Photo/Carolyn Kaster

A volunteer petitions people outside a polling place at which voters are deciding whether to allow the teaching of intelligent design as an alternative to the theory of evolution.

held that the stickers conveyed a "message of endorsement of religion," thus violating the First Amendment.

EVOLUTION VERSUS INTELLIGENT DESIGN. Some schools have adopted the concept of "intelligent design" as an alternative to the teaching of evolution. Advocates of intelligent design believe that an intelligent cause, and not an undirected process such as natural selection, lies behind the creation and development of the universe and living things. Proponents of intelligent design claim that it is a scientific theory and thus that its teaching should not violate the establishment clause in any way. Opponents of intelligent design theory claim that it is pseudoscience at best and that, in fact, the so-called theory masks its supporters' belief that God is the "intelligent cause."

AID TO PAROCHIAL SCHOOLS. Americans have long been at odds over whether public tax dollars should be used to fund activities in parochial schools—private schools that have religious affiliations. Over the years, the courts have often had to decide whether specific types of aid do or do not violate the establishment clause. Aid to church-related schools in the form of transportation, equipment, or special educational services for disadvantaged students has been held permissible. Other forms of aid, such as funding teachers' salaries and paying for field trips, have been held unconstitutional.

Since 1971, the Supreme Court has held that, to be constitutional, a state's school aid must meet three requirements: (1) the purpose of the financial aid must be clearly secular (not religious), (2) its primary effect must neither advance nor inhibit religion, and (3) it must avoid an "excessive government entanglement with religion." The Court first used this three-part test in *Lemon v. Kurtzman*,[10] and hence it is often referred to as the ***Lemon* test.** In the 1971 *Lemon* case, the Court denied public aid to private and parochial schools for the salaries of teachers of secular courses and for textbooks and instructional materials in certain secular subjects. The Court held that the establishment clause is designed to prevent three main evils: "sponsorship, financial support, and active involvement of the sovereign [the government] in religious activity."

Lemon test A three-part test enunciated by the Supreme Court in the 1971 case of *Lemon v. Kurtzman* to determine whether government aid to parochial schools is constitutional. To be constitutional, the aid must (1) be for a clearly secular purpose; (2) in its primary effect, neither advance nor inhibit religion; and (3) avoid an "excessive government entanglement with religion." The *Lemon* test has also been used in other types of cases involving the establishment clause.

school voucher An educational certificate, provided by the government, that allows a student to use public funds to pay for a private or a public school chosen by the student or his or her parents.

In 2000, the Supreme Court applied the *Lemon* test to a federal law that gives public school districts federal funds for special services and instructional equipment. The law requires that the funds be shared with all private schools in the district. A central issue in the case was whether using the funds to supply computers to parochial schools had a clearly secular purpose. Some groups claimed that it did not, because students in parochial schools could use the computers to access religious materials online. Others, including the Clinton administration (1993–2001), argued that giving high-tech assistance to parochial schools did have a secular purpose and was a religiously neutral policy. The Supreme Court sided with the latter argument and held that the law did not violate the establishment clause.[11]

SCHOOL VOUCHER PROGRAMS. Another contentious issue has to do with the use of **school vouchers**—educational certificates, provided by state governments, that students can use at any school, public or private. In an effort to improve their educational systems, several school districts have been experimenting with voucher systems. Six states and the District of Columbia now have limited voucher programs under which schoolchildren may attend private elementary or high schools using vouchers paid for by taxpayers' dollars.

In 2002, the United States Supreme Court ruled that a voucher program in Cleveland, Ohio, was constitutional. Under the program, the state provided up to $2,250 to low-income families, who could use the funds to send their children to either public or private schools. The Court concluded that the taxpayer-paid voucher program did not unconstitutionally entangle church and state because the funds went to parents, not to schools. The parents theoretically could use the vouchers to send their children to nonreligious private academies or charter schools, even though 95 percent used the vouchers at religious schools.[12]

THE FREE EXERCISE CLAUSE protects a person's right to worship or believe as he or she wishes without government interference.

Despite the 2002 Supreme Court ruling, several constitutional questions surrounding school vouchers remain unresolved. For example, some state constitutions are more explicit than the federal Constitution in denying the use of public funds for religious education. Even after the Supreme Court ruling in the Ohio case, a Florida court ruled in 2002 that a voucher program in that state violated Florida's constitution.[13]

The public is very closely divided on this issue. About 30 percent of those responding to a public opinion poll on the subject did not have strong feelings one way or the other; those with opinions were evenly split. Support for vouchers tended to come from Catholics and white evangelicals, which is not surprising—a large number of existing private schools represent either the Catholic or evangelical faiths. Public-school teacher unions oppose vouchers strongly, and they are a major constituency for the Democratic Party. With the Democrats in control of the presidency and both chambers of Congress, therefore, federal support for vouchers is unlikely in the near future.

THE FREE EXERCISE CLAUSE As mentioned, the second part of the First Amendment's statement on religion consists of the free exercise clause, which forbids the passage of laws "prohibiting the free exercise of religion." This clause protects a person's right to worship or believe as he or she wishes without government interference. No law or act of government may violate this constitutional right.

BELIEF AND PRACTICE ARE DISTINCT. The free exercise clause does not necessarily mean that individuals can act in any way they want on the basis of their religious beliefs. There is an important distinction between belief and practice. The Supreme Court has ruled consistently that the right to hold any *belief* is absolute. The government has no authority to compel you to accept or reject any particular religious belief. The right to *practice* one's beliefs, however, may have some limits. As the Court itself once asked, "Suppose one believed that human sacrifice were a necessary part of religious worship?"

The Supreme Court first dealt with the issue of belief versus practice

This proponent of a school voucher program in Cleveland, Ohio, believes that only the students of rich parents have much school choice. In other words, her implicit argument is that school vouchers will give the same school choice to children who are poor as to those who are rich.

AP Photo/Rick Bowmer

in 1878 in *Reynolds v. United States.*[14] Reynolds was a Mormon who had two wives. Polygamy, or the practice of having more than one spouse at a time, was encouraged by the customs and teachings of his religion. Polygamy was also prohibited by federal law. Reynolds was convicted and appealed the case, arguing that the law violated his constitutional right to freely exercise his religious beliefs. The Court did not agree. It said that to allow Reynolds to practice polygamy would make religious doctrines superior to the law.

RELIGIOUS PRACTICES AND THE WORKPLACE. The free exercise of religion in the workplace was bolstered by Title VII of the Civil Rights Act of 1964, which requires employers to accommodate their employees' religious practices unless such accommodation causes an employer to suffer an "undue hardship." Thus, if an employee claims that his or her religious beliefs prevent him or her from working on a particular day of the week, such as Saturday or Sunday, the employer must attempt to accommodate the employee's needs.

Several cases have come before lower federal courts concerning employer dress codes that contradict the religious customs of employees. For example, in 1999 the Third Circuit Court of Appeals ruled in favor of two Muslim police officers in Newark, New Jersey, who claimed that they were required by their faith to wear beards and would not shave them to comply with the police department's grooming policy. A similar case was brought in 2001 by Washington, D.C., firefighters.[15] Muslims, Rastafarians, and others have refused to change the grooming habits required by their religions and have been successful in court.

"FREE SPEECH is the whole thing, the whole ball game. Free speech is life itself."

~ SALMAN RUSHDIE ~
INDIAN-BORN BRITISH WRITER
B. 1947

Freedom of Expression

No one in this country seems to have a problem protecting the free speech of those with whom they agree. The real challenge is protecting unpopular ideas. The protection needed is, in Justice Oliver Wendell Holmes's words, "not free thought for those who agree with us but freedom for the thought that we hate." The First Amendment is designed to protect the freedom to express *all* ideas, including those that may be unpopular.

The First Amendment has been interpreted to protect more than merely spoken words; it also protects **symbolic speech**—speech involving actions and other nonverbal expressions. Some common examples include picketing in a labor dispute and wearing a black armband in protest of a government policy. Even burning the American flag as a gesture of protest has been held to be protected by the First Amendment.

THE RIGHT TO FREE SPEECH IS NOT ABSOLUTE Although Americans have the right to free speech, not *all* speech is protected under the First Amendment. Our constitutional rights and liberties are not absolute. Rather, they are what the Supreme Court—the ultimate interpreter of the Constitution—says they are. Although the Court has zealously safeguarded the right to free speech, at times it has imposed limits on speech in the interests of protecting other rights of Americans. These rights include security against harm to one's person or reputation, the need for public order, and the need to preserve the government.

Generally, throughout our history, the Supreme Court has attempted to balance our rights to free speech against these other needs of society. As Justice Holmes once said, even "the most stringent protection of free speech would not protect a man in falsely shouting fire in a theatre and causing a panic."[16] We look next at some of the ways that the Court has limited the right to free speech.

EARLY RESTRICTIONS ON EXPRESSION At times in our nation's history, various individuals have opposed our form of government. The government, however, has drawn a fine line between legitimate criticism and the expression of ideas that may seriously harm society. Clearly, the government may pass laws against violent acts. But what about **seditious speech,** which urges resistance to lawful authority or advocates overthrowing the government?

As early as 1798, Congress took steps to curb seditious speech when it passed the Alien and Sedition Acts, which made it a crime to utter "any false, scandalous, and malicious" criticism of the government.

symbolic speech The expression of beliefs, opinions, or ideas through forms other than speech or print; speech involving actions and other nonverbal expressions.

seditious speech Speech that urges resistance to lawful authority or that advocates the overthrowing of a government.

Library of Congress

More than 450 conscientious objectors were imprisoned as a result of the Espionage Act of 1917, including Rose Pastor Stokes, who was sentenced to ten years in prison for saying, in a letter to the *Kansas City Star*, that "no government which is for the profiteers can also be for the people, and I am for the people while the government is for the profiteers."

The acts were considered unconstitutional by many but were never tested in the courts. Several dozen individuals were prosecuted under the acts, and some were actually convicted. In 1801, President Thomas Jefferson pardoned those sentenced under the acts, and Congress soon repealed them.

During World War I, Congress passed the Espionage Act of 1917 and the Sedition Act of 1918. The 1917 act prohibited attempts to interfere with the operation of the military forces, the war effort, or the process of recruitment. The 1918 act made it a crime to "willfully utter, print, write, or publish any disloyal, profane, scurrilous [insulting], or abusive language" about the government. More than two thousand persons were tried and convicted under this act, which was repealed at the end of World War I.

commercial speech Advertising statements that describe products. Commercial speech receives less protection under the First Amendment than ordinary speech.

libel A published report of a falsehood that tends to injure a person's reputation or character.

slander The public utterance (speaking) of a statement that holds a person up for contempt, ridicule, or hatred.

In 1940, Congress passed the Smith Act, which forbade people from advocating the violent overthrow of the U.S. government. In 1951, the Supreme Court first upheld the constitutionality of the Smith Act in *Dennis v. United States,*[17] which involved eleven top leaders of the Communist Party who had been convicted of violating the act. The Court found that their activities went beyond the permissible peaceful advocacy of change. Subsequently, however, the Court modified its position. Since the 1960s, the Court has defined seditious speech to mean only the advocacy of imminent and concrete acts of violence against the government.[18]

LIMITED PROTECTION FOR COMMERCIAL SPEECH Advertising, or **commercial speech,** is also protected by the First Amendment, but not as fully as regular speech. Generally, the Supreme Court has considered a restriction on commercial speech to be valid as long as the restriction "(1) seeks to implement a substantial government interest, (2) directly advances that interest, and (3) goes no further than necessary to accomplish its objective." Problems arise, though, when restrictions on commercial advertising achieve one substantial government interest yet are contrary to the interest in protecting free speech and the right of consumers to be informed. In such cases, the courts have to decide which interest takes priority.

Liquor advertising is a good illustration of this kind of conflict. For example, in one case, Rhode Island argued that its law banning the advertising of liquor prices served the state's goal of discouraging liquor consumption (because the ban discouraged bargain hunting and thus kept liquor prices high). The Supreme Court, however, held that the ban was an unconstitutional restraint on commercial speech. The Court stated that the First Amendment "directs us to be especially skeptical of regulations that seek to keep people in the dark for what the government perceives to be their own good."[19]

UNPROTECTED SPEECH Certain types of speech receive no protection under the First Amendment. These types of speech include defamation (libel and slander) and obscenity.

LIBEL AND SLANDER. No person has the right to libel or slander another. **Libel** is a published report of a falsehood that tends to injure a person's reputation or character. **Slander** is the public utterance (speaking) of a statement that holds a person up for contempt, ridicule, or hatred. To prove libel or slander, however, certain criteria must be met. The statements made must be untrue,

Libel Tourism: A British Growth Industry

Americans pride themselves on having almost unlimited freedom of speech. Most of us believe that the British have similar freedoms. Although that perception may be true for most civil liberties, British libel law is quite different from libel law in the United States. As a result, some who don't like what others say or write about them have engaged in what has been called "libel tourism." Rather than filing a defamation lawsuit in the United States, where freedom of speech and the press are strongly protected, an aggrieved individual or company files the same lawsuit in a foreign jurisdiction—typically Britain, but sometimes Ireland—where the chances of winning are much greater.

Libel suits are relatively easy to win in Britain—even in cases that involve sham claims. British law on defamation requires that that the writer or author (the defendant) prove that what was written is true. In the United States and many other countries, the person suing for libel (the plaintiff) has the burden of proving that the statements were false. In the United States, the plaintiff must also prove that the statements caused an actual injury. If the plaintiff is a celebrity, he or she must also show that the statements were made with reckless disregard for accuracy.

The Chilling Effect of Libel Tourism on Free Speech

Some argue that libel tourism can have a chilling effect on the speech of U.S. journalists and authors because the fear of liability in other nations may prevent them from freely discussing topics of profound public importance.

The threat of libel tourism captured media attention when Khalid Bin Mahfouz, a Saudi businessman, sued U.S. citizen Dr. Rachel Ehrenfeld. In her book *Funding Evil: How Terrorism Is Financed—And How to Stop It,* Ehrenfeld claimed that Mahfouz had been involved in financing Islamic terrorist groups. Mahfouz filed a libel lawsuit in London, despite the fact that Ehrenfeld's book was never published outside the United States. Apparently, twenty-three copies of that book had been ordered online from the United States by British residents. Ehrenfeld made no attempt to defend, and the British court entered a judgment of $225,000 against her.

Critics of the British system say that London courts are all too ready to take jurisdiction over cases in which neither the plaintiff nor the defendant has serious links to Britain. In one case, an Icelandic bank sued a Danish tabloid in London over an article published in Denmark in the Danish language. A businessman in Libya successfully sued an Arabic-language television network located in Dubai, United Arab Emirates. A Ukrainian tycoon won a judgment against a Ukrainian newspaper as a result of a story written in Ukrainian and published in Kiev, the Ukrainian capital.

Some U.S. Reactions

In response to the Ehrenfeld case, the New York State legislature enacted the Libel Terrorism Protection Act in 2008. The act allows New York courts to assert jurisdiction over anyone who obtains a foreign libel judgment against a writer or publisher living in New York State. It also prevents courts from enforcing foreign libel judgments unless the foreign country provides free speech protection that is equal to or greater than what is available in the United States and in New York. Illinois has passed similar legislation. California and Florida may soon join them. Similar federal legislation is pending as well.

For Critical Analysis *Mahfouz made no attempt to collect the $225,000 judgment against Ehrenfeld. Given that fact, why might he have brought the libel suit in the first place?*

must stem from an intent to do harm, and must result in actual harm.

The Supreme Court has ruled that public figures (public officials and others in the public limelight) cannot collect damages for remarks made against them unless they can prove the remarks were made with "reckless" disregard for accuracy. Generally, it is believed that because public figures have greater access to the media than ordinary persons do, they are in a better position to defend themselves against libelous or slanderous statements. Other nations often have very different laws concerning defamation, as you can see in this chapter's *The Rest of the World* feature.

OBSCENITY. Obscene speech is another form of speech that is not protected under the First Amendment. Although the dictionary defines **obscenity** as that which is offensive and indecent, the courts have had difficulty

obscenity Indecency or offensiveness in speech, expression, behavior, or appearance. Whether specific expressions or acts constitute obscenity normally is determined by community standards.

katmere/Creative Commons

Before the Supreme Court held that the First Amendment applied to the states, many well-known works of literature were banned by various state and local governments. A number of famous works, such as *Ulysses,* were banned by the national government as well. In recent years, book banning has usually taken the form of removing a book from public or high school libraries, or from high school reading lists.

defining the term with any precision. Supreme Court justice Potter Stewart's famous statement, "I know it when I see it," certainly gave little guidance on the issue.

One problem in defining obscenity is that what is obscene to one person is not necessarily obscene to another; what one reader considers indecent, another reader might see as "colorful." Another problem is that society's views on obscenity change over time. Major literary works of such great writers as D. H. Lawrence (1885–1930), Mark Twain (1835–1910), and James Joyce (1882–1941), for example, were once considered obscene in most of the United States.

After many unsuccessful attempts to define obscenity, in 1973 the Supreme Court came up with a three-part test in *Miller v. California.*[20] The Court decided that a book, film, or other piece of material is legally obscene if it meets the following criteria:

1. The average person applying contemporary (present-day) standards finds that the work taken as a whole appeals to the prurient interest—that is, tends to excite unwholesome sexual desire.
2. The work depicts or describes, in a patently (obviously) offensive way, a form of sexual conduct specifically prohibited by an antiobscenity law.
3. The work taken as a whole lacks serious literary, artistic, political, or scientific value.

The very fact that the Supreme Court has had to set up such a complicated test shows how difficult defining obscenity is. The Court went on to state that, in effect, local communities should be allowed to set their own standards for what is obscene. What is obscene to many people in one area of the country might be perfectly acceptable to those in another area.

OBSCENITY IN CYBERSPACE. One of the most controversial issues concerning free speech in cyberspace is the question of obscene and pornographic materials. Such materials can be easily accessed by anyone of any age anywhere in the world at countless Web sites. Many people strongly believe that the government should step in to prevent obscenity on the Internet. Others believe, just as strongly, that speech on the Internet should not be regulated.

The issue came to a head in 1996, when Congress passed the Communications Decency Act (CDA). The law made it a crime to transmit "indecent" or "patently offensive" speech or images to minors (those under the age of eighteen) or to make such speech or images available online to minors. Violators of the act could be fined up to $250,000 or imprisoned for up to two years. In 1997, the Supreme Court held that the law's sections on indecent speech were unconstitutional. According to the Court, those sections of the CDA were too broad in their scope and significantly restrained the constitutionally protected free speech of adults.[21] Congress made a further attempt to regulate Internet speech in 1998 with the Child Online Protection Act. The act imposed criminal penalties on those who distribute material that is "harmful to minors" without using some kind of age-verification system to separate adult and minor Web users. In 2004, the Supreme Court barred enforcement of the act, ruling that the act likely violated constitutionally protected free speech, and sent the case back to the district court for a trial.[22] The district court found the act unconstitutional, and in 2008 a federal appellate court upheld the district court's ruling.

Having failed twice in its attempt to regulate online obscenity, Congress decided to try a different approach. In late 2000, it passed the Children's Internet Protection Act (CIPA). This act requires schools and libraries to use Internet filtering software to protect children from pornography or risk losing federal funds for technology upgrades. The CIPA was also challenged on

Reprinted with special permission of King Features Syndicate.

> "Be not intimidated,
> NOR SUFFER YOURSELVES TO BE WHEEDLED OUT OF YOUR LIBERTIES BY
> any pretense of politeness,
> DELICACY, OR DECENCY."
>
> ~ JOHN ADAMS ~
> SECOND PRESIDENT
> OF THE UNITED STATES
> 1797–1801

constitutional grounds, but in 2003 the Supreme Court held that the act did not violate the First Amendment. The Court concluded that because libraries can disable the filters for any patrons who ask, the system was reasonably flexible and did not burden free speech to an unconstitutional extent.[23]

In 1996, with the Child Pornography Prevention Act, Congress also attempted to prevent the distribution and possession of "virtual" child pornography—computer-generated images of children engaged in lewd and lascivious behavior. In 2002, the Supreme Court reviewed the 1996 act and found it unconstitutional. The Court ruled that the act did not establish the necessary link between "its prohibitions and the affront to community standards prohibited by the obscenity definition." The Court reaffirmed its position on this issue in 2008.[24]

The Free Speech Movement at the University of California at Berkeley campus made national headlines during the 1964–1965 academic year. Its leaders demanded that the university lift its on-campus ban on political activities. At the time, the largest student demonstrations ever essentially shut down large parts of that university. Some historians believe that the Free Speech Movement formed the basis of the civil rights movement in the 1960s.

Bettmann/Corbis

FREE SPEECH FOR STUDENTS? America's schools and college campuses experience an ongoing tension between the guarantee of free speech and the desire to restrain speech that is offensive to others. Typically, cases involving free speech in the schools raise the following question: Where should the line between unacceptable speech and merely offensive speech be drawn? Schools at all levels—elementary schools, high schools, and colleges and universities—have grappled with this issue.

Generally, the courts allow elementary schools wide latitude to define what students may and may not say to other students. At the high school level, the Supreme Court has allowed some restraints to be placed on the freedom of expression. For example, as you will read shortly, in the discussion of freedom of the press, the Court does allow school officials to exercise some censorship over high school publications. And, in a controversial 2007 case, the Court upheld a school principal's decision to suspend a high school student who unfurled a banner reading "Bong Hits 4 Jesus" at an event off the school premises. The Court sided with the school officials, who maintained that the banner appeared to advocate illegal drug use in violation of school policy. Many legal commentators and scholars strongly criticized this decision.[25]

A difficult question that many universities face today is whether the right to free speech includes the right to make hateful remarks about others based on their race, gender, or sexual orientation. Some claim that allowing people with extremist views to voice their opinions can lead to violence. In response to this question, several universities have gone so far as to institute speech codes to minimize the disturbances that hate speech might cause. Although these speech codes have often been ruled unconstitutional on the ground that they restrict freedom of speech,[26] such codes continue to exist on many college campuses. For example, the student assembly at Wesleyan University passed a resolution in 2002 stating that the "right to speech comes with implicit responsibilities to respect community standards."[27] Campus rules governing speech and expression, however, can foster the idea that "good" speech should be protected, but "bad" speech should not. Furthermore, who should decide what is considered "hate speech"?

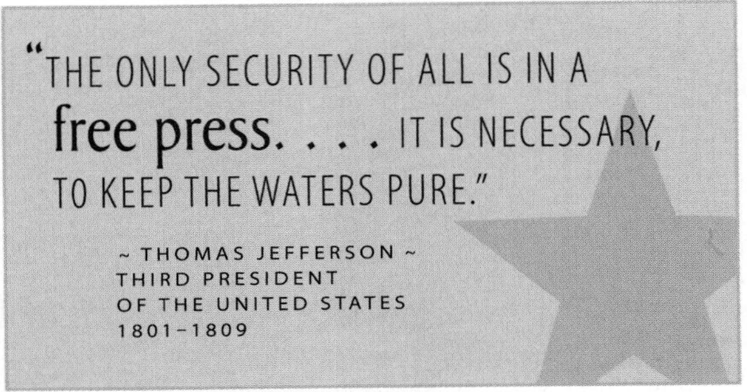

Freedom of the Press

The framers of the Constitution believed that the press should be free to publish a wide range of opinions and information, and generally the free speech rights just discussed also apply to the press. The courts have placed certain restrictions on the freedom of the press, however. Over the years, the Supreme Court has developed various guidelines and doctrines to use in deciding whether freedom of speech and the press can be restrained.

CLEAR AND PRESENT DANGER One guideline the Court has used resulted from a case in 1919, *Schenck v. United States.*[28] Charles T. Schenck was convicted of printing and distributing leaflets urging men to resist the draft during World War I. The government claimed that his actions violated the Espionage Act of 1917, which made it a crime to encourage disloyalty to the government or resistance to the draft. The Supreme Court upheld both the law and the convictions. Justice Holmes, speaking for the Court, stated as follows:

> The question in every case is whether the words used are used in such circumstances and are of such a nature as to create a *clear and present danger* that they will bring about the substantive evils that Congress has a right to prevent. It is a question of proximity [closeness] and degree. [Emphasis added.]

Thus, according to the *clear and present danger test,* government should be allowed to restrain speech only when that speech clearly presents an immediate threat to public order. It is often hard to say when speech crosses the line between being merely controversial and being a "clear and present danger," but the principle has been used in many cases since *Schenck*.

The clear and present danger principle seemed too permissive to some Supreme Court justices. Several years after the *Schenck* ruling, in the case of *Gitlow v. New York,*[29] the Court held that speech could be curtailed even if it had only a *tendency* to lead to illegal action. Since the 1920s, however, this guideline, known as the *bad-tendency test,* generally has not been supported by the Supreme Court.

THE PREFERRED-POSITION DOCTRINE Another guideline, called the *preferred-position doctrine,* states that certain freedoms are so essential to a democracy that they hold a preferred position. According to this doctrine, any law that limits these freedoms should be presumed unconstitutional unless the government can show that the law is absolutely necessary. Thus, freedom of speech and the press should rarely, if ever, be diminished, because spoken and printed words are the prime tools of the democratic process.

PRIOR RESTRAINT Stopping an activity before it actually happens is known as *prior restraint.* With respect to freedom of the press, prior restraint involves *censorship,* which occurs when an official removes objectionable materials from an item before it is published or broadcast. An example of censorship and prior restraint would be a court's ruling that two paragraphs in an upcoming article in the local newspaper had to be removed before the article could be published. The Supreme Court has generally ruled against prior restraint, arguing that the government cannot curb ideas *before* they are expressed.

On some occasions, however, the Court has allowed prior restraint. For example, in a 1988 case, *Hazelwood School District v. Kuhlmeier,*[30] a high school principal deleted two pages from the school newspaper just before it was printed. The pages contained stories on students' experiences with pregnancy and discussed the impact of divorce on students at the school. The Supreme Court, noting that students in school do not have exactly the same rights as adults in other settings, ruled that high school administrators *can* censor school publications. The Court said that school newspapers are part of the school curriculum, not a public forum. Therefore, administrators have the right to censor speech that promotes conduct inconsistent with the "shared values of a civilized social order."

All groups—even the racially intolerant Ku Klux Klan—are guaranteed the freedom of assembly under the First Amendment.

Freedom of Assembly

The First Amendment also protects the right of the people "peaceably to assemble" and communicate their ideas on public issues to government officials, as well as to other individuals. Parades, marches, protests, and other demonstrations are daily events in this country and allow groups to express and publicize their ideas. The Supreme Court has often put this freedom of assembly, or association, on a par with freedom of speech and freedom of the press. In the interests of public order, however, the Court has allowed municipalities to require permits for parades and sound trucks.

Like unpopular speech, unpopular assemblies or protests often generate controversy. One controversial case arose in 1977, when the American Nazi Party decided to march through the largely Jewish suburb of Skokie, Illinois. The city of Skokie enacted three ordinances designed to prohibit the types of demonstrations that the Nazis planned to undertake. The American Civil Liberties Union (ACLU) sued the city on behalf of the Nazis, defending their right to march (in spite of the ACLU's opposition to the Nazi philosophy). A federal district court agreed with the ACLU and held that the city of Skokie had violated the Nazis' First Amendment guarantees by denying them a permit to march. The appellate court affirmed that decision. The Supreme Court refused to review the case, thus letting the lower court's decision stand.[31]

What about laws that prevent gang members from assembling on city streets? Do such laws violate the gang members' First Amendment rights or other constitutional guarantees? Courts have answered this question differently, depending in part on the nature of the laws in question.

In some cases, for example, "antiloitering" laws have been upheld by the courts. In others, they have not. In 1999, the Supreme Court held that Chicago's antiloitering ordinance violated the right to due process because, among other things, it left too much "lawmaking" power in the hands of the police, who had to decide what constitutes "loitering."[32] How a particular court balances gang members' right of assembly against the rights of society may also come into play. In 1997, for example, the California Supreme Court had to decide whether court injunctions barring gang members from appearing in public together in certain areas of San Jose, California, were constitutional. The court upheld the injunctions, declaring that society's rights to peace and quiet and to be free from harm outweighed the gang members' First Amendment rights to gather together in public.[33]

The Right to Petition the Government

The First Amendment also guarantees the right of the people "to petition the government for a redress of grievances." This important right sometimes gets lost among the other, more well-known First Amendment guarantees, such as the freedoms of religion, speech, and the press. Nonetheless, the right to petition the government is as important and fundamental to our democracy as the other First Amendment rights.

The right to petition the government allows citizens to lobby members of Congress and other government officials, to sue the government, and to submit petitions to the government. A petitioner may be an individual or a large group. In the past, Americans have petitioned the government to ban alcohol, give the vote to women, and abolish slavery. They have petitioned the government to improve roads and obtain economic relief. Whenever someone writes to her or his congressional representative for help with a problem, such as not receiving a Social Security payment, that person is petitioning the government.

LO3 *The Right to Privacy*

Supreme Court justice Louis Brandeis stated in 1928 that the right to privacy is "the most comprehensive of rights and the right most valued by civilized men."[34] The majority of the justices on the Supreme Court at that time did not agree. In 1965, however, in the landmark case of *Griswold v. Connecticut,*[35] the justices on the Supreme Court held that a right to privacy is implied by other constitutional rights guaranteed in the First, Third, Fourth, Fifth, and Ninth Amendments. For example, consider the words of the Ninth Amendment: "The enumeration in the Constitution, of certain rights, shall not be construed to deny or disparage others retained by the people." In other words, just because the Constitution, including its amendments, does not specifically mention the right to privacy does not mean that this right is denied to the people.

> **"THE RIGHT TO BE LET ALONE** – the most comprehensive of the rights and the right most valued by civilized men."
>
> ~ LOUIS BRANDEIS ~
> ASSOCIATE JUSTICE OF THE UNITED STATES SUPREME COURT
> 1916–1939

Since then, the government has also passed laws ensuring the privacy rights of individuals. For example, in 1966 Congress passed the Freedom of Information Act, which, among other things, allows any person to request copies of any information about her or him contained in government files. In 1974, Congress passed the Privacy Act, which restricts government disclosure of data to third parties. In 1994, Congress passed the Driver's Privacy Protection Act, which prevents states from disclosing or selling a driver's personal information without the driver's consent.[36] In late 2000, the federal Department of Health and Human Services issued a regulation ensuring the privacy of a person's medical information. Health-care providers and insurance companies are restricted from sharing confidential information about their patients.

Although Congress and the courts have acknowledged a constitutional right to privacy, the nature and scope of this right are not always clear. For example, Americans continue to debate whether the right to privacy includes the right to have an abortion or the right of terminally ill persons to commit physician-assisted suicide. Since the terrorist attacks of September 11, 2001, another pressing privacy issue has been how to monitor potential terrorists to prevent another attack without violating the privacy rights of all Americans.

The government is not the only entity that can threaten our privacy. Information collected by private corporations can be just as much of a concern, as explained in this chapter's *Join the Debate* feature on the facing page.

The Abortion Controversy

One of the most divisive and emotionally charged issues being debated today is whether the right to privacy means that women can choose to have abortions.

ABORTION AND PRIVACY In 1973, in the landmark case of *Roe v. Wade,*[37] the Supreme Court, using the *Griswold* case as a precedent, held that the "right of privacy . . . is broad enough to encompass a woman's decision whether or not to terminate her pregnancy." The right is not absolute throughout pregnancy, however.

¡DERECHOS REPRODUCTIVOS SON DERECHOS HUMANOS
plannedparenthood.org
KEEP ABORTION LEGAL
FOR U CHOICE
IT'S YOUR CHOICE ...NOT THEIRS.

Mark Peterson/Redux

Mark Peterson/Redux

Abortion continues to be extremely controversial in the United States. On the left, pro-choice supporters demonstrate their desire that abortion remain legal. In stark contrast, on the right, an antiabortion activist protests in front of the United States Supreme Court building in Washington, D.C. Before the *Roe v. Wade* decision in 1973, whether abortion was legal depended on state legislation.

JOIN THE DEBATE

Should the Use of Cameras in Public Places Be Regulated?

You might spot them in Singapore, Mexico City, or Bemidji, Minnesota. Around the world, a fleet of cars, including Chevrolet Cobalts, Opel Astras, and Toyota Priuses, cruise the streets with a startling array of gear mounted on their roofs. The equipment currently in use includes nine directional cameras for 360-degree views, global positioning system (GPS) units, and three laser range scanners that can measure distances of up to fifty yards. Antennas search for 3G/GSM and Wi-Fi hotspots. These are the vehicles of Google Street View. The cameras take simultaneous photographs in different directions. The photos are indexed to locations using the GPS equipment. Google can even photograph narrow streets that cars cannot reach, which are common in the Far East. It does so by mounting its equipment on adult tricycles.

Through Street View, you can engage in virtual travel down various streets in hundreds of U.S. towns and cities, both large and small. Street View shows you more than just streets and buildings—people and personal property are also visible. You might even see someone slipping into a seedy business. Are Google's actions violating privacy rights? And Google is not alone. What about the cameras surrounding Citibank's ATM machines? Do they invade our privacy? In New York City's Time Square alone, more than two thousand cameras automatically photograph everybody and everything.

Fogging the Faces

Street View was introduced in 2007 with shots of San Francisco and four other U.S. cities. It didn't take long before privacy advocates became alarmed. Google's cameras caught shots of people and personal property that could be accessed by millions of Internet users. Privacy advocates argued that individual citizens have a right to prevent personal information from being revealed on the Internet by snooping cameras. Images of sunbathers, drunks, persons entering "adult" bookstores, and people picking up prostitutes have been widely republished. Some of these shots are still visible through Street View. Due to criticisms, though, in May 2008 Google introduced a system that blurred faces in its images. (Because the system is automated, it also blurs faces on posters, such as the face of Colonel Sanders, used to advertise KFC restaurants.)

Mark Wallace/Creative Commons

What the Law Says

On the other side of this debate are history and the First Amendment right to free speech. Muckrakers and tabloids have been taking pictures in public places since the advent of photography. The Google photographs shown on Street View are taken on public streets. Someone in a public place has no reasonable expectation of privacy. Although you can prevent others from making money by using your name and face (to advertise products or services, for example), photographing you or anybody else in public is protected by the First Amendment. Anyone has the right to "ogle" in public spaces and then turn this action into "speech" and publish it in newspapers, in magazines, and, of course, on the Internet. The federal courts are not going to block Google or any competing organization from photographing every street in the country. Consider also that Street View has been known to help victims of crime. For example, a boy in the Netherlands found a photo on Street View showing him with two men immediately before they mugged him. Authorities were able to use these photos to arrest the suspects.

Blog On *It's simple to use Google Street View. Just go to maps.google.com. You'll see a map of North America. The control on the left-hand side of the map lets you zoom in or out. To change your location, you can click on the map itself and drag it about. When you've reached a spot where you'd like to use Street View, click on the little orange person at the top of the control and drag it to the street you'd like to see. For a collection of interesting Street View photos, visit* ***streetviewgallery.corank.com****.*

The Court also said that any state could impose certain regulations to safeguard the health of the mother after the first three months of pregnancy and, in the final stages of pregnancy, could act to protect potential life.

Since the *Roe v. Wade* decision, the Supreme Court has adopted a more conservative approach and has upheld restrictive state laws requiring counseling, waiting periods, notification of parents, and other actions prior to abortions.[38] Yet the Court has never overturned the *Roe* decision. In fact, in 1997 and again in 2000, the Supreme Court upheld laws requiring "buffer zones" around abortion clinics to protect those entering the clinics from unwanted counseling or harassment by antiabortion groups.[39] In 2000, the Supreme Court invalidated a Nebraska statute banning "partial-birth" abortions, a procedure used during the second trimester of pregnancy.[40] Undeterred by the fate of the Nebraska law, President George W. Bush signed the Partial Birth Abortion Ban Act in 2003. In a close (five-to-four) and controversial 2007 decision, the Supreme Court upheld the constitutionality of the 2003 act.[41]

Many were surprised at the Court's decision on partial-birth abortion, given that the federal act banning this practice was quite similar to the Nebraska law that had been struck down by the Court in 2000, just seven years earlier. Since that decision was rendered, however, the Court has generally become more conservative with the appointment of two new justices. Dissenting from the majority opinion in the case, Justice Ruth Bader Ginsburg said that the ruling was an "alarming" departure from three decades of Supreme Court decisions on abortion.

ABORTION AND POLITICS

American opinion on the abortion issue is more nuanced than the labels "pro-life" and "pro-choice" would indicate. For example, a 2008 Gallup poll found that 45 percent of the respondents considered themselves pro-choice and 45 percent called themselves pro-life. Yet when respondents were asked whether abortion should be legal or illegal, public opinion was more conservative than the attachments to these labels would suggest. About 58 percent thought that abortion should either be limited to only a few circumstances or be illegal in all circumstances; 41 percent thought that it should be legal in all or most circumstances.

Some have contended that President George W. Bush's appointment of more than 250 federal judges caused a rightward shift in the judiciary and that this shift will result in more conservative abortion rulings in the future. President Barack Obama's appointees, however, are likely to push the courts back toward the left.

Do We Have the "Right to Die"?

Whether it is called euthanasia (mercy killing), assisted suicide, or a dignified way to leave this world, it all comes down to one basic question: Do terminally ill persons have, as part of their civil liberties, a right to die and to be assisted in the process by physicians or others? Phrased another way, are state laws banning physician-assisted suicide in such circumstances unconstitutional?

In 1997, the issue came before the Supreme Court, which characterized the question as follows: Does the liberty protected by the Constitution include a right to commit suicide, which itself includes a right to assistance in doing so? The Court's clear and categorical answer to this question was no. To hold otherwise, said the Court, would be "to reverse centuries of legal doctrine and practice, and strike down the considered

Supreme Court Chief Justice John Roberts swears in the first Hispanic (and third female) supreme court justice in the over two-hundred-year history of that institution. Justice Sonia Sotomayor faced hostile questions from some members of Congress during her nomination hearings. Why?

AP Photo/J. Scott Applewhite

policy choice of almost every state."[42] Although the Court upheld the states' rights to ban such a practice, the Court did not hold that state laws *permitting* assisted suicide were unconstitutional. In 1997, Oregon became the first state to implement such a law. In 2008, Washington and Montana became the second and third states, respectively, to allow the practice. Oregon's law was upheld by the Supreme Court in 2006.[43]

The Supreme Court's enunciation of its opinion on this topic has not ended the debate, though, just as the debate over abortion did not stop after the 1973 *Roe v. Wade* decision legalizing abortion. Americans continue to be at odds over this issue.

Personal Privacy and National Security

Since the terrorist attacks of September 11, 2001, one of the most common debates in the news media and on Capitol Hill has been how the United States can address the urgent need to strengthen national security while still protecting civil liberties, particularly the right to privacy. As you will read throughout this book, various programs have been proposed or attempted, and some have already been dismantled after public outcry. For example, the Homeland Security Act passed in late 2002 included language explicitly prohibiting a controversial program called Operation TIPS (Terrorism Information and Prevention System). Operation TIPS was proposed to create a national reporting program for "citizen volunteers" who regularly work in neighborhoods and communities, such as postal carriers and meter readers, to report suspicious activity to the government. The public backlash against the program was quick and resolute—neighbors would not spy on neighbors.

FBI director Robert Mueller often faces questioning in front of congressional hearings on national security. What limits his decisions?

AP Photo/Gerald Herbert

Other laws and programs that infringe on Americans' privacy rights were also created in the wake of 9/11 in the interests of protecting the nation's security. For example, the USA Patriot Act of 2001 gave the government broad latitude to investigate people who are only vaguely associated with terrorists. Under this law, the government can access personal information on American citizens to an extent heretofore never allowed by law. The Federal Bureau of Investigation was also authorized to use "National Security Letters" to demand personal information about individuals from private companies (such as banks and phone companies). In one of the most controversial programs, the National Security Agency (NSA) was authorized to monitor certain domestic phone calls without first obtaining a warrant. When Americans learned of the NSA's actions in 2005, the ensuing public furor forced the Bush administration to agree to henceforth obtain warrants for such monitoring activities.

Some Americans, including many civil libertarians, are so concerned about the erosion of privacy rights that they wonder why the public outcry has not been even more vehement. They point out that trading off even a few civil liberties, including our privacy rights, for national security is senseless. After all, these liberties are at the heart of what this country stands for. When we abandon any of our civil liberties, we weaken our country rather than defend it. Essentially, say some members of this group, the federal government has achieved what the terrorists were unable to accomplish—the destruction of our freedoms. Other Americans believe that we have little to worry about. Those who have nothing to hide should not be concerned about government surveillance or other privacy intrusions undertaken by the government to make our nation more secure against terrorist attacks. To what extent has the Obama administration revised the policies established under President Bush? We examine that question in this chapter's *Perception versus Reality* feature on the following page.

Obama's Antiterrorism Stance Compared With Bush's

During much of the Bush administration, civil libertarians denounced the antiterrorism policies of President George W. Bush and his vice president, Dick Cheney. Certainly, after 9/11, the administration's view of civil liberties, especially those relating to privacy, changed substantially. The USA Patriot Act, which Bush signed into law on October 26, 2001, authorized a major expansion in the "snooping" activities of the federal government. In addition, the National Security Agency (NSA) was allowed to engage in domestic wiretapping without obtaining search warrants.

The Perception

During the Bush administration, Bush and Cheney ran a counterterrorism program that violated the civil liberties of Americans, tortured enemy combatants, and committed a variety of other illegal actions. According to Cheney, these practices saved "thousands, perhaps hundreds of thousands" of lives. They were also "legal, essential, justified, successful and the right thing to do." President Obama made the country "less safe," said Cheney, by eliminating them and by attempting to close the prison holding suspected terrorists at the Guantánamo Bay Naval Base.

In contrast, Obama called the Guantánamo prison a "misguided experiment" that actually increased the threats to American national security. "The Supreme Court that invalidated the system of prosecution at Guantánamo in 2006 was overwhelmingly appointed by Republican presidents," Obama said. "In other words, the problem of what to do with Guantánamo detainees was not caused by my decision to close the facility; the problem exists because of the decision to open Guantánamo in the first place."

The Reality

At most, the excessive antiterrorism policies of the Bush administration lasted for three years following 9/11. This nation had been blindsided—our intelligence officials knew almost nothing about the threats against us. The Bush administration frantically attempted to discover and prevent any further threats. It was in this environment that officials such as Cheney could demand—and obtain—policies that violated traditional American standards.

By 2005, however, members of the Bush administration were trying to rein in the excesses of the earlier post-9/11 period. Secretary of State Condoleezza Rice, National Security Advisor Stephen Hadley, and other officials sought to wean the administration away from the Cheney approach. In 2007, Rice refused to support an executive order reviving the "enhanced" interrogation program. Throughout Bush's second term, officials tried to close Guantánamo and pleaded with foreign governments to take some of its prisoners.

The most famous "enhanced" interrogation technique—water boarding—was halted long before Obama came to power. Obama castigated the military-commission system used to try captured enemy combatants, but in fact he revived this system with only cosmetic changes. Harvard law professor Jack Goldsmith puts it this way: "The main difference between the Obama and Bush administrations concerns not the substance of terrorism policy, but rather its packaging." In reality, Obama's policies largely represented a continuation of the policies adopted during Bush's second term. Cheney, Bush, and Obama all had an interest in glossing over that fact.

Blog On *National security blogs may outnumber the stars you can see on a cloudless night. We can mention only a few. At* **voices.washingtonpost.com/earlywarning,** *the* Washington Post *hosts moderators with experience in journalism, public service, and the military. The* National Journal *offers expert posts at* **security.nationaljournal.com.** *The Heritage Foundation takes a strongly conservative line at* **blog.nationalsecurity.org.** *Finally, these two blogs defend the rights of Guantánamo detainees:* **gtmoblog.blogspot.com** *and* **www.bradblog.com/?cat=263.**

LO4 *The Rights of the Accused*

The United States has one of the highest murder rates in the industrialized world. It is therefore not surprising that many Americans have extremely strong opinions about the rights of persons accused of criminal offenses. Indeed, some Americans complain that criminal defendants have too many rights.

Why do criminal suspects have rights? The answer is that all persons are entitled to the protections afforded by the Bill of Rights. If criminal suspects were deprived of their basic constitutional liberties, all people would suffer the consequences, because there is nothing to stop the government from accusing anyone of being a criminal. In a criminal case, a state official (such as the district attorney, or D.A.) prosecutes the defendant, and the state has immense resources that it can bring to bear against the accused person. By protecting the rights of accused persons, the Constitution helps to prevent the arbitrary use of power by the government.

The Rights of Criminal Defendants

The basic rights, or constitutional safeguards, provided for criminal defendants are set forth in the Bill of Rights. These safeguards include the following:

- The Fourth Amendment protection from unreasonable searches and seizures.
- The Fourth Amendment requirement that no warrant for a search or an arrest be issued without **probable cause**—cause for believing that there is a substantial likelihood that a person has committed or is about to commit a crime.
- The Fifth Amendment requirement that no one be deprived of "life, liberty, or property, without due process of law." As discussed earlier in this chapter, this requirement is also included in the Fourteenth Amendment, which protects persons against actions by state governments.
- The Fifth Amendment prohibition against **double jeopardy**—being tried twice for the same criminal offense.
- The Fifth Amendment provision that no person can be required to be a witness against (incriminate) himself or herself. This is often referred to as the constitutional protection against **self-incrimination.** It is the basis for a criminal suspect's "right to remain silent" in criminal proceedings.
- The Sixth Amendment guarantees of a speedy trial, a trial by jury, a public trial, and the right to confront witnesses.
- The Sixth Amendment guarantee of the right to counsel at various stages in some criminal proceedings. The right to counsel was strengthened in 1963 in *Gideon v. Wainwright.*[44] The Supreme Court held that if a person is accused of a felony and cannot afford an attorney, an attorney must be made available to the accused person at the government's expense.
- The Eighth Amendment prohibitions against excessive bail and fines and against cruel and unusual punishments.

The Exclusionary Rule

Any evidence obtained in violation of the constitutional rights spelled out in the Fourth Amendment normally is not admissible at trial. This rule, which has been applied in the federal courts since at least 1914, is known as the **exclusionary rule.** The rule was extended to state court proceedings in 1961.[45] The reasoning behind the exclusionary rule is that it forces law enforcement personnel to gather evidence properly. If they do not, they will be unable to introduce the evidence at trial to convince the jury that the defendant is guilty.

The *Miranda* Warnings

In the 1950s and 1960s, one of the questions facing the courts was not whether suspects had constitutional rights—that was not in doubt—but how and when those rights could be exercised. For example, could the right to remain silent (under the Fifth Amendment's prohibition against self-incrimination) be exercised during pretrial interrogation proceedings or only during the trial? Were confessions obtained from suspects admissible in court if the suspects had not been advised of their right to remain silent and other constitutional rights? To clarify these issues, in 1966 the Supreme Court issued a landmark decision in *Miranda v. Arizona.*[46] In that case, the Court enunciated the ***Miranda* warnings** that are now familiar to virtually all Americans:

> Prior to any questioning, the person must be warned that he has a right to remain silent, that any statement he does make may be used against him, and that he has a right to the presence of an attorney, either retained or appointed.

The Erosion of *Miranda*

As part of a continuing attempt to balance the rights of accused persons against the rights of society, the Supreme Court

probable cause Cause for believing that there is a substantial likelihood that a person has committed or is about to commit a crime.

double jeopardy The prosecution of a person twice for the same criminal offense; prohibited by the Fifth Amendment in all but a few circumstances.

self-incrimination Providing damaging information or testimony against oneself in court.

exclusionary rule A criminal procedural rule requiring that any illegally obtained evidence not be admissible in court.

***Miranda* warnings** A series of statements informing criminal suspects, on their arrest, of their constitutional rights, such as the right to remain silent and the right to counsel; required by the Supreme Court's 1966 decision in *Miranda v. Arizona.*

has made a number of exceptions to the *Miranda* ruling. In 1986, for example, the Court held that a confession need not be excluded even though the police failed to inform a suspect in custody that his attorney had tried to reach him by telephone.[47] In an important 1991 decision, the Court stated that a suspect's conviction will not be automatically overturned if the suspect was coerced into making a confession. If the other evidence admitted at trial was strong enough to justify the conviction without the confession, then the fact that the confession was obtained illegally can be, in effect, ignored.[48] In yet another case, in 1994 the Supreme Court ruled that a suspect must unequivocally and assertively state his right to counsel in order to stop police questioning. Saying "Maybe I should talk to a lawyer" during an interrogation after being taken into custody is not enough. The Court held that police officers are not required to decipher the suspect's intentions in such situations.[49]

Elena Rooraid/PhotoEdit

This police officer is reading the accused his *Miranda* warnings. Since the 1966 *Miranda* decision, the Supreme Court has relaxed its requirements in some situations, such as when a criminal suspect who is not under arrest enters a police station voluntarily.

Miranda may eventually become obsolete regardless of any decisions made in the courts. A relatively new trend in law enforcement has been for agencies to digitally record interrogations and confessions. Thomas P. Sullivan, a former U.S. attorney in Chicago, and his staff interviewed personnel in more than 230 law enforcement agencies in thirty-eight states that record interviews of suspects who are in custody. Sullivan found that nearly all police officers said the procedure saved time and money, created valuable evidence to use in court, and made it more difficult for defense attorneys to claim that their clients had been illegally coerced.[50] Some scholars have suggested that recording all custodial interrogations would satisfy the Fifth Amendment's prohibition against coercion and in the process render the *Miranda* warnings unnecessary.

Michael Stravato/*The New York Times*/Redux

Recently arrested men are searched before being moved into a cell in the Inmate Processing Center at the Harris County jail in Houston Texas. What right do these men have?

AMERICA AT ODDS Civil Liberties

For more than two hundred years, Americans have been among the freest people in the world. This is largely because our courts have upheld, time and again, the liberties set forth in the Bill of Rights and because the government has enforced the courts' decisions. Every generation of Americans has given strength to the Bill of Rights by bringing pressure to bear on the government when these liberties have been violated. If either the courts or the government fails to enforce these liberties, then the Bill of Rights itself becomes irrelevant—a useless piece of paper. Many nations with written constitutions that set forth generous rights and liberties for their citizens nonetheless are ruled by oppressive dictatorships. The constitution of Saddam Hussein's Iraq, for example, specified numerous rights and liberties, but they remained largely fictional.

At times in our nation's history, typically in wartime, the government has placed restraints on certain rights and liberties. You read about one example in this chapter—the Alien and Sedition Acts of 1798, which criminalized speech critical of government. Another example is the internment of Japanese Americans in the 1940s during World War II, which stemmed from a fear that this group of Americans could aid one of our enemies in that war—Japan. Today, many argue that more of our civil liberties have been sacrificed than ever before to protect against a "war on terrorism" that is not even a war in any traditional sense. Are such sacrifices necessary? Some Americans, including President George W. Bush and his supporters, believed they were. Others, including many members of Congress, did not agree. Generally, Americans remain divided on this important issue.

ISSUES FOR DEBATE & DISCUSSION

Since 9/11, cities across America have become much more vigilant in monitoring people's activities on the streets and at bridges, tunnels, airports, and subways. Since 2003, the New York City Police Department has gone even further. It has been videotaping political assemblies and other public events, including a march in Harlem and a demonstration by homeless people before the mayor's home, even without any evidence showing that these gatherings would be anything but peaceful. The New York City police have also used undercover police officers to infiltrate political gatherings. Some believe that such monitoring activities are justified because of the threat of terrorism. Others claim that they go too far in intruding on our right to privacy. What is your position on this issue?

TAKE ACTION

If you are ever concerned that your civil liberties are being threatened by a government action, you can exercise one of your liberties—the right to petition the government—to object to the action. Often, those who want to take action feel that they are alone in their struggles until they begin discussing their views with others. Brenda Koehler, a writing student attending college in Kutztown, Pennsylvania, relates how one of her friends, whom we will call "Charyn," took action in response to the USA Patriot Act of 2001. Concerned about the extent to which this act infringed on Americans' civil liberties, Charyn began e-mailing her friends and others about the issue. Eventually, a petition against the enforcement of the act in her town was circulated, and the city council agreed to consider the petition. Charyn did not expect anything to come from the review and assumed that the council would dismiss the petition without even reading the three-hundred-page Patriot Act. On the day of the hearing, the council chambers were packed with town citizens who shared Charyn's and her friends' concerns. The council adjourned the meeting for a week so that it could review the act, and when it met the next week, the resolution to oppose enforcing the act was adopted. Although one person's efforts are not always so successful, there will certainly be no successes at all if no one takes action.[51]

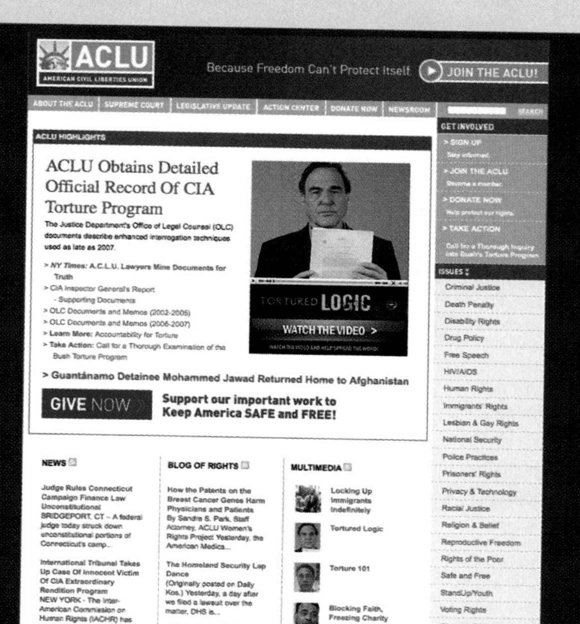

The American Civil Liberties Union has a Web site that tracks all kinds of issues pertaining to the protection of civil liberties. To see what your fellow citizens are doing to protect civil liberties, go to www.aclu.org.

POLITICS ON THE WEB

- Almost three dozen First Amendment groups have launched the Free Expression Network Clearinghouse, which is a Web site designed to feature legislation updates, legal briefings, and news on cases of censorship in local communities. Go to **www.freeexpression.org**
- The Website for the leading civil liberties organization, the American Civil Liberties Union (ACLU), can be found at **www.aclu.org**
- The Liberty Counsel is "a nonprofit religious civil liberties education and legal defense organization established to preserve religious freedom." Its take on civil liberties is definitely right of center. You can access this organization's home page at **www.lc.org**
- For information on the effect of new computer and communications technologies on the constitutional rights and liberties of Americans, go to the Center for Democracy and Technology at **www.cdt.org**
- For information on privacy issues relating to the Internet, go to the Electronic Privacy Information Center's Web site at **www.epic.org/privacy**
- To access United States Supreme Court decisions on civil liberties, go to the Court's official Web site at **www.supremecourtus.gov**

Online resources for this chapter

This text's Companion Web site, at **www.4ltrpress.cengage.com/govt**, offers links to numerous resources that you can use to learn more about the topics covered in this chapter.

civil liberties
www.aclu.org
writ of *habeas corpus*
due process of law
Miranda warnings
exclusionary rule
obscenity
www.freeexpression.org

David Freund/Photodisc/Getty Images

Civil Rights

GOVT 5

LEARNING OBJECTIVES

LO1 Explain the constitutional basis for our civil rights and for laws prohibiting discrimination.

LO2 Discuss the reasons for the civil rights movement and the changes it caused in American politics and government.

LO3 Describe the political and economic achievements of women in this country over time and identify some obstacles to equality that they continue to face.

LO4 Summarize the struggles for equality faced by other groups in America.

LO5 Explain what affirmative action is and why it has been so controversial.

AMERICA AT ODDS

Should Employers Be Able to Demand That Their Employees Speak Only English?

Do you believe that the Constitution makes English the official language of the United States? Sixty-four percent of Americans believe that. The Constitution, though, contains not one word about the English language. Other countries have official languages though.

To be sure, in the United States, English is the language of choice in most transactions. Less than 1 percent of the population cannot speak English at all. At least thirty states have made English their official language, and other states are considering such legislation. Still, English is not universally spoken. Spanish is the native language of at least 30 million Americans. Others may speak Cantonese, German, or Italian. More than 325 languages are in use in the United States. About 175 are Native American languages, so there are actually many more languages spoken in the United States than in Europe.

In this environment, a number of private businesses have instituted English-only rules. A Connecticut-based sheet metal manufacturing company, with a labor force that is 75 percent Latino, instituted such a policy a few years ago. At least one staff member who objected to the policy was fired. Five employees sued in federal district court. Their lawyers argued that there was no justifiable reason for an English-only policy and that it would lead to less safety and efficiency in the plant. Americans remain at odds about the necessity and validity of requiring English in the workplace.

This Is America, and We Speak English

Those in favor of English-only rules in the workplace argue that America became a great country because its immigrants quickly learned English and assimilated. English-only rules in the workplace are a useful counterweight to government policies that allow and even encourage the use of other languages. In the workplace, safety requires that everyone understand and speak English. If managers are to have control of the workplace, they must be able to understand what employees are saying. Clearly, too, if employees have face-to-face contact with the public, they must be able to communicate in English.

Federal appeals courts have generally held that English-only policies are not inherently discriminatory. As far back as 1980, the federal courts have upheld English-only workplace rules. In New York, a federal court upheld a taxi company's English-only policy as being a justifiable business necessity. Also in New York, another federal court ruled that a retail company had a justifiable reason for its English-only policy. This reason was to curb hostility among employees and to assist supervisors in understanding what those employees were saying in the workplace.

This Is a Free Country, So Let People Speak as They Wish

Even if workplace English-only rules are not intentionally discriminatory, their effect, or impact, is discriminatory. They violate the Civil Rights Act of 1964. English-only rules are widely—and correctly—perceived as an attack on Hispanic Americans. More than 30 million Americans speak Spanish, and we should not force them to speak only English.

Many English-only workplace rules have nothing to do with safety or communication. For example, the EEOC filed a suit on behalf of two Salvation Army workers in Framingham, Massachusetts, who were fired because they did not comply with an English-only rule. The two people involved were isolated in a back room, and there was absolutely no need for them to speak English. Consider also that new, legal immigrants who speak English poorly need time to learn it. During this assimilation period, English-only laws prevent such individuals from being able to work. It makes no sense for employers who have large numbers of Spanish-speaking employees to require English only. Such a knee-jerk reaction against Spanish on the job actually leads to less efficiency, less safety, and more strained employer-employee relations.

WHERE DO YOU STAND?

1. **Do you believe that Congress should adopt legislation making English the country's official language? Why or why not?**
2. **In private businesses, should the owners be allowed to establish whatever requirements they want for their employees? Why or why not?**

EXPLORE THIS ISSUE ONLINE

- **ProEnglish is the most prominent organization lobbying to make English the sole language officially recognized by the national and state governments. Its Web site is at www.proenglish.org.**
- **English-only rules are one of many issues taken up by advocates for the immigrant population. The Catholic Church defends immigrants' rights at www.justiceforimmigrants.org. The ACLU addresses these issues at www.aclu.org/immigrants.**

Introduction

As noted in Chapter 4, people sometimes confuse civil rights with civil liberties. Generally, though, the term **civil rights** refers to the rights of all Americans to equal treatment under the law, as provided for by the Fourteenth Amendment. One of the functions of our government is to ensure—through legislation or other means—that this constitutional mandate is upheld.

All Americans are entitled to **EQUAL TREATMENT UNDER THE LAW** as provided for by the Fourteenth Amendment.

Although the democratic ideal is for all people to have equal rights and equal treatment under the law, and although the Constitution guarantees those rights, this ideal has often remained just that—an ideal. It is people who put ideals into practice, and as James Madison (1751–1836) once pointed out (and as we all know), people are not angels. As you will read in this chapter, the struggle of various groups in American society to obtain equal treatment has been a long one, and it still continues. One such group is made up of immigrants, both legal and illegal. We discussed an issue that concerns them in this chapter's opening *America at Odds* feature.

In a sense, the history of civil rights in the United States is a history of discrimination against various groups. Discrimination against women, African Americans, and Native Americans dates back to the early years of this nation, when the framers of the Constitution did not grant these groups rights that were granted to others (that is, to white, property-owning males). During our subsequent history, as peoples from around the globe immigrated to this country at various times and for various reasons, each of these immigrant groups faced discrimination in one form or another. More recently, other groups, including older Americans, persons with disabilities, and gay men and lesbians, have struggled for equal treatment under the law.

Central to any discussion of civil rights is the interpretation of the equal protection clause of the Fourteenth Amendment to the Constitution. For that reason, we look first at that clause and how the courts, particularly the United States Supreme Court, have interpreted it and applied it to civil rights issues.

LO1 The Equal Protection Clause

Equal in importance to the due process clause of the Fourteenth Amendment is the **equal protection clause** in Section 1 of that amendment, which reads as follows: "No State shall . . . deny to any person within its jurisdiction the equal protection of the laws." Section 5 of the amendment provides a legal basis for federal civil rights legislation: "The Congress shall have power to enforce, by appropriate legislation, the provisions of this article."

The equal protection clause has been interpreted by the courts, and especially the Supreme Court, to mean that states must treat all persons in

Reuters/Chip East/Landov

These demonstrators are making sure that the residents of New York City remember the goals of Martin Luther King, Jr.—equality for all minorities in America.

civil rights The rights of all Americans to equal treatment under the law, as provided for by the Fourteenth Amendment to the Constitution.

equal protection clause Section 1 of the Fourteenth Amendment, which states that no state shall "deny to any person within its jurisdiction the equal protection of the laws."

an equal manner and may not discriminate *unreasonably* against a particular group or class of individuals unless there is a sufficient reason to do so. The task of distinguishing between reasonable discrimination and unreasonable discrimination is difficult. Generally, in deciding this question, the Supreme Court balances the constitutional rights of individuals to equal protection against government interests in protecting the safety and welfare of citizens. Over time, the Court has developed various tests, or standards, for determining whether the equal protection clause has been violated.

Strict Scrutiny

If a law or action prevents some group of persons from exercising a **fundamental right** (such as one of our First Amendment rights), the law or action will be subject to the "strict-scrutiny" standard. Under this standard, the law or action must be necessary to promote a *compelling state interest* and must be narrowly tailored to meet that interest. A law based on a **suspect classification,** such as race, is also subject to strict scrutiny by the courts, meaning that the law must be justified by a compelling state interest.

fundamental right A basic right of all Americans, such as First Amendment rights. Any law or action that prevents some group of persons from exercising a fundamental right is subject to the "strict-scrutiny" standard, under which the law or action must be necessary to promote a compelling state interest and must be narrowly tailored to meet that interest.

suspect classification A classification, such as race, that provides the basis for a discriminatory law. Any law based on a suspect classification is subject to strict scrutiny by the courts—meaning that the law must be justified by a compelling state interest.

rational basis test A test (also known as the "ordinary-scrutiny" standard) used by the Supreme Court to decide whether a discriminatory law violates the equal protection clause of the Constitution. Few laws evaluated under this test are found invalid.

Intermediate Scrutiny

Because the Supreme Court had difficulty deciding how to judge cases in which men and women were treated differently, another test was developed—the "intermediate-scrutiny" standard. Under this standard, laws based on gender classifications are permissible if they are "substantially related to the achievement of an important governmental objective." For example, a law punishing males but not females for statutory rape is valid because of the important governmental interest in preventing teenage pregnancy in those circumstances and because almost all of the harmful and identifiable consequences of teenage pregnancies fall on young females.[1] A law prohibiting the sale of beer to males under twenty-one years of age and to females under eighteen years would not be valid, however.[2]

Generally, since the 1970s, the Supreme Court has scrutinized gender classifications closely and has declared many gender-based laws unconstitutional. In 1979, the Court held that a state law allowing wives to obtain alimony judgments against husbands but preventing husbands from receiving alimony from wives violated the equal protection clause.[3] In 1982, the Court declared that Mississippi's policy of excluding males from the School of Nursing at Mississippi University for Women was unconstitutional.[4] In a controversial 1996 case, *United States v. Virginia,*[5] the Court held that Virginia Military Institute, a state-financed institution, violated the equal protection clause by refusing to accept female applicants. The Court said that the state of Virginia had failed to provide a sufficient justification for its gender-based classification.

The Rational Basis Test (Ordinary Scrutiny)

A third test used to decide whether a discriminatory law violates the equal protection clause is the **rational basis test.** When applying this test to a law that classifies or

Tim Schaffer/Reuters/Corbis

For many years, the Virginia Military Institute did not allow female students. That changed in 1996 when the United States Supreme Court ruled that this state-financed institution violated the equal protection clause by refusing to admit women.

treats people or groups differently, the justices ask whether the discrimination is rational. In other words, is it a reasonable way to achieve a legitimate government objective? Few laws tested under the rational basis test—or the "ordinary-scrutiny" standard, as it is also called—are found invalid, because few laws are truly unreasonable. A municipal ordinance that prohibits certain vendors from selling their wares in a particular area of the city, for example, will be upheld if the city can meet this rational basis test. The rational basis for the ordinance might be the city's legitimate government interest in reducing traffic congestion in that particular area.

Library of Congress

Homer Plessy.

LO2 *African Americans*

The equal protection clause was originally intended to protect the newly freed slaves after the Civil War (1861–1865). In the early years after the war, the U.S. government made an effort to protect the rights of blacks living in the former states of the Confederacy. The Thirteenth Amendment (which granted freedom to the slaves), the Fourteenth Amendment (which guaranteed equal protection under the law), and the Fifteenth Amendment (which stated that voting rights could not be abridged on account of race) were part of that effort. By the late 1880s, however, southern legislatures had begun to pass a series of segregation laws—laws that separated the white community from the black community. Such laws were commonly called "Jim Crow" laws (from a song that was popular in minstrel shows that caricatured African Americans). Some of the most common Jim Crow laws called for racial segregation in the use of public facilities, such as schools, railroads, and later, buses. These laws were also applied to housing, restaurants, hotels, and many other facilities.

This man is picketing in front of a variety store in downtown Atlanta in the fall of 1960. What did he mean when he referred to eliminating Jim Crow?

AP Photo

Separate but Equal

In 1892, a group of Louisiana citizens decided to challenge a state law that required railroads to provide separate railway cars for African Americans. A man named Homer Plessy, who was seven-eighths Caucasian and one-eighth African, boarded a train in New Orleans and sat in the railway car reserved for whites. When Plessy refused to move at the request of the conductor, he was arrested for breaking the law.

Four years later, in 1896, the Supreme Court provided a constitutional basis for segregation laws. In *Plessy v. Ferguson,*[6] the Court held that the law did not violate the equal protection clause if *separate* facilities for blacks were *equal* to those for whites. The lone dissenter, Justice John Marshall Harlan, disagreed: "Our Constitution is colorblind, and neither knows nor tolerates classes among citizens." The majority opinion, however, established the **separate-but-equal doctrine,** which was used to justify segregation in many areas of American life for nearly sixty years. Separate facilities for African Americans, when they were provided at all, were in practice almost never truly equal.

In the late 1930s and the 1940s, the United

separate-but-equal doctrine A Supreme Court doctrine holding that the equal protection clause of the Fourteenth Amendment did not forbid racial segregation as long as the facilities for blacks were equal to those for whites. The doctrine was overturned in the *Brown v. Board of Education of Topeka* decision of 1954.

***de jure* segregation** Racial segregation that occurs because of laws or decisions by government agencies.

***de facto* segregation** Racial segregation that occurs not as a result of deliberate intentions but because of past social and economic conditions and residential patterns.

busing The transportation of public school students by bus to schools physically outside their neighborhoods to eliminate school segregation based on residential patterns.

States Supreme Court gradually moved away from this doctrine. The major breakthrough, however, did not come until 1954, in a case involving an African American girl who lived in Topeka, Kansas.

AP Photo

These troops from the 101st Airborne division were sent to keep order at Central High School in Little Rock, Arkansas, during a tense integration period in the fall of 1957. Why were federal troops used?

The *Brown* Decisions and School Integration

In the 1950s, Topeka's schools, like those in many cities, were segregated. Mr. and Mrs. Oliver Brown wanted their daughter, Linda Carol Brown, to attend a white school a few blocks from their home instead of an all-black school that was twenty-one blocks away. With the help of lawyers from the National Association for the Advancement of Colored People (NAACP), Linda's parents sued the board of education to allow their daughter to attend the nearby school.

In *Brown v. Board of Education of Topeka,*[7] the Supreme Court reversed *Plessy v. Ferguson.* The Court unanimously held that segregation by race in public education was unconstitutional. Chief Justice Earl Warren wrote as follows:

> Does segregation of children in public schools solely on the basis of race, even though the physical facilities and other "tangible" factors may be equal, deprive the children of the minority group of equal educational opportunities? We believe that it does. . . . [Segregation generates in children] a feeling of inferiority as to their status in the community that may affect their hearts and minds in a way unlikely ever to be undone. . . . We conclude that in the field of public education the doctrine of "separate but equal" has no place. Separate educational facilities are inherently unequal.

In 1955, in *Brown v. Board of Education*[8] (sometimes called *Brown II*), the Supreme Court ordered desegregation to begin "with all deliberate speed," an ambiguous phrase that could be (and was) interpreted in a variety of ways.

REACTIONS TO SCHOOL INTEGRATION The Supreme Court ruling did not go unchallenged. Bureaucratic loopholes were used to delay desegregation. Another reaction was "white flight." As white parents sent their children to newly established private schools, some formerly white-only public schools became 100 percent black. In Arkansas, Governor Orval Faubus used the state's National Guard to block the integration of Central High School in Little Rock in 1957, which led to increasing violence in the area. A federal court demanded that the troops be withdrawn. Only after President Dwight D. Eisenhower federalized the Arkansas National Guard and sent in troops to help quell the violence did Central High finally become integrated.

By 1970, school systems with ***de jure* segregation**—segregation that is established by law—had been abolished. But that meant only that no public school could legally identify itself as being reserved for all whites or all blacks. It did not mean the end of ***de facto* segregation** (segregation that is not imposed by law but is produced by circumstances, such as the existence of neighborhoods or communities populated primarily by African Americans). Attempts to overcome *de facto* segregation included redrawing school district lines, reassigning pupils, and busing.

BUSING **Busing** is the transporting of students by bus to schools physically outside their neighborhoods in an effort to achieve racially desegregated schools. The Supreme Court first endorsed busing in 1971 in a case involving the school system in Charlotte, North Carolina.[9] Following this decision, the Court upheld busing in several northern cities.[10] Proponents believed that busing improved the educational and career opportunities of minority children and also enhanced the ability of children from different ethnic groups to get along with one another.

Nevertheless, busing was unpopular with many groups from its inception. By the mid-1970s, the courts had begun to retreat from their former support for busing. In 1974, the Supreme Court rejected the idea of busing children across school district lines.[11] In 1986, the Court refused to review a lower court decision that ended a desegregation plan in Norfolk, Virginia.[12] Today, busing orders to end *de facto* segregation are not upheld in court. Indeed, *de facto* segregation in America's schools is still widespread.

The Civil Rights Movement

In 1955, one year after the first *Brown* decision, an African American woman named Rosa Parks, a longtime activist in the NAACP, boarded a public bus in Montgomery, Alabama. When it became crowded, she refused to move to the "colored section" at the rear of the bus. She was arrested and fined for violating local segregation laws. Her arrest spurred the local African American community to organize a year-long boycott of the entire Montgomery bus system. The protest was led by a twenty-seven-year-old Baptist minister, the Reverend Dr. Martin Luther King, Jr. During the protest period, he was jailed and his house was bombed. Despite the hostility and what appeared to be overwhelming odds against them, the protesters were triumphant.

MPI/Getty Images

These Arkansas African American college students participate in a "sit-in" at a diner's counter. Why did they feel the need to demonstrate in this fashion? Why don't we see such pictures in the news today?

"INJUSTICE anywhere is a threat to justice everywhere."

~ MARTIN LUTHER KING, JR. ~
U.S. BLACK CIVIL RIGHTS LEADER
1929–1968

In 1956, a federal court prohibited the segregation of buses in Montgomery, and the era of the **civil rights movement**—the movement by minorities and concerned whites to end racial segregation—had begun. The movement was led by a number of groups and individuals, including Martin Luther King and his Southern Christian Leadership Conference (SCLC). Other groups, such as the Congress of Racial Equality (CORE), the NAACP, and the Student Nonviolent Coordinating Committee (SNCC), also sought to secure equal rights for African Americans.

Bettmann/Corbis

The Reverend Dr. Martin Luther King, Jr., shakes hands with President Lyndon B. Johnson just after Johnson signed the Civil Rights Act of 1964. At the signing, Johnson asked all Americans to join in the effort "to bring justice and hope to all our people and to bring peace to our land."

NONVIOLENCE AS A TACTIC Civil rights protesters in the 1960s began to apply the tactic of nonviolent **civil disobedience**—the deliberate and public refusal to obey laws considered unjust—in civil rights actions throughout the South. For example, in 1960, in Greensboro, North Carolina, four African American students sat at the "whites only" lunch counter at Woolworth's and ordered food. The waitress refused to serve them, and the store closed early, but more students returned the next day to sit at the counter, with supporters picketing

civil rights movement The movement in the 1950s and 1960s, by minorities and concerned whites, to end racial segregation.

civil disobedience The deliberate and public act of refusing to obey laws thought to be unjust.

sit-in A tactic of nonviolent civil disobedience. Demonstrators enter a business, college building, or other public place and remain seated until they are forcibly removed or until their demands are met. The tactic was used successfully in the civil rights movement and in other protest movements in the United States.

outside. **Sit-ins** spread to other lunch counters across the South. In some instances, students were heckled or even dragged from the store by angry whites. But the protesters never reacted with violence. They simply returned to their seats at the counter, day after day. Within months of the first sit-in, lunch counters began to reverse their policies of segregation.

Civil rights activists were trained in the tools of nonviolence—how to use nonthreatening body language, how to go limp when dragged or assaulted, and how to protect themselves from clubs or police dogs. As the civil rights movement gained momentum, the media images of nonviolent protesters being attacked by police, sprayed with fire hoses, and attacked by dogs shocked and angered Americans across the country. This public backlash led to nationwide demands for reform. The March on Washington for Jobs and Freedom, led by Martin Luther King in 1963, aimed in part to demonstrate the widespread public support for legislation to ban discrimination in all aspects of public life.

CIVIL RIGHTS LEGISLATION IN THE 1960s

As the civil rights movement demonstrated its strength, Congress began to pass civil rights laws. While the Fourteenth Amendment prevented the *government* from discriminating against individuals or groups, the private sector—businesses, restaurants, and so on—could still freely refuse to employ and serve nonwhites. Therefore, Congress sought to address this issue.

The Civil Rights Act of 1964 was the first and most comprehensive civil rights law. It forbade discrimination on the basis of race, color, religion, gender, and national origin. The major provisions of the act were as follows:

- It outlawed discrimination in public places of accommodation, such as hotels, restaurants, snack bars, movie theaters, and public transportation.
- It provided that federal funds could be withheld from any federal or state government project or facility that practiced any form of discrimination.
- It banned discrimination in employment.
- It outlawed arbitrary discrimination in voter registration.
- It authorized the federal government to sue to desegregate public schools and facilities.

Other significant laws passed by Congress during the 1960s included the Voting Rights Act of 1965, which made it illegal to interfere with anyone's right to vote in any election held in this country (see Chapter 8 for a discussion of the historical restrictions on voting that African Americans faced), and the Civil Rights Act of 1968, which prohibited discrimination in housing.

THE BLACK POWER MOVEMENT Not all African Americans embraced nonviolence. Several outspoken leaders in the mid-1960s were outraged at the slow pace of change in the social and economic status of blacks. Malcolm X, a speaker and organizer for the Nation of Islam (also called the Black Muslims), rejected the goals of integration and racial equality espoused by the civil rights movement. He called instead for black separatism and black pride. Although he later moderated some of his views, his rhetorical style and powerful message influenced many African American young people.

By the late 1960s, with the assassinations of Malcolm X in 1965 and Martin Luther King in 1968,

Library of Congress

Black Muslim leader Malcolm X speaks to an audience at a Harlem rally in 1963. His talk, in which he restated the Black Muslim theme of complete separation of whites and African Americans, outdrew a nearby rally sponsored by a civil rights group by ten to one.

the era of mass acts of civil disobedience in the name of civil rights had come to an end. Some civil rights leaders ceased to believe that further change was possible. Others entered politics and worked to advance the cause of civil rights from within the system.

Political Participation

As you will read in Chapter 8, in many jurisdictions African Americans were prevented from voting for years after the Civil War, despite the Fifteenth Amendment (1870). These discriminatory practices persisted in the twentieth century. In the early 1960s, only 22 percent of African Americans of voting age in the South were registered to vote, compared with 63 percent of voting-age whites. In Mississippi, the most extreme example, only 6 percent of voting-age African Americans were registered to vote. Such disparities led to the enactment of the Voting Rights Act of 1965, which ended discriminatory voter-registration tests and gave federal voter registrars the power to prevent racial discrimination in voting.

Today, the percentages of voting-age blacks and whites registered to vote are nearly equal. As a result of this dramatic change, political participation by African Americans has increased, as has the number of African American elected officials. Today, more than nine thousand African Americans serve in elective office in the United States. At least one congressional seat in each southern state is held by an African American, as are more than 15 percent of the state legislative seats in the South. A number of African Americans have achieved high government office, including Colin Powell, who served as President George W. Bush's first secretary of state, and Condoleezza Rice, his second secretary of state. Of course, in 2008 Barack Obama, a U.S. senator from Illinois, became the first African American president of the United States. Obama's election reflects a significant change in public opinion. Fifty years ago, only 38 percent of Americans said that they would be willing to vote for an African American as president; today, this number has risen to more than 90 percent.

Nonetheless, only two African Americans have been elected to a state governorship, and only a handful of African Americans have been elected to the U.S. Senate since 1900. Thirty-eight African Americans are seated in the House, along with two nonvoting delegates. In all, just over 7 percent of the members of Congress are African American, less than their share of the nation's total population.

AP Photo/Alex Brandon

President Obama often accepts public speaking engagements. While he has stumped for health care reform, increased regulation of business and of banks, and other causes, he has rarely talked about race relations. Why not?

Continuing Challenges

Although African Americans no longer face *de jure* segregation, they continue to struggle for income and educational parity with whites. Recent census data show that incomes in white households are two-thirds higher than those in black households. And the poverty rate for blacks is roughly three times that for whites.

The education gap between blacks and whites also persists despite continuing efforts by educators—and by government, through programs such as the federal No Child Left Behind Act—to reduce it. Recent studies show that on average, African American students in high school can read and do math at only the average level of whites in junior high school. While black adults have narrowed the gap with white adults in earning high school diplomas, the disparity has widened for college degrees.

These problems tend to feed on one another. Schools in poorer neighborhoods generally have fewer educational resources available, resulting in lower achievement levels for their students. Thus, some educational experts suggest that it all comes down to money. In fact, many parents of minority students in struggling school districts are less concerned about integration than they are about funds for their children's schools. A number of these parents have initiated lawsuits against their state governments, demanding that the states give poor districts more resources.

Researchers have known for decades that when students enrolled at a particular school come almost entirely from impoverished families, regardless of race, the performance of the students at that school is seriously depressed. When low-income students attend schools where the majority of the students are middle class, again regardless of race, their performance improves dramatically—without dragging down the performance of the middle-class students. Because of this research and recent U.S. Supreme Court rulings that have struck down some racial integration plans, several school systems have adopted policies that integrate students on the basis of socioeconomic class, not race.[13]

"THE RIGHT OF CITIZENS OF THE UNITED STATES TO VOTE shall not be denied or abridged . . . on account of sex."

~ THE NINETEENTH AMENDMENT TO THE UNITED STATES CONSTITUTION ~ 1920

VOTES FOR WOMEN

Library of Congress

A recent issue for African Americans and members of other minority groups is the impact of the Great Recession. Minority group members have been disproportionately affected by housing foreclosures. We discuss that problem in this chapter's *Our Government's Response to the Economic Crisis* feature.

LO3 *Women*

In 1776, Abigail Adams, wife of future president John Adams, wrote her husband a letter while he served as a Massachusetts representative to the Continental Congress in Philadelphia: "In the new Code of Laws which I suppose it will be necessary for you to make I desire you would Remember the Ladies, and be more generous and favorable to them than your ancestors." Abigail called for greater legal recognition of women and laws against domestic violence. Although John was greatly fond of Abigail and indeed reliant upon her, he dismissed this appeal out of hand. Not until the 1840s did women begin to organize groups to push for women's rights.

suffrage The right to vote; the franchise.

The Struggle for Voting Rights

In 1848, Lucretia Mott and Elizabeth Cady Stanton organized the first "woman's rights" convention in Seneca Falls, New York. The three hundred people who attended approved a Declaration of Sentiments: "We hold these truths to be self-evident: that all men *and women* are created equal." In the following years, other women's groups held conventions in various cities in the Midwest and the East. With the outbreak of the Civil War, though, women's rights advocates devoted their energies to the war effort.

The movement for political rights gained momentum again in 1869, when Susan B. Anthony and Elizabeth Cady Stanton formed the National Woman Suffrage Association. **Suffrage**—the right to vote—became their goal. Members of this association, however, saw suffrage as only one step on the road toward greater social and political rights for women. Lucy Stone and other women, who founded the American Woman Suffrage Association, thought that the right to vote should be the only goal. By 1890, the two organizations had joined forces, and the resulting National American Woman Suffrage Association had indeed only one goal—the enfranchisement of women. When little progress was made, small, radical splinter groups took to the streets. Parades, hunger strikes, arrests, and jailings soon followed.

World War I (1914–1918) marked a turning point in the battle for women's rights. The war offered many opportunities for women. Thousands of women served as volunteers, and about a million women joined the workforce, holding jobs vacated by men who entered military service. After the war, President Woodrow Wilson wrote to Carrie Chapman Catt, one of the leaders of the women's movement, "It is high time that [that] part of our debt should be acknowledged." Two years later, in 1920, seventy-two years after the Seneca Falls convention, the Nineteenth Amendment to the Constitution was ratified: "The right of citizens of the United States to vote shall not be denied or abridged by

Stabilizing the Housing Sector and Helping Minorities, Too

It's generally known that the origins of the Great Recession date back to 2006, when housing prices stopped rising and started to fall. The result of the bursting of the home-price bubble was a mushrooming rate of mortgage foreclosures. A foreclosure occurs when a homeowner is no longer making his or her mortgage payments and the owner of the mortgage—the lender—takes possession of the property. Typically, the former homeowner must leave the house. From late 2006 until recently, about 4.5 million homes went into foreclosure. The massive wave of foreclosures destroyed the value of financial securities that were based on these mortgages, and that in turn threatened to ruin the financial institutions that held these securities.

The Impact on Minority Group Members

A disproportionate share of foreclosures occurred in low-income and minority neighborhoods. That should come as no surprise, for from 1995 to the middle of the next decade, home ownership rates rose more rapidly among minority groups than among whites. When the bubble burst, home ownership rates fell faster for African Americans and Latinos than for the rest of the population. In addition, during the housing boom in the early 2000s, African Americans and Hispanics borrowed larger amounts than did whites with similar incomes. At the same time, many minority group members were steered into loans meant for subprime borrowers (borrowers with poor credit ratings), which have higher interest rates, even though their incomes and credit ratings made them eligible for less costly prime mortgages. As a consequence, African Americans and Hispanics were more exposed to debt relative to their incomes when the housing bubble burst.

What Caused the Foreclosures?

While there have been many theories about what caused the housing crisis, most of those theories are contradicted by the facts. For example, many people blamed the rise of foreclosures on subprime mortgage lenders, who purportedly misled borrowers into taking on mortgage loans with "teaser" interest rates. These rates started low but rose, sometimes substantially, after a certain period—often a few years. When the interest rates rose, the home buyers were unable to make the higher monthly payments. That sounds logical, but the foreclosure rate for prime loans—provided to households with good credit—grew by almost 500 percent, compared with growth of less than 200 percent for subprime foreclosures. By 2009, 51 percent of all homes foreclosed since mid-2006 had been financed by prime loans, not subprime ones.

University of Texas at Dallas professor Stan Liebowitz has proposed that the most important factor causing foreclosures was whether the home buyer had any money at risk. If there was no money down—if the entire cost of the home plus any other fees were included in the mortgage—the home buyer had nothing to lose if he or she walked away when the payments became too great. In many instances, the buyer was a small-time speculator who sought to resell the house at a profit and could not afford to sell the house at a loss. Liebowitz has argued that no federal government policy will work in the long run if it continues to allow house purchases involving no down payments (or very low down payments).

How the Government Tried to Keep Minorities and Others in Their Homes

One of the federal government's main tools in fighting the Great Recession was for the Federal Reserve to force down interest rates, and that did have some impact on housing. A substantial number of people were able to refinance their homes at a lower interest rate. Unfortunately, those who owed more than the value of their house could not refinance. No bank would write a new loan on a house for more money than the house was worth.

One federal program to deal with such problems was a $50 billion fund to encourage home loan modifications. This program was designed to encourage lenders to restructure mortgages so that the payments were more in line with the incomes of the borrowers. A program announced in 2009 authorized payments to lenders who let a homeowner sell a property for less than the balance owed on the loan. As a result, homeowners would make serious attempts to sell their homes rather than just walking away from them in foreclosures. The Obama administration also unveiled a program that would allow an individual to refinance even when the market value of the house was 25 percent less than the value of the old mortgage.

Finally, the government significantly stepped up the activity of the Federal Housing Authority (FHA). The FHA does not make loans. Rather, it is in effect a government-run insurance company. A person who qualifies for an FHA-backed loan pays a small percentage of the loan—an up-front mortgage insurance premium—so that the FHA will guarantee it. Additional insurance payments follow. The lending bank assumes no risk. Needless to say, an FHA guarantee makes it much easier to get a loan.

For Critical Analysis *In many countries, a majority of citizens rent rather than buy their apartments or homes. Why do you think that home ownership is so important in the United States?*

Table 5–1

Years, by Country, in Which Women Gained the Right to Vote

Year	Country
1893	New Zealand
1902	Australia
1913	Norway
1918	Britain
1918	Canada
1919	Germany
1920	United States
1930	South Africa
1932	Brazil
1944	France
1945	Italy
1945	Japan
1947	Argentina
1950	India
1952	Greece
1953	Mexico
1956	Egypt
1963	Kenya
1971	Switzerland
1984	Yemen

AP Photo/Carolyn Kaster (Right)
AP Photo/Qilai Shen, Pool (Left)

Nancy Pelosi (D., Calif.) was the first female Speaker of the House of Representatives. She frequently presents her agenda to the media. She has opposed the wars in Iraq and Afghanistan and has championed health-care reform and more stimulus spending. Why did it take over two hundred years before this nation had a woman as the leader of the House of Representatives?

Barack Obama named New York senator Hillary Clinton, his rival for the Democratic presidential nomination, to be secretary of state.

the United States or by any State on account of sex." Although it may seem that the United States was slow in giving women the right to vote, it was not really behind the rest of the world (see Table 5–1 above).

Women in American Politics Today

More than ten thousand members have served in the U.S. House of Representatives. Only 1 percent of them have been women. Women continue to face a "men's club" atmosphere in Congress, although in 2002, for the first time, a woman, Nancy Pelosi (D., Calif.), was elected minority leader of the House of Representatives. Pelosi again made history when, after the Democratic victories in the 2006 elections, she was elected Speaker of the House of Representatives, the first woman ever to hold that position.

In the 111th Congress, 17 percent of the 435 members of the House of Representatives and 16 percent of the 100 members of the Senate are women. Considering that eligible female voters outnumber eligible male voters, women continue to be vastly underrepresented in the U.S. Congress.

FEDERAL OFFICES The same can be said for the number of women receiving presidential appointments to federal offices. Franklin D. Roosevelt (1933–1945) appointed the first woman to a cabinet post—Frances Perkins, who was secretary of labor from 1933 to 1945. Several women have held cabinet posts in more recent administrations, however. All of the last three presidents have appointed women to the most senior cabinet post—secretary of state. Bill Clinton (1993–2001) appointed Madeleine Albright to this position, George W. Bush (2001–2009) picked Condoleezza Rice for the post in his second term, and most recently, Barack Obama chose New York senator Hillary Clinton to be secretary of state.

In addition, Ronald Reagan (1981–1989) appointed the first woman to sit on the Supreme Court, Sandra Day O'Connor. Bill Clinton appointed Ruth Bader Ginsburg to the Supreme Court, and in 2009 Barack Obama selected Sonia Sotomayor for the Court.

STATE POLITICS Women have made greater progress at the state level, and the percentage of women in state legislatures has been rising steadily. Women now constitute nearly one-fourth of state legislators. Notably, in 1998, women won races for each of the top five offices in Arizona, the first such occurrence in U.S. history. Generally, women have been more successful politically in the western states than elsewhere. In Washington State, more than one-third of the state's legislative seats are now held by women. At the other end of the spectrum, though, are states such as Alabama. In that state, fewer than 10 percent of the lawmakers are women.

Women in the Workplace

An ongoing challenge for American women is to obtain equal pay and equal opportunity in the workplace. In spite of federal legislation and programs to promote equal treatment of women in the workplace, women continue to face various forms of discrimination.

WAGE DISCRIMINATION In 1963, Congress passed the Equal Pay Act. The act requires employers to pay an equal wage for substantially equal work—males cannot be paid more than females who perform essentially the same job. The following year, Congress passed the Civil Rights Act of 1964, Title VII of which prohibits employment discrimination on the basis of race, color, national origin, gender, and religion. Women, however, continue to face wage discrimination.

It is estimated that for every dollar earned by men, women earn about 76 cents. Although the wage gap has narrowed significantly since 1963, when the Equal Pay Act was enacted (at that time, women earned 58 cents for every dollar earned by men), it still remains. This is particularly true for women in management positions and older women. Female managers now earn, on average, only 70 percent of what male managers earn. And women between the ages of forty-five and fifty-four make, on average, only 73 percent of what men in that age group earn. Notably, when a large number of women are in a particular occupation, the wages that are paid in that occupation tend to be relatively low.

Additionally, even though an increasing number of women now hold business and professional jobs once held only by men, relatively few of these women are able to rise to the top of the career ladder in their firms due to the lingering bias against women in the workplace. This bias has been described as the **glass ceiling**—an invisible but real discriminatory barrier that prevents women (or minorities) from rising to top positions of power or responsibility. Today, less than one-sixth of the top executive positions in the largest American corporations are held by women.

SEXUAL HARASSMENT Title VII's prohibition of gender discrimination has also been extended to prohibit sexual harassment. **Sexual harassment** occurs when job opportunities, promotions, salary increases, or even the ability to retain a job depend on whether an employee complies with demands for sexual favors. A special form of sexual harassment, called hostile-environment harassment, occurs when an employee is subjected to sexual conduct or comments in the workplace that interfere with the employee's job performance or that create an intimidating, hostile, or offensive environment.

The Supreme Court has upheld the right of persons to be free from sexual harassment on the job on a number of occasions. In 1986, the Court indicated that creating a hostile environment by sexual harassment violates Title VII, even when job status is not affected, and in 1993 the Court held that to win damages in a suit for sexual harassment, a victim does not need to prove that the harassment caused psychological harm.[14] In 1998, the Court made it clear that sexual harassment includes harassment by members of the same sex.[15] In the same year, the Court held that employers are liable for the harassment of employees by supervisors unless the employers can show that (1) they exercised reasonable care in preventing such problems (by implementing antiharassment policies and procedures, for example) and (2) the employees failed to take advantage of any corrective opportunities provided by the employers.[16] Additionally, the Civil Rights Act of 1991 greatly expanded the remedies available for victims

"I feel like a man trapped in a woman's salary."

glass ceiling An invisible but real discriminatory barrier that prevents women and minorities from rising to top positions of power or responsibility.

sexual harassment Unwanted physical contact, verbal conduct, or abuse of a sexual nature that interferes with a recipient's job performance, creates a hostile environment, or carries with it an implicit or explicit threat of adverse employment consequences.

of sexual harassment. Under the act, victims can seek damages as well as back pay, job reinstatement, and other compensation.

LO4 *Securing Rights for Other Groups*

In addition to African Americans and women, a number of other groups in U.S. society have faced discriminatory treatment. To discuss all of these groups would require volumes.

Here, we look first at three significant ethnic groups that have had to struggle for equal treatment—Hispanics, Asian Americans, and Native Americans. Then we examine the struggles of several other groups of Americans—elderly people, persons with disabilities, and gay men and lesbians.

Hispanics

Hispanics, or Latinos, constitute the largest ethnic minority in the United States. Whereas African Americans represent about 13 percent of the U.S. population, Hispanics now constitute more than 15 percent. Each year, the Hispanic population grows by nearly 1 million people, one-third of whom are newly arrived legal immigrants. By 2050, Hispanics are expected to constitute about one-fourth of the U.S. population.

Hispanics can be of any race, and to classify them as a single minority group is misleading. Spanish-speaking individuals tend to identify themselves by their country of origin, rather than as Hispanics. As you can see in Figure 5–1 alongside this page, the largest Hispanic group consists of Mexican Americans, who constitute about 64 percent of the Hispanic population living in the United States. About 9 percent of Hispanics are Puerto Ricans, and 3.5 percent are Cuban Americans. A significant number of the remaining Hispanics are from Central and South American countries.

Economically, Hispanic households are often members of this country's working poor. About 22 percent of Hispanic families live below the poverty line, compared with 8 percent of non-Hispanic white families. Hispanic leaders tend to attribute the low income levels to language problems, lack of job training, and continuing immigration. Immigration disguises statistical progress because language problems and lack of job training are usually more notable among new immigrants than among those who have lived in the United States for many years.

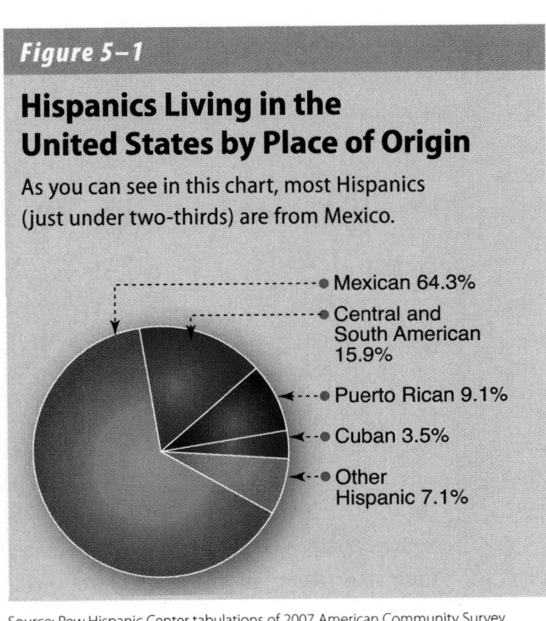

Source: Pew Hispanic Center tabulations of 2007 American Community Survey.

PARTY IDENTIFICATION AND ELECTORAL SIGNIFICANCE In their party identification, Hispanics tend to follow some fairly well-established patterns. Traditionally, Mexican Americans and Puerto Ricans identify with the Democratic Party, which has favored more government assistance and support programs for disadvantaged groups. Cubans, in contrast, tend to identify with the Republican Party. This is largely because of a different history. Cuban émigrés fled from Cuba during and after the Communist revolution led by Fidel Castro. The strong anti-Communist sentiments of the Cubans propelled them toward the more conservative party—the Republicans. Today, relations with Communist Cuba continue to be the dominant political issue for Cuban Americans.

Immigration reform was the subject of heated debate in the months leading up to the 2006 midterm elections, and this debate had a significant impact on Hispanic voters, especially in California. Exit polls conducted during the elections showed that for 69 percent of Hispanic voters, immigration was the number-one priority. Before the 2006 elections, to appeal to the party base, Republican ads attacked proposed legislation that would have made it possible for illegal immigrants to obtain legal status. According to some observers, many Hispanics perceived the ads as attacking all Hispanics and were motivated to vote against Republicans in the 2006 elections.

By 2008, immigration had receded as a national issue—it did not come up at all in the presidential debates. For Hispanics, along with everyone else, economic troubles were the number-one issue. In the fall elections, only 31 percent of Hispanic voters chose

Republican John McCain, even though he had been a major proponent of immigration reform. This was down sharply from the 40 percent of the Hispanic vote won by George W. Bush in 2004.

POLITICAL PARTICIPATION Generally, Hispanics in the United States have a comparatively low level of political participation. This is understandable, given that one-third of Hispanics are below voting age and another one-fourth are not citizens and thus cannot vote. Although voter turnout among Hispanics is generally low compared with the population at large, the Hispanic voting rate is rising as more immigrants become citizens and as more Hispanics reach voting age. Indeed, when comparing citizens of equal incomes and educational backgrounds, Hispanic citizens' participation rate is higher than average.

Increasingly, Hispanics hold political office, particularly in those states with large Hispanic populations. Today, more than 5 percent of the state legislators in Arizona, California, Colorado, Florida, New Mexico, and Texas are of Hispanic ancestry. Cuban Americans have been notably successful in gaining local political power, particularly in Dade County, Florida.

President George W. Bush appointed a number of Hispanics to federal offices, including cabinet positions. For example, he named Alberto Gonzales to head the Justice Department and Carlos Gutierrez as secretary of commerce. Barack Obama appointed Senator Ken Salazar (D., Colo.) to head the Interior Department and Representative Hilda Solis (D., Calif.) as secretary of labor. Hispanics are also increasing their presence in Congress, albeit slowly.

HISPANICS IN CONGRESS AFTER THE 2008 ELECTIONS Following the 2008 elections, there were twenty-three Hispanics in the House of Representatives and three Hispanics in the Senate. In all, though, Hispanics constitute only about 5 percent of the members of the 111th Congress. As with African Americans and women, Hispanic representation in Congress does not reflect the size of the Hispanic population in the United States.

Asian Americans

Asian Americans have also suffered, at times severely, from discriminatory treatment. The Chinese Exclusion Act of 1882 prevented persons from China and Japan from coming to the United States to prospect for gold or to work on the railroads or in factories in the West. After 1900, immigration continued to be restricted—only limited numbers of individuals from China and Japan were allowed to enter the United States. Those who were allowed into the country faced racial prejudice from Americans who had little respect for their customs and culture. In 1906, after the San Francisco earthquake, Japanese American students were segregated into special schools so that white children could use their buildings.

AP Photo/J. Scott Applewhite

Sonia Sotomayor was grilled by Republicans during her nomination hearing before the Senate Judiciary Committee. (Here you can see that she didn't always feel under pressure.) Her nomination was easily approved by the Senate, making her the first Hispanic to become a Supreme Court justice.

The Japanese bombing of Pearl Harbor in 1941, which launched the entry of the United States into World War II (1939–1945), intensified Americans' fear of the Japanese. Actions taken under an executive order issued by President Franklin D. Roosevelt in 1942 subjected many Japanese Americans to curfews, excluded them from certain "military areas," and evacuated most of the West Coast Japanese American population to internment camps (also called "relocation centers").[17] In 1988, Congress provided funds to compensate former camp inhabitants—$1.25 billion for approximately 60,000 people.

Today, Japanese Americans and Chinese Americans lead other ethnic groups in median income and median education. Indeed, Asians who have immigrated to the United States since 1965 (including immigrants from India) represent the most highly skilled immigrant groups in American history. Nearly 40 percent of

Joerg Modrow/laif/Redux

Asian American students routinely score higher on their entrance SATs than do other groups. Also, Asian Americans graduate at a higher rate than do other groups. Because they are in a minority, should they nonetheless benefit from affirmative action programs in college admissions and job hiring?

Asian Americans over the age of twenty-five have college degrees. The image of Asian Americans as a "model minority" has created certain problems for its members, however. Some argue that leading colleges and universities have discriminated against Asian Americans in admissions because so many of them apply. We discuss that issue in this chapter's *Join the Debate* feature on the facing page.

More than a million Indochinese war refugees, most from Vietnam, have immigrated to the United States since the 1970s. Many came with relatives and were sponsored by American families or organizations. Thus, they had support systems to help them get started. Some immigrants from other parts of Indochina, however, have experienced difficulties because they come from cultures that have had very little contact with the practices of developed industrial societies.

Native Americans

When we consider population figures since 1492, we see that the Native Americans experienced one catastrophe after another. We cannot know exactly how many people lived in America when Columbus arrived. Current research estimates the population of what is now the continental United States to have been anywhere from 3 to 8 million, out of a total New World population of 40 to 100 million. The Europeans brought with them diseases to which these Native Americans had no immunity. As a result, after a series of terrifying epidemics, the population of the continental United States was reduced to perhaps eight hundred thousand people by 1600. Death rates elsewhere in the New World were comparable. When the Pilgrims arrived at Plymouth, the Massachusetts coast was lined with abandoned village sites.[18]

In subsequent centuries, the American Indian population continued to decline, bottoming out at about half a million in 1925. These were centuries in which the European American—and African American—populations experienced explosive growth. By 2000, the Native American population had recovered to about 2 million, or about 3.5 million if we count individuals who are only part Indian.

In 1789, Congress designated the Native American tribes as foreign nations so that the government could sign land and boundary treaties with them. As members of foreign nations, Native Americans had no civil rights under U.S. laws. This situation continued until 1924, when the citizenship rights spelled out in the Fourteenth Amendment to the Constitution were finally extended to American Indians.

EARLY POLICIES TOWARD NATIVE AMERICANS

The Northwest Ordinance, passed by the Congress of the Confederation in 1787, stated that "the utmost good faith shall always be observed towards the Indians; their lands and property shall never be taken from them without their consent; and in their property, rights, and liberty, they shall never be invaded or disturbed, unless in just and lawful wars authorized by Congress." Over the next hundred years, these principles were violated more often than they were observed.

In the early 1830s, boundaries were established between lands occupied by Native Americans and those occupied by white settlers. In 1830, Congress instructed the Bureau of Indian Affairs (BIA), which Congress had established in 1824 as part of the War Department, to remove all tribes to lands (reservations) west of the Mississippi River in order to free land east of the Mississippi for white settlement.

In the late 1880s, the U.S. government changed its policy. The goal became the "assimilation" of Native Americans into American society. Each family was given a parcel of land within the reservation to farm. The remaining acreage was sold to whites, thus reducing the number of acres in reservation status from 140 million

JOIN THE DEBATE

Are Admissions at Top Schools Unfair to Asian Americans?

There are 14 million Asian Americans, about 4.5 percent of the U.S. population. They are a diverse group. Outside of the United States, people from China, India, Japan, and Korea have little in common. Only in America are they lumped together—and in this country, people from East and South Asia do have a few things in common. Their average family income is higher than that of whites. They are also well educated. By one estimate, Asian Americans make up as many as 30 percent of the top college candidates as determined by SAT scores, National Merit and AP Scholar awards, and grades. Asian American admissions to top schools, however, have not kept up with these figures. In the Ivy League, Asian admissions have consistently run below 20 percent. In other words, many excellent Asian American students are being turned away.

When the University of California (UC) abolished affirmative action in 1995, the percentage of Asian Americans admitted into the UC system jumped to 37 percent, even though they represent only 12 percent of the state's population. In 2009, however, the UC regents voted to lower the academic standards for admission and rely more on personal interviews. The obvious motivation for the changes was to bring in more African American and Hispanic students. UC's own projections, though, suggest that the plan will do almost nothing to expand Black enrollment and will benefit Latinos very modestly. The major beneficiaries will be non-Hispanic whites. The big losers will be Asian Americans, whose numbers will be reduced by 10 to 20 percent.

Colleges Admission Isn't Just about Grades and Test Scores

While it may appear to high-scoring Asian Americans who don't get into their college of choice that they have suffered from discrimination, it is not necessarily true. Universities routinely manage admissions to obtain the freshman classes they wish to have. They try to include the right number of football and basketball players, dancers, minorities, and men (the latter are favored in some universities because otherwise campuses might become "too female"). Only if you believe that high test scores should be the only basis for admission can you argue that university admission preferences constitute discrimination.

The goal of a diverse freshman class is to expose all students to a mix of races, ethnicities, and viewpoints. Such diversity is commendable. Vincent Pan, head of Chinese for Affirmative Action, argues that universities "have a public responsibility to prepare future leaders, and we need to prepare a generation of leaders that will look like America." A freshman class that is, say, 40 percent Asian American does not look like America, just as a class that is 80 percent women would not look like America.

Discrimination Is Discrimination—Period

Lately, Ivy League–level universities have established techniques to limit the number of Asian American students admitted to their institutions. These same techniques were used before World War II (and sometimes even after) to limit the number of Jewish students. The basic scheme, then and now, is to award lots of extra points for being "well-rounded" and then to define well-rounded as everything that young Asian Americans aren't (or that the young Jews weren't). A more labor-intensive method of accomplishing the same goal is through a "holistic" review process for all candidates. Schools using this process rely on admissions officers' subjective views of students, which yields an assessment that supposedly evaluates the "whole person." Lee Cheng, the co-founder of the Asian American Legal Foundation, believes that such a system is designed to "fulfill a distorted and unlawful view of what constitutes diversity . . . the bottom line is: If you hold people to a different standard, it is discrimination."

Furthermore, there is no need to set Asian Americans in competition with other minorities in admissions. More than 20 percent of the spaces at top private universities are currently set aside for legacy students, children of the rich and famous, and athletes. (Legacy students are the children of alumni or alumnae.) If the number of these unjustified preferences were merely cut in half, there would be enough room for qualified Asian youths.

Blog On *For background information on the Asian-American community in the U.S., go to* **www.asian-nation.org.**

Duke University/The Special Collections Library

Young men from a variety of tribes pose for a photograph in 1872 on their arrival at a Virginia boarding school for Native Americans. Later, they donned school uniforms, and another photo was taken (to be used for "before and after" comparisons). This was a typical practice at Native American boarding schools.

to about 47 million. Tribes that would not cooperate with this plan lost their reservations altogether. The BIA also set up Native American boarding schools for children to remove them from their parents' influence. In these schools, American Indian children were taught to speak English, to practice Christianity, and to dress like white Americans.

NATIVE AMERICANS TODAY Native Americans have always found it difficult to obtain political power. In part, this is because the tribes are small and scattered, making organized political movements difficult. Today, American Indians remain fragmented politically because large numbers of their population live off the reservations. Nonetheless, in the 1960s, some Native Americans formed organizations to strike back at the U.S. government and to reclaim their heritage, including their lands.

In the late 1960s, a small group of Indians occupied Alcatraz Island, claiming that the island was part of their ancestral lands. Other militant actions followed. For example, in 1973, supporters of the American Indian Movement took over Wounded Knee, South Dakota, where about 150 Sioux Indians had been killed by the U.S. Army in 1890.[19] The occupation was undertaken to protest the government's policy toward Native Americans and to call attention to the injustices they had suffered.

COMPENSATION FOR PAST INJUSTICES As more Americans became aware of the sufferings of Native Americans, Congress began to compensate them for past injustices. In 1990, Congress passed the Native American Languages Act, which declared that Native American languages are unique and serve an important role in maintaining Indian culture and continuity. Courts, too, have shown a greater willingness to recognize Native American treaty rights. For example, in 1985, the Supreme Court ruled that three tribes of Oneida Indians could claim damages for the use of tribal land that had been unlawfully transferred in 1795.[20]

The Indian Gaming Regulatory Act of 1988 allows Native Americans to have gambling operations on their reservations. Although the profits from casino gambling operations have helped to improve the economic and social status of many Native Americans, some Indians feel that the casino

Many Native Americans work at locally owned casinos, such as this one in Biloxi, Mississippi. Has gambling on reservations changed the standard of living of all Native Americans? Why or why not?

Justin Sullivan/Getty Images

industry has seriously injured their traditional culture. Poverty and unemployment remain widespread on the reservations.

Protecting Older Americans

Today, about 38 million Americans, nearly 13 percent of the population, are aged sixty-five or over. By the year 2040, this figure will almost double. Clearly, as the American population grows older, the problems of aging and retirement will become increasingly important national issues. Because many older people rely on income from Social Security, the funding of Social Security benefits continues to be a major issue on the national political agenda.

Many older people who would like to work find it difficult because of age discrimination. Some companies have unwritten policies against hiring, retaining, or promoting people they feel are "too old," making it impossible for some older workers to find work or to continue with their careers. At times, older workers have fallen victim to cost-cutting efforts by employers. To reduce expenses, companies may replace older, higher-salaried employees with younger workers who are willing to work for less pay. Employers who offer health benefits have a particular incentive to avoid older employees, who are likely to have greater health problems.

As part of an effort to protect the rights of older Americans, Congress passed the Age Discrimination in Employment Act (ADEA) in 1967. This act prohibits employers, employment agencies, and labor organizations from discriminating against individuals over the age of forty on the basis of age.

In 2000, the Supreme Court limited the applicability of the ADEA somewhat when it held that lawsuits under this act could not be brought against a state government employer.[21] Essentially, this means that the act does not protect state employees against age-based discrimination by their state employers. Most states, however, have laws prohibiting age-based discrimination against state employees, and employees can sue in state courts under those laws.

Obtaining Rights for Persons with Disabilities

Like age discrimination, discrimination based on disability crosses the boundaries of race, ethnicity, gender, and religion. Persons with disabilities, especially those with physical deformities or severe mental impairments, have to face social bias. Although attitudes toward persons with disabilities have changed considerably in the last several decades, such persons continue to suffer from discrimination in all its forms.

Roger L. Wollenberg/UPI/Landov

In the fall of 2008, Representative Jim Langevin (D., R.I.), in the center of the photo, speaks at a rally after Congress passed important amendments to the Americans with Disabilities Act.

Persons with disabilities first became a political force in the 1970s, and in 1973, Congress passed the first legislation protecting this group of persons—the Rehabilitation Act. This act prohibited discrimination against persons with disabilities in programs receiving federal aid. The Individuals with Disabilities Education Act (formerly called the Education for All Handicapped Children Act of 1975) requires public schools to provide children with disabilities with free, appropriate, and individualized education in the least restrictive environment appropriate to their needs. Further legislation in 1978 led to regulations for ramps, elevators, and the like in all federal buildings. The Americans with Disabilities Act (ADA) of 1990, however, is by far the most significant legislation protecting the rights of this group of Americans.

The ADA requires that all public buildings and public services be accessible to persons with disabilities. The act also mandates that employers "reasonably accommodate" the needs of workers or job applicants with disabilities who are otherwise qualified for particular jobs unless to do so would cause the employer to suffer an "undue hardship." The ADA defines persons with disabilities as persons who have physical or mental impairments that "substantially limit" their everyday activities. Health conditions that have been considered disabilities under federal law include blindness, alcoholism, heart disease, cancer, muscular dystrophy, cerebral palsy, paraplegia, diabetes, and acquired immune deficiency syndrome (AIDS). The ADA, however, does not require employers to hire or retain workers who, because of their disabilities, pose a "direct threat to the health or safety" of their co-workers.

"The liberty protected by the Constitution ALLOWS HOMOSEXUAL PERSONS THE RIGHT TO CHOOSE TO ENTER UPON RELATIONSHIPS IN THE CONFINES OF THEIR HOMES AND THEIR OWN PRIVATE LIVES AND STILL RETAIN THEIR dignity as free persons."

~ UNITED STATES SUPREME COURT ~
LAWRENCE V. TEXAS, 2003

In 2001, the Supreme Court reviewed a case raising the question of whether suits under the ADA could be brought against state employers. The Court concluded, as it did with respect to the ADEA, that states are immune from lawsuits brought to enforce rights under this federal law.[22]

Gay Men and Lesbians

Until the late 1960s and early 1970s, gay men and lesbians tended to keep quiet about their sexual preferences because exposure usually meant facing harsh consequences. This attitude began to change after a 1969 incident in New York City, however. When the police raided the Stonewall Inn—a bar popular with gay men and lesbians—on June 27 of that year, the bar's patrons responded by throwing beer cans and bottles at the police. The riot continued for two days. The Stonewall Inn uprising launched the gay power movement. By the end of the year, gay men and lesbians had formed fifty organizations, including the Gay Activist Alliance and the Gay Liberation Front.

A CHANGING LEGAL LANDSCAPE The number of gay and lesbian organizations has grown from fifty in 1969 to several thousand today. These groups have exerted significant political pressure on legislatures, the media, schools, and churches. In the decades following Stonewall, more than half of the forty-nine states that had sodomy laws—laws prohibiting homosexual conduct and certain other forms of sexual activity—repealed them. In seven other states, the courts invalidated such laws. Then, in 2003, the United States Supreme Court issued a ruling that effectively invalidated all remaining sodomy laws in the country. In *Lawrence v. Texas*,[23] the Court ruled that sodomy laws violated the Fourteenth Amendment's due process clause. According to the Court, "The liberty protected by the Constitution allows homosexual persons the right to choose to enter upon relationships in the confines of their homes and their own private lives and still retain their dignity as free persons."

Today, twenty-one states and more than 140 cities and towns in the United States have laws prohibiting discrimination against homosexuals in housing, education, banking, employment, or public accommodations. In a landmark case in 1996, *Romer v. Evans*,[24] the Supreme Court held that a Colorado amendment that would have invalidated all state and local laws protecting homosexuals from discrimination violated the equal protection clause of the Constitution. The Court stated that the amendment would have denied to homosexuals in Colorado—but to no other Colorado residents—"the right to seek specific protection from the law."

CHANGING ATTITUDES Laws and court decisions protecting the rights of gay men and lesbians reflect social attitudes that are much changed from the 1960s. Liberal political leaders have been supporting gay rights for at least two decades. In 1984, presidential candidate Walter Mondale openly sought the gay vote, as did Jesse Jackson in his 1988 presidential campaign. As president, Bill Clinton strongly supported gay rights.

Even some conservative politicians have softened their stance on the issue. For example, during his 2000 presidential campaign, George W. Bush met with representatives of gay groups to discuss issues important to them. Although Bush stated that he was opposed to gay marriage, he promised that he would not disqualify anyone from serving in his administration on the basis of sexual orientation.

According to a Gallup poll taken in 2009, public support for gay and lesbian rights has continued to rise. The survey showed that 56 percent of respondents believed that gay or lesbian relations between consenting adults should be legal, up from 43 percent in 1978.

Support for employment and domestic partnership rights ran even higher. Among those interviewed, 69 percent believed that openly gay or lesbian individuals should be able to serve in the military, and the same number believed that such persons should be allowed to teach children. Giving domestic partners access to health insurance and other employee benefits was endorsed by 67 percent of Americans, and inheritance rights by 73 percent. Only 40 percent of those interviewed endorsed same-sex marriage, but that was up substantially from 27 percent in 1996.

SAME-SEX MARRIAGE Today, same-sex marriage is legal in six states—Connecticut, Iowa, New Hampshire, Maine, Massachusetts, and Vermont. It was temporarily legal in California during 2008, between a state supreme court ruling in May that legalized the practice and a constitutional amendment passed by the voters in November that banned it again. California, however, continues to recognize those same-sex couples who married between May and November as lawfully wedded. New York State does not perform same-sex marriages but recognizes those performed elsewhere.

A number of states have civil union or domestic partnership laws that grant most of the benefits of marriage to registered same-sex couples. These include California, Nevada, New Jersey, Oregon, and Washington, plus the District of Columbia. More limited benefits are provided in Colorado, Hawaii, Maryland, and Wisconsin. Either through a constitutional amendment or through legislation, same-sex marriage is explicitly banned in most states without domestic partnership laws—and even in some of the states just mentioned.

A woman holds up a protest placard during a gay rights rally in Hollywood, California, after the state supreme court upheld Proposition 8, which redefined marriage in California as being unions between men and women only.

Mark Ralston/AFP/Getty Images

GAYS AND LESBIANS IN THE MILITARY For gay men and lesbians who wish to join the military, one of the battlefields they face is the "Don't ask, don't tell" policy. This policy, which bans openly gay men and lesbians from the military, was implemented in 1993 by President Bill Clinton when it became clear that any other alternative would not be accepted. During his presidential campaign, Barack Obama pledged to abolish the policy. Later, however, gay and lesbian rights activists accused him of "putting the issue on a back burner."

Generally, attitudes toward accepting gay men and lesbians in the military divide along party lines—with the Democrats approving such a policy and the Republicans opposing it. What do soldiers themselves think about serving alongside gay men and lesbians? According to a 2007 Zogby poll of service members returning from Afghanistan and Iraq, three-quarters of those polled said that they would have no problem serving with gay men or lesbians.

LO5 *Beyond Equal Protection—Affirmative Action*

One provision of the Civil Rights Act of 1964 called for prohibiting discrimination in employment. Soon after the act was passed, the federal government began to legislate programs promoting *equal employment opportunity.* Such programs require that employers' hiring and promotion practices guarantee the same opportunities to all individuals. Experience soon showed that minorities often had fewer opportunities to obtain education and relevant work experience

AP Photo/Rich Pedroncelli

Proponents of a constitutional amendment that defines marriage as a relationship between one man and one woman demonstrate their support for this concept. So far, they have not been successful.

than did whites. Because of this, they were still excluded from many jobs. Even though discriminatory practices were made illegal, the change in the law did not make up for the results of years of discrimination. Consequently, under President Lyndon B. Johnson (1963–1969), a new policy was developed.

Called **affirmative action,** this policy requires employers to take positive steps to remedy *past* discrimination. Affirmative action programs involve giving special consideration, in jobs and college admissions, to members of groups that have been discriminated against in the past. Until recently, all public and private employers who received federal funds were required to adopt and implement these programs. Thus, the policy of affirmative action has been applied to all agencies of the federal, state, and local governments and to all private employers who sell goods to or perform services for any agency of the federal government. In short, it has covered nearly all of the nation's major employers and many of its smaller ones.

affirmative action A policy calling for the establishment of programs that give special consideration, in jobs and college admissions, to members of groups that have been discriminated against in the past.

reverse discrimination Discrimination against those who have no minority status.

quota system A policy under which a specific number of jobs, promotions, or other types of placements, such as university admissions, must be given to members of selected groups.

Affirmative Action Tested

The Supreme Court first addressed the issue of affirmative action in 1978 in *Regents of the University of California v. Bakke.*[25] Allan Bakke, a white male, had been denied admission to the University of California's medical school at Davis. The school had set aside sixteen of the one hundred seats in each year's entering class for applicants who wished to be considered as members of designated minority groups. Many of the students admitted through this special program had lower test scores than Bakke. Bakke sued the university, claiming that he was a victim of **reverse discrimination**—discrimination against whites. Bakke argued that the use of a **quota system,** in which a specific number of seats were reserved for minority applicants only, violated the equal protection clause.

The Supreme Court was strongly divided on the issue. Some justices believed that Bakke had been denied equal protection and should be admitted. A majority on the Court concluded that although both the Constitution and the Civil Rights Act of 1964 allow race to be used as a factor in making admissions decisions, race cannot be the *sole* factor. Because the university's quota system was based solely on race, it was unconstitutional. For more affirmative action problems elsewhere, see *The Rest of the World* feature on the facing page.

Strict Scrutiny Applied

In 1995, the Supreme Court issued a landmark decision in *Adarand Constructors, Inc. v. Peña.*[26] The Court held that any federal, state, or local affirmative action program that uses racial classifications as the basis for making decisions is subject to "strict scrutiny" by the courts. As discussed earlier in this chapter, this means that, to be constitutional, a discriminatory law or action must be narrowly tailored to meet a *compelling* government interest. In effect, the *Adarand* decision narrowed the application of affirmative action programs. An affirmative action program can no longer make use of quotas or preferences and cannot be maintained simply to remedy past discrimination by society in general. It must be narrowly tailored to remedy actual discrimination that has occurred, and once the program has succeeded, it must be changed or dropped.

THE REST OF THE WORLD

India Faces an Affirmative Action Nightmare

Affirmative action in the United States has involved a relatively small number of groups, even if some of them have many members—women, for example, make up more than half the population. In India, however, affirmative action is much more complicated due to the caste tradition. Under this millennia-old system, Indians are grouped into thousands of castes and subcastes. Formerly, some groups were considered outside the caste system altogether—these were the "untouchables," or Dalits. In 1950, after India became independent from Britain, the new constitution abolished the practice of untouchability, or discrimination against Dalits, and established a program of rights and quotas for the former untouchables, now officially called the Scheduled Castes. Discrimination remains widespread in rural India, however.

Quotas for Scheduled Castes

Together with the Scheduled Tribes (generally located in the far east of the country), the Scheduled Castes make up about 25 percent of India's population. Quotas were established to bring members of these groups into universities and government jobs in a program that is now about sixty years old. Several years ago, the government expanded the quota program to include the Other Backward Castes, groups that have suffered impoverishment or discrimination, but not to the degree of the Scheduled Castes and Scheduled Tribes. With the addition of the Other Backward Castes, the favored groups swelled to constitute half of India's population. A nationwide furor resulted.

A Caste of Shepherds Demands to Be Downgraded

In 2007, tens of thousands of members of the Gujjar caste, who traditionally worked as shepherds, blocked the roads in an Indian farming region. The Gujjars were one of the Other Backward Castes, and they were demanding reclassification as one of the Scheduled Castes, or untouchables. Why? The Gujjars realized that if they were classified as Dalits, they would benefit from more generous quotas in schooling and employment, and they would be eligible for more government welfare. This shepherd caste made their demand even though a lower status might result in increased discrimination, such as not being allowed to use the same water pumps as their neighbors.

For Critical Analysis *An Indian sociologist, Dipankar Gupta, commented, "If you play the caste game, you will end up with caste war." What might he have meant?*

These members of India's Gujjar caste are demonstrating in the Indian state of Rajasthan. They wanted their status to be downgraded from "Other Backward Caste" to "Untouchable" so that they could benefit from more generous quotas and receive increased welfare benefits.

AP Photo/Aman Sharma

The Diversity Issue

Following the *Adarand* decision, several lower courts faced cases raising the question of whether affirmative action programs designed to achieve diversity on college campuses were constitutional. For example, in a 1996 case, *Hopwood v. State of Texas,*[27] two white law school applicants sued the University of Texas School of Law in Austin, claiming that they had been denied admission because of the school's affirmative action program. The program allowed admissions officials to take racial and other factors into consideration when determining which students would be admitted. A federal appellate court held that the program violated the equal protection clause because it discriminated in favor of minority applicants. In its decision, the court directly challenged the *Bakke* decision by stating that the use of race even as a means of achieving diversity on college campuses "undercuts the Fourteenth Amendment." In other words, race could never be a factor, even if it was not the sole factor, in such decisions.

In 2003, the United States Supreme Court reviewed two cases involving issues similar to that in the *Hopwood* case. Both cases involved admissions programs at the University of Michigan. In *Gratz v. Bollinger*,[28] two white applicants who were denied undergraduate admission to the university alleged reverse discrimination. The school's policy gave each applicant a score based on a number of factors, including grade point average, standardized test scores, and personal achievements. The system *automatically* awarded every "underrepresented" minority (African American, Hispanic, and Native American) applicant twenty points—one-fifth of the points needed to guarantee admission. The Court held that this policy violated the equal protection clause.

In contrast, in *Grutter v. Bollinger*,[29] the Court held that the University of Michigan Law School's admissions policy was constitutional. In that case, the Court concluded that "[u]niversities can, however, consider race or ethnicity more flexibly as a 'plus' factor in the context of individualized consideration of each and every applicant." The significant difference between the two admissions policies, in the Court's view, was that the law school's approach did not apply a mechanical formula giving "diversity bonuses" based on race or ethnicity. In short, the Court concluded that diversity on college campuses was a legitimate goal and that limited affirmative action programs could be used to attain this goal.

The Supreme Court Revisits the Issue

The Michigan cases were decided in 2003. By 2007, when another case involving affirmative action came before the Court, the Court had a new chief justice, John G. Roberts, Jr., and a new associate justice, Samuel Alito, Jr. Both men were appointed by President George W. Bush, and the conservative views of both justices have moved the Court significantly to the right. Justice Alito replaced Sandra Day O'Connor, who had often been the "swing" vote on the Court, sometimes voting with the more liberal justices and sometimes joining the conservative bloc. Hers was the deciding vote in the five-to-four decision upholding the University of Michigan Law School's affirmative action program.

Some claim that the more conservative composition of today's Court strongly influenced the outcome in a case that came before the Court in 2007: *Parents Involved in Community Schools v. Seattle School District No. 1*.[30] The case concerned the policies of two school districts, one in Louisville, Kentucky, and one in Seattle, Washington. Both schools were trying to achieve a more diversified student body by giving preference to minority students if space in the schools was limited and a choice among applicants had to be made. Parents of white children who were turned away from schools in these districts because of these policies sued the school districts, claiming that the policies violated the equal protection clause. Ultimately, the case reached the Supreme Court, and the Court, in a five-to-four vote, held in favor of the parents, ruling that the policies violated the equal protection clause. The Court's decision did not overrule the 2003 case involving the University of Michigan Law School, however, for the Court did not say that race could *not* be used as a factor in university admissions policies. Nonetheless, some claim that the decision represents a significant change on the Court with respect to affirmative action policies.

With the election of an African American as president of the United States in 2008, some have argued that affirmative action has become unnecessary. After all, if an African American can be elected to the nation's highest office, what barriers remain? We

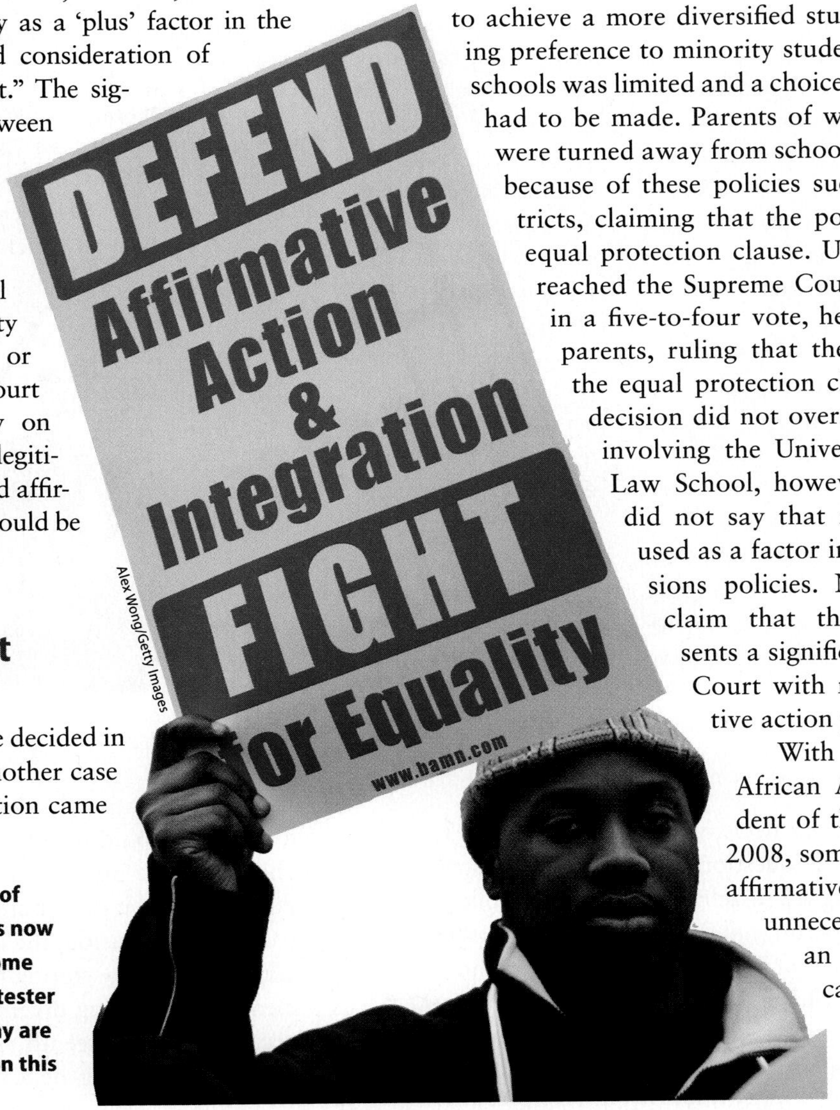

Alex Wong/Getty Images

Even some past supporters of affirmative action programs now believe that the time has come to eliminate them. This protester does not agree, though. Why are there still opposing views on this subject?

Obama's Election Means That Affirmative Action Is Obsolete

No one denies that discrimination is part of this country's past. In the 1960s, the federal government began to take serious steps to combat the problem. President John F. Kennedy first used the phrase *affirmative action* in a 1961 executive order that required federal contractors to "take affirmative action to ensure that applicants are employed, and that employees are treated during employment, without regard to their race, creed, color, or national origin." Under President Lyndon B. Johnson, the term was applied to attempts to rectify the "negative results of past discrimination," first for African Americans and other minority group members, and then for women as well.

From the very beginning, white males claimed that affirmative action programs made them the victims of "reverse discrimination." Now that the United States has its first African American president, have affirmative action programs done their job? Are they no longer necessary?

The Perception

It would appear, according to the media, that virtually all Americans are in favor of eliminating affirmative action programs. Already, several states have abolished such programs at public universities and in state employment. Clearly, the voters have spoken. They believe the time for affirmative action policies is past. And now an African American holds the most prestigious and important elective office in the land. This must surely mean that opportunity is unlimited in the United States.

The Reality

Obama graduated from Columbia University and later from Harvard Law School. At Harvard, he became the editor of the *Harvard Law Review*, the most prestigious position available to any law student. Yet when asked by the *Journal of Blacks in Higher Education* whether affirmative action was important, Obama replied: "I would argue that affirmative action is important precisely because those who benefit typically rise to the challenge when given an opportunity." In other words, even the African American president of the United States does not think that affirmative action programs should be eliminated entirely.

True, such programs have helped many African Americans move up the economic ladder. Nonetheless, only 40 percent of blacks can be considered middle class, compared with 60 percent of whites. While many whites favor abolishing affirmative action programs, almost 60 percent of African Americans in recent surveys agree that the United States should make "every effort to improve the position of Blacks and minorities, even if it means giving preferential treatment." And white opposition to affirmative action is far from monolithic. In the latest election cycle, a proposed ban on affirmative action in university admissions and state employment failed in Colorado—a predominately white state.

Blog On *"Does the Success of Barack Obama Mean We No Longer Need Affirmative Action?" This is the title of a page that the Public Broadcasting System hosts at* **www.pbs.org/now/shows/434.** *The page provides more than a dozen links to resources on the affirmative action issue.* The Washington Post *provides a variety of informative links at* **www.washingtonpost.com/wp-srv/politics/special/affirm/affirm.htm.**

examine that question in this chapter's *Perception versus Reality* feature above.

State Actions

Beginning in the mid-1990s, some states have taken actions to ban affirmative action programs or replace them with alternative policies. For example, in 1996, by a ballot initiative, California amended its state constitution to prohibit any "preferential treatment to any individual or group on the basis of race, sex, color, ethnicity, or national origin in the operation of public employment, public education, or public contracting."

Two years later, voters in the state of Washington approved a ballot measure ending all state-sponsored affirmative action. Florida has also ended affirmative action. In 2006, a ballot initiative in Michigan—just three years after the Supreme Court decisions discussed above—banned affirmative action in that state. In the 2008 elections, Nebraska also banned affirmative action, but voters in Colorado rejected such a measure. The

2008 initiatives were spearheaded by Ward Connerly, an opponent of affirmative action. Connerly, a libertarian businessman, is himself African American.

In the meantime, many public universities are trying to find "race-blind" ways to attract more minority students to their campuses. For example, Texas has established a program under which the top students at every high school in the state are guaranteed admission to the University of Texas–Austin. This policy ensures that the top students at minority-dominated inner-city schools can attend the state's leading public university. It also guarantees admission to the best white students from rural, often poor, communities. Previously, these students could not have hoped to attend the University of Texas. The losers are students from upscale metropolitan neighborhoods or suburbs who have high test scores but are not the top students at their schools. One result is that more students with high test scores enroll in less-famous schools, such as Texas Tech University and the University of Texas, Dallas—to the benefit of these schools' reputations.

Suzanne DeChillo/*The New York Times*/Redux

These high school students are attending a college fair in Queens, New York. Depending on where they are applying, some may benefit from affirmative action admissions policies. There has been a backlash in some states because majority students have argued that affirmative action is equivalent to reverse discrimination.

AMERICA AT ODDS Civil Rights

As noted in Chapter 4, our civil liberties are guaranteed in the Bill of Rights. Our civil rights, however, have evolved only slowly over time, as various groups pressured the public and Congress to make the Constitution's equal protection clause a reality. Today, we tend to take civil rights for granted. But consider that even as late as 1960, which is relatively recent in the long span of our nation's history, few of the rights discussed in this chapter existed. In 1960, the prevailing view was that "a woman's place is in the home," and there was no such thing as a lawsuit for gender discrimination or sexual harassment. In 1960, racial segregation was pervasive—and legal. African Americans were denied the right to vote in many jurisdictions. At that time, there were no legal protections for older Americans who were fired from their jobs because of their age; nor were there any laws protecting persons with disabilities and gay men and lesbians from discrimination. Equal employment opportunity was not required by law, and few civil and political rights were guaranteed for minority groups.

Clearly, our nation has come a long way since the time when only white males enjoyed the right to vote and to fully participate in American political life. This is not to say that there isn't a long way still to go. As you read in this chapter, minorities in this country continue to struggle for equal rights and opportunities, and women continue to face gender discrimination in the workplace, in politics, and in other areas. How to ensure equal treatment for all Americans continues to be a major challenge facing the nation's lawmakers—and all Americans.

ISSUES FOR DEBATE & DISCUSSION

1. **Some claim that racial or ethnic profiling can sometimes be justified. For example, if Arab truck drivers hauling loads of hazardous materials were ten times as likely to be terrorists as non-Arab truck drivers hauling such loads, then it might make sense to stop the drivers and interrogate them simply because of their ethnicity. Others argue that racial or ethnic profiling cannot be justified in any circumstances. What is your position on this issue?**
2. **Native American casinos first appeared on the American scene in the 1980s. Proponents of the casinos argue that these lucrative gambling establishments are an economic necessity for tribal groups and that the income the casinos generate has helped Native Americans gain self-respect and economic self-sufficiency. Opponents of Native American casinos contend that gambling leads to increased crime, alcoholism, drug addiction, and corruption. These critics also maintain that Native Americans should not be permitted to hold exclusive rights to operate casinos in states that otherwise restrict gambling. What is your position on this issue?**

TAKE ACTION

As mentioned in the introduction to this feature, despite the progress that has been made toward attaining equal treatment for all groups of Americans, much remains to be done. Countless activist groups continue to pursue the goal of equality for all Americans. If you wish to contribute your time and effort toward this goal, there are hundreds of ways to go about it. You can easily find activist opportunities just by going to the Web sites of the groups listed in this chapter's *Politics on the Web* section on the next page. There, you will find links to groups that seek to protect and enhance the rights of African Americans, Latinos, women, elderly persons, persons with disabilities, and others. Another source of information is the Justice for Immigrants Web site at **www.justiceforimmigrants.org**, where you can sign up to receive e-mails from the Immigrant Justice Action Network. If there are any gatherings or events planned for your neighborhood, such as a demonstration for immigrants' rights, you can participate in them—or volunteer to help organize them. Finally, you can search the Web for blogs on a civil rights issue that particularly interests you, read about what others on that site are saying, and "tell the world" your opinion on the issue.

Lee Celano/*The New York Times*/Redux

Some Native American tribes have benefited from laws that allow them to have casinos on reservations. What are the arguments against these casinos?

POLITICS ON THE WEB

- Stanford University's Web site contains primary documents written by Martin Luther King, Jr., as well as secondary documents written about King. The URL for the "Martin Luther King Directory" is **mlk-kpp01.stanford.edu**
- If you are interested in learning more about the Equal Employment Opportunity Commission (EEOC), the laws it enforces, and how to file a charge with the EEOC, go to **www.eeoc.gov**
- The home page for the National Association for the Advancement of Colored People (NAACP), which contains extensive information about African American civil rights issues, is **www.naacp.org**
- For information on Hispanics in the United States, the League of United Latin American Citizens is a good source. You can find it at **www.lulac.org**
- The most visible and successful advocacy group for older Americans is AARP (formerly known as the American Association of Retired Persons). Its home page contains helpful links and much information. Go to **www.aarp.org**
- The home page of the National Organization for Women (NOW) has links to numerous resources containing information on the rights and status of women both in the United States and around the world. You can find NOW's home page at **www.now.org**
- You can access the Web site of the Feminist Majority Foundation, which focuses on equality for women, at **www.feminist.org**
- For information on the Americans with Disabilities Act, including the text of the act, go to **www.jan.wvu.edu/links/adalinks.htm**
- The Gay and Lesbian Alliance against Defamation has an online news bureau. To find this organization's home page, go to **www.glaad.org**

Online resources for this chapter

This text's Companion Web site, at **www.4ltrpress.cengage.com/govt**, offers links to numerous resources that you can use to learn more about the topics covered in this chapter.

Paul Burns/Getty Images

Interest Groups

GOVT 6

LEARNING OBJECTIVES

LO1 Explain what an interest group is, how interest groups form, and how interest groups function in American politics.

LO2 Indicate how interest groups differ from political parties.

LO3 Identify the various types of interest groups.

LO4 Discuss how the activities of interest groups help to shape government policymaking.

LO5 Describe how interest groups are regulated by government.

AMERICA AT ODDS

Are Secret Ballots Essential in Union Elections?

The National Labor Relations Act of 1935 established the right of employees to form unions and the right of those unions to engage in collective bargaining—negotiation of contracts for the workers the unions represent—along with the right to strike. That act also created the National Labor Relations Board (NLRB) to oversee the unionization of workplaces. The decision on whether or not employees should be represented by a union is typically made though a secret-ballot election supervised by the NLRB.

In the early 2000s, with union membership declining, unions began pressuring members of Congress to pass legislation to help unions organize. The result was the proposed Employee Free Choice Act (EFCA), which has commonly been referred to as "card-check" legislation. The card-check system would in most instances replace privately held, federally supervised secret-ballot voting in decisions to form unions. Currently, elections are not mandatory, and an employer may voluntarily recognize a union if the union presents evidence that most employees support unionization. This evidence may include cards signed by a majority of employees. But the employer always has a right to ask for an election in spite of this evidence. Under the proposed law, that would no longer be the case. Organizers would simply need to gather signatures from more than 50 percent of the employees in a workplace. Once 50 percent of the workers had signed those cards, the employer would be required to recognize the union and negotiate with it.

Secret Ballots Are a Democracy's Only Choice

In 2001, a group of congressional representatives who were concerned about workers' rights in Mexico wrote to officials in that country stating, "We are writing to encourage you to use the secret ballot in all union recognition elections. . . . We feel that the secret ballot is absolutely necessary in order to ensure that workers are not intimidated into voting for a union they might not otherwise choose." Former Democratic presidential candidate George McGovern had this to say about the card-check legislation: "Workers would lose the freedom to express their will in private, the right to make a decision without anyone peering over their shoulder, free from fear of reprisal."

A major reason why unions spent half a billion dollars in the 2008 elections is because they were unified behind one driving goal—passing card-check legislation. In response to the unions' actions, McGovern stated that "part of being a steward of democracy means telling our friends 'no' when they press for a course that in the long run may weaken labor and disrupt a tried and trusted method for conducting honest elections."

Card-Check Union Organizing Will Level the Playing Field

The late senator Ted Kennedy (D., Mass.), claimed that card-check legislation was necessary to "level the playing field" between unions and management. He argued that there are large loopholes in today's labor laws that allow employers to intimidate their employees prior to and during secret elections. Representative George Miller (D., Calif.) contended that management in nonunion companies can "browbeat" workers about unions anytime and anywhere in the workplace. Union backers point out that it may be illegal to fire an employee for supporting a union drive, but it happens again and again. It is very difficult for an employee to prove that he or she was fired for supporting a union and not for some other reason.

Proponents of the EFCA agree that it will help increase union membership. They argue that this is good not only for union workers but also for other workers. Workers in general, they say, benefit when some of them strengthen their negotiating positions. Whenever a union effectively organizes another workplace, nonunion workers' bargaining positions are strengthened as well.

WHERE DO YOU STAND?

1. **How important is it for union elections to be held in secret?**
2. **Do you believe that an expansion in union membership can benefit all workers? Why or why not?**

EXPLORE THIS ISSUE ONLINE

- **Employer and conservative groups have organized the Coalition for a Democratic Workplace, a broad umbrella group, to oppose the EFCA card-check legislation. You can find that group's Web site at www.myprivateballot.com.**
- **The two largest union federations support the EFCA, of course. Find out what the American Federation of Labor–Congress of Industrial Organizations (AFL-CIO) says about it at www.aflcio.org/joinaunion/voiceatwork/efca. Change to Win, the nation's second-largest union alliance, argues for the EFCA at www.changetowin.org/index.php?id=268.**

Introduction

The groups supporting and opposing card checks for unionization provide but one example of how Americans form groups to pursue or protect their interests. All of us have interests that we would like to have represented in government: farmers want higher prices for their products, young people want good educational opportunities, and environmentalists want clean air and water.

The old adage that there is strength in numbers is certainly true in American politics. As discussed in Chapter 4, the right to organize groups is protected by the Constitution, which guarantees people the right "peaceably to assemble, and to petition the Government for a redress of grievances." The United States Supreme Court has defended this important right over the years.

Special interests significantly influence American government and politics. Indeed, some Americans think that this influence is so great that it jeopardizes representative democracy. Others maintain that interest groups are a natural consequence of democracy. After all, throughout our nation's history, people have organized into groups to protect special interests. Because of the important role played by interest groups in the American system of government, in this chapter we examine such groups. We look at what they are, why they are formed, and how they influence policymaking.

On any given day in Washington, D.C., you can see national interest groups in action. If you eat breakfast in the Senate dining room, you might see congressional committee staffers reviewing testimony with representatives from women's groups. Later that morning, you might visit the Supreme Court and watch a civil rights lawyer arguing on behalf of a client in a discrimination suit. Lunch in a popular Washington restaurant might find you listening in on a conversation between an agricultural lobbyist and a congressional representative.

That afternoon you might visit an executive department, such as the Department of Labor, and watch bureaucrats working out rules and regulations with representatives from a business interest group. Then you might stroll past the headquarters of the National Rifle Association (NRA), AARP (formerly the American Association of Retired Persons), or the National Wildlife Federation.

interest group An organized group of individuals sharing common objectives who actively attempt to influence policymakers.

"Politics is about **PEOPLE** not politicians."

~ SCOTT SIMMS ~
CANADIAN POLITICIAN
B. 1969

LO1 Interest Groups and American Government

An **interest group** is an organization of people sharing common objectives who actively attempt to influence government policymakers through direct and indirect methods. Whatever their goals—more or fewer social services, higher or lower prices—interest groups pursue these goals on every level and in every branch of government.

AP Photo/Tom Uhlman

This organizer from the United Food and Commercial Workers union gives a speech at a labor rally in downtown Cincinnati. He was supporting service workers, who include janitors and hotel workers.

How Interest Groups Form

Interest groups may form in response to change: a political or economic change, a dramatic shift in population or technology that affects how people live or work, or a change in social values or cultural norms. Some groups form to support the change or even speed it along, while others form to fight change. For example, during the economic boom of the 1990s, interest groups formed to support easing immigration restrictions on highly skilled workers, who were in great demand in technology industries. After the terrorist attacks of September 11, 2001, however, other groups formed to support more restrictions on immigration.

As you will read shortly, there are many different types of interest groups. Some represent the interests of a particular industry, while others lobby on behalf of employees. Some promote policies to protect the environment, and others seek to protect consumers. Other groups form in response to a single issue, such as a potential highway project. These groups are sometimes more successful than multi-issue groups.

FINANCING To have much success in gaining members and influencing policy, an interest group must have **patrons**—people or organizations willing to finance the group. Although groups usually collect fees or donations from their members, few can survive without large grants or donations. The level of financing required to form and expand an interest group successfully depends on the issues involved and the amount of lobbying the group needs to do. A group that pays professional lobbyists to meet with lawmakers in Washington, D.C., will require more funding than a group that operates with leaflets printed out from a Web site and distributed by volunteers.

As you can see in Figure 6–1 on the facing page, the budgets of different interest groups can vary widely. AARP has a budget of more than a billion dollars, while the League of Women Voters operates with only about $6.5 million. Some interest groups can become very powerful very quickly if they have wealthy patrons. Other groups can raise money in a hurry if a particular event galvanizes public attention on an issue.

INCENTIVES TO JOIN A GROUP The French political observer and traveler Alexis de Tocqueville wrote in 1835 that Americans have a tendency to form "associations" and have perfected "the art of pursuing in common the object of their common desires." "In no other country of the world," said Tocqueville, "has the principle of association been more successfully used or applied to a greater multitude of objectives than in America."[1] Of course, Tocqueville could not foresee the thousands of associations that now exist in this country. Surveys show that more than 85 percent of Americans belong to at least one group. Table 6–1 on page 134 shows the percentage of Americans who belong to various types of groups today.

Joining groups to pursue common goals is only part of the story. Americans have other incentives for

patron An individual or organization that provides financial backing to an interest group.

> "The health of a democratic society
> MAY BE MEASURED BY THE QUALITY OF FUNCTIONS PERFORMED BY PRIVATE CITIZENS."
>
> ~ ALEXIS DE TOCQUEVILLE ~
> FRENCH HISTORIAN AND POLITICAL SCIENTIST
> 1805–1859

Alexis de Tocqueville (1805–1859) was a well-known French political historian. He lived during a time of political upheaval in France and took a keen interest in the new democracy in America. He toured the United States and Canada as a young man and collected his observations in *Democracy in America,* which was published in 1835.

The Granger Collection

Figure 6–1

Profiles of Selected Interest Groups

AARP

Name: AARP
Founded: 1958
Membership: 40 million working or retired persons 50 years of age or older.
Description: AARP strives to better the lives of older people, especially in the areas of health care, worker equity, and minority affairs. AARP sponsors community crime prevention programs, research on the problems of aging, and a mail-order pharmacy.
Budget: $1,140,000,000
Address: 601 E St. N.W., Washington, DC 20049
Phone: (888) 687-2277 **Web site:** www.aarp.org

LWV

Name: League of Women Voters of the United States (LWVUS)
Founded: 1920
Membership: 150,000 members and supporters.
Description: The LWVUS promotes active and informed political participation. It distributes candidate information, encourages voter registration and voting, and takes action on issues of public policy. The group's national interests include international relations, natural resources, and social policy.
Budget: $6,560,000
Address: 1730 M St. N.W., Washington, DC 20036
Phone: (202) 429-1965 **Web site:** www.lwv.org

Name: National Education Association (NEA)
Founded: 1857
Membership: 3.2 million elementary and secondary school teachers, college and university professors, academic administrators, and others.
Description: The NEA's committees investigate and take action in the areas of benefits, civil rights, educational support, personnel, higher education, human relations, legislation, minority affairs, and women's concerns. Many NEA locals function as labor unions.
Budget: $307,000,000
Address: 1201 16th St. N.W., Washington, DC 20036
Phone: (202) 833-4000 **Web site:** www.nea.org

Name: National Rifle Association (NRA)
Founded: 1871
Membership: Nearly 4 million.
Description: The NRA promotes rifle, pistol, and shotgun shooting, as well as hunting, gun collecting, and home firearm safety. It educates police firearm instructors and sponsors teams to participate in international competitions.
Budget: $200,000,000
Address: 11250 Waples Mill Road, Fairfax, VA 22030
Phone: (800) 672-3888 **Web site:** www.nra.org

Name: The Sierra Club (SC)
Founded: 1892
Membership: 1.3 million.
Description: The Sierra Club protects and conserves natural resources; saves endangered areas; and resolves problems associated with wilderness, clean air, energy conservation, and land use. Its committees are concerned with agriculture, economics, environmental education, hazardous materials, the international environment, Native American sites, political education, and water resources.
Budget: $40,000,000
Address: 85 2d St., 2d Floor, San Francisco, CA 94105
Phone: (415) 977-5500 **Web site:** www.sierraclub.org

joining interest groups as well. Some people enjoy the camaraderie and sense of belonging that comes from associating with other people who share their interests and goals. Some groups offer their members material incentives for joining, such as discounts on products, subscriptions, or group insurance programs. But sometimes none of these incentives is enough to persuade people to join.

Table 6–1

Percentage of Americans Belonging to Various Groups

Group	Percentage
Health organizations	16%
Social clubs	17
Neighborhood groups	18
Hobby, garden, and computer clubs	19
PTA and school groups	21
Professional and trade associations	27
Health, sport, and country clubs	30
Religious groups	61

Source: AARP.

THE FREE RIDER PROBLEM This world in which we live is one of scarce resources that can be used to create *private goods* and *public goods.* Most of the goods and services that you use are private goods. If you consume them, no one else can consume them at the same time. For example, when you are using your computer, no one else can sit in front of it and type at the same time. With the other class of goods, called public goods, however, your use of a good does not diminish its use by someone else. National defense is a good example. If this country is protected through its national defense system, your protection from enemy invasion does not reduce anybody else's protection.

People cannot be excluded from enjoying a public good, such as national defense, just because they did not pay for it. If an interest group is successful in lobbying for laws that will improve air quality, for example, everyone who breathes that air will benefit, whether they paid for the lobbying effort or not. The existence of persons who benefit but do not contribute is called the **free rider problem.**

In some instances, the free rider problem can be overcome. For example, social pressure may persuade some people to join or donate to a group for fear of being ostracized. The government can also step in to ensure that the burden of lobbying for the public good is shared by all. When the government classifies interest groups as nonprofit organizations, it confers on them tax-exempt status. The groups' operating costs are reduced because they do not have to pay taxes, and the impact of the government's lost revenue is absorbed by all taxpayers.

free rider problem The difficulty that exists when individuals can enjoy the outcome of an interest group's efforts without having to contribute, such as by becoming members of the group.

How Interest Groups Function in American Politics

Despite the bad press that interest groups tend to get in the United States, they do serve several purposes in American politics:

- Interest groups help bridge the gap between citizens and government and enable citizens to explain their views on policies to public officials.
- Interest groups help raise public awareness and inspire action on various issues.
- Interest groups often provide public officials with specialized and detailed information that might be difficult to obtain otherwise. This information may be useful in making policy choices.
- Interest groups serve as another check on public officials to make sure that they are carrying out their duties responsibly.

Volunteers of the Vermont Public Interest Research Group are filling ten thousand cups of water at the statehouse's steps. This interest group wants Vermont legislators to pass clean water legislation.

AP Photo/Toby Talbot

ACCESS TO GOVERNMENT In a sense, the American system of government invites the participation of interest groups by offering many points of access for groups wishing to influence policy. Consider the possibilities at just the federal level. An interest group can lobby members of Congress to act in the interests of the group. If the Senate passes a bill opposed by the group, the group's lobbying efforts can shift to the House of Representatives. If the House passes the bill, the group can try to influence the new law's application by lobbying the executive agency that is responsible for implementing the law. The group might even challenge the law in court, directly (by filing a lawsuit) or indirectly (by filing a brief as an *amicus curiae,*[2] or "friend of the court").

PLURALIST THEORY The **pluralist theory** of American democracy focuses on the participation of groups in a decentralized government structure that offers many points of access to policymakers. According to the pluralist theory, politics is a contest among various interest groups. These groups vie with one another—at all levels of government—to gain benefits for their members. Pluralists maintain that the influence of interest groups on government is not undemocratic because individual interests are indirectly represented in the policymaking process through these groups. Although not every American belongs to an interest group, inevitably some group will represent each individual's interests. Each interest is satisfied to some extent through the compromises made in settling conflicts among competing interest groups.

Pluralists also contend that because of the extensive number of interest groups vying for political benefits, no one group can dominate the political process. Additionally, because most people have more than one interest, conflicts among groups do not divide the nation into hostile camps. Not all scholars agree that this is how interest groups function, however.

During the congressional recess in August 2009, many Americans showed their concerns about changing our health care system. This couple is worried about the "socialization" of health care. Why did their signs refer to Canada's system?

AP Photo/Hans Pennink

LO2 *How Do Interest Groups Differ from Political Parties?*

Although interest groups and political parties are both groups of people joined together for political purposes, they differ in several important ways. As you will read in Chapter 7, a political party is a group of individuals who organize to win elections, operate the government, and determine policy. Interest groups, in contrast, do not seek to win elections or operate the government, although they do seek to influence policy. Interest groups differ from political parties in the following ways:

- Interest groups are often policy *specialists,* whereas political parties are policy *generalists.* Political parties are broad-based organizations that must attract the support of many opposing groups and consider a large number of issues. Interest groups, in contrast, have only a handful of key policies to push. An environmental group will not be as concerned about the economic status of Hispanics as it is about polluters. A manufacturing group is more involved with pushing for fewer regulations than it is with inner-city poverty.

pluralist theory A theory that views politics as a contest among various interest groups—at all levels of government—to gain benefits for their members.

These members of AARP attend a rally in Richmond, Virginia, to demonstrate in favor of long-term health-care services.

AP Photo/Steve Helber

- Interest groups are usually more tightly organized than political parties. They are often financed through contributions or dues-paying memberships. Organizers of interest groups communicate with members and potential members through conferences, mailings, newsletters, and electronic formats, such as e-mail.
- A political party's main sphere of influence is the electoral system; parties run candidates for political office. Interest groups try to influence the outcome of elections, but unlike parties, they do not compete for public office. Although a candidate for office may be sympathetic to—or even be a member of—a certain group, he or she does not run for election as a candidate of that group.

LO3 *Different Types of Interest Groups*

public-interest group An interest group formed for the purpose of working for the "public good." Examples of public-interest groups are the American Civil Liberties Union and Common Cause.

trade organization An association formed by members of a particular industry, such as the oil industry or the trucking industry, to develop common standards and goals for the industry. Trade organizations, as interest groups, lobby government for legislation or regulations that specifically benefit their groups.

American democracy embraces almost every conceivable type of interest group, and the number is increasing rapidly. No one has ever compiled a *Who's Who* of interest groups, but you can get an idea of the number and variety by looking through the annually published *Encyclopedia of Associations*. Look again at Figure 6–1 on page 133 to see profiles of some selected important interest groups.

Some interest groups have large memberships. AARP, for example, has about 40 million members. Others, such as the Colorado Auctioneers Association, have barely a hundred members. Some, such as the NRA, are household names and have been in existence for many years, while others crop up overnight. Some are highly structured and are run by full-time professionals, while others are loosely structured and informal.

The most common interest groups are those that promote private interests. These groups seek public policies that benefit the economic interests of their members and work against policies that threaten those interests. Other groups, sometimes called **public-interest groups,** are formed with the broader goal of working for the "public good"; the American Civil Liberties Union and Common Cause are examples. Let there be no mistake, though, about the name *public interest.* There is no such thing as a clear public interest in a nation of more than 300 million diverse people. The two so-called public-interest groups just mentioned do not represent all American people but only a relatively small part of the American population. In reality, all lobbying groups, organizations, and other political entities always represent special interests.

Business Interest Groups

Business has long been well organized for effective action. Hundreds of business groups are now operating in Washington, D.C., in the fifty state capitals, and at the local level across the country. Two umbrella organizations that include small and large corporations and businesses are the U.S. Chamber of Commerce and the National Association of Manufacturers (NAM). In addition to representing about 3 million individual businesses, the Chamber has more than three thousand local, state, and regional affiliates. It has become a major voice for millions of small businesses.

The hundreds of **trade organizations** are far less visible than the Chamber of Commerce and the NAM, but they are also important in seeking policies that assist their members. Trade organizations usually support policies that benefit specific industries. For example, people in the oil industry work for policies that favor the development of oil as an energy resource.

Other business groups work for policies that favor the development of coal, solar power, and nuclear power. Trucking companies work for policies that would lower their taxes. Railroad companies would, of course, not want other forms of transportation to receive special tax breaks, because that would hurt their business.

Traditionally, business interest groups have been viewed as staunch supporters of the Republican Party. This is because Republicans are more likely to promote a "hands-off" government policy toward business. Over the last decade, however, donations from corporations to the Democratic National Committee have more than doubled. Why would business groups make contributions to the Democratic National Committee? Fred McChesney, a professor of law and business, offers an interesting answer to this question. He argues that campaign contributions are often made not to gain political favors but rather to avoid political disfavor. Just as government officials can take away wealth from citizens (in the form of taxes, for example), politicians can extort from private enterprises payments *not* to damage their business.[3]

Business interests have often wielded great power. In recent years, the financial industry has been especially successful in influencing the government. We discuss that issue in this chapter's *Our Government's Response to the Economic Crisis* feature on page 138.

These retired Army veterans march up 5th Avenue in New York City on Veterans' Day, November 11. Why has the political power of veterans as a lobbying group lessened in recent years compared to, say, during the 1950s?

AP Photo/Dima Gavrysh

Labor Interest Groups

Interest groups representing labor have been some of the most influential groups in our country's history. They date at least back to 1886, when the American Federation of Labor (AFL) was formed. The largest and most powerful labor interest group today is the AFL-CIO (the American Federation of Labor–Congress of Industrial Organizations), a confederation of fifty-six national and international labor unions representing 11 million members. Unions not affiliated with the AFL-CIO also represent millions of members. The Change to Win federation consists of seven unions and 6 million workers. These unions were formerly part of the AFL-CIO; most of them withdrew from the larger federation in 2005. Dozens of other unions have always been independent or have been so for many decades. Examples include the National Education Association, the United Electrical Workers (UE), and the Major League Baseball Players Association.

Like labor unions everywhere, American labor unions press for policies to improve working conditions and ensure better pay for their members. On some issues, however, unions may take opposing sides. For example, separate unions of bricklayers and carpenters may try to change building codes to benefit their own members even though the changes may hurt other unions. Unions may also compete for new members. In many states, the National Education Association and the AFL-CIO's American Federation of Teachers compete fiercely for members.

Although unions were highly influential in the 1930s, 1940s, and 1950s, their strength and political power have waned in the last several decades, as you can see in Figure 6–2. Today, members of organized

Figure 6–2

Union Membership, 1952 to Present

This figure shows the percentage of the workforce who are members of unions from 1952 to the present. As you can see, union membership has declined significantly over the past several decades.

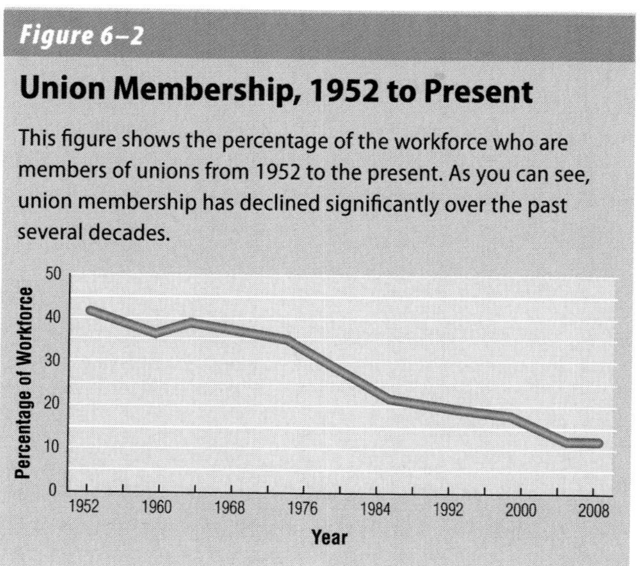

How the Financial Industry Has Affected Federal Policy

From the very beginning, helping out the financial industry has been a key part of our government's response to the current economic crisis. This seems appropriate, you might say, because finance is the lifeblood of our economy. Moreover, when the crisis caused by the subprime mortgage meltdown became acute in 2008, financial institutions were the ones immediately threatened. Investment banks were among the hardest hit.

A Little History, First

On April 28, 2004, the heads of five major investment banks gathered in the basement hearing room of the Securities and Exchange Commission (SEC) for a brief meeting. The bankers convinced the SEC to lift a rule that required them to hold reserves as a cushion against losses on their investments. Those five investment banks, which included Goldman Sachs, then went on an investment-selling spree the likes of which the world had never seen. They created trillions of dollars worth of mortgage-backed securities and credit derivatives, which are a form of insurance for investors. The head of Goldman Sachs at that time was Henry M. Paulson, Jr.

Fast-forward four years. All of these five investment banks had either gone bankrupt or been bailed out by the federal government. Who made the bailout decisions? None other than Henry M. Paulson, Jr., who had become secretary of the treasury under President George W. Bush. A huge share of the $700 billion bank bailout bill that Paulson championed was used to help his friends and colleagues in the investment-banking business. Critics soon complained that Paulson had helped bankers, rather than the banking industry.

A second example of successful lobbying by the financial industry involves Fannie Mae and Freddie Mac, institutions that were implicitly backed by the federal government. These two companies were in the business of buying mortgages, and in 2006 and 2007, they bought up every mortgage offered to them no matter how great the risk. Freddie and Fannie also spent hundreds of millions of dollars in lobbying to make sure that their preferred status continued and that they were allowed to expand their investments. They succeeded, right up to the day when they went broke and had to be taken over by the federal government.

The Investment-Banker Mentality Continues

Some commentators argue that paid lobbyists are not the most important reason for the financial industry's influence. They believe that financial institutions have gained political power through "cultural capital." That is, policymakers have come to believe that what is good for Wall Street is good for the United States. So-called Washington insiders continue to believe that the welfare of the nation's largest financial institutions is crucial to America's economic health.

Henry Paulson is by no means the only example of the easy passage from financial industry leader to Washington insider and back again. Another head of Goldman Sachs, Robert Rubin, was treasury secretary under President Bill Clinton. Before Paulson, Bush's treasury secretary was John Snow. He left to become chair of Cerberus, a large private equity firm. Former vice president Dan Quayle runs one of that company's international units. When Alan Greenspan, formerly the head of the Federal Reserve System, retired, he became a consultant to Pimco, a large international bond-trading firm.

The ties between Washington, D.C., and Wall Street have grown stronger over the last three presidential administrations. Today's leading financiers have very easy access to the highest U.S. government officials. Inevitably, throughout this economic crisis, whether the president has been George W. Bush or Barack Obama, the government has been careful not to upset the interests of major U.S. financial institutions.

The More Complex It Is, the Less the Public Will Understand

As the economic crisis deepened, U.S. financial institutions needed more and more help, and the federal government has assisted them in ways that the ordinary citizen cannot hope to understand. How has it done this? By providing banks with subsidies that are just too complex for the public at large to grasp.

Consider the Citigroup and Bank of America bailouts. They included complex guarantees of assets that in effect provided these two companies with insurance at below-market rates. As part of the bank bailouts, the government also took ownership of a special kind of nonvoting stock, called preferred stock. In February 2009, the government converted Citigroup preferred stock into common stock at a price that was enormously advantageous to the bank. As a result, U.S. taxpayers ended up owning 34 percent of Citigroup. If Citigroup's stock had been appropriately valued, however, the federal government would have become the majority owner.

For Critical Analysis *What does it mean to say that you, as a taxpayer, own part of a private banking company such as Citigroup? What does it mean when we say that U.S. taxpayers own a majority interest in General Motors?*

AP Photo/Michael Conroy

A number of national interest groups protect the interests of farmers. Through their lobbying efforts and campaign contributions, these groups have wielded significant influence on how Congress handles agricultural subsidies and other forms of assistance. Many political analysts contend that such subsidies harm the poor in developing countries. Why?

labor make up only 12.4 percent of the **labor force**—defined as all of the people over the age of sixteen who are working. While labor groups have generally experienced a decline in lobbying power, public employee unions have grown in both numbers and political clout in recent years. Public employees enjoy some of the nation's best health-care and retirement benefits because of the efforts of their labor groups.

Agricultural Interest Groups

Many groups work for general agricultural interests at all levels of government. Three broad-based agricultural groups represent millions of American farmers, from peanut farmers to dairy producers to tobacco growers. They are the American Farm Bureau Federation (Farm Bureau), the National Grange, and the National Farmers Union. The Farm Bureau, representing more than 5.5 million families (a majority of whom are not actually farm families), is the largest and generally the most effective of the three. Founded in 1919, the Farm Bureau achieved one of its greatest early successes when it helped to obtain government guarantees of "fair" prices during the Great Depression of the 1930s.[4] The Grange, founded in 1867, is the oldest group. It has units in 3,600 communities in thirty-seven states, with a total membership of about 300,000. The National Farmers Union comprises approximately 250,000 farm and ranch families.

Producers of various specific farm commodities, such as dairy products, soybeans, grain, fruit, corn, cotton, beef, and sugar beets, have formed their own organizations. These specialized groups, such as the Associated Milk Producers, Inc., also have a strong influence on farm legislation. Like business and labor groups, farm organizations sometimes find themselves in competition. In some western states, for example, barley farmers, cattle ranchers, and orchard owners may compete to influence laws governing water rights. Different groups also often disagree over the extent to which the government should subsidize or regulate farmers.

Consumer Interest Groups

Groups organized for the protection of consumer rights were very active in the 1960s and 1970s. Some are still active today. The best known and perhaps the most effective are the public-interest groups organized under the leadership of consumer activist Ralph Nader. Another well-known group is Consumers Union, a nonprofit organization started in 1936. In addition to publishing *Consumer Reports,* Consumers Union has been influential in pushing for the removal of phosphates from detergents, lead from gasoline, and pesticides from food. Consumers Union strongly criticizes government agencies when they appear to act against consumer interests.

Consumer groups have been organized in every city. They deal with such problems as poor housing, discrimination against minorities and women, discrimination in the granting of credit, and business inaction on consumer complaints.

Senior Citizen Interest Groups

While the population of the nation as a whole has tripled since 1900, the number of elderly persons has increased eightfold. Persons over the age of sixty-five now account for 13 percent of the population, and many of these people have united to call attention to their

labor force All of the people over the age of sixteen who are working or actively looking for jobs.

special needs and concerns. Senior citizens have a great deal at stake in debates over certain programs, such as Social Security and Medicare. Interest groups formed to promote the interests of elderly persons have been very outspoken and persuasive. As pointed out before, AARP has about 40 million members and is a potent political force.

Environmental Interest Groups

With the current concern for the environment, the membership of established environmental groups has blossomed, and many new groups have formed. They are becoming some of the most powerful interest groups in Washington, D.C. The National Wildlife Federation, one of the largest groups, has about 4 million members. Table 6–2 lists some of the major environmental groups and the number of members in each group.

Environmental groups have organized to support pollution controls, wilderness protection, and clean-air legislation. They have opposed strip-mining, nuclear power plants, logging, chemical waste dumps, and many other potential environmental hazards. Environmental groups are greatly concerned about global warming and have supported recent attempts to control pollutants that contribute to the problem. One issue—carbon taxes on imports—has united environmentalists with U.S. industries, such as steel manufacturing, that worry about foreign competition. We examine that topic in this chapter's *Join the Debate* feature on the facing page.

Table 6–2

Selected Environmental Interest Groups

Name of Group	Year Founded	Number of U.S. Members
Environmental Defense Fund	1967	500,000
Greenpeace USA	1971	250,000
Izaak Walton League of America	1922	40,000
League of Conservation Voters	1970	40,000
National Audubon Society	1905	500,000
National Wildlife Federation	1936	4,000,000
The Nature Conservancy	1951	1,000,000
The Sierra Club	1892	1,300,000
The Wilderness Society	1935	300,000
The World Wildlife Fund	1948	1,200,000

Sources: Foundation for Public Affairs, 1996; and authors' updates.

Professional Interest Groups

Most professions that require advanced education or specialized training have organizations to protect and promote their interests. These groups are concerned mainly with the standards of their professions, but they also work to influence government policy. Some also function as labor unions. Four major professional groups are the American Medical Association, representing physicians; the American Bar Association, representing lawyers; and the National Education Association and the American Federation of Teachers, both representing teachers. In addition, there are dozens of less well known and less politically active professional groups, such as the Screen Actors Guild, the National Association of Social Workers, and the American Political Science Association.

Single-Issue Interest Groups

Numerous interest groups focus on a single issue. For example, Mothers Against Drunk Driving (MADD) lobbies for stiffer penalties for drunk-driving convictions. Formed in 1980, MADD now boasts more than 3 million members and supporters. The abortion debate has created various single-issue groups, such as the Right to Life organization (which opposes abortion) and NARAL Pro-Choice America (which supports abortion rights). Other examples of single-issue groups are the NRA and the American Israel Public Affairs Committee (a pro-Israel group).

AP Photo/Rogelio V. Solis

What groups in the United States benefit from our buying goods "Made in America"?

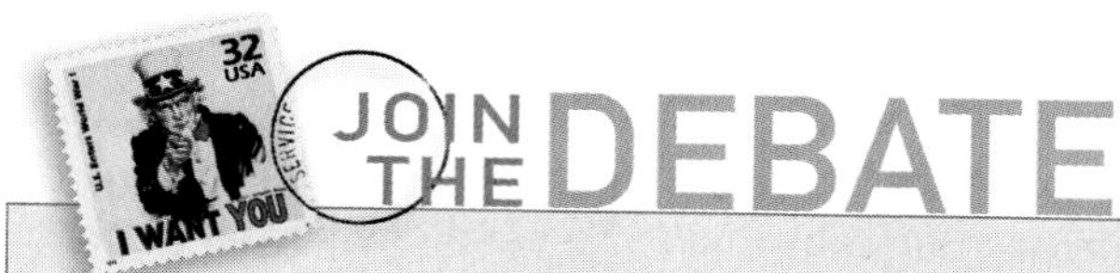

Should We Punish Countries That Don't Limit Carbon Emissions?

Many Americans and their elected officials are concerned about global warming. Scientists have argued that certain types of pollutants are causing a general rise in the earth's average temperature. They have identified carbon dioxide (CO_2) emissions as a major culprit. Presumably, manufacturing processes that generate large amounts of CO_2 are putting us at risk. Not surprisingly, our policymakers have focused on passing laws that would penalize CO_2 emitters. Congress is developing "cap-and-trade" legislation that would have the practical effect of taxing CO_2 emissions. Indeed, the Supreme Court ruled that the Environmental Protection Agency has the legal authority to regulate CO_2 emissions in the United States.

A House energy bill proposed in 2009 contained a clause aimed at making the rest of the world follow our lead on CO_2. It would tax goods coming from other countries where policymakers have yet to take global warming seriously. If we believed that certain goods from China, say, were manufactured in facilities that generate too much CO_2, we would place a " carbon tax" on those Chinese imports. (Taxes on imported goods are called tariffs.) As a euphemism, the energy bill calls these tariffs "border adjustments."

Many people who worry about global warming still wonder if such legislation isn't really just a disguised form of protectionism that will hinder world trade. Obviously, if goods from China are taxed, American producers of those same goods will gain a competitive advantage.

So-Called Carbon Tariffs Are Just a Tricky Way to Help American Industry

Let's face it—any tax on imported goods is a way to benefit domestic producers at the expense of foreign producers. We call these trade restrictions "protectionism." Yet the benefits of increased world trade are well known. Economists of every stripe, liberal as well as conservative, have long argued that free trade makes all countries better off. President Obama, who is no conservative, spoke out against the House bill provision. He pointed out that during the current recession, we have experienced a significant and damaging drop in global trade. "I think we have to be careful about sending any protectionist signals out there," he said.

Further, the United States cannot be the world's global pollution cop. Together with other countries, we might be able to use diplomacy to encourage polluting nations such as China to "clean up their act," but that is about it.

If We Tax Carbon Emissions, U.S. Companies Will Simply Go Offshore

Those in favor of "border adjustment" tariffs believe that they constitute a necessary safeguard. Consider the oil industry. If U.S. oil companies have to pay carbon taxes, they will react. If oil companies must pay a dollar in carbon taxes for each gallon of gasoline produced domestically, but can import gasoline that's not taxed, the companies are likely to shut down U.S. refineries. Rather than reducing dependence on overseas oil suppliers, a U.S. carbon tax will result in even more imports. The way to avoid this is to impose a carbon tax on imports from other countries that matches what we're imposing domestically.

Moreover, the World Trade Organization has already approved this concept: "Rules permit, under certain conditions, the use of border tax adjustments on imported products. The objective of a border tax adjustment is to level the playing field between taxed domestic industries and untaxed foreign competition by insuring that internal taxes on products are trade neutral." One way to think about this is that when the cost of production in the United States includes a carbon tax, consumers ultimately pay it. Why shouldn't consumers pay the same tax on carbon emissions caused by imports that they do on emissions resulting from domestic production?

Blog On *What groups in the United States would favor imposing higher tariffs on imports?*

Government Interest Groups

Efforts by state and local governments to lobby the federal government have escalated in recent years. When states experience budget shortfalls, these governments often lobby in Washington, D.C., for additional federal funds. The federal government has sometimes lobbied in individual states, too. During the 2004 elections, for example, the U.S. Attorney General's office lobbied against medical marijuana use in states that were considering ballot measures on the issue.

LO4 *How Interest Groups Shape Policy*

Interest groups operate at all levels of government and use a variety of strategies to steer policies in ways beneficial to their interests. Sometimes, they attempt to influence policymakers directly, but at other times they try to exert indirect influence on policymakers by shaping public opinion. The extent and nature of the groups' activities depend on their goals and their resources.

Direct Techniques

Lobbying and providing election support are two important **direct techniques** used by interest groups to influence government policy.

LOBBYING Today, **lobbying** refers to all of the attempts by organizations or by individuals to influence the passage, defeat, or contents of legislation or to influence the administrative decisions of government. (The term *lobbying* arose because, traditionally, individuals and groups interested in influencing government policy would gather in the foyer, or lobby, of the legislature to corner legislators and express their concerns.) A **lobbyist** is an individual who handles a particular interest group's lobbying efforts. Most of the larger interest groups have lobbyists in Washington, D.C. These lobbyists often include former members of Congress or former employees of executive bureaucracies who are experienced in the methods of political influence and who "know people." Many lobbyists also work at state and local levels. In fact, lobbying at the state level has increased in recent years as states have begun to play a more significant role in policymaking. Table 6–3 summarizes some of the basic methods by which lobbyists directly influence legislators and government officials.

Lobbying is one of the most widely used and effective ways to influence legislative activity. For example, Mothers Against Drunk Driving has had many lobbying successes at both the state and the federal levels. The NRA has successfully blocked most proposed gun control laws, even when a majority of Americans have favored such laws. An NRA brochure describes its lobbying operation as "the strongest, most formidable

direct technique Any method used by an interest group to interact with government officials directly to further the group's goals.

lobbying All of the attempts by organizations or by individuals to influence the passage, defeat, or contents of legislation or to influence the administrative decisions of government.

lobbyist An individual who handles a particular interest group's lobbying efforts.

Table 6–3

Direct Lobbying Techniques

Technique	Description
Making Personal Contacts with Key Legislators	A lobbyist's personal contacts with key legislators or other government officials—in their offices, in the halls of Congress, or on social occasions, such as dinners, boating expeditions, and the like—are one of the most effective direct lobbying techniques. The lobbyist provides the legislators with information on a particular issue in an attempt to convince them to support the interest group's goals.
Providing Expertise and Research Results for Legislators	Lobbyists often have knowledge and expertise that are useful in drafting legislation, and this expertise can be a major strength for an interest group. Because harried members of Congress cannot possibly be experts on everything they vote on and therefore eagerly seek information to help them make up their minds, some lobbying groups conduct research and present their findings to those legislators.
Offering "Expert" Testimony before Congressional Committees	Lobbyists often provide "expert" testimony before congressional committees for or against proposed legislation. A bill to regulate firearms, for example, might concern several interest groups. The NRA would probably oppose the bill, and representatives from that interest group might be asked to testify. Groups that would probably support the bill, such as law enforcement personnel, might also be asked to testify. Each side would offer as much evidence as possible to support its position.
Providing Legal Advice to Legislators	Many lobbyists assist legislators in drafting legislation or prospective regulations. Lobbyists are a source of ideas and sometimes offer legal advice on specific details.
Following Up on Legislation	Because executive agencies responsible for carrying out legislation can often increase or decrease the scope of the new law, lobbyists may also try to influence the bureaucrats who implement the policy. For example, beginning in the early 1960s, regulations outlawing gender discrimination were broadly outlined by Congress. Both women's rights groups favoring the regulations and interest groups opposing the regulations lobbied for years to influence how those regulations were carried out.

Jamie Rose/MCT/Landov

Senator Roger Wicker (R., Miss.) has just finished a meeting with lobbyists. In such meetings, members of Congress can obtain information that they otherwise would not have available.

grassroots lobby in the nation." Nevertheless, the NRA has occasionally been defeated in its lobbying efforts by interest groups that support gun regulation.

Lobbying can be directed at the legislative branch of government, at administrative agencies, and even at the courts. For example, pharmaceutical companies may lobby the Food and Drug Administration to speed up the process of approving new prescription drugs. Lobbying can also be directed at changing international policies. For instance, after political changes had opened up Eastern Europe to business in the late 1980s and early 1990s, intense lobbying by Western business groups helped persuade the United States and other industrial powers to reduce controls on the sale of high-technology products, such as personal computers, to Eastern European countries.

PROVIDING ELECTION SUPPORT Interest groups often become directly involved in the election process. Many interest group members join and work with political parties to influence party platforms and the nomination of candidates. Interest groups provide campaign support for legislators who favor their policies and sometimes encourage their own members to try to win posts in party organizations. Most important, interest groups urge their members to vote for candidates who support the views of the group. They can also threaten legislators with the withdrawal of votes. No candidate can expect to have support from all interest groups, but if the candidate is to win, she or he must have support (or little opposition) from the most powerful ones.

Since the 1970s, federal laws governing campaign financing have allowed corporations, labor unions, and special interest groups to raise funds and make campaign contributions through **political action committees (PACs).** Both the number of PACs and the amount of money PACs spend on elections have grown astronomically in recent years. There were about 1,000 PACs in 1976; today, there are more than 4,500 PACs. In 1973, total spending by PACs amounted to $19 million; in the 2007–2008 presidential election cycle, total spending by PACs exceeded $400 million. We will discuss PACs in more detail in Chapter 9.

Although campaign contributions do not guarantee that officials will vote the way the groups wish, contributions usually do ensure that the groups will have the ear of the public officials they have helped to elect.

Indirect Techniques

Interest groups also try to influence public policy indirectly through third parties or the general public. The effects of such **indirect techniques** may appear to be spontaneous, but indirect techniques are generally as well planned as the direct lobbying techniques just discussed. Indirect techniques can be particularly effective because public officials are often more impressed by contacts from voters than from lobbyists.

SHAPING PUBLIC OPINION Public opinion weighs significantly in the policymaking process, so interest groups cultivate their public images carefully. If public opinion favors a certain group's interests, then public officials will

political action committee (PAC) A committee that is established by a corporation, labor union, or special interest group to raise funds and make contributions on the establishing organization's behalf.

indirect technique Any method used by interest groups to influence government officials through third parties, such as voters.

Stan Honda/AFP/Getty Images

Immigration reform never happened during the Bush administration. These protesters want Barack Obama to address the issue. Which groups might favor allowing undocumented workers to remain in the United States? Which groups oppose any type of "amnesty"?

be more ready to listen and more willing to pass legislation favoring that group. To cultivate public opinion, an interest group's efforts may include online campaigns, television publicity, newspaper and magazine advertisements, mass mailings, and the use of public relations techniques to improve the group's public image.

For example, environmental groups often run television ads to dramatize threats to the environment. Oil companies may respond to criticism about increased gasoline prices with advertising showing their concern for the public welfare. The goal of all these activities is to influence public opinion and bring grassroots pressure to bear on officials.

Some interest groups also try to influence legislators through **rating systems.** A group selects legislative issues that it believes are important to its goals and rates legislators according to the percentage of times they vote favorably on that legislation. For example, a score of 90 percent on the Americans for Democratic Action (ADA) rating scale means that the legislator supported that liberal group's position to a high degree. Other groups tag members of Congress who support (or fail to support) their interests to a significant extent with telling labels. For instance, the Communications Workers of America refers to policymakers who take a position consistent with its members' own views as "Heroes" and those who take the opposite position as "Zeroes." Needless to say, such tactics can be an effective form of indirect lobbying, particularly with legislators who do not want to earn a low ADA score or be placed on the "Zeroes" list.

rating system A system by which a particular interest group evaluates (rates) the performance of legislators based on how often the legislators have voted with the group's position on particular issues.

ISSUE ADS AND "527s" One of the most powerful indirect techniques used by interest groups is the "issue ad"—a television or radio ad taking a position on a particular issue. The Supreme Court has made it clear that the First Amendment's guarantee of free speech protects interest groups' rights to set forth their positions on issues. Nevertheless, issue advocacy is controversial because the funds spent to air issue ads have had a clear effect on the outcome of elections.

Both parties have benefited from such interest group spending. As you will read in Chapter 9, the Bipartisan Campaign Reform Act of 2002 banned unlimited donations to campaigns and political parties, called *soft money.* In subsequent years, interest groups that had previously given soft money to parties set up new groups called "527s" (after the provision of the tax code that covers them). The 527s engaged in such practices as voter registration, but they also began making large expenditures on issue ads—which were legal so long as the 527s did not coordinate their activities with candidates' campaigns.

In the run-up to the 2008 presidential elections, clever campaign finance lawyers hit upon a new type of group, the 501(c)4 organization, also named after a section of the tax code. Lawyers argued that a 501(c)4 group could spend some of its funds on direct campaign contributions as long as most of the group's spending was on issue advocacy. Further, a 501(c)4 group could conceal the identity of its contributors. It was not possible to determine the legality of these claims in time for the 2008 elections. We will discuss this issue in greater depth in Chapter 9.

MOBILIZING CONSTITUENTS Interest groups sometimes urge members and other constituents to contact government officials—by letter, e-mail, or telephone—to show their support for or opposition to a certain policy. Large interest groups can generate hundreds of thousands of letters, e-mail messages, and phone calls. Interest groups often provide form letters or postcards for constituents to fill out and mail. The NRA has successfully used this tactic to fight strict federal gun control legislation by delivering half a million letters to Congress within a few weeks. Policymakers recognize that such communications are initiated by interest groups, however, and are impressed only when the volume of letters or e-mail communications is very large.

GOING TO COURT The legal system offers another avenue for interest groups to influence the political process. Civil rights groups paved the way for interest group litigation in the 1950s and 1960s with major victories in cases concerning equal housing, school desegregation, and employment discrimination. Environmental groups, such as the Sierra Club, have also successfully used litigation to press their concerns. For example, an environmental group might challenge in court an activity that threatens to pollute the environment or that will destroy the natural habitat of an endangered species. The legal challenge forces those engaging in the activity to bear the costs of defending themselves and may delay the project. In fact, much of the success of environmental groups has been linked to their use of lawsuits.

Interest groups can also influence the outcome of litigation without being a party to a lawsuit. Frequently, an interest group files an *amicus curiae* ("friend of the court") brief in an appellate (reviewing) court. The brief states the group's legal argument in support of its desired outcome in a case. For example, in the case *Metro-Goldwyn-Mayer Studios, Inc. v. Grokster, Ltd.*[5]—involving the legality of file-sharing software—hundreds of *amicus* briefs were filed by various groups on behalf of the petitioners. Groups filing *amicus* briefs for the case, which was heard by the Supreme Court in 2005, included the National Basketball Association, the National Football League, the National Association of Broadcasters, the Association of American Publishers, and numerous state governments. Often, interest groups have statistics and research that support their position on a certain issue, and this research can have considerable influence on the justices deciding the case.

"Never doubt that a small group of thoughtful, committed citizens can **CHANGE THE WORLD;** indeed, it's the only thing that ever has."

~ MARGARET MEAD ~
AMERICAN ANTHROPOLOGIST
1901–1978

DEMONSTRATIONS Some interest groups stage protests to make a statement in a dramatic way. The Boston Tea Party of 1773, in which American colonists dressed as Native Americans and threw tea into Boston Harbor to protest British taxes, is testimony to how long this tactic has been around. Over the years, many groups have organized protest marches and rallies to support or oppose such issues as legalized abortion, busing, gay and lesbian rights, government assistance to farmers, the treatment of Native Americans, restrictions on the use of federally owned lands in the West, trade relations with China, and the activities of global organizations, such as the World Trade Organization. Not all demonstration techniques are peaceful. Some environmental groups, for example, have used such dangerous tactics as spiking trees and setting traps on logging roads that puncture truck tires. Pro-life groups have bombed abortion clinics, and members of the Animal Liberation Front have broken into laboratories and freed animals being used for experimentation.

LO5 *Today's Lobbying Establishment*

Without a doubt, interest groups and their lobbyists have become a permanent feature in the landscape of American government. The major interest groups all have headquarters in Washington, D.C., close to the center of government. Professional lobbyists and staff members of various interest groups move freely between their groups' headquarters and congressional offices and committee rooms. Interest group representatives are routinely consulted when Congress drafts new legislation. As already mentioned, interest group representatives are frequently asked to testify before congressional committees or subcommittees on the effect or potential effect of particular legislation or regulations. In sum, interest groups have become an integral part of the American government system.

As interest groups have become a permanent feature of American government, lobbying has developed into a profession. A professional lobbyist—one who has mastered the techniques of lobbying discussed earlier in this chapter—is a valuable ally to any interest group seeking to influence government. Professional lobbyists can and often do represent a number of different interest groups over the course of their careers.

> "An honest politician IS ONE WHO, WHEN HE IS BOUGHT, WILL STAY BOUGHT."
>
> ~ SIMON CAMERON ~
> U.S. FINANCIER AND POLITICIAN
> 1799–1889

In recent years, it has become increasingly common for those who leave positions with the federal government to become lobbyists or consultants for the private-interest groups they helped to regulate. In spite of legislation and regulations that have been created in an attempt to reduce this "revolving door" syndrome, it is still functioning quite well.

Why Do Interest Groups Get Bad Press?

Despite their importance to democratic government, interest groups, like political parties, are often criticized by both the public and the press. Our image of interest groups and their special interests is not very favorable. You may have run across political cartoons depicting lobbyists standing in the hallways of Congress with briefcases stuffed with money.

These cartoons are not entirely factual, but they are not entirely fictitious either. President Richard Nixon (1969–1974) was revealed to have yielded to the campaign contributions of milk producers by later authorizing a windfall increase in milk subsidies. In 1977, "Koreagate," a scandal in which a South Korean businessman was accused of offering lavish "gifts" to several members of Congress, encouraged the belief that politicians are too easily susceptible to the snares of special interests. In the early 1990s, it was revealed that a number of senators who received generous contributions from a particular savings and loan association subsequently supported a "hands-off" policy by savings and loan regulators. The savings and loan association in question later got into financial trouble, costing the taxpayers billions of dollars. (One of the senators criticized for having exercised poor judgment during the savings and loan scandal was John McCain, the 2008 Republican presidential candidate. It may have been this painful experience that inspired McCain to become an ardent advocate of campaign-finance reform.) See this chapter's *Perception versus Reality* feature for another view of lobbyists.

"MY GREATEST ASSET IS I'M SO RICH, I CAN'T BE BOUGHT BY ANY INTEREST GROUP."

As you will read shortly, Congress has tried to impose stricter regulations on lobbyists. The most important legislation regulating lobbyists was passed in 1946 and was revised in 1995 and again in 2007. A problem with stricter regulation is that it could abridge First Amendment rights.

The Regulation of Interest Groups

In an attempt to control lobbying, Congress passed the Federal Regulation of Lobbying Act in 1946. The major provisions of the act are as follows:

- Any person or organization that receives money to be used principally to influence legislation before Congress must register with the clerk of the House and the secretary of the Senate.
- Any group or person registering must identify the group's or person's employer, salary, amount and purpose of expenses, and duration of employment.
- Every registered lobbyist must give quarterly reports on his or her activities, which are to be published in the *Congressional Quarterly*.
- Anyone failing to satisfy the specific provisions of this act can be fined up to $10,000 and be imprisoned for up to five years.

The act was very limited and did not succeed in regulating lobbying to any great degree for several reasons. First, the Supreme Court restricted the application of the law to only those lobbyists who sought to influence federal legislation directly.[6] Any lobbyist seeking to influence legislation indirectly through public opinion did not fall within the scope of the law. Second, only persons or organizations whose principal purpose was to influence legislation were required to register. Many

PERCEPTION VERSUS REALITY

Do Lobbyists Deserve All the Blame?

Just mention the word *lobbyist,* and red flags pop up. Most Americans have a negative opinion about those in the lobbying industry. Not surprisingly, when a congressional scandal involving kickbacks and bribery surfaces, cries for lobbying reforms are heard around the country. The last set of lobbying reforms, in 2007, occurred after a scandal involving Jack Abramoff, a lobbyist who is now in prison.

The Perception

By definition, a lobbyist is hired by a special interest group or a corporation to influence government policies. Lobbyists are professionals, and as such, they are paid by special interests and corporations to ply their skills. They are not paid to act in the national interest. Rather, a lobbyist's job is to convince government officials to undertake actions that are beneficial to the single industry or group that the lobbyist represents. This can mean supporting measures that unjustly divert wealth from the taxpayers or the economy in general into the pockets of favored individuals and industries. When dealing with members of Congress or the executive branch, "shady" lobbyists wheel and deal for the best possible outcome for the groups they represent. Typically, whenever lobbyists become involved in unethical or even illegal dealings in Washington, D.C., the public tends to blame the lobbyists rather than members of Congress.

The Reality

It takes two to tango. Lobbyists don't just walk into the offices of members of Congress with sacks of cash (although this has occasionally happened, to be sure). First and foremost, the job of the lobbyist is to inform members of Congress about the effects of proposed legislation on the interest group the lobbyist represents—or even to suggest legislation. After all, members of Congress cannot be on top of every problem that faces America.

Let's not forget that Benjamin Franklin was once the lobbyist in England for Pennsylvania and other colonies. During her attempt to become the Democratic presidential candidate in 2008, Senator Hillary Clinton (D., N.Y.) stated that "a lot of those lobbyists, whether you like it or not, represent real Americans. They represent nurses. They represent social workers. They represent . . . yes, they represent corporations. They employ lots of people."

Members of Congress, especially in the House of Representatives, spend much of their time making sure that they are reelected. Consequently, members of Congress require large sums for their reelection campaigns. On many occasions, members have either implicitly or explicitly "shaken down" lobbyists for campaign contributions. In this sense, lobbyists are victims as much as they are perpetrators. Former majority leader of the House of Representatives Tom DeLay (R., Tex.) ran an operation that ensured that only Republicans were hired for big lobbying jobs and that they were paid well. Once hired, every one of them was expected to contribute some of his or her income to Republican campaign chests. (Operations of this type were banned in 2007.)

Blog On *Most conservative blogs argue that restrictions on campaign contributions place unacceptable limits on the freedom of speech. The Liberty Papers at* **www.thelibertypapers.org** *is one such blog. In contrast, Common Cause at* **www.commonblog.com** *advocates strong measures to limit the political influence of well-funded groups.*

groups avoided registration by claiming that their principal function was something else. Third, the act did not cover those whose lobbying was directed at agencies in the executive branch or lobbyists who testified before congressional committees. Fourth, the public was almost totally unaware of the information in the quarterly reports filed by lobbyists, and Congress created no agency to oversee interest group activities. Not until 1995 did Congress finally address those loopholes by enacting new legislation.

The Lobbying Disclosure Act of 1995

In 1995, Congress passed new lobbying legislation—the Lobbying Disclosure Act—that reformed the 1946 act in the following ways:

- Strict definitions now apply to determine who must register with the clerk of the House and the secretary of the Senate as a lobbyist. A lobbyist is anyone who either spends at least 20 percent of his or her time lobbying members of Congress, their staffs, or executive-branch officials, or is paid more than

$5,000 in a six-month period for such work. Any organization that spends more than $20,000 in a six-month period conducting such lobbying activity must also register. These amounts have since been altered to $2,500 and $10,000 per quarter, respectively.

- Lobbyists must report their clients, the issues on which they lobbied, and the agency or chamber of Congress they contacted, although they do not need to disclose the names of those they contacted.

Tax-exempt organizations, such as religious groups, were exempted from these provisions, as were organizations that engage in grassroots lobbying, such as a media campaign that asks people to write or call their congressional representative. Nonetheless, the number of registered lobbyists nearly doubled in the first few years of the new legislation.

Lobbying Scandals in the 2000s

In 2005, a number of lobbying scandals in Washington, D.C., came to light. A major figure in the scandals was Jack Abramoff, an influential lobbyist who had ties to many Republicans (and a few Democrats) in Congress and to various officials in the Bush administration. Abramoff gained access to the power brokers in the capital by giving them campaign contributions, expensive gifts, and exotic trips.

Eventually, Abramoff pleaded guilty to charges of fraud, tax evasion, and conspiracy to bribe public officials. Abramoff received a prison sentence in 2006. The following year, Congressman Robert Ney (R., Ohio) and former Bush administration official Steven Griles also received prison sentences for their part in the scandal. One result of these events was a renewed interest in lobbying reform.

Lobbying Reform Efforts in 2007

Following the midterm elections of 2006, the new Democratic majority in the Senate and House of Representatives undertook a lobbying reform effort. The goal of the reforms was to force lobbyists to disclose their expenditures on House and Senate election campaigns above and beyond straight campaign contributions.

Bundled campaign contributions, in which a lobbyist arranges for contributions from a variety of sources, would have to be reported. Expenditures on the sometimes lavish parties to benefit candidates would have to be reported as well. (Of course, partygoers were expected to pay for their food and drink with a check written out to the candidate.) The new rules covered PACs as well as registered lobbyists, which led one lobbyist to observe sourly that this wasn't lobbying reform but campaign-finance reform.

President Bush signed the resulting Honest Leadership and Open Government Act in September 2007. The new law increased lobbying disclosure and placed further restrictions on the receipt of gifts and travel by members of Congress paid for by lobbyists and the organizations they represent. The act also strengthened rules governing bundled political contributions from lobbyists and included provisions requiring the disclosure of lawmakers' requests for earmarks in legislation. (We discuss earmarks in more depth in Chapter 11.)

Lobbyists and the Obama Administration

During his campaign for the presidency, Barack Obama pledged that "lobbyists won't find a job in my White House." Given how many talented individuals with experience in government have served as lobbyists, that pledge turned out to be unenforceable. Out of 267 senior administration officials appointed by May 2009, 30 had served as lobbyists within the past five years.

Appointees signed a pledge not to work on issues for which they lobbied in the previous two years, but given the positions that many of these appointees filled, such a pledge was probably unworkable as well. Interest groups represented among these former lobbyists included the Campaign for Tobacco-Free Kids, the mortgage giant Fannie Mae, the investment bank Goldman Sachs, Mothers Against Drunk Driving, the National Council of La Raza, the defense industry giant Raytheon, and the Service Employees International Union.

Other restrictions imposed by the new administration included a rule that all communications with lobbyists over economic stimulus projects had to be in writing. When Obama spoke at a congressional fund-raiser in June 2009, lobbyists were banned from attending. At breakfast the next morning, however, with Obama no longer present, the lobbyists returned with a rush. Many old hands in Washington considered Obama's policies toward lobbyists absurd and predicted that they would not last.

AMERICA AT ODDS *Interest Groups*

Interest groups were a cause of concern even before the Constitution was written. Recall from Chapter 2 that those opposed to the Constitution (the Anti-Federalists) claimed that a republican form of government could not work in a country this size because so many factions—interest groups—would be contending for power. The result would be anarchy and chaos. James Madison attempted to allay these fears (in *Federalist Paper* No. 10—see Appendix F) by arguing that the "mischiefs of factions" could be controlled. The large size of the United States would mean that so many diverse interests and factions would be contending for power that no one faction would be able to gain control of the government.

What Madison did not foresee was the extent to which money would become intertwined with lawmaking in this country. Wealthy pharmaceutical companies, insurance companies, financial firms, and other entities have often been far too influential in Congress and in the executive branch. On some occasions, they have virtually written the bills enacted by Congress. The challenge for our political leaders today is to somehow distance political decisions from the influence of wealthy, elite groups. As you will read in Chapter 9, Congress has tried on several occasions to regulate campaign spending and contributions to address this problem. The trouble is, some of the very people addressing the issue—members of Congress—benefit from the status quo, which hampers the prospect of any aggressive campaign-finance reform.

ISSUES FOR DEBATE & DISCUSSION

1. **One of the most controversial issues of our time with respect to interest groups has to do with issue advocacy. Issue ads paid for by certain groups, such as a pro-life organization or an antiwar group, can often be clearly in support of or against a specific candidate, even though the candidate's name is not mentioned. Yet, as you will read in Chapter 9, the funds used to pay for this type of campaign advertising are not regulated by the government. Some believe that there should be a cap on the amount of funds that any one group can spend for issue ads. Others assert that such a limit would violate the constitutional guarantee of freedom of expression, and free political speech is a core requirement of any true democracy. What is your position on this issue?**
2. **Some claim that companies that receive government contracts without a bidding procedure are often well-established, wealthy firms. Such firms make campaign contributions to government leaders so that the companies can receive profitable contracts for war-related and other work. Others claim that in time of war, it is so important to ensure that contractors do an acceptable job that it is often necessary to award contracts to experienced companies without bidding. What is your position on this issue?**

TAKE ACTION

An obvious way to get involved in politics is to join an interest group whose goals you endorse, including one of the organizations on your campus. You can find lists of interest groups operating at the local, state, and national levels by simply going to a search engine online, such as Google, and keying in the words "interest groups." If you have a particular interest or goal that you would like to promote, consider forming your own group, as some Iowa students did when they formed a group called Students Toward Environmental Protection. In the photo below, students from Grinnell College in Iowa stage a protest rally at the state capitol. The students wanted Iowa's lawmakers to issue tougher regulations governing factory farms and to expand the state's bottle deposit requirements.

AP Photo/Charlie Neibergall

POLITICS ON THE WEB

- To find particular interest groups online, a good point of departure is the Internet Public Library Association, which provides links to hundreds of professional and trade associations. Go to **www.ipl.org/div/aon**
- You can access the National Rifle Association online at **www.nra.org**
- AARP's Web site can be found at **www.aarp.org**
- To learn about the activities of the National Education Association, go to **www.nea.org**
- You can find information on environmental issues and the activities of the National Resources Defense Council at **www.nrdc.org**

Online resources for this chapter

This text's Companion Web site, at **www.4ltrpress.cengage.com/govt**, offers links to numerous resources that you can use to learn more about the topics covered in this chapter.

trade organization
free rider problem
rating system
labor force
www.igc.org
public-interest group
lobbyist
political action committee (PAC)

Pankaj & Insy Shah/Gulfimages/Getty Images

GOVT 7

Political Parties

LEARNING OBJECTIVES

LO1 Summarize the origins and development of the two-party system in the United States.

LO2 Describe the current status of the two major parties.

LO3 Explain how political parties function in our democratic system.

LO4 Discuss the structure of American political parties.

LO5 Describe the different types of third parties and how they function in the American political system.

AMERICA AT ODDS

Should the Republican Party Change Its Views?

The elections of 2006 and 2008 were not good ones for the Republican Party. In 2006, the Republicans lost control of the U.S. House and Senate. In 2008, the Republicans lost more seats in Congress and the presidency as well. Ominously, more than two out of three voters in the 19–29 age group cast their ballots for Democrat Barack Obama. In mid-2009, only 28 percent of the public told the Gallup poll that they were Republicans, compared with 34 percent who called themselves Democrats. Not surprisingly, these results have touched off a debate within the Republican Party. Should the Republicans moderate their conservative views to attract more independent voters? Should the party instead stand by its conservative principles, or even move further to the right?

The Republicans Must Stand by Their Principles

Those who believe that the Republicans must "stick to their guns" argue that support for conservatism is not merely a matter of political expediency. These activists argue that conservative values are not only popular but also "correct" in a very deep sense. Values such as religious belief, strong families, and individual self-reliance are the foundation of our civilization. Liberalism erodes these values and paves the road to cultural collapse.

Even though only 28 percent of voters call themselves Republicans, 40 percent say they are conservatives. In 2009, 39 percent of respondents said that they were becoming more conservative, not less. Support for such conservative positions as the right to bear arms and opposition to abortion is rising, not falling. On one set of issues, the Republicans are well advised to move further to the right. In a recent poll, both Republicans *and independents* agreed that economic conservatives did not have enough influence in the party. What did these people mean? Under President George W. Bush, Republicans in Congress abandoned their traditional opposition to government spending. Millions of Americans, including independents, were alarmed at Bush's budget deficits, and they are appalled at the deficits run up under Obama. In time, Americans will rebel against big government and cultural corruption. If Republicans don't continue to stand for true conservatism, then when the American people realize that it is what the country really needs, they won't have anyone to vote for.

To Win, the Republicans Need More Supporters

"Big tent" Republicans argue that a policy of relying on Democratic mistakes is bankrupt. Even if the Democrats fail, the resulting Republican advantage may only be temporary. The face of America is changing. Support for gay rights has risen dramatically, especially among young voters. The number of Hispanic voters rises year by year, and by 2050 at the latest, non-Hispanic whites will be a minority of the U.S. population. Despite these changes, some conservatives seem intent on ensuring that the Republicans are seen as the "nasty party"—the party that hates people. Conservatives say they want to return to the principles of Ronald Reagan, but they forget Reagan's sunny disposition. Even ardent liberals did not get the sense that Reagan was mad at them.

Those who want the Republicans to change do not necessarily have a long list of alternative policies. Support gay marriage? Obama doesn't even do that. And Republicans won't gain votes by changing their position on abortion. What the Republicans do need is to break with the ultra-right and stop antagonizing the very people they need to form a majority. As one Republican leader pointed out, referring to talk show host Rush Limbaugh, a 15 percent share of the radio audience is a phenomenally successful business model. In electoral politics, you require 50 percent plus one.

Republicans need young voters, but tirades against gays are poison to that constituency. If the overwhelming majority of Latinos come to reject the Republicans, eventually the party will have to kiss even Texas good-bye. Yet some conservatives demonize not only illegal immigrants but also Hispanic influence on American culture in general. If voters conclude that Republicans see large numbers of their fellow Americans as "the enemy," Republicans will lose.

WHERE DO YOU STAND?

1. **Pastor Rick Warren, author of *The Purpose Driven Life,* accepts that homosexuality is a sin, but he also emphasizes his belief in God's love for all people. Why might some members of the religious right reject Warren's formula?**
2. **American-style cultural conservatism is not popular in much of Europe. Many of these nations are also facing declines in their populations. Some conservatives would argue that these facts are connected. Is this argument reasonable? Why or why not?**

EXPLORE THIS ISSUE ONLINE

- **Web sites that advocate a more moderate Republican Party include David Frum's www.newmajority.com. For full-throttle conservatism, try www.rushlimbaugh.com.**

Introduction

Political ideology can spark heated debates among Americans, as you read in the chapter-opening *America at Odds* feature. A **political party** can be defined as a group of individuals who organize to win elections, operate the government, and determine policy. Political parties serve as major vehicles for citizen participation in our political system. It is hard to imagine democracy without political parties. Political parties provide a way for the public to choose who will serve in government and which policies will be carried out. Even citizens who do not identify with any political party or who choose not to participate in elections are affected by the activities of parties and their influence on government.

"Both of our political parties . . . agree conscientiously in the same object: **THE PUBLIC GOOD;** but they differ essentially in what they deem the means of promoting that good."

~ THOMAS JEFFERSON ~
IN A LETTER TO
ABIGAIL ADAMS
1804

Political parties were an unforeseen development in American political history. The founders defined many other important institutions, such as the presidency and Congress, and described their functions in the Constitution. Political parties, however, are not even mentioned in the Constitution. In fact, the founders decried factions and parties. Thomas Jefferson probably best expressed the founders' antiparty sentiments when he declared, "If I could not go to heaven but with a party, I would not go there at all."[1]

If the founders did not want political parties, though, who was supposed to organize political campaigns and mobilize supporters of political candidates? Clearly, there was a practical need for some kind of organizing group to form a link between citizens and their government. Even our early national leaders, for all their antiparty feelings, realized this; several of them were active in establishing or organizing the first political parties.

LO1 A Short History of American Political Parties

Throughout the course of our history, several parties have formed, and some have disappeared. Even today, although we have only two major political parties, numerous other parties have been organized, as will be discussed later in this chapter.

The First Political Parties

The founders rejected the idea of political parties because they believed, in the words of George Washington, that the "spirit of party . . . agitates the community with ill-founded jealousies and false alarms, kindles the animosity of one part against another, foments occasionally riot and insurrection."[2] At some point in the future, the founders feared, a party leader might even seize power as a dictator. Nonetheless, two major political factions—the Federalists and Anti-Federalists—were formed even before the Constitution was ratified. Remember from Chapter 2 that the Federalists pushed for the ratification of the Constitution because they wanted a stronger national government than the one that had existed under the Articles of Confederation. The Anti-Federalists argued against ratification. They supported states' rights and feared a too-powerful central government.

These two national factions continued, in somewhat altered form, after the Constitution was ratified. Alexander Hamilton, the first secretary of the Treasury, became the leader of the Federalist Party, which supported a strong central government that would encourage the development of commerce and manufacturing. The Federalists generally thought that a republic should be ruled by its wealthiest and best-educated citizens. Opponents of the Federalists and Hamilton's policies referred to themselves as Republicans. Today, they are often referred to as Jeffersonian Republicans, or Democratic Republicans (a name never used at the time), to distinguish this group from the later Republican Party. The Jeffersonian Republicans favored a more limited role for government. They believed that the nation's welfare would be best served if the states had more power than the central government. In their view, Congress should dominate the government, and government policies should serve farming interests, rather than promote commerce and manufacturing.

From 1796 to 1860

The nation's first two parties clashed openly in the elections of 1796, in which John Adams, the Federalists' candidate

political party A group of individuals who organize to win elections, operate the government, and determine policy.

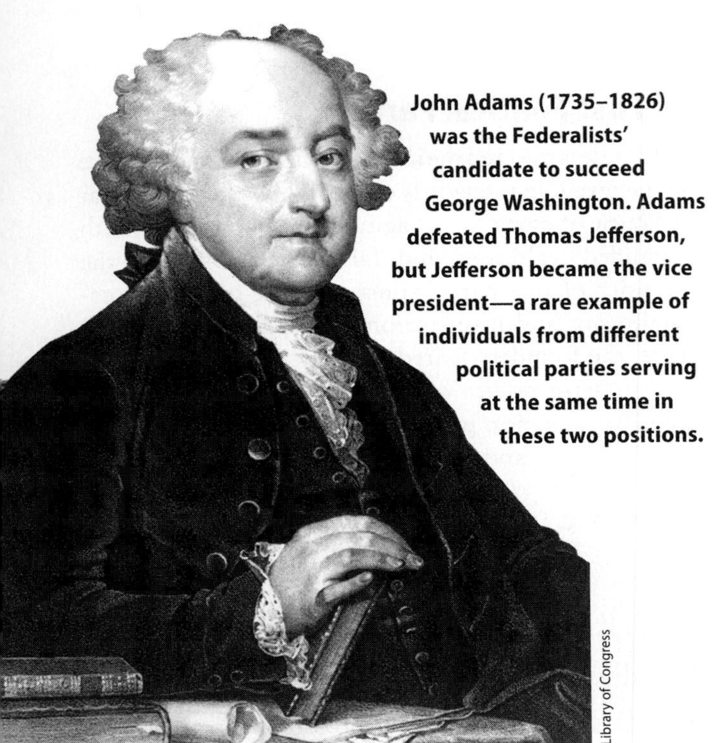

John Adams (1735–1826) was the Federalists' candidate to succeed George Washington. Adams defeated Thomas Jefferson, but Jefferson became the vice president—a rare example of individuals from different political parties serving at the same time in these two positions.

Library of Congress

to succeed George Washington as president, defeated Thomas Jefferson. Over the next four years, Jefferson and James Madison worked to extend the influence of the Jeffersonian Republican Party. In the presidential elections of 1800 and 1804, Jefferson won the presidency, and his party also won control of Congress. The Federalists never returned to power and thus became the first (but not the last) American party to go out of existence. (See the time line of American political parties in Figure 7–1 on the facing page.)

The Jeffersonian Republicans dominated American politics for the next twenty years. Jefferson was succeeded in the White House by two other members of the party—James Madison and James Monroe. In the mid-1820s, however, the Republicans split into two groups. Supporters of Andrew Jackson, who was elected president in 1828, called themselves Democrats. The Democrats appealed to small farmers and the growing class of urbanized workers. The other group, the National Republicans (later the Whig Party), was led by John Quincy Adams, Henry Clay, and the great orator Daniel Webster. It had the support of bankers, business owners, and many southern planters.

As the Whigs and Democrats competed for the White House throughout the 1840s and 1850s, the two-party system as we know it today emerged. Both parties were large, with well-known leaders and supporters across the nation. Both had grassroots organizations of party workers committed to winning as many political offices (at all levels of government) for the party as possible. Both the Whigs and the Democrats tried to avoid the issue of slavery. By the mid-1850s, the Whig coalition had fallen apart, and most northern Whigs were absorbed into the new Republican Party, which opposed the extension of slavery into new territories. Campaigning on this platform, the Republicans succeeded in electing Abraham Lincoln as the first president of the new Republican Party in 1860.

Thomas Jefferson (1743–1826) was a Republican who became our third president and served two terms. The Jeffersonian Republicans, not to be confused with the later Republican Party led by Abraham Lincoln, dominated American politics for more than two decades.

Library of Congress

Andrew Jackson (1767–1845) was part of the newly named party of Democrats. Jackson won the presidential election in 1828, defeating the candidate of the National Republicans.

Library of Congress

Figure 7–1

A Time Line of U.S. Political Parties

Many of these parties—including the Constitutional Union Party, Henry Wallace's Progressive Party, and the States' Rights Democrats—were important during only one presidential election.

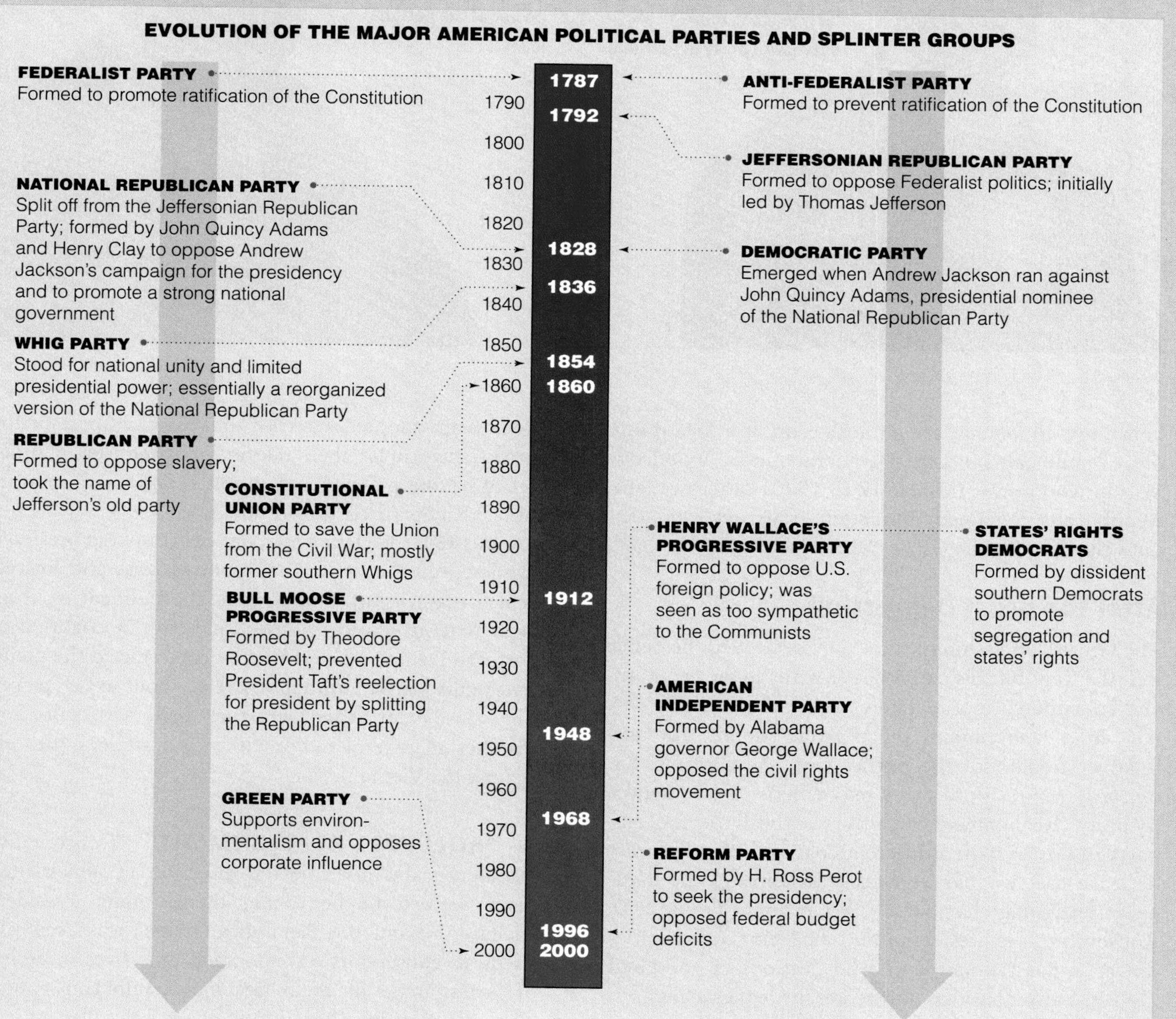

From the Civil War to the Great Depression

When the former Confederate states rejoined the Union after the Civil War, the Republicans and Democrats were roughly even in strength, although the Republicans were more successful in presidential contests. In the 1890s, however, the Republicans gained a decisive advantage. In that decade, the Democrats allied themselves with the Populist movement, which consisted largely of indebted farmers in the West and South. The Populists advocated inflation as a way of lessening their debts. Urban workers in the Midwest and East strongly opposed this program, which would erode the value of their paychecks. After the election of 1896, the Republicans established themselves in the minds of many Americans as the party that

From the election of Abraham Lincoln (shown here) in 1860 until the election of Franklin Delano Roosevelt in 1932, the Republican Party was the more successful party in national politics.

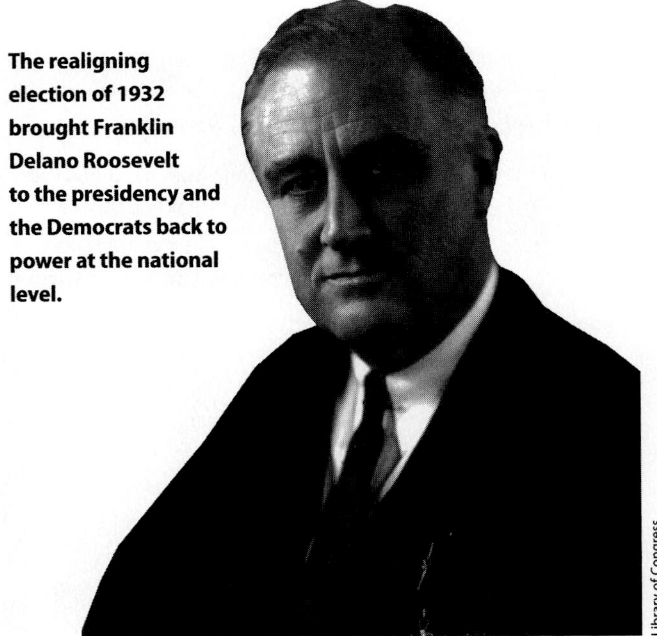

The realigning election of 1932 brought Franklin Delano Roosevelt to the presidency and the Democrats back to power at the national level.

knew how to manage the nation's economy. As a result of a Republican split, the Democrats under Woodrow Wilson won power from 1912 to 1920. Otherwise, the Republicans remained dominant in national politics until the onset of the Great Depression.

After the Great Depression

The Great Depression of the 1930s destroyed the belief that the Republicans could better manage the economy and contributed to a realignment in the two-party system. In a **realignment,** the popular support for and relative strength of the parties shift. As a result, the minority (opposition) party may emerge as the majority party. (Realignment can also reestablish the majority party in power with a different coalition of supporters or leave the two parties closely balanced.) The landmark realigning election of 1932 brought Franklin D. Roosevelt to the presidency and the Democrats back to power at the national level. The elections of 1860 and 1896 are also considered to represent realignments.

A CIVIL RIGHTS PLANK Those who joined the Democrats during Roosevelt's New Deal included a substantial share of African Americans—Roosevelt's relief programs were open to people of all races. (Until the 1930s, African Americans had been overwhelmingly Republican.) In 1948, for the first time ever, the Democrats adopted a civil rights plank as part of the party platform at their national convention. A number of southern Democrats revolted and ran a separate States' Rights ticket for president.

realignment A process in which the popular support for and relative strength of the parties shift and the parties are reestablished with different coalitions of supporters.

In 1964, the Democrats, under incumbent president Lyndon Johnson, won a landslide victory, and liberals held a majority in Congress. In the political environment that produced this election result, a coalition of northern Democrats and Republicans crafted the major civil rights legislation that you read about in Chapter 5. The subsequent years were turbulent, with riots and marches in several major cities and student protests against the Vietnam War.

A "ROLLING REALIGNMENT" Conservative Democrats did not like the direction in which their party seemed to be taking them. Under President Richard Nixon, the Republican Party was receptive to these conservative Democrats, and over a period of years, most of them became Republican voters. This was a major alteration in the political landscape, although it was not exclusively associated with a single election. Republican president Ronald Reagan helped cement the new Republican coalition. The Democrats continued to hold majorities in the House and Senate until 1994, but partisan labels were somewhat misleading. During the 1970s and 1980s, a large bloc of Democrats in Congress, mostly from the South, sided with the Republicans on almost all issues. In time, these conservative Democrats were replaced by conservative Republicans.

The result of this "rolling realignment" was that the two major parties were now fairly evenly matched. The Republicans appeared to have an edge during George W. Bush's first term (2001–2005). In 2006, however, the Democrats regained control of both chambers of Congress. The Democrats increased their margins in 2008, in both the House and the Senate, and reclaimed the presidency.

LO2 America's Political Parties Today

Historically, political parties drew together like-minded individuals. Today, too, individuals with similar characteristics tend to align themselves more often with one or the other major party. Such factors as race, age, income, education, marital status, and geography all influence party identification.

Normally, slightly more men than women identify with the Republican Party, and more women than men identify themselves as Democrats. While whites are slightly more likely to identify with the Republican Party, people in the other categories (black, other nonwhite, and Hispanic) overwhelmingly classify themselves as Democrats. In recent years, voters under the age of thirty have increasingly come to favor the Democrats. What impact did this development have on the 2008 presidential elections? We look for the answer to that question in this chapter's *Perception versus Reality* feature on the following page.

Red States versus Blue States

As just mentioned, geography is one of the many factors that can determine party identification. Examine the national electoral map shown on the right. In 2008, Republican John McCain did well in the South, on the Great Plains, and in parts of the Mountain West. Democrat Barack Obama did well in the Northeast, in the Midwest, and on the West Coast. Beginning with the presidential elections of 2000, the press has made much of the supposed cultural differences between the "blue" states that vote for the Democratic candidate and the "red" states that vote for the Republican. In reality, though, many states could better be described as "purple"—that is, a mixture of red and blue. These states could give their electoral votes to either party.

For another way to consider the influence of geography, see the map of Ohio on the next page. Most of Ohio is red, and a quick glance might lead you to believe that McCain carried the state. In fact, Obama carried Ohio by a margin of 4.6 percentage points. Ohio looks red because McCain carried almost all of the rural parts of the state. The Obama counties had larger populations. This pattern was seen all over the country: the more urban the county, the more likely it was to vote Democratic.

A Changing Electorate?

In recent years, polls on party identification showed a rough parity in the support for the two major political parties. About a third of the voters identified themselves as Democrats, a third as Republicans, and a third as independents. Many of the independents showed a strong inclination to favor one or the other of the major parties—they were independents in name only. But the number of independents leaning toward the Democrats and leaning toward the Republicans was about the same.

Since 2006, though, pollsters have noted a shift in party identification. A poll taken by the Pew Research Center for the People and the Press in 2008 found that

This map shows the 2008 presidential election results by state. Note that Obama won a single electoral vote in Nebraska, which is represented by a symbol.

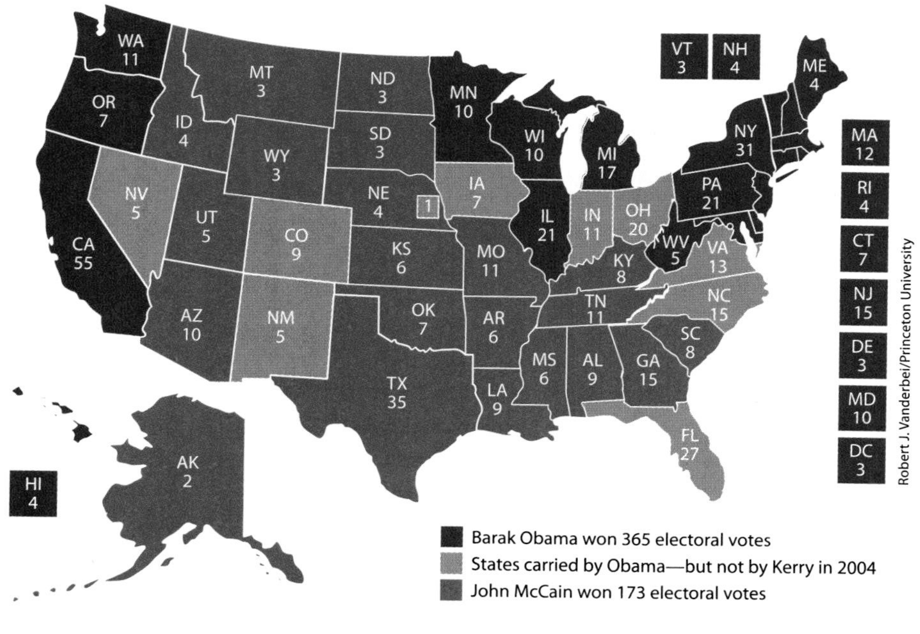

The Youth Vote Elected Barack Obama

He was young, dynamic, and hip. His name was Barack Obama. He understood how to use technology in campaigning better than any candidate ever had before. He reached out to the youth of America, and they responded. College campuses were filled with Obama supporters.

The Perception

To this day, many Obama supporters believe that the youth vote put him into office. On college campuses across the country, MySpace and Facebook users devoted many electrons to Obama's campaign. How could they not vote for such a young, athletic candidate? When all the results were in, voters under thirty supported Obama by a margin of 66 percent to 32 percent. Sixty-nine percent of first-time voters chose Obama as their president. In addition, young voters supported Democratic candidates for U.S. House seats by a margin of 63 percent to 34 percent.

The Reality

The young Americans who voted for Obama may believe that they made the key difference, but the facts do not support that belief. Voters under the age of thirty made up 18 percent of the electorate in 2008. That amounts to an increase of just one percentage point over 2004. True, almost a quarter of Obama's vote came from those under thirty years of age, but 77 percent of his supporters were over thirty. Consider the following: if everyone in the country under thirty years of age had stayed home, Obama would have lost only two of the states that he carried—Indiana and North Carolina.

Blog On *One of the largest collections of information on young voters is maintained by the Center for Information & Research on Civic Learning and Engagement, or CIRCLE. Located at* **www.civicyouth.org**, *CIRCLE is a project of Tufts University. The National Youth Rights Association, at* **www.youthrights.org**, *advocates greater rights for young people. It supports discussion forums that you can join.*

This map displays the Ohio counties carried by Barack Obama (blue) and John McCain (red) in the 2008 presidential elections. The cities shown on the map are the ten most populous municipalities in Ohio. Obama did well in urban and suburban counties, but poorly in nonmetropolitan regions. (Note that one nonmetropolitan county that Obama carried contains a major university.)

51 percent of those surveyed identified with or leaned toward the Democratic Party. In contrast, only 37 percent identified with or leaned toward the Republicans. Surveys have also found that public attitudes are drifting toward Democratic values, as reflected in increased support for government aid to the disadvantaged. Support for traditional family values, which helped fuel Republican victories over the years, has decreased.

The 2008 Elections

The changing political landscape just described made 2008 a promising year for the Democrats. New York senator Hillary Clinton was the initial Democratic presidential favorite, but by March 2008 she had fallen behind the well-organized and well-funded campaign of Illinois senator Barack Obama. The contest between the two remained close until the very end—Obama did not prevail until the first week of June. Leading Republicans included Arizona senator John McCain and former Massachusetts governor Mitt Romney. A late addition was former Arkansas governor Mike Huckabee, supported by evangelical Christians who were not happy with the other contenders. McCain clinched the race on March 4.

By 2008, Obama had spent only three years as a U.S. senator. His résumé was thin, and he was relatively unknown. McCain, in contrast, had a long-standing reputation as a maverick who would challenge his own party on issues such as immigration and campaign-finance reform. He had a proven record of appealing to independents, and he was widely seen as the one Republican who might hold the presidency for his party. Throughout the summer, McCain sought to portray Obama as dangerously inexperienced. By September, McCain had established a slight lead.

The hurricane that swept through the financial world after September 15 doomed McCain's candidacy. It also made many voters question basic Republican philosophies. Obama argued, with some success, that the crisis was due to the anti-regulation policies of the Republicans, which McCain also espoused. By Election Day, a majority of the voters wanted strong government action to right the economy, and they saw the Democrats as the party traditionally able to supply such policies. As you can see in the map on page 157, Obama added nine states to the number carried by Democrat John Kerry in 2004. With almost 53 percent of the popular vote, Obama won the strongest personal mandate of any Democrat in a generation.

LO3 *What Do Political Parties Do?*

As noted earlier, the Constitution does not mention political parties. Historically, though, political parties have played a vital role in our democratic system. Their main function has been to link the people's policy preferences to actual government policies. Political parties also perform many other functions.

Selecting Candidates

One of the most important functions of the two political parties is to recruit and nominate candidates for political office. This function simplifies voting choices for the electorate. Political parties take the large number of people who want to run for office and narrow the field. They accomplish this by the use of the **primary,** which is a preliminary election to choose a party's final candidate. This candidate then runs against the opposing party's candidate in the general election.

Informing the Public

Political parties help educate the public about important political issues. In recent years, these issues have included defense and environmental policies, health insurance, our tax system, welfare reform, crime, education, and Social Security. Each party presents its view of these issues through television announcements, newspaper articles or ads, Web site materials, campaign speeches, rallies, debates, and leaflets. These activities help citizens learn about the issues, form opinions, and consider proposed solutions.

Coordinating Policymaking

In our complex government, parties are essential for coordinating policy among the various branches of the government. The political party is usually the major institution through which the executive and legislative branches cooperate with each other. Each president, cabinet head, and member of Congress is normally a member of the Democratic or the Republican Party. The president works through party leaders in Congress to promote the administration's legislative program. Ideally, the parties work together to fashion compromises—legislation that is acceptable to both parties and that serves the national interest. In recent years, however, there has been little bipartisanship in Congress. (For a more detailed discussion of the role played by political parties in Congress, see Chapter 11.) Parties also act as the glue of our federal structure by connecting the various levels of government—state and national—with a common bond.

Checking the Power of the Governing Party

The party with fewer members in the legislature is the **minority party.** The party with more members is the **majority party.** The party that does not control Congress or a state legislature, or the presidency or a state governorship, also plays a vital function in American politics. The "out party" does what it can to influence the "in party" and its policies, and to check the actions of the

primary A preliminary election held for the purpose of choosing a party's final candidate.

minority party The political party that has fewer members in the legislature than the opposing party.

majority party The political party that has more members in the legislature than the opposing party.

AP Photo/Al Goldis

Political parties are constantly contacting potential supporters, especially prior to elections. That's what these volunteers are doing.

party in power. For example, depending on how evenly Congress is divided, the out party, or minority party, may be able to attract to its side some of the members of the majority party to pass or defeat certain legislation. The out party will also work to inform the voters of the shortcomings of the in party's agenda and to plan strategies for winning the next election.

coalition An alliance of individuals or groups with a variety of interests and opinions who join together to support all or part of a political party's platform.

electorate All of the citizens eligible to vote in a given election.

Balancing Competing Interests

Political parties are often described as vast umbrellas under which Americans with diverse interests can gather. Political parties are essentially **coalitions**—individuals and groups with a variety of interests and opinions who join together to support the party's platform, or parts of it.

> "Democracy is
> THE RECURRRENT SUSPICION THAT MORE THAN HALF OF THE PEOPLE ARE RIGHT MORE THAN HALF OF THE TIME."
>
> ~ E. B. WHITE ~
> AMERICAN WRITER
> 1900–1965

The Republican Party, for example, includes a number of groups with different views on such issues as health care, immigration, and global warming. The role of party leaders in this situation is to adopt a broad enough view on these issues that the various groups will not be alienated. In this way, different groups can hold their individual views and still come together under the umbrella of the Republican Party. Leaders of both the Democratic Party and the Republican Party modify contending views and arrange compromises among different groups. In so doing, the parties help to unify, rather than divide, their members.

Running Campaigns

Through their national, state, and local organizations, parties coordinate campaigns. Political parties take care of a large number of small and routine tasks that are essential to the smooth functioning of the electoral process. For example, they work at getting party members registered and at conducting drives for new voters. Sometimes, party volunteers staff the polling places.

LO4 *How American Political Parties Are Structured*

Each of the two major American political parties consists of three components: the party in the electorate, the party organization, and the party in government.

1. The party in the **electorate** is the largest component, consisting of all of those people who describe themselves as Democrats or Republicans. Members of the party in the electorate never need to work on a campaign or attend a party meeting. In most

states, they may register as Democrats or Republicans, but registration can be changed at will.

2. Each major party has a national organization with national, state, and local offices. As will be discussed later in this section, the party organizations include several levels of people who maintain the party's strength between elections, make its rules, raise money, organize conventions, help with elections, and recruit candidates.

3. The party in government consists of all of the party's candidates who have won elections and now hold public office. Even though members of Congress, state legislators, presidents, and all other officeholders almost always run for office as either Democrats or Republicans, members of any one party do not always agree with each other on government policy. The party in government helps to organize the government's agenda by coaxing and convincing its own party members to vote for its policies. If the party is to translate its promises into public policies, the job must be done by the party in government.

"Under democracy one party always devotes its chief energies to trying to prove that the other party is **UNFIT TO RULE**—and both commonly succeed."

~ H. L. MENCKEN ~
AMERICAN JOURNALIST
1880–1956

The Party in the Electorate

Let's look more closely at the largest component of each party—the party in the electorate. What does it mean to belong to a political party? In many European countries, being a party member means that you actually join a political party. You get a membership card to carry in your wallet, you pay dues, and you vote to select your local and national party leaders. In the United States, becoming a member of a political party is far less involved. To be a member of a political party, an American citizen has only to think of herself or himself as a Democrat or a Republican (or a member of a third party, such as the Green Party, the Libertarian Party, or the American Independent Party). Members of parties do not have to work for the party or attend party meetings. Nor must they support the party platform.[3]

IDENTIFIERS AND ACTIVISTS Generally, the party in the electorate consists of **party identifiers** (those who identify themselves as being members of a particular party) and **party activists**—party members who choose to work for the party and even become candidates for office. Political parties need year-round support from the latter group to survive. During election campaigns in particular, candidates depend on active party members or volunteers to mail literature, answer phones, conduct door-to-door canvasses, organize speeches and appearances, and, of course, donate money. Between elections, parties also need active members to plan the upcoming elections, organize fund-raisers, and stay in touch with party leaders in other communities to keep the party strong. The major functions of American political parties are carried out by the party activists.

WHY PEOPLE JOIN POLITICAL PARTIES Generally, in the United States people belong to a political party because they agree with many of its main ideas and support some of its candidates. In a few countries, such as the People's Republic of China, people belong to a political party because they are required to do so to get ahead in life, regardless of whether they agree with the party's ideas and candidates.

People join political parties for a multitude of reasons. One reason is that people wish to express their **solidarity,** or mutual agreement, with the views of friends, loved ones, and other like-minded people. People also join parties because they enjoy the excitement of politics. In addition, many believe they will benefit materially from joining a party through better employment or personal career advancement. The traditional institution of **patronage**—rewarding the party faithful with government jobs or contracts—lives on, even though it has been limited to prevent abuses.[4] Finally, some join political parties because they wish to actively promote a set of ideals and principles that they feel are important to American politics and society.

As a rule, people join political parties because of their overall agreement with what a particular party stands for. Thus, when

party identifier A person who identifies himself or herself as being a member of a particular political party.

party activist A party member who helps to organize and oversee party functions and planning during and between campaigns.

solidarity Mutual sympathy among the members of a particular group.

patronage A system of rewarding the party faithful and workers with government jobs or contracts.

Most colleges and universities have mascots that represent their athletic teams. So, too, do the two major political parties. On the left, you see the donkey that became the Democratic Party mascot. On the right, you see the elephant that became the Republican Party mascot. Whatever might have been the meaning behind these cartoon figures when they were created, the two mascots for the major parties in the United States have no particular meaning today. Americans simply know that a donkey is the symbol of the Democratic Party and an elephant is the symbol of the Republican Party.

interviewed, people may make the following remarks when asked why they support the Democratic Party: "It seems that the economy is better when the Democrats are in control." "The Democrats are for the working people." People might say about the Republican Party: "The Republicans help small businesses more than the Democrats." "The Republicans deal better with foreign policy and defense issues."

The Party Organization

In theory, each of the major American political parties has a standard, pyramid-shaped organization. This theoretical structure is much like that of a large company, in which the bosses are at the top and the employees are at various lower levels.

Actually, neither major party is a closely knit or highly organized structure. Both parties are fragmented and *decentralized,* which means there is no central power with a direct chain of command. If there were, the national chairperson of the party, along with the national committee, could simply dictate how the organization would be run, just as if it were Microsoft or General Electric. In reality, state party organizations are all very different and are only loosely tied to the party's national structure. Local party organizations are often quite independent from the state organization. There is no single individual or group who directs all party members. Instead, a number of personalities, frequently at odds with one another, form loosely identifiable leadership groups.

STATE ORGANIZATIONS The powers and duties of state party organizations differ from state to state. In general, the state party organization is built around a central committee and a chairperson. The committee works to raise funds, recruit new party members, maintain a strong party organization, and help members running for state offices.

The state chairperson is usually a powerful party member chosen by the committee. In some instances, however, the chairperson is selected by the governor or a senator from that state.

LOCAL ORGANIZATIONS Local party organizations differ greatly, but generally there is a party unit for each district in which elective offices are to be filled. These districts include congressional and legislative districts, counties, cities and towns, wards, and precincts.

AP Photo/Paul Sancya

Democratic presidential candidate Barack Obama shares the stage with his vice-presidential choice, Joe Biden, who had just presented his acceptance speech to thousands of cheering delegates in Denver. How important was Obama's choice of his vice-presidential running mate?

Ethan Miller/Getty Images

Alaska's then governor, Sarah Palin, gave her vice-presidential nomination speech at the 2008 Republican National Convention in St. Paul, Minn. She ran with U.S. Senator John McCain from Arizona. Millions saw her for the first time on TV.

A **ward** is a political division or district within a city. A **precinct** can be either a political district within a city, such as a block or a neighborhood, or a rural portion of a county. Polling places are located within the precincts. The local, grassroots foundations of politics are formed within voting precincts.

THE NATIONAL PARTY ORGANIZATION On the national level, the party's presidential candidate is considered to be the leader of the party. Well-known members of Congress may also be viewed as national party leaders. In addition to the party leaders, the structure of each party includes four major elements: the national convention, the national committees, the national chairperson, and the congressional campaign committee.

THE NATIONAL CONVENTION Much of the public attention that the party receives comes at the **national convention,** which is held every four years during the summer before the presidential elections. The news media always cover these conventions, and as a result, they have become quite extravagant. They are often described as the party's national voice and are usually held in major cities. Are these extravaganzas worth the cost? We look at that question in this chapter's *Join the Debate* feature on page 164.

The national conventions are attended by delegates chosen by the states in various ways, which we describe in Chapter 9. The delegates' most important job is to choose the party's presidential and vice-presidential candidates, who together make up the **party ticket.** The delegates also write the **party platform,** which sets forth the party's positions on national issues. Essentially, through its platform, the party promises to initiate certain policies if it wins the presidency. Despite the widespread perception that candidates can and do ignore these promises once they are in office, in fact, many of them become law.

ward A local unit of a political party's organization, consisting of a division or district within a city.

precinct A political district within a city, such as a block or a neighborhood, or a rural portion of a county; the smallest voting district at the local level.

national convention The meeting held by each major party every four years to select presidential and vice-presidential candidates, write a party platform, and conduct other party business.

party ticket A list of a political party's candidates for various offices. In national elections, the party ticket consists of the presidential and vice-presidential candidates.

party platform The document drawn up by each party at its national convention that outlines the policies and positions of the party.

JOIN THE DEBATE

Are National Party Conventions Worth the Cost?

For many decades, national party conventions were important to the nomination of each party's presidential candidate. In modern times, however, each party has already chosen its candidates for president and vice president before the conventions begin. Nonetheless, state delegates continue to attend the four-day extravaganzas that each party holds every four years, and so do the media, political commentators, and quite a few entertainers. The traditional media broadcast live from the conventions a few hours a day—covering speeches by major political figures and the candidates—and all of the convention can be seen on the Internet.

What cannot be seen, except in person and by invitation only, are the hundreds of parties held at the conventions. At the 2008 Democratic Party convention in Denver, members of Congress were able to hear singer Kanye West, courtesy of the recording industry. Others were given $5,000 to play poker at a tournament that featured actor Ben Affleck. At the 2008 Republican Party convention, some lucky delegates were invited to the Aqua Nightclub in Minneapolis to hear the band Smash Mouth. Both conventions cost over $100 million. The debate still rages: Are national party conventions worth the cost?

It's Not Just Flash and Partying

Sure, the fireworks, hoopla, bands, parties, and other activities seem to be beside the point. But in addition to formalizing the nominations for president and vice president at the national party conventions, delegates conduct important party business, such as approving the party platform. The conventions serve to inspire and mobilize party members throughout the nation. They provide the voters with an opportunity to see and hear the candidates directly, rather than through the filter of the media or through characterizations provided by supporters and opponents. Candidate speeches draw huge audiences. For example, in 2008, more than 38 million people watched the acceptance speeches of Barack Obama and John McCain. Conventions can sway undecided voters to support one or the other of the presidential candidates.

Don't forget the unifying nature of most national party conventions. At the 2008 Democratic convention in Denver, supporters of Hillary Clinton were not necessarily convinced that they should support Barack Obama. By the end of that convention, many of these voters had decided that they could indeed endorse him. At the 2008 Republican convention in St. Paul, a humorous and aggressive acceptance speech by vice-presidential candidate Sarah Palin not only electrified the attending delegates but also served as a way to unify the party behind the ticket. In short, conventions are well worth their costs.

No More Wretched Excess

Who needs multimillion-dollar national conventions to ratify the nominations of presidential and vice-presidential candidates who have already been chosen? What party business is there that cannot be done with less time and expense? The party platforms can be hashed out in meetings, perhaps with the use of teleconferencing systems, without the costs of a convention. In 2008, during a period of economic struggle for many Americans, the spending of millions of dollars on superfluous activities in Denver and St. Paul certainly did not send the right signals.

And where did all that money come from? You guessed it—lobbyists, big business, and labor unions. In spite of new congressional ethics rules designed to curb the influence of these groups, they spent more in 2008 than ever before. Qwest Communications gave $6 million to each party for the conventions. Union Pacific gave $1 million to the Democrats, as did Xcel Energy. UnitedHealth Group gave $1.5 million to the Republicans. U.S. Bancorp gave another million, as did St. Jude Medical. Three big unions each gave $500,000 to the Democrats. Those millions are not spent to further the general welfare—they come from companies and associations that depend on government subsidies, tax breaks, or regulatory favors from Washington, D.C.

For Critical Analysis ***The parties often pick the states that host their national conventions in the hope of enhancing their performance in those states. In 2008, the Democrats sought to improve their prospects in Colorado, and the Republicans hoped to do better in Minnesota. Do you think that holding a party's convention in a particular state will win votes? Why or why not?***

THE NATIONAL COMMITTEE. Each state elects a number of delegates to the **national party committee**. The Republican National Committee and the Democratic National Committee direct the business of their respective parties during the four years between national conventions. The committees' most important duties, however, are to organize the next national convention and to plan how to obtain a party victory in the next presidential elections.

THE NATIONAL CHAIRPERSON. Each party's national committee elects a **national party chairperson** to serve as administrative head of the national party. The main duty of the national chairperson is to direct the work of the national committee from party headquarters in Washington, D.C. The chairperson is involved in raising funds, providing for publicity, promoting party unity, encouraging the development of state and local organizations, recruiting new voters, and other activities. In presidential election years, the chairperson's attention is focused on the national convention and the presidential campaign.

THE CONGRESSIONAL CAMPAIGN COMMITTEES. Each party has a campaign committee, made up of senators and representatives, in each chamber of Congress. Members are chosen by their colleagues and serve for two-year terms. The committees work to help reelect party members to Congress.

Tim Kaine (left) is currently the chair of the Democratic National Committee and also the governor of Virginia until January 2010. Michael Steele is the chair of the Republican National Committee. What do these men do?

William B. Plowman/NBC NewsWire via AP Images

The Party in Government: Developing Issues

When a political party wins the presidency or control of one or more chambers of Congress, it has the opportunity to carry out the party platform it developed at its national convention. The platform represents the official party position on various issues, although as just mentioned, neither all party members nor all candidates running on the party's ticket are likely to share these positions exactly.

HOW PRESIDENTS RESPOND TO PARTY PLATFORMS Party platforms do not necessarily tell you what candidates are going to do when they take office. For example, although the Democratic Party generally favors social legislation to help low-income individuals, it was a Democratic president, Bill Clinton, who signed a major welfare reform bill in 1996, forcing many welfare recipients off the welfare rolls. The Democrats usually have the support of labor unions, yet President Clinton approved the North American Free Trade Agreement, despite bitter opposition from most of the nation's unions. Additionally, the Democrats have traditionally been associated with "big government" and deficit spending, but under President Bill Clinton there was a budget surplus for several years in a row.

Similarly, although the Republican Party has long advocated "small government" and states' rights, federal government spending was taken to new heights during the Bush administration, budget surpluses disappeared, and legislation such as the No Child Left Behind Act effectively transferred power from the states to the federal government. How did the two major parties respond to the issues raised by the Great Recession? We examine that question in this chapter's *Our Government's Response to the Economic Crisis* feature on the following page.

national party committee The political party leaders who direct party business during the four years between the national party conventions, organize the next national convention, and plan how to obtain a party victory in the next presidential elections.

national party chairperson An individual who serves as a political party's administrative head at the national level and directs the work of the party's national committee.

Our Government's Response to the Economic Crisis

Partisan Politics More Than Ever

It used to be that Republicans could count on conservative Democrats to agree with them. Today, for the first time ever, the most conservative Democrats are now demonstrably to the left of the most moderate Republicans. Not surprisingly, when Congress debates how to pull America out of its greatest economic crisis since the Great Depression, bipartisanship is scarce. When President Obama's February 2009 stimulus bill was brought to a vote in the House, not one Republican voted "yea."

Taxes, Taxes, Taxes

As a candidate, Barack Obama promised that he would give 95 percent of Americans a tax break. The stimulus package did contain a variety of modest tax cuts for many taxpayers. Since then, however, the talk among Democrats in Congress has been of nothing but tax increases. The Democrats have attempted to load most of their proposed increases on upper-income individuals. Marginal tax rates on the highest-earning Americans are slated to rise from 35 percent to 39.6 percent. Additional taxes on the highest-earning Americans will undoubtedly be needed to pay for the Democratic program of universal health care. Beyond that, to help fund health care, senate Democrats have considered taxing medical benefits paid by employers. Such a tax would violate Obama's pledge to spare middle-income taxpayers. Several states also increased the marginal tax rates on high-earning residents.

In contrast, Republicans in Congress have kept up their long-time drumbeat in favor of lower taxes. For example, their alternative to the stimulus package would have consisted entirely of tax cuts. Called the Economic Recovery and Middle-class Tax Relief Act of 2009, the Republican plan would have:

1. Reduced individual income tax rates by 5 percent retroactive to 2008.
2. Capped the 15 percent capital gains tax rate permanently.
3. Prevented individual income tax rates from automatically rising in 2011.
4. Reduced the top corporate income tax rate from 35 percent to 25 percent.

Of course, tax cuts, like spending programs, may increase the federal budget deficit. For that reason, many rank-and-file conservatives are not as keen on tax cuts as the Republicans in Congress.

Spending, Spending, Spending

Democrats have been united in their belief in the necessity of a stimulus program. Before his inauguration, Obama observed: "There is no disagreement that we need action by our government, a recovery plan that will help to jumpstart our economy." In fact, though, the Republicans do not necessarily agree. After Obama made these remarks, the libertarian-leaning Cato Institute obtained the signatures of three hundred sympathetic economists on an advertisement that said: "notwithstanding reports that all economists are now Keynesians and that we all support a big increase in the burden of government, we do not believe that more government spending is a way to improve economic performance." (We described Keynesian economics in the *Our Government's Response to the Economic Crisis* feature in Chapter 3.)

The Cato advertisement was a big hit among many congressional Republicans. When a few Democrats raised the idea of a second stimulus bill in the summer of 2009, Republicans claimed that the first bill had not helped the economy. In fact, unemployment had risen to over 9.8 percent since Obama signed the $787 billion stimulus package.

Freshwater versus Saltwater Economics

Keynesianism has been called "saltwater economics" because it is popular at many universities on the East and West coasts. Some Republicans say that the approach is old fashioned. These Republicans now look to "freshwater economics" to understand our problems. Freshwater economists, many of whom work on the shores of the Great Lakes, look more at changes in incentives that face families and businesses than at government spending or tax cuts. According to freshwater economists, all deficits have to be paid for by the private sector (unless the funding is coming from Mars). Ultimately, workers, savers, investors, and business owners must pay for any stimulus package. Freshwater advocates argue that individuals will react to federal budget deficits by spending less and saving more in preparation for higher taxes in the future. Indeed, saving in the United States is at record levels.

For Critical Analysis ***If households save more, isn't that a good thing? Why would an increased saving rate slow down progress in solving the current economic crisis?***

THE PARTY PLATFORMS IN 2008 The two presidential candidates in 2008, Democrat Barack Obama and Republican John McCain, had contrasting relationships with the platforms of their parties. Obama had no problem standing on the Democratic Platform, key planks of which are given in Table 7–1 on the next page. Indeed, Obama was responsible for many of the planks, and the platform praised him repeatedly. It is reasonable to expect that, in office, President Obama will try to implement the proposals in the platform.

The Republican Platform mentioned McCain exactly once, on page one. The activists who wrote this document inserted dozens of planks that they knew McCain could not support. Consider the items listed in Table 7–1. The planks on Iran, earmarks, and free trade were clear endorsements of McCain's stands on these issues. The immigration plank, however, did not represent his views at all. McCain additionally wanted to do far more to fight global warming than the platform advocated—he proposed a "cap-and-trade" plan similar to the one included in the Democratic Platform. Although McCain supported the "right-to-life" cause, he did not favor a constitutional amendment on the issue, or on gay marriage. Finally, McCain did not favor banning all embryonic stem-cell research. Anyone who wondered what McCain would have done, had he been elected, would find the answer on the senator's own Web site, not in the Republican Platform.

"I AM NOT A MEMBER OF ANY ORGANIZED POLITICAL PARTY. I am a democrat."

~ WILL ROGERS ~
AMERICAN HUMORIST
1879–1935

Texas delegates at the 2008 Republican Party national convention bow their heads during the invocation on the last day. **Do these delegates have any real power to elect their party's presidential candidate when attending this convention?**

Sara Krulwich/*The New York Times*/Redux

LO5 *The Dominance of Our Two-Party System*

In the United States, we have a **two-party system.** (For an example of a multiparty system, see this chapter's *The Rest of the World* feature on page 169.) This means that the two major parties—the Democrats and the Republicans—dominate national politics. Why has the two-party system become so firmly entrenched in the United States? According to some scholars, the first major political division between the Federalists and the Anti-Federalists established a precedent that continued over time and ultimately resulted in the domination of the two-party system.

As noted earlier, about a third of the voters identify themselves as independents (although they may lean toward one party or the other). For these individuals, both of the major parties evidently fail to address issues that are important to them or represent their views. Nonetheless, the two-party system continues to thrive. A number of factors help to explain this phenomenon.

The Self-Perpetuation of the Two-Party System

One of the major reasons for the perpetuation of the two-party system is simply that there is no alternative. Minor parties, called **third parties,**[5] have found it extremely difficult to compete with the major parties for votes. There are many reasons for this, including election laws and institutional barriers.

ELECTION LAWS FAVORING TWO PARTIES American election laws tend to favor the major parties. In many states, for example, the established major parties need relatively few signatures to place their candidates on the ballot, whereas a third party must get many more signatures. The

two-party system A political system in which two strong and established parties compete for political offices.

third party In the United States, any party other than one of the two major parties (Republican and Democratic).

Table 7–1

The 2008 Platforms of the Democratic and Republican Parties

Democratic Platform (selected planks)	Republican Platform (selected planks)
• Provide $50 billion in economic stimulus, largely for infrastructure.	• Keep Congress from "micromanaging" the president on foreign policy and military issues.
• Extend health-care insurance to all Americans; ban "preexisting condition" exclusions.	• Have no discussions with Iran until it ends uranium enrichment and support of terrorism.
• End most Bush tax cuts for those earning more than $250,000 per year.	• Provide no amnesty for illegal immigrants; strengthen border security.
• Eliminate the income tax for seniors who earn less than $50,000 per year.	• "Recognize and promote" the English language.
• Expand tax rebates for the working poor; raise the minimum wage and index it to inflation.	• End earmarks, or "pork"—provisions in which lawmakers specify funding for specific projects.
• Provide $4,000 toward college tuition for any student who performs community service.	• Oppose activist judges; appoint judges who respect the Constitution.
• Invest major funds in renewable energy and energy conservation.	• Extend all Bush tax cuts; reduce corporate tax rates.
• Set a goal of reducing U.S. oil consumption by 35 percent by 2030.	• Create tax-free Lost Earnings Buffer Accounts and Farm Savings Accounts.
• Institute a "cap-and-trade" plan (in effect, a tax on corporate carbon dioxide emissions) to combat global warming.	• Support free trade.
• Rebuild relationships with America's allies.	• Stop government bailouts of private financial institutions.
• End the war in Iraq; send two more combat brigades to Afghanistan.	• Address increased carbon dioxide emissions in ways that do not hurt the economy.
• Improve veterans' benefits; let gay men and lesbians serve in the military.	• Encourage offshore oil drilling and new nuclear power plants; provide tax breaks for alternative energy sources.
• Let unions organize by collecting signed cards instead of winning secret-ballot elections.	• Pass a constitutional amendment to ban all abortions, without exception.
• Reform immigration; allow undocumented immigrants in good standing to join society.	• Pass a constitutional amendment to ban gay marriage.
• Restore civil liberties curtailed by the Bush administration.	• Ban all embryonic stem-cell research, public or private.

number of signatures required is often based on the total party vote in the last election, which penalizes a new party competing for the first time.

The rules governing campaign financing also favor the major parties. As you will read in Chapter 9, both major parties receive federal funds for presidential campaigns and for their national conventions. Third parties, in contrast, receive federal funds only if they garner 5 percent of the vote, and they receive the funds only *after* the election.

"Let us not seek the Republican answer or the Democratic answer, but the **RIGHT ANSWER.**"

~ JOHN FITZGERALD KENNEDY ~
THIRTY-FIFTH PRESIDENT OF THE UNITED STATES
1961–1963

INSTITUTIONAL BARRIERS TO A MULTIPARTY SYSTEM

The structure of many of our institutions prevents third parties from enjoying electoral success. One of the major institutional barriers is the winner-take-all feature of the electoral college system for electing the president (discussed in more detail in Chapter 9). In a winner-take-all system, which applies in all but two of the states (Maine and Nebraska), the winner of a state's popular vote gets all of that state's electoral votes. Thus, third-party candidates have little incentive to run for president, because they are unlikely to get enough popular votes to receive any state's electoral votes.

Another institutional barrier to a multiparty system is the single-member district. Today, all federal and most state legislative districts are single-member districts—that is, voters elect one member from their district to

THE REST OF THE WORLD

Re-Branding Political Parties in the United Kingdom

In the United Kingdom, the House of Commons, which is part of the British Parliament, exercises the nation's legislative power. (There is a House of Lords, but it has been politically insignificant since 1911.) Just as in the United States, legislators are elected in single-member districts. This system makes it difficult for third parties to organize, but over the last century, Britain has always had important third parties.

In the nineteenth century, the two major parties were the Conservatives and the Liberals. In the early twentieth century, however, the Liberals lost their position as a major party to the Labour Party. The Liberals never vanished entirely and are considered Britain's third party today. Other minor parties contest seats only in particular regions. These include the Scottish National Party, Plaid Cymru from Wales, and a variety of parties in Northern Ireland.

The Labour Party is the main left-of-center party in Britain. It was originally organized to defend labor unions, but it soon grew into a broader left-wing movement. The Liberal Party is also left of center. On the right is the Conservative Party, often called the Tories.

Labour Moves to the Middle

From the time of its founding in 1900, the Labour Party was an explicitly socialist organization. For Labour, socialism meant state ownership of major corporations, a generous welfare system, and extremely high taxes on the rich. From 1945 until 1979, Labour and the Conservatives regularly traded places as Her Majesty's Government and Her Majesty's Loyal Opposition.

In 1979, however, Margaret Thatcher became prime minister at the head of a radically renovated Conservative Party. The Conservatives were no longer an upper-class body with wishy-washy politics. Thatcher, the daughter of a grocer, stood squarely for free markets, free enterprise, and relatively unrestrained capitalism. Thatcherism, as it is now called, meant the privatization of state-owned industries and less state intervention in the economy. Thatcher broke the power of the Mineworkers Union and tried to curb the size of the welfare state. Labour spent the Thatcher years in the wilderness and at times seemed in danger of losing its major-party status to the Liberals.

In 1994, Tony Blair took the leadership of the Labour Party under the slogan "New Labour, New Life for Britain." Blair and his followers explicitly rejected the principle of state ownership of corporations. Blair's New Labour moved the party toward the political center. Blair was not antibusiness and was not particularly enamored of labor unions. He offered a supposed "middle way" between Thatcherism and socialism. Labour won the 1997 election in a landslide. In 2007, Blair resigned as prime minister in favor of his chief deputy, Gordon Brown.

The Conservative Party Remakes Itself

After Blair's victory, the Conservatives seemed to be in serious trouble, just as Labour had been earlier. Many British voters saw the Conservatives as too hard-edged. In time, though, a new leader sought to change that image. Upon taking over the Conservatives in 2005, David Cameron let it be known that he wanted the party to alter the way it looked, felt, thought, and behaved. His goal has been to move the Conservative Party closer to the center and to make the Conservative brand attractive to young, socially liberal voters. Not surprisingly, Conservative Party policy has increasingly focused on social and quality-of-life issues, such as health care, schools, and the environment. Cameron has called for fixing the "broken" British society. Cameron's reforms have been held up as a model by some U.S. Republicans who would like to change their party—see this chapter's *America at Odds* feature on page 152. The Conservatives now seem likely to win the next British general election, which must be held on or before June 3, 2010.

For Critical Analysis *Some say that it is a mistake for any party to move to the center. How might they explain this argument?*

the House of Representatives and to their state legislature.[6] In most European countries, by contrast, districts are drawn as multimember districts and are represented by multiple elected officials from different parties, according to the proportion of the vote their party received.

Third Parties in American Politics

Despite difficulties, throughout American history, third parties have competed for influence in the nation's two-party system. Indeed, as mentioned earlier, third parties have been represented in most of our national elections. These parties are as varied as the causes they represent, but all have one thing in common: their members and leaders want to challenge the major parties because they believe that certain needs and values are not being properly addressed.

Some third parties have tried to appeal to the entire nation; others have focused on particular regions, states, or local areas. Most third parties have been short lived. A few, however, such as the Socialist Party (founded in

1901 and disbanded in 1972), lasted for a long time. The number and variety of third parties make them difficult to classify, but most fall into one of the general categories discussed in the following subsections.

ISSUE-ORIENTED PARTIES An issue-oriented third party is formed to promote a particular cause or timely issue. For example, the Free Soil Party was organized in 1848 to oppose the expansion of slavery into the western territories. The Prohibition Party was formed in 1869 to advocate banning the use and manufacture of alcoholic beverages.

Most issue-oriented parties fade into history as the issue that brought them into existence fades from public attention, is taken up by a major party, or is resolved. Some issue-oriented parties endure, however, when they expand their focus beyond a single area of concern. For example, the Green Party was founded in 1972 to raise awareness of environmental issues, but it is no longer a single-issue party. Ralph Nader, the presidential candidate for the Green Party in 2000, campaigned against alleged corporate greed and the major parties' ostensible indifference to a number of issues, including universal health insurance, child poverty, the excesses of globalism, and the failure of the drug war.

IDEOLOGICAL PARTIES As discussed in Chapter 1, a *political ideology* is a system of political ideas rooted in beliefs about human nature, society, and government. An ideological party supports a particular political doctrine or a set of beliefs. For example, a party such as the (still-existing) Socialist Workers Party may believe that our free enterprise system should be replaced by one in which government or workers own all of the factories in the economy. The party's members may believe that competition should be replaced by cooperation and social responsibility so as to achieve an equitable distribution of income. In contrast, an ideological party such as the Libertarian Party may oppose virtually all forms of government interference with personal liberties and private enterprise.

SPLINTER OR PERSONALITY PARTIES A splinter party develops out of a split within a major party. This split may be part of an attempt to elect a specific person. For example, when Theodore Roosevelt did not receive the Republican Party's nomination for president in 1912, he created the Bull Moose Party (also called the Progressive Party) to promote his candidacy. From the Democrats have come Henry Wallace's Progressive Party and the States' Rights (Dixiecrat) Party, both formed in 1948. In 1968, the American Independent Party was formed to support George Wallace's campaign for president.

Most splinter parties have been formed around a leader with a strong personality, which is why they are sometimes called personality parties. When that person steps aside, the party usually collapses. An example of a personality party is the Reform Party, which was formed in 1996 mainly to provide a campaign vehicle for H. Ross Perot.

The Effects of Third Parties

Although most Americans do not support third parties or vote for their candidates, third parties have influenced American politics in several ways, some of which we examine here.

THIRD PARTIES BRING ISSUES TO THE PUBLIC'S ATTENTION Third parties have brought many political issues to the public's attention. They have exposed and focused on unpopular or highly debated issues that major parties have preferred to ignore. Third parties are in a position to take bold stands on issues that major parties avoid, because third parties are not trying to be all things to all people. Progressive social reforms such as the minimum wage, women's right to vote, railroad and banking legislation, and old-age pensions were first proposed by third parties. The Free Soilers of the 1850s, for example, were the first true antislavery party, and the Populists and Progressives put many social reforms on the political agenda.

Theodore Roosevelt and his Progressive (Bull Moose) Party changed the outcome of the 1912 election.

Bettmann/Corbis

Figure 7–2

The Effect of Third Parties on Vote Distribution, 1848–1992

In eight presidential elections, a third party's candidate received more than 10 percent of the popular vote—and in six of those elections, the incumbent party lost. As shown here, only in 1856 and 1924 did the incumbent party manage to hold on to the White House in the face of a significant third-party showing.

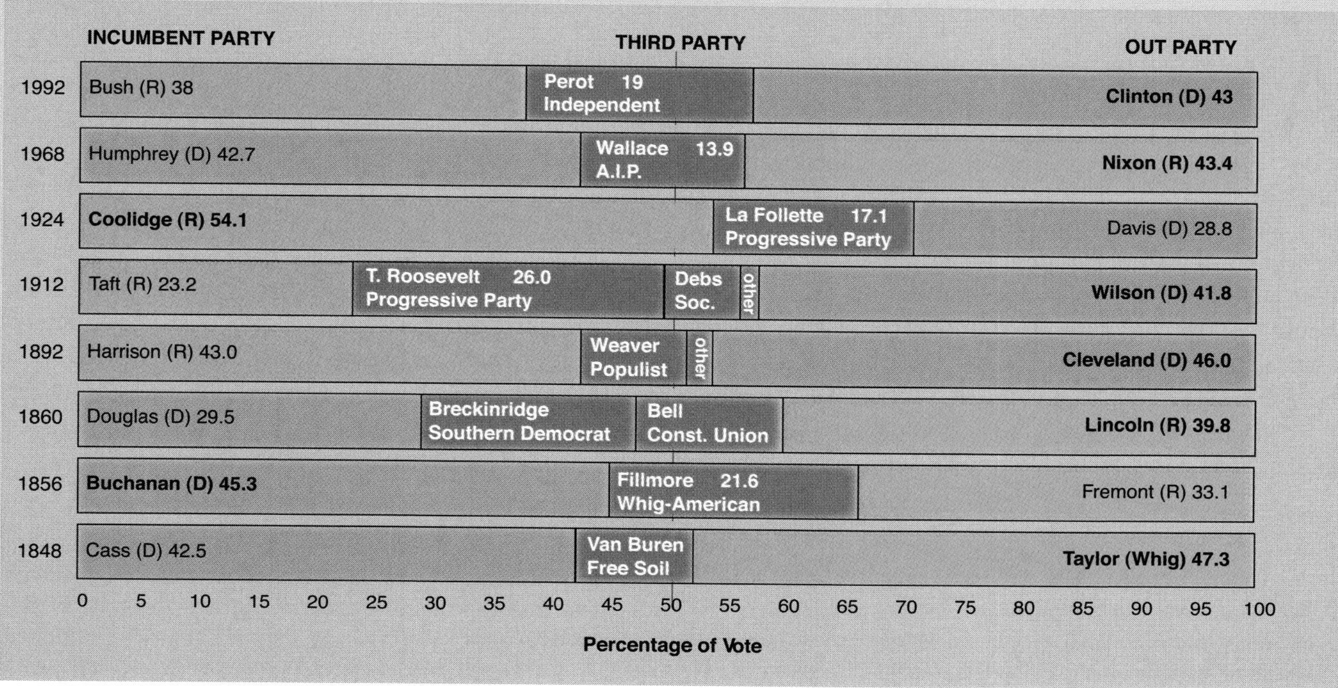

Source: *Congressional Quarterly Weekly Report*, June 13, 1992, p. 1729.

Some people have argued that third parties are often the unsung heroes of American politics, bringing new issues to the forefront of public debate. Some of the ideas proposed by third parties were never accepted, while others were taken up by the major parties as those ideas became increasingly popular.

THIRD PARTIES CAN AFFECT THE VOTE Third parties can influence not only voter turnout but also election outcomes. Third parties have occasionally taken victory from one major party and given it to another, thus playing the "spoiler" role.

For example, in 1912, when the Progressive Party split off from the Republican Party, the result was three major contenders for the presidency: Woodrow Wilson, the Democratic candidate; William Howard Taft, the regular Republican candidate; and Theodore Roosevelt, the Progressive candidate. The presence of the Progressive Party "spoiled" the Republicans' chances for victory and gave the election to Wilson, the Democrat. Without Roosevelt's third party, Taft might have won. Similarly, some commentators contended that Ralph Nader "spoiled" the chances of Democratic candidate Al Gore in the 2000 elections, because many of those who voted for Nader would have voted Democratic had Nader not been a candidate.

A significant showing by a minor party also reduces an incumbent party's chances of winning the election, as you can see in Figure 7–2 above. In 1992, for example, third-party candidate H. Ross Perot captured about 19 percent of the vote. Had those votes been distributed between the candidates of the major parties, incumbent George H. W. Bush and candidate Bill Clinton, the outcome of the election might have been different.

THIRD PARTIES PROVIDE A VOICE FOR DISSATISFIED AMERICANS Third parties also provide a voice for voters who are frustrated with and alienated from the Republican and Democratic parties. Americans who are unhappy with the two major political parties can still participate in American politics through third parties that reflect their opinions on political issues. For example, many new Minnesota voters turned out during the 1998 elections to vote for Jesse Ventura, a Reform Party candidate for governor in that state. Ventura won.

Finally, third parties find it difficult to break through in an electoral system that perpetuates their own failure. Because third parties normally do not win elections, Americans tend not to vote for them or to contribute to their campaigns, so they continue not to win elections. As long as Americans hold to the perception that third parties can never win big in an election, the current two-party system is likely to persist.

AMERICA AT ODDS *Political Parties*

As noted in this chapter, nowhere in the Constitution are political parties even mentioned. Yet, since the beginning of this nation, they have been at the heart of our political landscape. An early division of political attitudes among Americans was clearly reflected in the debate between the Federalists and the Anti-Federalists over the ratification of the Constitution. Today, Americans continue to be divided in their opinions as to what the government should—or should not—do. Generally, the two major political parties—the Republicans and the Democrats—represent, at least in part, this division of political attitudes.

How does our two-party system measure up? Has it been good or bad for this country? Some say simply that the two-party system has provided—and continues to provide—effective and stable leadership. After all, "the proof is in the pudding"—the "pudding" being the nation's ability to endure for more than two hundred years. Others are very dissatisfied with the parties today. Much of this dissatisfaction has to do with the serious problems that have no easy solutions, including the economic crisis and the health-care challenge. Finding solutions to these problems will be difficult for whichever party gains control of the government. Until those solutions are found and implemented, it is unlikely that either political party will receive high marks from the American electorate.

ISSUES FOR DEBATE & DISCUSSION

1. **At the national level, divided government exists when the president is from one political party and Congress is controlled by the other party. Some believe that divided government is better for the country, because Congress can better exercise "checks" on the presidential administration. These people assert that such checks are necessary to prevent Congress from endorsing the president's agenda, regardless of its merits, out of party loyalty. Others claim that unified government (which exists when one party controls both the presidency and Congress) is better because it allows the government to implement its policies more quickly and effectively. What is your position on this issue?**
2. **An ongoing controversy among Americans has to do with whether third-party presidential candidates should be allowed to participate in televised debates. Under the rules of the Commission for Presidential Debates (CPD) that were applied to the 2004 presidential elections, only candidates who had a level of support of at least 15 percent of the national electorate could participate. Critics of this rule point out that free elections mean little if minor-party candidates do not have realistic access to public forums, such as televised debates. Supporters of the CPD's position argue that opening up the presidential debates to third-party candidates, even to those with virtually no electoral support, would lead to chaos and that some standards for deciding who can and cannot participate in the debates are necessary. What is your position?**

TAKE ACTION

Getting involved in political parties is as simple as going to the polls and casting your vote for the candidate of one of the major parties—or of a third party. If you want to go a step further, you can attend a speech given by a political candidate or even volunteer to assist a political party or a specific candidate's campaign activities.

AP Photo/Charles Krupa

The government provides election materials in a variety of languages other than English.

POLITICS ON THE WEB

- For a list of political Web sites available on the Internet, sorted by country and with links to parties, organizations, and governments throughout the world, go to **www.politicalresources.net**
- Ron Gunzburger's Politics1 Web site contains a vast amount of information on American politics. Click on "Political Parties" in the directory box at the top of the home page to see one of the most complete descriptions of major and minor parties to be found anywhere. Gunzburger's site is at **www.politics1.com**
- The Democratic Party is online at **www.democrats.org**
- The Republican National Committee is online at **www.gop.org**
- The Libertarian Party has a Web site at **www.lp.org**
- The Green Party's Web site can be accessed by going to **www.greenparty.org**

Online resources for this chapter

This text's Companion Web site, at **www.4ltrpress.cengage.com/govt**, offers links to numerous resources that you can use to learn more about the topics covered in this chapter.

Stockbyte/Getty Images

GOVT

8 Public Opinion and Voting

LEARNING OBJECTIVES

LO1 Explain what public opinion is and how it is measured.

LO2 Describe the political socialization process.

LO3 Summarize the history of polling in the United States, and explain how polls are conducted and how they are used in the political process.

LO4 Indicate some of the factors that affect voter turnout, and discuss what has been done to improve voter turnout and voting procedures.

LO5 Discuss the different factors that affect voter choices.

AMERICA AT ODDS

Is the 1965 Voting Rights Act Obsolete?

In theory, African Americans have had the right to vote since the Reconstruction period following the Civil War. In practice, though, Southern whites found ways to prevent them from exercising that right. As one example, in many southern states, African Americans faced "literacy" tests that were impossible to pass.

In 1965, as a response to the Civil Rights movement, Congress passed the Voting Rights Act. The most controversial part of the Voting Rights Act is Section 5. It requires districts with a history of voter discrimination to win approval from the federal Justice Department before they change any electoral rule, even by moving a polling station. Section 5 was designed to prevent local jurisdictions from changing the rules to the disadvantage of black voters. Section 5 was set to expire in 1970 but has been extended, most recently in 2007 for twenty-five years. Since 1982, only 17 of the more than 12,000 political subdivisions subject to Section 5 have been allowed to "bail out" and escape from coverage by the act.

Many believe that the 1965 Voting Rights Act is obsolete in a nation that has elected an African American president.

Almost Fifty Years Later, We Do Not Need the Voting Rights Act

The Fifteenth Amendment guarantees the right to vote and grants Congress the power to enforce that right with appropriate legislation. Certainly, tight federal control of local electoral rules was justified in 1965, but not today. In those days, state and local governments were ingenious in devising tactics to suppress voting by African Americans, but that no longer happens.

Moreover, the electoral data used to justify the latest extension of the Voting Rights Act dates from 1972. At that time, gasoline cost thirty-five cents a gallon, and the winner of the Academy Award for Best Picture was *The Godfather*. Much has changed since then. Today, African Americans register and vote at rates comparable to those of whites.

The Voting Rights Act—in particular Section 5—has served its purpose. Punishment for ancient sins is not a legitimate basis for keeping it. Whites no longer vote in lockstep against black candidates. Among white voters, Barack Obama outperformed both Al Gore and John Kerry (the previous two Democratic candidates) in Georgia, North and South Carolina, Texas, and Virginia. In the South, as in the rest of the nation, African American politicians have been able to win office in districts with white majorities. Racially polarized voting habits are clearly on the wane.

Much Must Still Be Done

Those who support the continuation of the Voting Rights Act argue that much must still be done to ensure that citizens of all races have truly equal opportunities to participate in our democratic process. Without a federal leash, there are still forces that would deny the vote to as many African Americans as they could. According to Benjamin Jealous, the leader of the National Association for the Advancement of Colored People (NAACP), "Jim Crow might be dead but James Crow Esquire is alive and well, and while we may not see fire hoses and police dogs any longer, they have been replaced by false e-mails and polling station trickery."

It's true that in 2008 some states covered by Section 5 of the Voting Rights Act saw African Americans register and vote at rates that matched or even exceeded the rates of whites. But that does not mean that we should abolish Section 5—or the rest of the Voting Rights Act. Section 2 of the Voting Rights Act, for example, bars practices that "deny or abridge the right of any citizen of the United States to vote on account of race or color." Why would we want to eliminate a law that protects such basic rights? Any decrease in the effectiveness of the Voting Rights Act will likely have negative effects beginning in 2011. In that year, state legislatures across the country will draw new election district boundaries based on the 2010 census. Let's make sure that southern politicians aren't tempted to use the redistricting process to reduce the effectiveness of the African American vote.

WHERE DO YOU STAND?

1. **Does the election of the United States' first African American president mean that African Americans have full and equal voting rights? Why or why not?**
2. **Even if Barack Obama had not been elected, does the increase in the number of elected black officials throughout the country indicate that African Americans are no longer prevented from freely expressing their will at polling places? Justify your answer.**

EXPLORE THIS ISSUE ONLINE

- **In 2009, the United States Supreme Court weighed in on the question of whether Section 5 of the Voting Rights Act was still necessary. The Court upheld the act, but limited its effect slightly. You can visit the *National Law Journal* at www.law.com/jsp/nlj/index.jsp. To read its coverage of the Voting Rights Act, just type "voting rights act" (quotes included) into the site's search box. You can find the full text of Supreme Court opinions at the Court's own Web site: www.supremecourtus.gov.**

Introduction

> "A government can be no better than the **PUBLIC OPINION** that sustains it."
>
> ~ FRANKLIN DELANO ROOSEVELT ~ THIRTY-SECOND PRESIDENT OF THE UNITED STATES 1933–1945

For a democracy to be effective, members of the public must form opinions and openly express them to their elected officials. Only when the opinions of Americans are communicated effectively to elected representatives can those opinions form the basis of government action. As President Franklin D. Roosevelt once said, "A government can be no better than the public opinion that sustains it."

What exactly is *public opinion*? How do we form our opinions on political issues? How can public opinion be measured accurately? Finally, what factors affect voter participation?

Researchers and scholars have addressed these questions time and again. They are important questions because the backbone of our democracy has always been civic participation—taking part in the political life of the country. Civic participation means many things, but perhaps the most important way that Americans participate in their democracy is through voting—expressing their opinions in the polling places. Protecting the right to vote is therefore an important issue, as explained in this chapter's opening *America at Odds* feature.

LO1 What Is Public Opinion?

People hold opinions—sometimes very strong ones—about a variety of issues, ranging from the ethics of capital punishment to the latest trends in fashion. In this chapter, however, we are concerned with only a portion of those opinions. For our purposes here, we define **public opinion** as the sum total of a complex collection of opinions held by many people on issues in the public arena, such as taxes, health care, Social Security, clean-air legislation, and unemployment.

When you hear a news report or read a magazine article stating that "a significant number of Americans" feel a certain way about an issue, you are probably hearing that a particular opinion is held by a large enough number of people to make government officials turn their heads and listen. For example, public opinion surveys in 2008 revealed that the poor state of the economy was the number-one issue for Americans. By late fall, despite an economic stimulus package involving income tax rebates and a $700 billion banking bailout, the economy was even worse. Because of the economic crisis, both presidential candidates in the 2008 races were pressured to set forth their views on the issue and propose solutions. Many blamed the government's lack of oversight over the financial industry for the crisis. This made it difficult for Republican candidate Senator John McCain, who had been a proponent of deregulation for years, to compete effectively with his Democratic opponent, Senator Barack Obama.

public opinion The views of the citizenry about politics, public issues, and public policies; a complex collection of opinions held by many people on issues in the public arena.

LO2 How Do People Form Political Opinions?

When asked, most Americans are willing to express an opinion on political issues. Not one of us, however, was born with such opinions. Most

As the number of first-time claims for unemployment benefits rose in late 2009, many Americans had to look for a job. The man in the middle is giving résumé-writing advice at a San Francisco job fair. How does a serious recession change public opinion?

AP Photo/Marcio Jose Sanchez

people acquire their political attitudes, opinions, beliefs, and knowledge through a complex learning process called **political socialization.** This process begins early in childhood and continues throughout life.

Most political socialization is informal, and it usually begins during early childhood, when the dominant influence on a child is the family. Although parents normally do not sit down and say to their children, "Let us explain to you the virtues of becoming a Republican," their children nevertheless come to know the parents' feelings, beliefs, and attitudes. The strong early influence of the family later gives way to the multiple influences of school, peers, television, co-workers, and other groups. People and institutions that influence the political views of others are called **agents of political socialization.**

The Importance of Family

As just suggested, most parents or caregivers do not deliberately set out to form their children's political ideas and beliefs. They are usually more concerned with the moral, religious, and ethical values of their offspring. Yet a child first sees the political world through the eyes of his or her family, which is perhaps the most important force in political socialization. Children do not "learn" political attitudes the same way they learn to master in-line skating. Rather, they learn by hearing their parents' everyday conversations and stories about politicians and issues and by observing their parents' actions. They also learn from watching and listening to their siblings, as well as from the kinds of situations in which their parents place them.

The family's influence is strongest when children clearly perceive their parents' attitudes. Parents commonly do communicate their political attitudes to their children, however. For example, in one study, more high school students could identify their parents' political party affiliation than their parents' other attitudes or beliefs. In many situations, the political party of the parents becomes the political party of the children, particularly if both parents support the same party.

The Schools and Educational Attainment

Education also strongly influences an individual's political attitudes. From their earliest days in school, children learn about the American political system. They say the Pledge of Allegiance and sing patriotic songs. They celebrate national holidays, such as Presidents' Day and Veterans' Day, and learn about the history and symbols associated with them. In the upper grades, young people acquire more knowledge about government and democratic procedures through civics classes and through student government and various clubs. They also learn citizenship skills through school rules and regulations. Generally, those with more education have more knowledge about politics and policy than those with less education. The level of education also influences a person's political values, as will be discussed later in this chapter.

Although the schools have always been important agents of political socialization, many Americans today believe that our schools are not fulfilling this mission. Too many students are graduating from high school—and even college—with too little knowledge of the American system of government.

This Native American boy poses with his Cub Scout manual. He hopes to obtain a Cub Scout Religious Emblem that recognizes his faith in traditional Navajo spiritual way of life. Both his family and the Cub Scouts are socializing influences on him.

AP Photo/Navajo Nation, George Hardeen

political socialization The learning process through which most people acquire their political attitudes, opinions, beliefs, and knowledge.

agents of political socialization People and institutions that influence the political views of others.

Michael Newman/PhotoEdit

Students learn about the political process early on when they participate in class elections.

The Media

The **media**—newspapers, magazines, television, radio, and the Internet—also have an impact on political socialization. The most influential of these media is, of course, television. Television continues to be a leading source of political and public affairs information for most people.

Some contend that the media's role in shaping public opinion has increased to the point at which the media are as influential as the family, particularly among high school students. For example, in her analysis of the media's role in American politics, media scholar Doris A. Graber points out that high school students, when asked where they obtain the information on which they base their attitudes, mention the mass media far more than they mention their families, friends, and teachers.[1] Graber's conclusion takes on added significance in view of a 2006 Gallup poll showing that only about half of the parents polled were concerned about their children's TV-viewing habits, even when their children watched TV "a great deal" or a "fair amount" of time. Also, only about half of the respondents were aware that their television sets were equipped with parental controls, and most within that group rarely, if ever, used those functions.

Other studies have shown that the media's influence on people's opinions may not be as great as some have thought. Generally, people watch television, read articles, or access online sites with preconceived ideas about the issues. These preconceived ideas act as a kind of perceptual screen that blocks out information that is not consistent with those ideas. For example, if you are already firmly convinced that daily meditation is beneficial for your health, you probably will not change your mind if you watch a TV show that asserts that those who meditate live no longer on average than people who do not. Generally, the media tend to wield the most influence over the views of persons who have not yet formed opinions about certain issues or political candidates. (See Chapter 10 for a more detailed discussion of the media's role in American politics.)

media Newspapers, magazines, television, radio, the Internet, and any other printed or electronic means of communication.

Opinion Leaders

Every state or community has well-known citizens who are able to influence the opinions of their fellow citizens. These people may be public officials, religious leaders, teachers, or celebrities. They are the people to whom others listen and from whom others draw ideas and convictions about various issues of public concern.

Senator Ted Kennedy (D., Mass.) is shown here shortly before his death in 2009. Kennedy was a major opinion leader for decades while he served in the Senate. He especially tried to form others' opinions on the need for health care reform. How does a politician become an opinion leader?

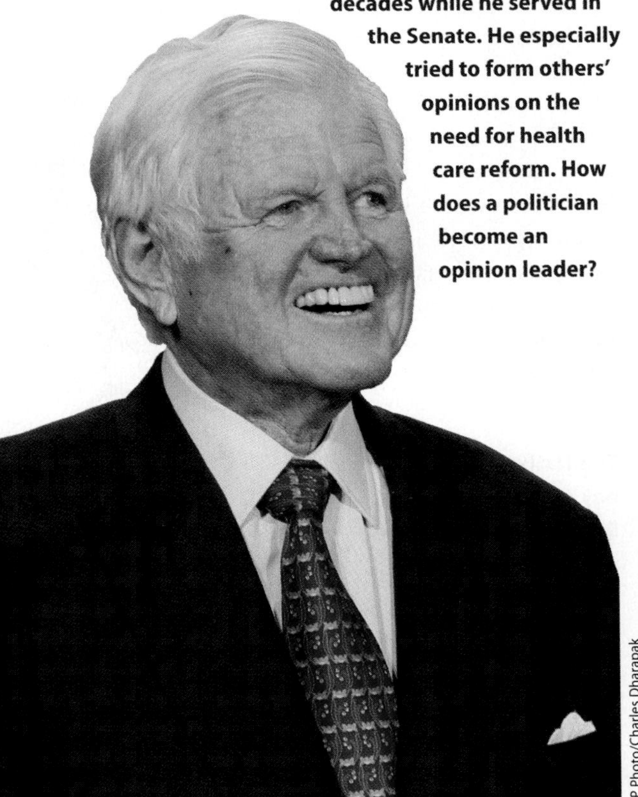

AP Photo/Charles Dharapak

These opinion leaders play a significant role in the formation of public opinion.

Opinion leaders often include politicians or former politicians. For example, President George W. Bush asked former U.S. presidents George H. W. Bush (2001–2009) and Bill Clinton to lead a nationwide fund-raising drive following the 2004 Indian Ocean earthquake and tsunami, which killed almost a quarter of a million people. (George H. W. Bush is George W. Bush's father.) Certainly, Americans' attitudes are influenced by the public statements of important government leaders such as the president or secretary of state. Sometimes, however, opinion leaders can fall from grace when they express views radically different from what most Americans believe. This was true for President George W. Bush. His insistence on continuing the widely unpopular war in Iraq was a major factor in causing his approval ratings to dip to historically low levels. Another example is former president Jimmy Carter (1977–1981), who lost much popularity after he published a book that harshly criticized Israel's actions toward the Palestinians.[2] (Most Americans of both parties are strongly pro-Israel.)

"I HAVE EXPERIENCED MANY INSTANCES OF BEING OBLIGED TO **change opinions**, EVEN ON IMPORTANT SUBJECTS, WHICH I ONCE THOUGHT RIGHT BUT FOUND TO BE OTHERWISE."

~ BENJAMIN FRANKLIN ~
AMERICAN STATESMAN
1706–1790

These volunteers and students from Tulane University paint a school in New Orleans after that city's destruction due to Hurricane Katrina. How do groups such as these help form political opinions?

AP Photo/Nam Y. Huh

Americans do not often look to other countries for opinion leaders, but the president of the United States is frequently an opinion leader in other nations. We examine the impact of a new president on citizens of other countries in this chapter's *The Rest of the World* feature on the next page.

Major Life Events

Often, the political attitudes of an entire generation of Americans are influenced by a major event. For example, the Great Depression (1929–1939), the most severe economic depression in modern U.S. history, persuaded many Americans who lived through it that the federal government should step in when the economy is in decline. Many citizens believed that increased federal spending and federal job-creation programs contributed to the economic recovery.

The generation that lived through World War II (1939–1945) tends to believe that American intervention in foreign affairs is good. In contrast, the generation that came of age during the Vietnam War (1964–1975) is more skeptical of American interventionism. A national tragedy, such as the terrorist attacks of September 11, 2001, is also likely to influence the political attitudes of a generation, though in what way is difficult to predict. Certainly, the U.S. government's response to 9/11, and particularly the war in Iraq, has elicited deep concern on the part of Americans. Opposition to the war, however, did not lead to the widespread antiwar demonstrations that took place during another unpopular war—in Vietnam—years ago. The recent Great Recession and the financial crisis that struck in September 2008 will surely affect popular attitudes in years to come.

Peer Groups

Once children enter school, the views of friends begin to influence their attitudes and beliefs. From junior high school on, the **peer group**—friends, classmates, co-workers, club members, or religious group members—becomes a significant factor in the political socialization process. Most of this socialization occurs when the peer group is

peer group Associates, often close in age to one another; may include friends, classmates, co-workers, club members, or religious group members. Peer group influence is a significant factor in the political socialization process.

An Improved Image of the United States Abroad?

During George W. Bush's eight years as president, foreign public opinion about the United States in general and Bush in particular fell dramatically. Since the election of Barack Obama, however, the world's view of the United States has, on average, undergone measurable improvement.

U.S. "Favorability" Ratings

While citizens of most countries look at the United States more favorably since President Obama took office, attitudes vary from region to region. In Western Europe, "favorability" ratings have soared. According to the Pew Research Center's Global Attitudes Project, the number of Germans with a favorable opinion of the United States jumped from 31 percent in 2008 to 64 percent in 2009. In France, the number climbed from 42 percent to 75 percent. Opinions of America have also become more positive in many nations of Latin America.

It should be understood that in quite a few countries, Bush was never particularly unpopular. These include the nations of Eastern Europe, which for many years were dominated by the Soviet Union. This experience made Eastern Europeans strong supporters of the United States, the longtime rival of the Soviets during the Cold War. By 2008 and 2009, the United States was still popular enough in Eastern Europe that there was little room for improvement. Other nations that did not exhibit strong negativity toward Bush included India, China, South Korea, and Japan.

Bush was actually quite popular in sub-Saharan Africa. Many Americans may not realize that Bush increased foreign aid to Africa dramatically, but Africans know it. Of course, as the son of an African father, Obama has been more popular still.

In contrast, opinions of the United States among Muslims in the Middle East have remained extremely unfavorable. An exception: favorability ratings have gone up substantially in Indonesia, a predominantly Muslim nation. Obama is something of a "favorite son" in that country—he lived there as a boy and has Indonesian relatives. Russian opinions of the United States have risen somewhat, but remain very low.

Will the United States Do the Right Thing in World Affairs?

Much of the resurgence in favorable opinion follows from confidence that President Obama's foreign policy judgments will be correct. Again, in Western Europe, there was almost universal agreement that Obama will "do the right thing in world affairs." France and Germany, for example, believed so to the extent of 90 percent of the polled population. Even in some Middle Eastern countries, such as Egypt and Jordan, a rising number of citizens thought that Obama would choose the correct foreign policy.

What about the Economy?

The United States has the world's largest economy, and people in the rest of the world have opinions about its impact on their own economies. Throughout much of the world, people thought that the Great Recession in the United States hurt them. This belief was even stronger in 2009 than in 2008. Some countries, such as Nigeria and Russia, were of the opinion in 2008 that they were immune to the international economic contagion. By 2009, they realized that they were not. In India, in contrast, over 55 percent of those interviewed believed that the United States was having a positive effect on their economy. The Chinese were evenly divided on the question.

For Critical Analysis *Will President Obama's Nobel Peace Price help improve the United State's image in the rest of the world? Why or why not?*

involved in political activities. For example, your political beliefs might be influenced by a peer group with which you are working on a common political cause, such as preventing the clear-cutting of old-growth forests or campaigning for a favorite candidate. Your political beliefs probably would not be as strongly influenced by peers with whom you snowboard regularly or attend concerts.

Economic Status and Occupation

A person's economic status may influence her or his political views. For example, poorer people are more likely to favor government assistance programs. On an issue such as abortion, lower-income people are more likely to be conservative—that is, to be against abortion—than are higher-income groups (of course, there are many exceptions).

Where a person works also affects her or his opinion. Co-workers who spend a great deal of time working together tend to influence one another. For example, labor union members working together for a company may have similar political opinions, at least on issues of government involvement in the economy. Individuals working for a nonprofit agency that depends on government funds will tend to support government spending in that area. Business managers are more likely to favor tax laws helpful to businesses than are factory workers.

LO3 *Measuring Public Opinion*

If public opinion is to affect public policy, then public officials must be made aware of it. They must know which issues are of current concern to Americans and how strongly people feel about those issues. They must also know when public opinion changes. Public officials commonly learn about public opinion through election results, personal contacts, interest groups, and media reports. Other than elections, however, the only relatively precise way to measure public opinion is through the use of public opinion polls.

A **public opinion poll** is a numerical survey of the public's opinion on a particular topic at a particular moment. The results of opinion polls are most often cast in terms of percentages: 62 percent feel this way, 27 percent do not, and 11 percent have no opinion. Of course, a poll cannot survey the entire U.S. population. Therefore, public opinion pollsters have devised scientific polling techniques for measuring public opinion through the use of **samples**—groups of people who are typical of the general population.

Early Polling Efforts

Since the 1800s, magazines and newspapers have often spiced up their articles by conducting **straw polls** of readers' opinions. Straw polls try to read the public's collective mind by simply asking a large number of people the same question. The early straw polls were mail surveys. Today, many newspapers and magazines still run "mail-in" polls. Increasingly, though, straw polls make use of telephone technology—encouraging people to call "900" numbers, for example—or the Internet. Visitors to a Web page can instantly register their opinion on an issue with the click of a mouse. The problem with straw polls is that the opinions expressed usually represent an atypical subgroup of the population, or a **biased sample.** A survey of those who read the *Reader's Digest* will most likely produce different results than a survey of those who read *Rolling Stone.*

The most famous of all straw-polling errors was committed by the *Literary Digest* in 1936 when it tried to predict the outcome of that year's presidential elections. The *Digest* had accurately predicted the winning candidates in several earlier presidential elections, but in 1936 the *Digest* forecast that Alfred Landon would easily defeat incumbent Franklin D. Roosevelt. Instead, Roosevelt won by a landslide. The editors of the *Digest* had sent mail-in cards to citizens whose names appeared in telephone directories, to its own subscribers, and to automobile owners—in all, to a staggering 2,376,000 people. In the mid-Depression year of 1936, however, people who owned a car or a telephone or who subscribed to the *Digest* were not representative of the majority of Americans. The vast majority of Americans could not afford such luxuries. Despite the enormous number of people surveyed, the sample was unrepresentative and consequently inaccurate.

Several newcomers to the public opinion poll industry, however, did predict Roosevelt's landslide victory. Two of these organizations are still at the forefront of the polling industry today: the Gallup Organization, started by George Gallup; and Roper Associates, founded by Elmo Roper and now known as the Roper Center.

Former Arkansas governor Mike Huckabee speaks during the Iowa Straw Poll, a year before the last presidential elections. Straw polls are wholly unscientific, and can be compared to the bad polling techniques used in the early days of polling. Why are such polls called "straw" polls?

AP Photo/Charlie Neibergall

Polling Today

Today, polling is used extensively by political candidates and policymakers. Politicians and the news media generally place a great deal of faith in the accuracy of poll results. Polls can be remarkably accurate when they are conducted

public opinion poll A numerical survey of the public's opinion on a particular topic at a particular moment.

sample In the context of opinion polling, a group of people selected to represent the population being studied.

straw poll A nonscientific poll; a poll in which there is no way to ensure that the opinions expressed are representative of the larger population.

biased sample A poll sample that does not accurately represent the population.

properly. In the last fourteen presidential elections, Gallup polls conducted early in September predicted the eventual winners in eleven of the fourteen races. Even polls taken several months in advance have been able to predict the eventual winner quite well. This success is largely the result of careful sampling techniques.

> "A popular government without popular information, or the means of acquiring it, is but **A PROLOGUE TO A FARCE OR A TRAGEDY,** or perhaps both."
>
> ~ JAMES MADISON ~
> FOURTH PRESIDENT
> OF THE UNITED STATES
> 1809–1817

SAMPLING Today, most Gallup polls sample between 1,500 and 2,000 people. How can interviewing such a small group possibly indicate what millions of voters think? To be successful, a sample must consist of people who are typical of the general population. If the sample is properly selected, the opinions of those in the sample will be representative of the opinions held by the population as a whole. If the sample is not properly chosen, then the results of the poll may not reflect the beliefs of the general population.

The most important principle in sampling is randomness. A **random sample** means that each person within the entire population being polled has an equal chance of being chosen. For example, if a poll is trying to measure how women feel about an issue, the sample should include respondents from all groups within the female population in proportion to their percentage in the entire population. A properly drawn random sample, therefore, would include appropriate numbers of women in terms of age, racial and ethnic characteristics, occupation, geography, household income level, and religious affiliation.

BIAS In addition to trying to secure a random sample, poll takers also want to ensure that there is no bias in their polling questions. How a question is phrased can significantly affect how people answer it. Consider a question about whether high-speed connections to the Internet should be added to the school library's computer center. One way to survey opinions on this issue is simply to ask, "Do you believe that the school district should provide high-speed connections to the Internet?" Another way to ask the same question is, "Are you willing to pay higher property taxes so that the school district can have high-speed connections to the Internet?" Undoubtedly, the poll results will differ depending on how the question is phrased.

Polling questions also sometimes reduce complex issues to questions that simply call for "yes" or "no" answers. For example, a survey question might ask respondents whether they favor giving aid to foreign countries. A respondent's opinion on the issue might vary depending on the recipient country or the purpose and type of the aid. The poll would nonetheless force the respondent to give a "yes" or "no" answer that does not fully reflect his or her opinion.

Respondents to such questions sometimes answer "I don't know" or "I don't have enough information to answer," even when the poll does not offer such answers. Interestingly, a study of how polling is conducted on the complex issue of school vouchers (school vouchers were discussed in Chapter 4) found that about 4 percent volunteered the answer "I don't know" when asked if they favored or opposed vouchers. When respondents were offered the option of answering "I haven't heard or read enough to answer," however, the proportion choosing that answer jumped to about 30 percent.[3] One current issue on which members of the public often have complicated opinions is health-care reform, as we explain in this chapter's *Our Government's Response to the Economic Crisis* feature on the facing page.

RELIABILITY OF POLLS In addition to potential bias, poll takers must also be concerned about the general reliability of their polls. Respondents interviewed may be influenced by the interviewer's personality or tone of voice. They may answer without having any information on the issue, or they may give the answer that they think will please the interviewer. Additionally, any opinion poll contains a **sampling error,** which is the difference between what the sample results show and what the true results would have been had everybody in the relevant population been interviewed. (For a further look at how polling can lead to misleading results, see this chapter's *Perception versus Reality* feature on page 184.)

random sample In the context of opinion polling, a sample in which each person within the entire population being polled has an equal chance of being chosen.

sampling error In the context of opinion polling, the difference between what the sample results show and what the true results would have been had everybody in the relevant population been interviewed.

The Public's Complicated Attitude toward Health-Care Reform

During the long campaign for the White House, all presidential candidates from both parties agreed that America's health-care system needed reform. After all, we are currently spending about 17 percent of our total national income on health care. Moreover, health-care costs have been rising faster than the rate of inflation. A substantial share of the population also lacks insurance. Upon taking office, President Barack Obama served notice that one of his major economic and social goals was to reform our health-care system as quickly as possible. He argued that we cannot have a booming economy unless we change the way medical services are paid for in this country.

The First Setback—High Costs

Obama gave Congress a deadline of August 1, 2009, to pass health-care reform legislation. The deadline was not met. One problem facing Congress as it attempted to address health care was the number of Congressional committees with jurisdiction over the topic. By the end of July, committees in the House of Representatives had settled on a proposed bill. Two Senate committees were still at work, however, which meant that three possible bills were in play, each of them substantially different from the others. It was not clear, at this point, exactly what the Democratic health-care reform proposal would look like.

One thing was clear: health-care reform was likely to cost around a trillion dollars over a ten-year period, and paying for it would require substantial new taxes. The House proposed to load these new taxes onto the richest taxpayers. Senators, in contrast, were considering a tax on existing employer-provided benefits. A tax on these benefits was widely considered rational by economists. It would violate Obama's campaign pledges, however, and millions of Americans considered it to be radically unfair. Furthermore, while all of the proposals would expand the number of people covered, the Congressional Budget Office found that none of the proposals would seriously reduce health-care costs. With such enormous new expenditures proposed in an environment of huge federal budget deficits, public opinion about health-care reform grew complicated in the hot days of the summer of 2009.

But Will Reform Help Me?

By the end of July, the nation was split in its view of how well President Obama was handling health-care reform, according to a survey by *Time* magazine. This was a significant decline in public approval of Obama's efforts. Months before, when Obama first announced his health-care objectives, a clear majority of Americans polled thought he was doing a great job.

In the same survey, 55 percent of those polled said they thought that the health-care system in the United States was either poor or only fair. Yet when respondents who currently have health-care coverage were asked, "How satisfied are you with the health-care plan you now have?" fully 86 percent were either very or somewhat satisfied. The paradox is that relatively few Americans believe we have a good health-care system, but among those currently insured, only 14 percent were dissatisfied.

A further paradox: even though 55 percent of respondents in the *Time* poll agreed that the health-care system needed a major overhaul, those polled were pessimistic about what effect reform might have on their own circumstances. Of those polled, 62 percent believed that proposed legislation would raise their own health-care costs, and 56 percent thought that reform would limit their freedom to choose physicians and coverage. The health-care reform campaign, in short, suffered from a serious weakness—a large number of people believed that reform might help someone else, but not them.

What about Congress?

A Gallup poll conducted on July 26, 2009, revealed that Americans do not have much faith that members of Congress can reform health care. Respondents were asked, "Would you say that members of Congress have a good understanding of the issues involved in the current debate over national health-care reform?" Fully 66 percent answered in the negative. In another poll, Ipsos/McCoatchy asked, "Which of the parties involved in health-care reform do you trust the most to make sure that all Americans have access to quality health care?" The Democrats in Congress garnered only 14 percent support. Republicans in Congress scored even lower—10 percent. Even so, Congress outscored the insurance and pharmaceutical companies. President Obama came in first, with a modest 26 percent.

Who Will Pay for Government-Provided Universal Health Care?

For the most part, Americans understand that expanded health-care services will not come free of charge. No matter how much politicians talk about reducing health-care costs, universal coverage is bound to increase these costs. How should this increase be paid for? The House proposal was clear: tax the rich more. A *USA Today*/Gallup poll on July 10, 2009, showed that increasing income taxes on upper-income Americans was strongly or somewhat favored by 58 percent of those polled. In contrast, 64 percent opposed taxing employer-provided health insurance.

For Critical Analysis *How might it be possible to have increased health-care coverage and lower health-care costs?*

PERCEPTION VERSUS REALITY

The Accuracy of Public Opinion Polls

Today, more than ever before, Americans are bombarded with the results of public opinion polls. If you can think of a political candidate, topic, issue, or concept, chances are one or more public polling organizations can tell you what "Americans really think" about that candidate or topic. Polling organizations increasingly use telephone interviews and the Internet to conduct their polls. Because these polls are much cheaper to conduct than "feet on the street" polling, it is not surprising that more poll results are available every day. If you subscribe to the online services of the Gallup poll, for example, at least once a week Gallup will send you information on approximately a dozen topics on which that organization has sought to discover Americans' opinions.

The Perception

Americans who hear or read about the results of public opinion polls naturally assume that polling organizations undertook those polls in a scientific way and presented accurate results. Those who know a little bit about polling also assume that the small numbers of people polled represented a random sample.

The Reality

Many polls are not based on a random sample, however. Consider a poll published by the *Military Times* in 2008, which found that 58 percent of respondents opposed military service by openly gay individuals. Further, 10 percent claimed that they would not reenlist if the ban on open gay service were lifted. The press gave this survey widespread coverage without questioning its methodology. One pundit claimed, on the basis of the poll, that gays in the military would "destroy" the institution. In fact, the poll was not based on a random sample but on a self-selected pool of *Military Times* readers, who tended to be older and more conservative than the military as a whole. Further, opinions do not necessarily predict behavior. Before Britain and Canada ended their service bans, polls found widespread resistance to openly gay and lesbian soldiers. Upon integration, however, almost no one actually resigned from service.

Think also about how respondents answer interviewers' questions. Consider one *New York Times*/CBS News poll in which voters were asked if they had voted in a specific presidential election. Although 73 percent said yes, the U.S. Census Bureau later determined that only 64 percent of eligible voters actually voted in that election. Analysts concluded that those who had been interviewed wanted to appear to be "good citizens," so not all of them told the truth.

Do not forget about sampling error. For example, say that two candidates for president are neck and neck in the opinion polls, but the sampling error is 4 percent. That means that either candidate could actually be ahead by 54 percent to 46 percent.

Blog On • *You'll find a poll-lover's dream at Mark Blumenthal's* **www.pollster.com/blogs,** *where readers debate about all the recent polls.* **Pollster.com's** *main page,* **www.pollster.com,** *is also a trove of information about polls. Another site that collects polls and analyzes them is* **www.electionprojection.com,** *run by Scott Elliott, who is known as the "blogging Caesar."*

Opinion polls of voter preferences cannot reflect rapid shifts in public opinion unless they are taken frequently. During the 2004 presidential elections, polls showed George W. Bush ahead at times and John Kerry ahead at other times. The media reported extensively on the many polls conducted and their discrepancies. In the weeks prior to Election Day, a poll from Gallup, *USA Today,* and CNN showed Bush leading Kerry by a margin of eight points. Meanwhile, a poll by ABC News and the *Washington Post* showed Bush leading by a three-point margin. Yet another poll by the *New York Times* and CBS News showed the race as a tie. (In the end, Bush's margin of victory was about 2.5 percent.)

EXIT POLLS The reliability of polls was also called into question by the use of exit polls in the 2000 presidential elections. The Voter News Service (VNS)—a consortium of news networks that no longer exists—conducted polls of people exiting polling places on Election Day. These exit polls were used by the news networks to predict the winner of the Florida race—and they were wrong, not just once, but twice. First, they claimed that the Florida vote had gone to Al Gore. Then, a few hours later, they said it had gone to George W. Bush. Finally, they said the Florida race was too close to call.

These miscalls of the election outcome in Florida caused substantial confusion—and frustration—for the candidates as well as for the voters. They also led to a significant debate over exit polls: Should exit polls be banned, even though they provide valuable information on voter behavior and preferences?

Exit polls were employed during the 2004 presidential elections. Again the results were troublesome. During the early hours of the elections, exit polls caused the media to conclude that Democratic candidate John Kerry was leading in the race. Preliminary results of exit polls were leaked to the Internet by midafternoon. After the votes were tallied, however, the exit poll results were shown to have inflated Kerry's support by 6.5 percent—the largest margin of error in decades.

In 2008, the television networks were careful about making predictions based on exit polls. It was clear early that Obama was winning, but the networks wanted viewers to keep watching, so they maintained the suspense. Print media exit polls, used to determine the voting preferences of various groups, did better in 2008 than in 2004, when they contained some major errors.

Table 8–1

Checklist for Evaluating Public Opinion Polls

Because public opinion polls are so widely used by the media and policymakers, and their reliability is so often called into question, several organizations have issued guidelines for evaluating polls. Below is a list of questions that you can ask to evaluate the quality and reliability of a poll. You can find the answers to many, if not all, of these questions in the polling organization's report accompanying the poll results.

1. Who conducted the poll, and who sponsored or paid for it?
2. How many people were interviewed for the survey, and what part of the population did they represent (for example, registered voters, likely voters, persons over age eighteen)?
3. How were these people chosen, and how random was the sample?
4. How were respondents contacted and interviewed (by telephone, by mail-in survey)?
5. Who should have been interviewed but was not (what was the "nonresponse" rate—people who should have been part of the random sample but who refused to be interviewed, do not have telephones, or do not have listed telephone numbers, for example)?
6. What is the margin of error for the poll? (The acceptable margin of error for national polls is usually plus or minus 4 percent.)
7. What questions did the poll ask?
8. In what order were the questions asked?
9. When was the poll conducted?
10. What other polls were conducted on this topic, and do they report similar findings?

MISUSE OF POLLS Today, a frequently heard complaint is that, instead of measuring public opinion, polls can end up creating it. For example, to gain popularity, a candidate might claim that all the polls show that he is ahead in the race. People who want to support the winner may back this candidate despite their true feelings. This is often called the "bandwagon" effect. Presidential approval ratings lend themselves to the bandwagon effect.

The media also sometimes misuse polls. Many journalists take the easy route during campaigns and base their political coverage almost exclusively on poll findings, with no mention of the chance for bias or the margin of error in the poll. A useful checklist for evaluating the quality of opinion polls is presented in Table 8–1. An increasingly common misuse of polls by politicians is the *push poll,* discussed next.

DEFINING A PUSH POLL One tactic in political campaigns is to use **push polls,** which ask "fake" polling questions that are actually designed to "push" voters toward one candidate or another. The use of push polls has become so prevalent today that many states are taking steps to ban them. The problem with trying to ban push polls, or even to report accurately on which candidates are using them, is that defining a push poll can be difficult.

The National Council on Public Polls describes push polls as outright political manipulation, the spreading of rumors and lies by one candidate about another. For example, a push poll might ask, "Do you believe the rumor that Candidate A misused campaign funds to pay for a family vacation to Hawaii?" Push pollsters usually do not give their name or identify the poll's sponsor. The interviews last less than a minute, whereas legitimate pollsters typically interview a respondent for five to thirty minutes. Based on these characteristics, it is sometimes possible to distinguish a push poll from a legitimate poll conducted by a respected research organization. The checklist in Table 8–1 can also help you distinguish between a legitimate poll and a push poll.

Some researchers argue that identifying a push poll is not that straightforward, however. Political analyst Charlie Cook points out that "there are legitimate polls that can ask push

push poll A campaign tactic used to feed false or misleading information to potential voters, under the guise of taking an opinion poll, with the intent to "push" voters away from one candidate and toward another.

Bob Daemmrich/Sygma/Corbis

An African American does his part to "get out the vote" before an election. African Americans faced significant restrictions on voting until the 1950s and 1960s, when new laws and policies helped to end both formal and informal barriers to voting for them. Voter turnout among African Americans is increasing, and in 2008 their share of the vote rose from 11 percent to 13 percent.

questions, which test potential arguments against a rival to ascertain how effective those arguments might be in future advertising. . . . These are not only legitimate tools of survey research, but any political pollster who did not use them would be doing his or her clients a real disservice."[4] Distinguishing between push polls and push questions, then, can be challenging—which is usually the intent of the push pollsters. A candidate does not want to be accused of conducting push polls, because the public considers them a "dirty trick" and may turn against the candidate who uses them. In several recent campaigns, candidates have accused each other of conducting push polls—accusations that could not always be proved or disproved.

LO4 *Voting and Voter Turnout*

Voting is arguably the most important way in which citizens participate in the political process. Because we do not live in a direct democracy, Americans use the vote to elect politicians to represent their interests, values, and opinions in government. In many states, public-policy decisions—for example, access to medical marijuana—are decided by voters. Our right to vote also helps keep elected officials accountable to campaign promises because they must face reelection.

Factors Affecting Voter Turnout

If voting is so important, then why do so many Americans fail to exercise their right to vote? Why is voter turnout—the percentage of those eligible to vote who actually turn out to vote—relatively low? As you will read shortly, in the past, legal restrictions based on income, gender, race, and other factors kept a number of people from voting. In the last decades of the twentieth century, these restrictions were almost completely eliminated, and yet voter turnout in presidential elections still hovered around 55 percent, as shown in Figure 8–1 on the facing page. In the last two presidential elections, however, turnout has exceeded 60 percent—a welcome, if modest, improvement.

According to a Pew Research Center survey of voter turnout, one of the reasons for low voter turnout is that many nonvoters (close to 40 percent) do not feel that they have a duty to vote. The survey also found that nearly 70 percent of nonvoters said that they did not vote because they lacked information about the candidates.[5] Finally, some people believe that their vote will not make any difference, so they do not bother to become informed about the candidates and issues or go to the polls.

The Legal Right to Vote

In the United States today, all citizens who are at least eighteen years of age have the right to vote. This was not always true, however. Recall from Chapter 5 that restrictions on *suffrage,* the legal right to vote, have existed since the founding of our nation. Expanding the right to vote has been an important part of the gradual democratization of the American electoral process. Table 8–2 on page 188 summarizes the major amendments, Supreme Court decisions, and laws that extended the right to vote to various American groups.

HISTORICAL RESTRICTIONS ON VOTING Those who drafted the Constitution left the power to set suffrage qualifications to the individual states. Most states limited suffrage to adult white males who owned property, but these restrictions were challenged early on in the history of the republic. By 1828, laws

Figure 8–1

Voter Turnout since 1968

The figures in this chart show voter turnout as a percentage of the population that is eligible to vote.

Sources: *Statistical Abstract of the United States*, various issues; the Committee for the Study of the American Electorate; and authors' updates.

restricting the right to vote to Christians were abolished in all states, and property ownership and tax-payment requirements gradually began to disappear as well. By 1850, all white males were allowed to vote. Restrictions based on race and gender continued, however.

The Fifteenth Amendment, ratified in 1870, guaranteed suffrage to African American males. Yet, for many decades, African Americans were effectively denied the ability to exercise their voting rights. Using methods ranging from mob violence to economic restrictions, groups of white southerners kept black Americans from voting. Some states required citizens to pass **literacy tests** and to answer complicated questions about government and history before they could register to vote. Registrars made sure that African Americans would always fail such tests. The **poll tax,** a fee of several dollars, was another device used to prevent African Americans from voting. At the time, this tax was a sizable burden, not only for most blacks but also for poor whites. Another restriction was the **grandfather clause,** which had the effect of restricting voting rights to those whose ancestors had voted before the 1860s. This technique was prohibited by the United States Supreme Court in 1915.[6]

Still another voting barrier was the **white primary**—African Americans were prohibited from voting in the primary elections. The Supreme Court initially upheld this practice on the grounds that the political parties were private entities, not public, and thus could do as they wished. Eventually, in 1944, the Court banned the use of white primaries.[7]

VOTING RIGHTS TODAY Today, these devices for restricting voting rights are explicitly outlawed by constitutional amendments and by the Voting Rights Act of 1965, as discussed in Chapter 5. Furthermore, the Nineteenth Amendment gave women the right to vote in 1920. In 1971, the Twenty-sixth Amendment reduced the minimum voting age to eighteen.

literacy test A test given to voters to ensure that they could read and write and thus evaluate political information; a technique used in many southern states to restrict African American participation in elections.

poll tax A fee of several dollars that had to be paid before a person could vote; a device used in some southern states to prevent African Americans from voting.

grandfather clause A clause in a state law that had the effect of restricting the franchise (voting rights) to those whose ancestors had voted before the 1860s; one of the techniques used in the South to prevent African Americans from exercising their right to vote.

white primary A primary election in which African Americans were prohibited from voting. The practice was banned by the Supreme Court in 1944.

Some restrictions on voting rights still exist. Every state except North Dakota requires voters to register with the appropriate state or local officials before voting. Residency requirements are also usually imposed for voting. Since 1970, however, no state can impose a residency requirement of more than thirty days. Twenty-five states require that length of time, while the other twenty-five states require fewer or no days. Another voting requirement is citizenship. Aliens may not vote in any public election held anywhere in the United States. Most states also do not permit prison inmates, mentally ill people, convicted felons, or election-law violators to vote.

Attempts to Improve Voter Turnout

Attempts to improve voter turnout typically have a partisan dimension. This is because the kinds of people who find it difficult to register to vote tend to be disproportionately Democratic in their sympathies. Many, for example, are African Americans, a reliably Democratic voting bloc. As a result, Republicans are generally wary of efforts to make registration easier. For example, most Republicans opposed the passage of the National Voter Registration Act (the "Motor Voter Law") of 1993, which simplified the voter-registration process. The act requires states to provide all eligible citizens with the opportunity to register to vote when they apply for or renew a driver's license. The law also requires that states allow mail-in registration, with forms given at certain public assistance agencies. The law, which took effect on January 1, 1995, has facilitated millions of registrations.

In 1998, Oregon voters approved a ballot initiative requiring that all elections in that state, including presidential elections, be conducted exclusively by mail. In the 2008 presidential elections, 66 percent of Oregonians eligible to vote cast ballots, a figure that is somewhat higher than the national average but not exceptionally so. Some argue that if mail-in voting were allowed nationwide, voter turnout would increase. Others believe that voting by mail has a number of disadvantages, including greater possibilities for voter fraud.

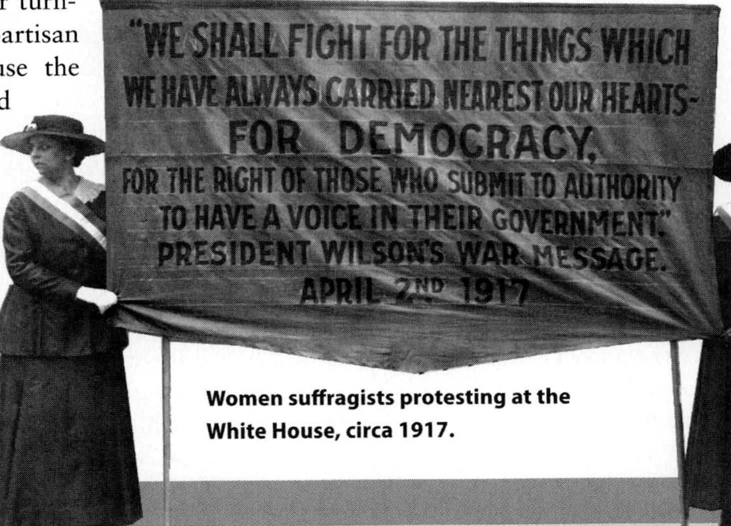

Women suffragists protesting at the White House, circa 1917.

Corbis

Table 8–2

Extension of the Right to Vote

Year	Action	Impact
1870	Fifteenth Amendment	Discrimination based on race outlawed.
1920	Nineteenth Amendment	Discrimination based on gender outlawed.
1924	Congressional act	All Native Americans given citizenship.
1944	*Smith v. Allwright*	Supreme Court prohibits white primary.
1957	Civil Rights Act of 1957	Justice Department can sue to protect voting rights in various states.
1960	Civil Rights Act of 1960	Courts authorized to appoint referees to assist voter-registration procedures.
1961	Twenty-third Amendment	Residents of District of Columbia given right to vote for president and vice president.
1964	Twenty-fourth Amendment	Poll tax in national elections outlawed.
1965	Voting Rights Act of 1965	Literacy tests prohibited; federal voter registrars authorized in seven southern states.
1970	Voting Rights Act Amendments of 1970	Voting age for federal elections reduced to eighteen years; maximum thirty-day residency required for presidential elections; state literacy tests abolished.
1971	Twenty-sixth Amendment	Minimum voting age reduced to eighteen for all elections.
1975	Voting Rights Act Amendments of 1975	Federal voter registrars authorized in ten more states; bilingual ballots to be used in certain circumstances.
1982	Voting Rights Act Amendments of 1982	Extended provisions of Voting Rights Act amendments of 1970 and 1975; private parties allowed to sue for violations.

Voter Fraud—A Real Problem or Much Ado about Nothing?

Cries of voter fraud came from the Democrats in 2000 and again in 2004. The Democrats believed that votes were handled improperly in Florida in 2000 and that this kept Democratic presidential candidate Al Gore from carrying the state and winning the presidency. In 2004, some believed that fraud cost Democratic presidential candidate John Kerry the state of Ohio and the presidency. In 2008, accusations of voter fraud became a major campaign issue when Republican John McCain claimed that a group called Acorn was "on the verge of maybe perpetrating one of the greatest frauds in voter history." Acorn is a nonprofit group that advocates for the poor. It mounted a voter-registration drive in 2008, and some of its employees handed in registration forms that bore the names of cartoon characters and out-of-state major-league athletes. Strictly speaking, this was not voter fraud, but registration fraud. Voter fraud would occur only if someone using the name Mickey Mouse actually turned up at the polls and tried to vote. Acorn said that it had fired the offending employees and that state laws required it to hand in even obviously bogus registration forms, which it marked as suspect.

Voter Fraud Is a Myth

Political analyst Harold Meyerson of the *Los Angeles Times* wrote, "Voter fraud is a myth—not an urban or a real myth, as such, but a Republican one." The Justice Department's Ballot Access and Voting Integrity Initiative has obtained only eighty-six convictions for voter fraud over a five-year period. Many Americans contend that voter fraud will always exist on a small scale, but it is not a serious problem today. Rather, the Republicans have raised the specter of voter fraud in order to pass laws, such as those requiring photo IDs, that make it harder for disadvantaged persons (mostly Democrats) to vote.

Voter Fraud Is a Real Problem

Other Americans believe that voter fraud is a significant problem. The Election Assistance Commission issued a report indicating that the extent of voter fraud is still open to debate. Lapses in enforcing voting and registration rules continue to occur. Thousands upon thousands of ineligible voters are allowed to vote. Many convicted felons—who are not allowed to vote in most states—end up voting anyway. The only effective method of reducing voter fraud is to require photo IDs at polling places, as is done in states such as Indiana.

For Critical Analysis *Those concerned about voter fraud contend that felons who are ineligible to vote sometimes do so anyway. Is it appropriate to ban felons who have completed their time in prison from voting? Why or why not?*

Civil rights protesters, led by Martin Luther King, Jr., march on the road from Selma to Montgomery, Alabama, in March 1965. During the five-day, fifty-mile march, federal troops were stationed every one hundred yards along the route to protect the marchers from violent attacks by segregationists.

AP Photo/Matt Heron/Smithsonian

Attempts to Improve Voting Procedures

Because of serious problems in achieving accurate vote counts in recent elections, particularly in the 2000 presidential elections, steps have been taken to attempt to ensure more accuracy in the voting process. In 2002, Congress passed the Help America Vote Act, which, among other things, provided funds to the states to help them purchase new electronic voting equipment. Concerns about the possibility of fraudulent manipulation of electronic voting machines then replaced the worries over inaccurate vote counts caused by the previous equipment.

PROBLEMS IN 2006 In the 2006 elections, about half of the states that were using new electronic voting

AP Photo/John Gress

A worker moves bundled vote-by-mail ballots in Portland, Oregon. Oregon, which is the only state in the country to conduct all elections exclusively by mail.

systems reported problems. Some systems "flipped" votes from the selected candidate to the opposing candidate. In one Florida district, about eighteen thousand votes apparently were unrecorded by electronic equipment, and this may have changed the outcome of a congressional race. Many experts have demanded that electronic systems create a "paper trail" so that machine errors can be tracked and fixed.

VOTING SYSTEMS IN THE 2008 ELECTIONS Because of problems with electronic systems, fewer polling places used them in 2008. Indeed, more than half of all votes cast in 2008 used old-fashioned paper ballots. As a result, vote counting was slow. One feature of the elections was the large number of states that allowed early voting at polling places that opened weeks before Election Day. A benefit of early voting was that it allowed election workers time to ensure that all systems were working properly by Election Day.

Who Actually Votes

Just because an individual is eligible to vote does not necessarily mean that the person will actually go to the polls on Election Day and vote. Why do some eligible voters go to the polls while others do not? Although nobody can answer this question with absolute conviction, certain factors, including those discussed next, appear to affect voter turnout.

EDUCATIONAL ATTAINMENT Among the factors affecting voter turnout, education appears to be the most important. The more education a person has, the more likely it is that she or he will be a regular voter. People who graduated from high school vote more regularly than those who dropped out, and college graduates vote more often than high school graduates.

INCOME LEVEL AND AGE Differences in income also lead to differences in voter turnout. Wealthy people tend to be overrepresented among regular voters. Generally, older voters turn out to vote more regularly than younger voters do, although participation tends to decline among the very elderly. Participation likely increases with age because older people tend to be more settled, are already registered, and have had more experience with voting.

MINORITY STATUS Racial and ethnic minorities traditionally have been underrepresented among the ranks of voters. In several recent elections, however, participation by these groups, particularly African Americans and Hispanics, has increased.

This voter is using an accessible voting machine, which provides audio and touch-screen ballots in several languages, depending on the area's demographics. Are there ways to improve voting procedures? Do so-called accessible voting machines create any new problems?

AP Photo/Elaine Thompson

It was expected that with an African American running for president on the Democratic ticket in 2008, voter turnout among African Americans would go through the roof. African American turnout was indeed high, but not as high as some had expected. About 20 percent more African Americans voted in 2008 than in 2004, and their share of the vote rose from 11 percent to 13 percent. African Americans were essential to Obama's victories in North Carolina and Virginia.

In part because the number of Hispanic citizens has grown rapidly, the increase in the Hispanic vote—more than 30 percent—was even larger than the increase in the black vote. Hispanics helped Obama carry Colorado, Indiana, Nevada, and New Mexico.

IMMIGRATION AND VOTER TURNOUT The United States has experienced high rates of immigration in recent decades, and that has had an effect on voter turnout figures. In the past, voter turnout was often expressed as a percentage of the **voting-age population,** the number of people residing in the United States who are at least eighteen years old. Due to legal and illegal immigration, however, there are many people of voting age who are not eligible to vote because they are not citizens. Millions more cannot vote because they are felons. Additionally, the voting-age population excludes Americans abroad, however, they can cast absentee ballots.

Today, political scientists calculate the **vote-eligible population,** the number of people who are actually entitled to vote in American elections. They have found that there may be 20 million fewer eligible voters than the voting-age population suggests. Therefore, voter turnout is actually greater than the percentages sometimes cited. Some experts have argued that the relatively low levels of voter turnout often reported for the years between 1972 and 2000 were largely due to immigration.[8] Beginning in 2004, voter turnout has improved by any calculation method.

LO5 *Why People Vote as They Do*

What prompts some citizens to vote Republican and others to vote Democratic? What persuades voters to choose certain kinds of candidates? Obviously, more is involved than measuring one's own position against the candidates' positions and then voting accordingly. Voters choose candidates for many

© 2009 Harley L. Schwadron

reasons. Researchers have collected more information on voting than on any other form of political participation in the United States. These data shed some light on why people decide to vote for particular candidates.

Party Identification

Many voters have a standing allegiance to a political party, or a party identification, although the proportion of the population that does so has fallen in recent decades. For established voters, party identification is one of the most important and lasting predictors of how a person will vote. Party identification is an emotional attachment to a party that is influenced by family, age, peer groups, and other factors that play a role in the political socialization process discussed earlier.

A large number of voters call themselves independents. Despite this label, many independents actually support one or the other of the two major parties quite regularly. Figure 8–2 on the following page shows how those who identified themselves as Democrats, Republicans, and independents voted in the 2008 presidential elections.

Perception of the Candidates

Voters often base their decisions on the perceived character of the candidates rather than on their qualifications or policy positions. Such perceptions were important in the 2008 presidential elections. At first, some observers saw Democrat Barack Obama as aloof or even arrogant. During

voting-age population The number of people residing in the United States who are at least eighteen years old.

vote-eligible population The number of people who are actually eligible to vote in an American election.

Figure 8–2

Party Identification and Voting Behavior in the 2008 Presidential Elections

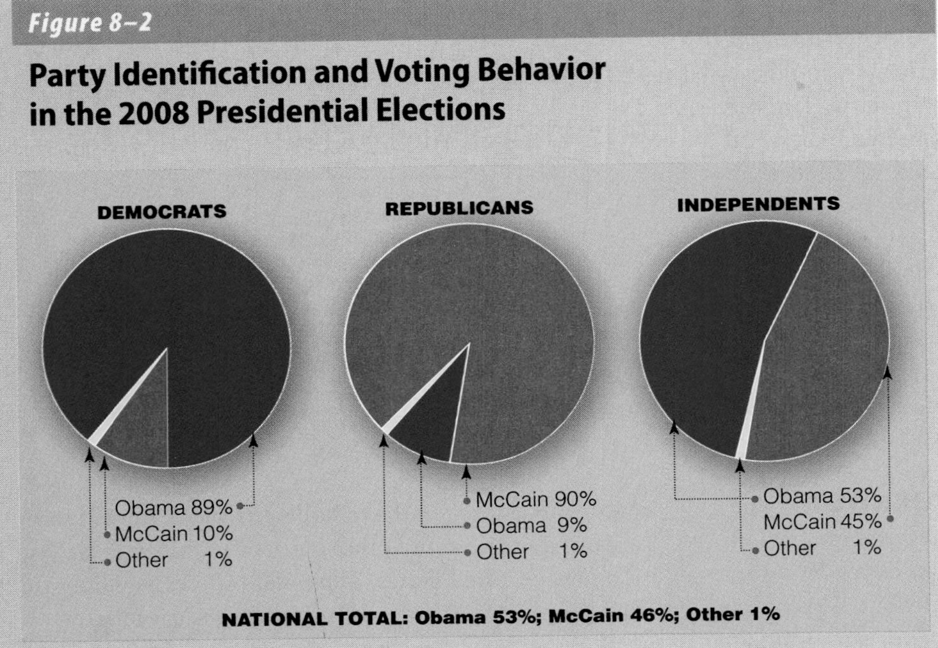

Source: National Election Pool; Dave Leip's Atlas of U.S. Presidential Elections (**www.uselectionsatlas.org**); and authors' estimates.

the economic crisis, however, Obama's calm temperament was viewed as "presidential." Six out of ten voters reported that they had no idea what Obama would do to get the country out of its financial mess, but they were sure he could do it. Republican John McCain sought to portray himself as a fighter for America. Sometimes he simply came across as angry, however. As Republican strategist Karl Rove put it, "When was the last time Americans elected an angry president?" Falling behind in the polls, McCain repeatedly changed direction in an attempt to alter the nature of the race. These moves, however, played into the impression that he was erratic and unpredictable. His choice of Sarah Palin as a running mate also seemed impulsive.

Policy Choices

When people vote for candidates who share their positions on particular issues, they are engaging in policy voting. If a candidate for senator in your state opposes gun control laws, for example, and you decide to vote for her for that reason, you have engaged in policy voting.

Historically, economic issues have had the strongest influence on voters' choices. When the economy is doing well, it is very difficult for a challenger, particularly at the presidential level, to defeat the incumbent. In contrast, when the country is experiencing inflation, rising unemployment, or high interest rates, the incumbent will likely be at a disadvantage. The main issue in the 2008 presidential elections was the financial crisis facing all Americans.

Some of the most heated debates in American political campaigns have involved social issues, such as abortion, gay and lesbian rights, the death penalty, and religion in the schools. Often, presidential candidates prefer to avoid publicizing their stand on these types of issues, because voters who have strong opinions about such issues are likely to be offended if a candidate does not share their views.

Socioeconomic Factors

Some factors that influence how people vote can be described as socioeconomic. These factors include educational attainment, income level, age, gender, religion, and geographic location. Some of these factors have to do with the circumstances into which individuals are born; others have to do with personal choices. Figure 8–3 on the facing page shows how various groups voted in the 2008 presidential elections.

EDUCATIONAL ATTAINMENT As a general rule, people with more education are more likely to vote Republican, although in recent years, voters with postgraduate degrees have tended to vote Democratic. Typically, those with less education are also more inclined to vote for the Democratic nominee. Educational attainment, of course, can be linked to income level. Recent studies show that among students from families with income in the bottom fifth of the population, only 12 percent earn a bachelor's degree by the age of twenty-four. In the top fifth, the figure is 73 percent.

OCCUPATION AND INCOME LEVEL Businesspersons tend to vote Republican and have done so for many years. Recently, professionals (such as attorneys, professors, and physicians) have been more likely to vote Democratic than in years past. Manual laborers, factory workers, and especially union members are more likely to vote Democratic. In the past, the higher the income, the more likely it was that a person would vote Republican. Conversely, a much larger percentage of low-income individuals voted Democratic. But this pattern is also breaking down, and there are no hard-and-fast

Figure 8–3

Voting by Groups in the 2008 Presidential Elections

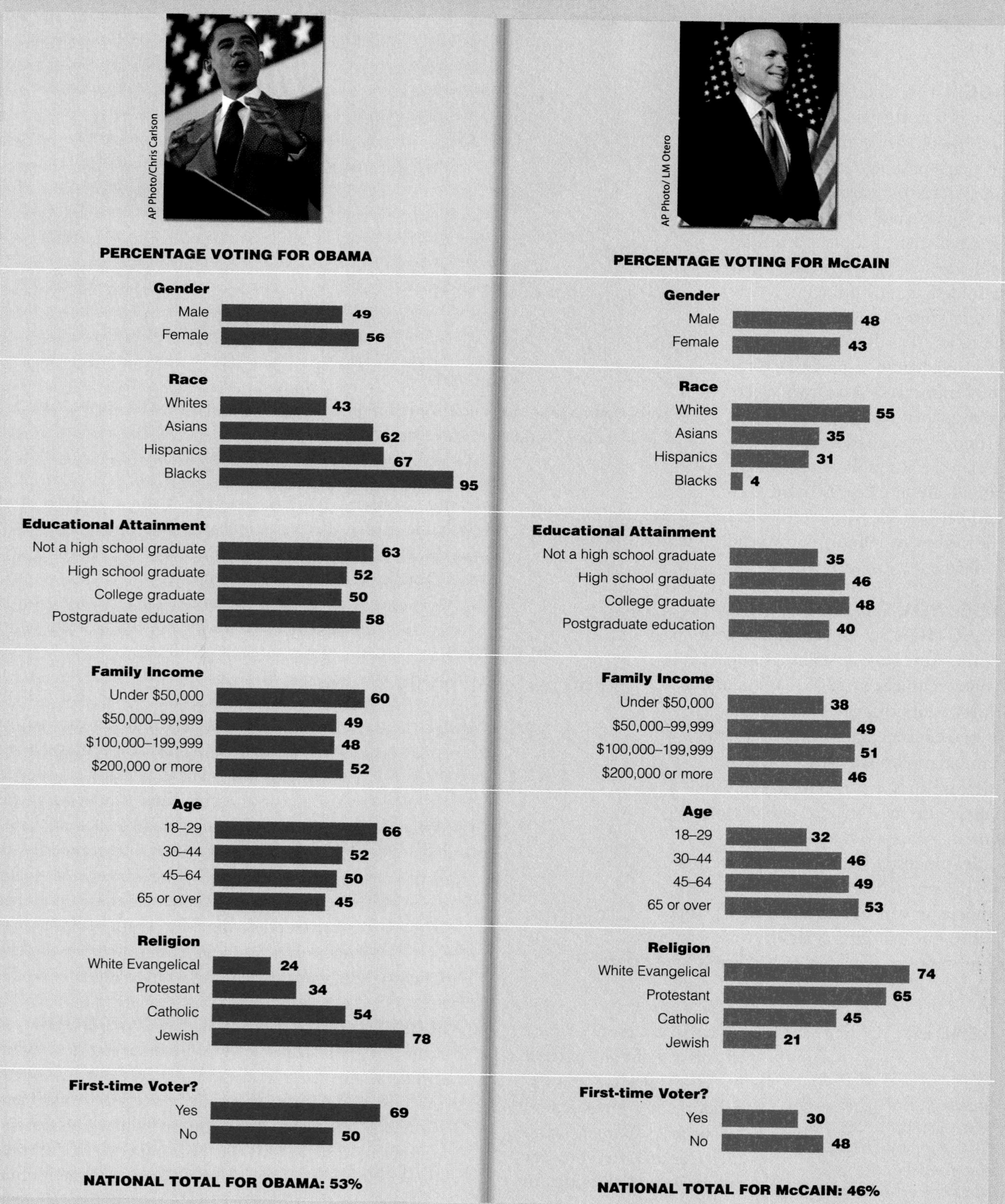

Source: The National Election Pool.

rules. Some very poor individuals are devoted Republicans, just as some extremely wealthy persons are supporters of the Democratic Party.

Emmanuel Dunand/AFP/Getty Images

Barack Obama supporters hold signs during a "Women's Rally for the Change We Need" in Coral Gables, Florida, in September 2008.

AGE The conventional wisdom is that the young are liberal and the old are conservative, yet in years past age differences in support for the parties have often been quite small. One age-related effect is that people's attitudes are shaped by the events that unfolded as they grew up. Many voters who came of age during Franklin D. Roosevelt's New Deal held onto a preference for the Democrats. Voters who were young when Ronald Reagan was president have had a tendency to prefer the Republicans. Younger voters are noticeably more liberal on one set of issues, however—those dealing with the rights of minorities, women, and gay males and lesbians.

THE YOUTH VOTE IN THE 2008 ELECTIONS In contrast with past years, age had a striking impact on voters' choices in 2008. Voters under thirty years of age chose Obama by a two-to-one margin. The Obama campaign hoped for a massive increase in the turnout of younger voters. In the end, though, young voters' share of the electorate rose only modestly, from 17 percent to 18 percent. What made the youth vote important was not turnout, but Obama's enormous margin, a result with ominous implications for the Republicans in future years.

> "In politics, an organized minority is A POLITICAL MAJORITY."
>
> ~ REV. JESSE JACKSON ~
> CIVIL RIGHTS ACTIVIST
> 1941–PRESENT

GENDER Until about thirty years ago, there seemed to be no fixed pattern of voter preferences by gender in presidential elections. Women and men tended to vote for the various candidates in roughly equal numbers. Some political analysts believe that a **gender gap** became a major determinant of voter decision making in the 1980 presidential elections, however. In that year, Ronald Reagan outdrew Jimmy Carter by 16 percentage points among male voters, whereas women gave about an equal number of votes to each candidate.

gender gap The difference between the percentage of votes cast for a particular candidate by women and the percentage of votes cast for the same candidate by men.

THE GENDER GAP IN 2008 In 2008, Barack Obama carried the male vote by one percentage point and the female vote by a 13 percent margin. This gender gap was close to the average seen since 1980. John McCain hoped to make inroads among women by naming Sarah Palin as his running mate. He especially hoped to attract disgruntled supporters of Obama's defeated opponent in the primaries, Hillary Clinton. This strategy does not seem to have worked.

RELIGION AND ETHNIC BACKGROUND A century ago, at least in the northern states, white Catholic voters were likely to be Democrats and white Protestant voters were likely to be Republicans. There are a few places around the country where this pattern continues to hold, but for the most part, white Catholics are now almost as likely as their Protestant neighbors to support the Republicans.

In recent years, a different religious variable has become important in determining voting behavior. Regardless of their denomination, white Christian voters who attend church regularly have favored the Republicans by substantial margins. White voters who attend church rarely or who find religion less important in their lives are more likely to vote Democratic. Jewish voters are strongly Democratic, regardless of whether they attend services.

> "Whenever a fellow tells me he is bipartisan, I KNOW HE IS GOING TO VOTE AGAINST ME."
>
> ~ HARRY TRUMAN ~
> THIRTY-THIRD PRESIDENT OF THE UNITED STATES 1945–1953

Most African Americans are Protestants, but African Americans are perhaps the most solidly Democratic constituency in the United States. This is a complete reversal of the circumstances that existed a century ago. As noted in Chapter 7, for many years after the Civil War, those African Americans who could vote were overwhelmingly Republican. Not until President Franklin Roosevelt's New Deal did black voters begin to turn to the Democrats. Hispanic voters have supported the Democrats by margins of about two to one, with some exceptions: Cuban Americans are strongly Republican. Asian Americans also tend to favor the Democrats, although Vietnamese Americans are strongly Republican.

GEOGRAPHIC REGION In today's presidential contests, states in the South, the Great Plains, and parts of the Rocky Mountains are strongly Republican. The Northeast, the West Coast, and Illinois are firmly Democratic. Many of the swing states that decide elections are located in the Midwest, although several Rocky Mountain states swing between the parties as well. This pattern is an almost complete reversal of the one that existed a century ago. In those years, most white southerners were Democrats, and people spoke of the **Solid South**—solidly Democratic, that is. The Solid South lasted for a century after the Civil War and in large part was the result of southern resentment of the Republicans for their role in the "War between the States" and their support of African Americans in the postwar era. At the end of the nineteenth century, the Republicans were strong in the Northeast and much of the Midwest, while the Democrats were able to find support outside of the South in the Great Plains and the Far West.

The ideologies of the two parties have likewise undergone something of a reversal. One hundred years ago, the Democrats were seen as *less* likely than the Republicans to support government intervention in the economy. The Democrats were also the party that opposed civil rights. Today, the Democrats are often regarded as the party that supports "big government" and affirmative action programs.

Ideology

Ideology is another indicator of voting behavior. A significant percentage of Americans today identify themselves as moderates. Recent polls indicate that 44 percent of Americans consider themselves to be moderates, 22 percent consider themselves liberals, and 34 percent identify themselves as conservatives.

For many Americans, where they fall in the political spectrum is a strong indicator of how they will vote: liberals vote for Democrats, and conservatives vote for Republicans. The large numbers of Americans who fall in the political center do not adhere strictly to an ideology. In most elections, the candidates compete aggressively for these voters because they know their "base"—on the left or right—is secure.

THE VITAL CENTER In 1949, historian Arthur Schlesinger, Jr., described the position between the political extremes as the **vital center.** The center is vital because without it, necessary compromises may be difficult, if not impossible, to achieve. One problem with activating the vital center is that voter apathy and low voter turnout are found most commonly among those in the center. The most motivated voters are the "ideologically zealous."[9]

IDEOLOGY IN THE 2008 ELECTIONS According to 2008 exit polls, 89 percent of voters who identified themselves as liberals voted for Barack Obama, who also received the votes of 20 percent of self-identified conservatives. Obama carried self-described moderates by 60 percent to 49 percent, a result that was crucial to his victory.

Solid South A term used to describe the tendency of the southern states to vote Democratic after the Civil War.

vital center The center of the political spectrum; those who hold moderate political views. The center is vital because without it, it may be difficult, if not impossible, to reach the compromises that are necessary to a political system's continuity.

These figures raise some interesting questions. John McCain tried very hard to portray Obama as "too liberal," and to a certain extent he succeeded. Among all voters, 42 percent thought that Obama was too liberal, compared with 50 percent who thought that his positions were about right. Only 4 percent of those questioned thought that he was too conservative. In another poll, average respondents believed that McCain's ideological positions were closer to their own than Obama's. Still, a majority of these voters supported Obama.

It is clear from these results that there are limits to the power of ideology to determine election outcomes. Many moderate and even some conservative voters supported Obama because they thought he was better suited to be president—regardless of ideology. In this sense, Obama won the support of the vital center.

Voting patterns often depend on geography. Usually, states in the South, the Great Plains, and parts of the Rocky Mountains vote Republican.

AP Photo/Harry Cabluck

AMERICA AT ODDS *Public Opinion and Voting*

At the time the Constitution was drafted, the phrase *public opinion* meant something quite different from what it means today. At that time, the "public" referred to a narrow sphere of elite, educated gentlemen. According to John Randolph in a 1774 political pamphlet, "When I mention the public, I mean to include only the rational part of it. The ignorant vulgar are as unfit to judge of the modes, as they are unable to manage the reins of government."[10] During the 1800s, this elitist view gave way to one that included all white men as part of the "public," and public opinion came to be regarded as "the vital principle underlying American government, society, and culture."[11] Today, the public opinion of all adults remains a "vital principle" throughout the political sphere.

The framers of the U.S. Constitution left the power to establish voting qualifications to the individual states. Under that arrangement, initially only property-owning white males were able to vote. As discussed in this chapter, over time the franchise was extended to other groups, and now all Americans over the age of eighteen—with certain exceptions, such as felons—have the right to vote. Typically, however, only around one-half of voting-age Americans actually do vote. The fact that voter turnout among older Americans is higher than among younger Americans clearly has an effect on the policies adopted by our government, as does the relatively low turnout among poorer and disadvantaged groups of Americans. Because the views of the latter groups tend to be more liberal than conservative, liberal Democrats have been in the forefront of efforts to increase voter turnout among these groups.

ISSUES FOR DEBATE & DISCUSSION

1. **Some Americans argue that all states should implement vote-by-mail systems for all elections. Vote-by-mail systems would increase voter participation; allow voters more time for deliberation; avoid the problems caused by voting equipment, including the new electronic voting systems; and provide for accurate vote counting. Additionally, the blitz of last-minute, largely negative advertising before elections would likely be reduced because many mail-in voters would have already sent in their ballots two or three weeks before the election. Opponents of mail-in voting contend that going to the polling place on Election Day generates political energy and facilitates personal contact with other concerned citizens. These critics also point out that mail-in voting would allow voters to be strongly influenced by their families or friends. Finally, this group believes that voting by mail would almost certainly increase fraudulent voting during elections. Where do you stand on this issue?**
2. **Many Americans believe that our government representatives, when creating policies, should be guided by the public's views on the issues at hand. After all, in a democracy, the elected leaders should ensure that their decisions are consistent with the will of the citizenry. Others contend that elected officials should not be led by public opinion but by their own expertise and convictions in a given policy area. Consider that racial segregation was at one time supported by a majority of Americans. Was segregation therefore a reasonable policy? Where do you stand on this issue?**

TAKE ACTION

"Citizens at the polls are the most powerful agents of change." Thus say political analysts Thomas Mann and Norman Ornstein.[12] But if citizens are not informed about the political issues of the day or the candidates' qualifications, there is little sense in going to the polls. Indeed, as mentioned in this chapter, one of the reasons for the relatively low voter turnout in this country is a sense on the part of some citizens that they lack information. As also noted, peer groups are important in the political socialization process. But just as you might be influenced by your peers, you can also influence them.

If you would like to take action to increase interest in our political life, one thing you might do is host a political salon. This would be a gathering, either in your home or at some other place, that would focus on learning about political issues and opinions. You could invite friends, other students, co-workers, or other persons who might be interested to attend the salon, which could be held weekly, monthly, or at some other interval. At the first meeting, you could set the "rules" for the salon. What topics do you want to discuss? How much time do you want to devote to each topic? What reading or research, if any, should be undertaken before the meetings? Depending on the views and energies of those who attend the salon, you might also devise an activist agenda to increase voter turnout. For example, you could plan a get-out-the-vote drive for the next election.

POLITICS ON THE WEB

- Recent polls conducted and analyzed by the Roper Center for Public Opinion Research can be found at **www.ropercenter.uconn.edu**
- American National Election Studies (ANES) is a good source of information on public opinion. To reach this site, go to **www.electionstudies.org**
- At the Gallup Organization's Web site, you can find the results of recent polls, as well as an archive of past polls and information on how polls are conducted. Go to **www.gallup.com**
- You can find poll data and material on major issues at the following site: **www.publicagenda.org**
- In addition to its enormous collection of recent articles on politics, the Real Clear Politics Web site has one of the most comprehensive collections of election polls available. For the polls, go to **www.realclearpolitics.com/polls**
- PBS features a section on its Web site titled "PBS by the People," which provides some good tips on how to analyze a poll. Go to **www.pbs.org/elections/savvyanalyze.html**

Online resources for this chapter

This text's Companion Web site, at **www.4ltrpress.cengage.com/govt**, offers links to numerous resources that you can use to learn more about the topics covered in this chapter.

Ken Seet/Flame/Corbis

Campaigns and Elections

LEARNING OBJECTIVES

LO1 Explain how elections are held and how the electoral college functions in presidential elections.

LO2 Discuss how candidates are nominated.

LO3 Indicate what is involved in launching a political campaign today, and describe the structure and functions of a campaign organization.

LO4 Describe how the Internet has transformed political campaigns.

LO5 Summarize the laws that regulate campaign financing and the role of money in modern political campaigns.

LO6 Describe what took place during recent presidential elections and what these events tell us about the American electoral system.

AMERICA AT ODDS

Are Early Primaries Really Such a Bad Thing?

Campaigning to become the presidential candidate of either major party used to be a relatively clear-cut affair. The Iowa caucuses came first, then the New Hampshire primary. A few states would hold their primaries in February; others would vote in March and April. The "stragglers" would hold their primaries in May and June.

The "stragglers," however, began to realize that they no longer counted in choosing the major parties' candidates because they held their primaries so late. Therefore, state after state moved its primary election date toward the beginning of the year. In the most recent presidential primary season, a majority of the states, controlling a majority of the delegates to the national party conventions, held their primary contests in the three weeks between January 14 and February 5. More than twenty primaries were held on February 5 alone. It is no wonder that the presidential campaign had already been under way for a full year when the Iowa caucuses were held on January 3.

Many political observers contend that having so many primaries so early has defeated the purpose of the primary season. It is no longer a season, these critics say, but is more like a one-inning baseball game. Others are not so sure.

Candidates Cannot Present Themselves Properly if the Primary Season Is Short

One major complaint about having primaries in so many states in January and February is that candidates cannot campaign in all of these states. Furthermore, it may no longer be possible for a "dark horse" to come from behind and surprise everyone, eventually becoming a major party's presidential candidate. After all, early primaries could mean that by February 5, one candidate would already have enough convention delegates to become the candidate. That's only thirty-three days after the January 3 Iowa caucuses.

In our political system, parties are loose affiliations of people whose views may differ considerably. As a result, it can be hard to assess the many candidates running in each party. This is not something that should be done in just a few weeks. Inevitably, the early primaries have created a two-year presidential campaign. In 2007, the many presidential hopefuls engaged in a variety of debates, events, and fund-raisers.

Big sums have to be raised much earlier than in the past. By the end of the first quarter of 2007, candidates had already raised a third as much in campaign funds as their counterparts did during the entire 1996 campaign. Never before have we seen so much money-chasing begin so early.

An Early Primary Season Means a Longer General Election Campaign

Those in favor of the early primary season argue that as a result, much more time can be spent campaigning in the general elections. Why not give the voters the most exposure possible to the major candidates before the general elections? In European countries, for example, a political party's entire set of potential cabinet members is usually decided well before a national election, sometimes years in advance. Politicians have plenty of time to make their mark on public opinion.

Also, early primaries do not necessarily mean that one party's candidate can wrap up the nomination early in the year. Witness what happened in the Democratic Party in the last election. Hillary Clinton entered the primaries expecting an easy victory, but Barack Obama matched her effort, and the campaign lasted longer than any in decades. During these many months, voters in the straggler states saw far more of the two Democratic candidates than voters in the states that held their primaries early. Ultimately, of course, Obama prevailed.

Critics of the early primaries argue that this system favors politicians who have high name recognition and big bankrolls. Yet on the basis of the 2008 experience, that argument does not appear to hold water. Barack Obama overcame such obstacles as lesser name recognition. On the Republican side, John McCain, the winner, was not the candidate who started with the most campaign funds.

WHERE DO YOU STAND?

1. **Do you believe that it is better to have more campaign time devoted to the primaries than the general election? Or should it be the other way around? Why?**
2. **What would be the effect on the campaigns if the national parties took complete control of the primary elections calendar and scheduled a series of regional primaries at regular intervals?**

EXPLORE THIS ISSUE ONLINE

- **Anyone interested in alternative voting systems and how they might influence the political process should visit the FairVote Web site at www.fairvote.com.**
- **The Pew Center on the States sponsors a Web site devoted to elections reform at www.electionline.org.**

Introduction

During elections, candidates vie to become representatives of the people in both national and state offices. The population of the United States is now more than 300 million. Clearly, all citizens who are eligible to vote cannot gather in one place to make laws and run the government. We have to choose representatives to govern the nation and to act on behalf of our interests. We accomplish this through popular elections.

Campaigning for election has become an arduous task for every politician. As you will see in this chapter, American campaigns are long, complicated, and very expensive undertakings. They can also be wearing on the citizens who are not running for office. In particular, as you read in the chapter-opening *America at Odds* feature, some people believe that the existing system of presidential primary elections creates problems for candidates and voters alike. Yet America's campaigns are an important part of our political process because it is through campaigns that citizens learn about the candidates and decide how they will cast their votes.

LO1 *How We Elect Candidates*

The ultimate goal of a political campaign and the associated fund-raising efforts is, of course, winning the election. The most familiar kind of election is the **general election,** which is a regularly scheduled election held in even-numbered years on the Tuesday after the first Monday in November. During general elections, the voters decide who will be the U.S. president, vice president, and senators and representatives in Congress. The president and vice president are elected every four years, senators every six years, and representatives every two years. General elections are also held to choose state and local government officials, often at the same time as those for national offices. A **special election** is held at the state or local level when the voters must decide an issue before the next general election or when vacancies occur by reason of death or resignation.

Types of Ballots

Since 1888, all states in the United States have used the **Australian ballot**—a secret ballot that is prepared, distributed, and counted by government officials at public expense. Two variations of the Australian ballot are used today. Most states use the **party-column ballot** (also called the Indiana ballot), which lists all of a party's candidates together in a single column under the party label. In some states, the party-column ballot allows voters to vote for all of a party's candidates for local, state, and national offices by making a single "X" or pulling a single lever. The major parties favor this ballot form because it encourages straight-ticket voting.

Other states use the **office-block ballot,** (also called the Massachusetts ballot) which lists together all of the candidates for each

This voter casts her secret ballot in the 2008 primaries on Super Tuesday.

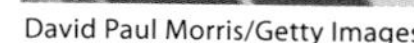

David Paul Morris/Getty Images

general election A regularly scheduled election to choose the U.S. president, vice president, and senators and representatives in Congress. General elections are held in even-numbered years on the Tuesday after the first Monday in November.

special election An election that is held at the state or local level when the voters must decide an issue before the next general election or when vacancies occur by reason of death or resignation.

Australian ballot A secret ballot that is prepared, distributed, and counted by government officials at public expense; used by all states in the United States since 1888.

party-column ballot A ballot (also called the Indiana ballot) that lists all of a party's candidates under the party label. Voters can vote for all of a party's candidates for local, state, and national offices by making a single "X" or pulling a single lever.

office-block ballot A ballot (also called the Massachusetts ballot) that lists together all of the candidates for each office.

poll watcher A representative from one of the political parties who is allowed to monitor a polling place to make sure that the election is run fairly and to avoid fraud.

elector A member of the electoral college.

electoral college The group of electors who are selected by the voters in each state to elect officially the president and vice president. The number of electors in each state is equal to the number of that state's representatives in both chambers of Congress.

winner-take-all system A system in which the candidate who receives the most votes wins. In contrast, proportional systems allocate votes to multiple winners.

office. Parties tend to dislike the office-block ballot because it places more emphasis on the office than on the party and thus encourages split-ticket voting.

Conducting Elections and Counting the Votes

Recall from Chapter 8 that local units of government, such as cities, are divided into smaller voting districts, or precincts. Within each precinct, voters cast their ballots at one polling place.

An election board supervises the polling place and the voting process in each precinct. The board sets hours for the polls to be open according to the laws of the state and sees that ballots or voting machines are available. In most states, the board provides the list of registered voters and makes certain that only qualified voters cast ballots in each precinct. When the polls close, staff members count the votes and report the results, usually to the county clerk or the board of elections. Representatives from each party, called **poll watchers,** are allowed at each polling place to make sure the election is run fairly and to avoid fraud.

Presidential Elections and the Electoral College

When citizens vote for president and vice president, they are not voting directly for the candidates. Instead, they are voting for **electors** who will cast their ballots in the **electoral college.** The electors are selected during each presidential election year by the states' political parties, subject to the laws of the state. Each state has as many electoral votes as it has U.S. senators and representatives (see Figure 9–1). In addition, there are three electors from the District of Columbia, even though it is not a state. Should D.C. also have the right to a representative with a full vote in the House of Representatives? We look at that question in this chapter's *Join the Debate* feature on the facing page.

The electoral college system is primarily a **winner-take-all system,** in which the candidate who receives the largest popular vote in a state is credited with all that state's electoral votes. The only exceptions are Maine and Nebraska.[1]

Figure 9–1

State Electoral Votes in 2004 and 2008

This map of the United States is distorted to show the relative weights of the states in terms of their electoral votes in 2004 and 2008, following changes required by the 2000 census. A candidate must win 270 electoral votes, cast by the electors, to become president through the electoral college system.

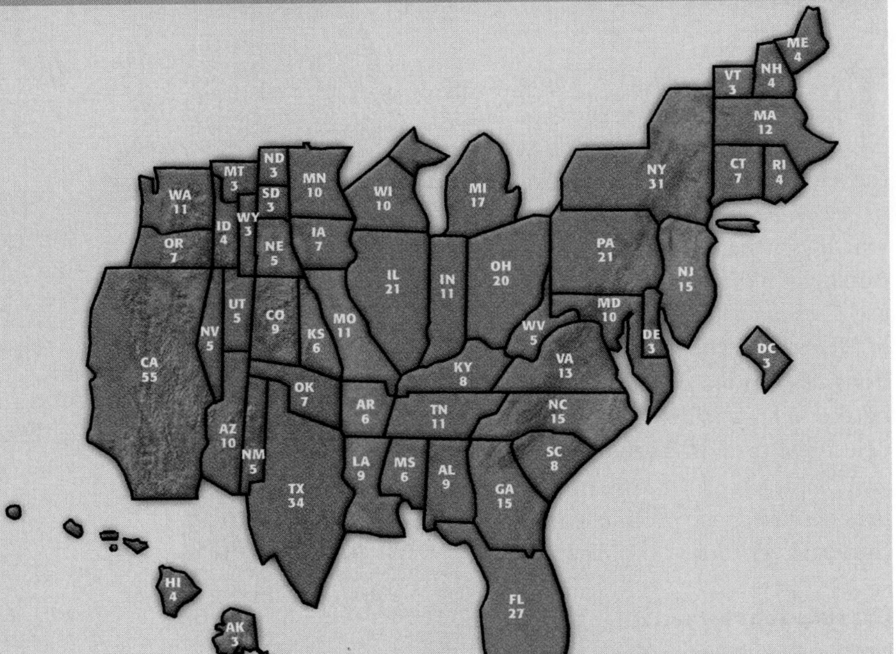

JOIN THE DEBATE

Should D.C. Residents Have a Representative?

If you are a resident of Washington, D.C., you can vote for president. You also can vote for a delegate who sits in the House of Representatives. That delegate, though, is not a full member. She or he cannot vote on any issues that come before the full House. The District of Columbia has no voting representation in Congress.

It's Only Fair

Back in 1978, Congress approved a constitutional amendment that would have provided the District with two senators and a representative. The amendment was never ratified. In 2009, Congress debated the D.C. Voting Rights Act. That act would make the District's current delegate a voting member of the House.

Such a change seems quite fair, especially to those who live in the District. After all, everybody else who lives in the fifty states is represented by a voting member of the House (and two senators to boot). Whether or not granting full voting privileges to the delegate from the District is fair, one thing is certain. Any representative from D.C. will probably be a Democrat. Why? Because the District has an African American majority, and African Americans for many years have been the Democrats' most loyal supporters.

Please Respect the Constitution

On the other side of the debate are those who argue that the U.S. Constitution simply does not allow District residents to have a voting member in the House. The framers of the Constitution deliberately established the federal capital as a non-state over which Congress would have exclusive legislative authority. Article I, Section 8, Clause 17, provides for the creation of a permanent "Seat of Government of the United States," located in a "District." This geographic and political entity has become Washington, D.C., a territory of sixty-eight square miles that has been the nation's capital since 1800.

The Constitution requires that House members be elected by the people of the states. The District is not a state, and therefore its residents cannot have a voting member of the House. In other words, the D.C. Voting Rights Act is unconstitutional, and the legislation could never withstand even the first judicial test of its legitimacy. Congress should not waste its time on unconstitutional measures.

AP Photo/Lauren Burke

"Taxation without representation" and statehood are perennial political issues in Washington, D.C.

Why the Real Solution Won't Work

There's an obvious solution to the D.C. representation issue: admit the District as a state. Such a proposal would work its way through Congress as ordinary legislation. It is, in fact, the solution that D.C. residents prefer. If the District became a state, it would join Wyoming as one of the most overrepresented states in the Senate. A second possible solution would be to give the District back to Maryland. The Maryland legislature would probably have to vote to accept it. As a result, though, the city of Washington would have enough people to dominate its own House district, and Washington residents could vote for Maryland's U.S. senators.

If the District were a state or part of a state, the national government would still have full authority over all federal facilities, just as it controls such facilities in the states today. What Congress would give up, however, is the right to interfere in the District's business when federal questions are not involved. Clearly, Congress finds that right too precious to lose.

For Critical Analysis *In what ways might Congress want to interfere with the government of the District? What kinds of votes by District residents might it overturn? Recall from Chapter 3 the difference between a unitary and a federal government. If the United States had a unitary government, on what issues might Congress wish to exert control over the states?*

caucus A meeting held to choose political candidates or delegates.

In December, after the general election, electors (either Republicans or Democrats, depending on which candidate has won the state's popular vote) meet in their state capitals to cast their votes for president and vice president. When the Constitution was drafted, the framers intended that the electors would use their own discretion in deciding who would make the best president. Today, however, the electors usually vote for the candidates to whom they are pledged. The electoral college ballots are then sent to the U.S. Senate, which counts and certifies them before a joint session of Congress held early in January. The candidates who receive a majority of the electoral votes are officially declared president and vice president. To be elected, a candidate must receive more than half of the 538 electoral votes available. Thus, a candidate needs 270 votes to win. If no presidential candidate gets an electoral college majority (which has happened twice—in 1800 and 1824), the House of Representatives votes on the candidates, with each state delegation casting only a single vote. If no candidate for vice president gets a majority of electoral votes, the vice president is chosen by the Senate, with each senator casting one vote.

"A politician should have three hats: ONE FOR THROWING INTO THE RING, ONE FOR TALKING THROUGH, AND ONE FOR PULLING RABBITS OUT OF IF ELECTED."

~ CARL SANDBURG ~
AMERICAN POET AND HISTORIAN
1878–1967

Even when a presidential candidate wins by a large margin in the electoral college and in the popular vote—a *landslide election*—it does not follow that the candidate has won the support of the majority of those eligible to vote. We explore this paradox in this chapter's *Perception versus Reality* feature on the facing page.

LO2 *How We Nominate Candidates*

The first step on the long road to winning an election is the nomination process. Nominations narrow the field of possible candidates and limit each political party's choice to one person. For many local government posts, which are often nonpartisan, self-nomination is the most common way to become a candidate. Such a procedure is frequently used in lightly populated areas. A self-proclaimed candidate usually files a petition to be listed on the ballot. Each state has laws that specify how many signatures a candidate must obtain to show that he or she has some public support. An alternative is to be a write-in candidate—voters write the candidate's name on the ballot on Election Day.

Candidates for major offices are rarely nominated in these ways, however. As you read in Chapter 7, most candidates for high office are nominated by a political party and receive considerable support from party activists throughout their campaigns.

Party Control over Nominations

The methods used by political parties to nominate candidates have changed during the course of American history. Broadly speaking, the process has grown more open over the years, with the involvement of ever-greater numbers of local leaders and ordinary citizens. Today, any voter can participate in choosing party candidates. This was not true as recently as 1968, however, and was certainly not possible during the first years of the republic.

George Washington was essentially unopposed in the first U.S. presidential elections in 1789—no other candidate was seriously considered in any state. By the end of Washington's eight years in office, however, political divisions among the nation's leaders had solidified into political parties, the Federalists and the Jeffersonian (or Democratic) Republicans (see Chapter 7). These early parties were organized by gatherings of important persons, who often met in secret. These meetings came to be called **caucuses.**[2] Beginning in 1800, members of Congress who belonged to the two parties held caucuses to nominate candidates for president and vice president. The Republican caucus chose Thomas Jefferson in 1800, as expected, and the Federalist caucus nominated the incumbent president, John Adams. By 1816, the Federalist Party had ceased to exist, and the Jeffersonian Republican congressional caucus was in complete control of selecting the president of the United States.

The congressional caucus system collapsed in 1824.[3] It was widely seen as undemocratic; opponents derided it as "King Caucus." A much-diminished caucus nominated a candidate who then came in third in the

PERCEPTION VERSUS REALITY

Presidents and the "Popular Vote"

Every four years, American citizens go to the polls to cast their votes for the presidential candidate of their choice. Some presidential contests are very close, such as the 2000 race between Al Gore and George W. Bush and the 2004 race between John Kerry and Bush. Others are less so, such as the one between Lyndon B. Johnson and Barry Goldwater in 1964. When a presidential candidate wins the race by a wide margin, as Johnson did, we may hear the result referred to as a *landslide election* or a *landslide victory* for the winning candidate.

The Perception

The traditional perception has been that, in general, our presidents are elected by a majority of eligible American voters. As the people's choice, the president is beholden to the wishes of the broad American electorate that voted him or her into office. A president who has been swept into office by a so-called landslide victory may claim to have received a "mandate from the people" to govern the nation. A president may assert that a certain policy or program she or he endorsed in campaign speeches is backed by popular support simply because she or he was elected to office by a majority of the voters.

The Reality

In reality, the "popular vote" is not all that popular, in the sense of representing the wishes of a majority of American citizens who are eligible to vote. In fact, the president of the United States has never received the votes of a majority of all eligible adults. Lyndon Johnson, in 1964, came the closest of any president in history to gaining the votes of a majority of the eligible public, and even he won the votes of less than 40 percent of those citizens who were eligible to cast a ballot.

The hotly contested presidential elections of 2000 and 2004 were divisive, leaving the millions of Americans who had voted for the losing candidates unhappy with the results. Indeed, in winning the elections of 2000 and 2004, Bush received the votes of a mere 26.0 percent and 30.5 percent of those with the right to vote, respectively. Nonetheless, Bush assumed that his reelection was a signal from the American people to push his controversial domestic ideas, such as Social Security reform, as well as an endorsement of his foreign policy and the war on terrorism. Yet 69.5 percent of the electorate did not vote for him. Even though Barack Obama did better, slightly less than one-third of all Americans who are eligible to vote gave him their support.

AP Photo

Lyndon B. Johnson came the closest of any candidate ever to winning a majority of the votes of all citizens eligible to cast a ballot. Even then, though, he received less than 40 percent of the votes of all eligible citizens.

It is useful to keep these figures in mind whenever a president claims to have received a mandate from the people. The truth is, no president has ever been elected with sufficient popular backing to make this a serious claim.

Blog On *Dave Leip's Atlas of U.S. Presidential Elections hosts a major discussion site at* **www.uselectionatlas.org**, *where hundreds of guests discuss election results. You can find detailed figures to back up your arguments elsewhere on Dave's site, along with an electoral college calculator that lets you figure out how many electoral votes a candidate will receive if he or she carries a particular share of the states.*

nominating convention An official meeting of a political party to choose its candidates. Nominating conventions at the state and local levels also select delegates to represent the citizens of their geographic areas at a higher-level party convention.

delegate A person selected to represent the people of one geographic area at a party convention.

primary election An election in which voters choose the candidates of their party, who will then run in the general election.

direct primary An election held within each of the two major parties—Democratic and Republican—to choose the party's candidates for the general election. Voters choose the candidate directly, rather than through delegates.

electoral vote. The other three major candidates were essentially self-nominated.[4] The four candidates split the electoral vote so completely that the House of Representatives had to decide the contest. It picked John Quincy Adams, even though Andrew Jackson had won more popular and electoral votes.

The Party Nominating Convention

In the run-up to the 1828 elections, two new parties grew up around the major candidates. Adams's supporters called themselves the National Republicans (later known as the Whigs). Jackson's supporters organized as the Democratic Party, which won the election. In 1832, both parties settled on a new method of choosing candidates for president and vice president—the national nominating convention. A number of state parties had already adopted the convention system for choosing state-level candidates. New Jersey held conventions as early as 1800.

A **nominating convention** is an official meeting of a political party to choose its candidates. Those who attend the convention are called **delegates,** and they are chosen to represent the people of a particular geographic area. Conventions can take place at multiple levels. A county convention might choose delegates at a state convention. The state convention in turn might select delegates to the national convention. By 1840, the convention system was the most common method of nominating political party candidates at the state and national levels.

While the convention system drew in a much broader range of leaders than had the caucus, it was not a particularly democratic institution. Convention delegates were rarely chosen by a vote of the party's local members. Typically, they were appointed by local party officials, who were often, with good reason, called bosses. These local leaders often gained their positions in ways that were far from democratic. Not until 1972 did ordinary voters in all states gain the right to select delegates to the national presidential nominating conventions.

Primary Elections and the Loss of Party Control

The corruption that so often accompanied the convention system led reformers to call for a new way to choose candidates—the **primary election,** in which voters go to the polls to decide among candidates who seek the nomination of their party. Candidates who win a primary election then go on to compete against the candidates from other parties in the general election. The first primary election may have been held in 1842 by Democrats in Crawford County, Pennsylvania. The technique was not widely used, however, until the end of the nineteenth century and the beginning of the twentieth. These were years in which reform was a popular cause.

DIRECT AND INDIRECT PRIMARIES The rules for conducting primary elections are highly variable, and a number of different types of primaries exist. One major distinction is between a direct primary and an indirect primary. In a **direct primary,** voters cast their ballots directly for candidates. In an *indirect primary,* voters choose delegates, who in turn choose the candidates. The delegates may be pledged to a particular candidate but sometimes run as *unpledged delegates.* The major parties use indirect primaries to elect delegates to the national nominating conventions that choose candidates for president and vice president. The elections that nominate candidates for Congress and for state or local offices are almost always direct primaries.

THE ROLE OF THE STATES Primary elections are normally conducted by state governments. States set the dates and conduct the elections. They provide polling places, election officials, and registration lists, and they then count the votes. By sponsoring the primaries, state governments have obtained considerable influence over the rules by which the primaries are conducted. The power of the states is limited, however, by the parties' First Amendment right to freedom of association, a right that has been repeatedly confirmed by the United States Supreme Court.[5] On occasion, parties that object to the rules imposed by state governments have opted out of the state-sponsored primary system altogether.[6] Note that third parties typically do not participate in state-sponsored primaries, but hold nominating conventions instead. The major parties rarely opt out of

AP Photo/Mary Ann Chastain

During the latest presidential primaries, there were three main Republican hopefuls: former Massachusetts Governor Mitt Romney (left), Arizona Senator John McCain (center), and former Arkansas Governor Mike Huckabee (right).

AP Photo/John Raoux

The final two contenders for the Democratic presidential nomination were Illinois Senator Barack Obama and New York Senator Hillary Clinton. Both candidates represented historical firsts for a major party.

state elections, however, because the financial—and political—costs of going it alone are high. (When primary elections are used to choose candidates for local *nonpartisan* positions, state control is uncontested.)

INSURGENT CANDIDATES Primary elections were designed to take nominations out of the hands of the party bosses, and indeed, the most important result of the primary system has been to dramatically reduce the power of elected and party officials over the nominating process. Ever since primary elections were established, the insurgent candidate who runs against the party "establishment" has been a common phenomenon. Running against the "powers that be" is often a very effective campaign strategy, and many insurgents have won victories at the local, state, and national levels.

Insurgent campaigns often replace incumbent leaders who are out of touch with the party rank and file, sometimes because the incumbents are too liberal or too conservative. Occasionally, an insurgent's platform is strikingly different from that of the party as a whole. Yet even when an insurgent's politics are abhorrent to the rest of the party—for example, an insurgent might make an outright appeal to racism—the party has no way of denying the insurgent the right to the party label in the general election.

OPEN AND CLOSED PRIMARIES Primaries can be classified as closed or open. In a **closed primary,** only party members can vote to choose that party's candidates, and they may vote only in the primary of their own party. Thus, only registered Democrats can vote in the Democratic primary to select candidates of the Democratic Party. Only registered Republicans can vote for the Republican candidates. A person usually establishes party membership when she or he registers to vote. Some states have a *semiclosed* primary, which allows voters to register with a party or change their party affiliations on Election Day. Regular party workers favor the closed primary because it promotes party loyalty. Independent voters usually oppose it because it forces them to select a party if they wish to participate in the nominating process.

In an **open primary,** voters can vote for a party's candidates regardless of whether they belong to the party. In most open primaries, all voters receive both a Republican ballot and a Democratic ballot. Voters then choose either the Democratic or the Republican ballot in the privacy of the voting booth. In a *semiopen* primary, voters request the ballot for the party of their choice.

The fifty states have developed dozens of variations on the open and closed primary plans. In some states, primaries are closed only to persons registered to another party, and independents can vote in either primary. In several states, an independent who votes in

closed primary A primary in which only party members can vote to choose that party's candidates.

open primary A primary in which voters can vote for a party's candidates regardless of whether they belong to the party.

AP Photo/Harry Cabluck

Texas Democrats convened in 2008 to divide caucus delegates between presidential hopefuls Barack Obama and Hillary Clinton. The Texas delegate selection system culminated at the state Democratic convention in June.

a party primary is automatically enrolled in that party; in other states, the voter remains an independent. The two major parties often have different rules. For example, in two states, the Democrats allow independents to vote in the primaries, but the Republicans do not.

Until 2000, California and a few other states employed a *blanket primary,* in which voters could choose candidates of more than one party. In that year, however, the Supreme Court ruled that the blanket primary violated the parties' right to freedom of association.[7] Louisiana has for many years had a unique system in which all candidates participate in the same primary, regardless of party. The two candidates receiving the most votes then proceed on to the general election. In 2008, Louisiana abandoned this system for the U.S. House and Senate, but kept it for state and local offices.

Nominating Presidential Candidates

In some respects, being nominated for president is more difficult than being elected. The nominating process narrows a very large number of hopefuls down to a single candidate from each party. Choosing a presidential candidate is unlike nominating candidates for any other office. One reason for this is that the nomination process combines several different methods.

PRESIDENTIAL PRIMARIES Most of the states hold presidential primaries, beginning early in the election year. For a candidate, a good showing in the early primaries results in plenty of media attention as television networks and newspaper reporters play up the results. Subsequent state primaries tend to serve as contests to eliminate unlikely candidates. Sometimes, the political parties have tried to manipulate primary dates to maximize their candidates' media attention. The order and timing of primary dates also influence the candidates' fund-raising.

The presidential primaries do not necessarily follow the same rules the states use for nominating candidates for the U.S. Congress or for state and local offices. Often, the presidential primaries are not held on the same date as the other primaries. States frequently hold the presidential primaries early in hopes of exercising greater influence on the outcome.

CAUCUSES The caucus system is an alternative to primary elections. Strictly speaking, the caucus system is a convention system. The caucuses are party conventions held at the local level that elect delegates to conventions at the county or congressional district level. These mid-level conventions then choose the delegates to the state convention, which finally elects the delegates to the national party convention. Unlike the caucuses of two centuries ago, modern caucuses are open to all party members. It is not hard to join a party. At the famous Iowa caucuses, you become a party member simply by attending a local caucus.

While some states, such as Iowa and Minnesota, rely on the caucus/convention system to nominate candidates for state and local positions, the system is more frequently used only to choose delegates to the Democratic and Republican national conventions. Most states with presidential caucuses use primaries to nominate state and local candidates. Twelve states choose national convention delegates through caucuses. Four states use caucuses to allocate some of the national convention delegates and use primaries to allocate the others.

PRIMARIES—THE RUSH TO BE FIRST Traditionally, states have held their presidential primaries at various times over the first six months of a presidential election year. In an effort to make their primaries prominent in the media and influential in the political process, however, many states have moved the date of their primary to earlier in the year—a practice known as *front-loading.* In 1988, a group of southern states created a "Super Tuesday" by holding their primaries on the same day in early March. Then, many states in the Midwest, New England, and the West Coast (including California) moved their primaries to an earlier date, too.

After Illinois Senator Barack Obama became the Democratic Party candidate, he chose Delaware Senator Joe Biden as his vice-presidential running mate.

The practice of front-loading primaries has gained momentum over the last decade. The states with later primary dates found that most nominations were decided early in the season, leaving their voters "out of the action." As more states moved up their primary dates, however, the early primaries became even more important, and other states, to compete, also moved up their primaries.

This rush to be first was particularly notable in the year or so preceding the 2008 presidential primaries. By 2007, about half the states had moved their primaries to earlier dates. Many of these states opted for February 5—or "Super-Super Tuesday," as some called it—as the date for their primaries.

THE IMPACT OF FRONT-LOADING

Many Americans worried that with a shortened primary season, long-shot candidates would no longer be able to propel themselves into serious contention by doing well in small, early-voting states, such as New Hampshire and Iowa. Traditionally, for example, a candidate who had a successful showing in the New Hampshire primary had time to obtain enough financial backing to continue in the race. The fear was that an accelerated schedule of presidential primaries would favor the richest candidates.

In practice, front-loading did not have this effect in 2008. On the Republican side, the early primaries might have benefited a front-runner—if there had been a Republican front-runner in January 2008. As it happened, the candidate with the most funds, former Massachusetts governor Mitt Romney, did not win the most votes. After February 5, Arizona senator John McCain had a clear lead. The Republican primaries were mostly conducted on a winner-take-all basis, a rule that allowed McCain to wrap up the nomination on March 4.

The Democrats, however, allocated delegates on a proportional basis, so that each candidate received delegates based on his or her share of the vote. That rule made an early decision impossible, and Barack Obama did not obtain a majority of the Democratic delegates until June 3. As a result, many of the most important Democratic primaries took place late in the season. States that had moved their primaries to February 5 discovered that they were lost in the crowd of early contests. Front-loading, in other words, had become counterproductive.

After Arizona Senator John McCain became the Republican Party's presidential candidate, he chose relatively unknown Alaskan Governor Sarah Palin as his vice-presidential running mate.

NATIONAL PARTY CONVENTIONS Born in the 1830s, the American national political convention is unique in Western democracies. Elsewhere, candidates for prime minister or chancellor are chosen within the confines of party councils. That is actually the way the framers wanted it done—the Constitution does not mention nominating conventions. Indeed, Thomas Jefferson feared that if the presidential race became a popularity contest, it would develop into "mobocracy."

At one time, the conventions were indeed often giant free-for-alls. It wasn't always clear who the winning presidential and vice-presidential candidates would be until the delegates voted. As more states opted to hold presidential primaries, however, the drama of national conventions diminished. Today, the conventions have been described as massive pep rallies. Nonetheless, each convention's task remains a serious one. In late summer, two thousand to three thousand delegates gather at each convention to represent the wishes of the voters and political leaders of their home states. They adopt the official party platform and declare their support for the party's presidential and vice-presidential candidates.

On the first day of the convention, delegates hear the reports of the **Credentials Committee,** which inspects each prospective delegate's claim to be seated as a legitimate representative of her or his state. When the eligibility of delegates is in question, the committee decides who will be seated. In the evening, there is usually a keynote speaker to whip up enthusiasm among the delegates. The second day includes committee reports and debates on the party platform. The third day is devoted to nominations and voting. Balloting begins with an alphabetical roll call in which states and territories announce their votes. By midnight, the convention's real work is over, and the presidential candidate has been selected. The vice-presidential nomination and the acceptance speeches occupy the fourth day.

Some people have complained that the national conventions are now little more than prolonged infomercials. In recent years, the major broadcast networks (ABC, CBS, NBC, and Fox) have covered only the most important speeches and events, although gavel-to-gavel coverage has been available on several cable channels. For millions of voters, however, the conventions are an invaluable opportunity to learn about the two major tickets. In 2008, more than 42 million people watched Barack Obama's acceptance speech, and John McCain's numbers may have been even higher. Alaska governor Sarah Palin, the Republican vice-presidential nominee, drew an audience of at least 37 million people who were eager to see a candidate who had previously been little known outside her home state. Following each of the two conventions, the party in question received a substantial, if temporary, boost in the polls.

Credentials Committee
A committee of each national political party that evaluates the claims of national party convention delegates to be the legitimate representatives of their states.

"THERE IS NO EXCITEMENT anywhere in the world . . . to match the excitement of an American presidential campaign."

~ THEODORE H. WHITE ~
AMERICAN JOURNALIST AND HISTORIAN
1915–1986

LO3 *The Modern Political Campaign*

Once nominated, candidates focus on their campaigns. The term *campaign* originated in the military context. Generals mounted campaigns, using their scarce resources (soldiers and materials) to achieve military objectives. Using the term in a political context is apt. In a political campaign, candidates also use scarce resources (time and funds) in an attempt to defeat their adversaries in the battle to win votes.

Responsibilities of the Campaign Staff

To run a successful campaign, the candidate's campaign staff must be able to raise funds for the effort, get media coverage, produce and pay for political ads, schedule the candidate's time effectively with constituent groups and potential supporters, convey the candidate's position on the issues, conduct research on the opposing candidate, and get the voters to go to the polls. When party identification was stronger and TV campaigning was still in its infancy, a strong party organization on the local, state, or national level could furnish most of the services and expertise that the candidate needed. Less effort was spent on advertising each candidate's position and character, because the party label communicated that information to many of the voters.

Today, party labels are no longer as important as they once were. In part, this is because fewer people identify with the major parties, as evidenced by the rising number of independent voters. Instead of relying so extensively on political parties, candidates now turn to professionals to manage their campaigns.

The Professional Campaign Organization

With the rise of candidate-centered campaigns in the past two decades, the role of the political party in managing campaigns has declined. Professional **political consultants** now manage nearly all aspects of a presidential candidate's campaign. President Barack Obama, for example, relied heavily on his longtime political adviser David Axelrod in crafting his 2008 election victory. Most candidates for governor, the House, and the Senate also rely on consultants. Political consultants generally specialize in a particular area of the campaign, such as researching the opposition, conducting polls, developing the candidate's advertising, or organizing "get out the vote" efforts. Nonetheless, most candidates have a campaign manager who coordinates and plans the **campaign strategy.** Figure 9–2 on the next page shows a typical presidential campaign organization. The political party also continues to play an important role in recruiting volunteers and getting out the vote.

A major development in contemporary American politics is the focus on reaching voters through effective use of the media, particularly television. At least half of the budget for a major political campaign is consumed by television advertising. Media consultants are therefore pivotal members of the campaign staff. The nature of political advertising is discussed in more detail in Chapter 10.

In recent years, the Internet has become a political playing field that is in some ways more important than any other. Candidates such as Barack Obama have parlayed their Internet strength into powerful, well-funded campaigns. In this chapter's *The Rest of the World* feature on page 15, we describe how American campaigning techniques, especially use of the Internet, have impressed young visitors from Europe. In the next section, we discuss the use of the Internet in political campaigns.

LO4 *The Internet Campaign*

Over the years, political leaders have benefited from understanding and using new communications technologies. In the 1930s, command of a new medium—radio—gave President Franklin D. Roosevelt an advantage. In 1960, Democratic presidential candidate John F. Kennedy gained an edge on Republican Richard Nixon because Kennedy had a better understanding of the visual requirements of television. Today, the ability to make effective use of e-mail and the Web is essential to a candidate. In the 2008 presidential elections, Barack Obama gained a margin over his rivals in part because of his use of the new technologies. His team relied on the Internet for several tasks, which included fund-raising, targeting potential supporters, and creating local political organizations.

Fund-Raising on the Internet

Internet fund-raising grew out of an earlier technique: the direct-mail campaign. In direct mailings, campaigns send solicitations to large numbers of likely prospects, typically seeking contributions. Developing good lists of prospects is central to an effective direct-mail operation. Postage, printing, and the rental of address lists push the marginal cost of each additional letter well above a dollar. Response rates are low; a 1 percent response rate is a tremendous success. In many direct-mail campaigns, most of the funds raised are used up by the costs of the campaign itself. From the 1970s on, conservative organizations became especially adept at managing direct-mail campaigns. This expertise gave conservative causes and candidates a notable advantage over liberals.

To understand the old system is to recognize the superiority of the new one. The marginal cost of each additional e-mail message is essentially zero. Lists of prospects need not be prepared as carefully, because e-mail sent to unlikely prospects does not waste resources. E-mail fund-raising did face one problem when it was new—many people were not yet online. Today, that issue is no longer important.

HOWARD DEAN'S FUND-RAISING CAMPAIGN The new technology brought with it a change in the groups that benefited the most. Conservatives were no longer the most effective fund-raisers. Instead, liberal and libertarian

political consultant A professional political adviser who, for a fee, works on an area of a candidate's campaign. Political consultants include campaign managers, pollsters, media advisers, and "get out the vote" organizers.

campaign strategy The comprehensive plan for winning an election developed by a candidate and his or her advisers. The strategy includes the candidate's position on issues, slogan, advertising plan, press events, personal appearances, and other aspects of the campaign.

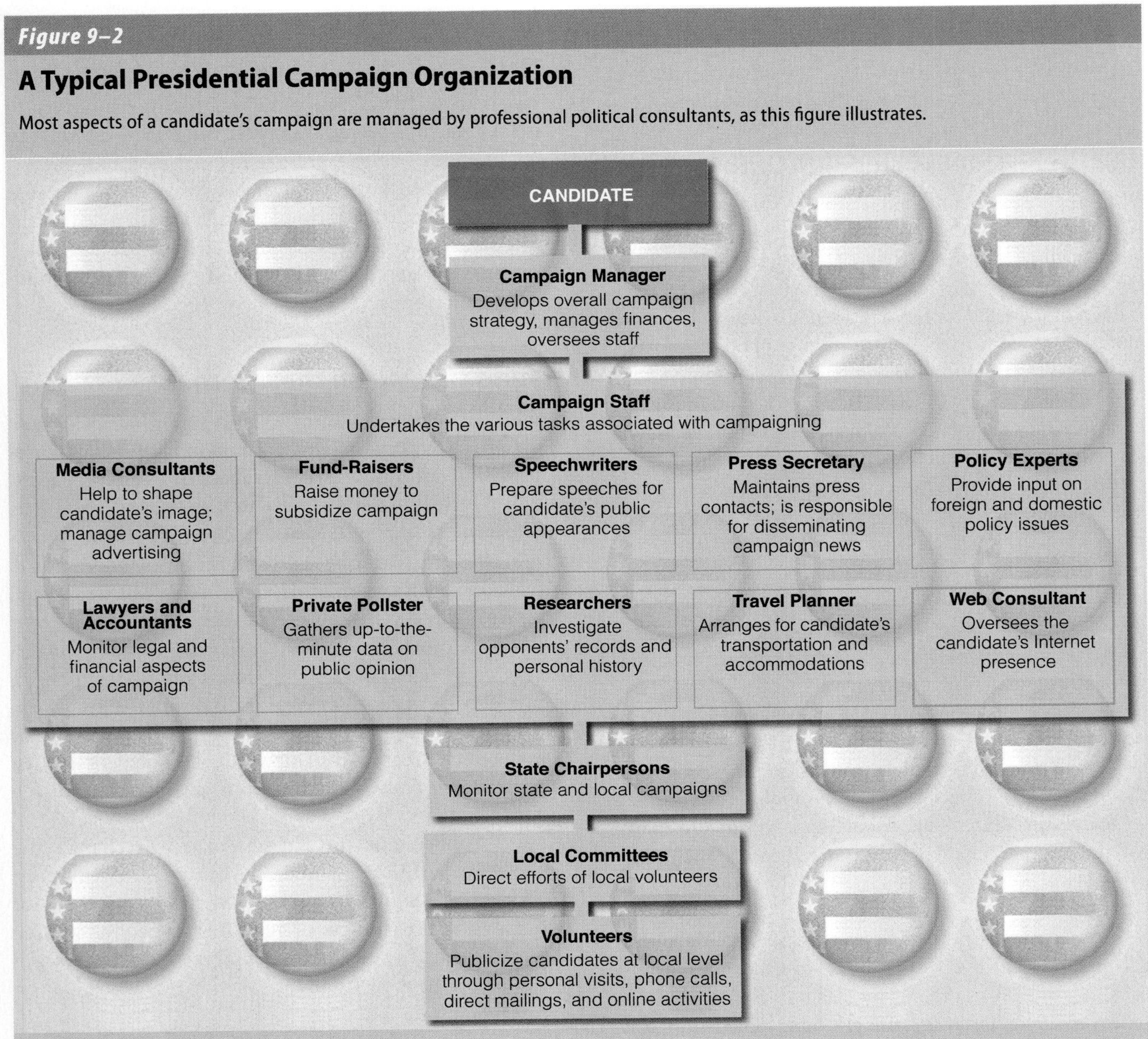

Figure 9–2

A Typical Presidential Campaign Organization

Most aspects of a candidate's campaign are managed by professional political consultants, as this figure illustrates.

organizations enjoyed some of the greatest successes. A well-known example was the 2004 presidential campaign of Howard Dean, formerly a Democratic governor of Vermont. While other presidential candidates relied heavily on contributions from wealthy, established political donors, Dean focused on collecting small donations over the Internet—his average donation was about $80. Because most donations were well under the legal limit of $2,000 per individual, Dean could continue to solicit his supporters throughout the election season. Indeed, many supporters made multiple donations. In the third quarter of 2003, Dean raised $14.8 million, at that time the largest sum ever raised by a Democratic primary candidate in a single quarter. By the time Dean ceded the nomination to Massachusetts senator John Kerry, Dean's campaign had raised about $50 million.

OBAMA ONLINE Barack Obama took Internet fund-raising to a new level during his 2008 presidential bid. One of the defining characteristics of his fund-raising was its decentralization. The Obama campaign attempted to recruit as many supporters as possible

European Students Learn U.S. Campaign Methods

Today, there's not the slightest chance that a relatively unknown politician (let alone one from a minority race) will become head of a European government. Political campaigns on the Old Continent are, well, pretty old-fashioned. Most European parties put forth seasoned political players as potential members of the nation's cabinet. Candidates for prime minister in European countries have had many years of experience in their parties and within government. The established political parties are not worried about an upstart obtaining millions of euros in campaign contributions through a savvy Internet operation. A few young Europeans going to college in the United States, however, would like to shake up the system.

Young Europeans Learn Some Valuable Lessons

Not many foreigners participate in American campaigns. During the last presidential elections, however, more young Europeans were active than ever before. Young volunteers worked not only for Barack Obama, but also for Hillary Clinton, John McCain, and Ralph Nader. Many of these volunteers were recruited by the Bertelsmann Foundation, a German nonprofit organization. Bertelsmann provided dozens of foreign students with encouragement and help that allowed them to work in U.S. presidential campaigns. Those young Europeans knocked on doors, stuffed envelopes, and answered phones.

To be sure, donations by foreign nationals to American campaigns are banned, but volunteer work is permitted. The Federal Election Commission has ruled that foreign students can engage in "uncompensated volunteer services." Still, a few foreign volunteers encountered unwelcoming attitudes from some Americans, who did not think it appropriate for them to be involved in campaigns.

The Amazing Efficacy of the Internet

What most young Europeans who joined our political campaigns noticed was how effectively volunteers used the Internet. A handful of activists in any small town in America could use Facebook and MySpace pages to gather local residents to promote a candidate. College students, more than any other group, informed themselves about political issues through the Internet. Some foreign students stated that they would take their knowledge of online social networking back to their home countries to help underdog candidates wrest control from established politicians.

Germany as an Example

German students were amazed to see American college students take an afternoon off to staff phone lines in support of their chosen candidates. They were also impressed at how engaged Americans in general were in the political process. Jenny Weinkoph, a German student at Johns Hopkins University, observed that "in Germany, our generation does not feel that they have a lot to say in political debates."

For Critical Analysis *One student observed that "European politics seems more oriented to content [issues], while in the United States the campaigns are often more about candidates' personalities." Do you think that Americans are excessively concerned with politicians' personalities? Explain.*

AP Photo/Mel Evans

These college student volunteers worked the phones at a Metuchen, New Jersey, Obama campaign office.

to act as fund-raisers who would solicit contributions from their friends and neighbors. As a result, Obama was spared much of the personal fund-raising effort that consumes the time of most national politicians. In the first half of 2007, Obama's campaign raised $58 million, $16.4 million of which was made up of donations of less than $200. The total sum was a record, and the small-donation portion was unusually large. In August 2008, the Obama campaign set another record, raising $66 million—the most ever raised in one month by a presidential campaign. By then, 2.5 million people had donated to Obama's campaign. Most of them had been contacted through the Internet.

Targeting Supporters

In 2004, President George W. Bush's chief political adviser, Karl Rove, pioneered a new campaign technique known as *microtargeting*. The process involves collecting as much information as possible about voters in a gigantic database and then filtering out various groups for special attention. Through microtargeting, for example, the Bush campaign could identify Republican prospects living in heavily Democratic neighborhoods—potential supporters whom the campaign might have neglected because the neighborhood as a whole seemed so unpromising.

"IN CONSTANT PURSUIT OF MONEY to finance campaigns, the political system is simply unable to function. Its deliberative powers are paralyzed."

~ JOHN RAWLS ~
AMERICAN EDUCATOR
1921–2000

Microtargeting could also reveal groups that might be receptive to specific appeals. For example, the Republican campaign identified a group of education-conscious Hispanic mothers in New Mexico, and it plied them with mailings and phone calls that touted Bush's No Child Left Behind legislation. Although Rove's operation frequently contacted such voters in traditional ways, much of the data necessary for microtargeting was collected through the Internet. In 2004, the Democrats had nothing to match Rove's efforts. By 2008, however, microtargeting was employed by all major candidates.

In 2008, both the Democratic and Republican general election campaigns supplemented microtargeting with a new and somewhat controversial targeting method—behavioral targeting. This technique is entirely Web-based. It uses information about people's online behavior, such as the pages they visit and the searches they make, to tailor the advertisements that they see. What is controversial about the practice is that it involves placing a cookie in the cookie folder of a person's computer, without that person's knowledge, to collect information on the person's online behavior. Later, the person may see online advertisements based on what the cookie "knows" about the person's preferences. Behavioral targeting raises privacy concerns, and both Congress and the Federal Trade Commission have held hearings on the practice.

Support for Local Organizing

Perhaps the most effective use of the Internet has been as an organizing tool. Again, Howard Dean's supporters were among the first to see the possibilities. A crucial step undertaken by the Dean campaign was to use the site Meetup.com to organize real-world meetings. In this way, Dean was able to gather supporters and bypass the existing party and activist infrastructure.

As with fund-raising, Barack Obama took Web-based organizing to a new level. In part, his campaign used existing sites such as Facebook and MySpace. By June 2008, Obama had 953,000 Facebook backers to John McCain's 142,000. He also had 394,000 supporters on MySpace, seven times McCain's total. On YouTube, Obama's videos were viewed 50 million times, compared with 4 million for McCain's. Obama's own Web site was especially important to the campaign. My.BarackObama.com eventually racked up more than a million members.

By gathering information on large numbers of potential supporters, the Obama campaign was able to create local support groups in towns and counties across the country. For example, the Obama campaign assembled a group of forty volunteers in Avery County, North Carolina, a locality in the Blue Ridge Mountains traditionally carried by Republican presidential candidates at rates of more than three to one. The volunteers were often surprised to discover that neighbors they had known for years were fellow Democrats. Several had thought they were the only Democrats in town. The group coordinated its activities by e-mail, in part because of rugged terrain and poor local cell phone reception. Obama's national Internet fund-raising success meant that he could field hundreds of paid organizers in North Carolina, some of whom supported local groups of volunteers such as this one. In the end, McCain easily carried Avery County, but Obama carried the state.[8]

LO5 *What It Costs to Win*

The modern political campaign is an expensive undertaking. Huge sums must be spent for professional campaign managers and consultants, television and radio ads, the printing of campaign literature, travel, office rent, equipment, and other necessities.

To get an idea of the cost of waging a campaign for Congress today, consider that in the 2006 election cycle, candidates for the House of Representatives and the Senate spent close to $1.3 billion. The most expensive race in 2006 was for the Senate seat representing New York. In that race, the candidates spent a total of $62.8 million, $40.8 million of which was spent by the winner, Hillary Clinton. In the 2008 cycle, even with the presidential contest soaking up much of the political funding, congressional candidates spent an estimated $2.9 billion, a new record. The most expensive 2008 senate race, in Minnesota, cost well over $40 million.

Presidential campaigns are even more costly. In 1992, Americans were stunned to learn that about $550 million had been spent in the presidential campaigns. In 2004, presidential campaign expenditures climbed to nearly $830 million. In the 2007–2008 election cycle, these costs reached about $2.4 billion, making the 2008 presidential campaigns the most expensive in history.

The high cost of campaigns gives rise to the fear that campaign contributors may be able to influence people running for office. Another possibility is that special interest groups will try to buy favored treatment from those who are elected to office. In an attempt to prevent these abuses, the government regulates campaign financing.

The Federal Election Campaign Act

Congress passed the Federal Election Campaign Act (FECA) of 1971[9] in an effort to curb irregularities and abuses in the ways political campaigns were financed. The 1971 act placed no limit on overall spending but restricted the amount that could be spent on mass media advertising, including television. It limited the amount that candidates and their families could contribute to their own campaigns and required disclosure of all contributions and expenditures of more than $100. In principle, the 1971 act limited the role of labor unions and corporations in political campaigns. Also in 1971, Congress passed a law that provided for a $1 checkoff on federal income tax returns for general campaign funds to be used by major-party presidential candidates. This law was first applied in the 1976 campaign. (Since then, the amount of the checkoff has been raised to $3.)

AMENDMENTS IN 1974 Amendments to the act passed in 1974 did the following:

- *Created the Federal Election Commission (FEC) to administer and enforce the act's provisions.*
- *Provided public financing for presidential primaries and general elections.* Presidential candidates who raise some money on their own can get funds from the U.S. Treasury to help pay for primary campaigns. For the general election campaign, presidential candidates receive federal funding for almost all of their expenses if they are willing to accept campaign-spending limits.
- *Limited presidential campaign spending.* Any candidate accepting federal support must agree to limit expenditures to amounts set by law.
- *Required disclosure.* Candidates must file periodic reports with the FEC that list the contributors to the campaign and indicate how the funds were spent.
- *Limited contributions.* Limits were placed on how much individuals and groups could contribute to candidates. (These limits have changed over time—we discuss the current limits later in this section.)

A recent development in presidential campaign finance has been the tendency of candidates to reject public funding on the grounds that they can raise larger sums outside the system. By 2008, a majority of the leading Democratic and Republican presidential candidates were refusing public funding for the primaries. That year, Barack Obama became the first major-party candidate in decades to refuse federal funding for the general election as well.

BUCKLEY v. VALEO In a 1976 case, *Buckley v. Valeo,*[10] the United States Supreme Court declared unconstitutional the provision in the 1971 act that limited the amount each individual could spend on his or her own campaign. The Court held that a "candidate, no less than any other person, has a First Amendment right to engage in the discussion of public issues and vigorously and tirelessly to advocate his own election."

THE RISE OF PACS The FECA allows corporations, labor unions, and special interest groups to set up national *political action committees (PACs)* to raise money for candidates. For a PAC to be legitimate, the money must be raised from at least fifty volunteer donors and must be given to at least five candidates in the national elections. PACs can contribute up to $5,000 per candidate in each election, but there is no limit on the total amount of PAC contributions during an election cycle. As discussed in Chapter 6, the number of PACs has grown significantly since the 1970s, as have their campaign contributions. In the 2004 election cycle, about 36 percent of campaign funds spent on House races came from PACs.[11] Since 2004, however, other methods of raising campaign funds have reduced the relative importance of PACs.

> "A promising young man SHOULD GO INTO POLITICS SO THAT HE CAN GO ON PROMISING FOR THE REST OF HIS LIFE."
>
> ~ ROBERT BYRNE ~
> AMERICAN AUTHOR
> 1930–PRESENT

Skirting the Campaign-Financing Rules

Individuals and corporations have found **loopholes**—legitimate ways of evading legal requirements—in the federal laws limiting campaign contributions.

SOFT MONEY The biggest loophole in the FECA and its amendments was that they did not prohibit individuals or corporations from contributing to political *parties*. Contributors could make donations to the national parties to cover the costs of such activities as registering voters, printing brochures and fliers, advertising, developing campaigns to "get out the vote," and holding fund-raising events. Contributions to political parties were called **soft money.** Even though soft money clearly was used to support the candidates, it was difficult to track exactly how this was happening.

By 2000, the use of soft money had become standard operating procedure, and the parties raised nearly $463 million through soft money contributions. Soft dollars became the main source of campaign money in the presidential race. They far outpaced PAC contributions and federal campaign funds until after the 2002 elections, when they were banned, as you will read shortly.

loophole A legitimate way of evading a certain legal requirement.

soft money Campaign contributions not regulated by federal law, such as some contributions that are made to political parties instead of to particular candidates.

independent expenditure An expenditure for activities that are independent from (not coordinated with) those of a political candidate or a political party.

INDEPENDENT EXPENDITURES Another major loophole in campaign-financing laws was that they did not prohibit corporations, labor unions, and special interest groups from making **independent expenditures** in an election campaign. Independent expenditures, as the term implies, are expenditures for activities that are independent from (not coordinated with) those of the candidate or a political party. In other words, interest groups can wage their own "issue" campaigns so long as they do not go so far as to say "Vote for Candidate X."

The problem is, where do you draw the line between advocating a position on a particular issue and contributing to the campaign of a candidate who endorses that position? In addressing this thorny issue, the United States Supreme Court has developed two determinative tests. Under the first test, a group's speech is a campaign "expenditure" only if it explicitly calls for the election of a particular candidate. Using this test, the courts repeatedly have held that interest groups have the right to advocate their positions. For example, the Christian Coalition has the right to publish voter guides informing voters of candidates' positions. The second test applies when a group or organization has made expenditures explicitly for the purpose of endorsing a candidate. Such expenditures are permissible unless they were made in "coordination" with a campaign. According to the Supreme Court, an issue-oriented group has a First Amendment right to advocate the election of its preferred candidates as long as it acts independently.

In 1996, the Supreme Court held that these guidelines apply to expenditures by political parties as well. Parties may spend money on behalf of candidates if they do so independently—that is, if they do not let the candidates know how, when, or for what the money was spent.[12] As critics of this decision have pointed out, parties generally work closely with candidates, so establishing the "independence" of such expenditures is difficult.

The Bipartisan Campaign Reform Act of 2002

Demand for further campaign-finance reform had been growing for several years, and in 2000 a Republican presidential candidate, John McCain, made it one of the cornerstones of his campaign. McCain lost to George W. Bush in the 2000 Republican presidential primaries, but his legislative campaign was successful. In 2002, Congress passed, and the president signed, the Bipartisan Campaign Reform Act.

CHANGES UNDER THE 2002 LAW The new law banned soft money. It also regulated campaign ads paid for by interest groups and prohibited any such issue advocacy commercials within thirty days of a primary election or sixty days of a general election.

The 2002 act set the amount that an individual can contribute to a federal candidate at $2,000 and the amount that an individual can give to all federal candidates at $95,000 over a two-year election cycle. (Under the law, some individual contribution limits are indexed for inflation and thus may change slightly with every election cycle.) Individuals can still contribute to state and local parties, so long as the contributions do not exceed $10,000 per year per individual. The new law went into effect the day after the 2002 general elections.

CONSTITUTIONAL CHALLENGES TO THE 2002 LAW Several groups immediately filed lawsuits challenging the constitutionality of the new law. Supporters of the restrictions on campaign ads by special interest groups argued that the large amounts of funds spent on these ads create an appearance of corruption in the political process. In contrast, an attorney for the National Rifle Association (NRA) argued that because the NRA represents "millions of Americans speaking in unison . . . [it] is not a *corruption* of the democratic political process; it *is* the democratic political process."[13] In December 2003, the Supreme Court upheld nearly all of the clauses of the act in *McConnell v. Federal Election Commission*.[14]

In 2007, however, the Supreme Court invalidated a major part of the 2002 law and overruled a portion of its own 2003 decision upholding the act. In the four years since the earlier ruling, Chief Justice John Roberts, Jr., and Associate Justice Samuel Alito, Jr., had been appointed, and both were conservatives. In a five-to-four decision, the Court held that issue ads could not be prohibited in the time period preceding elections (thirty days before primary elections and sixty days before general elections) *unless* they were "susceptible of no reasonable interpretation other than as an appeal to vote for or against a specific candidate."[15] The Court concluded that restricting *all* television ads paid for by corporate or union treasuries in the weeks before an election amounted to censorship of political speech. "Where the First Amendment is implicated," said the Court, "the tie goes to the speaker, not the censor."

INDEPENDENT EXPENDITURES AFTER 2002 As you read in Chapter 6, "issue advocacy" groups soon attempted to exploit loopholes in the 2002 act. A major technique was to establish independent 527 committees, named after the provision of the tax code that covers them. Spending by 527s rose rapidly after 2002, and in the 2004 election cycle, the committees spent about $612 million to "advocate positions."

By 2008, the relative importance of 527 committees began to decline. The reason was the creation of a new kind of body, the 501(c)4 organization. According to some lawyers, a 501(c)4 could make limited contributions directly to campaigns and—perhaps more importantly—could conceal the identity of its donors. A ruling on the legality of this technique has yet to be issued.

Campaign Contributions and Policy Decisions

Considering the passion on both sides of the debate about campaign-finance reform, one might wonder how much campaign contributions actually influence policy decisions. Table 9–1 on the next page lists leading industries and other groups contributing to either party in the 2008 election cycle. These contributors must want something in return for their dollars, but what, exactly, do their contributions buy? Do these donations influence government policymaking?

Despite popular suspicions, we cannot assume that a member of Congress who received

AP Photo/Dennis Cook

Senator John McCain (R., Ariz.) was a major sponsor of campaign-finance reform. He succeeded in getting Congress to pass the Bipartisan Campaign Reform Act of 2002.

financial contributions from certain groups while campaigning for Congress will vote differently on policy issues than she or he would otherwise vote. After all, many groups make contributions not so much to influence a candidate's views as to ensure that a candidate whose views the group supports will win the elections.

Many groups routinely donate to candidates from both parties so that, regardless of who wins, the groups will have access to the officeholder. Note that some of the groups listed in Table 9–1 contributed to both parties. Not surprisingly, campaign contributors find it much easier than other constituents to get in to see politicians or get them to return phone calls. Because politicians are more likely to be influenced by those with whom they have personal contacts, access is important for those who want to influence policymaking.

Table 9–1

Selected Industries and Other Groups Contributing Funds in the 2008 Presidential Election Cycle

Industry/Group	Total	To Democrats	To Republicans
Retired	$303,935,912	48%	51%
Lawyers/Law Firms	236,460,041	76	23
Securities/Investments	154,920,873	57	43
Real Estate	136,732,529	49	51
Health Professionals	97,275,179	53	47
Miscellaneous Business	81,856,314	63	37
Business Services	66,578,728	64	35
Education	57,696,138	82	18
TV/Movies/Music	47,968,669	78	22
Insurance	46,938,387	45	55
Communications/Electronics	45,794,358	78	22
Computers/Internet	41,159,467	67	33
Democratic/Liberal	40,772,513	100	0
Commercial Banks	37,126,707	48	52
General Contractors	29,414,262	33	67
Civil Servants/Public Officials	29,406,719	69	30
Printing and Publishing	26,672,171	77	22
Construction	20,389,766	45	55
Republican/Conservative	18,780,431	0	100
Energy/Natural Resources	11,078,167	38	62
Hedge Funds	10,012,816	60	40

Data through March 2, 2009.
Source: Center for Responsive Politics.

LO6 *The Closeness of Recent Elections*

The events surrounding the 2000 presidential elections are still fresh in the minds of some Americans. It was the first time since 1888 that the electoral college system gave Americans a president who had not won the popular vote. The events of the 2000 elections will undoubtedly be recounted in history books, but was the outcome an anomaly? The 2004 elections again were close, but in 2008, the pattern changed.

The 2000 Presidential Elections

In 2000, then vice president Al Gore won the popular vote by 540,000 votes. Nonetheless, on election night, the outcome in Florida, which would have given Gore the winning votes in the electoral college, was deemed "too close to call." Controversy erupted over the types of ballots used, and some counties in Florida began recounting ballots by hand. This issue ultimately came before the United States Supreme Court: Did manual recounts of some ballots but not others violate the Constitution's equal protection clause? On December 12, five weeks after the election, the Supreme Court ruled against the manual recounts.[16] The final vote tally in Florida gave Bush a 537-vote lead, all of Florida's twenty-five electoral votes, and the presidency.

The 2004 Presidential Elections

The 2004 presidential elections produced another close race, with President Bush edging out Democratic challenger John Kerry by a mere thirty-five electors. In contrast to the situation in 2000, Bush won the popular vote in 2004, defeating Kerry by a 2.5 percentage point margin. Many commentators argued that the elections were decided by the closely contested vote in Ohio.

From early in the 2004 election cycle, Ohio had been viewed as a *battleground state*—a state where voters were not clearly leaning toward either

"IT'S NOT THE VOTING THAT'S DEMOCRACY;
it's the counting."

~ TOM STOPPARD ~
PLAYWRIGHT
1938–PRESENT

major candidate leading up to the elections. Political analysts and news media outlets placed a great deal of emphasis on the battleground states, arguing that these states could potentially decide the outcome.

The 2008 Presidential Elections

At times during the campaign, the 2008 presidential contest appeared to be close. The financial panic that struck on September 15, however, tipped the elections decisively, as we explain in this chapter's feature *Our Government's Response to the Economic Crisis* on the following page.

Barack Obama's decisive victory in 2008 reversed the trend of extremely close elections established in 2000 and 2004. Obama's popular-vote margin over John McCain was about 7.2 percentage points, nearly a 10-point swing to the Democrats from the elections of 2004. With approximately 52.9 percent of the total popular vote, Obama was the first Democrat to win an absolute majority (more than 50 percent) of the popular vote since Jimmy Carter did so in 1976. Indeed, Obama won a larger share of the popular vote than any Democrat since Lyndon Johnson's 61 percent victory in 1964. Clearly, Obama had secured the strongest personal mandate of any Democrat in a generation.

The results did not quite amount to a landslide, as most analysts would define such an event. For example, Obama's popular vote percentage did not reach the 58.8 percent enjoyed by Republican Ronald Reagan in his 1984 reelection bid, and Obama's 365 electoral votes certainly did not match Reagan's 1984 total of 525. Obama's popular vote win was comparable to Reagan's 1980 victory over Jimmy Carter, however—and many commentators thought that the elections of 2008 had many similarities to the 1980 contest. One such similarity was the need of both Reagan and Obama to reassure the public that they were not dangerously radical and that they had the proper temperament to succeed as president.

In 2012, if the voters believe that Obama's presidency has been a success, he may win a true landslide in that year's presidential elections, as Reagan did in 1984. If Obama's administration is widely seen as a failure, however, the voters could reject his reelection bid, just as they turned out Carter in 1980.

AP Photo/Pablo Martinez Monsivais

Barack Obama, his wife, Michelle, and their children, Malia and Sasha, as they appeared on stage at the victory celebration held in Chicago's Grant Park on November 4, 2008. Hundreds of thousands of supporters turned out to see the future First Family and to hear Barack Obama deliver his first speech as president-elect of the United States.

After claims of voting irregularities and improper voting procedures, many counties in Florida began manually recounting the votes cast for president in the 2000 elections. Here, these Florida officials attempted to establish the actual votes cast for the two candidates by holding up the voting punch cards to see if the "chads" had been clearly punched out or not.

AP Photo/Charles Rex Arbogast

The Great Recession in the 2008 Presidential Elections

Many elections are won or lost on the basis of whether the electorate is experiencing good or bad economic times. One year before the 2008 presidential elections, most observers thought that the war in Iraq would be the defining issue of the campaign. For many months, it was. Little by little, though, the deteriorating state of the economy came to the fore. As unemployment grew and as home foreclosures began to mount, Democratic candidate Barack Obama found a theme that would allow him to win the presidency. That theme was that the Republicans, specifically George W. Bush, had fostered the worst recession since the Great Depression.

The Bank Bailout Bill

One of our government's most important responses to the economic crisis took place in the final months before the general elections—the passage of the Emergency Economic Stabilization Act of 2008, better known as the bank bailout bill. After the failure of the Lehman Brothers investment bank on September 15, the financial community pleaded with the government to "do something." Along with other Bush administration officials, Secretary of the Treasury Henry Paulson thought that the crisis was due to the collapse in value of mortgage-backed securities held by banks and other financial firms. Paulson proposed to restore confidence by buying up those assets with federal dollars.

The bill Paulson proposed to the House of Representatives—which was all of three pages long—would have given Paulson $700 billion of federal monies to buy mortgage-related assets. (No one knew where the $700 billion figure came from—it was simply "pulled out of a hat.") Members of the House were astounded by the bill, but they dutifully went to work. A House committee reported a 110-page bill out to the full House, which promptly voted it down. The Senate then took up the issue, and it passed a measure that was 451 pages long and loaded with pork-barrel spending projects. The House accepted the Senate bill, and President Bush signed it into law on October 3, 2008. The key part of the package was the creation of the Troubled Asset Relief Program (TARP).

By October 14, President Bush and Secretary Paulson had completely changed the purpose of the new law. TARP was now a hodgepodge of federal government purchases of preferred stock in banks. These purchases were supposed to give the banks more capital and hence the ability to start lending again.

The Dilemma for the Two Presidential Candidates

Many people considered the legislation to be a plan to bail out the bankers instead of the banks. Both major-party candidates, Barack Obama and John McCain, concluded that they had to support the bill while at the same time displaying their anger over it to the voters. For example, Obama said: "This financial crisis is a direct result of the greed and irresponsibility that has dominated Washington and Wall Street for years." To ensure there was no doubt about whom he meant, Obama named them: "Speculators who gamed the system. Regulators who looked the other way. Lobbyists who bought their way into our government."

Did the Bailout Affect the Election?

In responding to the immediate crisis, Obama may have led on points. His unruffled demeanor, which some had seen as remote, now seemed reassuring. In contrast, McCain seemed "hair-triggered." But those perceptions did not seriously alter the election results.

The economic crisis itself was definitive for the elections, however. Republicans could argue that congressional Democrats helped bring on the crisis by encouraging the government-backed mortgage giants Freddie Mac and Fannie Mae to take on risky loans. Such arguments, however, could not overcome the decades-old popular perception of the Republicans as the party of finance, and big finance seemed to be the villain in the economic meltdown. Most importantly, the Republicans were still seen as the party in power because they held the presidency. Consequently, they took the blame for the bad economy.

For Critical Analysis *Paulson's three-page proposed bill ultimately ballooned to more than 450 pages. Why do you think it became so long in such a short period of time? How might the bill have attracted enough support to finally pass?*

AMERICA AT ODDS Campaigns and Elections

The U.S. Constitution includes some provisions about elections, but it says nothing about how candidates will be selected or run for political office. In the very early years of the nation, many of the founders wondered how candidates would be nominated after George Washington left the presidency. Most envisioned that candidates would simply "stand" for election, rather than actively run for office. Instead of shaking hands and making speeches, candidates would stay on their farms and wait for the people's call, as Washington had done. Some of the framers believed that the electors of the electoral college would put forward candidates' names. Some observers believe that if the founders could see how presidential campaigns are conducted today, they would be shocked at how candidates "pander to the masses."

Whether they would be shocked at the costliness of modern campaigns is not as clear. After all, the founders themselves were an elitist, wealthy group, as are today's successful candidates for high political offices. In any event, Americans today are certainly shocked at how much money it takes to win political office. Seats in Congress and the presidency are increasingly held by millionaires. This means that someone without independent wealth or the ability to attract significant amounts of campaign contributions simply has no chance to compete, no matter how qualified that person may be. Campaign-finance reform laws have attempted to ease this problem by providing funds for presidential candidates. Yet to accept government funds, presidential candidates must forgo other financial backing. If a candidate has alternative sources of funds and wants to compete effectively in a presidential race, he or she is likely to refuse federal funding—as Barack Obama did during the 2008 presidential campaigns.

Also, attempts to curb the influence of money in elections through campaign-finance reform may violate the constitutional right to free political expression—a value at the heart of our democracy. The old saying that "anyone can become president" in this country, if it was ever true, is certainly not a reality today. In fact, fewer and fewer Americans can even hope to win a seat in Congress.

ISSUES FOR DEBATE & DISCUSSION

1. In democratically held elections in Palestine in 2006, the terrorist group known as Hamas won a majority of the legislative seats and thus majority control of the Palestinian government. Because of Hamas's terrorist activities and its stated desire to destroy the state of Israel, however, the Western powers refused to deal with Hamas as a legitimate governing force. Some Americans believe that any government elected by a majority of the people in a democratic election should be recognized as legitimate, regardless of that government's agenda, and that the decision of the United States not to recognize Hamas was contrary to the U.S. goal of supporting elections and spreading democracy to the Middle East. Others maintain that a terrorist group such as Hamas, regardless of how it came to power, should not be recognized as legitimate by other nations. What is your position on this issue?

2. Some political commentators argue strongly that campaign contributions are a form of expression and that limits on such contributions, such as those contained in the Bipartisan Campaign Reform Act of 2002, violate our constitutionally protected right to freedom of speech. Others contend that, in practice, campaign contributions are often little more than thinly disguised attempts to bribe public officials. An alternative danger is that elected leaders might threaten various business interests with adverse legislation unless they "cough up." Under what circumstances do campaign contributions seem to be most similar to speech? Under what circumstances do they threaten to corrupt the political process? Can you think of any principles or guidelines that would distinguish legitimate contributions from troublesome ones?

TAKE ACTION

Many groups have worked toward reforming the way campaign funds are raised and spent in politics today. One nonprofit, nonpartisan, grassroots organization that lobbies for campaign-finance reform is Common Cause. In the photo below, a participant in Colorado Common Cause's effort to reform campaign financing displays a mock-up of a TV remote control with a large mute button at a news conference. The group was asking voters to "mute" attack ads directed against a Colorado initiative to amend the state constitution to limit campaign financing and set contribution limits.

AP Photo/Ed Andrieski

POLITICS ON THE WEB

- You can find out exactly what the laws are that govern campaign financing by accessing the Federal Election Commission's Web site. The commission has provided an online "Citizen's Guide" that spells out what is and is not legal. You can also download actual data on campaign donations from the site. Go to **www.fec.gov**
- To look at data from the Federal Election Commission presented in a more user-friendly way, you can access the following nonpartisan, independent site that allows you to type in an elected official's name and receive large amounts of information on contributions to that official. Go to **www.moneyline.cq.com/pml/home.do**
- Another excellent source for information on campaign financing, including who's contributing what amounts to which candidates, is the Center for Responsive Politics. You can access its Web site at **www.opensecrets.org**
- Common Cause offers additional information about campaign financing on its Web site at **www.commoncause.org**
- Project Vote Smart offers information on campaign financing, as well as voting, on its Web site at **www.votesmart.org**

Online resources for this chapter

This text's Companion Web site, at **www.4ltrpress.cengage.com/govt**, offers links to numerous resources that you can use to learn more about the topics covered in this chapter.

Politics and the Media

LEARNING OBJECTIVES

LO1 Explain the role of a free press in a democracy.

LO2 Summarize how television influences the conduct of political campaigns.

LO3 Explain why talk radio has been described as the "Wild West" of the media.

LO4 Describe types of media bias and explain how such bias affects the political process.

LO5 Indicate the extent to which the Internet is reshaping news and political campaigns.

AMERICA AT ODDS

Can We Do Without Newspapers?

The *New York Times.* The *Washington Post.* The *Wall Street Journal.* The *Christian Science Monitor.* These and hundreds of other major and minor newspapers have generated and disseminated the nation's news for more than one hundred years. Already in 1783, at the end of the Revolutionary War, America had forty-three newspapers. Not until 1910, though, did all of the essential features that we recognize in today's newspapers become commonplace.

Gradually, radio and television supplanted newspapers as this country's primary information source. Today, some great newspapers have already filed for bankruptcy protection, including the *Journal Register* in Philadelphia, the *Chicago Tribune,* and the *Star Tribune* in Minneapolis. Others will certainly have gone bankrupt by the time you read this. The following newspapers no longer exist: the *Tucson Citizen,* the *Rocky Mountain News,* the *Baltimore Examiner,* the *Cincinnati Post,* and the *Albuquerque Tribune.* Additional newspapers have reduced their printing schedules or have gone completely online.

The online revolution has certainly changed the newspaper business—and perhaps will eventually eliminate it. The godfather of the U.S. investing community, Warren Buffet, recently said that the newspaper business faces "just unending losses." His recommendation to investors—stay away. With newspapers in so much trouble, the question arises: Does it matter if newspapers disappear?

Who Cares About Newspapers When Free Content Is Everywhere?

Those who do not mourn the loss of newspapers—particularly the younger generation—point out the obvious. Americans have more access to more news than ever before. Online news is available and updated day and night. An enormous number of citizen bloggers will help you find out what is happening anywhere in the world any time you want. So who needs newspapers?

Even if your hometown newspaper shuts down, local Web sites are increasingly available to deliver local news. Many of these sites are organized by companies such as EveryBlock, Outside.In, Placeblogger, and Patch.

Newspapers have always had a "slant," anyway, and in the past most Americans had to put up with whatever point of view their local newspaper provided. That is no longer the case. You can find the news—presented in whatever way you like—on thousands of Internet news sites and millions of blogs (short for "Web logs"). Variety is the spice of life, and we certainly have more variety in news gathering and presentation than ever before.

Newspapers are dead. Long live the news.

Without Newspapers, the News Is Just Background Noise

The reality of this world, is that people have to be paid to do a good job no matter what that job is. Journalists have families to feed. Rarely are they independently wealthy amateurs. Where does all that free content on the Web come from? Most of it can ultimately be traced back to journalists working for the print media. Even today, newspapers employ the overwhelming majority of all journalists. How many bloggers bother to attend city council meetings and report what happens? Precious few do.

Dan Kennedy, writing in the British newspaper The *Guardian,* sums up the entire argument: "The real value that newspapers provide, whether in print or online, is organization, editing, and reputation." Kennedy observes that the issue is not the survival of the newspaper industry. Rather, it is the survival of an informed citizenry. If citizens believe that information, no matter where it comes from—blogs, tweets, Web sites that promote conspiracy theories—is all of the same value, then these citizens are in trouble.

We need to change the way newspapers work. We need to figure out ways in which online versions of publications can earn enough revenue to be self-supporting. If we do this, we can ensure that newspapers remain the mainstay of American news gathering and distribution.

WHERE DO YOU STAND?

1. **Most young people rarely, if ever, read a newspaper. Does that mean they are not getting any news? Why or why not?**
2. **How much do you think the reputation of a news source really matters?**

EXPLORE THIS ISSUE ONLINE

- **Newspapers have been harder hit in Michigan than in any other state. Ann Arbor, home of the University of Michigan, with a metro population of almost 350,000, may be the largest urban area in the country to lose its only daily newspaper. Papers in Flint, Saginaw, and Bay City, Michigan, now publish only three times a week. The Detroit papers have drastically cut back their distribution as well. Statewide coverage is now provided by the online service www.mlive.com. For details of how the *Ann Arbor News* came to close its doors, see www.mlive.com/annarbornews.**

Introduction

"The press may not be successful much of the time in telling people what to think, but it is stunningly successful in telling its audience **WHAT TO THINK ABOUT.**"

~ BERNARD C. COHEN ~
AMERICAN POLITICAL SCIENTIST
1926–PRESENT

mass media Communication channels, such as newspapers and radio and television broadcasts, through which people can communicate to mass audiences.

print media Communication channels that consist of printed materials, such as newspapers and magazines.

electronic media Communication channels that involve electronic transmissions, such as radio, television, and the Internet.

The debate over the survival of newspapers is just one aspect of an important topic that you will read about in this chapter: the role of the media in American politics. Strictly defined, the term *media* means communication channels. It is the plural form of *medium,* as in medium of communication. In this strict sense, any method used by people to communicate—including the telephone—is a communication medium. In this chapter, though, we look at the **mass media**—channels through which people can communicate to mass audiences. These channels include the **print media** (newspapers and magazines) and the **electronic media** (radio, television, and the Internet).

The media are a dominant presence in our lives largely because they provide entertainment. Americans today enjoy more leisure time than at any time in history, and we fill it up with books, movies, Web surfing, and television—a huge amount of television. But the media play a vital role in our political lives as well, particularly during campaigns and elections. Politicians and political candidates have learned—often the hard way—that positive media exposure and news coverage are essential to winning votes.

As you read in Chapter 4, one of the most important civil liberties protected in the Bill of Rights is freedom of the press. Like free speech, a free press is considered a vital tool of the democratic process. If people are to cast informed votes, they must have access to a forum in which they can discuss public affairs fully and assess the conduct and competency of their officials. The media provide this forum. In contrast, government censorship of the press is

Larry Busacca/WireImage

Jim Watson/AFP/Getty Images

Walter Cronkite was considered the "voice of America" for decades. He presented the *CBS Evening News* from 1962 to 1981. Today, Katie Couric is the CBS News anchor. Why is it harder today for a news anchor to become as well known and influential as was Cronkite?

China's Mastery of Internet Censorship

Most people have heard of the Great Wall of China, which was built about 2,500 years ago. Today, the Chinese government has created the Great Firewall of China, also called the Golden Shield Project. China has an estimated 40,000 Internet police who monitor Web sites, blogs, and online traffic. Their mission? To find offending content, especially instances of political dissent. Chinese Internet police monitor a long list of "politically offensive" words, terms, and topics. These include Taiwanese independence, the religious group Falun Gong, the Dalai Lama, and the Tiananmen Square protests and massacre of 1989. Indeed, terms that the Chinese Internet police find suspicious number in the thousands.

Monitoring Internet "Phone Calls"

An activist group called Citizen Lab, based at the University of Toronto, has discovered that there is also a surveillance system built into an Internet portal called TOM-Skype. TOM is a Chinese media company with headquarters in Hong Kong; Skype is both a software application that lets users make voice calls over the Internet and the name of the company that provides the service. TOM-Skype is a joint venture between the two companies. An encrypted list of words is stored within the TOM-Skype software. If those words show up in a message, the transmission of the message is blocked, and a copy of the message is sent to one of eight message-logging computers maintained by the Chinese government. These computers are used to monitor a wide variety of systems, not just TOM-Skype. Citizen Lab has determined that the eight computers contain more than a million censored messages.

Blocking YouTube in China

YouTube has become ubiquitous. When the Chinese government does not like particular clips on YouTube, however, it is prepared to block the entire site. For example, the official Chinese news agency, Xinhua, recently claimed that supporters of the Dalai Lama had fabricated a video that showed Chinese police beating Tibetans. When the government was unable to block that particular video on YouTube, it shut down the site—and then denied that it had done so.

The Game of Cat and Mouse

Internet users, particularly those who understand the Chinese system, are creating "escape hatch" systems that allow Chinese citizens (as well as those in other countries where there is censorship, such as Iran) to access blocked Web sites. Chinese computer experts working for the religious group Falun Gong created one of these systems. Downloaded software allows users to contact a series of computers and data centers around the world that reroute Web requests in ways that the Great Firewall of China (and similar firewalls in Iran) cannot detect. Citizen Lab has developed an alternative escape hatch system called Psiphon. It allows just about anyone to evade national Internet firewalls.

For Critical Analysis *What prevents the United States government from blocking Web sites in this country?*

common in many nations around the globe. One example is China, where the Web is heavily censored even though China now has more Internet users than any other country on earth. We discuss that in this chapter's *The Rest of the World* feature above.

LO1 *The Role of the Media in a Democracy*

What the media say and do has an impact on what Americans think about political issues. But just as clearly, the media also *reflect* what Americans think about politics. Some scholars argue that the media is the fourth "check" in our political system—checking and balancing the power of the president, the Congress, and the courts. The power of the media today is enormous, but how the media use their power is an issue about which Americans are often at odds.

The Agenda-Setting Function of the Media

One of the criticisms often levied against the media is that they play too large a role in determining the issues, events, and personalities that are in the public eye. When people take in the day's top news stories, they usually assume automatically that these stories concern the most important issues facing the nation. In actuality, the media

Is the Press Living Up to Its Role as a "Watchdog"?

Thomas Jefferson said in 1787 that he'd rather have newspapers without a government than a government without newspapers. Not surprisingly, the First Amendment to the Constitution upholds the important role of a free press. The news media have been placed in a specially protected position in our complicated country to serve as a watchdog against abuses of government. Some Americans believe that the press has lost its ability to act in this way. Others, however, believe that the government scandals unearthed by the media in years past show that the media are doing their job.

The Press Is Not Doing Its Job

Americans who believe that the media are not acting as proper watchdogs contend that journalists are frequently intimidated by the politicians and public officials that they cover. To write stories that catch the reader's eye, journalists must have access to government officials and political candidates. If the journalists are excessively critical, they may lose this access. Journalists are also addicted to "balanced" coverage that "gives both sides" of an issue. The problem is, sometimes there aren't two sides to a story. If a politician makes a statement that is obviously untrue, reporters do the public no favors by neglecting to point that out. Yet it is very rare for the media to challenge a politician on even the most preposterous falsehoods.

During the run-up to the Iraq War, most journalists were reluctant to dispute the Bush administration's arguments in favor of military action. A number of reporters later admitted that they were afraid of being characterized as "unpatriotic" if they questioned the administration's actions. Later, both before the 2008 elections and after President Barack Obama took office, conservatives argued that mainstream journalists were so personally enamored of Obama that they were giving him a "free ride." For their part, liberals complained that the press had largely failed to challenge a series of obviously false statements that Republican leaders made about Democratic health-care proposals.

The Truth Will Come Out Eventually

Those who take the other side of this debate believe that we still have the freest press in the world. Currently, few regulations control what members of the media can say, report, or film. Even if the traditional media do not do a good job, the truth will come out in the blogosphere. Indeed, bloggers have done a better job of investigating some news stories than have the mainstream media. In some instances, the mainstream press has been forced to publish information on stories that first became big in the blogosphere.

When reporting is erroneous, it is quickly exposed—first by bloggers and then by the established media—and the perpetrators are often punished. Some former media superstars, such as Dan Rather, have been relieved of their duties when critics determined that their news reports were unfounded. Also, let's not forget the role of media watchdog groups. They are numerous and represent both conservative and liberal viewpoints. All in all, it's hard to imagine that with current communications possibilities, our government is not being watched enough.

For Critical Analysis *We discussed the crisis of the newspaper business in the chapter-opening America at Odds feature. What impact might these problems have on the ability of the press to serve as a watchdog?*

decide the relative importance of issues by publicizing some issues and ignoring others, and by giving some stories high priority and others low priority. By helping to determine what people will talk and think about, the media set the *political agenda*—the issues that politicians will address. In other words, to borrow from Bernard Cohen's classic statement on the media and public opinion, the press (media) may *not* be successful in telling people what to think, but it is "stunningly successful in telling its readers what to think about."[1]

For example, television played a significant role in shaping public opinion about the Vietnam War (1964–1975), which has been called the first "television war." Part of the public opposition to the war in the late 1960s came about as a result of the daily portrayal of the war's horrors on TV news programs. Film footage and narrative accounts of the destruction, death, and suffering in Vietnam brought the war into living rooms across the United States. (To examine whether the press is doing its job, see *Join the Debate* feature above.)

Figure 10–1

Media Usage by Consumers, 1988 to Present

Hours shown for Internet usage include only those for "pure-play Internet services"—that is, they do not include time spent at the Web sites of TV networks or print media, including e-books. They also do not include hours for Internet services provided by cable TV companies. All of these hours are included in the totals for the traditional media. If they were included with Internet services, the number of Internet hours in 2009 would approximately double. Internet services would then be in the same range as network TV.

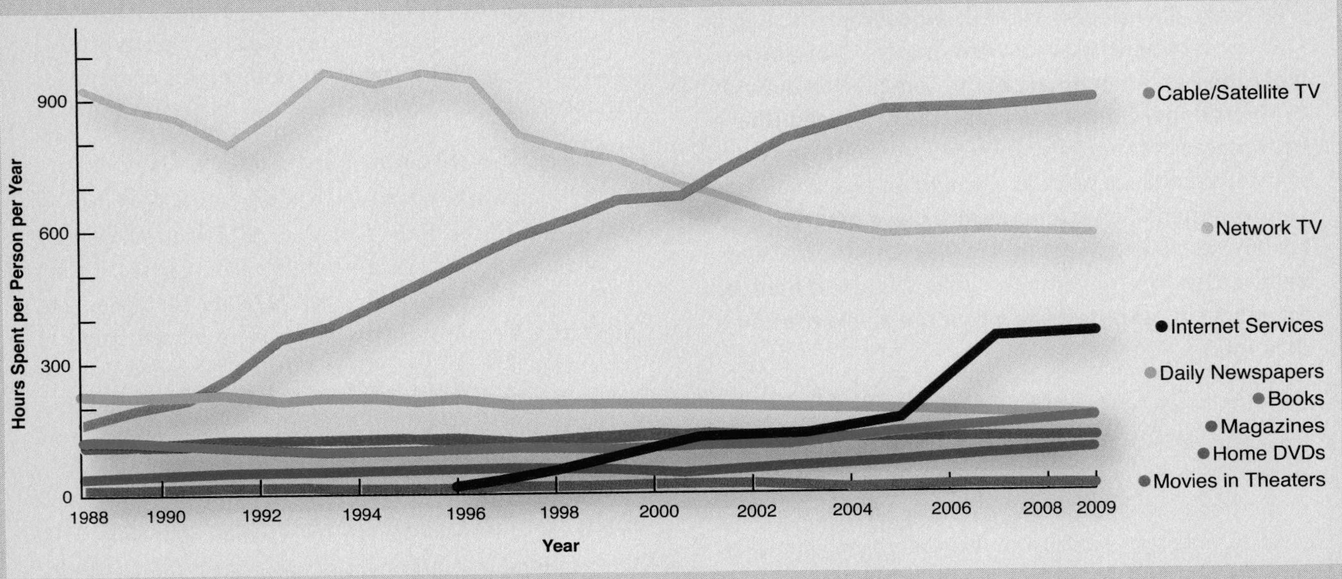

Sources: U.S. Department of Commerce, *Statistical Abstract of the United States, 2008* (Washington, D.C.: U.S. Government Printing Office, 2008), p. 709; and authors' updates.

Events in Iraq were also the subject of constant news coverage. Some believe that the media played a crucial role in influencing public opinion at the outset of the war. Indeed, recently the media have been sharply criticized by media watchdog groups for failing to do more fact checking prior to the invasion of Iraq. Instead of investigating the Bush administration's assertions that Iraq had weapons of mass destruction and links to al Qaeda, the media just passed this information on to the public. If the media had done their job, claim these critics, there would have been much less public support for going to war with Iraq.

The degree to which the media influence public opinion is not always all that clear, however. As you read in Chapter 8, some studies show that people filter the information they receive from the media through their own preconceived ideas about issues. Scholars who try to analyze the relationship between American politics and the media inevitably confront the chicken-and-egg conundrum: Do the media cause the public to hold certain views, or do the media merely reflect views that are formed independently of the media's influence?

The Medium Does Affect the Message

Of all the media, television has the greatest impact. Television reaches into almost every home in the United States. Virtually all homes have televisions. Even outside their homes, Americans can watch television—in airports, shopping malls, golf clubhouses, and medical offices. People can view television shows on their computers, and they can download TV programs to their iPods or iPhones and view the programs whenever and wherever they want.

For some time, it was predicted that as more people used the Internet, fewer people would turn to television for news or entertainment. This prediction turned out to be off the mark. Today, Americans watch more television than ever, and it is the primary news source for more than 65 percent of the citizenry. Figure 10–1 above shows the prominence of television when compared with other media.

As you will read shortly, politicians take maximum advantage of the power and influence of television. But does the television medium alter the presentation of political information in any way? Compare the coverage given to an important political issue by the print media—including the online sites of major newspapers and magazines—with the coverage provided by broadcast and cable TV networks. You will note some striking differences. For one thing, the print media (particularly leading newspapers such as the *Washington Post,* the *New York Times,* and the *Wall Street Journal*) treat an important issue in much more detail. In addition to news stories based on reporters' research, you will find editorials taking positions on the issue and arguments supporting those positions. Television news, in contrast, is often criticized as being too brief and too superficial.

TIME CONSTRAINTS The medium of television necessarily imposes constraints on how political issues are presented. Time is limited. News stories must be reported quickly, in only a few minutes or occasionally in only a **sound bite,** a brief comment lasting for just a few seconds that captures a thought or a perspective and has an immediate impact on the viewers.

A VISUAL MEDIUM Television reporting also relies extensively on visual elements, rather than words, to capture the viewers' attention. Inevitably, the photos or videos selected to depict a particular political event have exaggerated importance. The visual aspect of television contributes to its power, but it also creates a potential bias. Those watching the news presentation do not know what portions of a video being shown have been deleted, what other photos may have been taken, or whether other records of the event exist. This kind of "selection bias" will be discussed in more detail later in this chapter.

TELEVISION IS BIG BUSINESS Today's TV networks compete aggressively with one another to air "breaking news" and to produce interesting news programs. Competition in the television industry understandably has had an effect on how the news is presented. To make profits, or even stay in business, TV stations need viewers. And to attract viewers, the news industry has turned to "infotainment"—programs that inform and entertain at the same time. Slick sets, attractive reporters, and animated graphics that dance across the television screen are now commonplace on most news programs, particularly on the cable news channels.

TV networks also compete with one another for advertising income. Although the media in the United States are among the freest in the world, their programming nonetheless remains vulnerable to the influence of their advertising sponsors.

Concentrated ownership of media is another concern. Many mainstream media outlets are owned by giant corporations, such as Time Warner, Rupert Murdoch's News Corporation, and even General Electric. Concentrated ownership may be a more serious problem at the local level than at the national level. If only one or two companies own a city's newspaper and its TV stations, these outlets may not present a diversity of opinion. Further, the owners are unlikely to air information that could be damaging either to their advertisers or to themselves, or even to publicize views that they disagree with politically. For example, TV networks have refused to run antiwar commercials created by religious groups. Still, some media observers are not particularly concerned about concentrated ownership of traditional outlets, because the Internet has generated a massive diversification of media.

LO2 *The Candidates and Television*

Given the TV-saturated environment in which we live, it should come as no surprise that candidates spend a great deal of time—and money—obtaining a TV presence through political ads, debates, and general news coverage. Candidates and their campaign managers realize that the time and money are well spent because television has an important impact on the way people see the candidates, understand the issues, and cast their votes.

Political Advertising

Today, televised **political advertising** consumes at least half of the total budget for a major political campaign. In the 2000 election cycle, $665 million was spent for political advertising on broadcast TV. In the 2004 election cycle, the amount reached $1.4 billion. As you can see in Figure 10–2, on page 230 this was almost five

sound bite In televised news reporting, a brief comment, lasting for only a few seconds, that captures a thought or a perspective and has an immediate impact on the viewers.

political advertising Advertising undertaken by or on behalf of a political candidate to familiarize voters with the candidate and his or her views on campaign issues; also advertising for or against policy issues.

Figure 10–2

Political Ad Spending on Broadcast Television, 1992–2008

As you can see in this figure, spending for political advertising has increased steadily over the last nine elections.

Sources: Television Bureau of Advertising, as presented in Lorraine Woellert and Tom Lowry, "A Political Nightmare: Not Enough Airtime," *BusinessWeek*, November 23, 2000, p. 111; and authors' updates.

times the amount spent in the 1992 election cycle. For the 2006 elections, the figure climbed to $1.7 billion. According to an estimate by the research firm PQ Media, spending on all forms of political advertising reached $4.5 billion in the 2007–2008 election cycle, including $2.3 billion for broadcast TV in 2008 alone.

Political advertising first appeared on television during the 1952 presidential campaign. At that time, there were only about 15 million television sets; today, there are almost as many TV sets as people. Initially, political TV commercials were more or less like any other type of advertising. Instead of focusing on the positive qualities of a product, thirty-second or sixty-second ads focused on the positive qualities of a political candidate. Within the decade, however, **negative political advertising** began to appear on TV.

negative political advertising Political advertising undertaken for the purpose of discrediting an opposing candidate in the eyes of the voters. Attack ads and issue ads are forms of negative political advertising.

personal attack ad A negative political advertisement that attacks the character of an opposing candidate.

issue ad A political advertisement that focuses on a particular issue. Issue ads can be used to support or attack a candidate.

ATTACK ADS Despite the barrage of criticism levied against the candidates' use of negative political ads during recent election cycles, such ads are not new. Indeed, **personal attack ads**—advertising that attacks the character of an opposing candidate—have a long tradition. In 1800, an article in the *Federalist Gazette of the United States* described Thomas Jefferson as having a "weakness of nerves, want of fortitude, and total imbecility of character." After the terrorist attacks of September 11, 2001, candidates found that ads involving fear of terrorism resonated with voters. As a result, they routinely accused their opponents of lacking the fortitude to wage war on terrorism.

In 2008, the Republicans understood that after eight years of President Bush, voters wanted something new. For John McCain to win, voters had to see Democrat Barack Obama as an unacceptable alternative. The McCain campaign therefore aired a series of personal attack ads that portrayed Obama as a dangerous radical with unsavory associates. The ads by the McCain camp may have enhanced voter turnout among Republicans at the cost of alienating some independent voters. On the Democratic side, the Obama campaign generally employed issue ads, which were also largely negative. We discuss issue ads next.

ISSUE ADS Candidates use negative **issue ads** to focus on flaws in the opponents' positions on issues. Candidates level criticisms at each other's stated positions on various issues, such as the war in Iraq and the bank-bailout legislation. Candidates also try to undermine their opponents' credibility by pointing to discrepancies between what the opponents say in their campaign speeches and their political records, such as voting records, which are available to the public and thus can easily be verified. As noted in Chapters 6 and 9,

"The thing to do now, Senator, is to hit back with some negative advertising of our own."

www.OurCountryPAC.org

Negative advertising has become a staple in American political campaigns, whether for political races or for issues to be decided by Congress and the president. As much as voters claim that negative ads are offensive, they are effective. Why?

issue ads are also used by interest groups to gather support for candidates who endorse the groups' causes.

Issue ads can be even more devastating than personal attacks—as Barry Goldwater learned in 1964 when his opponent in the presidential race, President Lyndon Johnson, aired the "daisy girl" ad. This ad, a new departure in negative advertising, showed a little girl standing quietly in a field of daisies. She held a daisy and pulled off the petals, counting to herself. Suddenly, a deep voice was heard counting: "10, 9, 8, 7, 6 . . . ." When the countdown hit zero, the unmistakable mushroom cloud of an atomic explosion filled the screen. Then President Johnson's voice was heard saying, "These are the stakes: to make a world in which all of God's children can live, or to go into the dark. We must either love each other or we must die." A message on the screen then read: "Vote for President Johnson on November 3." The implication, of course, was that Goldwater would lead the country into a nuclear war.[2]

NEGATIVE ADVERTISING—IS IT GOOD OR BAD FOR OUR DEMOCRACY? The debate over the effect of negative advertising on our political system is ongoing. Some observers argue that negative ads can backfire. Extreme ads may create sympathy for the candidate being attacked rather than support for the attacker, particularly when the charges against the candidate being attacked are not credible. Many people fear that attack ads and "dirty tricks" used by both parties during a campaign may alienate citizens from the political process itself and thus lower voter turnout in elections.

Yet candidates and their campaign managers typically assert that they use negative advertising simply because it works. Negative TV ads are more likely than positive ads to grab the viewers' attention and make an impression. Also, according to media expert Shanto Iyengar, "the more negative the ad, the more likely it is to get free media coverage. So there's a big incentive to go to extremes."[3] Others believe that negative advertising is a force for the good because it sharpens public debate, thereby enriching the democratic process. This is the position taken by Vanderbilt University political science professor John Geer. He contends that negative ads are likely to focus on substantive political issues instead of candidates' personal characteristics. Thus, negative ads do a better job of informing the voters about important campaign issues than positive ads do.[4]

Television Debates

Televised debates have been a feature of presidential campaigns since 1960, when presidential candidates Republican Richard M. Nixon and Democrat John F. Kennedy squared off in four great TV debates. Television debates provide an opportunity for voters to find out how candidates differ on issues. They also allow candidates to capitalize on the power of television to improve their images or point out the failings of their opponents.

It is widely believed that Kennedy won the first of the 1960 debates in large part because of Nixon's haggard appearance and poor makeup—many people who heard the debate on the radio thought that Nixon had done well. No presidential debates were held during the general election campaigns of 1964, 1968, or 1972, but the debates have been a part of every election since 1976. The 1992 debates, which starred Republican George H. W. Bush and Democrat Bill Clinton, also included a third-party candidate, H. Ross Perot. Since 1996, however, the Commission on Presidential Debates, which now organizes the events, has limited the participants to candidates of the two major parties.[5] The commission also organizes debates between the vice-presidential candidates.

Many contend that the presidential debates help shape the outcome of the elections. Others doubt that the

Mario Tama/Getty Images

Obama and McCain faced each other for three separate debates during the 2008 campaign season. Here they are shown at Hofstra University in the last one that occurred just three weeks before the November 4 elections. How important are these debates in making up voters' minds?

debates—or the postdebate "spin" applied by campaign operatives and political commentators—have changed many votes. Evidence on this question is mixed.

Gallup polling figures suggest that in 1960 the debates helped Kennedy to victory. In 1980, Republican Ronald Reagan did well in a final debate with Democratic incumbent Jimmy Carter. Reagan impressed many voters with his sunny temperament, which helped dispel fears that he was a right-wing radical. In Gallup's opinion, however, Reagan would have won the election even without the debate.

The 2000 debates between Republican George W. Bush and Democrat Al Gore may have tipped the election results in Bush's favor—some voters thought that Gore was condescending. In 2004, Democrat John Kerry improved his chances during debates with Bush, who was now the incumbent. Kerry appeared confident, while Bush seemed somewhat nervous. In the end, however, Bush won reelection.

The 2008 Presidential Debates

managed news coverage News coverage that is manipulated (managed) by a campaign manager or political consultant to gain media exposure for a political candidate.

The first debate between Republican John McCain and Democrat Barack Obama was supposed to focus on foreign policy. It took place, however, in one of the worst weeks of the 2008 credit crisis, when Congress was struggling to agree on a $700 billion Wall Street bailout package. Inevitably, much time was spent on economics. Some journalists considered the first debate to be a draw. Some voters, however, thought that McCain displayed a patronizing attitude toward Obama and were put off by it.

The second debate was steered by questions from undecided voters in a town hall format, which was usually McCain's strong suit. Because the financial meltdown in the economy had gotten worse, many questions related to economics. The debate had a tougher tone than the first one, with McCain frequently raising questions about Obama's plans, record, and attitudes. Obama, in turn, blamed the economic crisis on the failed policies of McCain and the Republicans.

In the third and final debate, Obama appeared to be "playing it safe," given that he was so far ahead in the polls. McCain accused Obama of advocating too much redistribution of wealth—in his opinion, a socialist idea. In the end, surveys showed that Obama's performance in all three debates was better received than McCain's.

News Coverage

Whereas political ads are expensive, coverage by the news media is free. Accordingly, the candidates try to take advantage of the media's interest in campaigns to increase the quantity and quality of news coverage. This is not always easy. Often, the media devote the lion's share of their coverage to polls and other indicators of which candidate is ahead in the race.

In recent years, candidates' campaign managers and political consultants have shown increasing sophistication in creating newsworthy events for journalists and TV camera crews to cover, an effort commonly referred to as **managed news coverage.** For example, typically one of the jobs of the campaign manager is to create newsworthy events that demonstrate the candidate's

Peter Kramer/Getty Images

Dana Edelson/NBCU Photo Bank via AP Images

Left Photo: Jon Stewart hosts *The Daily Show* on the Comedy Central channel. A significant percentage of young people obtain their political ideas from this show. Right Photo: Tina Fey depicts Republican vice-presidential candidate Sarah Palin on the *Saturday Night Live* show, accompanied by Will Ferrell, who portrays President George W. Bush. Why do comedy shows devote so much time to politics?

strong points so that the media can capture this image of the candidate.[6]

Besides considering how camera angles and lighting affect a candidate's appearance, the political consultant plans political events to accommodate the press. The campaign staff attempts to make what the candidate is doing appear interesting. The staff also knows that journalists and political reporters compete for stories and that they can be manipulated. Hence, they often are granted favors, such as exclusive personal interviews with the candidate. Each candidate's press advisers, often called **spin doctors,** also try to convince reporters to give the story or event a **spin,** or interpretation, that is favorable to the candidate.[7]

"Popular" Television

Although not normally regarded as a forum for political debate, television programs such as dramas, sitcoms, and late-night comedy shows often use political themes. For example, the popular courtroom drama *Law & Order* regularly broaches controversial topics such as the death penalty, the USA Patriot Act, and the rights of the accused. For years, the sitcom *Will and Grace* consistently brought to light issues regarding gay and lesbian rights. The dramatic *West Wing* series gave viewers a glimpse into national politics as it told the story of a fictional presidential administration. Late-night shows and programs such as *The Daily Show with Jon Stewart* provide a forum for politicians to demonstrate their lighter sides.

LO3 *Talk Radio—The Wild West of the Media*

Ever since Franklin D. Roosevelt held his first "fireside chats" on radio, politicians have realized the power of that medium. From the beginning, radio has been a favorite outlet for the political right. During the 1930s, for example, the nation's most successful radio commentator was Father Charles Edward Coughlin, a Roman Catholic priest based at the National Shrine of the Little Flower church in Royal Oak, Michigan. Coughlin's audience numbered more than 40 million listeners—this in a nation that had only 123 million inhabitants in 1930. Coughlin started out as a Roosevelt supporter, but he soon moved to the far right, advocating anti-Semitism and expressing sympathy for Adolf Hitler. Coughlin's fascist connections eventually destroyed his popularity.

Modern talk radio took off in the United

spin doctor A political candidate's press adviser, who tries to convince reporters to give a story or event concerning the candidate a particular "spin" (interpretation, or slant).

spin A reporter's slant on, or interpretation of, a particular event or action.

Conservative talk-radio personality Sean Hannity has broadened his audience by also appearing on Fox TV five nights a week.

Kevin Winter/Getty Images

Rush Limbaugh is considered the dean of conservative talk-show hosts.

AP Photo/Eric Risberg

States during the 1990s. In 1988, there were 200 talk-show radio stations. Today, there are more than 1,200. The growth of talk radio was made possible by the Federal Communications Commission's repeal of the *fairness doctrine* in 1987. Introduced in 1949, the fairness doctrine required the holders of broadcast licenses to present controversial issues of public importance in a manner that was (in the commission's view) honest, equitable, and balanced. That doctrine would have made it difficult for radio stations to broadcast conservative talk shows exclusively, as many now do. All of the top ten talk-radio shows, as measured by Arbitron ratings, are politically conservative. No liberal commentator ranks higher than twentieth place in the ratings. (Several of the shows ranked tenth through twentieth, however, are not political, but deal with subjects such as personal finance, paranormal activities, computers, and sports.)

Audiences and Hosts

The Pew Research Center for the People and the Press reports that 17 percent of the public regularly listen to talk radio. This audience is predominantly male, middle-aged, and conservative. Among those who regularly listen to talk radio, 41 percent consider themselves Republicans and 28 percent, Democrats.

Talk radio is sometimes characterized as the Wild West of the media. Talk-show hosts do not attempt to hide their political biases; if anything, they exaggerate them for effect. No journalistic conventions are observed. Leading shows, such as those of Rush Limbaugh, Sean Hannity, Glenn Beck, Andrew Wilkow, and Michael Savage, espouse a brand of conservatism that is robust, even radical. Opponents are regularly characterized as Nazis, Communists, or both at the same time. Limbaugh, for example, consistently refers to feminists as "feminazis." Talk-show hosts care far more about the entertainment value of their statements than whether they are, strictly speaking, true. Hosts often publicize fringe beliefs such as the contention that President Barack Obama was not really born in the United States. The government of Britain actually banned Michael Savage from entry into that country based on his remarks about Muslims.

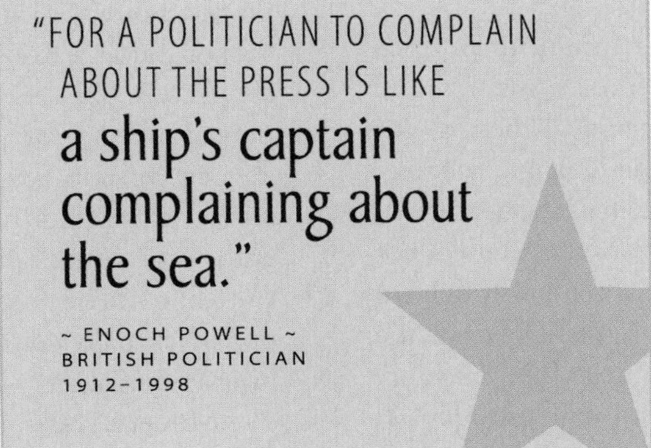

The Impact of Talk Radio

The overwhelming dominance of strong conservative voices on talk radio is justified by supporters as a good way to counter what they perceive as the liberal bias in the mainstream print and TV media (we discuss the question of bias in the media in the following section). Supporters say that such shows are simply a response to consumer demand. Those who think that talk radio is good for the country argue that talk shows, taken together, provide a great populist forum. Others are uneasy because they fear that talk shows empower fringe groups, perhaps magnifying their rage. Certainly, prominent hosts have had great fun organizing potentially disruptive activities. For example, during the 2008 presidential primaries, Limbaugh called for conservatives to reregister as Democrats and vote for Obama. The theory was that Obama would be easier for a Republican to beat than Hillary Clinton. In 2009, Glenn

Beck promoted attempts to shout down Democratic members of Congress at town hall meetings set up to discuss health-care reform.

Those who claim that talk-show hosts go too far ultimately have to deal with the constitutional issue of free speech. While the courts have always given broad support to freedom of expression, broadcast media have been something of an exception, as was explained in Chapter 4. The United States Supreme Court, for example, upheld the fairness doctrine in a 1969 ruling.[8] Presumably, the doctrine could be reinstated. In 2009, after the Democratic victories in the 2008 elections, a few liberals advocated doing just that. President Obama and the Democratic leadership in Congress, however, quickly put an end to this notion. Americans have come to accept talk radio as part of the political environment, and any attempt to curtail it would be extremely unpopular.

LO4 *The Question of Media Bias*

The question of media bias is important in any democracy. After all, for our political system to work, citizens must be well informed. And they can be well informed only if the news media, the source of much of their information, do not slant the news. Today, however, relatively few Americans believe that the news media are unbiased in their reporting. Accompanying this perception is a notable decline in the public's confidence in the news media in recent years. In a 2008 Gallup poll measuring the public's confidence in various institutions, only 24 percent of the respondents stated that they had "a great deal" or "quite a lot" of confidence in either newspapers or television news. Because of this low percentage, some analysts believe that the media are facing a crisis of confidence.

"A nation that is afraid to let its people judge truth and falsehood in an **OPEN MARKET** is a nation that is afraid of its people."

~ JOHN FITZGERALD KENNEDY ~
THIRTY-FIFTH PRESIDENT
OF THE UNITED STATES
1961–1963

Partisan Bias

For years, conservatives have argued that there is a liberal bias in the media, and liberals have complained that the media reflect a conservative bias. The majority of Americans think that the media reflect a bias in one direction or another. According to a recent poll, 64 percent of the respondents believed that the news media leaned left, whereas only 28 percent thought that the news media had a conservative bias.

Surveys and analyses of the attitudes and voting habits of reporters have suggested that journalists do indeed hold liberal views. In 1992, Bill Clinton beat George H. W. Bush by 5 percent among the general public but, according to a Roper poll, by 82 percent among journalists. Still, members of the press are likely to view themselves as moderates. In a 2005 study, the Pew Research Center for the People and the Press found that 64 percent of reporters in both national and local media applied the term "moderate" to themselves. Among journalists working for national outlets, 22 percent described themselves as liberal and only 5 percent as conservative. In contrast, 14 percent of local reporters called themselves liberals, and 18 percent adopted the conservative label. There is substantial evidence that top journalists working for the nation's most famous newspapers and networks do tend to be liberal. Many journalists themselves perceive the *New York Times* as liberal (although an even larger number view Fox News as conservative).

Nonetheless, a number of media scholars, including Kathleen Hall Jamieson, suggest that even if many reporters hold liberal views, these views are not reflected in their reporting. Based on an extensive study of media coverage of presidential campaigns, Jamieson, director of the Annenberg Public Policy Center of the University of Pennsylvania, concludes that there is no systematic liberal or Democratic bias in news coverage.[9] Media analysts Debra and Hubert van Tuyll have similarly concluded that left-leaning reporters do not automatically equate to left-leaning news coverage. They point out that reporters are only the starting point for news stories. Before any story goes to print or is aired on television, it has to go through a progression of editors and perhaps even the publisher. Because employees at the top of the corporate ladder in news organizations are more right leaning than left leaning, the end result of the editorial and oversight process is more balanced coverage.[10]

The Bias against Losers

Kathleen Hall Jamieson believes that media bias does play a significant role in shaping presidential campaigns and elections, but she argues that it is not a partisan bias. Rather, it is a bias against losers. A candidate who

AP Photo/Charles Dharapak

President George W. Bush holds a press conference in front of the White House press corps. Bush gave fewer such conferences than most presidents.

falls behind in the race is immediately labeled a "loser," making it even more difficult for the candidate to regain favor in the voters' eyes.[11]

Jamieson argues that the media use the winner-loser paradigm to describe events throughout the campaigns. Even a presidential debate is regarded as a "sporting match" that results in a winner and a loser. Before the 2008 debates, reporters focused on what each candidate had to do to "win" the debate. When the debate was over, reporters immediately speculated about who had "won" as they waited for postdebate polls to answer that question. According to Jamieson, this approach "squanders the opportunity to reinforce learning." The debates are an important source of political information for the voters, and this fact is eclipsed by the media's win-lose focus.

"Selection Bias"

As mentioned earlier, television is big business, and maximizing profits from advertising is a major consideration in what television stations choose to air. After all, a station or network that incurs losses will eventually go bankrupt. The expansion of the media universe to include cable channels and the Internet has also increased the competition among news sources. As a result, news directors select programming they believe will attract the largest audiences and garner the highest advertising revenues.

Competition for viewers and readers has become even more challenging in the wake of a declining news audience. A recent survey and analysis of reporters' attitudes conducted by the Pew Research Center's Project for Excellence in Journalism found that all media sectors except two are losing popularity. The two exceptions are the ethnic press, such as Latino newspapers and TV programs, and online sources—and even the online sector has stopped growing.[12]

SELECTION BIAS AND THE BOTTOM LINE The Pew study also indicates that news organizations' struggles to stay afloat are having a notable effect on news coverage. The survey showed that a larger number of reporters than ever before (about 66 percent) agreed that "increased bottom-line pressure is seriously hurting the quality of news coverage." About one-third of the journalists—again, more than in previous surveys—stated that they have felt pressure from either advertisers or corporate owners concerning what to write or broadcast. In other words, these journalists believe that economic pressure—the need for revenues—is making significant inroads on independent editorial decision making. Generally, the study found that news reporters are not too confident about the future of journalism.

A CHANGING NEWS CULTURE A number of studies, including the Pew study just cited, indicate that today's news culture is in the midst of change. News organizations are redefining their purpose and increasingly looking for special niches in which to build their audiences. According to the Pew study, for some markets, the niche is *hyperlocalism*—that is, narrowing the focus of news to the local area. For others, it is personal commentary, revolving around such TV figures as Bill O'Reilly, Larry King, and Keith Olbermann. In a sense, news organizations have begun to base their appeal less on *how* they cover the news and more on *what* they cover. Traditional journalism—fact-based reporting instead of opinion and punditry—is becoming a smaller part of this mix. Additionally, as already mentioned, bloggers and others on the Web are having an impact on the popularity of traditional news.

AP Photo/Jeff Christensen

Today, news organizations look for special niches around which to build their audiences. At the left, you see Bill O'Reilly of *The O'Reilly Factor,* a Fox News cable program where O'Reilly covers news stories and provides commentary on them. At the right is Keith Olbermann of *Countdown,* an MSNBC news program that highlights the day's top stories with interviews and commentary by Olbermann. O'Reilly is widely considered to be politically conservative, and Olbermann is seen as a liberal. The two men are often critical of one another.

LO5 *Political News and Campaigns on the Web*

Cyberspace is getting bigger every day. Internet World Stats reports that more than one-fifth of the world's inhabitants now use the Internet, a total that approaches 1.5 billion people. In 1995, there were fewer than 20,000 Web sites. Today, the Internet supports 180 million individual host names, and millions more are added every month. According to Technorati, bloggers around the world update their blogs with new posts in eighty-one languages at a rate of almost a million posts every day. Among U.S. Internet users, 77 percent read blogs, and one blog tracker, Universal McCann, has identified more than 26 million blogs in the United States. In addition, popular networking sites have enormous numbers of personalized pages—MySpace has 117 million members, and Facebook has 250 million.

Not surprisingly, the Internet is now a major source of information for many people. Gone are the days when you and your friends tromped to the library to research a paper. Why should you? You can go online and in a matter of seconds look up practically any subject. Of course, all major newspapers are online, as are transcripts of major television news programs. About two-thirds of Internet users consider the Internet to be an important source of news. Certainly, news abounds on the Web, and having an Internet strategy has become an integral part of political campaigning.

News Organizations Online

Almost every major news organization, both print and broadcast, delivers news via the Web. Indeed, an online presence is required to compete effectively with other traditional news companies for revenues. Studies of the media, including the study by the Pew Research Center's Project for Excellence in Journalism mentioned earlier, note that the online share of newspaper company revenues has increased over the years. Today, for example, 14 percent of the *Washington Post*'s revenues are from online revenues. For the *New York Times,* this share is 8 percent.

Web sites for newspapers, such as the *Washington Post* and the *New York Times,* have a notable advantage over their printed counterparts. They can add breaking news to their sites, informing readers of events that occurred just minutes ago. Another advantage is that they can link the reader to more extensive reports on particular topics. According to the Pew study, though, many papers shy away from in-text linking, perhaps fearing that if readers leave the news organization's site, they may not return.

Although some newspaper sites simply copy articles from their printed versions, the Web sites for major newspapers, including those for the *Washington Post* and the *New York Times,* offer a different array of

FOX News Poll: Americans Prefer Current System to Obama's Health Care Plan

Thursday, September 17, 2009
FOX NEWS

Print | ShareThis

By Dana Blanton

Aug. 12: Opponents of health care reform voice their opinions during the town hall meeting at the Casselton Fire Department in Casselton, N.D.

Most Americans see no upside for their family in the health care reforms being considered in Washington and don't believe President Obama when he says his plan won't add "one dime" to the federal deficit. The majority of Americans believe they will have to make changes to their health care coverage if the president's plan is passed.

These are just some of the findings of a new FOX News poll released Thursday.

More Americans would rather Congress do nothing than pass Obama's plan: 46 percent to 37 percent of people polled say they prefer the current health care system to the one the president has proposed.

http://www.foxnews.com

"The citizen CAN BRING OUR POLITICAL AND GOVERNMENTAL INSTITUTIONS BACK TO LIFE, MAKE THEM RESPONSIVE AND ACCOUNTABLE, AND KEEP THEM HONEST. No one else can."

~ JOHN GARDNER ~
AMERICAN NOVELIST
1933–1982

coverage and options than their printed counterparts. Indeed, the Pew study noted that the online versions of competing newspapers tend to be much more similar than their printed versions are.

A major problem facing these news organizations is that readers or viewers of online newspapers and news programs are typically the same people who read the printed news editions and view news programs on TV. Web-only readers of a particular newspaper make up a relatively small percentage of those going online for their news. Therefore, investing heavily in online news delivery may not be a solution for news companies seeking to increase readership and revenues.

In fact, the additional revenues that newspapers have gained from their online editions do not come close to making up for the massive losses in advertising revenue suffered by their print editions. In many instances, publications have not sold enough advertising in their online editions even to make up for the additional expense of publishing on the Web.

Blogs and the Emergence of Citizen Journalism

citizen journalism The collection, analysis, and dissemination of information online by independent journalists, scholars, politicians, and the general citizenry.

podcasting The distribution of audio or video files to a personal computer or a mobile device, such as an iPod.

As mentioned earlier, the news culture is changing, and at the heart of this change—and of most innovation in news delivery today—is the blogosphere. There has been a virtual explosion of blogs in recent years. To make their Web sites more competitive and appealing, and to counter the influence of blogs run by private citizens and those not in the news business, the mainstream news organizations have themselves been adding blogs to their Web sites.

Blogs are offered by independent journalists, various scholars, political activists, and the citizenry at large. Anyone who wants to can create a blog and post news or information, including videos, to share with others. Many blogs are political in nature, both reporting political developments and discussing politics. Taken as a whole, the collection, analysis, and dissemination of information online by the citizenry is referred to as **citizen journalism.** (Other terms that have been used to describe the news blogosphere include *people journalism* and *participatory journalism.* When blogs focus on news and developments in a specific community, the term *community journalism* is often applied.)

The increase in news blogs and do-it-yourself journalism on the Web clearly poses a threat to mainstream news sources. Compared with the operational costs faced by a major news organization, the cost of creating and maintaining blogs is trivial. How can major news sources adhere to their traditional standards and still compete with this new world of news generated by citizens?

Podcasting the News

Another nontraditional form of news distribution is **podcasting**—the distribution of audio or video files to personal computers or mobile devices, such as iPods.[13] Though still a relatively small portion of the overall news-delivery system, podcasts are becoming increasingly popular. Almost anyone can create a podcast and make it available for downloading onto computers or mobile devices, and like blogging, podcasting is inexpensive. As you will read next, political candidates are

PERCEPTION VERSUS REALITY

Twitter and Tweets—Much Ado about Nothing?

Back in 2006, Jack Dorsey created Twitter, a free social networking and microblogging service. As just about everyone now knows, Twitter posts—or tweets—are text-based messages that cannot exceed 140 characters. Today, Twitter users can send and receive messages through Twitter.com as well as through other media and applications.

The Perception

What can be more useless than twittering about what you are doing? What can be more superfluous than accessing Paris Hilton's Twitter site to find out that she thinks Jimmy Kimmel is funny, or discovering that Denise Richards just had her breakfast coffee? Twitter appears to be for those who don't value their time very highly—it's even more of a time waster than text messaging and blogging. Just because Twitter.com is ranked as one of the fifty most popular Web sites in the world doesn't mean that it has much value to the world. Some believe that twittering has simply replaced reading *People* magazine and talking on the phone about, well, nothing.

The Reality

Today, Twitter is an important news and political vehicle. Often, breaking news stories are first reported on Twitter and then picked up by major media sources. In addition, many media outlets use Twitter to measure public sentiment on various issues. And Twitter was used by both candidates in the 2008 U.S. presidential campaign, particularly by Barack Obama.

Look at some of the important messages Twitter made possible. When graduate journalism student James Buck was arrested in Egypt for photographing an antigovernment protest, he used Twitter to get out the message. He was able to send updates about his condition while being detained. He was released the next day. During the 2008 terrorist attacks in Mumbai, India, eyewitnesses twittered every five seconds, letting the rest of the world know what was happening. After the presidential elections in Iran were deemed fraudulent by many citizens, the Iranian government shut off most Internet outlets. But it wasn't able to shut off Twitter. Indeed, Twitter was almost the only communication medium for protesters in Iran. Much of what the rest of the world saw came through TwitPics.

Blog On *You can sign up for Twitter at* **twitter.com.** *Want to know the demographics of who's on Twitter? The site Quantcast has the answer—go to* **www.quantcast.com/twitter.com.** *You can follow in-depth reporting on Twitter at* **www.telegraph.co.uk/technology/twitter.**

using both blogging and podcasting as part of their Internet campaign strategy.

Still another new Internet technology is Twitter, a method for sending short messages to large numbers of people. How useful is Twitter? We discuss that question in this chapter's *Perception versus Reality* feature above.

Cyberspace and Political Campaigns

Today's political parties and candidates realize the benefits of using the Internet to conduct online campaigns and raise funds. Voters also are increasingly using the Web to access information about parties and candidates, promote political goals, and obtain political news. Generally, the use of the Internet is an inexpensive way for candidates to contact, recruit, and mobilize supporters, as well as disseminate information about their positions on issues. In effect, the Internet can replace brochures, letters, and position papers. Individual voters or political party supporters can use the Internet to avoid having to go to special meetings or to a campaign site to do volunteer work or obtain information on a candidate's positions.

That the Internet is now a viable medium for communicating political information and interacting with voters was made clear in the campaigns preceding the 2004, 2006, and 2008 elections. According to a Pew Research Center survey following the 2004 presidential elections, 29 percent of Americans said that they went online for election news, up from 4 percent who did so in the 1996 campaign. Nearly seven in ten of this group went online to seek information on the candidates' positions. Moreover, 43 percent of this group claimed that the information they found online affected their voting decisions.

ONLINE FUND-RAISING The Internet can be an effective—and inexpensive—way to raise campaign funds. Fund-raising on the Internet by presidential

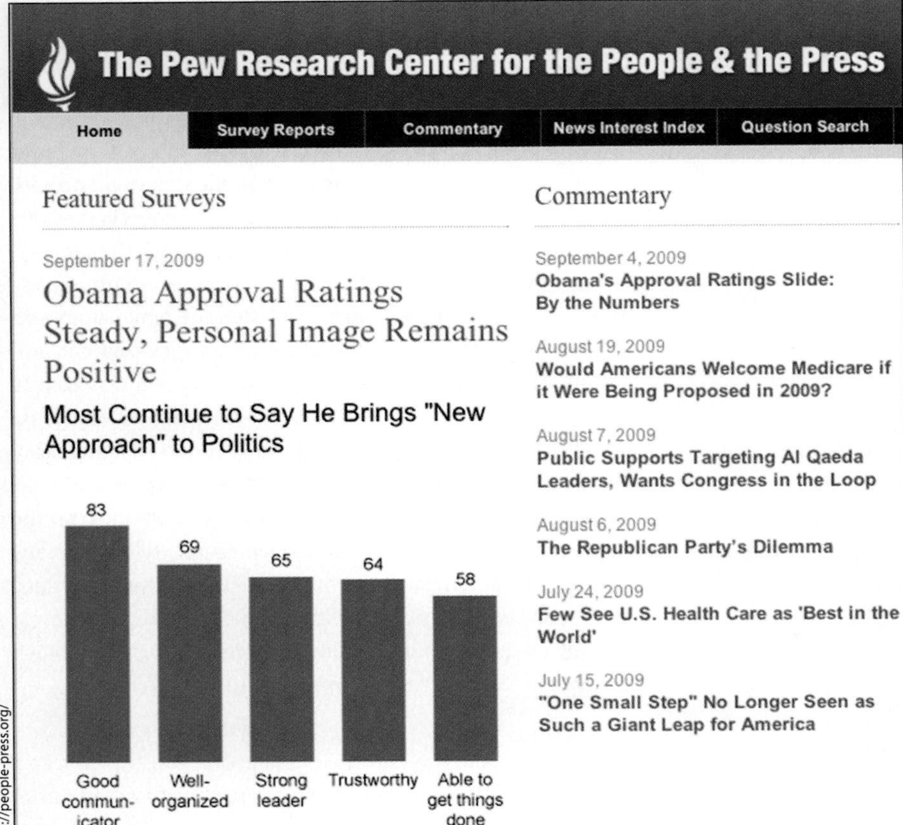

http://people-press.org/

candidates became widespread after the Federal Election Commission decided, in June 1999, that the federal government could distribute matching funds for credit-card donations received by candidates via the Internet. In 2003, Democratic presidential hopeful Howard Dean showed the fund-raising power of the Internet by raising more than $20 million online. Political analysts marveled at Dean's success, especially in shifting the focus of campaign finance from a few large donors to countless small donors. These important new Internet strategies were then adopted by the presidential campaigns of John Kerry and George W. Bush in 2004.

In the run-up to the 2006 midterm elections, both Democrats and Republicans increased the size of their campaign chests through online contributions. In the 2008 presidential contest, however, the candidates took online fund-raising to an entirely new level, especially in the Democratic primaries. The fund-raising effort of Hillary Clinton would have been considered outstanding in any previous presidential election cycle. Yet it was eclipsed by the organization put together by Barack Obama.

Obama's online operation was the heart of his fund-raising success. One of its defining characteristics was its decentralization. The Obama campaign attempted to recruit as many supporters as possible to act as fund-raisers who solicited contributions from their friends and neighbors. As a result, Obama personally was spared much of the fund-raising effort that consumes the time of most national politicians. In the first half

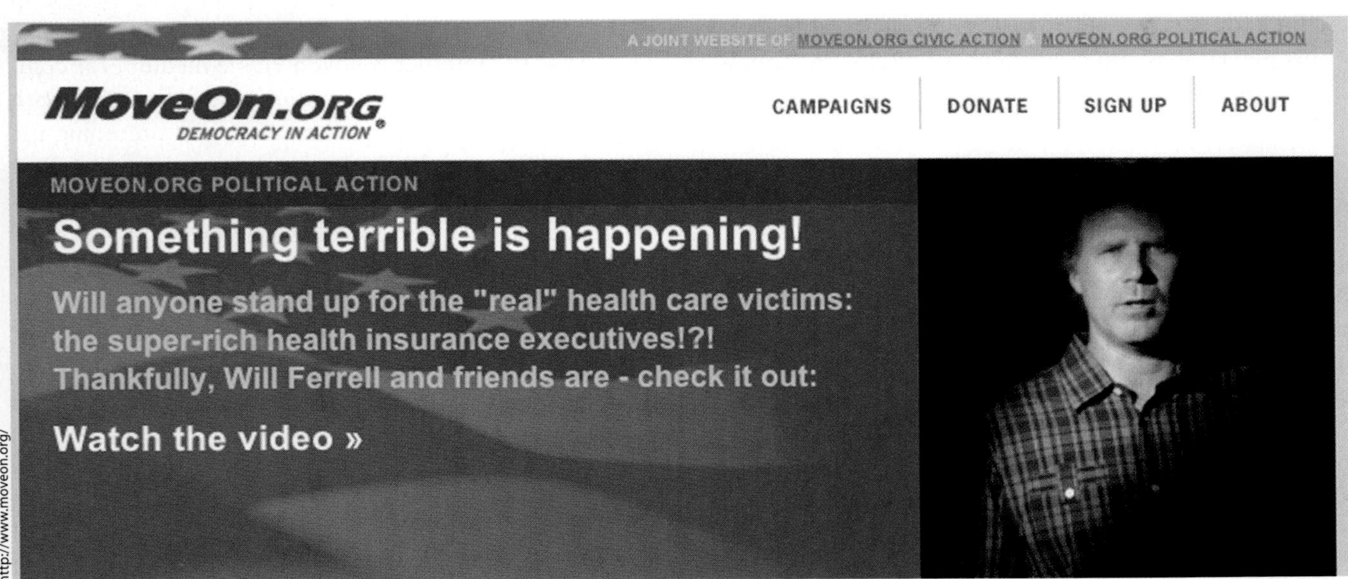

http://www.moveon.org/

www.youtube.com

Top Photo: YouTube has become an unwitting political force. In 2007, millions of people heard Hillary Clinton sing the national anthem off-key. Center Photo: Republican presidential candidate Mitt Romney saw his own inconsistencies on a YouTube video. Bottom Photo: Democratic presidential candidate Barack Obama laid out his plans on YouTube for the 2008 presidential elections.

of 2007, Obama's campaign raised $58 million, $16.4 million of which was made up of donations of less than $200. The total sum was a record, and the small-donation portion was unusually large. In September 2008, the Obama campaign set another fund-raising record with $150 million, the most ever raised in one month by a presidential campaign. By then, 2.9 million people had donated to Obama's campaign.

THE RISE OF THE INTERNET CAMPAIGN An increasingly important part of political campaigning today is the Internet campaign. Candidates typically hire Web managers to manage their Internet campaigns. The job of the Web manager, or Web strategist, is to create a well-designed, informative, and user-friendly campaign Web site to attract viewers, hold their attention, manage their e-mail, and track their credit-card contributions. The Web manager also hires bloggers to promote the candidate's views, arranges for podcasting of campaign information and updates to supporters, and hires staff to monitor the Web for news about the candidates and to track the online publications of *netroots groups*—online activists who support the candidate but are not controlled by the candidate's organization.

CONTROLLING THE "NETROOTS." One of the challenges facing candidates today is trying to deliver a consistent campaign message to voters. Netroots groups may publish online promotional ads or other materials that do not represent a candidate's position. Similarly, online groups may attack the candidate's opponent in ways that the candidate does not approve. Yet no candidate wants to alienate these groups, because they can raise significant sums of money and garner votes for the candidate. For example, the group MoveOn.org raised $28 million for Democrats prior to the 2006 elections. Yet MoveOn.org is more left leaning on issues than the most competitive Democratic presidential candidates in 2008 wanted to appear—because those candidates hoped to gain the votes of more moderate voters.

CANDIDATES' 24/7 EXPOSURE. Just as citizen journalism, discussed earlier, has altered the news culture, so have citizen videos changed the traditional campaign. For example, a candidate can never know when a comment that she or he makes may be caught on camera by someone with a cell phone or digital camera and published on the Internet for all to see. At times, such exposure can be devastating, as George Allen, the former Republican senator from Virginia, learned in the 2006 midterm elections. He was captured on video making a racial slur about one of his opponent's campaign workers. The video was posted on YouTube, and within a short time the major news organizations picked up the story. Many news commentators claimed that this video exposé gave Allen's Democratic opponent, Jim Webb, enough votes to win the race. A candidate's opponents may also post on YouTube or some other Web site a compilation of video clips showing the candidate's inconsistent comments over time on a specific topic, such as abortion or the war in Iraq. The effect can be very damaging by making the candidate's "flip-flopping" on the issue apparent.

This 24/7 exposure of the candidates also makes it difficult for the candidates to control their campaigns. Even videos on the lighter side, such as a video showing Hillary Clinton singing the "Star-Spangled Banner" when she didn't know that her lapel microphone was on, can be embarrassing. The potential for citizen videos to destroy a candidate's chances is always there, creating a new type of uncertainty in political campaigning. In 2007, noted political commentator Andrew Sullivan concluded that "one can safely predict that at some point in the wide-open race for the American presidency in 2008 at least one candidate will be destroyed by video-blogs and one may be handed a victory. Every gaffe will matter much more, and every triumph can echo for much longer."[14] Sullivan was wrong about 2008, but such an event will surely take place in years to come.

During the last Senate race in Virginia, incumbent George Allen (R) fought a close battle with Democratic challenger Jim Webb. Allen was caught on video making a distasteful remark to a spectator who was born in India. Some believe that this video, which millions saw on YouTube, allowed Webb to gain the advantage and win.

Photo by Mark Wilson/GettyImages

AMERICA AT ODDS Politics and the Media

The news business has been with us from the beginning of our republic. In the early years, the publication of ideas took place largely through political pamphleteering. Yet the price of pamphlets often put them beyond the reach of most citizens. Even Senator William Maclay of Pennsylvania said that he could not afford to buy a copy of the *Federalist* and hoped that someone would lend him one. Nonetheless, by 1800 newspapers had begun to circulate in large numbers. In contrast to the 1720s, when there were fewer than a half-dozen newspapers in the colonies, by 1800 there were more than 230. By 1810, Americans were buying more than 22 million copies of 376 newspapers every year. Media bias has also always been with us. The first presidents and their political parties all had run-ins with the press, and it was not too uncommon for a party to buy a newspaper operation and shut it down in an effort to control public opinion.

Today, as you have seen, the media continue to be accused of biased reporting. Conservatives accuse the news industry of reflecting a liberal bias, while liberals argue just the opposite. As one observer noted, though, if this is the case, then the news must be reflecting both liberal and conservative views. Generally, compared with people in other nations, Americans enjoy a news industry that is remarkably free from government interference. This is increasingly true in this new age of citizen journalism, in which any and all Americans, if they wish, can participate in the reporting and dissemination of news to the public.

ISSUES FOR DEBATE & DISCUSSION

1. **Some Americans, including many journalists, complain that the news media offer too much "shallow" coverage. For example, stories about Britney Spears abound in the national media, while an incident that resulted in the deaths of thirty-two Chicago schoolchildren—mostly black, Hispanic, or poor—received scant attention. Others believe that the media are forced to focus on flashy events, including those involving celebrities, in order to survive in an increasingly competitive industry. On the whole, this group claims, given their constraints the media do a relatively good job of delivering the news to Americans. What is your position on this issue?**
2. **Many people believe that bias in the media is a serious problem. In the media that you follow, have you seen examples of what you would call bias? If so, how was the bias expressed? If some media outlets are liberal and others are conservative, do they balance each other out, or does this situation just make the problem worse? Either way, why?**

TAKE ACTION

Today, the media are wide open for citizen involvement. You, too, can be a reporter of the news. You can create videos of events that you believe are newsworthy and post them online. You can podcast video or audio coverage of an event from a Web site that you have created. You can write a blog of your own on your Web site and invite others to participate. You, by yourself or with others, can set up a "radio station" to spread your views using the Internet. For example, in the photo shown here, two citizens who supported a proposed Tennessee state tax reform set up their own radio station in Nashville to mock local radio personalities who were opposed to the reform. Lining the street nearby are other supporters of the tax reform.

Local talk-radio and news programs abound. They are often irreverent and operated by young people.

AP Photo/John Russell

POLITICS ON THE WEB

- Newspapers.com features links to more than ten thousand newspapers nationwide. You can also search by categories, such as business, college newspapers, and industry. Go to **www.newspapers.com**
- Townhall.com provides political commentary from more than a hundred columnists. It seeks to amplify conservative voices in America's political debates. It can be found at **www.townhall.com**
- MoveOn.org, a liberal online group that promotes left-leaning values and Democratic candidates, is on the Web at **www.moveon.org**
- The Polling Report Web site provides polling results on a number of issues, organized by topics. The site is easy to use and up to date. Go to **www.pollingreport.com**
- A blog search engine with links to blogs in a variety of categories can be accessed at **www.blogsearchengine.com**

Online resources for this chapter

This text's Companion Web site, at **www.4ltrpress.cengage.com/govt**, offers links to numerous resources that you can use to learn more about the topics covered in this chapter.

Congress

GOVT

11

LEARNING OBJECTIVES

LO1 Explain how seats in the House of Representatives are apportioned among the states.

LO2 Describe the power of incumbency.

LO3 Identify the key leadership positions in Congress, describe the committee system, and indicate some important differences between the House of Representatives and the Senate.

LO4 Summarize the specific steps in the lawmaking process.

LO5 Identify Congress's oversight functions and explain how Congress fulfills them.

LO6 Indicate what is involved in the congressional budgeting process.

AMERICA AT ODDS

Should It Take Sixty Senators to Pass Important Legislation?

If there is a magic number in politics, it is sixty. Why? Because sixty is the number of Senate votes required to force an end to a filibuster. A filibuster takes place when senators use the chamber's tradition of unlimited debate to block legislation. In years past, filibustering senators would speak for hours—even reading names from the telephone book—to prevent a vote on a proposed bill. In recent decades, however, Senate rules have permitted filibusters in which actual continuous floor speeches are not required. Senators merely announce that they are filibustering. The threat of a filibuster has created an *ad hoc* rule that important legislation needs the support of sixty senators. (There are exceptions; budget bills are handled using a special "reconciliation" rule that does not permit filibusters.)

If one party can elect sixty or more U.S. senators, assuming they all follow the party line, they can force through any legislation they want by invoking "cloture," which ends filibusters. In mid-2009, the Democrats finally got what they had hoped for: a supermajority in the Senate. In April, Senator Arlen Specter of Pennsylvania left the Republicans to join the Democrats. In June, the Minnesota Supreme Court finally decided the hotly contested Senate race in that state and awarded the victory to Al Franken, the Democrat.

The question remains, though, whether the magic number of sixty is an appropriate requirement for passing important legislation in the Senate. Should the number be reduced to fifty-five or even to fifty-one—a simple majority of all sitting senators?

Don't Let the Majority Trample on the Minority

The long history of the filibuster in the United States Senate and the consequent need for a supermajority to pass legislation has served us well. Filibusters, or even the threat of filibusters, provide the minority with an effective means of preventing the majority from ramrodding legislation down the throats of American voters.

Rule by a simple majority can be scary. Support for a measure can shift between 49 percent and 51 percent very quickly. Should such small changes be the basis for passing major legislation? A simple majority does not signify an adequate degree of consensus. When it comes to major issues, something more weighty than simple majority rule should prevail.

Many states require supermajorities for passing any legislation that would raise taxes. In California, for example, a tax increase must win two-thirds approval in both chambers of the state legislature. It takes two-thirds of both chambers of Congress to override a veto by the president. That's another supermajority. Changing the Constitution requires a very substantial supermajority—three-quarters of the state legislatures. If these supermajority rules were good enough for the founders, then the principle still is good enough for the Senate.

Don't Let Obstructionists Determine Legislation

Just because supermajorities were required in jury deliberations in classical Rome and for the election of a pope in the Catholic Church does not mean they are necessary in the Senate. Supermajorities make it harder to achieve needed changes. Supermajorities allow a minority to block the preference of the majority. Even James Madison, who worried about the tyranny of the majority over the minority, recognized the opposite possibility. He said that "the fundamental principle of free government" might be reversed by supermajorities. "It would be no longer majority that would rule: the power would be transferred to the minority."

Furthermore, the sixty-vote requirement in the Senate has led to a significant increase in "pork"—that is, special spending provisions inserted into legislation. Senators working on bills find that they must fill them with pork to attract the votes of their colleagues. Without the pork, the bills won't pass. The bank bailout bill, which we describe later in this chapter, is an excellent example of this process. The Senate should reduce the votes required for cloture of a filibuster to fifty-five or even fifty-one. Let's get on with government by the majority, not the supermajority.

WHERE DO YOU STAND?

1. **Why might it be appropriate to require supermajority voting for important legislation?**
2. **Under what circumstances do supermajority voting rules prevent democracy from being fully realized?**

EXPLORE THIS ISSUE ONLINE

William Greider denounces the tradition of the filibuster in the pages of *The Nation*, a strongly liberal publication. See his article at www.thenation.com/doc/20081229/greider. Nick Dranias, a conservative, defends the supermajority concept at www.goldwaterinstitute.org/article/3244.

Introduction

Congress is the lawmaking branch of government. When someone says, "There ought to be a law," at the federal level it is Congress that will make that law. The framers had a strong suspicion of a powerful executive authority. Consequently, they made Congress—not the executive branch (the presidency)—the central institution of American government. Yet, as noted in Chapter 2, the founders created a system of checks and balances to ensure that no branch of the federal government, including Congress, could exercise too much power.

Many Americans view Congress as a largely faceless, anonymous legislative body that is quite distant and removed from their everyday lives. Yet the people you elect to Congress represent and advocate your interests at the very highest level of power. Furthermore, the laws created by the men and women in the U.S. Congress affect the daily lives of every American in one way or another. Getting to know your congressional representatives and how they are voting in Congress on issues that concern you is an important step toward becoming an informed voter. Even the details of how Congress makes law—such as the Senate rules described in the chapter-opening *America at Odds* feature—should be of interest to the savvy voter.

The Senate Health, Education, Labor, and Pensions Committee begins work on a health-care reform bill. Most of the work of Congress occurs in committees like this one. Some bills end up being over a thousand pages long. Why do you think they end up being so lengthy?

Stephen Crowley/The New York Times/Redux

LO1 The Structure and Makeup of Congress

The framers agreed that the Congress should be the "first branch of the government," as James Madison said, but they did not immediately agree on its organization. Ultimately, they decided on a *bicameral legislature*—a Congress consisting of two chambers. This was part of the Great Compromise, which you read about in Chapter 2. The framers favored a bicameral legislature so that the two chambers, the House and the Senate, might serve as checks on each other's power and activity. The House was to represent the people as a whole, or the majority. The Senate was to represent the states and would protect the interests of small states by giving them the same number of senators (two per state) as the larger states.

Apportionment of House Seats

The Constitution provides for the **apportionment** (distribution) of House seats among the states on the basis of their respective populations. States with larger populations, such as California, have many more representatives than states with smaller populations, such as Wyoming. California, for example, currently has fifty-three representatives in the House; Wyoming has only one.

Every ten years, House seats are reapportioned based on the outcome of the decennial (ten-year) census conducted by the U.S. Census Bureau. Figure 11–1 on the next page indicates the states that gained and lost seats based on population changes reported by the 2000 census. This redistribution of seats took effect with the 108th Congress, which was elected in 2002.

Each state is guaranteed at least one House seat, no matter what its population. Today, seven states have only one representative.[1] The District of Columbia, American Samoa, Guam, and the U.S. Virgin Islands all send nonvoting delegates to the House. Puerto Rico, a self-governing

apportionment The distribution of House seats among the states on the basis of their respective populations.

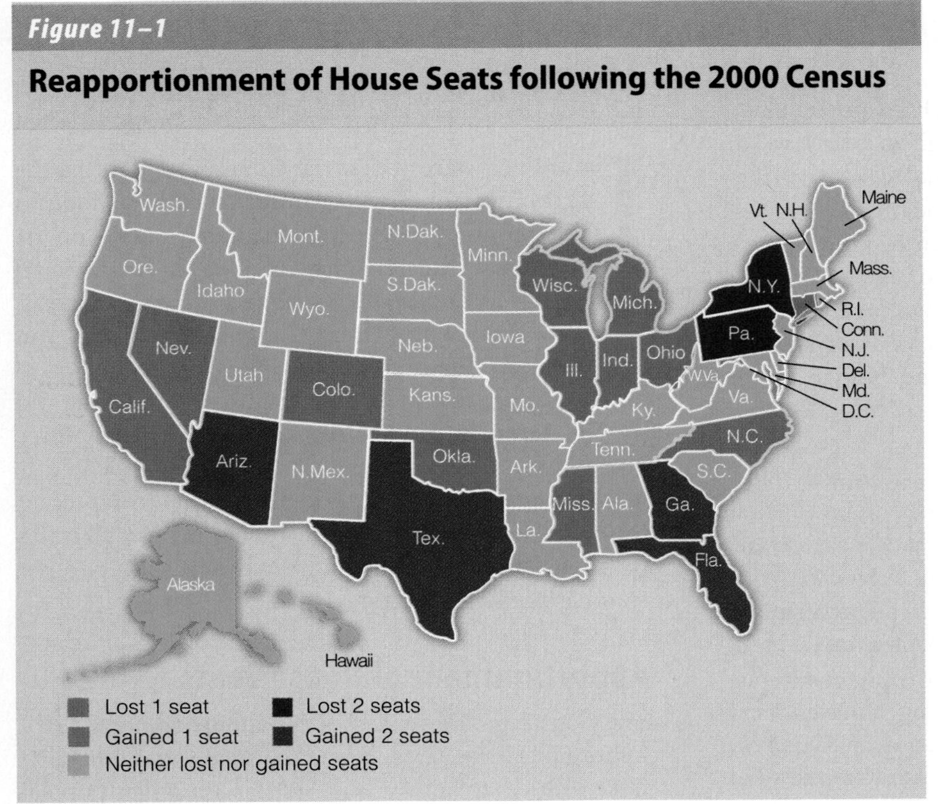

Figure 11–1

Reapportionment of House Seats following the 2000 Census

Source: U.S. Bureau of the Census.

possession of the United States, is represented by a nonvoting resident commissioner.

Congressional Districts

Whereas senators are elected to represent all of the people in the state, representatives are elected by the voters of a particular area known as a **congressional district.** The Constitution makes no provisions for congressional districts, and in the early 1800s each state was given the right to decide whether to have districts at all. Most states set up single-member districts, in which voters in each district elected one of the state's representatives. In states that chose not to have districts, representatives were chosen at large, from the state as a whole. In 1842, however, Congress passed an act that required all states to send representatives to Congress from single-member districts, as you read in Chapter 7.

congressional district
The geographic area that is served by one member in the House of Representatives.

malapportionment
A condition in which the voting power of citizens in one district is greater than the voting power of citizens in another district.

In the early 1900s, the number of House members increased as the population expanded. In 1929, however, a federal law fixed House membership at 435 members. Thus, today the 435 members of the House are chosen by the voters in 435 separate congressional districts across the country. If a state's population allows it to have only one representative, the entire state is one congressional district. In contrast, states with large populations have many districts. California, for example, because its population entitles it to send fifty-three representatives to the House, has fifty-three congressional districts.

By default, the lines of the congressional districts are drawn by the state legislatures. Alternatively, the task may be handed off to a designated body such as an independent commission. States must meet certain requirements in drawing district boundaries. To ensure equal representation in the House, districts must contain, as nearly as possible, equal numbers of people. Additionally, each district must have contiguous boundaries and must be "geographically compact," although this last requirement is not enforced very strictly.

THE REQUIREMENT OF EQUAL REPRESENTATION If congressional districts are not made up of equal populations, the value of people's votes is not the same. In the past, state legislators often used this fact to their advantage. For example, traditionally, many state legislatures were controlled by rural areas. By drawing districts that were not equal in population, rural leaders attempted to curb the number of representatives from growing urban centers. At one point in the 1960s, in many states the largest district had twice the population of the smallest district. In effect, this meant that a person's vote in the largest district had only half the value of a person's vote in the smallest district.

For some time, the United States Supreme Court refused to address this problem. In 1962, however, in *Baker v. Carr,*[2] the Court ruled that the Tennessee state legislature's **malapportionment** was an issue that could be heard in the federal courts because it affected the constitutional requirement of equal protection under the law. Two years later, in *Wesberry v. Sanders,*[3] the Supreme Court held that congressional districts must have equal populations. This principle has come to be known as the **"one person, one vote" rule.** In other words, one person's vote has to count as much as another's vote.

GERRYMANDERING Although in the 1960s the Supreme Court ruled that congressional districts must be equal in population, it continued to be silent on the issue of gerrymandered districts. **Gerrymandering** occurs when a district's boundaries are drawn to maximize the influence of a certain group or political party. Where a party's voters are scarce, the boundaries can be drawn to include as many of the party's voters as possible. Where the party is strong, the lines are drawn so that the opponent's supporters are spread across two or more districts, thus diluting the opponent's strength. (The term *gerrymandering* was originally used to describe the district lines drawn to favor the party of Governor Elbridge Gerry of Massachusetts prior to the 1812 election—see Figure 11–2 on the next page.)

Library of Congress

Elbridge Gerry, governor of Massachusetts, 1810–1812.

Although there have been constitutional challenges to political gerrymandering,[4] the practice continues. It was certainly evident following the 2000 census. Sophisticated computer programs can now analyze the partisan leanings of individual neighborhoods and city blocks. District lines are drawn to "pack" the opposing party's voters into the smallest number of districts or "crack" the opposing party's voters into several different districts. "Packing and cracking" makes congressional races less competitive. In 2003, for example, Texas adopted a controversial redistricting plan that was spearheaded by then House majority leader Tom DeLay (R., Tex.). DeLay and Texas Republicans used "pack and crack" tactics to redraw districts that had formerly leaned toward Democratic candidates. The plan effectively cost four Democratic representatives their seats in the 2004 elections.[5]

RACIAL GERRYMANDERING Although political gerrymandering has a long history, gerrymandering to empower minority groups is a relatively new phenomenon. In the early 1990s, the U.S. Department of Justice instructed state legislatures to draw district lines to maximize the voting power of minority groups. As a result, several **minority-majority districts** were created. Many of these districts took on bizarre shapes. For example, North Carolina's newly drawn Twelfth Congressional District was 165 miles long—a narrow strip that, for the most part, followed Interstate 85. Georgia's new Eleventh District stretched from Atlanta to the Atlantic, splitting eight counties and five municipalities. The practice of racial gerrymandering has generated heated argument on both sides of the issue.

Some groups contend that minority-majority districts are necessary to ensure equal representation of minority groups, as mandated by the Voting Rights Act of 1965. They further contend that these districts have been instrumental in increasing the number of African Americans holding political office. Minority-majority districts in the South contain, on average, 45 percent nonblack voters, whereas before 1990, redistricting plans in the South often created only white-majority districts.[6]

Opponents of racial gerrymandering argue that such race-based districting is unconstitutional because it violates the equal protection clause. In a series of cases in the 1990s, the Supreme Court agreed and held that when race is the dominant factor in the drawing of congressional district lines, the districts are unconstitutional and must be redrawn.[7]

In 2001, however, the Supreme Court issued a ruling that seemed—at least to some observers—to be out of step with its earlier rulings. North Carolina's Twelfth District, which had been redrawn in 1997, was again challenged in court as unconstitutional, and a lower court agreed. When the case reached the Supreme Court, however, the justices concluded that there was

"one person, one vote" rule A rule, or principle, requiring that congressional districts have equal populations so that one person's vote counts as much as another's vote.

gerrymandering The drawing of a legislative district's boundaries in such a way as to maximize the influence of a certain group or political party.

minority-majority district A district whose boundaries are drawn so as to maximize the voting power of minority groups.

Figure 11–2

The First "Gerrymander"

Prior to the 1812 elections, the Massachusetts legislature divided up Essex County in a way that favored Governor Elbridge Gerry's party; the result was a district that looked something like a salamander. A newspaper editor of the time referred to it as a "gerrymander," and the name stuck.

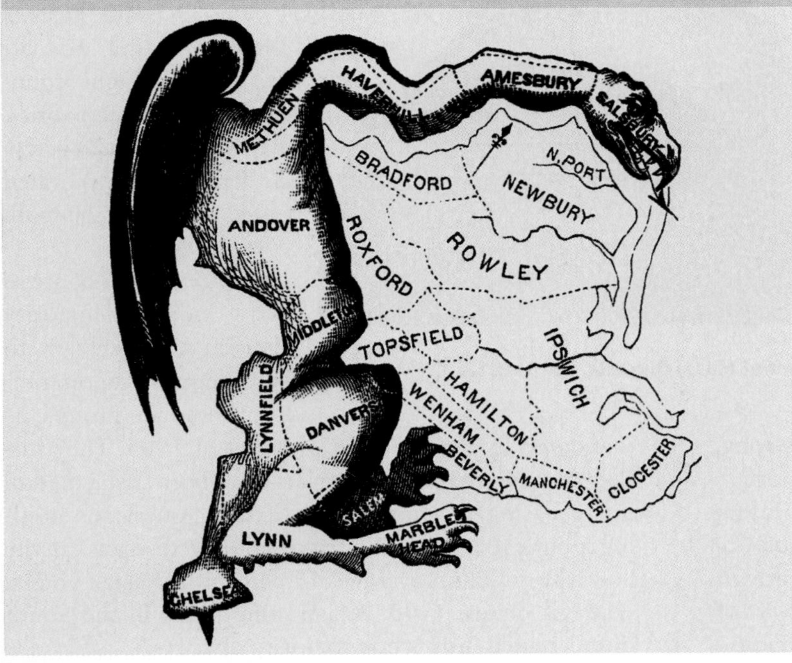

Source: *Congressional Quarterly's Guide to Congress,* 3d ed. (Washington, D.C.: Congressional Quarterly Press, 1982), p. 695.

"When a man assumes a public trust, he should consider himself a **PUBLIC PROPERTY.**"

~ THOMAS JEFFERSON ~
THIRD PRESIDENT OF THE UNITED STATES
1801–1809

insufficient evidence that race had been the dominant factor in redrawing the district's boundaries.[8]

The Representation Function of Congress

Of the three branches of government, Congress has the closest ties to the American people. Members of Congress represent the interests and wishes of the constituents in their home states. At the same time, they must also consider larger national issues such as the economy and the environment. Often, legislators find that the interests of their constituents are at odds with the demands of national policy. For example, limits on emissions of carbon dioxide might help reduce global warming, to the benefit of all Americans and the people of the world generally. Yet members of Congress who come from states where most electricity comes from coal-burning power plants might fear that new laws would hurt the local economy and cause companies to lay off workers. All members of Congress face difficult votes that set representational interests against lawmaking realities. There are several views on how legislators should decide such issues.

trustee A representative who tries to serve the broad interests of the entire society and not just the narrow interests of his or her constituents.

instructed delegate A representative who deliberately mirrors the views of the majority of his or her constituents.

THE TRUSTEE VIEW OF REPRESENTATION Some believe that representatives should act as **trustees** of the broad interests of the entire society rather than serving only the narrow interests of their constituents. Under the trustee view, a legislator should act according to her or his conscience and perception of national needs. For example, a senator from North Carolina might support laws regulating the tobacco industry even though the state's economy could be negatively affected.

THE INSTRUCTED-DELEGATE VIEW OF REPRESENTATION In contrast, others believe that members of Congress should behave as **instructed delegates.** The instructed-delegate view requires representatives to mirror the views of their constituents, regardless of their opinions. Under this view, a senator from Nebraska would strive to obtain subsidies for corn growers, and a representative from the Detroit area would seek to protect the automobile industry.

THE PARTISAN VIEW OF REPRESENTATION Because the political parties often take different positions on legislative issues, there are times when members of Congress are very attentive to the wishes of the party leadership. Especially on matters that are

These female members of the House of Representatives wave to the delegates at the National Democratic Convention in Denver in 2008. While women have made serious inroads into the halls of political power, they are still underrepresented relative to their 51 percent share of our population.

controversial, the Democratic members of Congress will be more likely to vote in favor of policies endorsed by a Democratic president, while Republicans will be more likely to oppose them.

THE POLITICO STYLE Typically, members of Congress combine these three approaches in what is often called the "politico" style. Legislators may take a trustee approach on some issues, adhere to the instructed-delegate view on other matters, and follow the party line on still others.

LO2 *Congressional Elections*

The U.S. Constitution requires that representatives to Congress be elected every second year by popular vote. Senators are elected every six years, also by popular vote (since the ratification of the Seventeenth Amendment). Under Article I, Section 4, of the Constitution, state legislatures control the "Times, Places and Manner of holding Elections for Senators and Representatives." Congress, however, "may at any time by Law make or alter such Regulations." As you read in Chapter 9, control over the process of nominating congressional candidates has largely shifted from party conventions to direct primaries in which the party's supporters select the candidates who will carry that party's endorsement into the general election.

Who Can Be a Member of Congress?

The Constitution sets forth only a few qualifications that those running for Congress must meet. To be a member of the House, a person must have been a citizen of the United States for at least seven years prior to his or her election, must be a legal resident of the state from which he or she is to be elected, and must be at least twenty-five years of age. To be elected to the Senate, a person must have been a citizen for at least nine years, must be a legal resident of the state from which she or he is to be elected, and must be at least thirty years of age. The Supreme Court has ruled that neither the Congress nor the states can add to these three qualifications.[9]

Once elected to Congress, a senator or representative receives an annual salary from the government, currently $174,000 for rank-and-file members. He or she also enjoys certain perks and privileges. Additionally, if a member of Congress wants to run for reelection in the next congressional elections, that person's chances are greatly enhanced by the power that incumbency brings to a reelection campaign.

Table 11–1

The Power of Incumbency

	Presidential-Year Elections								Midterm Elections						
House	1980	1984	1988	1992	1996	2000	2004	2008	1982	1986	1990	1994	1998	2002	2006
Number of incumbent candidates	398	411	409	368	384	403	404	404	393	394	406	387	402	393	405
Reelected	361	392	402	325	361	394	397	381	354	385	390	349	395	383	382
Percentage of total	90.7	95.4	98.3	88.3	94.0	97.8	98.3	94.3	90.1	97.7	96.0	90.2	98.3	97.5	94.3
Defeated	37	19	7	43	23	9	7	23	39	9	16	38	7	10	23
Senate															
Number of incumbent candidates	29	29	27	28	21	29	26	30	30	28	32	26	29	28	29
Reelected	16	26	23	23	19	23	25	26	28	21	31	24	26	24	23
Percentage of total	55.2	89.6	85.2	82.1	90.5	79.3	96.2	86.7	93.3	75.0	96.9	92.3	89.7	85.7	79.3
Defeated	13	3	4	5	2	6	1	4	2	7	1	2	3	4	6

Sources: Norman Ornstein, Thomas E. Mann, and Michael J. Malbin, *Vital Statistics on Congress, 2001–2002* (Washington, D.C.: The AEI Press, 2002); and authors' updates.

The Power of Incumbency

The power of incumbency has long been noted in American politics. Typically, incumbents win so often and by such large margins that some observers have claimed that our electoral system involves something similar to a hereditary entitlement. As you can see in Table 11–1 above, most incumbents in Congress are reelected if they run.

Incumbent politicians enjoy several advantages over their opponents. A key advantage is their fund-raising ability. Most incumbent members of Congress have a much larger network of contacts, donors, and lobbyists than their opponents. Incumbents raise, on average, twice as much in campaign funds as their challengers. Other advantages that incumbents can put to work to aid their reelection include:

- *Congressional franking privileges*—members of Congress can mail newsletters and other correspondence to their constituents at the taxpayers' expense.
- *Professional staffs*—members have large administrative staffs both in Washington, D.C., and in their home districts.
- *Lawmaking power*—members of Congress can back legislation that will benefit their states or districts, and then campaign on that legislative record in the next election.
- *Access to the media*—because they are elected officials, members have many opportunities to stage events for the press and thereby obtain free publicity.
- *Name recognition*—incumbent members are usually far better known to the voters than challengers are.

Critics argue that the advantage enjoyed by incumbents reduces the competition necessary for a healthy democracy. It also suppresses voter turnout. Voters are less likely to turn out when an incumbent candidate is virtually guaranteed reelection. The solution often proposed to eliminate the power of incumbency is term limits, a topic we discuss shortly.

Congressional Terms and Term Limits

As noted earlier, members of the House of Representatives serve two-year terms, and senators serve six-year terms. This means that every two years, we hold congressional elections: the entire House of Representatives and a third of the Senate are up for election. In January of every odd-numbered year, a "new" Congress convenes (of course, two-thirds of the senators are not new, and most House incumbents are reelected, so they are not new to Congress either). Each Congress has been numbered consecutively, dating back to 1789. The Congress that convened in 2009 is the 111th.

Each congressional term is divided into two regular sessions, or meetings—one for each year. Until about 1940, Congress remained in session for only four or five months, but the complicated rush of legislation and increased demand for services from the public in recent years have forced Congress to remain in session through most of each year.[10] Both chambers, however,

speaker.gov/newsroom/photogallery?id=0001

www.majorityleader.gov

johnboehner.house.gov

When the Democrats took control of the House of Representatives after the 2006 midterm elections, they elected Nancy Pelosi (D., Calif.) as Speaker of the House and Steny H. Hoyer (D., Md.) as House majority leader. John Boehner (R., Ohio), on the right, was named House minority leader by the Republicans. All three were reelected in 2008.

schedule short recesses, or breaks, for holidays and vacations. The president may call a *special session* during a recess, but because Congress now meets on nearly a year-round basis, such sessions are rare.

As you will read in Chapter 12, the president can serve for no more than two terms in office, due to the Twenty-second Amendment. There is no limit on the number of terms a senator or representative can serve, however. For example, Strom Thurmond (R., S.C.) served eight terms in the U.S. Senate, from 1955 until he retired, at the age of one hundred, in 2003.

As mentioned, some observers favor term limits for Congress. Persuading incumbent politicians to vote for term limits, however, is difficult. At the national level, the Supreme Court has ruled that state-level attempts to impose term limits on members of the U.S. House or Senate are unconstitutional.[11] Efforts to pass a constitutional amendment that would impose term limits on members of Congress have had little success.

LO3 *Congressional Leadership, the Committee System, and Bicameralism*

The Constitution provides for the presiding officers of both the House and the Senate, and each chamber has added other leadership positions as it has seen fit. Leadership and organization in both chambers are based on membership in the two major political parties. The majority party in each chamber chooses the major officers of that chamber, controls debate on the floor, selects all committee chairpersons, and has a majority on all committees.

House Leadership

The Constitution states that members of the House are to choose their Speaker and other officers but says nothing more about these positions. Today, important "other officers" include the majority and minority leaders and whips.

SPEAKER OF THE HOUSE Chief among the leaders in the House of Representatives is the **Speaker of the House.** This office is filled by a vote taken at the beginning of each congressional term. The Speaker has traditionally been a longtime member of the majority party who has risen in rank and influence through years of service in the House. The candidate for Speaker is selected by the majority-party caucus; the House as a whole then approves the selection.

As the presiding officer of the House and the leader of the majority party, the Speaker has a great deal of power. In the nineteenth century, the Speaker had even more

Speaker of the House The presiding officer in the House of Representatives. The Speaker has traditionally been a longtime member of the majority party and is often the most powerful and influential member of the House.

Within each party in the House of Representatives, there is a leadership position called the *whip*. The main job of the party whips is to assist party leaders in getting members to vote along party lines. On the left is House majority whip James E. Clyburn from South Carolina. On the right is House minority whip Eric Cantor from Virginia.

power and was known as the "king of the congressional mountain." Speakers known by such names as "Uncle Joe Cannon" and "Czar Reed" ruled the House with almost unchallengeable power. A revolt in 1910 reduced the Speaker's powers and gave some of those powers to various committees. Today, the Speaker still has many important powers, including the following:

- The Speaker has substantial control over what bills get assigned to which committees.
- The Speaker may preside over the sessions of the House, recognizing or ignoring members who wish to speak.
- The Speaker votes in the event of a tie, interprets and applies House rules, rules on points of order (questions about procedures asked by members), puts questions to a vote, and interprets the outcome of most of the votes taken.
- The Speaker plays a major role in making important committee assignments, which all members desire.
- The Speaker schedules bills for action.

majority leader The party leader elected by the majority party in the House or in the Senate.

minority leader The party leader elected by the minority party in the House or in the Senate.

whip A member of Congress who assists the majority or minority leader in the House or in the Senate in managing the party's legislative preferences.

The Speaker may choose whether to vote on any measure. If the Speaker chooses to vote, he or she appoints a temporary presiding officer (called a Speaker *pro tempore*), who then occupies the Speaker's chair. Under the House rules, the only time the Speaker *must* vote is to break a tie. Otherwise, a tie automatically defeats a bill. The Speaker does not often vote, but by choosing to vote in some cases, the Speaker can actually cause a tie and defeat a proposal.

MAJORITY LEADER The **majority leader** of the House is elected by the caucus of majority party members to act as spokesperson for the party and to keep the party together. The majority leader's job is to help plan the party's legislative program, organize other party members to support legislation favored by the party, and make sure the chairpersons on the many committees finish work on bills that are important to the party. The House majority leader makes speeches on important bills, stating the majority party's position.

MINORITY LEADER The House **minority leader** is the leader of the minority party. Although not as powerful as the majority leader, the minority leader has similar responsibilities. The primary duty of the minority leader is to maintain solidarity within the party. The minority leader persuades influential members of the party to follow its position and organizes fellow party members in criticism of the majority party's policies and programs.

WHIPS The leadership of each party includes assistants to the majority and minority leaders known as **whips.** Whips originated in the British House of Commons, where they were named after the "whipper in," the rider who keeps the hounds together in a fox hunt. The term is applied to assistant party leaders because of the pressure that they place on party members to uphold the party's positions. Whips try to determine how each member is going to vote on certain issues and then advise the party leaders on the strength of party support. Whips also try to see that members are present when important votes are to be taken and that they vote with the party leadership. For example, if the Republican Party strongly supports a tax-cut bill, the Republican Party whip might meet with other

In 2006, Republican senator Mitch McConnell of Kentucky, left, became Senate minority leader, and Democratic senator Harry Reid of Nevada, right, became the Senate majority leader. Both retained these offices after the 2008 elections.

Republican Party members in the House to try to persuade them to vote with the party.

Senate Leadership

The Constitution makes the vice president of the United States the president of the Senate. As presiding officer, the vice president may call on members to speak and put questions to a vote. The vice president is not an elected member of the Senate, however, and may not take part in Senate debates. The vice president may cast a vote in the Senate only in the event of a tie.

PRESIDENT PRO TEMPORE Because vice presidents are rarely available to preside over the Senate, senators elect another presiding officer, the president pro tempore ("pro tem"), who serves in the absence of the vice president. The president pro tem is elected by the whole Senate and is ordinarily the member of the majority party with the longest continuous term of service in the Senate. In the absence of both the president pro tem and the vice president, a temporary presiding officer is selected from the ranks of the Senate, usually a junior member of the majority party.

PARTY LEADERS The real power in the Senate is held by the majority leader, the minority leader, and their whips. The majority leader is the most powerful individual and chief spokesperson of the majority party. The majority leader directs the legislative program and party strategy. The minority leader commands the minority party's opposition to the policies of the majority party and directs the legislative strategy of the minority party.

Congressional Committees

Thousands of bills are introduced during every session of Congress, and no single member can possibly be adequately informed on all the issues that arise. The committee system is a way to provide for specialization, or a division of the legislative labor. Members of a committee concentrate on just one area or topic—such as agriculture or transportation—and develop sufficient expertise to draft appropriate legislation when needed. The flow of legislation through both the House and the Senate is determined largely by the speed with which the members of these committees act on bills and resolutions. The permanent and most powerful committees of Congress are called **standing committees;** their names are listed in Table 11–2 on the following page.

Before any bill can be considered by the entire House or Senate, it must be approved by a majority vote in the standing committee to which it was assigned. As mentioned, standing committees are controlled by the majority party in each chamber. Committee membership is generally divided between the parties according to the number of members in each chamber. In both the House and the Senate, committee *seniority*—the length of continuous service on a particular committee—typically plays a role in determining the committee chairpersons.

Most House and Senate committees also have **subcommittees** with limited areas of jurisdiction. Today, there are more than two hundred subcommittees. There are also other types of

standing committee A permanent committee in Congress that deals with legislation concerning a particular area, such as agriculture or foreign relations.

subcommittee A division of a larger committee that deals with a particular part committee's policy area. Most standing committees have several subcommittees.

committees in Congress. Special, or select, committees, which may be either permanent or temporary, are formed to study specific problems or issues. Joint committees are created by the concurrent action of both chambers of Congress and consist of members from each chamber. Joint committees have dealt with the economy, taxation, and the Library of Congress. There are also conference committees, which include members from both the House and the Senate. They are formed for the purpose of achieving agreement between the House and the Senate on the exact wording of legislative acts when the two chambers pass legislative proposals in different forms. No bill can be sent to the White House to be signed into law unless it first passes both chambers in identical form.

Most of the actual work of legislating is performed by the committees and subcommittees (the "little legislatures"[12]) within Congress. In creating or amending laws, committee members work closely with relevant interest groups and administrative agency personnel. (For more details on the interaction among these groups, see the discussion of "iron triangles" in Chapter 13.)

Table 11–2

Standing Committees in the 111th Congress, 2009–2011

House Committees	Senate Committees
Agriculture	Agriculture, Nutrition, and Forestry
Appropriations	Appropriations
Armed Services	Armed Services
Budget	Banking, Housing, and Urban Affairs
Education and Labor	Budget
Energy and Commerce	Commerce, Science, and Transportation
Financial Services	Energy and Natural Resources
Foreign Affairs	Environment and Public Works
Homeland Security	Finance
House Administration	Foreign Relations
Judiciary	Health, Education, Labor, and Pensions
Natural Resources	Homeland Security and Governmental Affairs
Oversight and Government Reform	Judiciary
Rules	Rules and Administration
Science and Technology	Small Business and Entrepreneurship
Small Business	Veterans' Affairs
Standards of Official Conduct	
Transportation and Infrastructure	
Veterans' Affairs	
Ways and Means	

The Differences between the House and the Senate

To understand what goes on in the chambers of Congress, we need to look at the effects of bicameralism. Each chamber of Congress has developed certain distinct features. The major differences between the House and the Senate are listed in Table 11–3.

Rules Committee A standing committee in the House of Representatives that provides special rules governing how particular bills will be considered and debated by the House. The Rules Committee normally proposes time limits on debate for any bill.

filibustering The Senate tradition of unlimited debate undertaken for the purpose of preventing action on a bill.

SIZE MATTERS Obviously, with 435 voting members, the House cannot operate the same way as the Senate, which has only 100 members. With its larger size, the House needs both more rules and more formality; otherwise, no work would ever get done. The most obvious formal rules have to do with debate on the floor.

The Senate normally permits extended debate on all issues that arise before it. In contrast, the House uses an elaborate system: the House **Rules Committee** normally proposes time limits on debate for any bill, which are accepted or modified by the House. Despite its greater size, as a consequence of its stricter time limits on debate, the House is often able to act on legislation more quickly than the Senate.

IN THE SENATE, DEBATE CAN JUST KEEP GOING AND GOING At one time, both the House and the Senate allowed unlimited debate, but the House ended this practice in 1811. The use of unlimited debate in the Senate to obstruct legislation is called **filibustering** (see the chapter-opening feature). The longest filibuster was waged by Senator Strom Thurmond of South Carolina, who held forth on the Senate floor for twenty-four hours and eighteen minutes in an attempt to thwart the passage of the 1957 Civil Rights Act.

Table 11–3

Major Differences between the House and the Senate

House*	Senate*
Members chosen from local districts	Members chosen from entire state
Two-year term	Six-year term
Always elected by voters	Originally (until 1913) elected by state legislatures
May impeach (accuse, indict) federal officials	May convict federal officials of impeachable offenses
Larger (435 voting members)	Smaller (100 members)
More formal rules	Fewer rules and restrictions
Debate limited	Debate extended
Floor action controlled	Unanimous consent rules
Less prestige and less individual notice	More prestige and media attention
Originates bills for raising revenues	Power of "advice and consent" on presidential appointments and treaties
Local or narrow leadership	National leadership

*Some of these differences, such as term of office, are provided for in the Constitution, while others, such as debate rules, are not.

Today, under Senate Rule 22, debate may be ended by invoking **cloture**—a method of closing debate and bringing the matter under consideration to a vote in the Senate. Sixteen senators must sign a petition requesting cloture, and then, after two days have elapsed, three-fifths of the entire membership must vote for cloture. Once cloture is invoked, each senator may speak on a bill for no more than one hour before a vote is taken. Additionally, a final vote must take place within one hundred hours after cloture has been invoked.

THE SENATE WINS THE PRESTIGE RACE, HANDS DOWN Because of the large number of representatives, few can garner the prestige that a senator enjoys. Senators have relatively little difficulty in gaining access to the media. Members of the House, who run for reelection every two years, have to survive many reelection campaigns before they can obtain recognition for their activities. Usually, a representative has to become an important committee leader before she or he can enjoy the consistent attention of the national news media.

Senators John Kerry (D., Mass.), Charles Schumer (D., N.Y.), and Jeff Bingaman (D., NM) confer during a Senate Finance Committee meeting. Much of the legislative process consists of compromise. No member of Congress can ever obtain everything that he or she wants in new legislation.

Mark Wilson/Getty Images

LO4 *The Legislative Process*

Look at Figure 11–3 on the next page, which shows the basic process through which a bill becomes law at the national level. Not all of the complexities of the process are shown, to be sure. For example, the figure does not indicate the extensive lobbying and media politics that are often involved in the legislative process. There is also no mention of the informal negotiations and "horse trading" that occur to get a bill passed. In this chapter's *Our Government's Response to the Economic Crisis* feature on page 259, we describe how one rather unusual measure—the bank bailout bill—passed through the legislative process.

The basic steps in the process are as follows:

1. ***Introduction of legislation.*** Most bills are proposed by the executive branch, although individual members of Congress or their staffs

cloture A method of ending debate in the Senate and bringing the matter under consideration to a vote by the entire chamber.

Figure 11–3

How a Bill Becomes a Law

This illustration shows the most typical way in which proposed legislation is enacted into law. The process is illustrated with two hypothetical bills, House bill No. 100 (HR 100) and Senate bill No. 200 (S 200). Bills must be passed by both chambers in identical form before they can be sent to the president. The path of HR 100 is traced by an orange line, and that of S 200 by a purple line. In practice, most bills begin as similar proposals in both chambers.

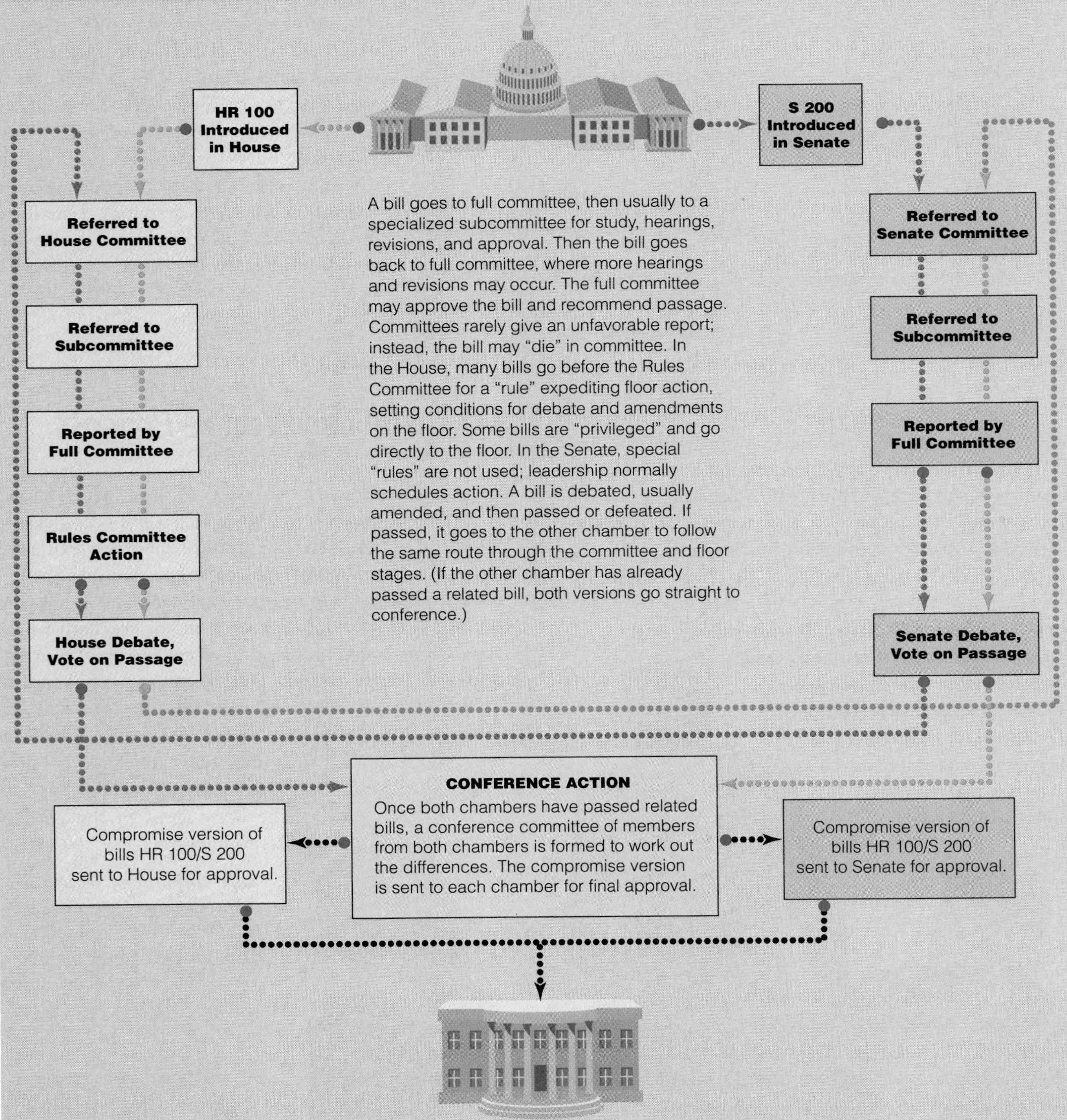

A compromise bill approved by both chambers is sent to the president, who can sign it, veto it, or let it become law without the president's signature. Congress may override a veto by a two-thirds majority vote in each chamber.

Bailing Out the Banks—Big Time

During the increasingly heated presidential campaign in 2008, the American economy was sliding quickly downhill. Major political issues, such as troop withdrawals from Iraq, troop insertions into Afghanistan, and even health-care reform, took a backseat to getting the economy back on track. Members of Congress—and the lame-duck president, George W. Bush—feared an economic meltdown that could rival the Great Depression of the 1930s. A key issue was the state of the financial system and, in particular, what to do to prevent wholesale bankruptcies of financial institutions and a freeze on credit.

Bailing Out the Banks

The bankers caused the problem—so let's bail out the banks. That's what critics of the bank bailout said, at any rate. The global financial system in 2008 was awash with so-called toxic assets. Massive numbers of mortgages were in default. These mortgages had been packaged into securities that were sold throughout the world. Portfolios that were once worth hundreds of billions were worth a fraction of that sum. The mortgage collapse soon revealed that everywhere, too many institutions and people had borrowed too much or invested in highly risky assets. Many banks, especially investment banks, were teetering. On September 15, 2008, the giant investment bank Lehman Brothers failed. It held more than $600 billion in assets and debts. That was the largest bankruptcy in U.S. history.

For the Bush administration, the Lehman Brothers bankruptcy was the last straw. Treasury secretary Henry Paulson immediately called on Congress to give him and his staff the ability to bail out financial institutions by purchasing their distressed mortgage-backed securities. Paulson quickly put together a three-page bill that would have authorized the U.S. Treasury to spend up to $700 billion in this process. (Where this number came from remains a mystery to this day. Why not $200 billion or $900 billion?)

Of course, the objective of this plan was not only to purchase bad assets but also to reduce uncertainty over how much the remaining assets in the financial world were worth. Ultimately, the goal was to restore confidence in credit markets and to get the world economy moving again.

Small Is Bad

No one had ever heard of a three-page bill before. Furthermore, Congress had never before granted such uncontrolled spending power to an executive department. Still, the congressional leadership went to work. Paulson's proposal was a "money" bill that, according to the Constitution, had to originate in the House. If it were sent to a standing committee, however, it would be held up for days, no matter how fast the members worked. Instead, the House Democratic leadership attached the measure to an existing bill as an amendment. The leadership also expanded Paulson's proposal to 110 pages by adding oversight mechanisms and a huge serving of pork. The amendment, however, was rejected in the House by a margin of 228 to 205. For the moment, the act was dead. In response, the value of stocks on Wall Street plunged radically.

Enter the Senate. It is not supposed to initiate spending bills, but it got around this restriction by attaching the legislation as an amendment to an existing bill already passed by the House. The Senate's amendment, called the Emergency Economic Stabilization Act of 2008, had ballooned to 451 pages. Within those pages you could find the newly created Troubled Assets Relief Program (TARP), a $700 billion fund to purchase bank assets—or to do almost anything else that the Treasury considered necessary. The bill passed the Senate on a vote of 74 to 25.

The bill was returned to the House, which this time accepted it by a vote of 263 to 171. Because the House endorsed the measure exactly as the Senate had written it, there was no need for a conference committee to reconcile the versions. The law was immediately sent to President Bush, who signed it that same day.

Don't Waste a Crisis

It was a crisis situation, and Congress made sure not to waste it. The 451-page bill contained almost $14 billion in various tax-break extensions for businesses. There were special provisions that benefited rural schools, film and television producers, makers of toy wooden arrows, victims of the 1989 *Exxon Valdez* oil spill in Alaska, rum distillers in the Virgin Islands and Puerto Rico, auto racetracks, and wool researchers. The bill also included a landmark health-care provision that requires health insurance companies to provide coverage for mental health treatment equivalent to that provided for treatment of physical illnesses. (That had been part of the original bill that the Senate hijacked and amended.)

For Critical Analysis ***Why does it seem that all legislation coming from Congress contains pork that is totally unrelated to the original purpose of the legislation?***

Alex Wong/Getty Images

Senator Max Baucus (D., Mont.) on the left discusses pending legislation with Senator Bill Nelson (D., Fla.) during a hearing on health-care reform in the fall of 2009. At the same moment, other committees in the House and the Senate were creating their own versions of that legislation.

can come up with ideas for new legislation; so, too, can private citizens or lobbying groups. Only a member of Congress can formally introduce legislation, however. In reality, an increasing number of bills are proposed, developed, and often written by the White House or an executive agency. Then a "friendly" senator or representative introduces the bill in Congress. Such bills are rarely ignored entirely, although they are often amended or defeated.

2. *Referral to committees.* As soon as a bill is introduced and assigned a number, it is sent to the appropriate standing committee. In the House, the Speaker assigns the bill to the appropriate committee. In the Senate, the presiding officer assigns the bill to the proper committee. For example, a farm bill in the House would be sent to the Agriculture Committee; a gun control bill would be sent to the Judiciary Committee. A committee chairperson will typically send the bill on to a subcommittee. For example, a Senate bill concerning additional involvement in NATO (the North Atlantic Treaty Organization) in Europe would be sent to the Senate Foreign Relations Subcommittee on European Affairs. Alternatively, the chairperson may decide to put the bill aside and ignore it. Most bills that are pigeonholed in this manner receive no further action.

   If a bill is not pigeonholed, committee staff members go to work researching the bill. The committee may hold public hearings during which people who support or oppose the bill can express their views. Committees also have the power to order witnesses to testify at public hearings. Witnesses may be executive agency officials, experts on the subject, or representatives of interest groups concerned about the bill.

   The subcommittee must meet to approve the bill as it is, add new amendments, or draft a new bill. This meeting is known as the **markup session.** If members cannot agree on changes, a vote is taken. When a subcommittee completes its work, the bill goes to the full standing committee, which then meets for its own markup session. The committee may hold its own hearings, amend the subcommittee's version, or simply approve the subcommittee's recommendations.

markup session A meeting held by a congressional committee or subcommittee to approve, amend, or redraft a bill.

3. *Reports on a bill.* Finally, the committee will report the bill back to the full chamber. It can report the bill favorably, report the bill with amendments, or report a newly written bill. It can also report a bill unfavorably, but usually such a bill will have been pigeonholed earlier instead. Along with the bill, the committee will send to the House or Senate a written report that explains the committee's actions, describes the bill, lists the major changes made by the committee, and gives opinions on the bill.
4. *The Rules Committee and scheduling.* Scheduling is an extremely important part of getting a bill enacted into law. A bill must be put on a calendar. Typically, the House Rules Committee plays a major role in the scheduling process. This committee, along with the House leaders, regulates the flow of the bills through the House. The Rules Committee will also specify the amount of time to be spent on debate and whether amendments can be made by a floor vote.

   In the Senate, a few leading members control the flow of bills. The Senate brings a bill to the floor

> "You've got to work things out in the cloakroom.
> AND WHEN YOU'VE GOT THEM WORKED OUT, YOU CAN DEBATE A LITTLE BEFORE YOU VOTE."
>
> ~ LYNDON BAINES JOHNSON ~
> THIRTY-SIXTH PRESIDENT
> OF THE UNITED STATES (1963–1969)
> AND MAJORITY LEADER OF THE SENATE (1955–1961)

by "unanimous consent," a motion by which all members present on the floor set aside the formal Senate rules and consider a bill. In contrast to the procedure in the House, individual senators have the power to disrupt work on legislation.

5. *Floor debate.* Because of its large size, the House imposes severe limits on floor debate. The Speaker recognizes those who may speak and can force any member who does not "stick to the subject" to give up the floor. Normally, the chairperson of the standing committee reporting the bill will take charge of the session during which it is debated. You can often watch such debates on C-SPAN.

   Only on rare occasions does a floor debate change anybody's mind. The written record of the floor debate completes the legislative history of the proposed bill in the event that the courts have to interpret it later on. Floor debates also give the full House or Senate the opportunity to consider amendments to the original version of the bill.

6. *Vote.* In both the House and the Senate, the members present generally vote for or against the bill. There are several methods of voting, including voice votes, standing votes, and recorded votes (also called roll-call votes). Since 1973, the House has had electronic voting. The Senate does not have electronic voting, however.

7. *Conference committee.* To become a law, a bill must be passed in identical form by both chambers. When the two chambers pass separate versions of the same bill, the measure is turned over to a special committee called a **conference committee**—a temporary committee with members from the two chambers, as mentioned earlier.

   Most members of the committee are drawn from the standing committees that handled the bill in both chambers. In theory, the conference committee can consider only those points in a bill on which the two chambers disagree; no proposals are supposed to be added. In reality, however, the conference committee sometimes makes important changes in the bill or adds new provisions.

   Once the conference committee members agree on the final compromise bill, a **conference report** is submitted to each house. The bill must be accepted or rejected by both houses as it was written by the committee, with no further amendments made. If the bill is approved by both chambers, it is ready for action by the president.

8. *Presidential action.* All bills passed by Congress have to be submitted to the president for approval. The president has ten days to decide whether to sign the bill or veto it. If the president does nothing, the bill goes into effect unless Congress has adjourned before the ten-day period expires. In that case, the bill dies in what is called a **pocket veto.**

9. *Overriding a veto.* If the president decides to veto a bill, Congress can still get the bill enacted into law. With a two-thirds majority vote in both chambers, Congress can override the president's veto.

LO5 *Investigation and Oversight*

Steps 8 and 9 of the legislative process described above illustrate the integral role that the executive and the legislative branches play in making laws. The relationship between Congress and the president is at the core of our system of government, although, to be sure, the judicial branch plays a vital role as well (see Chapter 14).

One of the most important functions of Congress is its oversight (supervision) of the executive branch and its many federal departments and agencies. The executive bureaucracy, which includes the president's cabinet departments, wields tremendous power, as you will read in Chapters 12 and 13. Congress can rein in that power by choosing not to provide the money necessary for the bureaucracy to function (the budgeting process will be discussed later in this chapter).

The Investigative Function

Congress also has the authority to investigate the actions of the executive branch, the need for certain legislation, and even the actions of its own members. The Congressional Research Service and the Congressional Budget Office, for example, provide members of Congress with vital information about policies and economic projections. The numerous congressional committees and subcommittees regularly hold

conference committee A temporary committee that is formed when the two chambers of Congress pass separate versions of the same bill. The conference committee, which consists of members from both the House and the Senate, works out a compromise form of the bill.

conference report A report submitted by a congressional conference committee after it has drafted a single version of a bill.

pocket veto A special type of veto power used by the chief executive after the legislature has adjourned. Bills that are not signed die after a specified period of time.

AP Photo

The House Judiciary Committee, shown here, approved three articles of impeachment against President Richard M. Nixon in late July 1974. The articles charged Nixon with obstruction of justice, abuse of power, and contempt of Congress. Nixon resigned on August 9, 1974, before the full House of Representatives voted on the articles. The Senate, therefore, was never able to try Nixon on any of the articles of impeachment.

hearings to investigate the actions of the executive branch. Congressional committees receive opinions, reports, and assessments on a broad range of issues. A widely held belief is that between 2001 and 2007, when Republicans controlled both the two chambers of Congress and the presidency, Congress neglected its oversight function out of deference to President Bush. Can oversight also become excessive? We look at this issue in this chapter's *Perception versus Reality* feature.

Impeachment Power

Congress has the power to impeach and remove from office the president, vice president, and other "civil officers," such as federal judges. To *impeach* means to accuse or charge a public official with improper conduct in office. The House of Representatives is vested with this power and has exercised it twice against a president; the House voted to impeach Andrew Johnson in 1868 and Bill Clinton in 1998. After a vote to impeach in the full House, the president is then tried in the Senate. If convicted by a two-thirds vote, the president is removed from office. Both Johnson and Clinton were acquitted by the Senate. A vote to impeach President Richard Nixon was pending before the full House of Representatives in 1974 when Nixon chose to resign. Nixon is the only president ever to resign from office.

Congress, as mentioned, can also take action to remove other officials. For example, the House of Representatives voted to impeach Judge Alcee Hastings in 1988, and the Senate removed him from the bench (he was later elected to the House in 1992). Only one United States Supreme Court justice has ever been impeached; the House impeached Samuel Chase in 1804, although he was later acquitted by the Senate.

Senate Confirmation

Article II, Section 2, of the Constitution states that the president may appoint ambassadors, justices of the Supreme Court, and other officers of the United States "with the Advice and Consent of the Senate." The Constitution leaves the precise nature of how the Senate will give this "advice and consent" up to the lawmakers. In practice, the Senate confirms the president's nominees for the Supreme Court, other federal judgeships, and members of the president's cabinet. Nominees appear first before the appropriate Senate committee—the Judiciary Committee for federal judges or the Foreign Relations Committee for the secretary of state, for example. If the individual committee approves the nominee, the full Senate will vote on the nomination.

As you will read further in Chapters 12 and 14, Senate confirmation hearings have been very politicized at times. Judicial appointments often receive the most intense scrutiny by the Senate, because the judges serve on the bench for life. The president has a somewhat freer hand with cabinet appointments, because the heads of executive departments are expected to be loyal to the president. Nonetheless, Senate confirmation

Congressional Oversight

Our political system relies on checks and balances. One of the checks on the executive branch is congressional oversight. This refers to the supervision and monitoring of federal programs, agencies, and activities, as well as of policy implementation by the executive branch. Congress has dozens of standing committees and subcommittees through which it carries out its oversight function. These standing committees and subcommittees routinely hold hearings on various issues that involve the executive branch. There are also select committees in Congress that are temporary and undertake specialized investigations. While nothing in the U.S. Constitution explicitly gives Congress oversight authority, Congress has taken on this duty as one of its implied powers.

Scott J. Ferrell/Congressional Quarterly/Getty Images

Robert B. Willumstad and Martin J. Sullivan, former CEOs of insurance giant AIG, testify during the House Oversight and Government Reform committee hearing on the events leading to the market breakdown on Wall Street. These former executives laid much of the blame on an accounting method that federal regulators had recently moved to relax.

The Perception

While few Americans doubt the value of congressional oversight of the executive branch, many believe that Congress engages in too little oversight. Certainly, until 2007, Congress seemed to have "rubber stamped" the Bush administration's agenda. Americans got the impression that the executive branch was out of control from 2001 until the Democrats took control of Congress in 2007. Now that a Democratic president is matched up with a Democratic Congress, many people fear that Congress will go back to sleep and oversight will again cease.

The Reality

With the election of President Obama, the biggest oversight problem faced by Congress has been evaluating the impact of the enormous spending measures advanced by the new administration. Certainly, the Democratic majority had a political interest in putting the best face possible on the Obama administration's proposals. One way in which Congress has "kept itself honest" is by establishing oversight bodies separate from—but responsible to—Congress. One of the most important of these agencies is the Congressional Budget Office (CBO), which evaluates the impact of proposed legislation on the federal budget and the budget deficit. The CBO was much in the news in 2009 due to its "scoring" of the various health-care reform proposals considered by standing committees in the House and Senate. Members of Congress found themselves tailoring the measures to earn a better score from the CBO.

It is also true that some parts of the executive branch have had so much oversight that they cannot run efficiently. Consider the Department of Homeland Security, which was created by combining more than twenty separate agencies. Each of those agencies had roughly four committees and subcommittees overseeing them. When those agencies were consolidated into one executive department, there was no parallel consolidation of the congressional oversight system. Consequently, about eighty committees and subcommittees now oversee Homeland Security. (Compare this with the Department of Defense, which deals with only four committees on a regular basis.) In a typical year, officials in the Department of Homeland Security must testify in over two hundred congressional hearings. They must also provide more than 2,500 briefings to legislators and their staffs. Much of this time could be used to devise more efficient agency policies.

Blog On *Virginia L. Thomas, a conservative, calls for strong oversight of the Internal Revenue Service at* **www.heritage.org/press/commentary/ed042899.cfm.** *For a left-leaning argument in favor of oversight, see Chuck Collins at* **www.thenation.com/blogs/congress2/154082.** *Business Executives for National Security argues for reforming the oversight of Homeland Security at* **www.bens.org/mis_support/White Paper_Final.pdf.**

remains an important check on the president's power. We will discuss the relationship between Congress and the president in more detail in Chapter 12.

LO6 *The Budgeting Process*

The Constitution makes it very clear that Congress has the power of the purse. Only Congress can impose taxes, and only Congress can authorize expenditures. To be sure, the president submits a budget, but all final decisions are up to Congress.

The congressional budget is, of course, one of the most important determinants of what policies will or will not be implemented. For example, the president might order executive agencies under presidential control to undertake specific programs, but these orders are meaningless if there is no money to pay for their execution. It is Congress that has the power of the "purse strings," and this power is significant. Congress can nullify a president's ambitious program by simply refusing to allocate the necessary money to executive agencies to implement it.

Authorization and Appropriation

The budgeting process is a two-part procedure. **Authorization** is the first part. It involves the creation of the legal basis for government programs. In this phase, Congress passes authorization bills outlining the rules governing the expenditure of funds. Limits may be placed on how much money can be spent and for what period of time.

Appropriation is the second part of the budgeting process. In this phase, Congress determines how many dollars will actually be spent in a given year on a particular set of government activities. Appropriations must never exceed the authorized amounts, but they can be less.

Many **entitlement programs** operate under open-ended authorizations that, in effect, place no limits on how much can be spent. The government is obligated to provide benefits, such as Social Security benefits, veterans' benefits, and the like, to persons who qualify under entitlement laws. The remaining federal programs fall under discretionary spending and can be altered at will by Congress. National defense is the most important item in the discretionary-spending part of the budget.

"The American Republic will endure UNTIL THE DAY CONGRESS DISCOVERS THAT IT CAN BRIBE THE PUBLIC WITH THE PUBLIC'S MONEY."

~ ALEXIS DE TOCQUEVILLE ~
FRENCH HISTORIAN AND POLITICAL SCIENTIST
1805–1859

authorization A part of the congressional budgeting process that involves the creation of the legal basis for government programs.

appropriation A part of the congressional budgeting process that involves determining how many dollars will be spent in a given year on a particular set of government activities.

entitlement program A government program (such as Social Security) that allows, or entitles, a certain class of people (such as elderly persons) to receive benefits. Entitlement programs operate under open-ended budget authorizations that, in effect, place no limits on how much can be spent.

During and after authorization and appropriation of federal monies, committees in Congress often ask for testimony from the administration. Here, Treasury secretary Tim Geithner (seated left), testifies before the Congressional Oversight Panel while protesters demonstrate their displeasure at the huge sums of taxpayer dollars his department has already spent.

AP Photo/Susan Walsh

JOIN THE DEBATE

Should "Earmarks" Be Banned?

In recent years, Congress has voted to fund a "bridge to nowhere" in Alaska, protection from blackbirds for sunflowers in North Dakota, a program to combat wild hogs in Missouri, and payment of storage fees for Georgia peanut farmers, among many other special projects. Every year, virtually every bill coming out of Congress includes "earmarked funds" for special interests or projects that are important to individual legislators. Much of this special interest spending consists of what is impolitely called *pork-barrel* spending. The term *pork* comes from the idea that members of Congress "bring home the bacon" to their home states, usually in the form of additional federal spending that benefits local businesses and workers. In 2008, earmarks cost taxpayers more than $18 billion. The total for 2009 was estimated to be higher still. Should earmarks be banned altogether?

We Must End the Pork

Yes, argue most Americans, it is time to end this unsightly "feeding frenzy" at every legislative session in Congress. Earmarks took off in Congress in the 1990s and have risen astronomically with members from both parties. The bridge to nowhere in Alaska mentioned earlier would have cost more than $200 million to link the small city of Ketchikan to Gravina Island—with a population of fifty. This would have been an obscene use of taxpayers' hard-earned dollars. (The bridge project was eventually killed.) If pork were banned, legislators would no longer be able to "bribe" other legislators by allowing them to include their pet projects in a bill if they agree to support certain legislation in return. In other words, so-called *logrolling* would be much more difficult without earmarks.

Not So Fast

Those in favor of keeping earmarks point out that every member of Congress has constituents. Those constituents

AP Photo/Hall Anderson/*Ketchikan Daily News*

Earmarked spending, or pork-barrel legislation, often involves local construction projects, some of dubious value, such as the famous "bridge to nowhere" across the Tongass Narrows in Alaska. The bridge would have connected the town of Ketchikan, on the left, with Gravina Island, on the right, which contains the town's airport and fifty inhabitants.

benefit from earmarked funds. Banning earmarks altogether would reduce the value of members of Congress to their own constituents and thereby weaken the ties between elected officials and their constituents. Also, without congressional earmarks, Congress would have to accept the decisions of the executive branch as to how each agency or program should allocate its funds among projects. Why should the president and the bureaucracy be the only ones allowed to identify specific worthy projects?

A less dramatic alternative is to provide for greater disclosure. In the past, earmarks have often been entirely anonymous, and the general public never learned which member of Congress demanded any particular piece of pork. Indeed, in 2007, the new Democratic majority in Congress changed the rules to require the disclosure of lawmakers' earmark requests. It turns out, however, that many members are quite proud of their pork and want their constituents to know all about it.

For Critical Analysis *Given that pork-barrel spending actually amounts to only a small percentage of the federal government's budget, why are these earmarks so controversial?*

The Actual Budgeting Process

Look at Figure 11–4 on the following page, which outlines the lengthy budgeting process. The process runs from January, when the president submits a proposed federal budget for the next **fiscal year,** to the start of that fiscal year on October 1. In actuality, about eighteen months prior to October 1, the executive agencies submit their requests to the Office of Management and Budget (OMB), and the OMB outlines a

fiscal year A twelve-month period that is established for bookkeeping or accounting purposes. The government's fiscal year runs from October 1 through September 30.

Figure 11–4

The Budgeting Process

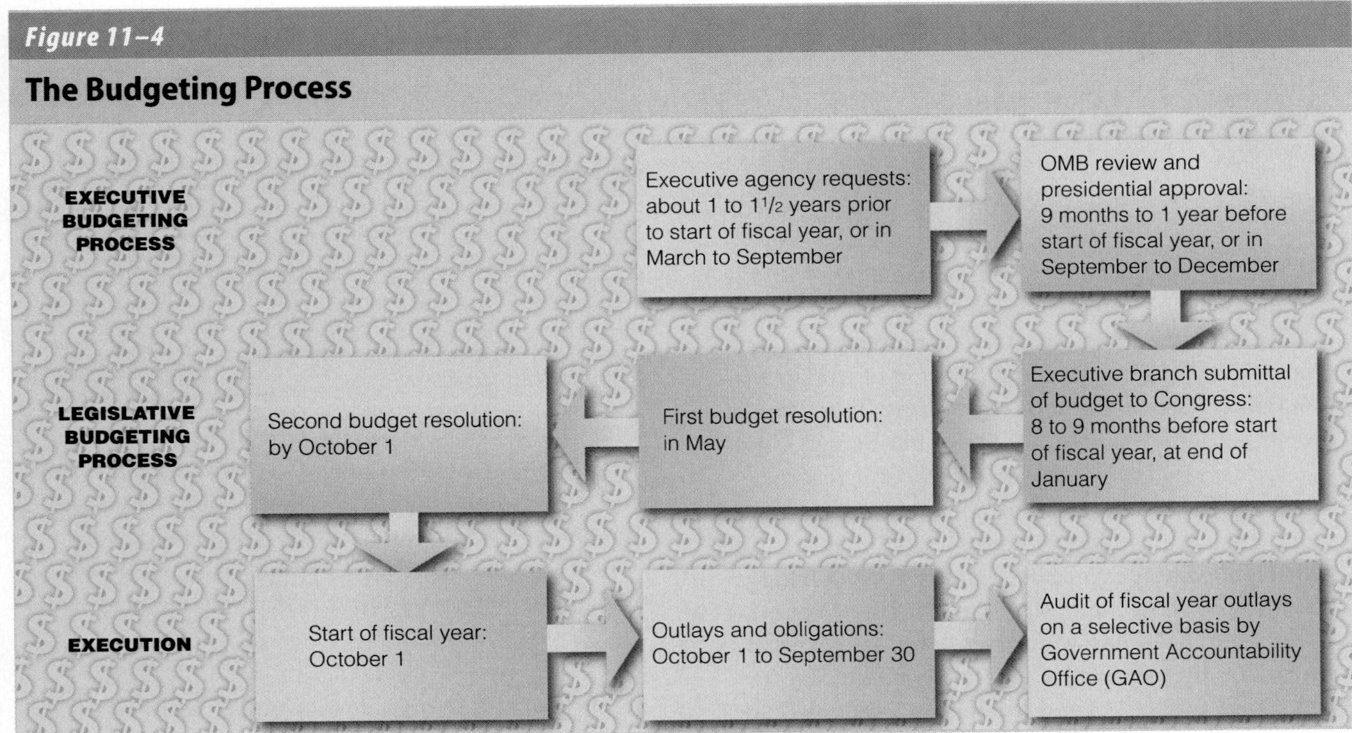

proposed budget. If the president approves it, the budget is officially submitted to Congress.

The legislative budgeting process begins eight to nine months before the start of the fiscal year. The **first budget resolution** is supposed to be passed in May. It sets overall revenue goals and spending targets and, by definition, the size of the federal budget deficit or surplus. The **second budget resolution,** which sets "binding" limits on taxes and spending, is supposed to be passed in September, before the beginning of the fiscal year on October 1. Whenever Congress is unable to pass a complete budget by October 1, it passes **continuing resolutions,** which enable the executive agencies to keep on doing whatever they were doing the previous year with the same amount of funding. Even continuing resolutions have not always been passed on time.

first budget resolution A budget resolution, which is supposed to be passed in May, that sets overall revenue goals and spending targets for the next fiscal year, which begins on October 1.

second budget resolution A budget resolution, which is supposed to be passed in September, that sets "binding" limits on taxes and spending for the next fiscal year.

continuing resolution A temporary resolution passed by Congress when an appropriations bill has not been passed by the beginning of the new fiscal year.

"WE THE PEOPLE are the rightful masters of both Congress and the courts."

~ ABRAHAM LINCOLN ~
SIXTEENTH PRESIDENT OF THE UNITED STATES
1861–1865

The budget process involves making predictions about the state of the U.S. economy for years to come. This process is necessarily very imprecise. Since 1996, both Congress and the president have attempted to make ten-year projections for income (from taxes) and spending, but no one can really know what the financial picture of the United States will look like in ten years. The workforce could grow or shrink, which would drastically alter government revenue from taxes. Any number of emergencies could arise that would require increased government spending—from going to war against terrorists to inoculating federal employees against smallpox.

In any event, when you read about what the administration predicts the budget deficit (or surplus) will be in five or ten years, take such predictions with a grain of salt. There has never been such a long-term prediction that has come close to being accurate. Moreover, most times, the longest-term predictions made by administrations will depend on decisions made when *another* administration is in office later on.

AMERICA AT ODDS Congress

When the founders drafted the Constitution, they envisioned that Congress would play the leading role in our national government. The founders, who were all too familiar with the treatment of the colonies by King George III of Britain, had a very real fear of tyranny and the arbitrary exercise of unchecked power by the executive. For the framers, the real governing was to be done by the legislative branch. For this reason, the powers of Congress are set forth in the first article of the U.S Constitution. The desire to prevent any one branch of government from becoming too powerful also caused the founders to include various checks and balances in the Constitution, as you read in Chapters 2 and 3.

Many Americans believe that the 109th Republican-led Congress, which stepped down in 2007 after the Democrats took control, largely failed in its oversight duties. Congress never made any serious attempt to check Republican president George W. Bush's legislative agenda and administrative policymaking, even though legal scholars point out that several of his antiterrorism programs were clearly unconstitutional and others possibly so. The Democratic majority that took control of Congress in 2007 attempted to resume congressional oversight by investigating many of Bush's policies and programs, but because the Democrats had only a narrow majority in Congress, they found it difficult to garner enough votes to bring proposed bills to the floor for a vote or to override threatened (or real) presidential vetoes. Now that a Democratic Congress faces a Democratic administration, Congress again may lose its appetite for oversight. Clearly, in recent years Congress has not played the strong and central role in the national government that was envisioned by the founders. Whether it can again exercise such powers remains to be seen.

ISSUES FOR DEBATE & DISCUSSION

1. **For some time, Americans have debated whether something should be done to reform the redistricting process to reduce the electoral advantage enjoyed by congressional incumbents. Some groups have argued that the responsibility of redrawing congressional district lines after each census should be taken away from political partisans in state legislatures and given to a panel of nonpartisan retired judges instead. Others believe that there is nothing wrong with drawing district lines to ensure that a maximum number of people in a particular district will have views similar to those of their representative. What is your position on this issue?**
2. **Review this chapter's discussion of racial gerrymandering on pages 249–250. There, we stated that some Americans believe that minority-majority districts are necessary to ensure equal representation of minority groups, as mandated by the Voting Rights Act of 1965, and that these districts have helped to increase the number of African Americans holding political office. Others argue that race-based districting is unconstitutional because it violates the equal protection clause. What is your position on this issue?**

TAKE ACTION

During each session of Congress, your senators and representative debate the pros and cons of proposed laws, some of which may affect your daily life or the lives of those you care about. If you want to let your voice be heard, you can do so simply by phoning or e-mailing your senators or your representative in the House. You can learn the names and contact information for the senators and representative from your area by going to the Web sites of the Senate and the House, which are given in this chapter's *Politics on the Web* feature. Your chances of influencing your members of Congress will be greater if you can convince others, including your friends and family members, to do likewise. Citizens often feel that such efforts are useless. Yet members of Congress *do* listen to their constituents and often *do* act in response to their constituents' wishes. Indeed, next to voting, contacting those who represent you in Congress is probably the most effective way to influence government decision making.

Kayte M. Deioma/PhotoEdit

Contacting U.S. representatives and senators is much easier today using the Internet. Next to voting, the most effective ways to influence decision making in Washington, D.C., are phoning, writing to, or e-mailing members of Congress.

POLITICS ON THE WEB

- There is an abundance of online information about Congress and congressional activities. The THOMAS site (named for Thomas Jefferson), maintained by the Library of Congress, provides a record of all bills introduced into Congress, information about each member of Congress and how he or she voted on specific bills, and other data. Go to **thomas.loc.gov**
- The U.S. Government Printing Office (GPO) Access on the Web offers information on the Congress in session, bills pending and passed, and a history of the bills at **www.gpoaccess.gov**
- To learn more about how a bill becomes a law, go to **www.vote-smart.org**

  Click on "Political Resources" and scroll down to "Vote Smart Classroom." Select "An Introduction to the U.S. Government," and then choose "How a Bill Becomes Law."
- You can find e-mail addresses and home pages for members of the House of Representatives at **www.house.gov**
- For e-mail addresses and home pages for members of the Senate, go to **www.senate.gov**
- To have your local congressional representative's votes e-mailed to you every week, to post letters online and read what others are saying about elected officials, or to create and post a "soapbox action alert" to get others on your side of an issue, explore your options at **www.congress.org**

Online resources for this chapter

This text's Companion Web site, at **www.4ltrpress.cengage.com/govt**, offers links to numerous resources that you can use to learn more about the topics covered in this chapter.

The Presidency

GOVT 12

LEARNING OBJECTIVES

LO1 List the constitutional requirements for becoming president.

LO2 Explain the roles that a president performs while in office.

LO3 Indicate the scope of presidential powers.

LO4 Describe key areas of advantages for Congress and for the president in their institutional relationship.

LO5 Discuss the organization of the executive branch and the role of cabinet members in presidential administrations.

AMERICA AT ODDS

Just How Liberal Is President Obama?

Clearly, during the 2008 presidential campaign, Senator Barack Obama of Illinois stood to the political left of his Republican opponent, Senator John McCain of Arizona. Nonetheless, one of Obama's messages was that of uniting this country and avoiding the divisive partisanship that had marked the eight years of George W. Bush's presidency. One of Obama's themes was "no more politics as usual." Presumably, Obama would seek counsel from both parties in Congress. He would be open to all arguments, suggestions, and ideas.

Soon after the election, President-elect Obama named a series of moderate personalities to his cabinet. Some observers thought that Obama truly did envision a new spirit in Washington, based on resolving conflicts between conservatives and progressives. Most conservatives are having none of that, though. They believe that Obama is the most left-leaning president we have ever had. Yet many Democrats believe that Obama has made too many compromises already.

Obama Is Compromising His Progressive Agenda

Liberals had little to complain about during President Obama's first one hundred days, but not long after, many became troubled. They believed that Obama was making too many compromises. For one example, Obama decided to maintain the Bush-era military commissions to judge some of the prisoners held at the Guantánamo Bay Naval Base. Obama was clearly keeping his word about setting a deadline for pulling out of Iraq. Antiwar activists, however, feared that he was simply moving military resources into an unwinnable war in Afghanistan.

Health-care reform turned out to be by far the most contentious issue of 2009, and progressives grew alarmed at the compromises that Obama was willing to make on this issue. In August, when public protests at congressional "town meetings" proved embarrassing, liberals became afraid that Obama was pulling away from the so-called public option—a government-run heath-insurance company that would compete with private insurance companies.

Obama's stands on gay rights also disturbed liberals. During his campaign, Obama had called for the repeal of the 1996 Defense of Marriage Act, which defines marriage as between a man and a woman and frees states from the need to recognize same-sex marriages performed in other states. Yet in the late summer of 2009, Obama's Justice Department defended the act in court. The department filed papers arguing for the dismissal of a federal suit brought by two California gay men who were married and who were challenging the act.

A More Left-Leaning President We Have Never Had

Conservatives paid little attention to liberal criticism of Obama's compromises. They firmly believed that he was indeed the most liberal president we have ever had—at least since Franklin Delano Roosevelt in the 1930s. Obama increased the size of the federal government even faster than Roosevelt did in the run-up to World War II. He was willing to make the federal government (that is, the taxpayers) the owner of banks, insurance companies, and automobile companies. Who knows what you, as a taxpayer, may own by the time you read this? If government ownership of private companies isn't a left-wing move, then what is?

Conservatives argued that Obama's version of health-care reform was no more than a road to the complete federal takeover of medical care—a slow or fast road, depending on what Congress does. Even before Obama took office, federal and state governments provided close to 50 percent of all medical care funding through Medicare, Medicaid, the State Children's Health Insurance Program (SCHIP), and medical care for veterans and federal employees. Conservatives feared that by the time Obama served four years as president, that percentage would be closer to 100 percent.

Obama's conservative critics argued that Obama wanted to fundamentally change the American social compact. Mainstream conservatives believed that Obama envisioned the kind of social democratic institutions we see in Western Europe. Radical conservatives went so far as to accuse Obama of seeking some kind of dictatorship.

WHERE DO YOU STAND?

1. **Has Obama made so many compromises with his original progressive agenda that he could be called a moderate?**
2. **Is Obama's desire to involve the government more deeply in health care an indication of his liberal ideals? Why or why not?**

EXPLORE THIS ISSUE ONLINE

- **Dozens of progressive bloggers are prepared to take Obama to task for compromises on health care and other issues. We can name only a few—www.talkingpointsmemo.com, www.politico.com, and www.democracyforamerica.com.**
- **A vast number of conservative sites vehemently oppose Obama's programs. Examples include www.americanthinker.com, www.clubforgrowth.org, and www.cwfa.org (Concerned Women for America).**

Introduction

President Lyndon B. Johnson (1963–1969) stated in his autobiography[1] that "[o]f all the 1,886 nights I was President, there were not many when I got to sleep before 1 or 2 A.M., and there were few mornings when I didn't wake up by 6 or 6:30." President Harry Truman (1945–1953) once observed that no one can really understand what it is like to be president: there is no end to "the chain of responsibility that binds him," and he is "never allowed to forget that he is president." These responsibilities are, for the most part, unremitting. Unlike Congress, the president never adjourns.

"No man will ever bring out of the Presidency the reputation which carries him into it. To myself personally, it brings nothing but increasing **DRUDGERY AND DAILY LOSS OF FRIENDS.**"

~ THOMAS JEFFERSON ~
THIRD PRESIDENT OF THE UNITED STATES
1801–1809

Given the demands of the presidency, why would anyone seek the office? There are some very special perks associated with the presidency. The president enjoys, among other things, the use of the White House. The White House has 132 rooms located on 18.3 acres of land in the heart of the nation's capital. At the White House, the president in residence has a staff of more than eighty persons, including chefs, gardeners, maids, butlers, and a personal tailor. Amenities also include a tennis court, a swimming pool, bowling lanes, and a private movie theater. Additionally, the president has at his or her disposal a fleet of automobiles, helicopters, and jets (including *Air Force One,* which costs more than $70,000 an hour to run). For relaxation, the presidential family can go to Camp David, a resort hideaway in the Catoctin Mountains of Maryland. Other perks include free dental and medical care.

These amenities are only a minor motivation for wanting to be president of the United States, of course. A greater motivation is that the presidency is at the apex of the political ladder. It is the most powerful and influential political office that any one individual can hold. Presidents can help to shape not only domestic policy but also global developments. Since the demise of the Soviet Union and its satellite Communist countries in the early 1990s, the president of the United States has been the leader of the most powerful nation on earth. The president heads the greatest military force anywhere. Presidents have more power to reach their political objectives than any other players in the American political system. (We discussed President Barack Obama's political goals in this chapter's opening *America at Odds* feature.) It is not surprising, therefore, that many Americans aspire to attain this office.

Ronald Reagan was an actor before he became a politician. Here he is shown with actresses Lucille Barkley on the left and Wanda Hendrix. They were promoting a movie in Hollywood in 1950. How did Reagan's acting career help him in politics?

AP Photo

LO1 *Who Can Become President?*

The notion that anybody can become president of this country has always been a part of the American mythology. Certainly, the requirements for becoming president set forth in Article II, Section 1, of the Constitution are not difficult to meet:

> No Person except a natural born Citizen, or a Citizen of the United States, at the time

JOIN THE DEBATE

A Foreign-Born President?

As you just read, Article II of the Constitution states that "[n]o Person except a natural born Citizen . . . shall be eligible to the Office of President." This restriction has long been controversial, for it has kept many otherwise qualified Americans from running for president. These persons include California governor Arnold Schwarzenegger, who was born in Austria, and Michigan governor Jennifer M. Granholm, who was born in Canada, both of whom have been U.S. citizens for decades. In all, some 13 million Americans born outside the United States are excluded by this provision. The requirement of native birth has come up most recently because of claims by political extremists that President Obama was not born in the United States. These individuals claim that Obama's Hawaiian birth certificate was forged, and they are undeterred by the fact that Obama's birth was also announced in Honolulu newspapers.

An Obsolete Provision

America is a nation of immigrants, so it strikes some as odd that a foreign-born person would be barred from aspiring to the presidency. Naturalized U.S. citizens are allowed to vote, to serve on juries, and to serve in the military. They are also allowed to serve as secretary of state and represent the nation in foreign affairs. Why can't they run for president? Critics of the Constitution's citizenship requirement think that the requirement should be abolished by a constitutional amendment. They point out that the clause was initially included in the Constitution to prevent European princes from attempting to force the young republic back under monarchical rule in the late 1700s. Clearly, the clause is now obsolete and should no longer apply.

A Requirement Still Valid Today

Other Americans believe that the constitutional ban should remain. They argue that national security could be compromised by a foreign-born president. With the immense power that the president wields, especially in the realm of foreign policy, loyalty is of the utmost concern. The current war on terrorism only heightens the need to ensure that the president does not have divided loyalties.

In addition, the Constitution is quite difficult to amend, requiring support from two-thirds of both chambers of Congress and ratification by three-fourths of the fifty states. The need for an amendment that would allow Schwarzenegger and other immigrants to run for president is hardly as pressing as the need for past antidiscrimination amendments such as those abolishing slavery and giving women the right to vote, opponents argue.

For Critical Analysis *Some have suggested that a foreign-born president probably would be more nationalistic than a president born in this country. Why might that be so?*

> of the Adoption of this Constitution, shall be eligible to the Office of President; neither shall any Person be eligible to that Office who shall not have attained to the Age of thirty-five Years, and been fourteen Years a Resident within the United States. (See *Join the Debate* above.)

It is true that modern presidents have included a haberdasher (Harry Truman), a peanut farmer (Jimmy Carter), and an actor (Ronald Reagan), although all of these men also had significant political experience before assuming the presidency. If you look at Appendix E, though, you will see that the most common previous occupation of U.S. presidents has been the legal profession. Out of forty-four presidents, twenty-seven have been lawyers, and many presidents have been wealthy. Additionally, although the Constitution states that anyone who is thirty-five years of age or older can become president, the average age at inauguration has been fifty-four. The youngest person elected president was John F. Kennedy (1961–1963), who assumed the presidency at the age of forty-three (the youngest person to hold the office was Theodore Roosevelt, who was forty-two when he became president after the assassination of William McKinley). The oldest was Ronald Reagan (1981–1989), who was sixty-nine years old when he became president.

For most of American history, all presidential candidates, even those of minor parties, were white, male, and of the Protestant religious tradition. In recent years, however, the pool of talent has expanded. In 1928, Democrat Al Smith became the first Catholic to run for president on a major-party ticket, and in 1960 Democrat John F. Kennedy became the first Catholic president.

Among recent unsuccessful Democratic presidential candidates, Michael Dukakis was Greek Orthodox and John Kerry was Catholic. In 2008, the doors swung wide in the presidential primaries as the Democrats chose between a white woman, Hillary Clinton, and an African American man, Barack Obama. By that time, about 90 percent of Americans told pollsters that they would be willing to support an African American for president, and the same number would support a woman.

LO2 *The President's Many Roles*

The president has the authority to exercise a variety of powers. Some of these are explicitly outlined in the Constitution, and some are simply required by the office—such as the power to persuade. In the course of exercising these powers, the president performs a variety of roles. For example, as commander in chief of the armed services, the president can exercise significant military powers. Which roles a president executes successfully usually depends on what is happening domestically and internationally, as well as on the president's personality. Some presidents, including Bill Clinton during his first term, have shown much more interest in domestic policy than in foreign policy. Others, such as George H. W. Bush (1989–1993), were more interested in foreign affairs than in domestic ones. Although George W. Bush might have wanted to spend more time on his domestic proposals, after 2003 he had to focus largely on the war in Iraq and then on the 2008 economic crisis.

Table 12–1 on the next page summarizes the major roles of the president. An important role is, of course, that of chief executive. Other roles include those of commander in chief, head of state, chief diplomat, chief legislator, and political party leader.

Chief Executive

According to Article II of the Constitution,

> The executive Power shall be vested in a President of the United States of America. . . . [H]e may require the Opinion, in writing, of the principal Officer in each of the executive Departments, upon any Subject relating to the Duties of their respective Offices . . . and he shall nominate, and by and with the Advice and Consent of the Senate, shall appoint . . . Officers of the United States . . . . [H]e shall take Care that the Laws be faithfully executed.

This constitutional provision makes the president of the United States the nation's **chief executive,** or the head of the executive branch of the federal government. When the framers created the office of the president, they created a uniquely American institution. Nowhere else in the world at that time was there a democratically elected chief executive. The executive branch is also unique among the branches of government because it is headed by a single individual—the president.

Commander in Chief

The Constitution states that the president "shall be Commander in Chief of the Army and Navy of the United States, and of the Militia of the several States, when called into the actual Service of the United States." As **commander in chief** of the nation's armed forces, the president exercises tremendous power.

National Photo Company Collection/Library of Congress

President Woodrow Wilson throwing out the first pitch on the opening day of the major league baseball season in 1916. This action is part of the president's role as head of state.

chief executive The head of the executive branch of government. In the United States, the president.

commander in chief The supreme commander of a nation's military force.

Table 12–1

Roles of the President

Role	Description	Examples
Chief executive	Enforces laws and federal court decisions, along with treaties signed by the United States	• Can appoint, with Senate approval, and remove high-ranking officers of the federal government • Can grant reprieves, pardons, and amnesty • Can handle national emergencies during peacetime, such as riots or natural disasters
Commander in chief	Leads the nation's armed forces	• Can commit troops for up to ninety days in response to a military threat (War Powers Resolution) • Can make secret agreements with other countries • Can set up military governments in conquered lands • Can end fighting by calling a cease-fire (armistice)
Head of state	Performs certain ceremonial roles as a personal symbol of the nation	• Decorates war heroes • Dedicates parks and post offices • Throws out first pitch of baseball season • Lights national Christmas tree
Chief diplomat	Directs U.S. foreign policy and is the nation's most important representative in dealing with foreign countries	• Can negotiate and sign treaties with other nations, with Senate approval • Can make pacts (executive agreements) with other heads of state, without Senate approval • Can accept the legal existence of another country's government (power of recognition) • Receives foreign heads of state
Chief legislator	Informs Congress about the condition of the country and recommends legislative measures	• Proposes legislative program to Congress in traditional State of the Union address • Suggests budget to Congress and submits annual economic report • Can veto a bill passed by Congress • Can call special sessions of Congress
Political party leader	Heads political party	• Chooses a vice president • Makes several thousand top government appointments, often to party faithful (patronage) • Tries to execute the party's platform • May attend party fund-raisers • May help reelect party members running for office as mayors, governors, or members of Congress

Under the Constitution, war powers are divided between Congress and the president. Congress was given the power to declare war and the power to raise and maintain the country's armed forces. The president, as commander in chief, was given the power to deploy the armed forces. The president's role as commander in chief has evolved over the last century. We will examine this shared power of the president and Congress in more detail later in this chapter.

head of state The person who serves as the ceremonial head of a country's government and represents that country to the rest of the world.

Head of State

Traditionally, a country's monarch has performed the function of **head of state**—the country's representative to the rest of the world. The United States, of course, has no king or queen to act as head of state. Thus, the president of the United States fulfills this role. The president engages in many symbolic or ceremonial activities, such as throwing out the first pitch to open the baseball season and turning on the lights of the national Christmas tree. The president also decorates war heroes, dedicates parks and post offices, receives visiting heads of state at the White House, and goes on official state visits to other countries. Some argue that presidents should not perform such ceremonial duties because they take time that the president should be spending on "real work." (See this chapter's *The Rest of the World* feature on the facing page for more information on how some other countries handle this issue.)

When the Head of State Is Not the Head of Government

In the United States, we take it for granted that our president dominates the political system. The president is the head of the government and also serves as head of state. The powers that our president has, however, are not common outside of the Western Hemisphere. Most European countries have a parliamentary system instead. In such a system, the head of state, whether a monarch or an elected president, has a ceremonial role. The head of government, who has real power, represents a majority or plurality in the "lower house" of the national legislature. (The upper house, or senate, in a parliamentary system usually has only limited powers.) In addition to Europe, parliamentary systems are found in Australia, Canada, India, Japan, and many other nations. A few countries have a third system, however—a kind of hybrid system that is part parliamentary and part presidential. You could call it a semi-presidential system. France is the most notable example of such a system.

The Presidential-Parliamentary System

France has a president, currently Nicolas Sarkozy, and a prime minister, now François Fillon. Both represent the "center-right" party in France, the Union for a Popular Movement. In France, the president names the prime minister and the members of the cabinet. The prime minister and the cabinet, though, are responsible to the legislature, not the president. The National Assembly, which is the lower house of Parliament, can force the entire cabinet to resign by passing a motion of no confidence. In other words, "the government"—the prime minister and the other cabinet members—cannot survive politically unless a majority in the National Assembly supports them, regardless of the president's preferences.

The Unique French Practice of Cohabitation

For much of the history of the modern French Republic, the legislature's ability to throw out the government was not important, because the president's party had a majority in the National Assembly. French legislators were willing to let the president—the head of their party—choose the government. In 1981, the French elected a Socialist president for the first time, but they also gave the Socialists a majority in the National Assembly. In the 1986 elections, however, France voted for a center-right Assembly majority. While the Socialist president, François Mitterrand, still had two years left in his term of office.

The French have a quaint term for the resulting situation: "cohabitation." During cohabitation, the prime minister and the rest of the cabinet are from one party and the president is from another. Consider what would happen if we had such a system in the United States. In 2006, following the Democratic takeover of Congress, President George W. Bush would have been forced to pick a cabinet consisting entirely of Democrats who enjoyed the support of their party. If the Democrats were to lose control of the House of Representatives in the 2010 elections, President Obama would be forced to fill his cabinet completely with Republicans loyal to their colleagues in the House. Obviously, in the United States, Congress does not have that kind of power.

Who Does What?

Nowhere in the French constitution is there an explicit statement of the division of powers between the president and the prime minister. The division of duties that exists today is a political convention that has evolved over time. Typically, the president is responsible for foreign policy and the prime minister for domestic policy. This distinction is most carefully observed during periods of cohabitation. When one party is in full control of the government, the president tends to take over completely. Consider President Sarkozy, the current incumbent. "Sarko," as he is known, meddles in every type of policy. Some of his critics argue that his prime minister is simply a puppet.

For Critical Analysis *Does our president fill too many roles? Would our government work better if a prime minister served under the president?*

President Nicolas Sarkozy is shown with his wife, Carla Bruni, who continues to have a singing career.

AP Photo/Charles Dharapak

Chief Diplomat

A **diplomat** is a person who represents one country in dealing with representatives of another country. In the United States, the president is the nation's **chief diplomat.** The Constitution did not explicitly reserve this role to the president, but since the beginning of this nation, presidents have assumed the role based on their explicit constitutional powers to recognize foreign governments and, with the advice and consent of the Senate, to appoint ambassadors and make treaties. As chief diplomat, the president directs the foreign policy of the United States and is our nation's most important representative.

Chief Legislator

Nowhere in the Constitution do the words *chief legislator* appear. The Constitution, however, does require that the president "from time to time give to the Congress Information of the State of the Union, and recommend to their Consideration such Measures as he shall judge necessary and expedient." The president has, in fact, become a major player in shaping the congressional agenda—the set of measures that actually get discussed and acted on. This was not always the case. In the nineteenth century, some presidents preferred to let Congress lead the way in proposing and implementing policy. Since the administration of Theodore Roosevelt (1901–1909), however, presidents have taken an activist approach. Presidents are now expected to develop a legislative program and propose a budget to Congress every year. This shared power often puts Congress and the president at odds.

Political Party Leader

The president of the United States is also the *de facto* leader of his or her political party. The Constitution, of course, does not mention this role because, in the eyes of the founders, parties should have no role in the American political system.

As party leader, the president exercises substantial powers. For example, the president chooses the chairperson of the party's national committee. The president can also exert political power within the party by using presidential appointment and removal powers. Naturally, presidents are beholden to the party members who put them in office, and usually presidents indulge in the practice of **patronage**—appointing individuals to government or public jobs—to reward those who helped them win the presidential contest. The president may also reward party members with fund-raising assistance (campaign financing was discussed in Chapter 9). The president is, in a sense, "fund-raiser in chief" for his or her party, and recent presidents, including Bill Clinton, George W. Bush, and Barack Obama, have proven themselves to be prodigious fund-raisers. Understandably, the use of patronage within the party system gives the president singular powers.

The current and last three presidents are shown in the Oval Office of the White House. What can a president do after she or he leaves office?

Doug Mills/*The New York Times*/Redux

diplomat A person who represents one country in dealing with representatives of another country.

chief diplomat The role of the president in recognizing and interacting with foreign governments.

patronage The practice of giving government jobs to individuals belonging to the winning political party.

LO3 *Presidential Powers*

The president exercises numerous powers. Some of these powers are set forth in the Constitution. Others, known as *inherent powers,* are those that are necessary to carry out the president's constitutional duties. We look next at these powers, as well as at the expansion of presidential powers over time.

The President's Constitutional Powers

As you have read, the constitutional source for the president's authority is found in Article II of the Constitution, which states, "The executive Power shall be vested in a President of the United States of America." The Constitution then sets forth the president's relatively limited constitutional responsibilities. Just how much power should be entrusted to the president was debated at length by the framers of the Constitution. On the one hand, they did not want a king. On the other hand, they believed that a strong executive was necessary if the republic was to survive. The result of their debates was an executive who was granted enough powers in the Constitution to balance those of Congress.

Article II grants the president broad but vaguely described powers. From the very beginning, there were different views as to what exactly the "executive Power" clause enabled the president to do. Nonetheless, Sections 2 and 3 of Article II list the following specific presidential powers. These powers parallel the roles of the president discussed in the previous section:

- To serve as commander in chief of the armed forces and the state militias.
- To appoint, with the Senate's consent, the heads of the executive departments, ambassadors, justices of the Supreme Court, and other top officials.
- To grant reprieves and pardons, except in cases of impeachment.
- To make treaties, with the advice and consent of the Senate.
- To deliver the annual State of the Union address to Congress and to send other messages to Congress from time to time.
- To call either house or both houses of Congress into special sessions.
- To receive ambassadors and other representatives from foreign countries.
- To commission all officers of the United States.

AP Photo

President John F. Kennedy (right) and Prime Minister Harold Macmillan of Great Britain stop just outside the White House office in 1961 to discuss problems in Southeast Asia. What role is the president playing here?

- To ensure that the laws passed by Congress "be faithfully executed."

In addition, Article I, Section 7, gives the president the power to veto legislation. We discuss some of these powers in more detail below. As you will see, many of these powers are balanced by the powers of Congress. We address the complex relationship between the president and Congress later in this chapter.

PROPOSAL AND RATIFICATION OF TREATIES

A **treaty** is a formal agreement between two or more sovereign states. The president has the sole power to negotiate

treaty A formal agreement between the governments of two or more countries.

President Jimmy Carter (center) met with Egyptian president Anwar Sadat (left) and Israeli prime minister Menachem Begin (right) at the White House for the signing of the Camp David Accords on September 18, 1978. Since then, Egypt and Israel have not been at war.

and sign treaties with other countries. The Senate, however, must approve a treaty by a two-thirds vote of the members present before it becomes effective. If the treaty is approved by the Senate and signed by the president, it becomes law.

Presidents have not always succeeded in winning the Senate's approval for treaties. Woodrow Wilson (1913–1921) lost his effort to persuade the Senate to approve the Treaty of Versailles,[2] the peace treaty that ended World War I in 1918. Among other things, the treaty would have made the United States a member of the League of Nations. In contrast, Jimmy Carter (1977–1981) convinced the Senate to approve a treaty returning the Panama Canal to Panama by the year 2000 (over such objections as that of Senator S. I. Hayakawa, a Republican from California, who said, "We stole it fair and square"). The treaty was approved by a margin of a single vote.

THE POWER TO GRANT REPRIEVES AND PARDONS The president's power to grant a pardon serves as a check on judicial power. A *pardon* is a release from punishment or the legal consequences of a crime; it restores a person to the full rights and privileges of citizenship. In 1925, the United States Supreme Court upheld an expansive interpretation of the president's pardon power in a case involving an individual convicted for contempt of court. The Court held that the power covers all offenses "either before trial, during trial, or after trial, by individuals, or by classes, conditionally or absolutely, and this without modification or regulation by Congress."[3] The president can grant a pardon for any federal offense, except in cases of impeachment.

veto A Latin word meaning "I forbid"; the refusal by an official, such as the president of the United States or a state governor, to sign a bill into law.

One of the most controversial pardons was that granted by President Gerald Ford (1974–1977) to former president Richard Nixon (1969–1974) after the Watergate affair (to be discussed later in the chapter), before any formal charges were brought in court. Sometimes pardons are granted to a class of individuals, as a general amnesty. For example, President Jimmy Carter granted amnesty to approximately 10,000 people who had resisted the draft during the Vietnam War. Just before he left office in 2001, President Bill Clinton (1993–2001) pardoned 140 individuals. Some of these pardons were controversial.

A more recent controversy surrounded President George W. Bush's decision, in 2007, to use his pardon powers to commute the prison sentence received by Lewis ("Scooter") Libby. Libby, who had served as Vice President Dick Cheney's chief of staff, was found guilty of several crimes in connection with a leak made to the press that exposed the identity of Central Intelligence Agency agent Valerie Plame. Plame's husband, Joseph Wilson, had earlier reported that key evidence cited by Bush as a justification for invading Iraq did not, in fact, exist. Bush administration critics alleged that the exposure of Plame's identity was an attempt to punish Wilson for this action.

THE PRESIDENT'S VETO POWER As noted in Chapter 11, the president can **veto** a bill passed by Congress. Congress can override the veto with a two-thirds vote by the members present in each chamber. The result of a veto override is that the bill becomes law against the wishes of the president. If the president does not send a bill back to Congress after ten congressional working days, the bill becomes law without the president's signature. If the president refuses to sign the bill and Congress adjourns within ten working days after the bill has been submitted to the president, however, the bill is killed for that session of Congress. As mentioned in Chapter 11, this is called a *pocket veto*.

Presidents used the veto power sparingly until the administration of Andrew Johnson (1865–1869).

Johnson vetoed twenty-one bills. Franklin D. Roosevelt (1933–1945) vetoed more bills by far than any of his predecessors or successors in the presidency. During his administration, there were 372 regular vetoes, 9 of which were overridden by Congress, and 263 pocket vetoes.

President George W. Bush, in contrast, used his veto power very sparingly. Indeed, during the first six years of his presidency, Bush vetoed only one bill—a proposal to expand the scope of stem-cell research. Bush vetoed so few bills, in large part, because the Republican-led Congress during those years strongly supported his agenda and undertook no actions to oppose it. After the Democrats took control of Congress in 2007, however, Bush vetoed eleven bills. Congress overrode four of these vetoes. With a Congress led by his own party, President Obama faces circumstances similar to those enjoyed by George W. Bush during most of his presidency. Obama is unlikely to make much use of the veto in his first two years of office, and in fact by late 2009 he had not yet employed this presidential power.

Many presidents have complained that they cannot control "pork-barrel" legislation—federal expenditures tacked onto bills to "bring home the bacon" to a particular congressional member's district. For example, expenditures on a specific sports stadium might be added to a bill involving crime. The reason is simple: the president would have to veto the entire bill to eliminate the pork—and that might not be feasible politically. Presidents have often argued in favor of a *line-item veto* that would enable them to veto just one (or several) items in a bill. In 1996, Congress passed and President Clinton signed a line-item veto bill. The Supreme Court concluded in 1998 that it was unconstitutional, however.[4]

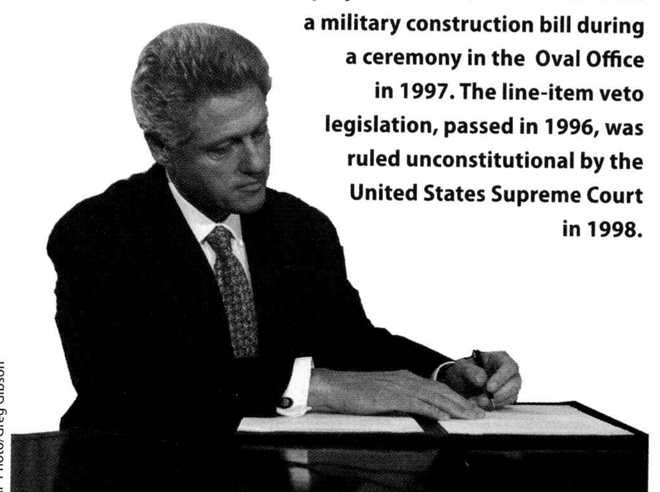

AP Photo/Greg Gibson

President Bill Clinton used line-item veto powers to eliminate nearly forty construction projects worth $287 million from a military construction bill during a ceremony in the Oval Office in 1997. The line-item veto legislation, passed in 1996, was ruled unconstitutional by the United States Supreme Court in 1998.

Jim Young/Reuters

When the president contemplates vetoing legislation, not all Americans are necessarily in agreement. In 2007, protesters—many of them children pulling wagons—gathered in front of the White House to ask President George W. Bush not to veto legislation expanding a health insurance program for low-income children.

The President's Inherent Powers

In addition to the powers explicitly granted by the Constitution, the president also has *inherent powers*—powers that are necessary to carry out the specific responsibilities of the president as set forth in the Constitution. The presidency is, of course, an institution of government, but it is also an institution that consists, at any one moment in time, of one individual. That means that the lines between the presidential office and the person who holds that office often become blurred. Certain presidential powers that today are considered part of the rights of the office were simply assumed by strong presidents to be inherent powers of the presidency, and their successors then continued to exercise these powers.

President Woodrow Wilson clearly indicated this interplay between presidential personality and presidential powers in the following statement:

> The President is at liberty, both in law and conscience, to be as big a man as he can. His capacity will set the limit; and if Congress be overborne by him, it will be no fault of the makers of the Constitution—it will be from no lack

As chief diplomat, George Washington made foreign policy decisions without consulting Congress. This action laid the ground-work for an active presidential role in the area of foreign policy.

By the time Abraham Lincoln gave his Inauguration Day speech, seven southern states had already seceded from the Union. Some scholars believe that Lincoln's skillful and vigorous handling of the Civil War increased the power and prestige of the presidency.

In its attempts to counter the effects of the Great Depression, Franklin D. Roosevelt's administration not only extended the role of the national government in regulating the nation's economic life but also further increased the power of the president.

> of constitutional powers on his part, but only because the President has the nation behind him, and Congress has not.[5]

In other words, because the Constitution is vague as to the actual carrying out of presidential powers, presidents are left to define the limits of their authority—subject, of course, to obstacles raised by the other branches of government.

The Expansion of Presidential Powers

The Constitution defines presidential powers in very general language, and even the founders were uncertain just how the president would perform the various functions. George Washington (1789–1797) set many of the precedents that have defined presidential power. For example, he removed officials from office, interpreting the constitutional power to appoint officials as implying power to remove them as well.[6] He established the practice of meeting regularly with the heads of the three departments that then existed and of turning to them for political advice. He set a precedent for the president to act as chief legislator by submitting proposed legislation to Congress. Abraham Lincoln (1861–1865), confronting the problems of the Civil War during the 1860s, took several important actions while Congress was not in session. He suspended certain constitutional liberties, spent funds that Congress had not appropriated, blockaded southern ports, and banned "treasonable correspondence" from the U.S. mail. Lincoln carried out all of these actions in the name of his power as commander in chief and his constitutional responsibility to "take Care that the Laws be faithfully executed."

Other presidents, including Thomas Jefferson, Andrew Jackson, Woodrow Wilson, Franklin D. Roosevelt, and George W. Bush, also greatly expanded the powers of the president. The power of the president continues to evolve, depending on the person holding the office, the relative power of Congress, and events at home and abroad.

THE PRESIDENT'S EXPANDED LEGISLATIVE POWERS Congress has come to expect the president to develop a legislative program. From time to time, the president submits special messages on certain subjects. These messages call on Congress to enact laws that the president thinks are necessary. The president also works closely with members of Congress to persuade them to support particular programs. The president writes, telephones, and meets with various congressional leaders to discuss pending bills. The president also sends aides to lobby on Capitol Hill. One study of the legislative process found that "no other single actor in the political system has quite the capability of the president to set agendas in given policy areas." As one lobbyist told a researcher, "Obviously, when a president sends up a bill [to Congress], it takes first place in the queue. All other bills take second place." Compared with some recent presidents, however, Barack Obama has shown a surprising willingness to let Congress determine the details of important legislation. We discuss that issue in this chapter's *Our Government's Response to the Economic Crisis* feature on the next page.

> "All the president is, is a glorified public relations man
> WHO SPENDS HIS TIME FLATTERING, KISSING, AND KICKING PEOPLE TO GET THEM TO DO WHAT THEY ARE SUPPOSED TO DO ANYWAY."
>
> ~ HARRY TRUMAN ~
> THIRTY-THIRD PRESIDENT OF THE UNITED STATES
> 1945–1953

THE POWER TO PERSUADE. The president's political skills and ability to persuade others play a large role in determining the administration's success. According to Richard Neustadt in his classic work *Presidential Power,* "Presidential power is the power to persuade."[7] For all of the resources at the president's disposal, the president still must rely on the cooperation of others if the administration's goals are to be accomplished. After three years in office, President Harry Truman made this remark about the powers of the president:

> The president may have a great many powers given to him in the Constitution and may have certain powers under certain laws which are given to him by the Congress of the United States; but the principal power that the president has is to bring people in and try to persuade them to do what they ought to do without persuasion. That's what the powers of the president amount to.[8]

For example, President Barack Obama embarked on an ambitious legislative agenda following his election in 2008. His ability to win congressional support for his plans depended largely on his persuasive power. Persuasive powers are particularly important when divided government exists. If a president from one political party faces a Congress dominated by the other party, the president must overcome more opposition than usual to get legislation passed.

GOING PUBLIC. The president may also use a strategy known as "going public"[9]—that is, using press conferences, public appearances, and televised events to arouse public opinion in favor of certain legislative programs. The public may then pressure legislators to support the administration's programs. A president who has the support of the public can wield significant persuasive power over Congress. Presidents who are voted into office through "landslide" elections have increased bargaining power because of their widespread popularity. Those with less popular support have less bargaining leverage.

THE POWER TO INFLUENCE THE ECONOMY. Some of the greatest expansions of presidential power occurred during Franklin D. Roosevelt's administration. Roosevelt claimed the presidential power to regulate the economy during the Great Depression in the 1930s. Since that time, Americans have expected the president to be actively involved in economic matters and social programs, and that expectation becomes especially potent during a major economic downturn, such as the Great Recession that began in December 2007. Congress annually receives from the president a suggested budget and the *Economic Report of the President.* The budget message suggests what amounts of money the government will need for its programs. The *Economic Report of the President* presents the state of the nation's economy and recommends ways to improve it.

THE LEGISLATIVE SUCCESS OF VARIOUS PRESIDENTS. Look at Figure 12–1 on page 283. It shows the success records of presidents in getting their legislation passed. Success is defined as how often the president won his way on roll-call votes on which he took a clear position. As you can see, typically a president's success record was very high when he first took office and then gradually declined. This is sometimes attributed to the president's "honeymoon period," when Congress may be most likely to work with the president to achieve the president's legislative agenda. The media often put a great deal of emphasis on how successful a president is during the "first hundred days" in office. Ironically, this is also the period when the president is least experienced in the ways of the White House, particularly if the president was a Washington outsider, such as a state governor, before becoming president.

Our Government's Response to the Economic Crisis

Has Obama Deferred to Congress Too Much?

One of the roles of the president is "legislator in chief." Many past presidents relished this role. The president's staff would write legislation, and the administration would find sponsors to introduce the measures in the House and the Senate. In the current economic crisis, however, President Obama seems to have taken a much more hands-off approach. Some critics—on both the political right and left—argue that he has gone too far in allowing Congress to shape important legislation.

The Economic Stimulus Act—One Example

When Obama took office, he faced the worst economic crisis in more than half a century, the Great Recession. Many economic policy analysts recommended a stimulus bill. In spite of a White House filled with first-rate policy "wonks," Obama largely subcontracted the stimulus bill to the Democratic leadership in Congress. The result was a bill of more than a thousand pages that included $284 billion in tax breaks and about half a trillion dollars in new spending.

Republicans claimed that this spending was dangerous and that the bill contained endless barrels of pork. Indeed, much of the spending was to be distributed to state and local governments in response to grant requests. Technically, this may not have been pork, but it certainly resembled it. And many of the line items in the bill clearly were pork. These included $2 billion for the domestic lithium ion battery industry, $100 million for shipyards in small cities, and $2 billion for a demonstration clean-coal plant in Illinois. Some argued that relying on Congress was essential to moving the stimulus bill out quickly. That argument would not apply to health-care reform, however.

The Keystone of Obama's "Change for America": Health-Care Reform

Obama argued during his campaign and after his inauguration that health-care reform, including cost controls, was essential to promote long-term economic growth and to address the federal budget deficit. As Obama and his staff made their plans for health-care reform, they clearly kept in mind what had happened the last time a president made a major push on this issue. In 1993, President Bill Clinton set up a Task Force on National Health Care Reform headed by his wife, Hillary Clinton. Working essentially in secret, the task force drafted an enormously complex, comprehensive plan for universal health insurance. The Clintons presented the plan to Congress almost on a take-it-or-leave-it basis. Congress left it. Obama and his team concluded that they must let Congress draft a health-care bill. Senators and representatives would then feel as if they "owned" the legislation and would support it.

Through the summer of 2009, Obama let Congress do its work. One resulting problem was that by August, when Congress took its annual recess, three versions of the health-care bill existed, one in the House and two in different committees in the Senate. It wasn't at all clear what Obama's health-care plan actually was. That made selling the plan to the public very difficult. Opinion polls revealed considerable confusion among members of the public about what health-care reform really entailed. Misinformation was rife. In this environment, Obama's approval ratings began to slip as well.

For Critical Analysis *What might some of the downsides be if President Obama resumes the role of "legislator in chief" instead of deferring to Congress?*

THE INCREASING USE OF EXECUTIVE ORDERS As the nation's chief executive, the president is considered to have the inherent power to issue **executive orders,** which are presidential orders to carry out policies described in laws that have been passed by Congress. These orders have the force of law. Presidents have issued executive orders for a variety of purposes, including to establish procedures for appointing noncareer administrators, restructure the White House bureaucracy, ration consumer goods and administer wage and price controls under emergency conditions, classify government information as secret, implement affirmative action policies, and regulate the export of certain items. Presidents issue executive orders frequently, sometimes as many as one hundred a year.

executive order A presidential order to carry out a policy or policies described in a law passed by Congress.

AN UNPRECEDENTED USE OF SIGNING STATEMENTS President George W. Bush made wide use of signing statements as a means to avoid

Figure 12–1

Presidential Success Records

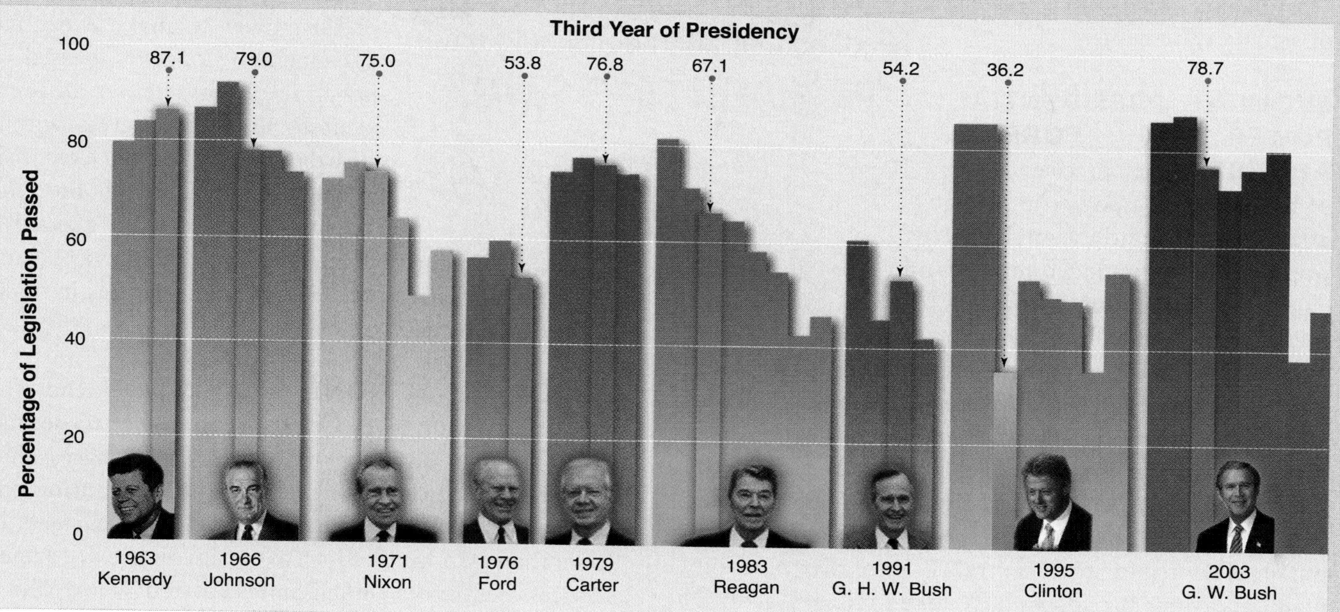

Source: *Congressional Quarterly Almanac.*

being constrained by legislation. A **signing statement** is a written statement, appended to a bill at the time the president signs it into law, indicating how the president interprets that legislation. For example, in 2005 Congress passed a law that prohibited the military from using torture when trying to gain information from detainees designated as "enemy combatants." Bush signed the legislation, but he also added a signing statement that read, in part, "The executive branch shall construe [the law banning torture] in a manner consistent with the constitutional authority of the President to supervise the unitary executive branch and as Commander in Chief and consistent with the constitutional limitations on the judicial power." In other words, this statement says that Bush had the constitutional authority, as commander in chief, to order torture if he wanted to.

President George W. Bush is shown here approving a signing statement attached to a piece of legislation. During his two terms as president, Bush issued more signing statements than all other previous presidents combined.

AP Photo/The White House/Chris Greenberg

Signing statements have been used by presidents in the past, but never to the extent that Bush used them. By the end of his second term, he had issued a total of more than 1,100 signing statements. According to a number of commentators, Bush used the signing statement as an alternative to the veto. In effect, the signing statement was like a line-item veto, allowing the president to disregard a specific provision in a bill if he chose to do so when the law was applied. A task force of the American Bar Association stated that Bush's use of signing statements to such a degree "raise[d] serious concerns crucial to the survival of our democracy." Barack Obama criticized Bush's use of signing

signing statement A written statement, appended to a bill at the time the president signs it into law, indicating how the president interprets that legislation.

statements and promised to cut back drastically on the practice. Within months of taking office, however, Obama had already issued dozens of signing statements.

> "If one morning I walked on top of the water across the Potomac River, the headline that afternoon would read: 'PRESIDENT CAN'T SWIM.'"
>
> ~ LYNDON B. JOHNSON ~
> THIRTY-SIXTH PRESIDENT OF THE UNITED STATES
> 1963–1969

EVOLVING PRESIDENTIAL POWER IN FOREIGN AFFAIRS The precise extent of the president's power in foreign affairs is constantly evolving. The president is commander in chief and chief diplomat, but only Congress has the power to formally declare war, and the Senate must ratify any treaty that the president has negotiated with other nations. George Washington laid the groundwork for our long history of the president's active role in foreign policy. For example, when war broke out between Britain and France in 1793, Washington chose to disregard a treaty of alliance with France and to pursue a course of strict neutrality. Since that time, on many occasions presidents have taken military actions and made foreign policy without consulting Congress.

EXECUTIVE AGREEMENTS. In foreign affairs, presidential power is enhanced by the ability to make **executive agreements,** which are pacts between the president and other heads of state. Executive agreements do not require Senate approval (even though Congress may refuse to appropriate the necessary money to carry out the agreements), but they have the same legal status as treaties.

Presidents form executive agreements for a wide range of purposes. Some involve routine matters, such as promises of trade or assistance to other countries. Others concern matters of great importance. In 1940, for example, President Franklin D. Roosevelt formed an important executive agreement with British prime minister Winston Churchill. The agreement provided that the United States would lend American destroyers to Britain to help protect that nation and its shipping during World War II. In return, the British allowed the United States to use military and naval bases on British territories in the Western Hemisphere.

To prevent presidential abuse of the power to make executive agreements, Congress passed a law in 1972 that requires the president to inform Congress within sixty days of making any executive agreement. The law did not limit the president's power to make executive agreements, however, and they continue to be used far more than treaties in making foreign policy.

MILITARY ACTIONS. As you have read, the U.S. Constitution gives Congress the power to declare war. Consider however, that although Congress has declared war in only five different conflicts during our nation's history,[10] the United States has engaged in more than two hundred activities involving the armed services. Before the United States entered World War II in 1941, Franklin D. Roosevelt ordered the Navy to "shoot on sight" any German submarine that appeared in the Western Hemisphere security zone. Without a congressional declaration of war, President Truman sent U.S. armed forces to Korea in 1950, thus involving American troops in the conflict between North and South Korea.

executive agreement A binding international agreement, or pact, that is made between the president and another head of state and that does not require Senate approval.

Franklin D. Roosevelt and Winston Churchill discuss matters relating to World War II aboard a British battleship in August 1941.

Library of Congress

In 1991, the United States, along with other nations, invaded Iraq after that country took over Kuwait. Here, President George H. W. Bush (left) meets with General Colin Powell (right) at the Pentagon to discuss whether the coalition forces should invade Baghdad, the capital of Iraq.

The United States also entered the Vietnam War (1964–1975) without a congressional declaration. President Nixon did not consult Congress when he made the decision to invade Cambodia in 1970. Neither did President Reagan when he sent troops to Lebanon and Grenada in 1983 and ordered American fighter planes to attack Libya in 1986 in retaliation for terrorist attacks on American soldiers. No congressional vote was taken before President George H. W. Bush sent troops into Panama in 1989. Bush did, however, obtain congressional approval to use American troops to force Iraq to withdraw from Kuwait in 1991. Without Congress, President Clinton made the decision to send troops to Haiti in 1994 and to Bosnia in 1995, as well as to bomb Iraq in 1998. In 1999, he also decided on his own authority to send U.S. forces under the command of NATO (North Atlantic Treaty Organization) to bomb Yugoslavia.

Harry Truman

THE WAR POWERS RESOLUTION. As commander in chief, the president can respond quickly to a military threat without waiting for congressional action. This power to commit troops and to involve the nation in a war upset many members of Congress as the undeclared war in Vietnam dragged on for years into the 1970s. Criticism of the president's role in the Vietnam conflict led to the passage of the War Powers Resolution of 1973, which limits the president's war-making powers. The law, which was passed over President Nixon's veto, requires the president to notify Congress within forty-eight hours of deploying troops. It also prevents the president from sending troops abroad for more than sixty days (or ninety days, if more time is needed for a successful withdrawal). If Congress does not authorize a longer period, the troops must be removed.

THE WAR ON TERRORISM. President George W. Bush did not obtain a declaration of war from Congress for the war against terrorism that began on September 11, 2001. Instead, Congress invoked the War Powers Resolution and passed a joint resolution authorizing the president to use "all necessary and appropriate force against those nations, organizations, or persons he determines planned, authorized, committed, or aided the terrorist attacks that occurred on September 11, 2001." Also, in October 2002, Congress passed a joint resolution authorizing the use of U.S. armed forces against Iraq.

The resolutions set no date for Bush to halt military operations, and as a consequence, the president was able to invoke certain emergency wartime measures. For example, through executive order the president created military tribunals for trying terrorist suspects. The president also held American citizens as "enemy combatants," denying them access to their attorneys. In late 2007, because of the strong public opinion against continuing the war in Iraq, the Democratic majority in Congress sought to repeal the 2002 authorization and pass legislation that would set a deadline for deploying U.S. troops. This attempt was unsuccessful, however.

NUCLEAR WEAPONS. Since 1945, the president, as commander in chief, has been responsible for the most difficult of all military decisions—if and when to use nuclear weapons. In 1945, Harry Truman made the awesome decision to drop atomic bombs on the

Japanese cities of Hiroshima and Nagasaki. "The final decision," he said, "on where and when to use the atomic bomb was up to me. Let there be no mistake about it." Today, the president travels at all times with the "football"—the briefcase containing the codes used to launch a nuclear attack.

"As to the presidency, the two happiest days of my life WERE THOSE OF MY ENTRANCE UPON THE OFFICE AND MY SURRENDER OF IT."

~ MARTIN VAN BUREN ~
EIGHTH PRESIDENT
OF THE UNITED STATES
1837–1841

"presidential approval ratings," and meeting with the press. Much of this activity is for the purpose of gaining leverage with Congress. The president can put all of his or her persuasive powers to work in achieving a legislative agenda, but Congress still retains the ultimate lawmaking authority.

LO4 *Congressional and Presidential Relations*

Despite the seemingly immense powers at the president's disposal, the president is limited in what he or she can accomplish, or even attempt. In our system of checks and balances, the president must share some powers with the legislative and judicial branches of government. The president's power is checked not only by these institutions but also by the media, public opinion, and the voters. The founders hoped that this system of shared power would lessen the chance of tyranny.

Some scholars believe the relationship between Congress and the president is the most important one in the American system of government. Congress traditionally has had the upper hand in some areas, primarily in passing legislation. In some other areas, though, particularly in foreign affairs, the president can exert tremendous power that Congress is virtually unable to check.

Advantage: Congress

Congress has the advantage over the president in the areas of legislative authorization, the regulation of foreign and interstate commerce, and some budgetary matters. Of course, as you have already read, the president today proposes a legislative agenda and a budget to Congress every year. Nonetheless, only Congress has the power to pass the legislation and appropriate the money. The most the president can do constitutionally is veto an entire bill if it contains something that the president does not like. As noted, however, modern presidents have frequently used signing statements in an attempt to avoid portions of bills that they did not approve.

Presidential popularity is a source of power for the president in dealings with Congress. Presidents spend a great deal of time courting public opinion, eyeing the

DIVIDED GOVERNMENT When government is divided—with at least one house of Congress controlled by a different party than the White House—the president can have difficulty even getting a legislative agenda to the floor for a vote. President Bill Clinton found this to be so after the congressional elections of 1994 brought the Republicans to power in Congress. Clinton's success rate in implementing his legislative agenda dropped to 36.2 percent in 1995, after a high of 86.4 the previous year (see Figure 12–1 on page 283).

President George W. Bush faced a similar problem in 2007, when the Democrats gained a majority in Congress. During his first six years as president, Bush had worked with an extremely cooperative Republican-led Congress. After the Democrats became the majority, however, divided government existed again.

DIFFERENT CONSTITUENCIES Congress and the president have different constituencies, and this fact influences their relationship. Members of Congress represent a state or a local district, and this gives them a regional focus. As we discussed in Chapter 11, members of Congress like to have legislative successes of their own to bring home to their constituents—military bases that remain operative, public-works projects that create local jobs, or trade rules that benefit a big local employer. Ideally, the president's focus should be on the nation as a whole: national defense, homeland security, the national economy. At times, this can put the president at odds even with members of his or her own party in Congress.

Furthermore, members of Congress and the president face different election cycles (every two years in the House, every six years in the Senate, and every four years for the president), and the president is limited to two terms in office. Consequently, the president and Congress sometimes feel a different sense of urgency about implementing legislation. For example, the president often senses the need to demonstrate legislative success during the first year in office, when the excitement over the elections is still fresh in the minds of politicians and the public.

Advantage: The President

The president has the advantage over Congress in dealing with a national crisis, in setting foreign policy, and in influencing public opinion. In times of crisis, the presidency is arguably the most crucial institution in government because, when necessary, the president can act quickly, speak with one voice, and represent the nation to the world. George W. Bush's presidency was unquestionably changed by the terrorist attacks of September 11, 2001. He represented the United States while it was under attack from foreign enemies and reeling from shock and horror. No member of Congress could wield the kind of personal power that accrues to a president in a time of national crisis.

Some scholars have argued that recent presidents have abused the powers of the presidency by taking advantage of crises. Others have argued that there is an unwritten "doctrine of necessity" under which presidential powers can and should be expanded during a crisis. When this has happened in the past, however, Congress has always retaken some control when the crisis was over, in a natural process of institutional give-and-take. A problem faced during the Bush administration was that the "war on terrorism" had no obvious end or conclusion. It was not clear when the crisis would be over and the nation could return to normal government relations and procedures.

Executive Privilege

As you read in Chapter 11, Congress has the authority to investigate and oversee the activities of other branches of government. Nonetheless, both Congress and the public have accepted that a certain degree of secrecy by the executive branch is necessary to protect national security. Some presidents have claimed an inherent executive power to withhold information from, or to refuse to appear before, Congress or the courts. This is called **executive privilege,** and it has been invoked by presidents from the time of George Washington to the present.

One of the problems with executive privilege is that it has been used for more purposes than simply to safeguard the national security. President Nixon invoked executive privilege in an attempt to avoid handing over taped White House conversations to Congress during the **Watergate scandal.** President Clinton invoked the privilege in an attempt to keep details of his sexual relationship with Monica Lewinsky a secret. President George W. Bush claimed executive privilege on numerous occasions. For example, the Bush administration refused to deliver information about Vice President Dick Cheney's meetings and other communications with certain industry representatives when Cheney was chairing a task force on energy policy.

After the Democrats took control of Congress in 2007 and began to investigate various actions undertaken by the Bush administration, they were frequently blocked in their attempts to obtain information by the claim of executive privilege. For example, during Congress's investigation of the Justice Department's firing of several U.S. attorneys for allegedly political reasons, the Bush administration raised the claim of executive privilege to prevent several people from testifying or submitting requested documents to Congress.

While campaigning, Barack Obama promised that his administration would be much more open than that of President Bush. Is Obama keeping his promise? We examine that question in this chapter's *Perception versus Reality* feature on the following page.

LO5 *The Organization of the Executive Branch*

In the early days of this nation, presidents answered their own mail, as George Washington did. Only in 1857 did Congress authorize a private secretary for the president, to be paid by the federal government. Even Woodrow Wilson typed most of his correspondence, although by that time several secretaries were assigned to the president. When Franklin D. Roosevelt became president in 1933, the entire staff consisted of thirty-seven employees. Only during Roosevelt's New Deal and World War II did the presidential staff become a sizable organization.

executive privilege An inherent executive power claimed by presidents to withhold information from, or to refuse to appear before, Congress or the courts. The president can also accord the privilege to other executive officials.

Watergate scandal A scandal involving an illegal break-in at the Democratic National Committee offices in 1972 by members of President Nixon's reelection campaign staff. Before Congress could vote to impeach Nixon for his participation in covering up the break-in, Nixon resigned from the presidency.

The President's Cabinet

The Constitution does not specifically mention presidential assistants

Obama and Open Government

Obama campaigned hard on many themes, but one of the most important was open government. If he was elected, the Bush era of government secrecy would end. Barack Obama promised that his presidency would be the most open in the history of this nation.

The Perception

The day after taking the oath of office, President Obama issued a much-publicized "transparency memo." No more secret meetings. No more secret deals. Openness would be the watchword. It looked as if President Obama would make good on his promise that the federal government would become an open book, in contrast to what his predecessor had done.

The Reality

Later the same year, a group of coal executives visited the White House to discuss Obama's "clean coal" policies. Public interest groups filed a Freedom of Information Act request for logs that would show the identities of the coal executives in attendance. The request was refused. Why? Because the disclosure of such records would impinge on privileged "presidential communications." White House counsel Greg Craig approved this refusal.

President Bush had famously refused to reveal which energy industry leaders met with Vice President Dick Cheney to chart the administration's energy policies. Now, by refusing to identify the coal executives, Obama appeared to be adopting the same policy of secrecy. David Sobel, a lawyer who argues Freedom of Information Act cases, claims that nothing has changed. All he sees is "the recycling of old Bush secrecy policies."

Surprisingly little has changed with respect to presidential signing statements either. These statements effectively negate certain aspects of legislation duly passed by Congress and signed into law by the president. While campaigning, Obama condemned the hundreds of signing statements made by Bush. In June 2009, however, Obama drafted a signing statement concerning a $108 billion loan guarantee to the International Monetary Fund (IMF). In the statement, Obama essentially disavowed deals his staff members had made with members of Congress to get the IMF legislation passed. Members of Congress, naturally, were furious. While Obama is not likely to reach Bush's record of more than a thousand signing statements, he is off to a good start.

Finally, one method the administration is using to bypass oversight is the appointment of more than forty "czars." These czars are White House staff members who report directly to the president on various topics. We have long had a drug czar, but now we have an auto czar, a technology czar, and many others. Unlike ordinary cabinet members, these White House czars and czarinas are not confirmed by Congress. As White House staff members, they can also hide behind the protection of executive privilege if Congress seeks to question them.

It would seem that transparency may not really be the watchword of the current administration, in spite of all those campaign promises.

Blog On *The Federation of American Scientists (FAS) is concerned about another type of openness that the Obama administration has addressed more with talk than with action—the declassification of secret documents. The Bush administration, after all, went wild with the classification stamp. See what FAS has to say at* **www.fas.org/blog/secrecy**. *Questions have also been raised about the degree to which Obama will protect whistleblowers, federal employees who "blow the whistle" on government abuses. Whistleblowers now have their own Web site at* **www.whistleblowers.org**.

and advisers. The Constitution states only that the president "may require the Opinion, in writing, of the principal Officer in each of the executive Departments." Since the time of our first president, however, presidents have had an advisory group, or **cabinet,** to turn to for counsel. Originally, the cabinet consisted of only four officials—the secretaries of state, treasury, and war and the attorney general. Today, the cabinet includes fourteen department secretaries, the attorney general, and a number of other officials. (See Table 12–2 for the names of the major executive departments represented in the cabinet.) Additional cabinet members vary from one presidency to the next. Typically, the vice president is

cabinet An advisory group selected by the president to assist with decision making. Traditionally, the cabinet has consisted of the heads of the executive departments and other officers whom the president may choose to appoint.

Table 12–2

The Major Executive Departments

The heads of all of these departments are members of the president's cabinet.

Department	Year of First Establishment
Department of State	1789
Department of the Treasury	1789
Department of Defense*	1789
Department of Justice (headed by the Attorney General)†	1789
Department of the Interior	1849
Department of Agriculture	1889
Department of Commerce‡	1903
Department of Labor‡	1903
Department of Health and Human Services§	1953
Department of Housing and Urban Development	1965
Department of Transportation	1967
Department of Energy	1977
Department of Education	1979
Department of Veterans Affairs	1989
Department of Homeland Security	2002

*Established in 1947 by merging the Department of War, created in 1789, and the Department of the Navy, created in 1798.
†Formerly the Office of the Attorney General; renamed and reorganized in 1870.
‡Formed in 1913 by splitting the Department of Commerce and Labor, which was created in 1903.
§Formerly the Department of Health, Education, and Welfare; renamed when the Department of Education was spun off in 1979.

a member. President Clinton added ten officials to the cabinet, and George W. Bush added five. Under Barack Obama, the members in addition to the vice president are:

- The administrator of the Environmental Protection Agency.
- The chair of the Council of Economic Advisers.
- The director of the Office of Management and Budget.
- The United States ambassador to the United Nations.
- The United States trade representative.
- The White House chief of staff.

Because the Constitution does not require the president to consult with the cabinet, the use of this body is purely discretionary. Some presidents have relied on the counsel of their cabinets. Other presidents solicited the opinions of their cabinets and then did what they wanted to do anyway. After a cabinet meeting in which a vote was seven nays against his one aye, President Lincoln supposedly said, "Seven nays and one aye, the ayes have it."[11] Still other presidents have sought counsel from so-called **kitchen cabinets.** A kitchen cabinet is a very informal group of persons, such as Ronald Reagan's trusted California coterie, to whom the president turns for advice. (Reagan had been governor of California.) The term *kitchen cabinet* originated during the presidency of Andrew Jackson, who relied on the counsel of close friends who allegedly met with him in the kitchen of the White House.

In general, few presidents have relied heavily on the advice of the formal cabinet. To a certain extent, the growth of other components of the executive branch has rendered the formal cabinet less significant as an advisory board to the president. Additionally, the department heads are at times more responsive to the wishes of their own staffs or to their own political ambitions than they are to the president. They may be more concerned with obtaining resources for their departments than with helping presidents achieve their goals. As a result, there is often a conflict of interest between presidents and their cabinet members.

The Executive Office of the President

In 1939, President Franklin D. Roosevelt set up the **Executive Office of the President (EOP)** to cope with the increased responsibilities brought on by the Great Depression. Since then, the EOP has grown significantly to accommodate the expansive role played by the national government, including the executive branch, in the nation's economic and social life.

The EOP is made up of the top advisers and assistants who help the president carry out major duties. Over the years, the EOP has changed according to the needs and leadership style of each president. It has become an increasingly influential and important part of the executive branch. Table 12–3 on the following page lists various offices within the

kitchen cabinet The name given to a president's unofficial advisers. The term was coined during Andrew Jackson's presidency.

Executive Office of the President (EOP) A group of staff agencies that assist the president in carrying out major duties. Franklin D. Roosevelt established the EOP in 1939 to cope with the increased responsibilities brought on by the Great Depression.

Table 12–3

The Executive Office of the President as of 2010

Department
Council of Economic Advisers
Council on Environmental Quality
Domestic Policy Council
National Economic Council
National Security Council
Office of Administration
Office of Management and Budget
Office of National Drug Control Policy
Office of Science and Technology Policy
Office of the U.S. Trade Representative
President's Intelligence Advisory Board
White House Military Office
White House Office

Source: www.whitehouse.gov.

EOP as of 2010. Note that the organization of the EOP is subject to change. Presidents have frequently added new bodies to its membership and subtracted others. President George W. Bush made a number of changes to the EOP's table of organization during his eight years in office, and President Obama has made further changes still.

White House Office The personal office of the president. White House Office personnel handle the president's political needs and manage the media.

chief of staff The person who directs the operations of the White House Office and advises the president on important matters.

press secretary A member of the White House staff holds news conferences for reporters and makes public statements for the president.

Office of Management and Budget (OMB) An agency in the Executive Office of the President that assists the president in preparing and supervising the administration of the federal budget.

THE WHITE HOUSE OFFICE Of all of the executive staff agencies, the **White House Office** has the most direct contact with the president. The White House Office is headed by the **chief of staff,** who advises the president on important matters and directs the operations of the presidential staff. In November 2008, President-elect Barack Obama named Rahm Emanuel, a longtime friend from Chicago and a member of the House of Representatives, as his chief of staff. A number of other top officials, assistants, and special assistants to the president also aid him or her in such areas as national security, the economy, and political affairs. The **press secretary** (under Obama, Robert Gibbs) meets with reporters and makes public statements for the president. The counsel to the president serves as the White House lawyer and handles the president's legal matters. The White House staff also includes speechwriters, researchers, the president's physician, and a correspondence secretary. Altogether, the White House Office has more than four hundred employees.

The White House staff has several duties. First, the staff investigates and analyzes problems that require the president's attention. Staff members who are specialists in certain areas, such as diplomatic relations or foreign trade, gather information for the president and suggest solutions. White House staff members also screen the questions, issues, and problems that people present to the president, so matters that can be handled by other officials do not reach the president's desk. Additionally, the staff provides public relations support. For example, the press staff handles the president's relations with the White House press corps and schedules news conferences. Finally, the White House staff ensures that the president's initiatives are effectively transmitted to the relevant government personnel. Several staff members are usually assigned to work directly with members of Congress for this purpose.

The White House Office also includes the staff of the president's spouse. First Ladies have at times taken important roles within the White House. For example, Franklin D. Roosevelt's wife, Eleanor, advocated the rights of women, labor, and African Americans. As First Lady, Hillary Clinton developed an unsuccessful plan for a national health-care system. In 2008, she was a leading contender for the Democratic presidential nomination. Had she won the presidency, Bill Clinton would have become the nation's First Gentleman.

THE OFFICE OF MANAGEMENT AND BUDGET The **Office of Management and Budget (OMB)** was originally the Bureau of the Budget. Under recent presidents, the OMB has become an important and influential unit of the Executive Office of the President. The main function of the OMB is to assist the president in preparing the proposed annual budget, which the president must submit to Congress in January of each year (see Chapter 11 for details). The federal budget lists the revenues and expenditures expected for the coming year. It indicates which programs the federal government will pay for and how much they will cost. Thus, the budget is an annual statement of the public policies of the United States translated into dollars and cents. Making changes in the budget is a key way for presidents to influence the direction and policies of the federal government.

The president appoints the director of the OMB with the consent of the Senate. The director oversees the OMB's work and argues the administration's positions before Congress. The director also lobbies members of Congress to support the president's budget or to accept key features of it. Once the budget is approved by Congress, the OMB has the responsibility of putting it into practice. The OMB oversees the execution of the budget, checking the federal agencies to ensure that they use funds efficiently.

Beyond its budget duties, the OMB also reviews new bills prepared by the executive branch. It checks all legislative matters to be certain that they agree with the president's own positions.

THE NATIONAL SECURITY COUNCIL The **National Security Council (NSC)** was established in 1947 to manage the defense and foreign policy of the United States. Its members are the president, the vice president, and the secretaries of state and defense; it also has several informal advisers. The NSC is the president's link to his or her key foreign and military advisers. The president's special assistant for national security affairs heads the NSC staff.

AP Photo/Jim Cole

Vice President Joe Biden is a close adviser to President Obama. Biden's years of experience in Congress make him a useful counselor.

The Vice Presidency and Presidential Succession

As a rule, presidential nominees choose running mates who balance the ticket or whose appointment rewards or appeases party factions. For example, to balance the ticket geographically, a presidential candidate from the South may solicit a running mate from the West. George W. Bush, who had little experience in national government, picked Dick Cheney, a well-known Republican with extensive political experience in Washington, D.C.

In 2008, unsuccessful Republican candidate John McCain chose as his running mate Alaska governor Sarah Palin. He hoped, in part, to capture a larger share of the female vote. Palin also shored up McCain's support among cultural conservatives. President Barack Obama picked Senator Joe Biden, who had thirty-five years of experience in Congress. Obama wished to counter detractors who claimed that he was too inexperienced.

THE ROLE OF VICE PRESIDENTS For much of our history, the vice president has had almost no responsibilities. Still, the vice president is in a position to become the nation's chief executive should the president die, be impeached, or resign the presidential office. Nine vice presidents have become president because of the death or resignation of the president.

In recent years, the responsibilities of the vice president have grown immensely. The vice president has become one of the most—if not *the* most—important of the president's advisers. The first modern vice president to act as a major adviser was Walter Mondale, who served under Jimmy Carter. Later, Bill Clinton relied heavily on Vice President Al Gore, who shared many of Clinton's values and beliefs.

Without question, however, the most powerful vice president in American history was Dick Cheney, who served under George W. Bush. A consummate bureaucratic strategist, Cheney

National Security Council (NSC) A council that advises the president on domestic and foreign matters concerning the safety and defense of the nation; established in 1947.

was able to place his supporters in important positions throughout the government, giving him access to information and influence. He sat in on all important meetings, usually read the president's briefings before the president saw them, and even oversaw the work of the OMB. This unprecedented delegation of power, of course, would not have been possible without the president's agreement, and Bush clearly approved of it. Vice President Joe Biden is one of President Barack Obama's most important advisers, but not at the level of Cheney.

PRESIDENTIAL SUCCESSION One of the questions left unanswered by the Constitution was what the vice president should do if the president becomes incapable of carrying out necessary duties while in office. The Twenty-fifth Amendment to the Constitution, ratified in 1967, filled this gap. The amendment states that when the president believes that he or she is incapable of performing the duties of the office, he or she must inform Congress in writing of this fact. Then the vice president serves as acting president until the president can resume his or her normal duties. For example, President George W. Bush invoked the Twenty-fifth Amendment in 2007 before undergoing a minor surgical procedure.

When the president is unable to communicate, a majority of the cabinet, including the vice president, can declare that fact to Congress. Then the vice president serves as acting president until the president resumes normal duties. If a dispute arises over the return of the president's ability to discharge the normal functions of the presidential office, a two-thirds vote of both chambers of Congress is required if the vice president is to remain acting president. Otherwise, the president resumes these duties.

The Twenty-fifth Amendment also addresses the question of how the president should fill a vacant vice presidency. Section 2 of the amendment states, "Whenever there is a vacancy in the office of the Vice President, the President shall nominate a Vice President who shall take office upon confirmation by a majority vote of both Houses of Congress."

In 1973, Gerald Ford became the first appointed vice president of the United States after Spiro Agnew was forced to resign. One year later, President Richard Nixon resigned, and Ford advanced to the office of president. President Ford named Nelson Rockefeller as his vice president. For the first time in U.S. history, neither the president nor the vice president had been elected to his position.

What if both the president and the vice president die, resign, or are disabled? According to the Succession Act of 1947, then the Speaker of the House of Representatives will act as president on his or her resignation as Speaker and as representative. If the Speaker is unavailable, next in line is the president pro tem of the Senate, followed by the permanent members of the president's cabinet in the order of the creation of their departments (see Table 12–2 on page 289).

In 1973, the vice president under President Richard Nixon resigned. Nixon appointed as his vice president Congressman Gerald Ford. In 1974, when Nixon resigned, Ford became president and appointed a vice president. For the first time in U.S. history, neither the president nor the vice president had been elected to his position.

Library of Congress

AMERICA AT ODDS *The Presidency*

Tench Coxe, a prominent Philadelphian at the time the Constitution was written, commented that the president's power over legislation "amounts to no more than a serious duty imposed upon him to request both houses to reconsider any matter on which he entertains doubts or feels apprehensions." This opinion was in keeping with the founders' views, which essentially gave the president only a "negative power"—that is, the veto power.

As you have read in this chapter, the powers of the presidency have expanded to the point at which the president engages in a significant amount of "lawmaking" through increasing use of executive orders and signing statements. Some political and legal scholars are deeply concerned about how President George W. Bush transformed the presidency. They claim that because Bush had a relatively free hand in determining and implementing national policy, without facing significant congressional or judicial checks on his asserted powers, he was able to set precedents that may be followed by the Obama administration and by subsequent presidents. Clearly, many members of Congress believed that the legal justifications given by the Bush administration for many of its actions were invalid. Whether Congress will act to restrain the Obama administration remains to be seen.

ISSUES FOR DEBATE & DISCUSSION

1. **Surveys have shown that voters, when choosing a president, are at least as concerned about a candidate's character as they are about the position that the candidate takes on the major issues of the day. In 1976, in the wake of the Watergate scandal, voters appeared to place a high value on moral character, to the benefit of Democratic candidate Jimmy Carter. Four years later, however, Carter was widely viewed as weak and ineffective. Voters seemed to approve of Ronald Reagan's optimism and, later, Bill Clinton's ability to "feel your pain." Clearly, the public has favored different presidential attributes in different years, depending on the state of the economy, foreign crises, and other developments. What characteristics might Americans seek in a president regardless of recent events? To what extent should a voter value the candidate's character, as opposed to his or her platform? Can you think of an instance in which voters—or even you—have supported a candidate based on character issues even when the other candidate's platform was more appealing?**
2. **Do you believe that a U.S. president should be the "moral leader" of this country and base national policies on religious beliefs? Or should the president avoid any intermingling of religious beliefs and policymaking? Explain your position.**

TAKE ACTION

President James Madison (1809–1817) once said, "The citizens of the United States are responsible for the greatest trust ever confided to a political society." Notice that Madison laid the responsibility for this trust on the "citizens," not the "government." Even though it may seem that one person can do little to affect government policymaking and procedures, this assumption has been proved wrong time and again. If you would like to influence the way things are done in Washington, D.C., you can do so by helping to elect a president and members of Congress whose views you endorse and who you think would do a good job of running the country. Clearly, you will want to vote in the next elections. Before then, though, you could join others who share your political beliefs and work on behalf of one of the candidates. You could support a candidate in your home state or join others in "adopting" a candidate from another state who is facing a close race for a congressional seat. You can access that candidate's Web site and offer your services, such as calling voters of the candidate's party and urging them to go to the polls and vote for the candidate. You can also help raise funds for the candidate's campaign and, if you can afford it, even donate some money yourself.

During the 2008 presidential campaigns, Democrat Barack Obama (left) debated his Republican opponent, John McCain (right), on three separate occasions. Here, the candidates are shown in a debate moderated by CBS broadcast journalist Bob Schieffer. The debate took place at Hofstra University in Hempstead, New York.

AP Photo/Ron Edmonds

POLITICS ON THE WEB

- The White House home page offers links to many sources of information on the presidency. You can access this site at **www.whitehouse.gov**
- If you are interested in reading the inaugural addresses of American presidents from George Washington to Barack Obama, go to **www.bartleby.com/124**. In addition to the full text of the inaugural addresses, this site provides biographical information on the presidents.
- If you would like to research documents and academic resources concerning the presidency, a good Internet site to consult is provided by the University of Virginia's Miller Center of Public Affairs at **millercenter.org/academic/americanpresident**
- To access the various presidential libraries, visit the National Archives site at **www.archives.gov/presidential-libraries**

Online resources for this chapter

This text's Companion Web site, at **www.4ltrpress.cengage.com/govt**, offers links to numerous resources that you can use to learn more about the topics covered in this chapter.

GOVT 13

The Bureaucracy

LEARNING OBJECTIVES

LO1 Describe the size and functions of the U.S. bureaucracy.

LO2 Discuss the structure and basic components of the federal bureaucracy.

LO3 Indicate when the federal civil service was established and explain how bureaucrats get their jobs.

LO4 Explain how regulatory agencies make rules and how "iron triangles" affect policymaking in government.

LO5 Identify some of the ways in which the government has attempted to curb waste and improve efficiency in the bureaucracy.

AMERICA AT ODDS

Do We Need More—or Less—Regulation?

During the financial crisis of 2008 and 2009, the hue and cry over regulation of financial enterprises—mainly the lack thereof—was heard not only in the United States but also throughout the world. For every economic problem that makes the headlines, there is some group in America that believes that the problem was caused by too little regulation of American (or foreign) businesses.

In this nation's distant past, there was very little government regulation. Consider the health-care industry. One hundred years ago, drugs were not tested before they were put on the market. Hospitals had no uniform standards. Physicians were licensed, but that's about it. Jump forward to the current situation. The gross cost of complying with federal government rules regulating U.S. health care has been estimated at about $350 billion per year. The U.S. health-care industry is not the only regulated sector of the economy. A variety of federal agencies spend directly about $50 billion a year controlling everything from milk production to nuclear power plants. Most of the growth in this spending has occurred since 1970. After 9/11, new national security regulations increased such spending even further. The federal government publishes its new regulations in the *Federal Register*. In a typical year, new regulations generate eighty thousand pages in that publication.

Unbridled Capitalism Is Dead

The law of the capitalist jungle is what got us into the biggest financial crisis since the Great Depression. The events leading up to the credit meltdown in 2008 and the massive federal bailout of banks and insurance companies were caused by unregulated financial entities. Investment banking firms created ever riskier financial assets, which they sold to unsuspecting individuals and even to local governments as solid, gold-plated investments. In the mortgage industry, unscrupulous salespeople who earned big commissions tricked unsuspecting families into buying homes that were too expensive for their modest means. When house payments went up, those families lost their homes and sometimes their life savings.

We have lived through a time when a president—George W. Bush—scornfully ignored a Supreme Court decision on the regulation of greenhouse gas emissions. Even with something as important as the drugs that we take, the government is not giving us enough protection. Recently, despite its staff members' misgivings, the Food and Drug Administration allowed a drug named Avandia to hit the market. That drug turned out to have potential cardiac side effects, and no safety statement on the drug's label warned of them. Regulation is here to stay. Indeed, we need more regulation to protect our lives and our pocketbooks.

Too Much of Anything is Bad

While no one argues that regulation should be eliminated, many today believe that it is too costly relative to the actual benefits received. Consider the health-care industry regulatory costs mentioned above. By one estimate, the dollar value of the benefits from those regulations is only $170 billion per year. That means that with a total cost of $350 billion, the regulations generate a net cost to society of about $180 billion, or about $1,500 per U.S. household.

Consider another example. We all want safer products, but the Consumer Product Safety Commission now requires that warning labels appear on even common products. A standard ladder has six hundred words of warning pasted on it, including a warning not to place it in front of a swinging door. What are we, idiots? Every toy has a warning that says, "Small parts may cause a choking risk." Parents don't know this? Studies indicate that virtually no one reads warning labels anymore because they are either obvious or too long. What happened to personal responsibility in America? With excessive regulation, the average American no longer appears to be responsible for any of her or his purchases, activities, or actions. Regulation has its place, but it shouldn't control the entire life of a nation.

WHERE DO YOU STAND?

1. **How much do you think you benefit from regulation in our economy? Give some examples.**
2. **Are there any circumstances under which warning labels on consumer products could help you? Give some examples.**

EXPLORE THIS ISSUE ONLINE

1. **For arguments that the FDA is not strict enough in approving medicines, go to the Public Citizen's Health Research Group site at www.citizen.org/hrg.**
2. **The Competitive Enterprise Institute believes the FDA is too slow to approve drugs. See its articles at cei.org/issue/65.**

Introduction

Did you eat breakfast this morning? If you did, **bureaucrats**—individuals who work in the offices of government—had a lot to do with that breakfast. If you had bacon, the meat was inspected by federal agents. If you drank milk, the price was affected by rules and regulations of the Department of Agriculture. If you looked at a cereal box, you saw fine print about minerals and vitamins, which was the result of regulations made by several other federal agencies, including the Food and Drug Administration. If you ate leftover pizza for breakfast, state or local bureaucrats made sure that the kitchen of the pizza eatery was sanitary and safe. Other bureaucrats ensured that the employees who put together (and perhaps delivered) the pizza were protected against discrimination in the workplace.

Today, the word *bureaucracy* often evokes a negative reaction. For some, it conjures up visions of depersonalized automatons performing their chores without any sensitivity toward the needs of those they serve. For others, it is synonymous with government "red tape." A **bureaucracy,** however, is simply a large, complex administrative organization that is structured hierarchically in a pyramid-like fashion.[1] Government bureaucrats carry out the policies of elected government officials. Members of the bureaucracy deliver our mail, clean our streets, teach in our public schools, run our national parks, and attempt to ensure the safety of our food and the prescription drugs that we take. Life as we know it would be quite different without government bureaucrats to keep our governments—federal, state, and local—in operation. Americans, however, disagree over how much regulation is necessary, as discussed in the chapter-opening *America at Odds* feature.

GOVERNMENT BUREAUCRACY:

"A marvelous labor-saving device which enables ten men to do the work of one."

~ JOHN MAYNARD KEYNES ~
BRITISH ECONOMIST
1883–1946

LO1 The Nature and Size of the Bureaucracy

The concept of a bureaucracy is not confined to the federal government. Any large organization has to have a bureaucracy. In each bureaucracy, everybody (except the head of the bureaucracy) reports to at least one other person. In the federal government, the head of the bureaucracy is the president of the United States, and the bureaucracy is part of the executive branch.[2]

A bureaucratic form of organization allows each person to concentrate on her or his area of knowledge and expertise. In your college or university, for example, you do not expect the basketball coach to solve the problems of the finance department. The reason the federal government bureaucracy exists is

These food inspectors work in the part of our federal bureaucracy that is responsible for the quality and safety of what we eat.

Mike Mergen/Bloomberg News/Landov

bureaucrat An individual who works in a bureaucracy. As generally used, the term refers to a government employee.

bureaucracy A large, complex, hierarchically structured administrative organization that carries out specific functions.

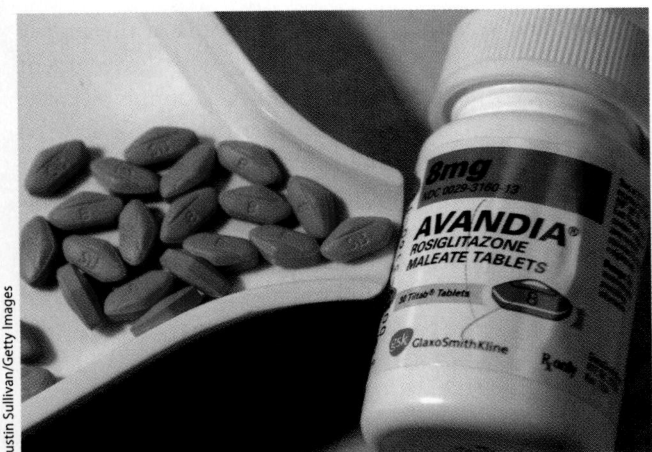

Justin Sullivan/Getty Images

The diabetes drug Avandia was approved by the Food and Drug Administration without any warning concerning cardiac side effects. These side effects were later made public.

that Congress, over time, has delegated certain tasks to specialists. For example, in 1914, Congress passed the Federal Trade Commission Act, which established the Federal Trade Commission to regulate deceptive and unfair trade practices. Those appointed to the commission were specialists in this area. Similarly, Congress passed the Consumer Product Safety Act in 1972, which established the Consumer Product Safety Commission to investigate the safety of consumer products placed on the market. The commission is one of many federal administrative agencies.

Another key aspect of any bureaucracy is that the power to act resides in the *position* rather than in the *person.* In your college or university, the person who is president now has more or less the same authority as any previous president. Additionally, bureaucracies usually entail standard operating procedures—directives on what procedures should be followed in specific circumstances. Bureaucracies normally also have a merit system, meaning that people are hired and promoted on the basis of demonstrated skills and achievements.

The Growth of Bureaucracy

The federal government that existed in 1789 was small. It had three departments, each with only a few employees: (1) the Department of State (nine employees), (2) the Department of War (two employees), and (3) the Department of the Treasury (thirty-nine employees). By 1798, nine years later, the federal bureaucracy was still quite small. The secretary of state had seven clerks. His total expenditures on stationery and printing amounted to $500, or about $8,700 in 2010 dollars. The Department of War spent, on average, a grand total of $1.4 million each year, or about $25.4 million in 2010 dollars.

Times have changed. Figure 13–1 shows the number of government employees at the local, state, and national levels from 1982 to 2009. Most growth has been at the state and local levels. All in all, the three levels of government employ more than 15 percent of the civilian labor force. Today, more Americans are employed by government (at all three levels) than by the entire manufacturing sector of the U.S. economy.

During election campaigns, politicians throughout the nation claim they will "cut big government and red tape" and "get rid of overlapping and wasteful bureaucracies." For the last several decades, virtually every president has campaigned on a platform calling for a reduction in the size of the federal bureaucracy. Yet, at the same time, candidates promise to establish programs that require new employees.

Figure 13–1

Government Employment at the Local, State, and National Levels

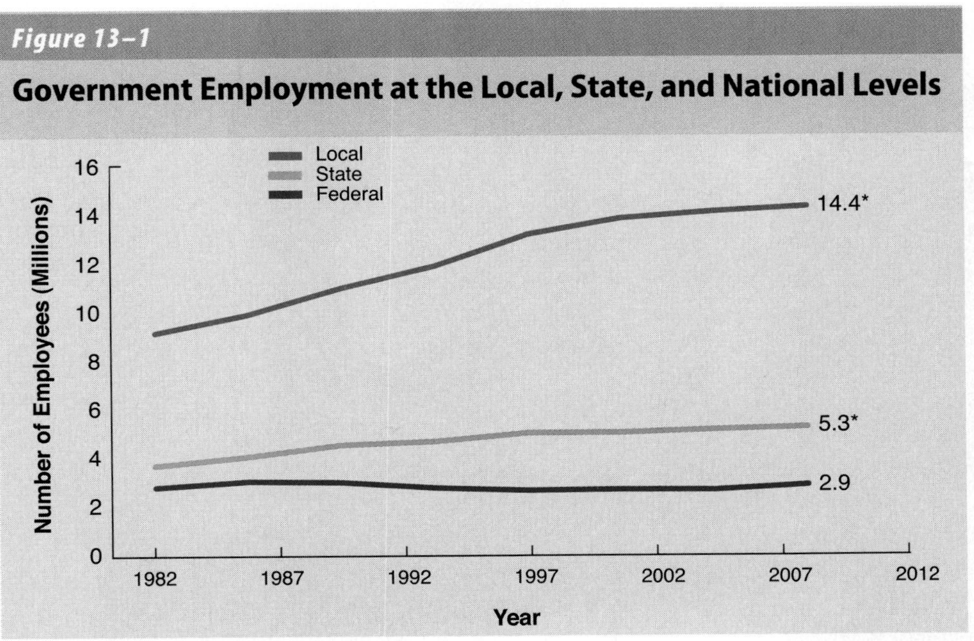

Source: U.S. Census Bureau.
* Estimated.

The Costs of Maintaining the Government

The costs of maintaining the government are high and growing. In 1929, government at all levels accounted for about 11 percent of the nation's gross domestic product (GDP). Today, that figure exceeds 40 percent. Average citizens pay a significant portion of their income to federal, state, and local governments. They do this by paying income taxes, sales taxes, property taxes, and many other types of taxes and fees. To fully understand the amount of money spent by federal, state, and local governments each year, consider that the same sum of money could be used to purchase all of the farmland in the United States plus all of the assets of the one hundred largest American corporations.

The government is costly, to be sure, but it also provides numerous services for Americans. Cutting back on the size of government inevitably means a reduction in those services. The trade-off between government spending and popular services is central to the debate over health-care reform. Even as the Obama administration advocated substantial new health-care spending, it also tried to limit costs. We discuss this issue in this chapter's *Our Government's Response to the Economic Crisis* feature on the following page.

Attorney General Eric Holder, Jr., heads the Department of Justice, which is part of the administration. Some believe that the attorney general should be insulated from partisan politics, much like the director of the F.B.I.

Doug Mills/*The New York Times*/Redux

LO2 *How the Federal Bureaucracy Is Organized*

A complete organization chart of the federal government would cover an entire wall. A simplified version is provided in Figure 13–2 on page 301. The executive branch consists of a number of bureaucracies that provide services to Congress, to the federal courts, and to the president directly.

The executive branch of the federal government includes four major types of structures:

- Executive departments.
- Independent executive agencies.
- Independent regulatory agencies.
- Government corporations.

Each type of structure has its own relationship to the president and its own internal workings.

The Executive Departments

You were introduced to the various executive departments in Chapter 12, when you read about how the president works with the cabinet and other close advisers. The fifteen executive departments, which are directly accountable to the president, are the major service organizations of the federal government. They are responsible for performing government functions, such as training troops (Department of Defense), printing money (Department of the Treasury), and enforcing federal laws setting minimum safety and health standards for workers (Department of Labor).

Table 13–1 on pages 302 and 303 provides an overview of each of the departments within the executive branch. The table lists a few of the many activities undertaken by each department. Because the president appoints the department heads, they are expected to help carry out the president's policy objectives. Often, they attempt to maximize the president's political fortunes as well. Is this a problem when the cabinet member in question is the U.S. attorney general? We discuss that issue in this chapter's *Join the Debate* feature on page 304.

Each executive department was created by Congress as the perceived need for it arose, and each department manages a specific policy area. In 2002, for example, Congress created the Department of Homeland Security to deal with the threat of terrorism. The head of each department is known as the secretary, except for the Department of Justice, which is headed by the attorney

Changing the Health-Care Spending Mix

Part of the Obama administration's thinking about how to solve the current economic crisis involves "rationalizing" health-care spending, particularly the spending undertaken by the federal government. In the past, most such spending went for two programs: Medicare, which provides health-care insurance to those aged sixty-five or older, and Medicaid, which funds health care for the poor. A White House fact sheet entitled "Paying for Health Care Reform" stated that the administration would cut $622 billion over ten years from Medicare and Medicaid, particularly from a program called Medicare Advantage. Why? To pay for overhauling our health-care system without adding hundreds of billions per year to the federal government budget deficit. The president stated in numerous speeches during August and September of 2009 that his health-care reform proposals would not add to the deficit, would not lead to health-care rationing, and would improve every family's health care.

Cost-Cutting Is Already Part of the System

In fact, attempts to restrain spending are already built into the existing system. During 2009, while Obama and Democratic members of Congress were arguing that the proposed health-care reforms would not affect the quality of services, a federal agency called the Centers for Medicare and Medicaid Services (CMS) was simultaneously proposing a rate reduction for more than one million physicians and nonphysician practitioners. This 13.5 percent rate reduction for 2010 would apply to all those paid under the Medical Physician Fee Schedule (MPFS). The MPFS determines Medicare and Medicaid payment rates for seven thousand types of services in physicians' offices and hospitals. Of course, some physicians were not happy. The American College of Cardiology, as an example, vowed to "fight these cuts."

Cutting Back on Medicare Advantage

The Medicare Advantage program was started in 2003. It allows seniors to use Medicare funds to buy private insurance plans. More than 20 percent of American seniors have enrolled in Medicare Advantage. When Obama attended a Colorado town hall meeting in the summer of 2009, he stated that over the next decade, roughly two-thirds of his $900 billion health-care reform program would be covered by "eliminating waste." He again cited Medicare Advantage. Medicare Advantage is somewhat more expensive than standard Medicare, but polls also show that its enrollees are more satisfied with their care than those who are enrolled in the regular Medicare program.

A Debate That Will Continue

After the U.S. economy finally weathers the Great Recession, the current debate about reducing inefficiencies in government-funded health care will undoubtedly continue. Those who currently view Medicare most favorably are in general over age sixty-five. A Kaiser Family Foundation poll and a CBS News/*New York Times* poll both discovered that well over 70 percent of seniors approve of Medicare, their government-administered health-insurance program. A majority consider it to be well run. In contrast, younger Americans not enrolled in Medicare are more skeptical. Only 45 percent rated Medicare favorably, and just 36 percent considered it well run. Clearly, the more familiar voters are with Medicare, the more likely they are to approve of it. The question is: Will Medicare enrollees continue to report high levels of satisfaction if the government continues to try to cut the program's costs?

For Critical Analysis *Why do you think health-care reform became such a major "hot button" issue so early in Obama's presidency?*

general. Each department head is appointed by the president and confirmed by the Senate.

A Typical Departmental Structure

Each cabinet department consists of the department's top administrators (the secretary of the department, deputy secretary, undersecretaries, and the like), plus a number of agencies. For example, the National Park Service is an agency within the Department of the Interior. The Drug Enforcement Administration is an agency within the Department of Justice.

Although there are organizational differences among the departments, each department generally

Figure 13–2

The Organization of the Federal Government

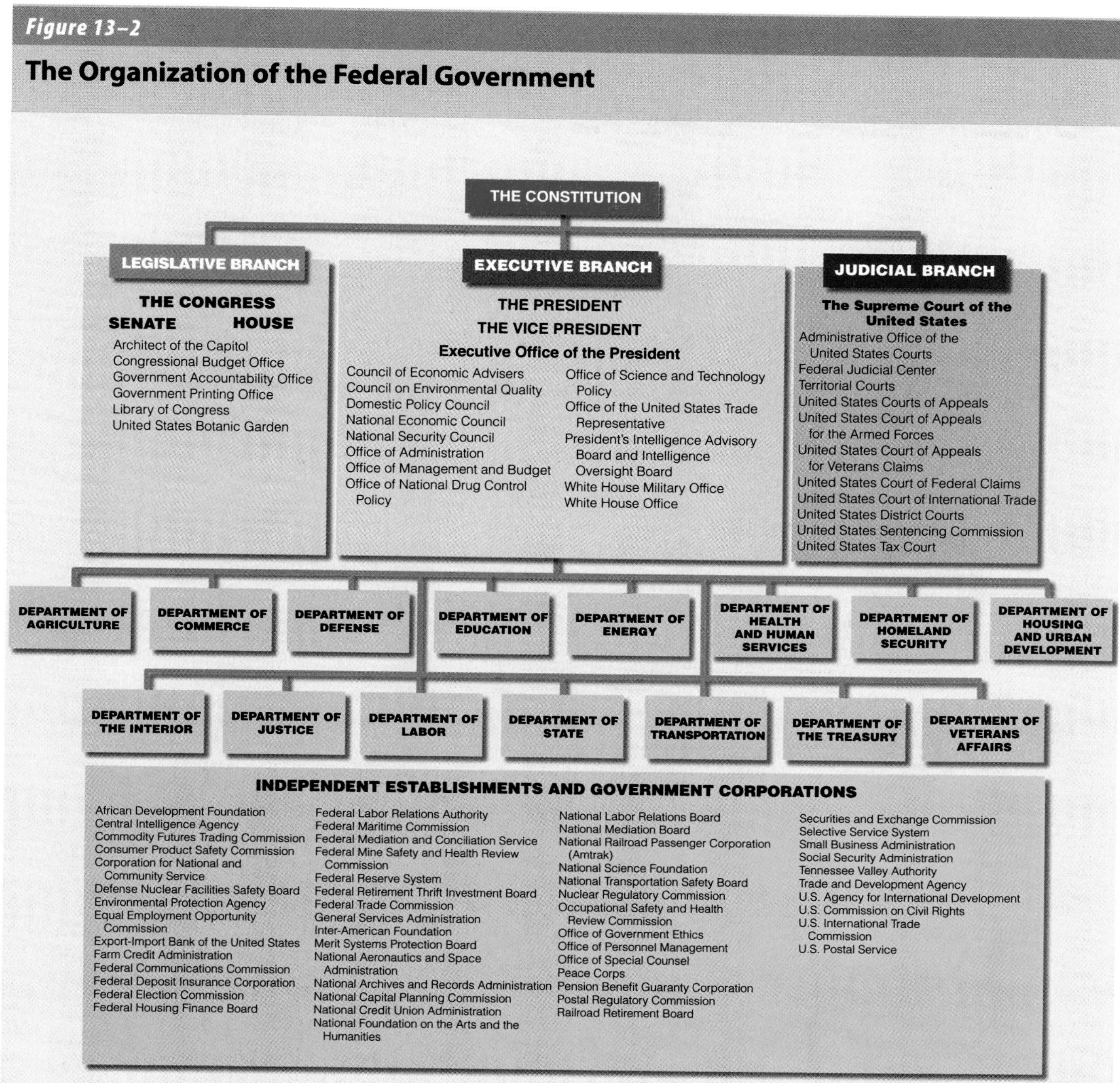

Source: *United States Government Manual*, 2008–09 (Washington, D.C.: U.S. Government Printing Office, 2008).

follows a typical bureaucratic structure. The Department of Agriculture provides a model for how an executive department is organized (see Figure 13–3 on page 305).

One aspect of the secretary of agriculture's job is to carry out the president's agricultural policies. Another aspect, however, is to promote and protect the department. The secretary spends time ensuring that Congress allocates enough money for the department to work effectively. The secretary also makes sure that constituents, or the people the department serves—farmers and major agricultural corporations—are happy. In general, the secretary tries to maintain or improve the status of the department with respect to all of the other departments and units of the federal bureaucracy.

The secretary of agriculture is assisted by a deputy secretary and several assistant secretaries and undersecretaries, all of whom are nominated by the president and put into office with Senate approval. The secretary

Table 13–1

Executive Departments

DEPARTMENT (Year of Original Establishment)		PRINCIPAL DUTIES	SELECTED SUBAGENCIES
State (1789)		Negotiates treaties; develops our foreign policy; protects citizens abroad.	Passport Services Office; Bureau of Diplomatic Security; Foreign Service; Bureau of Human Rights and Humanitarian Affairs; Bureau of Consular Affairs.
Treasury (1789)		Pays all federal bills; borrows money; collects federal taxes; mints coins and prints paper currency; supervises national banks.	Internal Revenue Service; U.S. Mint.
Defense (1789)*		Manages the armed forces (Army, Navy, Air Force, Marines); operates military bases.	National Security Agency; Joint Chiefs of Staff; Departments of the Air Force, Navy, Army; Defense Intelligence Agency; the service academies.
Justice (1789)†		Furnishes legal advice to the president; enforces federal criminal laws; supervises the federal corrections system (prisons).	Federal Bureau of Investigation; Drug Enforcement Administration; Bureau of Prisons; U.S. Marshals Service.
Interior (1849)		Supervises federally owned lands and parks; operates federal hydroelectric power facilities; supervises Native American affairs.	U.S. Fish and Wildlife Service; National Park Service; Bureau of Indian Affairs; Bureau of Land Management.
Agriculture (1889)		Provides assistance to farmers and ranchers; conducts research to improve agricultural activity and to prevent plant disease; works to protect forests from fires and disease.	Soil Conservation Service; Agricultural Research Service; Food Safety Inspection Service; Federal Crop Insurance Corporation; Forest Service.
Commerce (1903)‡		Grants patents and trademarks; conducts national census; monitors the weather; protects the interests of businesses.	Bureau of the Census; Bureau of Economic Analysis; Minority Business Development Agency; Patent and Trademark Office; National Oceanic and Atmospheric Administration.

Table 13–1

Executive Departments—(Continued)

DEPARTMENT (Year of Original Establishment)		PRINCIPAL DUTIES	SELECTED SUBAGENCIES
Labor (1903)[‡]		Administers federal labor laws; promotes the interests of workers.	Occupational Safety and Health Administration; Bureau of Labor Statistics; Employment Standards Administration; Employment and Training Administration.
Health and Human Services (1953)[§]		Promotes public health; enforces pure food and drug laws; sponsors health-related research.	Food and Drug Administration; Centers for Disease Control and Prevention; National Institutes of Health; Administration for Children and Families; Centers for Medicare and Medicaid Services.
Housing and Urban Development (1965)		Concerned with the nation's housing needs; develops and rehabilitates urban communities; oversees resale of mortgages.	Government National Mortgage Association; Office of Multifamily Housing Development; Office of Single Family Program Development; Office of Fair Housing and Equal Opportunity.
Transportation (1967)		Finances improvements in mass transit; develops and administers programs for highways, railroads, and aviation.	Federal Aviation Administration; Federal Highway Administration; National Highway Traffic Safety Administration; Federal Transit Administration.
Energy (1977)		Promotes the conservation of energy and resources; analyzes energy data; conducts research and development.	Office of Civilian Radioactive Waste Management; National Nuclear Security Administration; Energy Information Administration.
Education (1979)		Coordinates federal programs and policies for education; administers aid to education; promotes educational research.	Office of Special Education and Rehabilitation Services; Office of Elementary and Secondary Education; Office of Postsecondary Education; Office of Vocational and Adult Education.
Veterans Affairs (1989)		Promotes the welfare of veterans of the U.S. armed forces.	Veterans Health Administration; Veterans Benefits Administration; National Cemetery Administration.
Homeland Security (2002)		Works to prevent terrorist attacks within the United States, control America's borders, and minimize the damage from potential attacks and natural disasters.	U.S. Customs and Border Protection; U.S. Citizenship and Immigration Services; U.S. Coast Guard; Secret Service; Federal Emergency Management Agency.

* Established in 1947 by merging the Department of War, created in 1789, and the Department of the Navy, created in 1798.
† Formerly the Office of the Attorney General; renamed and reorganized in 1870.
‡ Formed in 1913 by splitting the Department of Commerce and Labor, which was created in 1903.
§ Formerly the Department of Health, Education, and Welfare; renamed when the Department of Education was spun off in 1979.

JOIN THE DEBATE

Should the Attorney General Be Independent of the President?

The attorney general is a member of the president's cabinet. As such, he or she is nominated by the president and must be approved by the Senate before taking office. Traditionally, the attorney general has been a close political ally of the president. Ronald Reagan and Jimmy Carter both named reliable cronies to head up the Justice Department. Richard Nixon's attorney general John Mitchell was even sentenced to prison for corrupt politicization of his office. George W. Bush's attorney general Alberto Gonzales deferred completely to the White House. One result was a politically motivated "midnight massacre" during which eight U.S. attorneys were fired for purely partisan reasons.

Is it right for the attorney general to be so close to the president? What if it becomes necessary to investigate members of the president's own administration? Shouldn't the nation's chief law enforcement officer be independent and nonpartisan? One way to accomplish this would be to remove the attorney general position from the president's cabinet and appoint that official for a fixed term of years that transcends the term of any one president. That is exactly what we have done with the position of Federal Bureau of Investigation (FBI) director, so why not do it with the position of attorney general?

Yes, Let's Make the Attorney General Independent

We do not need another attorney general like Alberto Gonzales or John Mitchell. Any president needs a personal attorney, but that official should be a member of the White House staff, not the head of the Justice Department. Presidents appoint FBI directors for a fixed term of ten years, which ensures that directors do not serve under a single president. If the FBI director wants to be reappointed, the director must consider that the president making the reappointment could belong to either political party. In the same way, if the attorney general were removed from the cabinet and appointed to a fixed term, the attorney general would have less political allegiance to any one president.

The attorney general should not be the handmaiden of presidential policy. The attorney general should be able to give the White House frank, independent advice whenever the administration is considering actions that might overreach the bounds of what is permitted by law. We should stop allowing our president to appoint cronies to such an important position.

We Don't Want a Nonpolitical Attorney General

Those who accept the current situation argue that we don't want a nonpolitical attorney general. We elect a president based on his or her policy proposals. We expect the agenda of the Justice Department to reflect the policies that got the president elected. If the president is an advocate of civil liberties, those who elected the president expect the attorney general to reflect this position. If a president has made a strong commitment to reduce illegal immigration, voters expect the attorney general to follow through on this pledge.

The comparison with an independent FBI director is not valid. The FBI director is in charge of the closest thing we have to a national police force. We obviously do not want that position to be politicized. The attorney general is a different type of creature. The president should be able to name an attorney general whose views reflect the president's.

For Critical Analysis *If a president does not like what the attorney general is doing, does the president have any recourse?*

and assistant secretaries have staffs that help with all sorts of jobs, such as hiring new people and generating positive public relations for the Department of Agriculture.

Independent Executive Agencies

independent executive agency A federal agency that is not located within a cabinet department.

Independent executive agencies are federal bureaucratic organizations that have a single function. They are independent in the sense that they are not located within a cabinet department; rather, independent executive agency heads report directly to the president. A new federal independent executive agency can be created only through cooperation between the president and Congress.

Prior to the twentieth century, the federal government did almost all of its work through the executive departments. In the twentieth century, in contrast, presidents began to ask for certain executive agencies to be

Figure 13–3

The Organization of the Department of Agriculture

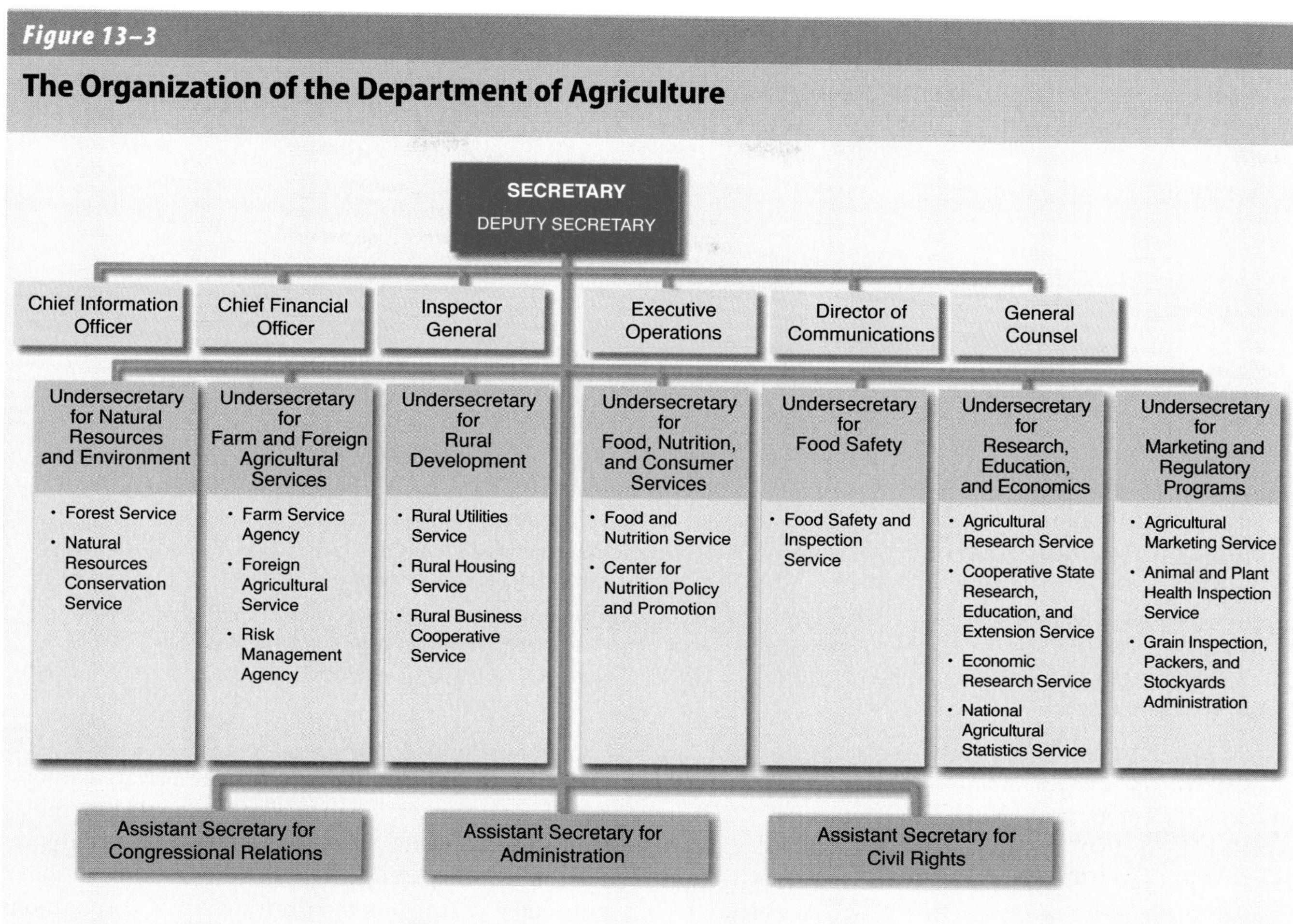

Source: *United States Government Manual, 2008–09* (Washington, D.C.: U.S. Government Printing Office, 2009).

kept separate, or independent, from existing departments. Today, there are more than two hundred independent executive agencies.

Sometimes, agencies are kept independent because of the sensitive nature of their functions; at other times, Congress creates independent agencies to protect them from **partisan politics**—politics in support of a particular party. The U.S. Commission on Civil Rights, which was created in 1957, is a case in point. Congress wanted to protect the work of the commission from the influences not only of Congress's own political interests but also of the president. The Central Intelligence Agency (CIA), which was formed in 1947, is another good example. Both Congress and the president know that the intelligence activities of the CIA could be abused if it were not independent. Finally, the General Services Administration (GSA) was created as an independent executive agency in 1949 to monitor federal government spending. To perform its function of overseeing congressional spending, it has to be an independent agency.

Among the more than two hundred independent executive agencies, a few stand out in importance either because of the mission they were established to accomplish or because of their large size. We list selected independent executive agencies in Table 13–2 on page 306.

Independent Regulatory Agencies

Independent regulatory agencies are responsible for a specific type of public policy. Their function is to create and implement rules that regulate private activity and protect the public interest in a particular sector of the economy. They are sometimes called the "alphabet soup" of government because most such agencies are known in Washington by their initials.

partisan politics Political actions or decisions that benefit a particular party.

independent regulatory agency A federal organization that is responsible for creating and implementing rules that regulate private activity and protect the public interest in a particular sector of the economy.

Table 13–2

Selected Independent Executive Agencies

Name	Date Formed	Principal Duties
Central Intelligence Agency (CIA)	1947	Gathers and analyzes political and military information about foreign countries so that the United States can improve its own political and military status; conducts covert activities outside the United States.
General Services Administration (GSA)	1949	Purchases and manages property of the federal government; acts as the business arm of the federal government, overseeing federal government spending projects; discovers overcharges in government programs.
National Science Foundation (NSF)	1950	Promotes scientific research; provides grants to all levels of schools for instructional programs in the sciences.
Small Business Administration (SBA)	1953	Promotes the interests of small businesses; provides low-cost loans and management information to small businesses.
National Aeronautics and Space Administration (NASA)	1958	Responsible for the U.S. space program, including building, testing, and operating space vehicles.
Environmental Protection Agency (EPA)	1970	Undertakes programs aimed at reducing air and water pollution; works with state and local agencies to fight environmental hazards.
Social Security Administration (SSA)*	1995	Manages the government's Social Security programs, including Retirement and Survivors Insurance, Disability Insurance, and Supplemental Security Income.

*Separated from the Department of Health and Human Services in 1979.

One of the earliest independent regulatory agencies was the Interstate Commerce Commission (ICC), established in 1887. (This agency was abolished in 1995.) After the ICC was formed, other agencies were created to regulate aviation (the Civil Aeronautics Board, or CAB, which was abolished in 1985), communication (the Federal Communications Commission, or FCC), the stock market (the Securities and Exchange Commission, or SEC), and many other areas of business. Table 13–3 on the facing page lists some major independent regulatory agencies.

Government Corporations

The newest form of federal bureaucratic organization is the **government corporation,** a business that is owned by the government. Government corporations are not exactly like corporations in which you buy stock, become a shareholder, and share in the profits by collecting dividends. The U.S. Postal Service is a government corporation, but it does not sell shares. If a government corporation loses money in the course of doing business, taxpayers, not shareholders, foot the bill.

government corporation
An agency of the government that is run as a business enterprise. Such agencies engage in primarily commercial activities, produce revenues, and require greater flexibility than that permitted in most government agencies.

Government corporations are like private corporations in that they provide a service that could be handled by the private sector. They are also like private corporations in that they charge for their services, though sometimes they charge less than private-sector corporations charge for similar services. Table 13–4 on the facing page lists selected government corporations.

Leon Panetta is the director of the Central Intelligence Agency. What are his responsibilities?

Ruth Fremson/*The New York Times*/Redux

Table 13–3

Selected Independent Regulatory Agencies

Name	Date Formed	Principal Duties
Federal Reserve System (Fed)	1913	Determines policy with respect to interest rates, credit availability, and the money supply.
Federal Trade Commission (FTC)	1914	Works to prevent businesses from engaging in unfair trade practices and to stop the formation of monopolies in the business sector; protects consumers' rights.
Securities and Exchange Commission (SEC)	1934	Regulates the nation's stock exchanges, where shares of stocks are bought and sold; requires full disclosure of the financial profiles of companies that wish to sell stocks and bonds to the public.
Federal Communications Commission (FCC)	1934	Regulates all communications by telegraph, cable, telephone, radio, and television.
National Labor Relations Board (NLRB)	1935	Protects employees' rights to join unions and to bargain collectively with employers; attempts to prevent unfair labor practices by both employers and unions.
Equal Employment Opportunity Commission (EEOC)	1964	Works to eliminate discrimination that is based on religion, gender, race, color, national origin, age, or disability; examines claims of discrimination.
Nuclear Regulatory Commission (NRC)	1974	Ensures that electricity-generating nuclear reactors in the United States are built and operated safely; regularly inspects operations of such reactors.

A number of intermediate forms of organization exist that fall between a government corporation and a private one. In some circumstances, the government can take control of a private corporation. When a company goes bankrupt, for example, it is subject to the supervision of a federal judge until it exits from bankruptcy or is liquidated. The government can purchase stock in a private corporation—the government used this technique to funnel funds into major banks during the financial crisis that began in September 2008. The government can also set up a corporation and sell stock to the public.

The Federal Home Loan Mortgage Corporation (Freddie Mac) and the Federal National Mortgage Association (Fannie Mae) are examples of stockholder-owned government-sponsored enterprises. Fannie Mae (founded in 1938) and Freddie Mac (created in 1970) buy, resell, and guarantee home mortgages. In September 2008, the government placed the two businesses into a

Table 13–4

Selected Government Corporations

Name	Date Formed	Principal Duties
Tennessee Valley Authority (TVA)	1933	Operates a Tennessee River control system and generates power for a seven-state region and for U.S. aeronautics and space programs; promotes the economic development of the Tennessee Valley region; controls floods and promotes the navigability of the Tennessee River.
Federal Deposit Insurance Corporation (FDIC)	1933	Insures individuals' bank deposits up to $250,000* and oversees the business activities of banks.
Export/Import Bank of the United States (Ex/Im Bank)	1933	Promotes American-made goods abroad; grants loans to foreign purchasers of American products.
National Railroad Passenger Corporation (Amtrak)	1970	Provides a national and intercity rail passenger service network; controls more than 23,000 miles of track with about 505 stations.
U.S. Postal Service (formed from the old U.S. Post Office department—the Post Office itself is older than the Constitution)	1971	Delivers mail throughout the United States and its territories; is the largest government corporation.

*This limit, previously $100,000, was raised in October 2008 in response to the financial crisis of that year.

conservatorship—effectively a bankruptcy overseen by the Federal Housing Finance Agency instead of a federal judge. The government also took an 80 percent share of the stock of each firm. Fannie Mae and Freddie Mac had become examples of almost every possible way that the government can intervene in a private company.

LO3 *How Bureaucrats Get Their Jobs*

As already noted, federal bureaucrats holding top-level positions are appointed by the president and confirmed by the Senate. These bureaucrats include department and agency heads, their deputy and assistant secretaries, and so on. The list of positions that are filled by appointments is published after each presidential election in a document called *Policy and Supporting Positions.* The booklet is more commonly known as the "Plum Book," because the eight thousand jobs it summarizes are known as "political plums." Normally, these jobs go to those who supported the winning presidential candidate.

The rank-and-file bureaucrats—the rest of the federal bureaucracy—are part of the **civil service** (nonmilitary employees of the government). They obtain their jobs through the Office of Personnel Management (OPM), an agency established by the Civil Service Reform Act of 1978. The OPM recruits, interviews, and tests potential government workers and determines who should be hired. The OPM makes recommendations to individual agencies as to which persons meet relevant standards (typically, the top three applicants for a position), and the agencies generally decide whom to hire. The 1978 act also created the Merit Systems Protection Board (MSPB) to oversee promotions, employees' rights, and other employment matters. The MSPB evaluates charges of wrongdoing, hears employee appeals from agency decisions, and can order corrective action against agencies and employees.

The idea that the civil service should be based on a merit system dates back more than a century. The Civil Service Reform Act of 1883 established the principle of government employment on the basis of merit through open, competitive examinations. Initially, only about 10 percent of federal employees were covered by the merit system. Today, more than 90 percent of the federal civil service is recruited on the basis of merit. Are public employees paid as well as workers in the private sector? For a discussion of this question, see this chapter's *Perception versus Reality* feature on the facing page.

civil service Nonmilitary government employees.

legislative rule An administrative agency rule that carries the same weight as a statute enacted by a legislature.

LO4 *Regulatory Agencies: Are They the Fourth Branch of Government?*

In Chapter 2, we considered the system of checks and balances among the three branches of the U.S. government—executive, legislative, and judicial. Recent history, however, shows that it may be time to regard the regulatory agencies as a fourth branch of the government. Although the U.S. Constitution does not mention regulatory agencies, these agencies can and do make **legislative rules** that are as legally binding as laws passed by Congress. With such powers, this administrative branch has an influence on the nation's businesses that rivals that of the president, Congress, and the courts. Indeed, most Americans do not realize how much of our "law" is created by regulatory agencies.

Regulatory agencies have been on the American political scene since the nineteenth century, but their golden age came during the regulatory explosion of the 1960s and 1970s. Congress itself could not have overseen the actual implementation of all of the laws that it was enacting at that time to control pollution and deal with other social problems. It therefore chose (and still chooses) to delegate to administrative agencies the tasks involved in implementing its laws. By delegating some of its authority to an administrative agency, Congress may indirectly monitor a particular area in which it has passed legislation without becoming bogged down in the details relating to the enforcement of that legislation—details that are often best left to specialists. In recent years, the government has been hiring

Lawrence Migdale/Stone/Getty

Working for the Government at Low Pay

Most parents do not jump for joy at the thought of their children going to work for the government. Government work in general in the United States has never been considered the road to riches. Indeed, the common picture of government employment is quite negative.

The Perception

It is often assumed that only individuals working in the private sector can hope to receive large paychecks. Even a member of Congress makes far less than most operations officers in mid-level corporations. Top-level staff members in the executive branch of the federal government also make much less than senior executives in the private sector. (This disparity is not really due to low pay for federal executives—it exists because the salaries of private-sector executives have skyrocketed in recent years.) Although even rank-and-file workers in the public sector receive paid-for medical insurance and a generous retirement program, the perception is that these benefits do not make up for the lower pay they earn.

The Reality

The Employee Benefit Research Institute has discovered that overall compensation costs for state and local governments are almost 50 percent higher than for private-sector employers. A recent study showed that a typical hour's work costs state and local governments almost $26 in wages and salaries, plus more than $13 in benefits. For that same hour of work, on average, a private-sector employer pays only about $19 in wages and salaries, plus about $8 in benefits.

Move now to the federal government. The U.S. Bureau of Economic Analysis estimates that federal civilian government workers earn an average of $119,982 a year in total compensation (salaries plus benefits), which is twice the $59,909 in compensation for the average private-sector worker. This is one reason why Washington, D.C.—which is loaded with federal employees—is the fourth richest among this nation's 360 metropolitan areas. The gap between federal and private wages appears to have grown in recent years. Public-sector workers also enjoy pay bonuses amounting to 30 percent more than the bonuses received in the private sector. In addition, federal civil service rules bestow lifetime job security in the sense that it is extremely difficult to fire a federal employee.

One reason why government workers are paid so well is that, on average, they don't do exactly the same kind of work as employees in the private sector. When federal and private salaries are compared on an occupation-by-occupation basis, much of the income disparity goes away. Of course, if many federal employees have jobs that are also well paid in the private sector, that is another reality that contradicts the negative myths concerning government employment.

Blog On *Arguments that government employees are overpaid are a constant theme of conservative blogs. Warren Meyer's Coyote Blog pays more attention to the topic than most. Visit it at* **www.coyoteblog.com/coyote_blog/government.** *The magazine* Government Executive *is a good place to find out how government employees, especially ones in the defense and technological fields, feel about their work. See it at* **www.govexec.com.**

increasing numbers of specialists to oversee its regulatory work.

Agency Creation

To create a federal administrative agency, Congress passes **enabling legislation,** which specifies the name, purpose, composition, and powers of the agency being created. The Federal Trade Commission (FTC), for example, was created in 1914 by the Federal Trade Commission Act, as mentioned earlier. The act prohibits unfair and deceptive trade practices. The act also describes the procedures that the agency must follow to charge persons or organizations with violations of the act, and it provides for judicial review of agency orders.

Other portions of the act grant the agency powers to "make rules and regulations for the purpose of carrying out the Act," to conduct investigations of business practices, to obtain reports on business practices from interstate corporations, to investigate possible violations of federal antitrust statutes, to publish findings of its investigations, and to recommend new legislation. The

enabling legislation A law enacted by a legislature to establish an administrative agency. Enabling legislation normally specifies the name, purpose, composition, and powers of the agency being created.

act also empowers the FTC to hold trial-like hearings and to **adjudicate** (formally resolve) certain kinds of disputes that involve FTC regulations or federal antitrust laws. When adjudication takes place, within the FTC or any other regulatory agency, an administrative law judge (ALJ) conducts the hearing and, after weighing the evidence presented, issues an *order.* Unless it is overturned on appeal, the ALJ's order becomes final.

Enabling legislation makes the regulatory agency a potent organization. For example, the Securities and Exchange Commission (SEC) imposes rules regarding the disclosures a company must make to those who purchase its stock. Under its enforcement authority, the SEC also investigates and prosecutes alleged violations of these regulations. Finally, the SEC sits as judge and jury in deciding whether its rules have been violated and, if so, what punishment should be imposed on the offender (although the judgment may be appealed to a federal court).

Rulemaking

A major function of a regulatory agency is **rulemaking**—the formulation of new regulations. The power that an agency has to make rules is conferred on it by Congress in the agency's enabling legislation. For example, the Occupational Safety and Health Administration (OSHA) was authorized by the Occupational Safety and Health Act of 1970 to develop and issue rules governing safety in the workplace. Under this authority, OSHA has issued various safety standards. For example, OSHA deemed it in the public interest to issue a rule regulating the health-care industry to prevent the spread of certain diseases, including acquired immune deficiency syndrome (AIDS). The rule specified various standards—on how contaminated instruments should be handled, for instance—with which employers in that industry must comply. Agencies cannot just make a rule whenever they wish, however. Rather, they must follow certain procedural requirements, particularly those set forth in the Administrative Procedure Act of 1946.

Agencies must also make sure that their rules are based on substantial evidence and are not "arbitrary and capricious." Therefore, before proposing a new rule, an agency may engage in extensive investigation (through research, on-site inspections of the affected industry, surveys, and the like) to obtain data on the problem to be addressed by the rule. Based on this information, the agency may undertake a cost-benefit analysis of a new rule to determine whether its benefits outweigh its costs. For example, when issuing new rules governing electrical equipment, OSHA predicted that they would cost business $21.7 billion annually but would save 60 lives and eliminate 1,600 worker injuries a year. The agency also estimated that its safety equipment regulations for manufacturing workers would cost $52.4 billion, save 4 lives, and prevent 712,000 lost workdays because of injuries each year.

Don't get the idea that rulemaking is isolated from politics. As you will read shortly, bureaucrats work closely with members of Congress, as well as interest groups, when making rules.

adjudicate To render a judicial decision. In regard to administrative law, the process in which an administrative law judge hears and decides issues that arise when an agency charges a person or firm with violating a law or regulation enforced by the agency.

rulemaking The process undertaken by an administrative agency when formally proposing, evaluating, and adopting a new regulation.

neutral competency The application of technical skills to jobs without regard to political issues.

Policymaking and the Iron Triangle

Bureaucrats in federal agencies are expected to exhibit **neutral competency,** which means that they are supposed to apply their technical skills to their jobs without regard to political issues. In principle, they should not be swayed by the thought of personal or political gain. In reality, each independent agency and each executive department is interested in its own survival and expansion. Each is constantly battling the others for a larger share of the budget. All agencies and departments wish to retain or expand their functions and staffs; to do this, they must gain the goodwill of both the White House and Congress.

Although administrative agencies of the federal government are prohibited from directly lobbying Congress, departments and agencies have developed techniques to help them gain congressional support. Each organization maintains a congressional information office, which specializes in helping members of Congress by supplying any requested information and solving casework problems. For example, if a member of the House of Representatives receives a complaint from a constituent that his Social Security checks are not arriving on time, that member of Congress may go to the Social Security Administration and ask that something be done. Typically, requests from members of Congress receive immediate attention.

Analysts have determined that one way to understand the bureaucracy's role in policymaking is to examine the **iron triangle,** which is a three-way alliance among legislators (members of Congress), bureaucrats, and interest groups. (Iron triangles are also referred to as *subgovernments* or *policy communities.*) Presumably, the laws that are passed and the policies that are established benefit the interests of all three sides of the iron triangle. Iron triangles are well established in almost every part of the bureaucracy.

AGRICULTURE AS AN EXAMPLE As an example, consider agricultural policy. Be aware first that the bureaucracy within the Department of Agriculture consists of almost 100,000 individuals working directly for the federal government and thousands of other individuals who work indirectly for the department as contractors, subcontractors, or consultants. Now think about the various interest groups and client groups that are concerned with what the bureaus and agencies in the Agriculture Department can do for them. Some of these groups are the American Farm Bureau Federation, the National Cattlemen's Beef Association, the National Milk Producers Federation, the National Corn Growers Association, and the various regional citrus growers associations. Finally, take a look at Congress, and you will see that two major committees are concerned with agriculture: the House Committee on Agriculture and the Senate Committee on Agriculture, Nutrition, and Forestry. Each committee has several specialized subcommittees.

The bureaucrats, interest groups, and legislators who make up this iron triangle cooperate to create mutually beneficial regulations and legislation. Because of the connections between agricultural interest groups and policymakers within the government, the agricultural industry has benefited greatly over the years from significant farm subsidies.

CONGRESS'S ROLE The Department of Agriculture is headed by the secretary of agriculture, who is nominated by the president (and confirmed by the Senate). But that secretary cannot even buy a desk lamp if Congress does not approve the appropriations for the department's budget. Within Congress, the responsibility for considering the Department of Agriculture's request for funding belongs first to the House and Senate appropriations committees and then to the agriculture subcommittees under them. The members of those subcommittees, most of whom represent agricultural states, have been around a long time and have their own ideas about what is appropriate for the Agriculture Department's budget. They carefully scrutinize the ideas of the president and the secretary of agriculture.

THE INFLUENCE OF INTEREST GROUPS The various interest groups—including producers of farm chemicals and farm machinery, agricultural cooperatives, grain dealers, and exporters—have vested interests in what the Department of Agriculture does and in what Congress lets the department do. Those interests are well represented by the lobbyists who crowd the halls of Congress. Many lobbyists have been working for agricultural interest groups for decades. They know the congressional committee members and Agriculture Department staff extremely well and routinely meet with them.

Issue Networks

The iron triangle relationship does not apply to all policy domains. When making policy decisions on environmental and welfare issues, for example, many members of Congress and agency officials rely heavily on "experts." Legislators and agency heads tend to depend on their staff members for specialized knowledge of rules, regulations, and legislation. These experts have frequently served variously as interest group lobbyists and as public-sector staff members during their careers, creating a revolving-door effect. They often have strong opinions and interests regarding the direction of policy and are thus able to exert a great deal of influence on legislators and bureaucratic agencies. The relationships among these experts, which are less structured than iron triangles, are often referred to as **issue networks.** Like iron triangles, issue networks are made up of people with similar policy concerns. Issue networks are less interdependent and unified than iron triangles, however, and often include more players, such as media outlets.[3] (See Figure 13–4 on the next page.)

LO5 *Curbing Waste and Improving Efficiency*

There is no doubt that our bureaucracy is costly. There is also little doubt that at times it can be wasteful and inefficient. Each year, it is possible to cull through the budgets of the various federal

iron triangle A three-way alliance among legislators, bureaucrats, and interest groups to make or preserve policies that benefit their respective interests.

issue networks Groups of individuals or organizations—which consist of legislators and legislative staff members, interest group leaders, bureaucrats, the media, scholars, and other experts—that support particular policy positions on a given issue.

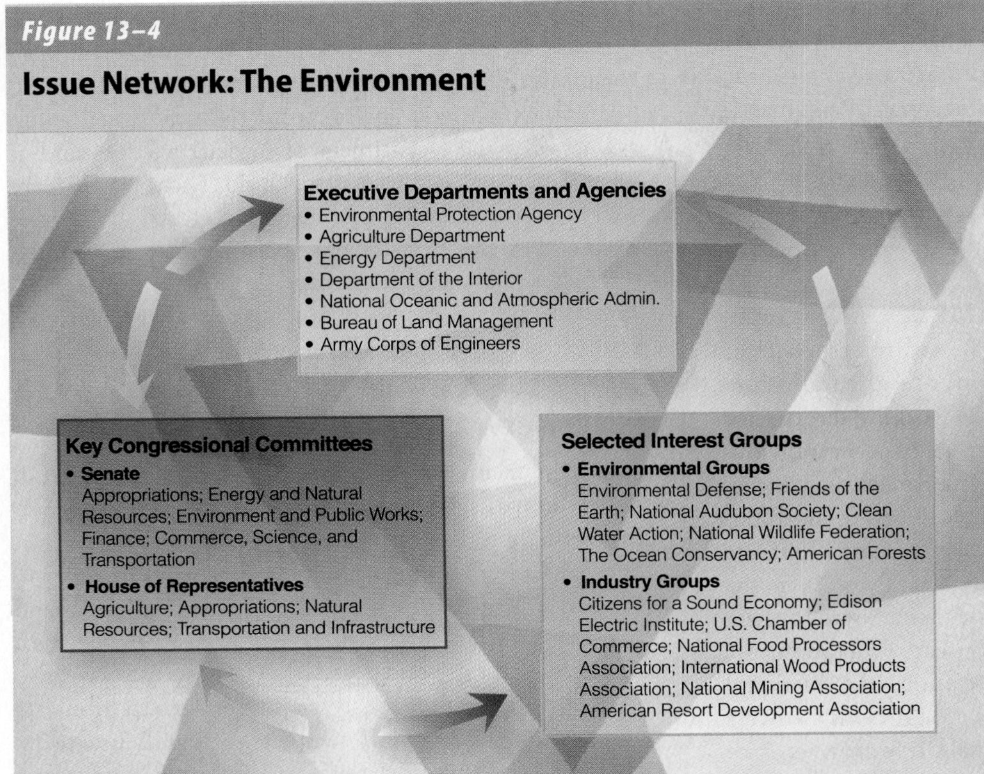

agencies and discover quite outrageous examples of government waste. Here are some of them:

- More than $11 million paid to psychics by the Pentagon and the Central Intelligence Agency to discover whether the psychics would offer insights about foreign threats to the United States.
- Payments of more than $20 million a year to thousands of prison inmates through the Social Security Administration's Supplemental Income Program.
- A total of $10 million per year paid by the Department of Energy to its employees to encourage them to lose weight.
- More than $30 million paid over two years by the Internal Revenue Service to tax filers claiming nonexistent slavery tax credits.
- A total of $1.1 million spent for a program that informed tenants of public housing about the types of gemstones, incense, and clothing colors that would best improve their self-esteem.

whistleblower In the context of government employment, someone who "blows the whistle" (reports to authorities) on gross governmental inefficiency, illegal action, or other wrongdoing.

The government has made several attempts to reduce waste, inefficiency, and wrongdoing. For example, over the years both the federal government and state governments have passed laws requiring more openness in government. Further attempts at bureaucratic reform have included, among other things, encouraging government employees to report to appropriate government officials any waste and wrongdoing that they observe.

Despite the difficulties involved in reforming the bureaucracy, our nation at least enjoys a civil service that is relatively impartial and free from corruption. This is not true of many nations. For example, Mexico, our immediate neighbor to the south, has had difficulties that would be almost unimaginable in the United States. We discuss that problem in this chapter's *The Rest of the World* feature.

Helping Out the Whistleblowers

The term **whistleblower,** as applied to the federal bureaucracy, has a special meaning: it is someone who blows the whistle, or reports, on gross governmental inefficiency, illegal action, or other wrongdoing. Federal employees are often reluctant to blow the whistle on their superiors, however, for fear of reprisals.

LEGISLATION PROTECTING WHISTLEBLOWERS To encourage federal employees to report government wrongdoing, Congress has passed laws to protect whistleblowers. The 1978 Civil Service Reform Act included some protection by prohibiting reprisals against whistleblowers by their superiors. The act set up the Merit Systems Protection Board as part of this protection. The Whistle-Blower Protection Act of 1989 authorized the Office of Special Counsel (OSC), an independent agency, to investigate complaints of reprisals against whistleblowers. From time to time, Congress considers more whistleblower legislation to protect special groups, such as employees of government contractors and federal workers who blow the whistle on officials who intentionally alter or distort scientific data. Many federal agencies also

THE REST OF THE WORLD

Mexico's Security Problem—The Drug Wars

The United States has 225 law enforcement officers for every 100,000 people. Mexico, in contrast, has 370 officers per 100,000 residents. You might think, then, that citizens of our neighbor to the south would enjoy even more personal security than we do in the United States. The reality is quite different. Crime rates in Mexico on average greatly exceed those in the United States. Why? For one thing, the United States has far more effective, professional, and trustworthy police forces than Mexico. In addition, Mexico is fighting drug cartels that are also fighting each other. Drug cartel enforcers in Mexico have at their disposal the highest-grade, most sophisticated weapons available—almost all purchased in the United States and smuggled across the border.

These drug cartels are so powerful that they have corrupted many of Mexico's customs agents, army commanders, and local police forces. For example, police in the city of Nuevo Laredo have reportedly participated in kidnapping members of the Gulf cartel and handing them over to the Zetas organization. The Zetas then hold them for ransom or torture them for information about drug deals. A report commissioned by the U.S. Congress states that in 2005, "federal officers arriving in Nuevo Laredo were fired on by municipal police leading to the arrest of 41 municipal police and the suspension of the entire 700-member Nuevo Laredo police force to investigate corruption." Mexico's Federal Investigative Agency (AFI) has 7,000 agents in total. Recently, almost 1,500 of these agents were under investigation, and 457 were facing criminal charges. Some agents were believed to work as enforcers for the Sinaloa cartel.[4]

The Mérida Initiative—U.S. Aid for What?

During the last few years, American taxpayers have provided the Mexican government with aid to combat drug trafficking under a program called the Mérida Initiative. Of the $1.4 billion in assistance, however, only about a third is targeted toward repairing Mexico's crumbling law-enforcement and judicial systems. Much of the rest goes to equipment. The results have not been encouraging. The killings and kidnappings continue. Let's face it; buying attack helicopters with the money (as the Mexican government has done) is not going to solve the drug-wars problem in the long run.

The conclusion of one study from the Rand Corporation, a California-based think tank, is that the United States "must engage in a strategic partnership with Mexico that emphasizes reform and longer-term institution-building." The lead author of that study, Agnes Schaefer, argues that the United States should help the Mexican government develop more sophisticated antidrug intelligence agencies and databases. In particular, the U.S. government could help prevent money laundering to cripple organized crime in that country.[5]

A House Cleaning

There are some signs that some institutional reform may be taking place in Mexico. In the summer of 2009, the Mexican federal government fired all 700 customs agents, a group notorious for corruption and dereliction of duty, and replaced them with 1,400 new personnel. The new agents had to take drug tests and undergo scrutiny to make sure that they did not have criminal records. Seventy percent of the new agents have a college education, compared with only 10 percent of the old group. Customs agents are responsible for curbing the smuggling of arms into the country.

For Critical Analysis *Will it ever be possible to eradicate police corruption in Mexico when the rewards can sometimes be ten to twenty times an average officer's annual salary? Why are the rewards so high?*

have toll-free hotlines that employees can use to anonymously report bureaucratic waste and inappropriate behavior.

WHISTLEBLOWERS CONTINUE TO FACE PROBLEMS In spite of these laws, there is little evidence that whistleblowers are adequately protected against retaliation. According to a study conducted by the Government Accountability Office, 41 percent of the whistleblowers who turned to the OSC for protection during a recent three-year period reported that they were no longer employed by the agencies on which they blew the whistle. Indeed, given how difficult it is to fire a federal employee under normal circumstances, it is amazing how quickly most whistleblowers are "shown the door."

In 2006, the United States Supreme Court rendered a decision that will likely make it even more difficult for whistleblowers to obtain protection. The case involved an assistant district attorney who inquired in a written memo about whether a county sheriff's deputy had lied in an affidavit. As a result, the attorney was demoted and denied a promotion. The attorney then sued his employer for violating his right to free speech. The Supreme Court held, in a five-to-four decision, that a public employee whose speech relates to official duties is not "speaking" as a citizen for First Amendment purposes.[6]

Many federal employees who have blown the whistle say that they would not do so again because it was so difficult to get help, and even when they did, the experience was a stressful ordeal. Creating more effective protection for whistleblowers remains an ongoing goal of the government. The basic problem, though, is that most organizations, including federal government agencies, do not like to have their wrongdoings and failings exposed, especially by insiders.

Improving Efficiency and Getting Results

The Government Performance and Results Act, which went into effect in 1997, has forced the federal government to change the way it does business. Since 1997, virtually every agency (except the intelligence agencies) has had to describe new goals and a method for evaluating how well those goals are met. A results-oriented goal of an agency could be as broad as lowering the number of highway traffic deaths or as narrow as trying to reduce the number of times an agency's phone rings before it is answered.

As one example, consider the National Oceanic and Atmospheric Adminstration (NOAA). It improved the effectiveness of its short-term forecasting services, particularly in issuing warnings of tornadoes. The warning time has increased from seven to nine minutes. This may seem insignificant, but it provides additional critical time for those in the path of a tornado.

"Performance-based budgeting," a system initiated by President George W. Bush, further extends the idea of focusing on results. Performance-based budgeting is designed to increase performance and accountability by linking the funding of federal agencies to their actual performance. Numerous federal programs now have to meet specific performance criteria. If they do, they will receive more funds. If they do not, their funding will be reduced or removed entirely. To determine the extent to which performance criteria have been met, the Office of Management and Budget "grades" each agency on how well it manages its operations, and these grades are considered during the budgeting process.

President Obama's contribution to the attempt to improve government effectiveness has been to create a chief performance officer. This individual reports directly to the president and works with other economic officials in an attempt to increase efficiency and eliminate waste in government.

Another Approach—Pay-for-Performance Plans

For some time, the private sector has used pay-for-performance plans as a means to increase employee productivity and efficiency. About one-third of the major firms in this country use some kind of alternative pay system, such as team-based pay, skill-based pay, profit-sharing plans, or individual bonuses. In contrast, workers for the federal government traditionally have received fixed salaries; promotions and salary increases are given on the basis of seniority, not output.

The federal government has been experimenting with pay-for-performance systems. For example, the U.S. Postal Service has implemented an Economic Value Added program, which ties bonuses to performance. As part of a five-year test of a new pay system, three thousand scientists working in Air Force laboratories received salaries based on actual results. Also, the Department of Veterans Affairs launched a skill-based pay project at its New York regional office.

This lab technician tests samples of H1N1 (swine) flu. Much of the research done about communicable diseases is performed by government agencies both at the federal and the state levels.

AP Photo/Matt York

Many hope that by offering such incentives, the government will be able to compete more effectively with the private sector for skilled and talented employees. Additionally, according to some, pay-for-performance plans will go a long way toward countering the entitlement mentality that has traditionally characterized employment within the bureaucracy.

Privatization

Another idea for reforming the federal bureaucracy is **privatization,** which means turning over certain types of government work to the private sector. Privatization can take place by contracting out (outsourcing) work to the private sector or by "managed competition," in which the task of providing public services is opened up to competition. In managed competition, both the relevant government agency and private firms can compete for the work. Vouchers are another way in which certain services traditionally provided by government, such as education, can be provided on the open market. The government pays for the vouchers, but the services are provided by the private sector.

State and local governments have been experimenting with privatization for some time. Virtually all of the states have privatized at least a few of their services, and some states, including California, Colorado, and Florida, have privatized more than one hundred activities formerly undertaken by government. In Scottsdale, Arizona, the city contracts for fire protection. In Baltimore, Maryland, nine of the city's schools are outsourced to private entities. In other cities, services ranging from janitorial work to managing recreational facilities are handled by the private sector.

> "The only thing that saves us from the bureaucracy IS ITS INEFFICIENCY."
>
> ~ EUGENE J. MCCARTHY ~
> U.S. SENATOR FROM MINNESOTA
> 1959–1971

The Bush administration attempted to follow the states' lead and privatize work undertaken by some 850,000 federal workers. Whether a host of other federal services should also be privatized was debated in think tanks and, to some extent, by policymakers. Under President Obama, however, privatization is no longer a major issue on the government's agenda.

Is It Possible to Reform the Bureaucracy?

Some claim that the bureaucracy is so massive, unwieldy, and self-perpetuating that it is impossible to reform. Attempts at reform, including those just discussed, can, at most, barely touch the surface of the problem.

In large part, this difficulty stems from the fact that the positions over which the president has direct or indirect control, through the appointment process, amount to fewer than 0.5 percent of the 2.9 million civilian employees who work for the executive branch. The bureaucracy is also deeply entrenched and is often characterized by inertia and by slow-moving responses to demands for change. As Laurence J. Peter, of "Peter Principle" fame, once said, a "bureaucracy defends the status quo long past the time when the quo has lost its status." It should come as no surprise, then, that virtually every president in modern times has found it difficult to exercise much control over the bureaucracy.

Complicating the problem is the fact that political appointees often know little about the work of the agency to which they are appointed and are rarely trained specifically in the areas that they supervise. Typically, they must look for assistance to the rank-and-file staff members, whose jobs do not come and go with each administration. Furthermore, federal employees have significant rights. Once a federal worker is hired, firing him or her is extremely difficult, regardless of job performance. Similarly, once a federal agency is created, it takes on a life of its own and tends to become permanent. Indeed, President Ronald Reagan (1981–1989) once commented that "a government bureau is the nearest thing to eternal life we'll ever see on this earth."[7]

Government in the Sunshine

The past four decades saw a trend toward more openness in government. The theory was that because Americans pay for the government, they own it—and they have a right to know what the government is doing with the taxpayers' dollars.

In response to pressure for more government openness and disclosure, Congress passed the Freedom of Information Act in 1966. This act requires federal agencies to disclose any information in agency files, with some exceptions, to any persons requesting it. Since the 1970s, "sunshine laws," which require government meetings to be open to the public, have been enacted at all levels of American government. During

privatization The transfer of the task of providing services traditionally provided by government to the private sector.

the Clinton administration (1993–2001), Americans gained even greater access to government information as federal and state agencies went online.

The trend toward greater openness in government came to an abrupt halt on September 11, 2001. In the wake of the terrorist attacks on the World Trade Center and the Pentagon, the government began tightening its grip on information. In the months following the attacks, hundreds of thousands of documents were removed from government Web sites. No longer can the public access plans of nuclear power plants, descriptions of airline security violations, or maps of pipeline routes. Agencies were instructed to be more cautious about releasing information in their files and were given new guidelines on what should be considered public information. State and local agencies followed the federal government's lead. Some states barred access to such information as emergency preparedness evacuation plans. Others established commissions or panels whose activities are exempt from state sunshine laws. All in all, the Bush administration made it much more difficult to obtain information about the government than it had been under previous administrations.

"BUREAUCRACY DEFENDS THE STATUS QUO long past the time when the quo has lost its status."

~ LAURENCE J. PETER ~
AMERICAN EDUCATOR
1919–1990

An Expanding Bureaucracy

The financial crisis that struck in September 2008 meant that even before a Democratic president and Democratic-dominated Congress were elected in November 2008, the federal bureaucracy was expanding. In early October, Congress passed, and the president signed, a $700 billion bank bailout bill. Implementing and managing this unprecedented spending program required the hiring of new government employees. At the same time, the Federal Reserve System (the Fed) was adding new regulations on the banking and finance sector. The Fed also was embarking on a lending program for businesses that it had never before undertaken. As a consequence, more employees were needed for the Fed.

These initial expansions of government to meet the crisis were dwarfed by the huge new spending programs implemented after Obama took office. The $787 billion stimulus bill was largely aimed at stabilizing and increasing employment in state and local government. An expansion of health insurance for low-income children—the State Children's Health Insurance Program, or SCHIP—helped safeguard employment in the health-care industry. Indeed, as the unemployment rate soared throughout 2009, only two industries were able to maintain or even increase their staffing levels—health care and government. Obama's ambitious plans for providing universal health insurance and reducing carbon dioxide emissions suggest that in the near future, the government's share of the nation's employment and output are likely to expand to a degree never before seen in peacetime.

This state official in Kansas is explaining to reporters and health-care providers the availability of swine flu vaccine in his state. Private pharmaceutical companies manufacture this vaccine. We often see such public-private sector cooperation.

AP Photo/Charlie Riedel

AMERICA AT ODDS *The Bureaucracy*

The bureaucracy is sometimes called the "fourth branch of government." It is not, of course, a part of the government established by the founders of this nation, and certainly the framers of the Constitution could not have anticipated the massive size of today's bureaucracy or the power that it wields over the life of the nation. Although the story is often told about the red tape and wasteful spending generated by our bureaucracy, all in all, the U.S. bureaucracy compares favorably with bureaucracies in other countries.

Presidential administrations have been challenged time and again by bureaucrats who resist reform measures in order to maintain or expand their "turf"—their jobs and responsibilities within the government. Laws governing federal workers make it extremely difficult to replace inefficient employees. Inadequate whistleblower protections make it difficult for bureaucrats who are aware of waste or wrongdoing to inform the relevant government office of such problems. Political appointments to offices within an administration may be based on loyalty to the president rather than on the appointees' expertise or qualifications in the relevant area. Almost inevitably, the U.S. government faces the same problems—sluggishness, inefficiency, and a certain degree of incompetence—with its bureaucracy that many large businesses and organizations throughout the country also face. The only major difference is the size and scope of the U.S. bureaucracy—and the effect that its actions can have on the daily lives of all Americans. Some attempts to reform the bureaucracy over the years have resulted in less waste and more efficiency; others have been less successful. One thing is certain: the need to reform the bureaucracy will be with us for a long time to come.

ISSUES FOR DEBATE & DISCUSSION

1. **Former surgeon general Richard H. Carmona testified to a congressional panel in 2007 that the Bush administration would not allow him to speak or issue reports about certain topics, including stem-cell research, emergency contraception, sex education, and mental and global health issues. Carmona said that he was also ordered to mention President Bush three times on every page of his speeches, to make speeches to support Republican political candidates, and to attend political briefings.[8] Some Americans believe that the Bush administration went too far in politicizing federal agencies and their activities. Others claim that if a president is to succeed in implementing a policy agenda, such control over agency leadership is essential. What is your position on this issue?**
2. **As you know, the Constitution authorized only Congress to make laws at the federal level. Congress, however, after enacting a statute, typically leaves it up to an administrative agency to interpret and apply the law. Consequently, through their rulemaking functions, regulatory agencies staffed by bureaucrats, not Congress, make much of the "law" in the United States. For example, much of the body of environmental law consists of regulations issued by the Environmental Protection Agency. Some believe that Congress should not delegate so much lawmaking authority to federal administrative agencies. After all, bureaucrats are not elected, as members of Congress are, so they should not, in fact, be "making the law." Others contend that if Congress did not delegate such work to agencies, it would get little done. Moreover, members of Congress normally do not have as much expertise in a given area, such as environmental science, as agency officials do. What is your position on this issue?**

TAKE ACTION

Although this chapter's focus is on the federal bureaucracy, realize that all levels of government require bureaucracies to implement their goals. In virtually every community, however, there are needs that government agencies cannot meet. Often, agencies simply lack the funds to hire more personnel or to provide assistance to those in need. To help address these needs, many Americans do volunteer work. If you want to take action in this way, check with your local government offices and find out which agencies or offices have volunteer programs. Volunteer opportunities on the local level can range from helping the homeless and mentoring children in a local school to joining a local environmental clean-up effort. Decide where your interests lie, and consider volunteering your time in a local bureaucracy.

AP Photo/Lennox McLendon

Volunteers answer hotlines that teenagers can call when they need help. Many volunteers at such hotline services have found this type of work especially rewarding.

POLITICS ON THE WEB

- For information on the government, including the Web sites for federal agencies, go to the federal government's "gateway" Web site at **www.usa.gov**
- The Web site of the Office of Management and Budget offers information on increasing the government's efficiency—and, of course, on the federal budget. You can access the OMB at **www.whitehouse.gov/omb**
- To learn more about the mission of the General Services Administration (GSA) and its role in managing the federal bureaucracy, go to **www.gsa.gov**
- If you want to see an example of what federal agencies are putting on the Web, you can go to the Department of Commerce's Web site at **www.commerce.gov**
- The *Federal Register* is the official publication for executive-branch documents. This publication, which includes the orders, notices, and rules of all federal administrative agencies, is online at **www.gpoaccess.gov**. From this home page, click on "A-Z Resource List." Scroll down until you see *Federal Register.*
- The *United States Government Manual* contains information on the functions, organization, and administrators of every federal department. You can access the most recent edition of the manual online at **www.gpoaccess.gov**. Click on "A-Z Resource List." Scroll down to the bottom, where you will see *U.S. Government Manual.*

Online resources for this chapter

This text's Companion Web site, at **www.4ltrpress.cengage.com/govt**, offers links to numerous resources that you can use to learn more about the topics covered in this chapter.

issue networks
adjudicate civil service
www.commerce.gov privatization
independent regulatory agency
WHISTLEBLOWER
www.usa.gov

GOVT 14

The Judiciary

LEARNING OBJECTIVES

LO1 Summarize the origins of the American legal system and the basic sources of American law.

LO2 Delineate the structure of the federal court system.

LO3 Indicate how federal judges are appointed.

LO4 Explain how the federal courts make policy.

LO5 Describe the role of ideology and judicial philosophies in judicial decision making.

LO6 Identify some of the criticisms of the federal courts and some of the checks on the power of the courts.

AMERICA AT ODDS

Are There Prisoners We Must Detain without Trial?

After the September 11, 2001, attacks in the United States, the George W. Bush administration interred hundreds of suspected terrorists at the Guantánamo Bay Naval Base in Cuba. Most of them were foreign fighters captured during the war in Afghanistan, a war initiated just after 9/11. A few suspected terrorists from elsewhere ended up at Guantánamo as well. All prisoners were labeled *unlawful enemy combatants* and therefore were afforded neither the legal protections guaranteed to prisoners of war (POWs) under the Geneva Conventions nor the protections required under the Conventions for dealing with civilians who commit crimes. Indeed, the Bush administration established the prison at Guantánamo in the belief that the facility would lie outside the reach of American law. President Barack Obama promised to close the Guantánamo prison, but he also stated that it may be necessary to hold some of the detainees more or less forever without bringing them to trial. There are those who object to this policy, but many who agree with it.

We Release Terrorists at the Civilized World's Peril

Look back over U.S. history. Federal judges never heard cases brought by Confederate prisoners of war held during the Civil War. During World War II, no civilian courts reviewed the cases of the thousands of German prisoners housed in the United States. At the end of that war, the Supreme Court agreed that enemy aliens held by the United States in Europe and Asia had no right to appear in front of an American judge.

Today, if the president deems that certain terrorist prisoners are too dangerous to be tried and perhaps freed, that is the president's prerogative. After all, under our Constitution, the president has wartime decision-making powers. We also have evidence that at least thirty detainees released from the Guantánamo prison rejoined terrorist organizations and have been responsible for the deaths of innocent people overseas.

Who will be responsible for the deaths caused by terrorists if they cannot be convicted and we then let them go? Terrorists do not deserve the civil liberties we offer to fellow Americans. If we cannot be sure that a trial will result in a conviction, we must not let these people stand trial at all.

Indefinite Detention Is Unconstitutional and Damages Our Image Abroad

It is wrong to hold persons deemed "dangerous" by the government indefinitely. How can we know that the government is correct in its allegations against these people? We have learned that some of the Afghans held at Guantánamo and elsewhere were arrested due to false accusations resulting from long-standing feuds between rival families. U.S. officials were reluctant to release these innocents because it meant admitting that the officials had made a mistake.

The way our government has handled POWs in the past is irrelevant. Traditional POWs were picked up during battle, on the field, in uniform. The potential for picking up a POW by mistake was minimal. In contrast, the danger of error when picking up an alleged unlawful enemy combatant is enormous. Most of the Guantánamo detainees were arrested nowhere near a battlefield. How can we know whether such detainees are truly dangerous if there is no trial? Furthermore, as the blog site Digby's Hullabaloo puts it: "There are literally tens of thousands of potential terrorists all over the world who could theoretically harm America. We cannot protect ourselves from that possibility by keeping the handful we have in custody locked up forever."

WHERE DO YOU STAND?

1. **Could Congress fashion a law providing a procedure to determine when an alleged terrorist should never be let out of prison?**
2. **Why is it easier to falsely arrest a purported terrorist than a regular military solder?**

EXPLORE THIS ISSUE ONLINE

- **The editorial page of the *Wall Street Journal* favors indefinite detention. One of the strongest voices on that page has been John Yoo, who served in President Bush's Justice Department when the detention policies were crafted. You'll find some of Yoo's articles if you perform a Google search on "john yoo wall street journal."**
- **Two of the many bloggers who oppose indefinite detentions are Digby and Glenn Greenwald. You can find their work at www.digbysblog.blogspot.com and www.salon.com/opinion/greenwald.**

Introduction

As you read in this chapter's opening *America at Odds* feature, the question of whether certain alleged terrorists should be imprisoned indefinitely without trial has elicited a great deal of controversy. Also controversial is the policymaking function of the United States Supreme Court. After all, when the Court renders an opinion on how the Constitution is to be interpreted, it is, necessarily, making policy on a national level. To understand the nature of this controversy, you first need to understand how the **judiciary** (the courts) functions in this country. We begin by looking at the origins and sources of American law. We then examine the federal court system, at the apex of which is the United States Supreme Court, and consider various issues relating to the courts.

LO1 *The Origins and Sources of American Law*

The American colonists brought with them the legal system that had developed in England over hundreds of years. Thus, to understand how the American legal system operates, we need to go back in time to the early English courts and the traditions they established.

U.S. attorneys are appointed by the president with the advice and consent of the Senate. They serve under the direction of the attorney general.

AP Photo/Dennis Cook

"It is confidence IN THE MEN AND WOMEN WHO ADMINISTER THE JUDICIAL SYSTEM that is the true backbone of the rule of law."

~ JOHN PAUL STEVENS ~
ASSOCIATE JUSTICE OF THE UNITED STATES SUPREME COURT 1975–PRESENT

The Common Law Tradition

After the Normans conquered England in 1066, William the Conqueror and his successors began the process of unifying the country under their rule. One of the methods they used was the establishment of the "king's courts," or *curiae regis*. Before the Norman Conquest, disputes had been settled according to the local legal customs and traditions in various regions of the country. The law developed in the king's courts, however, applied to the country as a whole. What evolved in these courts was the beginning of the **common law**—a body of general rules prescribing social conduct that was applied throughout the entire English realm. Trial by jury is a famous part of the common law tradition. Juries are less common outside the English-speaking world, but some countries with different legal traditions have begun to introduce them, as you will learn in this chapter's *The Rest of the World* feature on the next page.

THE RULE OF PRECEDENT The early English courts developed the common law rules from the principles underlying judges' decisions in actual legal controversies. Judges attempted to be consistent, and whenever possible, they based their decisions on the principles applied in earlier cases. They sought to decide similar cases in a similar way and considered new kinds of cases

judiciary The courts; one of the three branches of the federal government in the United States.

common law The body of law developed from judicial decisions in English and U.S. courts, not attributable to a legislature.

Jury Trials Finally Become a Reality in Asian Courts

The U.S. Constitution provides for jury trials in Article III and in the Bill of Rights, so most of us take jury trials for granted. Yet juries do not exist in most parts of the world, including many democracies. The right to a jury trial for a criminal defendant seems so obvious that it's hard for us to imagine how greatly the United States differs from many other countries on this issue.

South Korea and Japan Take the Plunge

Until 2008, South Korea had never had a jury trial in a criminal case. The first one was held in the small city of Taegu. It concerned a twenty-seven-year-old man who was charged with the petty criminal offenses of assault and trespass. A dozen South Korean citizens, who made up that country's first-ever jury, aided the presiding judge. The jury found the defendant guilty.

Until that special moment in South Korean judicial history, no one in that country could have imagined that citizens without legal training and with no accountability could decide the fate of a criminal defendant. The South Korean jury system is similar to that in the United States, but with some modifications. The more complex the case, the more jurors there are. Also, jury verdicts are based on majority vote rather than on unanimous decisions, as required in almost all American criminal cases. Finally, at least for the next few years, the vote of the jurors is not binding on the judge.

In 2009, Japan reinstated trials by jury after a sixty-five-year absence. The first individual to be tried under the new system was a seventy-two-year-old man who had confessed to stabbing a neighbor. A panel of ordinary citizens stood in judgment of the accused, alongside professional judges. Despite Japan's tradition of deferring to authority, the citizen judges participated actively, cross-examining the accused and the victim's son. The audience at the trial exceeded two thousand people. In Japan, those who are prosecuted are almost inevitably convicted—the conviction rate is over 99 percent. Confessions, made in police custody without a lawyer present, are very common. A spate of executions of persons later found to be innocent led to demands for the new system.

Why the Sudden Desire to Have Jury Trials?

Legal scholars analyzing the trend toward jury trials in Asia point out several reasons why they are now becoming more common. Many of these countries have opened themselves up to a growing influence from the United States. In South Korea particularly, U.S. influence may be important, because there has been a large U.S. military force on-site since the 1950s and the end of the Korean War.

Another possible explanation is that some formerly authoritarian countries that are now democracies believe that juries might be a way to foster stronger democratic values. The idea is obvious—individuals, rather than the government, should sit in judgment of citizens. Juries seem to serve as a check on governmental power. They build trust in legal institutions.

For Critical Analysis *In many jurisdictions in the United States, the defendant can waive his or her right to a jury trial. Why might a defendant waive this important right?*

This Japanese judicial officer participates in a seminar organized by that country's Justice Ministry. He is attempting to explain the most dramatic change in the justice system since the end of World War II. The big change involves the use of juries.

AP Photo/Katsumi Kasahara

precedent A court decision that furnishes an example or authority for deciding subsequent cases involving identical or similar facts and legal issues.

with care, because they knew that their decisions would make new law. Each interpretation became part of the law on the subject and served as a legal **precedent**—that is, a decision that furnished an example or authority for deciding subsequent cases involving identical or similar legal principles or facts.

The practice of deciding new cases with reference to former decisions, or precedents, eventually became a cornerstone of the English and American judicial systems. The practice forms a doctrine called ***stare decisis***[2] ("to stand on decided cases"). Under this doctrine, judges are obligated to follow the precedents established in their jurisdictions. For example, if the Supreme Court of Georgia holds that a state law requiring candidates for state office to pass drug tests is unconstitutional, that decision will control the outcome of future cases on that issue brought before the state courts in Georgia. Similarly, a decision on a given issue by the United States Supreme Court (the nation's highest court) is binding on all inferior (lower) courts. For example, if the Georgia case on drug testing is appealed to the United States Supreme Court and the Court agrees that the Georgia law is unconstitutional, the high court's ruling will be binding on *all* courts in the United States. In other words, similar drug-testing laws in other states will be invalid and unenforceable.

DEPARTURES FROM PRECEDENT Sometimes a court will depart from the rule of precedent if it decides that a precedent is simply incorrect or that technological or social changes have rendered the precedent inapplicable. Cases that overturn precedent often receive a great deal of publicity. For example, in 1954, in *Brown v. Board of Education of Topeka*,[3] the United States Supreme Court expressly overturned precedent when it concluded that separate educational facilities for African Americans, which had been upheld as constitutional in many earlier cases under the "separate-but-equal" doctrine[4] (see Chapter 5), were inherently unequal and violated the equal protection clause. The Supreme Court's departure from precedent in *Brown* received a tremendous amount of publicity as people began to realize the political and social ramifications of this change in the law.

More recently, the Supreme Court departed from precedent when it held in a 2003 case, *Lawrence v. Texas*,[5] that a Texas sodomy law (see Chapter 5) violated the U.S. Constitution. In that case, the Court concluded that consensual sexual conduct, including homosexual conduct, was part of the liberty protected by the due process clause of the Fourteenth Amendment. This decision overturned the Court's established precedent on such laws—specifically, its ruling in *Bowers v. Hardwick*,[6] a 1986 case in which the Court upheld a Georgia sodomy statute.

Sources of American Law

In any governmental system, the primary function of the courts is to interpret and apply the law. In the United States, the courts interpret and apply numerous sources of law when deciding cases. We look here only at the **primary sources of law**—that is, sources that *establish* the law—and the relative priority of these sources when particular laws come into conflict.

> "IT IS BETTER, so the Fourth Amendment teaches, THAT THE GUILTY SOMETIMES GO FREE than that citizens be subject to easy arrest."
>
> ~ WILLIAM O. DOUGLAS ~
> ASSOCIATE JUSTICE OF THE UNITED STATES SUPREME COURT
> 1939–1975

CONSTITUTIONAL LAW The U.S. government and each of the fifty states have separate written constitutions that set forth the general organization, powers, and limits of their respective governments. **Constitutional law** consists of the rights and duties set forth in these constitutions.

The U.S. Constitution is the supreme law of the land. As such, it is the basis of all law in the United States. Any law that violates the Constitution is invalid and unenforceable. Because of the paramount importance of the U.S. Constitution in the American legal system, the complete text of the Constitution is found in Appendix B.

The Tenth Amendment to the U.S. Constitution reserves to the states and to the people all powers not granted to the federal government. Each state in the union has its own constitution. Unless they conflict with the U.S. Constitution or a federal law, state constitutions are supreme within the borders of their respective states.

stare decisis A common law doctrine under which judges normally are obligated to follow the precedents established by prior court decisions.

primary source of law A source of law that establishes the law. Primary sources of law include constitutions, statutes, administrative agency rules and regulations, and decisions rendered by the courts.

constitutional law Law based on the U.S. Constitution and the constitutions of the various states.

STATUTORY LAW Statutes enacted by legislative bodies at any level of government make up another source of law, which is generally referred to as **statutory law.** Federal statutes—laws enacted by the U.S. Congress—apply to all of the states. State statutes—laws enacted by state legislatures—apply only within the state that enacted the law. Any state statute that conflicts with the U.S. Constitution, with federal laws enacted by Congress, or with the state's constitution will be deemed invalid, if challenged in court, and will not be enforced. Statutory law also includes the ordinances (such as local zoning or housing-construction laws) passed by cities and counties, none of which can violate the U.S. Constitution, the relevant state constitution, or any existing federal or state laws.

ADMINISTRATIVE LAW Another important source of American law consists of **administrative law**—the rules, orders, and decisions of administrative agencies. As you read in Chapter 13, at the federal level, Congress creates executive agencies, such as the Food and Drug Administration and the Environmental Protection Agency, to perform specific functions. Typically, when Congress establishes an agency, it authorizes the agency to create rules that have the force of law and to enforce those rules by bringing legal actions against violators. Rules issued by various government agencies now affect virtually every aspect of our economy. For example, almost all of a business's operations, including the firm's capital structure and financing, its hiring and firing procedures, its relations with employees and unions, and the way it manufactures and markets its products, are subject to government regulation.

Government agencies exist at the state and local levels as well. States commonly create agencies that parallel federal agencies. Just as federal statutes take precedence over conflicting state statutes, federal agency regulations take precedence over conflicting state regulations.

statutory law The body of law enacted by legislatures (as opposed to constitutional law, administrative law, or case law).

administrative law The body of law created by administrative agencies (in the form of rules, regulations, orders, and decisions) in order to carry out their duties and responsibilities.

case law The rules of law announced in court decisions. Case law includes the aggregate of reported cases that interpret judicial precedents, statutes, regulations, and constitutional provisions.

civil law The branch of law that spells out the duties that individuals in society owe to other persons or to their governments, excluding the duty not to commit crimes.

criminal law The branch of law that defines and governs actions that constitute crimes. Generally, criminal law has to do with wrongful actions committed against society for which society demands redress.

"Our Constitution is colorblind, AND NEITHER KNOWS NOR TOLERATES CLASSES AMONG CITIZENS."

~ JOHN MARSHALL HARLAN ~
ASSOCIATE JUSTICE OF THE UNITED STATES SUPREME COURT
1877–1911

CASE LAW As is evident from the earlier discussion of the common law tradition, another basic source of American law consists of the rules of law announced in court decisions, or **case law.** These rules of law include interpretations of constitutional provisions, of statutes enacted by legislatures, and of regulations issued by administrative agencies. Thus, even though a legislature passes a law to govern a certain area, how that law is interpreted and applied depends on the courts. The importance of case law, or judge-made law, is one of the distinguishing characteristics of the common law tradition.

Civil Law and Criminal Law

All of the sources of law just discussed can be classified in other ways as well. One of the most significant classification systems divides all law into two categories: civil law and criminal law. **Civil law** spells out the duties that individuals in society owe to other persons or to their governments, excluding the duty not to commit crimes. Typically, in a civil case, a private party sues another private party (although the government can also sue a party for a civil law violation). The object of a civil lawsuit is to make the defendant—the person being sued—comply with a legal duty (such as a contractual promise) or pay money damages for failing to comply with that duty.

Criminal law, in contrast, has to do with wrongs committed against the public as a whole. Criminal acts are prohibited by local, state, or federal government statutes. Thus, criminal defendants are prosecuted by public officials, such as a district attorney (D.A.), on behalf of the government, not by their victims or other private parties. In a criminal case, the government seeks to impose a penalty (a fine and/or imprisonment) on a person who has violated a criminal law. For example, when someone robs a convenience store, that person has committed a crime and, if caught and proved guilty, will normally spend some period of time in prison.

Basic Judicial Requirements

A court cannot decide just any issue at any time. Before any court can hear and decide a case, specific requirements must be met. To a certain extent, these requirements act as restraints on the judiciary because they limit the types of cases that courts can hear and decide. Courts also have procedural requirements that frame the judicial process.

JURISDICTION In Latin, *juris* means "law," and *diction* means "to speak." Therefore, **jurisdiction** literally refers to the power "to speak the law." Jurisdiction applies either to the geographic area in which a court has the right and power to decide cases, or to the right and power of a court to decide matters concerning certain persons, types of property, or subjects. Before any court can hear a case, it must have jurisdiction over the person against whom the suit is brought, the property involved in the suit, and the subject matter.

A state trial court, for example, usually has jurisdictional authority over the residents of a particular area of the state, such as a county or district. (A **trial court** is, as the term implies, a court in which a trial is held and testimony taken.) A state's highest court (often called the state supreme court)[7] has jurisdictional authority over all residents within the state. In some cases, if an individual has committed an offense such as injuring someone in an automobile accident or selling defective goods within the state, the court can exercise jurisdiction even if the individual is a resident of another state. State courts can also exercise jurisdiction over people who do business within the state. A New York company that distributes its products in California, for example, can be sued by a California resident in a California state court.

Because the federal (national) government is a government of limited powers, the jurisdiction of the federal courts is limited. Article III, Section 2, of the Constitution states that the federal courts can exercise jurisdiction over all cases "arising under this Constitution, the Laws of the United States, and Treaties made, or which shall be made, under their Authority." Whenever a case involves a claim based, at least in part, on the U.S. Constitution, a treaty, or a federal law, a federal question arises. Any lawsuit involving a **federal question** can originate in a federal court.

Federal courts can also exercise jurisdiction over cases involving **diversity of citizenship.** Such cases may arise when the parties in a lawsuit live in different states or when one of the parties is a foreign government or a foreign citizen. Before a federal court can take jurisdiction in a diversity case, the amount in controversy must be more than $75,000.

STANDING TO SUE To bring a lawsuit before a court, a person must have **standing to sue,** or a sufficient "stake" in the matter to justify bringing a suit.

jurisdiction The authority of a court to hear and decide a particular case.

trial court A court in which trials are held and testimony taken.

federal question A question that pertains to the U.S. Constitution, acts of Congress, or treaties. A federal question provides a basis for federal court jurisdiction.

diversity of citizenship A basis for federal court jurisdiction over a lawsuit that arises when (1) the parties in the lawsuit live in different states or when one of the parties is a foreign government or a foreign citizen, and (2) the amount in controversy is more than $75,000.

standing to sue The requirement that an individual must have a sufficient stake in a controversy before he or she can bring a lawsuit. The party bringing the suit must demonstrate that he or she has either been harmed or been threatened with a harm.

During many trials, the defense attorney asks or is asked to confer with the judge, often on procedural matters.

AP Photo/Zara Tzanev, Pool

Thus, the party bringing the suit must have suffered a harm or been threatened with a harm by the action at issue, and the issue must be justiciable. A **justiciable**[8] **controversy** is one that is real and substantial, as opposed to hypothetical or academic.

The requirement of standing clearly limits the issues that can be decided by the courts. Furthermore, both state and federal governments can specify by law when an individual or group has standing to sue. Variations in state laws have led to some interesting consequences. In New York State, for example, to have standing to sue a lawyer for making a mistake on a legal document, you must be the person who hired the lawyer. As a result, if an attorney makes a mistake when drafting a will, the beneficiaries have no standing to sue. In 2009, a New York lawyer did in fact make a mistake that cost the beneficiaries of a will millions of dollars, and a state judge affirmed the lawyer's immunity. The court ruled that the only person with standing was the deceased, who was obviously not going to sue anyone.

In complete contrast, the California legislature has placed no restrictions whatsoever on who has standing to file a suit seeking the appointment of a guardian for children. As a result, in 2009, Paul Petersen, a former child actor and head of a child advocacy group called A Minor Consideration, was able to proceed with a lawsuit calling for a guardian to protect the children of Nadya Suleman even though Petersen had no connection at all with the Suleman family. Suleman, also known as the "Octomom," gave birth to octuplets at a time when she was already the mother of six children. Suleman was single, unemployed, and receiving public assistance, and her fitness as a parent was widely questioned in the media.

COURT PROCEDURES Both the federal and the state courts have established procedural rules that apply in all cases. These procedures are designed to protect the rights and interests of the parties, ensure that the litigation proceeds in a fair and orderly manner, and identify the issues that must be decided by the court—thus saving court time and costs. Different procedural rules apply in criminal and civil cases. Generally, criminal procedural rules attempt to ensure that defendants are not deprived of their constitutional rights.

Parties involved in civil or criminal cases must comply with court procedural rules or risk being held in contempt of court. A party who is held in contempt of court can be fined, taken into custody, or both. A court must take care to ensure that the parties—and the court itself—comply with procedural requirements. Procedural errors often serve as grounds for a mistrial or for appealing the court's decision to a higher tribunal.

justiciable controversy A controversy that is not hypothetical or academic but real and substantial; a requirement that must be satisfied before a court will hear a case.

Figure 14–1

The Organization of the Federal Court System

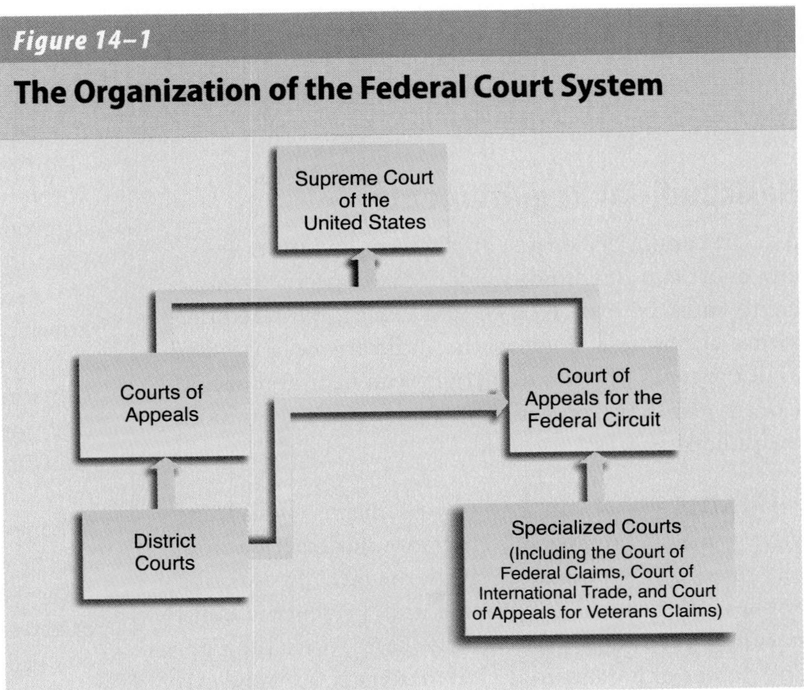

Note: Some specialized courts, such as the Tax Court, are not included in this figure.

LO2 *The Federal Court System*

The federal court system is a three-tiered model consisting of U.S. district courts (trial courts), U.S. courts of appeals, and the United States Supreme Court. Figure 14–1 above shows the organization of the federal court system.

Bear in mind that the federal courts constitute only one of the fifty-two court systems in the United States. Each of the fifty states has its own court system, as does the District of Columbia. No two state court systems are exactly the same, but usually each state has different levels, or tiers, of courts, just as the federal system does. Generally, state courts deal with questions of state law,

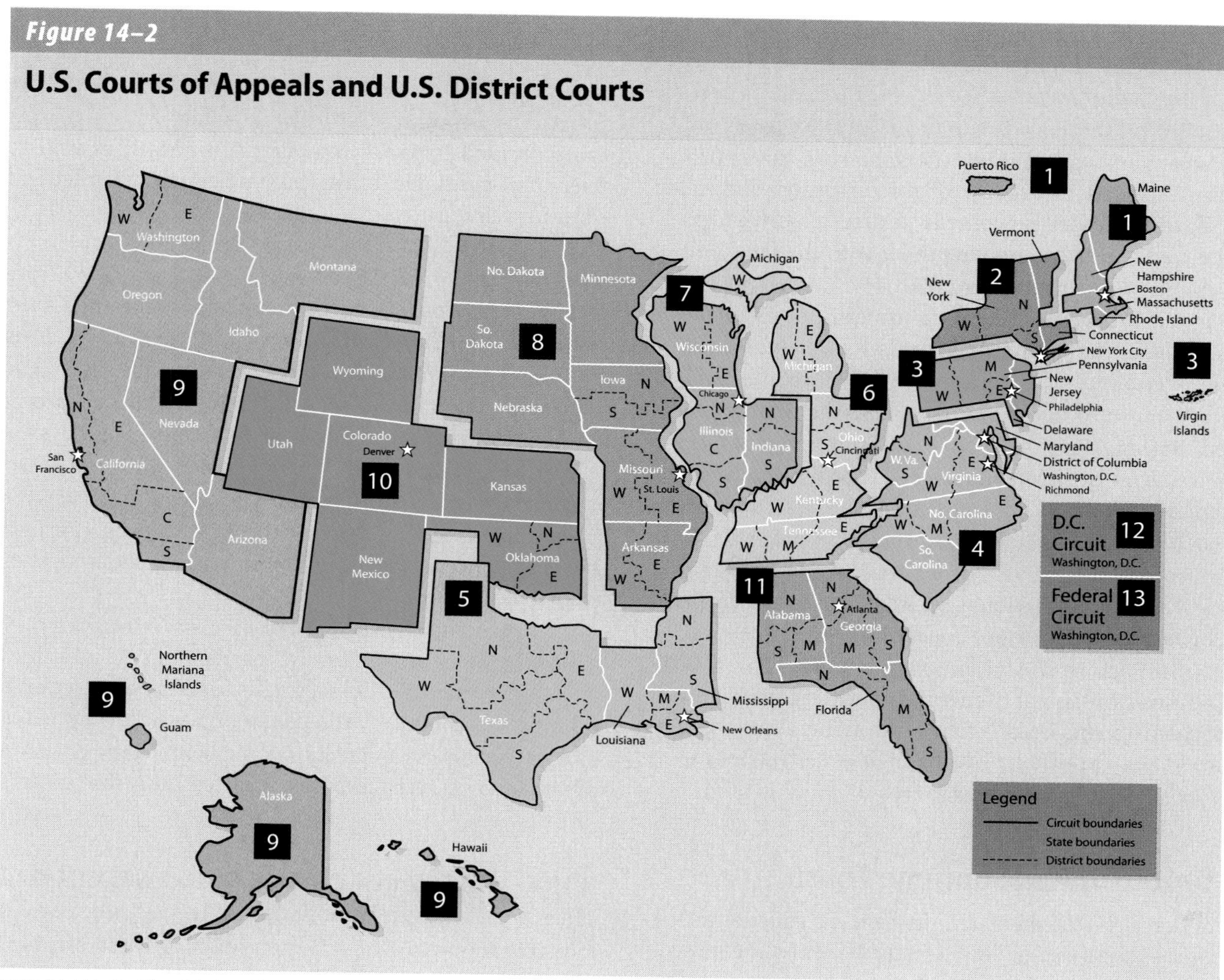

Figure 14–2

U.S. Courts of Appeals and U.S. District Courts

Source: Administrative Office of the United States Courts.

and the decisions of a state's highest court on matters of state law are normally final. If a federal question is involved, however, a decision of a state supreme court may be appealed to the United States Supreme Court. We will discuss the federal court system in the pages that follow.

U.S. District Courts

On the lowest tier of the federal court system are the U.S. district courts, or federal trial courts—the courts in which cases involving federal laws begin. The cases in these courts are decided by a judge or a jury (if it is a jury trial). There is at least one federal district court in every state, and there is one in the District of Columbia. The number of judicial districts varies over time, primarily owing to population changes and corresponding caseloads. Currently, there are ninety-four judicial districts; Figure 14–2 above shows their geographic boundaries. The federal system also includes other trial courts, such as the Court of International Trade and others shown in Figure 14–1. These courts have limited, or specialized, subject-matter jurisdiction; that is, they can exercise authority only over certain kinds of cases.

U.S. Courts of Appeals

On the middle tier of the federal court system are the U.S. courts of appeals. Courts of appeals, or **appellate courts,** do not hear evidence or testimony. Rather,

appellate court A court having appellate jurisdiction. An appellate court normally does not hear evidence or testimony but reviews the transcript of the trial court's proceedings, other records relating to the case, and attorneys' arguments as to why the trial court's decision should or should not stand.

an appellate court reviews the transcript of the trial court's proceedings, other records relating to the case, and attorneys' arguments as to why the trial court's decision should or should not stand. In contrast to a trial court, where normally a single judge presides, an appellate court consists of a panel of three or more judges. The task of the appellate court is to determine whether the trial court erred in applying the law to the facts and issues involved in a particular case.

There are thirteen federal courts of appeals in the United States. The courts of appeals for twelve of the circuits, including the Court of Appeals for the D.C. Circuit, hear appeals from the U.S. district courts located within their respective judicial circuits (see Figure 14–2 on the previous page). Appeals from decisions made by federal administrative agencies, such as the Federal Trade Commission, may also be made to the U.S. courts of appeals. The Court of Appeals for the Federal Circuit has national jurisdiction over certain types of cases, such as those concerning patent law and some claims against the national government.

The decisions of the federal appellate courts may be appealed to the United States Supreme Court. If a decision is not appealed, or if the high court declines to review the case, the appellate court's decision is final.

The United States Supreme Court

The highest level of the three-tiered model of the federal court system is the United States Supreme Court. According to Article III of the U.S. Constitution, there is only one national Supreme Court. Congress is empowered to create additional ("inferior") courts as it deems necessary. The inferior courts that Congress has created include the second tier in our model—the U.S. courts of appeals—as well as the district courts and any other courts of limited, or specialized, jurisdiction.

The United States Supreme Court consists of nine justices—a chief justice and eight associate justices—although that number is not mandated by the Constitution. The Supreme Court has original, or trial, jurisdiction only in rare instances (set forth in Article III, Section 2). In other words, only rarely does a case originate at the Supreme Court level. Most of the Court's work is as an appellate court. The Supreme Court has appellate authority over cases decided by the U.S. courts of appeals, as well as over some cases decided in the state courts when federal questions are at issue.

THE WRIT OF *CERTIORARI* To bring a case before the Supreme Court, a party may request that the Court issue a **writ of *certiorari*,**[9] often called "cert.," which is an order that the Supreme Court issues to a lower court requesting the latter to send it the record of the case in question. Parties can petition the Supreme Court to issue a writ of *certiorari,* but whether the Court will do so is entirely within its discretion. The Court will not issue a writ unless at least four of the nine justices approve. In no instance is the Court required to issue a writ of *certiorari.*[10]

Most petitions for writs of *certiorari* are denied. A denial is not a decision on the merits of a case, nor does it indicate that the Court agrees with a lower court's opinion. Furthermore, the denial of a writ has no value as a precedent. A denial simply means that the decision of the lower court remains the law within that court's jurisdiction.

WHICH CASES REACH THE SUPREME COURT? There is no absolute right to appeal to the United States Supreme Court. Although thousands of cases are filed with the Supreme Court each year, on average the Court hears fewer than one hundred. As Figure 14–3 below

writ of *certiorari* An order from a higher court asking a lower court for the record of a case.

Figure 14–3

The Number of Supreme Court Opinions

The number of Supreme Court opinions peaked at 151 in the Court's 1982 term and has been declining more or less steadily ever since. During the 2008 term (ending in June 2009), the Court issued 82 opinions.

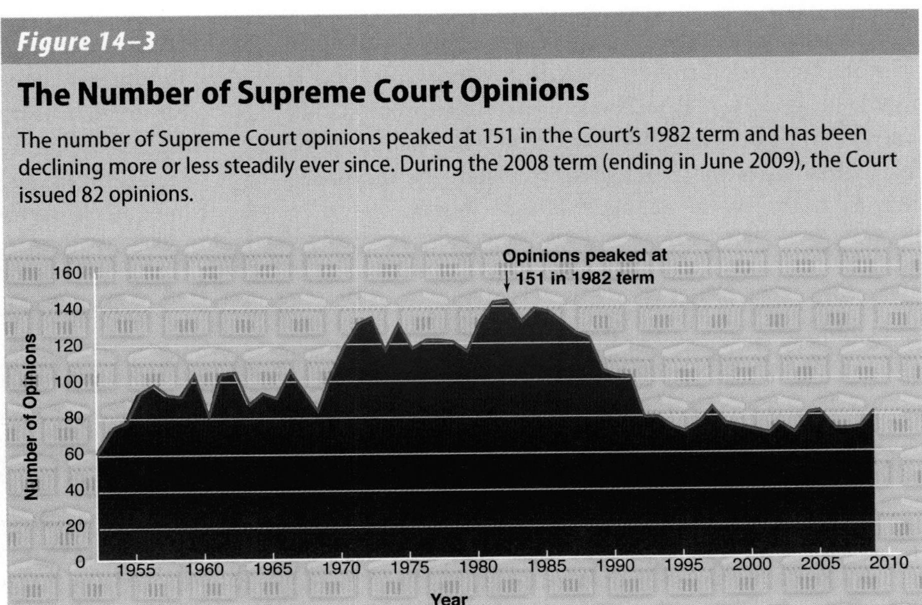

shows, the number of cases heard by the Court each year has declined significantly since the 1980s. In large part, this has occurred because the Court has raised its standards for accepting cases in recent years.

Typically, the Court grants petitions for cases that raise important policy issues that need to be addressed. In its 2007–2008 term, for example, the Court heard cases involving such pressing issues as:

- Whether individuals have a constitutional right to own guns for private use, rather than as members of a militia. (The Court determined that the right exists.)[11]
- Whether lethal injection, a method of carrying out the death penalty, constitutes cruel and unusual punishment. (The Court ruled that it does not.)[12]
- Whether alleged terrorists held at the Guantánamo Bay Naval Base in Cuba have *habeas corpus* rights—that is, the right to challenge the legitimacy of their detention in federal court. (The Court found that they do.)[13]

If the lower courts have rendered conflicting opinions on an important issue, the Supreme Court may review one or more cases involving that issue to define the law on the matter. For example, in 2002 the Court agreed to review two cases raising the issue of whether affirmative action programs (see Chapter 5) violate the equal protection clause of the Constitution. Different federal appellate courts had reached conflicting opinions on this issue.

SUPREME COURT OPINIONS Like other appellate courts, the United States Supreme Court normally does not hear any evidence. The Court's decision in a particular case is based on the written record of the case and the written arguments (legal briefs) that the attorneys submit. The attorneys also present **oral arguments**—spoken arguments presented in person rather than on paper—to the Court, after which the justices discuss the case in **conference.** The conference is strictly private—only the justices are allowed in the room.

When the Court has reached a decision, the chief justice, if in the majority, assigns the task of writing the Court's **opinion** to one of the justices. When the chief justice is not in the majority, the most senior justice voting with the majority assigns the writing of the Court's opinion. The opinion outlines the reasons for the Court's decision, the rules of law that apply, and the judgment.

Often, one or more justices who agree with the Court's decision do so for reasons different from those outlined in the majority opinion. These justices may write **concurring opinions,** setting forth their own legal reasoning on the issue. Frequently, one or more justices disagree with the Court's conclusion. These justices may write **dissenting opinions,** outlining the reasons they feel the majority erred in arriving at its decision. Although a dissenting opinion does not affect the outcome of the case before the Court, it may be important later. In a subsequent case concerning the same issue, a jurist or attorney may use the legal reasoning in the dissenting opinion as the basis for an argument to reverse the previous decision and establish a new precedent.

"AS NIGHTFALL DOESN'T COME AT ONCE, NEITHER DOES OPPRESSION. In both instances, . . . we must be aware of change in the air, however slight, lest we become unwitting victims of the darkness."

~ WILLIAM O. DOUGLAS ~
ASSOCIATE JUSTICE OF THE UNITED STATES SUPREME COURT
1939–1975

LO3 *Federal Judicial Appointments*

Unlike state court judges, who are often elected, all federal judges are appointed. Article II, Section 2, of the Constitution authorizes the president to appoint the justices of the Supreme Court with the advice and consent of the Senate. Laws enacted by Congress provide that the same procedure is to be used for appointing judges to the lower federal courts as well.

oral argument A spoken argument presented to a judge in person by an attorney on behalf of her or his client.

conference In regard to the Supreme Court, a private meeting of the justices in which they present their arguments concerning a case under consideration.

opinion A written statement by a court expressing the reasons for its decision in a case.

concurring opinion A statement written by a judge or justice who agrees (concurs) with the court's decision, but for reasons different from those in the majority opinion.

dissenting opinion A statement written by a judge or justice who disagrees with the majority opinion.

Federal judges receive lifetime appointments (because under Article III of the Constitution they "hold their Offices during good Behaviour"). Federal judges may be removed from office through the impeachment process, but such proceedings are extremely rare and are usually undertaken only if a judge engages in blatantly illegal conduct, such as bribery. In the history of this nation, only thirteen federal judges have been impeached, and only seven of them were removed from office. Normally, federal judges serve until they resign, retire, or die.

Although the Constitution sets no specific qualifications for those who serve on the Supreme Court, those who have done so share one characteristic: all have been attorneys. The backgrounds of the Supreme Court justices have been far from typical of the characteristics of the American public as a whole. Table 14–1 summarizes the backgrounds of all of the 111 United States Supreme Court justices through 2010.

The Nomination Process

The president receives suggestions and recommendations as to potential nominees for Supreme Court positions from various sources, including the Justice Department, senators, other judges, the candidates themselves, state political leaders, bar associations, and other interest groups. After selecting a nominee, the president submits her or his name to the Senate for approval. The Senate Judiciary Committee then holds hearings and makes its recommendation to the Senate, where it takes a majority vote to confirm the nomination.

When judges are nominated to the district courts (and, to a lesser extent, the U.S. courts of appeals), a senator of the president's political party from the state where there is a vacancy traditionally has been allowed to veto the president's choice. This practice is known as **senatorial courtesy.** At times, senatorial courtesy sometimes even permits senators from the opposing party to veto presidential choices. Because of senatorial courtesy, home-state senators of the president's party may be able to influence the choice of the nominee.

It should come as no surprise that partisanship plays a significant role in the president's selection of nominees to the federal bench, particularly to the Supreme Court, the crown jewel of the federal judiciary. Traditionally, presidents have attempted to strengthen their legacies by appointing federal

senatorial courtesy A practice that allows a senator of the president's party to veto the president's nominee to a federal court judgeship within the senator's state.

Table 14–1

Backgrounds of United States Supreme Court Justices through 2010

	Number of Justices (111 = Total)
Occupational Position before Appointment	
Private legal practice	25
State judgeship	21
Federal judgeship	31
U.S. attorney general	7
Deputy or assistant U.S. attorney general	2
U.S. solicitor general	2
U.S. senator	6
U.S. representative	2
State governor	3
Federal executive post	9
Other	3
Religious Affiliation	
Protestant	83
Roman Catholic	14
Jewish	6
Unitarian	7
No religious affiliation	1
Age on Appointment	
Under 40	5
41–50	32
51–60	60
61–70	14
Political Party Affiliation	
Federalist (to 1835)	13
Jeffersonian Republican (to 1828)	7
Whig (to 1861)	1
Democrat	45
Republican	44
Independent	1
Education	
College graduate	95
Not a college graduate	16
Gender	
Male	108
Female	3
Race	
White (non-Hispanic)	108
African American	2
Hispanic	1

Sources: *Congressional Quarterly, Congressional Quarterly's Guide to the U.S. Supreme Court* (Washington, D.C.: Congressional Quarterly Press, 1997); and authors' updates.

judges with similar political and philosophical views. In the history of the Supreme Court, fewer than 13 percent of the justices nominated by a president have been from an opposing political party.

Appointments to the U.S. courts of appeals can also have a lasting impact. Recall that these courts occupy the level just below the Supreme Court in the federal court system. Also recall that the decisions rendered by these courts—about 60,000 per year—are final unless overturned by the Supreme Court. Given that the Supreme Court renders opinions in fewer than one hundred cases a year, the decisions of the federal appellate courts have a wide-reaching impact on American society. For example, a decision interpreting the federal Constitution by the U.S. Court of Appeals for the Ninth Circuit, if not overruled by the Supreme Court, establishes a precedent that will be followed in the states of Alaska, Arizona, California, Hawaii, Idaho, Montana, Nevada, Oregon, and Washington.

Confirmation or Rejection by the Senate

The president's nominations are not always confirmed. In fact, almost 20 percent of presidential nominations for the Supreme Court have been either rejected or not acted on by the Senate. The process of nominating and confirming federal judges, especially Supreme Court justices, often involves political debate and controversy. Many bitter battles over Supreme Court appointments have ensued when the Senate and the president have disagreed on political issues.

From 1893 until 1968, the Senate rejected only three Court nominees. From 1968 through 1986, however, two presidential nominees to the highest court were rejected, and two more nominations, both by President Ronald Reagan, failed in 1987. First, Reagan nominated Robert Bork, who faced sometimes hostile questioning about his views on the Constitution during the confirmation hearings. When the Senate rejected Bork, Reagan nominated Douglas Ginsburg, who ultimately withdrew his nomination when the press leaked information about his alleged use of marijuana during the 1970s. Finally, the Senate approved Reagan's third choice, Anthony Kennedy. Although both of President George H. W. Bush's nominees to the Supreme Court—David Souter and Clarence Thomas—were confirmed by the Senate, Thomas's nomination aroused considerable controversy. Thomas's confirmation hearings were extremely volatile and received widespread publicity on national television. The nation watched as Anita Hill, a former aide, leveled charges of sexual harassment at Thomas.

In 1993, President Bill Clinton had little trouble gaining approval for his nominee to fill the seat left vacant by Justice Byron White. Ruth Bader Ginsburg became the second female Supreme Court justice, the first being Sandra Day O'Connor, who was appointed by President Reagan in 1981. When Justice Harry Blackmun retired in 1994, Clinton nominated Stephen Breyer to fill Blackmun's seat. Breyer was confirmed without significant opposition.

All federal judicial appointments must be approved by the Senate. Here, Senator Jeff Sessions (R., Ala.), on the right, and Senator Patrick Leahy (D., Vt.) greet Sonia Sotomayor during her nomination hearing to become a Supreme Court justice in July 2009. What happens when a nominee is rejected by the Senate?

Karen Bleier/AFP/Getty Images

Recent Judicial Appointments

Prior to the elections that elevated George W. Bush and then Barack Obama to the presidency, there was much conjecture about how the election outcomes might affect the federal judiciary—particularly the makeup of the United States Supreme Court. No justice retired from the Supreme Court during George W. Bush's first term as president. During his second term, however, the death of Chief Justice William Rehnquist and the retirement of Justice Sandra Day O'Connor allowed Bush to appoint two new justices to the Court. Bush nominated John G. Roberts, Jr., as chief justice to replace Chief Justice

AP Photo/Charles Dharapak

Justice Samuel Alito, Jr.

Rehnquist and Samuel A. Alito, Jr., as associate justice to replace Justice O'Connor. Both nominees were confirmed by the Senate with relatively little difficulty.

Bush also filled numerous vacancies on the lower courts, including vacancies on the benches of the U.S. courts of appeals. By 2009, Republican appointees made up about 60 percent of the federal judiciary.

On May 1, 2009, newly elected president Barack Obama announced that Justice David Souter intended to retire from the Supreme Court at the beginning of the Court's summer recess. On May 26, Obama named Sonia Sotomayor to replace Souter. Sotomayor had served for more than a decade as a judge of the U.S. Court of Appeals for the Second Circuit and was the first Hispanic woman ever nominated to the Supreme Court. Sotomayor was confirmed without difficulty, although conservative researchers turned up a number of statements she had made that were used to challenge the nomination. For example, Sotomayor had said that a "wise Latina woman" might, because of her background, be able to make better decisions in discrimination cases than a white man. On the basis of this remark, talk show host Rush Limbaugh called Sotomayor a racist. (See this chapter's *Join the Debate* on the facing page.)

AP Photo/Ron Edmonds

Sonia Sotomayor became only the third woman to serve on the Supreme Court and the first Latina (as she prefers to call herself).

LO4 *The Courts as Policymakers*

In the United States, judges and justices play a major role in government. Unlike judges in some other countries, U.S. judges have the power to decide on the constitutionality of laws or actions undertaken by the other branches of government.

Clearly, the function of the courts is to interpret and apply the law, not to make law—that is the function of the legislative branch of government. Yet judges can and do "make law"; indeed, they cannot avoid making law in some cases because the law does not always provide clear answers to questions that come before the courts. The text of the U.S. Constitution, for example, is set forth in broad terms. When a court interprets a constitutional provision and applies that interpretation to a specific set of circumstances, the court is essentially "making the law" on that issue. Examples of how the courts, and especially the United States Supreme Court, make law abound. Consider privacy rights, which we discussed in Chapter 4. Nothing in the Constitution or its amendments specifically states that we have a right to privacy. Yet the Supreme Court, through various decisions, has established such a right by deciding that it is implied by several constitutional amendments. The Court has also held that this right to privacy includes a number of specific rights, such as the right to have an abortion.

Statutory provisions and other legal rules also tend to be expressed in general terms, and the courts must decide how those general provisions and rules apply to specific cases. Consider the Americans with Disabilities Act of 1990. The act requires employers to reasonably accommodate the needs of employees with disabilities. But the act does not say exactly what employers must do to "reasonably accommodate" such persons. Thus, the courts must decide, on a case-by-case basis, what this phrase means. Additionally, in some cases there is no relevant law or precedent to follow. In recent years, for example, courts have been struggling with new kinds of legal issues stemming from new communications technology, including the Internet. Until legislative bodies enact laws governing these issues, it is up to the courts to fashion the law that will apply—and thus make policy.

The Impact of Court Decisions

As already mentioned, how the courts interpret particular laws can have a widespread impact on society. For example, in 1996, in *Hopwood v. Texas*,[14] the U.S.

JOIN THE DEBATE

Does Partisan Ideology Matter in Supreme Court Appointments?

President George W. Bush appointed not only a new chief justice, John Roberts, Jr., but also a new associate justice, Samuel Alito, Jr. Many believe that the conservative leanings of these two Supreme Court appointees will matter in both the short and the long run. Others are not so sure.

Conservative Appointments Mean Conservative Justices

The Rehnquist Court was considered conservative, but its decisions were not necessarily consistent. During the Roberts Court's first term (2005–2006), however, Roberts usually voted with the Court's most conservative justices, Clarence Thomas and Antonin Scalia. During its second term (2006–2007), the Roberts Court continued to issue conservative rulings. For example, Roberts voted with Kennedy, Scalia, Thomas, and Alito to uphold the 2003 federal law banning partial-birth abortion.[15] In its third term, in 2008, the Roberts Court issued the opinions mentioned on page 329, including conservative rulings on guns and the death penalty. The Court also upheld a law that criminalized offers to sell child pornography even if the pornography does not actually exist.[16] In its fourth term, in 2009, the Court avoided a ruling that would have invalidated the 1965 Voting Rights Act, as we explained in the chapter-opening *America at Odds* feature in Chapter 8. Nevertheless, the Court issued a stern warning to Congress to modernize the statute or face a more negative decision in the future.[17] Clearly, partisan ideology does matter when it comes to Supreme Court appointments.

AP Photo/Charles Dharapak

Chief Justice John Roberts, Jr.

Presidents Don't Always Get What They Want

Not everyone believes that the partisan views of Supreme Court appointees are that important. After all, presidents may nominate Supreme Court justices, but the Senate has to approve them. Moreover, in the past, some seemingly conservative nominees have not turned out to be conservative justices once on the bench. A good example is David Souter, who was appointed to the Court by Republican President George H. W. Bush (1989–1993). Bush thought that Souter would take a conservative approach when analyzing cases before the Court. In fact, Souter became a leading counterforce to the Court's conservatives. Consider also Sandra Day O'Connor, the first female justice, who was considered a conservative when she was appointed but gradually became less conservative as a justice. She became a pragmatic voice on the high court bench, even joining forces with the liberals on the Court on a number of issues, including abortion. Thus, the degree to which partisan ideology matters in Supreme Court appointments is greatly overrated.

For Critical Analysis *Now that Justice Sonia Sotomayor is on the Supreme Court and has begun to participate in rulings, do you think that President Obama got the kind of justice he hoped for when he appointed her? Why or why not?*

Court of Appeals for the Fifth Circuit held that an affirmative action program implemented by the University of Texas School of Law in Austin was unconstitutional. The court's decision in *Hopwood* set a precedent for all federal courts within the Fifth Circuit's jurisdiction (which covers Louisiana, Mississippi, and Texas).

Decisions rendered by the United States Supreme Court, of course, have an even broader impact, because all courts in the nation are obligated to follow precedents set by the high court. For example, in 2003 the Supreme Court issued two rulings on affirmative action programs at the University of Michigan. Unlike the appeals court in the *Hopwood* case, the Supreme Court held that diversity on college campuses is a legitimate goal and that affirmative action programs that take race into consideration as part of an examination of each applicant's background do not necessarily violate the equal protection clause of the Constitution.[18] This decision rendered any contrary ruling, including the ruling by the court in the *Hopwood* case, invalid. In 2007,

Photo by Mike Simons/Getty Images

The U.S. Supreme Court has often faced cases that deal with affirmative action questions. This University of Cincinnati student supports the continuation of affirmative action programs. What are the arguments in her favor? What are the arguments against?

however, the Court retreated somewhat from its position in the University of Michigan cases when it declared that Seattle schools could not use race as a determining factor when assigning students to schools.[19]

Thus, when the Supreme Court interprets laws, it establishes national policy. If the Court deems that a law passed by Congress or a state legislature violates the Constitution, for example, that law will be void and unenforceable in any court within the United States.

The Power of Judicial Review

judicial review The power of the courts to decide on the constitutionality of legislative enactments and of actions taken by the executive branch.

Recall from Chapter 2 that the U.S. Constitution divides government powers among the executive, legislative, and judicial branches. This division of powers is part of our system of checks and balances. Essentially, the founders gave each branch of government the constitutional authority to check the other two branches. The federal judiciary can exercise a check on the actions of either of the other branches through its power of **judicial review.**

The Constitution does not actually mention judicial review. Rather, the Supreme Court claimed the power for itself in *Marbury v. Madison.*[20] In that case, which was decided by the Court in 1803, Chief Justice John Marshall held that a provision of a 1789 law affecting the Supreme Court's jurisdiction violated the Constitution and was thus void. Marshall declared, "It is emphatically the province and duty of the judicial department [the courts] to say what the law is. . . . If two laws conflict with each other, the courts must decide on the operation of each. . . . So if a law be in opposition to the constitution . . . the court must determine which of these conflicting rules governs the case. This is the very essence of judicial duty."

Most constitutional scholars believe that the framers intended that the federal courts should have the power of judicial review. In *Federalist Paper* No. 78, Alexander Hamilton clearly espoused the doctrine. Hamilton stressed the importance of the "complete independence" of federal judges and their special duty to "invalidate all acts contrary to the manifest tenor of the Constitution." Without judicial review by impartial courts, there would be nothing to ensure that the other branches of government stayed within constitutional limits when exercising their powers, and "all the reservations of particular rights or privileges would amount to nothing." Chief Justice Marshall shared Hamilton's views and adopted Hamilton's reasoning in *Marbury v. Madison.*

Judicial Activism versus Judicial Restraint

As already noted, making policy is not the primary function of the federal courts. Yet it is unavoidable that courts do, in fact, influence or even establish policy when they interpret and apply the law. Further, the power of judicial review gives the courts, and particularly the Supreme Court, an important policymaking tool. When the Supreme Court upholds or invalidates a state or federal statute, the consequences for the nation can be profound.

One issue that is often debated is how the federal courts should wield their policymaking power, particularly the power of judicial review. Often, this debate is couched in terms of judicial activism versus judicial restraint.

ACTIVIST VERSUS RESTRAINTIST JUSTICES Although the terms *judicial activism* and *judicial restraint* do not have precise meanings, generally an activist judge or justice believes that the courts should actively use their powers to check the legislative and executive branches to ensure that they do not exceed their authority. A restraintist judge or justice, in contrast, generally assumes that the courts should defer to the decisions of the legislative and executive branches, because members of Congress and the president are elected by the people, whereas federal court judges are not. In other words, the courts should not thwart the implementation of legislative acts unless those acts are clearly unconstitutional.

POLITICAL IDEOLOGY AND JUDICIAL ACTIVISM/RESTRAINT One of the Supreme Court's most activist eras occurred during the period from 1953 to 1969 under the leadership of Chief Justice Earl Warren. The Warren Court propelled the civil rights movement forward by holding, among other things, that laws permitting racial segregation violated the equal protection clause (see Chapter 5).

Because of the activism of the Warren Court, the term *judicial activism* has often been linked with liberalism. Indeed, many liberals are in favor of an activist federal judiciary because they believe that the judiciary can "right" the "wrongs" that result from unfair laws or from "antiquated" legislation at the state and local levels. Neither judicial activism nor judicial restraint is necessarily linked to a particular political ideology, however. In fact, many observers claim that today's Supreme Court is actively pursuing a conservative agenda.

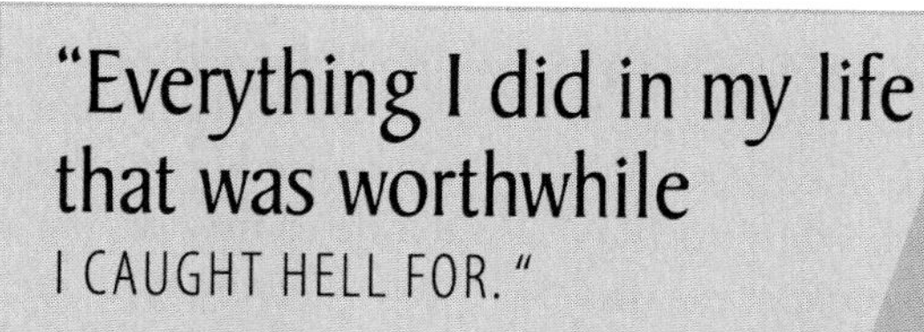

LO5 *Ideology and the Courts*

The policymaking role of the courts gives rise to an important question: To what extent do ideology and personal policy preferences affect judicial decision making? Numerous scholars have attempted to answer this question, especially with respect to Supreme Court justices.

Ideology and Supreme Court Decisions

In one study, conducted while William Rehnquist headed the Supreme Court, judicial scholars Jeffrey Segal and Harold Spaeth concluded that "the Supreme Court decides disputes in light of the facts of the case vis-à-vis the ideological attitudes and values of the justices. Simply put, Rehnquist votes the way he does because he is extremely conservative."[21] The authors maintained that Supreme Court justices base their decisions on policy preferences simply because they are free to do so—they are not accountable to the electorate because they are not elected to their positions. The desire to attain higher office is also not a factor in the Court's decision making because the justices are at the apex of the judicial career ladder.

Few doubt that ideology affects judicial decision making, although, of course, other factors play a role as well. Different courts (such as a trial court and an appellate court) can look at the same case and draw different conclusions as to what law is applicable and how it should be applied. Certainly, there are numerous examples of ideology affecting Supreme Court decisions. As new justices replace old ones and new ideological alignments are formed, the Court's decisions are affected. Yet many scholars argue that there is no real evidence that personal preferences influence Supreme Court decisions to an *unacceptable* extent.

Keep in mind that judicial decision making, particularly at the Supreme Court level, can be very complex. When deciding cases, the Supreme Court often must consider any number of sources, including constitutions, statutes, and administrative agency regulations—as well as cases interpreting relevant portions of those sources. At times, the Court may also take demographic data, public opinion, foreign laws, and other factors into account. How much weight is given to each of these sources or factors will vary from justice to justice. After all, reasoning of any kind, including judicial reasoning, does not take place in a vacuum. It is only natural that a justice's life experiences, personal biases, and intellectual abilities and predispositions will touch on the reasoning process. Nevertheless, when reviewing a case, a Supreme Court justice does not start out with a conclusion (such as "I don't like this particular law that Congress passed") and then look for legal sources to support that conclusion.

Ideology and the Roberts Court

In contrast to the liberal Supreme Court under Earl Warren today's Court is generally conservative. The Court began its rightward shift after President Ronald Reagan (1981–1989) appointed conservative William Rehnquist as chief justice in 1986, and the Court moved further to the right as other conservative appointments to the bench were made by Reagan and George H. W. Bush (1989–1993).

Many Supreme Court scholars believe that the appointments of John Roberts (as chief justice) and Samuel Alito (as associate justice) caused the Court to drift even further to the right.[22] Certainly, the five conservative justices on the bench during the Roberts Court's first three terms voted together and cast the deciding votes in numerous cases.[23] The remaining justices held liberal-to-moderate views and often formed an opposing bloc.

A notable change in the Court occurred when Alito replaced retiring justice Sandra Day O'Connor. O'Connor had often been the "swing" vote on the Court, sometimes voting with the liberal bloc and at other times siding with the conservatives. On the Roberts Court, the swing voter is Justice Anthony Kennedy, who is generally more conservative in his views than O'Connor was. Although Justice Kennedy dislikes being described as a swing voter, he often decides the outcome of a case. In the 2008–2009 term, for example, Kennedy was in the majority 92 percent of the time. According to the *New York Times,* "the Constitution now often means whatever Justice Kennedy says it means."

Today's Court is strongly divided ideologically. In the Court term ending in June 2007, one-third of the decisions rendered by the Court were reached by five-to-four votes—the highest portion of such votes in more than a decade. In the 2008–2009 term, twenty-three out of eighty-two cases were decided by five-to-four votes.[24]

AP Photo/Dan Loh

Although often considered a conservative when he served on the Rehnquist Court, Justice Anthony Kennedy has typically held the "swing" vote on the closely divided Roberts Court.

AP Photo/Charles Rex Arbogast

Justice John Paul Stevens is now the most senior member of the Court and is a voice of moderation on the increasingly conservative court.

Approaches to Legal Interpretation

It would be a mistake to look at the judicial philosophy of today's Supreme Court solely in terms of the political ideologies of liberalism and conservatism. In fact, some Supreme Court scholars have suggested that other factors are as important as, or even more important than, the justices' political philosophies in determining why they decide as they do. These factors include the justices' attitudes toward legal interpretation and their perceptions of the Supreme Court's role in the federal judiciary.

STRICT VERSUS BROAD CONSTRUCTION

Legal scholars have often used the terms *strict* and *broad* construction to describe how judges and justices interpret the law. Generally, strict constructionists look to the letter of the law as written when trying to decipher its meaning, whereas broad constructionists look more to the purpose and context of the law. Strict constructionists believe that the letter of the law should guide the courts' decisions. Broad constructionists believe that the law is an evolving set of standards and is not fixed in concrete. Generally, broad constructionists are more willing to "read between the lines" of a law to serve what they perceive to be the law's intent and purpose.

Strict construction of the law is often linked with conservative views, and broad construction with liberal views. The conservative justices on today's Supreme Court are often labeled strict constructionists because they give great weight to the text of the law. Of course, as with judicial activism and judicial restraint, it is possible for these links to be reversed. There have been cases in which the Court appeared to be taking a conservative broad-constructionist or a liberal narrow-constructionist approach.

THE ROLE OF THE SUPREME COURT How justices view the role of the Supreme Court in the federal judiciary also affects their decision making. Two of the Court's justices—Antonin Scalia and Stephen Breyer—have made public their different visions of the Court's role. For Justice Scalia, a conservative voice on the Court, the Court should establish clear rules for the lower courts to follow when they apply the law. For Justice Breyer, who holds moderate-to-liberal views, the Court's role should be to establish flexible standards for the lower courts to apply on a case-by-case basis. This rules-versus-standards debate is reflected in the justices' opinions.

In one case, for example, Breyer, who wrote the majority opinion, concluded that a seniority system in the workplace should "ordinarily" take priority over a disabled worker's right to "reasonable accommodation" under the Americans with Disabilities Act (ADA) of 1990—see Chapter 5. Yet, stated Breyer, there might be special circumstances that would make a disabled worker's reassignment to another position "reasonable" even though an employee with more seniority also had a right to the position. In other words, Breyer left the door open for the lower courts to deal with the question on a case-by-case basis, in light of the surrounding circumstances. Justice Scalia, in his dissent, concluded that a seniority system should always prevail. Saying that it should "ordinarily" prevail, he wrote, did not give any clear guidance to the lower courts and turned the "reasonable accommodation" provision in the ADA into a "standardless grab bag."[25]

These two positions reflect totally different concepts of the Court's role. For Scalia, it would be irresponsible to leave the law in such an indeterminate state. Therefore, the justices must provide strong guidance for the lower courts. For Breyer, an absolutist approach is unworkable. In a "participatory democracy," claims Breyer, the Court should not stand in the way of a new understanding of the law that "bubbles up from below."[26] Justice Clarence Thomas often agrees with Scalia on this issue, preferring that the Court give definite guidance to the lower courts when a case presents an opportunity to do so. The decisions of Chief Justice Roberts tend to reflect reasoning closer to Breyer's on this point. Yet Roberts's decisions also reflect a cautious and carefully reasoned approach to legal interpretation and a tendency to prefer only "incremental" changes in existing case law. Critics of the Court's 2007 decision on partial-birth abortion (see Chapter 4), for example, see this incremental approach at work. Although the Court did not overrule the *Roe v. Wade* decision outright, the decision on partial-birth abortion was seen by these critics as part of a process of "chipping away" at rights previously upheld by the Supreme Court.

AP Photo/Lawrence Jackson

Justice Stephen Breyer.

AP Photo/Mark Duncan

Justice Antonin Scalia.

AP Photo/Charles Dharapak

Justice Clarence Thomas.

Constitutional Interpretation: Original Intent versus Modernism

The terms *strict construction* and *broad construction* describe different approaches to interpreting the law generally. These approaches may be used when determining the meaning of any law, whether it be a statutory provision, a specific regulation, or a constitutional clause. When discussing *constitutional* interpretation, however, the terms *original intent* and *modernism* are also used to describe the differences in Supreme Court justices' reasoning.

ORIGINAL INTENT Some of the justices believe that to determine the meaning of a particular constitutional phrase, the Court should look to the intentions of the founders. What did the framers of the Constitution themselves intend when they included the phrase in the document? In other words, what was the "original intent" of the phrase? To discern the intent of the founders, the justices should look to sources that shed light on the founders'

AP Photo/Evan Vucci

Justice Ruth Bader Ginsburg.

views. These sources include contemporary writings by the founders, newspaper articles, the *Federalist Papers,* and notes taken during the Constitutional Convention. Justice Antonin Scalia, one of the Court's most conservative justices, gives some insight into this approach to constitutional interpretation in his book *A Matter of Interpretation.*[27] In response to those who maintain that the Constitution is a "living Constitution" and should be interpreted in light of society's needs and practices today, Scalia contends that constitutional principles are fixed, not evolving: "The Constitution that I interpret and apply is not living, but dead."

MODERNISM Other justices, sometimes referred to as "modernists," believe that the Constitution is indeed a living document that evolves to meet changing times and new social needs. Otherwise, how could the Constitution be relevant to today's society? How could the opinions of a small group of white men who drafted the document more than two hundred years ago possibly apply to today's large and diverse population? Moreover, the founders themselves often disagreed on what the Constitution should mean. Additionally, if original intent is the goal, what about the intentions of those who ratified the Constitution? Shouldn't they be taken into consideration also? The modernist approach to constitutional interpretation thus looks at the Constitution in the context of today's society and considers how today's life affects the words in the document. Modernists also defend their approach by stating that the founders intentionally left many constitutional provisions vague so that future generations could interpret the document in a manner that would meet the needs of a growing nation.

LO6 *Assessing the Role of the Federal Courts*

The federal courts have often come under attack, particularly in the last decade or so, for many reasons. This should come as no surprise in view of the policymaking power of the courts. After all, a Supreme Court decision can establish national policy on such issues as abortion, racial segregation, and online pornography. Critics, especially on the political right, frequently accuse the judiciary of "legislating from the bench." We discuss these criticisms in this chapter's *Perception versus Reality* feature on the facing page.

Criticisms of the Federal Courts

Certainly, policymaking by unelected judges and justices in the federal courts has serious implications in a democracy. Some Americans, including many conservatives, contend that making policy from the bench has upset the balance of powers envisioned by the framers of the Constitution. They cite Thomas Jefferson, who once said, "To consider the judges as the ultimate arbiters of all constitutional questions [is] a very dangerous doctrine indeed, and one which would place us under the despotism of an oligarchy."[28] This group believes that we should rein in the power of the federal courts, and particularly judicial activism.

Indeed, from the the mid-1990s until 2007, when the Republicans controlled Congress, a number of bills to restrain the power of the federal judiciary were introduced in Congress. Among other things, it was proposed that Congress, not the Supreme Court, should have the ultimate say in determining the meaning of the Constitution; that judges who ignore the will of Congress or follow foreign precedents should be impeached; that federal courts should not be allowed to decide certain types of cases, such as those involving abortion or the place of religion in public life; and that Congress should be empowered to use its control over the judiciary to punish judges who overstep their authority.

"THE CONSTITUTION ITSELF SHOULD BE OUR GUIDE, not our own concept of what is fair, decent, and right."

~ HUGO L. BLACK ~
ASSOCIATE JUSTICE OF THE UNITED STATES SUPREME COURT
1937–1971

PERCEPTION VERSUS REALITY

The Supreme Court Legislates from the Bench

Our constitution gives legislative powers to the Congress exclusively. All executive powers are granted to the president. And all judicial powers are given to the judiciary. The United States Supreme Court is the final arbiter and interpreter of what is and is not constitutional. Because of its power of judicial review, it has the ability to "make law," or so it seems.

The Perception

Using the power of judicial review, the Supreme Court creates new laws. In 1954, the Court determined that racial segregation is illegal, a position that is universally accepted today but was hugely controversial back in the 1950s. The Court has also legalized sexual acts between same-sex adults and, of course, abortion. These decisions, especially the legalization of abortion, remain very controversial today. Such decisions have had a major impact on the nature of American society. Because citizens elect members of Congress and the president only—and not members of the Supreme Court—it is undemocratic to allow these nine justices to determine laws for our nation.

The Reality

The Supreme Court cannot actually write new laws. It can only eliminate old ones. When the Court threw out laws that criminalized adult sexual activity by gay men and lesbians, it was abolishing laws, not creating them. The Court does not have the power to legislate—to create new laws. Consider what would happen if the Court decided that some basic level of health care is a constitutional right—a highly unlikely event. Could the Court establish mechanisms by which such a right could be enforced? It could not. It takes members of Congress months of hard work to craft bills that affect our health-care system. Such legislation fills thousands of pages and can only be developed with the assistance of large numbers of experts and lobbyists. The federal courts could not undertake such projects even if they wanted to.

Sonia Sotomayor, the most recently appointed Supreme Court justice, once said: "The courts of appeals are where policy is made." Indeed, most cases never make it to the Supreme Court, and this fact limits the ability of Supreme Court justices to make policy decisions. More to the point, however, in referring to policy, Sotomayor was speaking of judicial policy, not policy in general. The courts must decide how they will handle the cases that are brought before them. To do so establishes judicial policy. It does not constitute lawmaking.

In any event, we have no alternative to judicial review when it comes to determining what is or is not constitutional. Without the Supreme Court, Congress and the president could make all sorts of laws that violate our Constitution and infringe on our rights, and there would be nothing to stop them. As Chief Justice John Roberts said during his confirmation hearings, "Judges are like umpires. Umpires don't make the rules; they apply them."

Blog On *Plenty of bloggers follow the activities of the Supreme Court, but for sophisticated commentary, try* **www.scotusblog.com**, *produced by the law firm of Akin, Gump, Strauss, Hauer, and Feld. Another choice is* **ussc.blogspot.com**, *by Paul M. Rashkind, a Florida lawyer.*

The Case for the Courts

On the other side of the debate over the courts are those who argue in favor of leaving the courts alone. Several federal court judges have sharply criticized congressional efforts to interfere with their authority. They claim that such efforts violate the Constitution's separation of powers. Other critics of Congress's attacks on the federal judiciary include James M. Jeffords, a former independent senator from Vermont, who likened the federal court system to a referee: "The first lesson we teach children when they enter competitive sports is to respect the referee, even if we think he [or she] might have made the wrong call. If our children can understand this, why can't our political leaders?"[29]

Others argue that there are already sufficient checks on the courts, some of which we look at next.

JUDICIAL TRADITIONS AND DOCTRINES One check on the courts is judicial restraint. Supreme Court justices traditionally have exercised a great deal of self-restraint. Justices sometimes admit to making decisions that fly in the face of their personal values and policy preferences, simply because they feel obligated to do so in view of existing law. Self-restraint is also mandated by various judicially established traditions and doctrines, including the doctrine of *stare decisis,* which theoretically obligates the Supreme Court to follow its own precedents. Furthermore, the Supreme Court will not hear a meritless appeal just so it can rule on the issue. Finally, more often than not, the justices narrow their rulings to focus on just one aspect of an issue, even though there may be nothing to stop them from broadening their focus and thus widening the impact of their decisions.

OTHER CHECKS The judiciary is subject to other checks as well. Courts may make rulings, but they cannot force federal and state legislatures to appropriate the funds necessary to carry out those rulings. For example, if a state supreme court decides that prison conditions must be improved, the state legislature has to find the funds to carry out the ruling, or the improvements will not take place. Additionally, legislatures can rewrite (amend) old laws or pass new ones in an attempt to negate a court's ruling. This may happen when a court interprets a statute in a way that Congress did not intend. Congress may also propose amendments to the Constitution to reverse Supreme Court rulings, and Congress has the authority to limit or otherwise alter the jurisdiction of the lower federal courts. Finally, although it is most unlikely, Congress could even change the number of justices on the Supreme Court, in an attempt to change the ideological balance on the Court. (President Franklin D. Roosevelt proposed such a plan in 1937, without success.)

THE PUBLIC'S REGARD FOR THE SUPREME COURT As mentioned, some have proposed that Congress, not the Supreme Court, be the final arbiter of the Constitution. In debates on this topic, one factor is often overlooked: the American public's high regard for the Supreme Court and the federal courts generally. The Court continues to be respected as a fair arbiter of conflicting interests and the protector of constitutional rights and liberties. Even when the Court issued its decision to halt the manual recount of votes in Florida following the 2000 elections, which effectively handed the presidency to George W. Bush, Americans respected the Court's decision-making authority—although many disagreed with the Court's decision. Polls continue to show that Americans have more trust and confidence in the Supreme Court than they do in Congress.

AMERICA AT ODDS *The Judiciary*

"The Judicial Department comes home in its effect to every man's fireside: it passes on his property, his reputation, his life, his all." So stated John Marshall, chief justice of the United States Supreme Court from 1801 to 1835. If you reflect a moment on these words, you will realize their truth. A single Supreme Court decision can affect the lives of millions of Americans. For example, the Court's decision in *Brown v. Board of Education of Topeka* signaled a movement toward racial integration not only in the schools but in all of American society. In 1973, the Supreme Court, in *Roe v. Wade,* held that the constitutional right to privacy included the right to have an abortion. This decision has also affected the lives of millions of Americans.

The influence wielded by the Supreme Court today and the public's high regard for the Court are a far cry from the place that the Supreme Court held in public esteem at the beginning of this nation. Indeed, the Court's first chief justice, John Jay, thought that the Court had little stature and would never play an important role in American society. After resigning as chief justice and serving as governor of New York, Jay refused to return to the Court, even though President John Adams had appointed him for a second time. The third chief justice, Oliver Ellsworth, decided not to return to the bench after being sent as an envoy to France. When the nation's capital was moved to Washington, the Supreme Court was not even included in the plans for the new government buildings. Because of this oversight, the Court had to sit in various rooms of the Capitol building until it finally moved into its own building in 1935. Over time, however, the Court established its reputation as a branch of government capable of dispensing justice in a fair and reasonable manner. Although today's conservative Court may not have the admiration of more liberally inclined individuals (just as a more liberal-leaning Court led by Chief Justice Earl Warren frustrated conservatives in the 1950s and 1960s), by and large the Court continues to balance the scales of justice in a way acceptable to most Americans.

ISSUES FOR DEBATE & DISCUSSION

1. **On a few occasions in the last several years, the Supreme Court has looked to the decisions of foreign courts and international human rights laws when deciding cases. Some of these cases involved gay rights, affirmative action, and juveniles and the death penalty. Some jurists, politicians, and other Americans believe that it is inappropriate for our nation's highest court to look to foreign laws and decisions for guidance. This group also asserts that measuring the constitutionality of U.S. policies against the yardstick of foreign practices poses a threat to our national sovereignty. Others argue that we should not ignore the opinions and laws of the rest of our world and that it is vitally important to try to attain a deeper understanding of human rights on a worldwide level. What is your position on this issue?**
2. **Some Americans believe that partisanship should never be a factor in selecting Supreme Court justices, because their decisions have such a far-reaching effect on our society. Rather, Supreme Court nominees should be confirmed by a special Senate committee consisting of senators from both parties. Others claim that this is unnecessary because the ideology of Supreme Court justices is not that important—once on the high court bench, partisan ideology does not factor into the justices' decision making. What is your position on this issue?**

TAKE ACTION

In this chapter, you have read about the role played by the judiciary in our system of government. If you feel strongly about a particular judicial nominee, contact the U.S. senators from your state and voice your opinion. To get a better understanding of court procedures, consider visiting your local county court when a trial is in session (check with the clerk of the court before entering the trial room). If you have an opportunity to participate in a mock trial at your school, consider doing so.

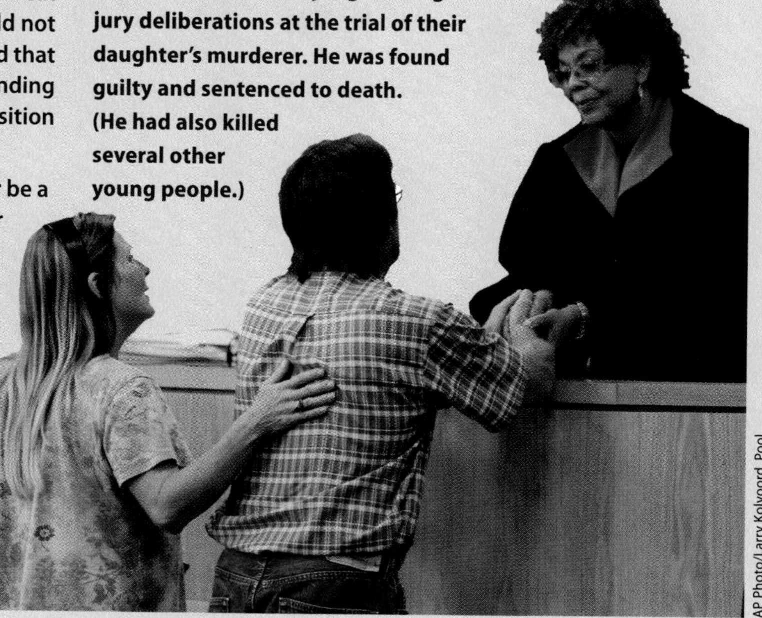

Parents confer with a judge during jury deliberations at the trial of their daughter's murderer. He was found guilty and sentenced to death. (He had also killed several other young people.)

AP Photo/Larry Kolvoord, Pool

POLITICS ON THE WEB

- An excellent Web site for information on the justices of the United States Supreme Court is **www.oyez.org**. This site offers biographies of the justices, links to opinions they have written, and, for justices who have served after 1920, video and audio materials. Oral arguments before the Supreme Court are also posted on this site.
- Another helpful Web site is **www.law.cornell.edu/supct**. This collection of United States Supreme Court cases includes recent Court decisions as well as selected historic decisions rendered by the Court.
- The Supreme Court makes its opinions available online at its official Web site. Go to **www.supremecourtus.gov**
- FindLaw offers a free searchable database of Supreme Court decisions since 1907 at **www.findlaw.com**
- Increasingly, decisions of the state courts are available online. You can search through the texts of state cases that are on the Internet, as well as federal cases, state and federal laws, and the laws of other countries, by accessing WashLaw at **www.washlaw.edu**
- To learn more about the federal court system, go to **www.uscourts.gov**. This is the home page for the federal courts. Among other things, you can follow the path a case takes as it moves through the federal court system.

Online resources for this chapter

This text's Companion Web site, at **www.4ltrpress.cengage.com/govt**, offers links to numerous resources that you can use to learn more about the topics covered in this chapter.

Domestic Policy

GOVT 15

LEARNING OBJECTIVES

LO1 Explain what domestic policy is and summarize the steps in the policymaking process.

LO2 Discuss the issue of health-care funding and recent proposals for universal health insurance.

LO3 Summarize the issues of energy independence, global warming, and cap-and-trade legislation.

LO4 Describe the two major areas of economic policymaking.

AMERICA AT ODDS

Is Cap-and-Trade a Helpful Way to Address Global Warming?

A large majority of climatologists believe that the major source of observed global warming is increased greenhouse gases. The most important of these is carbon dioxide (CO_2). Just about every production activity involves CO_2 emissions. So does breathing. The reason carbon dioxide is called a greenhouse gas is because when it is released into the atmosphere, it traps the sun's heat and slows its release into outer space.

One way to reduce CO_2 emissions would be for the federal government to establish a national target, or a "cap," for those emissions. Thereafter, major emitters, such as power plants and manufacturers, would need permits to engage in production. These permits could be bought and sold on an open market. That is where the "trade" part of cap-and-trade comes in. Over time, the federal government would reduce the target, or cap. This would force a reduction in overall CO_2 emissions.

For example, a U.S. House committee has reported a bill out to the floor of the House that calls for reducing overall national carbon dioxide emissions by 17 percent by 2020. Leaving aside the heated debate over whether global warming is as much of a problem as many contend, the question remains whether cap-and-trade is the right way to reduce greenhouse gases.

Cap-and-Trade Is Just a Disguised Way to Raise Taxes

Critics of proposed cap-and-trade legislation point out that, over time, an increasingly large share of permits would be offered for sale by the federal government. Therefore, this program would sharply increase government revenues. Indeed, at one point the Obama administration hoped to use the revenues from cap-and-trade to fund its universal health-insurance program. This new tax would be passed on to users of electricity, cars, and just about anything else that generates CO_2 during its production. The last thing we need is a new tax, especially one on productive activities. Also, cap-and-trade would force energy-intensive manufacturing companies to rely on more expensive energy sources. The increased costs would be passed on to consumers and could be a major drag on the economy indefinitely.

And what about the rest of the world? A major reduction in U.S. emissions of greenhouse gases will make little difference if developing countries, such as China and India, do not follow suit. Unless these countries join in this effort in a big way, the United States will be imposing higher costs on its own consumers for just about everything with no resulting benefits.

Cap-and-Trade Allows the Market to Work

Global warming is a real problem. Right now, private industry can emit as much CO_2 as it wants without paying for it. In other words, manufacturing and energy-generation industries impose a cost on the rest of society. The rest of us suffer as a result.

The cap-and-trade system puts a limit on overall emissions, and emitters have to pay a price for emitting. Under the cap-and-trade system, the market will prevail, with all the resulting efficiency that we can expect from relying on the market mechanism. Industries that can earn the most by using the permits will pay the highest prices for them. We know that cap-and-trade works because we have already used it for sulfur dioxide emissions from coal-burning power plants in the Midwest. The program started in 1990 to address acid rain problems in eastern states. No one talks about acid rain anymore because the sulfur dioxide cap-and-trade program was such a success. The same will be true for a cap-and-trade program for CO_2 emissions.

WHERE DO YOU STAND?

1. **An alternative to cap-and-trade is a simple carbon tax applied to everything, which varies according to the amount of CO_2 emitted during its production. Would such a tax be more efficient than a cap-and-trade system?**
2. **CO_2 is emitted by a much larger range of processes than sulfur dioxide. Basically, any time you burn carbon, you get CO_2. As a result, how might a CO_2 cap-and-trade program differ from the program implemented to control sulfur dioxide?**

EXPLORE THIS ISSUE ONLINE

- **Emissions trading now has its own trade association. See the site of the International Emissions Trading Association at www.ieta.org.**
- **The Institute for Energy Research opposes cap-and-trade and other measures that might interfere with existing energy markets. See its site at www.instituteforenergyresearch.org.**
- **Not all opponents of cap-and-trade are on the political right. For left-of-center objections, see articles collected by a British social justice organization at www.thecornerhouse.org.uk/summary.shtml?x=561412.**

Introduction

Whether cap-and-trade legislation is a solution to our global warming is just one of the issues that confront our nation's policymakers today. How are questions of national importance, such as this one, decided? Who are the major participants in the decision-making process?

To learn the answers to these questions, we need to delve into the politics of policymaking. Policy, or public policy, can be defined as a plan or course of action taken by the government to respond to a political issue or to enhance the social or political well-being of society. Public policy is the end result of the policymaking process, which will be described shortly. **Domestic policy,** in contrast to foreign policy, consists of public policy concerning issues *within* a national unit.

In this chapter, after discussing how policy is made through the policymaking process, we look at several aspects of domestic policy, including health-care policy, energy policy, and economic policy. We focus on these policy areas because they are the Obama administration's top priorities. An additional priority for the administration is immigration reform. Administration officials and leaders in Congress, however, have stated that this subject cannot be addressed until 2010 at the earliest. We consider immigration reform in this chapter's *Join the Debate* feature on the following page.

These New Jersey seniors express their opinions about health-care reform outside a town hall meeting in the city of Montclair. Why might seniors have different opinions about this important subject than, say, much younger Americans?

Mark Peterson/Redux

Bear in mind that although the focus here is on policy and policymaking at the national level, state and local governments also engage in policymaking and establish policies to achieve goals relating to activities within their boundaries.

LO1 The Policymaking Process

A new law does not appear out of nowhere. First, the problem addressed by the new law has to become part of the political agenda—that is, the problem must be defined as a political issue to be resolved by government action. Furthermore, once the issue gets on the political agenda, proposed solutions to the problem have to be formulated and then adopted. Issue identification and agenda setting, policy formulation, and policy adoption are all parts of the **policymaking process.** The process does not end there, however. Once the law is passed, it has to be implemented and then evaluated.

Each phase of the policymaking process involves interactions among various individuals and groups. The president and members of Congress are obviously important participants in the process. Remember from Chapter 6 that interest groups also play a key role. Groups that may be affected adversely by a new policy will try to convince Congress not to adopt the policy. Groups that will benefit from the policy will exert whatever influence they can on Congress to do the opposite. Congressional committees and subcommittees may investigate the problem to be addressed by the policy and, in so doing, solicit input from members of various groups or industries.

The participants in policymaking and the nature of the debates involved depend on the particular policy being proposed, formed, or implemented. Whatever the policy, however, debate over its pros and cons occurs during each stage of the policymaking process. Additionally, making policy

domestic policy Public policy concerning issues within a national unit, such as national policy concerning health care or the economy.

policymaking process The procedures involved in getting an issue on the political agenda; formulating, adopting, and implementing a policy with regard to the issue; and then evaluating the results of the policy.

JOIN THE DEBATE

Should Unauthorized Immigrants Be Given a Path to Citizenship?

The United States is a land of immigrants. Apart from Native Americans, all of us are either current immigrants or the descendants of immigrants. Yet immigration remains one of the most divisive issues facing Americans and their elected representatives today.

Congress has reacted in various ways to the issue of illegal immigration. At one time, it established an amnesty program to allow unauthorized immigrants who had been working in the United States for five years to obtain legal residency. More recently, it voted in favor of a large, secure fence on the U.S.-Mexican border to keep illegal immigrants out. Federal legislation proposed in 2007 included a complicated system that would allow current illegal immigrants to become legal, but the measure failed in the Senate. President Barack Obama's immigration proposal requires undocumented immigrants who do not otherwise violate the law to pay a fine, learn English, and go to the back of the line for the opportunity to become citizens. Obama also favors crackdowns on employers who hire illegal immigrants and steps to make legal immigration easier.

Today, there are about 12 million illegal immigrants living and working in this country. Should they be given a path to citizenship?

How Can Any American Be against Immigration?

Some find the "close the door after me" mentality to be very un-American. Just remember, standards of living in the United States have been improving for decades not in spite of immigration but because of it. It's true that an unauthorized immigrant is not playing by the rules. But that is because the rules are so difficult to follow. We should make it easier for current unauthorized immigrants to become legal. The vast majority of illegal immigrants are working and adding to this nation's well-being. The net taxpayer cost per immigrant is negative. They are normally not eligible to receive welfare benefits. They come here to work, not to receive government handouts.

A Path to Citizenship Sends the Wrong Signals

Illegal immigrants have broken the law. If we give them a path to citizenship or even to legal status, we are sending the wrong signals to the rest of the world. As a result, we will end up with even more illegal immigrants, all of them hoping to find a path to citizenship one day.

Most unauthorized immigrants have few job skills. Immigrants without high school diplomas now head about a third of immigrant households. Certainly, this country can use more high-skilled immigrants, those with scientific degrees and PhDs. Low-skilled immigrants, in contrast, simply take jobs away from Americans. To send the right signals to the rest of the world, we should also crack down on employers who hire illegal immigrants. These employers are making a real contribution to the problem. Then there is the issue of security. We have to protect our borders if we are to prevent terrorists from entering the United States.

For Critical Analysis ***How might we rationalize the inconsistency between our being a country of immigrants and wanting to keep out new ones?***

decisions inevitably involves *trade-offs,* in which policymakers must sacrifice one goal to achieve another because of budget constraints.

Issue Identification and Agenda Setting

agenda setting Getting an issue on the political agenda to be addressed by Congress; part of the first stage of the policymaking process.

If no one recognizes a problem, then no matter how important the problem may be, politically it does not yet really exist. Thus, *issue identification* is part of the first stage of the policymaking process. Some group—whether it be the media, the public, politicians, or even foreign commentators—must identify a problem that can be solved politically. The second part of this stage of the policymaking process involves getting the issue on the political agenda to be addressed by Congress. This is called **agenda setting,** or agenda building.

A problem in society can be identified as an issue and included on the political agenda in a number of different ways. An event or series of events may lead to a call for action. For example, the failure of a major bank may lead to the conclusion that the financial industry is in trouble and that the government should take action to rectify the problem. Dramatic increases in health-care costs may cause the media or other groups to consider health care a priority that should be on the national political agenda. Sometimes, the social or economic effects of a national calamity, such as the Great Depression of the 1930s or the terrorist attacks of September 11, 2001, create a pressing need for government action.

Policy Formulation and Adoption

The second stage in the policymaking process involves the formulation and adoption of specific plans for achieving a particular goal, such as health-care reform. The president, members of Congress, administrative agencies, and interest group leaders typically are the key participants in developing proposed legislation. Remember from Chapter 13 that iron triangles—alliances consisting of congressional committee members, interest group leaders, and bureaucrats in administrative agencies—work together in forming mutually beneficial policies. To a certain extent, the courts also establish policies when they interpret statutes passed by legislative bodies or make decisions concerning disputes not yet addressed by any law, such as disputes involving new technology.

Note that some issues may get on the political agenda but never proceed beyond that stage of the policymaking process. Usually, this happens when it is impossible to achieve a consensus over what policy should be adopted.

Policy Implementation

Because of our federal system, the implementation of national policies necessarily requires the cooperation of the federal government and the various state and local governments. A case in point is the 1996 Welfare Reform Act. The act required the states to develop plans for implementing the new welfare policy within their borders. The federal government, though, retained some authority over the welfare system by providing that state welfare plans had to be certified, or approved, by the federal government. In addition, successful implementation usually requires the support of groups outside the government. For example, the work requirements of the Welfare Reform Act meant that the business sector would also play a key role in the policy's implementation.

Policy implementation also involves agencies in the executive branch (see Chapter 13). Once Congress establishes a policy by enacting legislation, the executive branch, through its agencies, enforces the new policy. Furthermore, the courts are involved in policy implementation, because the legislation and administrative regulations enunciating the new policy must be interpreted and applied to specific situations by the courts.

Policy Evaluation

The final stage of policymaking involves evaluating the success of a policy during and following its implementation. Once a policy has been implemented, groups both inside and outside the government evaluate the policy. Congress may hold hearings to obtain feedback from different groups on how a statute or regulation has affected those groups. Scholars and scientists may conduct studies to determine whether a particular law, such as an environmental law designed to reduce air pollution, has actually achieved the desired result—less air pollution. Sometimes, feedback obtained in these or other ways indicates that a policy has failed, and a new policymaking process may be undertaken to modify the policy or create a more effective one.

> **"THE MORAL TEST OF GOVERNMENT** is how it treats those who are in the dawn of life, the children; those who are in the twilight of life, the elderly; and those who are in the shadows of life, the sick, the needy, and the handicapped."
>
> ~ HUBERT H. HUMPHREY ~
> SENATOR FROM MINNESOTA
> 1971–1978

Policymaking versus Special Interests

The policymaking steps just discussed seem straightforward, but they are not. Every bill that passes through Congress is a compromise. Every bill that passes through Congress is also an opportunity for individual members of Congress to help constituents, particularly those who were kind enough to contribute financially to the members' reelection campaigns.

Consider the Emergency Economic Stabilization Act of 2008, a $700 billion financial rescue plan that the Treasury Department urgently demanded on

September 19, 2008. After the U.S. House defeated the initial "clean" version of the bailout bill, the Senate drafted a second version. This second version included a landmark health-care provision requiring that insurance companies provide coverage for mental health treatment equivalent to that provided for the treatment of physical illnesses. The bill also contained almost $14 billion in tax-break extensions for businesses. Special provisions benefited rural schools, film and television producers, makers of toy wooden arrows, victims of the 1989 *Exxon Valdez* oil spill in Alaska, rum distillers in the Virgin Islands and Puerto Rico, auto racetracks, and wool researchers. The second bill passed the House on October 3. Clearly, policymaking, particularly on the economic front, remains a complicated process.

LO2 *Health-Care Policy*

There is no question as to why health-care policy is one of the most important issues facing the country. The federal government already pays the health-care costs of more than 100 million Americans. Even before President Barack Obama took office, the government was picking up the tab for more than 45 percent of the nation's health-care costs. Private insurance was responsible for about a third of all health-care payments, and the rest was met either by patients themselves or by charity. Paying for health-care expenses, in other words, was already a major federal responsibility, and questions about how the government should carry out that function in the future were unavoidable.

Our system for funding health care suffers from two major problems. One is that health care is expensive. About 16 percent of national spending in the United States goes to health care, compared with 10 percent in Canada, 9 percent in Sweden, and 8 percent in Japan. Also, more than 47 million Americans—about 16 percent of the population have no health-care insurance. Lack of coverage means that people may neglect preventive care, put off seeing a physician until it is too late, or be forced into bankruptcy due to large medical bills. One study has estimated that twenty thousand people each year die prematurely because they lack health insurance.[1] (Others dispute these findings.) All other economically advanced nations provide health insurance to everyone, typically through a government program similar to Social Security or Medicare in the United States.

Medicare A federal government program that pays for health-care insurance for Americans aged sixty-five years or over.

Medicaid A joint federal-state program that pays for health-care services for low-income persons.

State Children's Health Insurance Program (SCHIP) A joint federal-state program that provides health-care insurance for low-income children.

Before describing various proposals to deal with high costs and coverage, let's first look at the programs that are already in place. The most important of these is **Medicare,** which provides health-care insurance to Americans aged sixty-five or over, and **Medicaid,** which funds health-care coverage for the poor.

Medicaid and Medicare

The federal government pays for health care in a variety of ways. Like many major employers, it buys health-care insurance for its employees. In addition, members of the armed forces, veterans, and Native Americans receive medical services provided directly by the government. Most federal spending on health care, however, is accounted for by Medicare and Medicaid. Both are costly, and each, in its own way, poses a serious financial problem to the government.

MEDICAID A joint federal-state program, Medicaid provides health-care subsidies to low-income persons. The federal government provides about 60 percent of the Medicaid budget, and the states provide the rest. More than 60 million people are in the program, which currently costs all levels of government well over $300 billion per year. The cost of Medicaid has doubled in the last decade, and this has put a considerable strain on the budgets of many states. About 17 percent of the average state general fund budget now goes to Medicaid. Recent cost-containment measures have slowed the growth of Medicaid spending, however. Another program, the **State Children's Health Insurance Program (SCHIP),** covers children in families with incomes that are modest but too high to qualify for Medicaid.

The Great Recession put a considerable strain on the states' ability to pick up their share of Medicaid payments. The Obama administration's 2009 $787 billion stimulus package, therefore, included $87 billion to reduce temporarily the Medicaid burden on the states. Congressional Democrats also substantially increased the size of SCHIP within weeks of Obama's inauguration.

MEDICARE Medicare is the federal government's health-care program for persons over the age of sixty-five. Medicare is now the government's second-largest domestic spending program, after Social Security. In 1970, Medicare accounted for only 0.7 percent of total annual U.S. national income (gross domestic product, or GDP). It currently accounts for about 3.2 percent of GDP, and costs are expected to soar as millions of "baby boomers" retire over the next two decades. By 2030, the sixty-five-and-older population is expected to double. Further, technological developments in health care and the advancement of medical science are driving medical costs up every year. There are simply more things that medical science can do to keep people alive—and Americans naturally want to take advantage of these services. In the long run, therefore, Medicare is expected to put an enormous amount of pressure on the federal budget. Large tax increases to pay for this spending appear all too likely.

This senior lives in a nursing home in North Smithfield, Rhode Island. Most of her living and medical expenses are paid for by government. Rhode Island is one of many states that are facing record Medicaid expenses. Rhode Island may allow for elders to stay home with care instead of moving into an expensive assisted care facility.

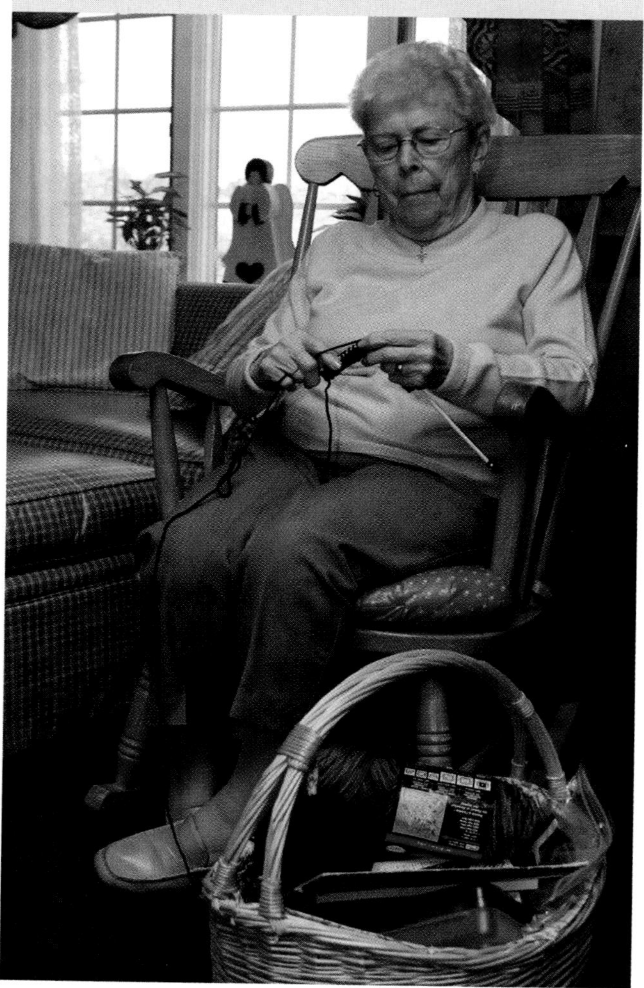

AP Photo/Stew Milne

Republican Health-Care Proposals: Let the Market Rule

During the 2008 presidential campaigns, both the Republican, John McCain, and the Democrat, Barack Obama, offered detailed programs for reforming the way we pay for health care. McCain's proposals can stand as a representative example of Republican health-care thinking. His program focused on cost containment, accomplished by relying on free-market mechanisms. The plan would grant any eligible family a $5,000 income tax break to pay for private health-care insurance. This break would be funded in part by taxing health-care insurance provided by employers (which is currently tax-free). Citizens would be permitted to buy from other states when shopping for private insurance, thus maximizing competition among plans. The only provision for increased coverage would be a federal subsidy to states that create insurance pools to cover the otherwise uninsurable.

McCain believed that competition among health-care plans would drive down costs and improve quality. Some people, however, argue that health care is not something that responds well to free-market competition. It can be hard to tell what you are really getting when you buy health insurance—plans are extremely complicated. Failure to obtain enough heath care, furthermore, can kill you. That's not a problem you face when shopping for a wide-screen television. Opponents of McCain's plan also had more specific criticisms. For example, employer-provided health insurance for a family costs about $12,000 on average, not $5,000.

Probably the biggest problem with the McCain proposal, in the minds of many people, was the plan to fund the $5,000 income tax break by taxing existing employer-provided insurance benefits. Abolishing the tax exemption of these benefits would make existing health-insurance plans more expensive to employers, leading many of them to drop the benefits. Employees would need to purchase individual coverage directly from insurance companies. To be sure, however, many supporters of the McCain plan saw this effect as desirable. Workers could change employers more easily if their health insurance was not tied to their existing jobs.

The Democrats Propose Universal Coverage

As noted earlier, the United States is the only economically advanced nation that does not provide universal health-insurance coverage to its citizens. Universal insurance is not a new idea. German chancellor Otto von Bismarck implemented the first such plan in Germany in 1883. (A staunch conservative, Bismarck sought to use social legislation to "steal the thunder" of the German socialists, who were quite popular.) Democratic president Bill Clinton (1993–2001) and then-First Lady Hillary Clinton made a serious push for a universal plan during Clinton's first term, but the project failed.

THE HOUSE OF REPRESENTATIVES PLAN

During the 2008 presidential elections, all Democratic candidates proposed universal health-insurance plans. The bills that were eventually debated in Congress, however, were only loosely based on the candidates' proposals. Three committees in the House of Representatives reported out similar proposals in July 2009. The bills assumed that employer-provided health insurance would continue to be a major part of the system. In fact, large employers who did not offer a plan would be required to pay a sizable penalty, that would be used to fund the overall system. Medicaid would be expanded. A new health-insurance marketplace, the Health Insurance Exchange, would allow individuals and small employers to shop for plans. The most controversial aspect of the proposed marketplace was that one of the competitors would be a government-sponsored insurance plan, known as the **public option.**

Insurance companies would not be allowed to deny anyone coverage. Most individuals would be required to obtain coverage or pay a penalty. Those with low-to-middle incomes would receive help in paying their premiums. The subsidy would dwindle in amount as income rose and would vanish for families making more than $88,000 a year. The requirement that all adults buy insurance, known as the **individual mandate,** contradicted an Obama campaign pledge, although it was part of then-candidate Hillary Clinton's platform.

To pay for the increased coverage, households with incomes in excess of $350,000 and individuals earning more than $280,000 would have to pay a health-care surcharge on their income taxes. The bill also sought to raise revenue by limiting increases in Medicare expenses in coming years. The **Congressional Budget Office (CBO),** an agency set up by Congress to evaluate the impact of proposed measures on the federal budget, estimated that the total cost of the measure over a ten-year period would be about a trillion dollars, or $100 billion per year. The proposed tax and revenue increases would cover much of the expense, but not all of it.

public option In the context of health-care reform, a government-sponsored health-care insurance program that would compete with private insurance companies.

individual mandate In the context of health-care reform, a requirement that all persons obtain health-care insurance from one source or another. Those failing to do so would pay a penalty.

Congressional Budget Office (CBO) An agency established by Congress to evaluate the impact of proposed legislation on the federal budget.

THE SENATE PLAN The Senate committee responsible for health care also reported out a bill in July that was quite similar to the House plan. Most attention, however, was focused on the Senate Finance Committee, chaired by Max Baucus of Montana. Many observers believed that a Finance Committee bill would have the best chance of passing the Senate and ultimately becoming law. The Baucus bill, as it came to be called, did not clear the committee until October. It also resembled the House bill in many respects, but it contained no public option. It also left out the income tax surcharge on the wealthy and sought instead to raise revenue through a complicated scheme that included taxes on insurance companies and on the most expensive employer-provided plans. The CBO priced this plan at $83 billion per year, with no increase in the federal deficit.

The Health-Care Debate

Much of the nation's political energy in 2009 was spent on the debate over the Democrats' health-care proposals. By then, the issue of an individual mandate, which had divided Democrats during the 2008 election campaigns, had been resolved. The individual mandate had been controversial because it would require all Americans to have health insurance whether they wanted it or not.

This requirement would impose a burden on some people, including those young, healthy persons who choose not to buy insurance—gambling, usually with success, that they will not be injured or become sick. Eventually, though, even moderate Democrats in Congress came to realize that without the individual mandate, the mathematics of a reform proposal would not work out. The premiums of those young, healthy Americans would be needed to a make a universal insurance system a reality.

THE PUBLIC OPTION Opposition to a government-backed insurance program that would compete with private insurers—the public option—was central to Republican hostility toward the Democratic proposals, and it divided the Democrats as well. A caucus of middle-of-the-road Democrats in the House, known as the **Blue Dog Coalition,** opposed the public option. A half-dozen centrist Democrats in the Senate were opposed to it as well.

Republicans and Democrats who rejected the public option were motivated, to a considerable degree, by opposition to the expansion of governmental power. As a matter of principle, they did not believe that the federal government should take over a function that could be managed by private enterprise. Popular opposition to the public option was less of a factor. Somewhat surprisingly, opinion polls reported more support among the general public for the public option than for health-care reform in general. On the broader issue, opinion was evenly split.

POSSIBLE CONSEQUENCES OF A PUBLIC OPTION Advocates of the public option contended that it would provide needed competition for private plans. Opponents argued that it could lead, in time, to the destruction of private-sector health insurance and a nearly complete federal takeover. Under the resulting government monopoly, health-care financing in the United States would resemble systems in Canada, France, and Germany. In these nations, the central government is responsible for providing basic health-care insurance coverage to everyone through a plan called **national health insurance.** Such programs are also called **single-payer plans,** because a single entity—the national government—issues the insurance. Many American liberals admire such systems and were quite willing to let a government insurance program drive private insurers out of the market. This was exactly the result that conservatives feared.

CONSERVATIVE OUTRAGE The Obama administration enjoyed considerable success in winning support for reform from interests that had opposed universal systems in the past. For the first time, the American Medical Association was on board. Pharmaceutical companies gave general support to the idea of reform. Even private insurance companies appeared willing to accept a universal program—provided that the public option was killed and benefit plans were not taxed. The private insurers, after all, would gain millions of new customers. The greater part of the opposition came not from interest groups but from the conservative movement and from the Republican Party.

Over the course of 2009, conservative hostility to the various Democratic plans grew in strength and fervor. During the August recess, when members of Congress returned to their districts to take the public's temperature, a number of them were shouted down by angry crowds at "town hall" meetings. Rhetoric on talk radio and on the Web, which is always exaggerated, reached new extremes. The motivations of the protesters went beyond hostility to Democratic health-care reform plans—their anger had broader sources. Most were upset over what they saw as the growing power of government in general. First, the Bush administration bailed out the banks. Then, Obama drastically increased spending to combat the recession. The government even took over General Motors. Many demonstrators believed that health-care reform was only one of several steps toward a vast federal leviathan that would crush individual freedoms.

In time, a second reason emerged for opposing reform—Democratic plans to curb increases in Medicare spending. Many people, especially older persons receiving Medicare, were afraid that their benefits would be cut. Democratic claims that large sums could be saved without cuts were met with disbelief. Indeed, many nonideological experts were also skeptical of the planned Medicare cuts. These observers, however, were not concerned that benefits would be reduced. Rather, they suspected

Blue Dog Coalition A caucus that unites most of the moderate-to-conservative Democrats in the House of Representatives.

national health insurance A program, found in many of the world's economically advanced nations, under which the central government provides basic health-care insurance coverage to everyone in the country. Some wealthy nations, such as the Netherlands and Switzerland, provide universal coverage through private insurance companies instead.

single-payer plan A system in which a single entity—usually the national government—has the sole responsibility for issuing health-care insurance policies.

that cuts in Medicare spending would prove to be politically impossible and that the hoped-for savings would simply evaporate.

LO3 *Energy Policy*

As a priority for the Obama administration, energy policy was second only to health-care policy. Energy policy is important because of two problems: (1) our reliance on imported oil and (2) global warming.

The Problem of Imported Oil

Our nation imports about three-fifths of its petroleum supply. Oil imports are a potential problem largely because many of the nations that export oil are not particularly friendly to the United States. Some, such as Iran, are outright adversaries. Other oil exporters that could pose difficulties include Iraq, Libya, Russia, and Venezuela. Even Saudi Arabia, nominally a U.S. friend, is something of a question mark. Most of the terrorists who attacked the United States on 9/11 were Saudis, and many Saudis have anti-Western attitudes. A change of regime in Saudi Arabia could spell big trouble. Some exporters, including Iraq, Nigeria, and Venezuela, have recently experienced drops in oil production due to internal disturbances. Fortunately for the United States, half of our oil imports come from Canada and Mexico, stable and friendly neighbors to the north and south. Venezuela, however, is also a major American supplier. In addition, many of our European and Asian allies are dependent on imports from questionable regimes.

THE PRICE OF OIL Until fairly recently, the price of oil was low, and the U.S. government was under little pressure to address our dependence on imports. In 1998, the price per barrel fell below $12. In July 2008, however, on the eve of the collapse of the Lehman Brothers investment bank, the price of oil spiked to more than $125 a barrel, forcing U.S. gasoline prices above $4 per gallon. Thereafter, oil prices fell dramatically when demand collapsed due to the global economic panic. Experts believe, however, that oil prices will rise again as economic activity resumes.

Corporate Average Fuel Economy (CAFE) standards A set of federal standards under which each manufacturer must meet a miles-per-gallon benchmark averaged across all cars or trucks that it sells.

U.S. ENERGY POLICIES The federal government responded to an earlier spurt in oil prices, in the 1970s, by imposing fuel-mileage standards on cars and trucks sold in this country. Under the **Corporate Average Fuel Economy (CAFE) standards,** each manufacturer had to meet a miles-per-gallon benchmark, which was averaged across all cars and trucks that it sold. Under the rules, trucks were allowed to consume more fuel. One unintended result was that when oil prices dropped in the 1980s, Americans began turning away from automobiles and toward pickups and SUVs, which were considered trucks under the standards.

Many economists have long argued that the best way to encourage fuel economy would be to impose a new federal tax on gasoline and diesel fuel, perhaps fifty cents per gallon. The resulting revenues could be used to lower other taxes. European nations have much higher taxes on fuel than the United States, and as a result, Europeans tend to favor smaller, more fuel-efficient vehicles. Very few American politicians have been willing to endorse such a concept, however. They rightly judged that it would be political poison.

> "NATURE PROVIDES A FREE LUNCH but only if we control our appetites."
>
> ~ WILLIAM DOYLE RUCKELSHAUS ~ FIRST HEAD OF THE ENVIRONMENTAL PROTECTION AGENCY 1970–1973

The steep rise in oil prices in 2007 and 2008, plus the election of a Democratic Congress and president, meant that measures to restrain U.S. fuel consumption were on the agenda again. In 2009, President Obama issued higher fuel-efficiency standards for cars and trucks. By 2016, the standards will be thirty-nine miles per gallon for cars and thirty miles per gallon for light trucks. The standards will begin to take effect in 2010. Because of this government mandate, along with expected high fuel prices, more fuel-efficient vehicles will almost certainly be part of America's future. Many of the new vehicles will run at least partially on electric power.

Global Warming

Observations collected by agencies such as the National Aeronautics and Space Administration (NASA) suggest that during the last century, average global temperatures

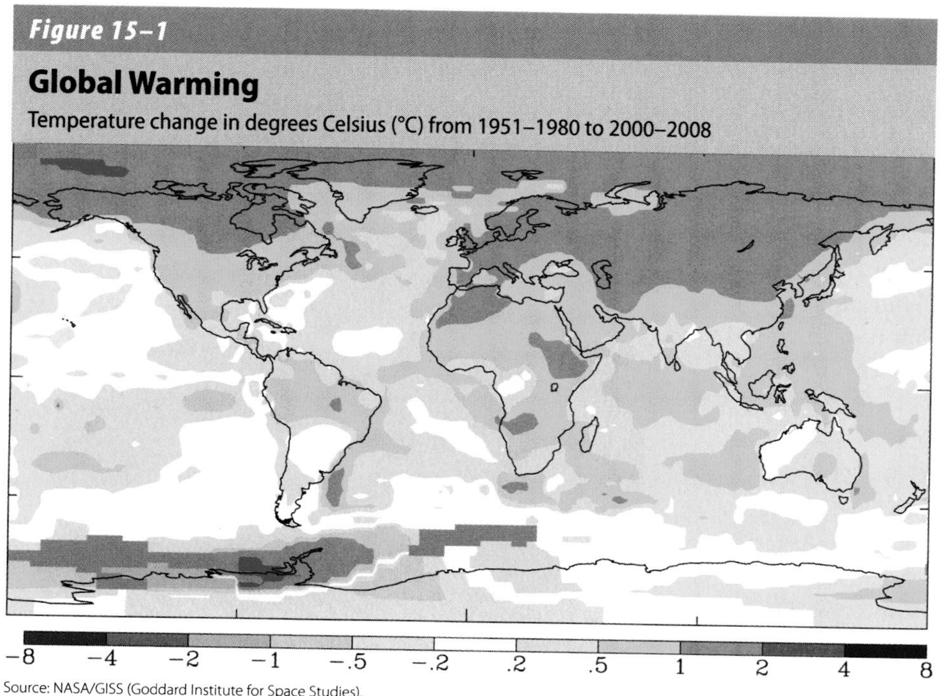

Figure 15–1

Global Warming

Temperature change in degrees Celsius (°C) from 1951–1980 to 2000–2008

Source: NASA/GISS (Goddard Institute for Space Studies).

increased by about 0.74 degrees Celsius (1.33 degrees Fahrenheit). Figure 15–1 above illustrates this phenomenon. Most climatologists believe that this **global warming** is the result of human activities, especially the release of **greenhouse gases** into the atmosphere. A United Nations body, the Intergovernmental Panel on Climate Change (IPCC), estimates that during the twenty-first century, global temperatures will probably rise an additional 1.1 to 6.4 degrees Celsius (2.0 to 11.5 degrees Fahrenheit). Warming may continue in subsequent centuries.

The predicted outcomes of global warming vary depending on the climate models on which they are based. If the oceans grow warmer, seawater will expand and polar ice will melt. These two developments will cause sea levels to rise, possibly drowning some coastal areas. Rainfall patterns are expected to change, turning some areas into desert but allowing agriculture to expand elsewhere. Other likely effects include increases in extreme weather and the extinction of some plants and animals.

THE GLOBAL WARMING DEBATE Few scientists actively working on climate issues dispute the consensus view of global warming. Those who dispute the consensus argue that any observed warming is due largely to natural causes and may not continue into the future. Although skepticism is rare (but growing) among relevant scientists, however, it is extremely common in the broader community. A Gallup poll in 2009 revealed that only 49 percent of those with an opinion believed that global warming is the result of human activities. Furthermore, attitudes toward global warming have become highly politicized. Some commentators on the political right contend that global warming is a giant liberal hoax designed to clear the way for increased government control of the economy and society. At the same time, many on the political left believe that the right-wing refusal to accept the existence of global warming threatens the very future of the human race. Members of Congress are influenced by these attitudes even if they do not necessarily share them, and as a result, congressional Republicans and Democrats have almost no common ground on questions of how global warming might be reduced or its effects mitigated.

RENEWABLE ENERGY Not all methods of supplying the economy with energy depend on burning carbon and thus releasing greenhouse gases into the environment. For example, hydroelectric energy, generated by water flowing through dams, is a widely used technology that employs no coal, natural gas, oil, or other fossil fuels. Energy from such technologies is referred to as **renewable energy,** because it does not rely on extracted resources, such as oil and coal, that can run out. Obviously, the use of renewable energy has many benefits. For one thing, it can be an effective method of reducing global warming. The problem is that most existing renewable technologies, such as solar power cells, are expensive. Hydropower is an exception, but the number of feasible locations for new dams in the United States is small, and dams create their own environmental problems.

global warming An increase in the average temperature of the Earth's surface over the last half century and its projected continuation.

greenhouse gas A gas that, when released into the atmosphere, traps the sun's heat and slows its release into outer space. Carbon dioxide (CO_2) is a major example.

renewable energy Energy from technologies that do not rely on extracted resources, such as oil and coal, that can run out.

One renewable technology that is almost as economical as conventional power sources is wind energy, and both the Bush and Obama administrations have subsidized wind power. Windmills are now under construction in many locations. Of course, even if the price is right, wind power suffers from one obvious problem: the wind does not always blow, so wind cannot provide more than a modest share of the nation's electrical needs. Still, Obama's $787 billion stimulus package set aside billions of dollars that could be used for high-tension lines to transport electricity from rural wind farms to major cities.

CAP-AND-TRADE LEGISLATION The chief Democratic proposal to respond to global warming is the **cap-and-trade** legislation described in the *America at Odds* feature that opened this chapter. The Obama administration hoped to see movement on cap-and-trade legislation as soon as work on health-care legislation was complete. The House of Representatives approved such legislation—the American Clean Energy and Security Act of 2009—in June of that year. The bill is better known as the Waxman-Markey Act, after its authors, Henry Waxman (D., Calif.) and Edward Markey (D., Mass.).

Under the bill, the government would establish a cap for CO_2 emissions. Major emitters would need permits, which they could buy and sell—or trade—on the open market. Over time, the cap would decline, resulting in a reduction in emissions. Initially, most of the permits would be distributed free to heavy emitters, but the free permits would be phased out over ten to fifteen years. Providing for free permits allowed the House Democratic leadership to win the support of energy industry leaders and Democrats representing states heavily reliant on coal-burning power plants. In September 2009, Senate Democrats proposed a similar measure.

cap-and-trade A method of restricting the production of a harmful substance. A cap is set on the volume of production, and permits to produce the substance can then be traded on the open market.

economic policy All actions taken by the national government to smooth out the ups and downs in the nation's overall business activity.

monetary policy Actions taken by the Federal Reserve Board to change the amount of money in circulation so as to affect interest rates, credit markets, the rate of inflation, the rate of economic growth, and the rate of unemployment.

fiscal policy The use of changes in government expenditures and taxes to alter national economic variables.

Photo by Mark Wilson/Getty Images

Henry M. Paulson was secretary of the treasury under President George W. Bush when the financial markets collapsed in September 2008. He argued for and received from Congress $700 billion dollars to "bail out" financial institutions.

LO4 *Economic Policy*

Economic policy consists of all actions taken by the government to smooth out the ups and downs in the nation's overall business activity. National economic policy is solely the responsibility of the national government.

One of the tools used in this process is **monetary policy,** which involves changing the amount of money in circulation so as to affect interest rates, credit markets, the rate of inflation, the rate of economic growth, and the rate of unemployment. You read about monetary policy in the *Our Government's Response to the Economic Crisis* feature in Chapter 2. There, we explained that monetary policy is under the control of the Federal Reserve System, an independent regulatory agency.

The national government also controls **fiscal policy,** which is the use of changes in government expenditures and taxes to alter national economic variables. These variables include the rate of unemployment, the total number of those in the labor market, labor force participation rates, and the rate of economic growth.

In this section, we look briefly at the politics of monetary and fiscal policy, as well as the federal tax system and the issue of deficit spending.

Monetary Policy

The Federal Reserve System (the Fed) was established by Congress as the nation's central banking system in 1913. The Fed is governed by a board of seven governors, including the very powerful chairperson. The president appoints the members of the board of governors, and the Senate must approve the nominations. Members of the board serve for fourteen-year terms. Although the Fed's board of governors acts independently, the Fed has, on occasion, yielded to presidential pressure, and the Fed's chairperson must follow a congressional resolution requiring the chairperson to report monetary targets over each six-month period. Nevertheless, to date, the Fed has remained one of the truly independent sources of economic power in the government.

The Fed and its **Federal Open Market Committee (FOMC)** make decisions about monetary policy several times each year. In theory, monetary policy is relatively straightforward. In periods of recession and high unemployment, we should pursue an **easy-money policy** to stimulate the economy by expanding the rate of growth of the money supply. An easy-money policy supposedly will lead to lower interest rates and induce consumers to spend more and producers to invest more. In periods of rising inflation, the Fed does the reverse: it reduces the rate of growth in the amount of money in circulation. This policy should cause interest rates to rise, thus inducing consumers to spend less and businesses to invest less. In theory, this sounds quite simple; the reality, however, is not simple at all. To give one example, if times are hard enough, people and businesses may not want to borrow even if interest rates go down to zero, and an easy-money policy will have little effect.

An additional difficulty is the length of time it takes for a change in monetary policy to become effective. There is usually a lag of about fourteen months between the time the economy slows down (or speeds up) and the time the economy begins to feel the effects of a policy change. Therefore, by the time a change in policy becomes effective, a different policy may be needed.

Federal Reserve chair Ben Bernanke (left) sits with U.S. Treasury secretary Tim Geithner at a meeting of twenty leading nations (the so-called G-20) in 2009. In the past, the Fed and the U.S. Treasury rarely worked together because the Fed is supposed to be an independent agency.

Photo by Geoff Caddick/WPA Pool/Getty Images

Fiscal Policy

The principle underlying fiscal policy, like the one that underlies monetary policy, is relatively simple: when unemployment is rising and the economy is going into a recession, fiscal policy should stimulate economic activity by increasing government spending, decreasing taxes, or both. When unemployment is decreasing and prices are rising (that is, when we have inflation), fiscal policy should curb economic activity by reducing government spending, increasing taxes, or both. In Chapter 3's *Our Government's Response to the Economic Crisis* feature, we explained that this view of fiscal

Federal Open Market Committee (FOMC) The most important body within the Federal Reserve System. The FOMC decides how monetary policy should be carried out by the Federal Reserve.

easy-money policy A monetary policy that involves stimulating the economy by expanding the rate of growth of the money supply. An easy-money policy supposedly will lead to lower interest rates and induce consumers to spend more and producers to invest more.

British economist John Maynard Keynes developed theories of how to pull the world out of the Great Depression in the 1930s. His work was cited frequently during the Great Recession that started in December 2007.

policy is an outgrowth of the economic theories of the British economist John Maynard Keynes (1883–1946). Keynes's theories were the result of his study of the Great Depression of the 1930s.

Keynesian economics suggests that the forces of supply and demand operate too slowly in recessions, and therefore the government should undertake actions to stimulate the economy during such periods. Keynesian economists maintain that the Great Depression resulted from a serious imbalance in the economy. The public was saving more than usual, and businesses were investing less than usual. According to Keynesian theory, at the beginning of the depression, the government should have filled the gap that was created when businesses began limiting their investments. The government could have done so by increasing government spending or cutting taxes.

Keynesian economics An economic theory proposed by British economist John Maynard Keynes that is typically associated with the use of fiscal policy to alter national economic variables.

action-reaction syndrome For every government action, there will be a reaction by the public. The government then takes a further action to counter the public's reaction—and the cycle begins again.

One of the problems with fiscal policy is that, just as with monetry policy, typically a lag exists between the government's decision to institute fiscal policy and the actual implementation of that policy. It is up to Congress, through its many committees, to enact the legislation necessary to implement fiscal policy.

The Federal Tax System

The government raises money to pay its expenses in two ways: through taxes levied on business and personal income and through borrowing. In 1960, individuals paid 52 percent of total federal tax revenues. By 2009, this proportion was more than 80 percent (adding income taxes and Social Security payments together). The American income tax system is progressive—meaning that as you earn more income, you pay a higher tax rate on the additional income earned. (The 2010 tax rates are shown in Table 15–1 below.) About 40 percent of American families earn so little that they have no income tax liability at all. (For a discussion of the amount of taxes paid by the rich versus other groups in American society, see this chapter's *Perception versus Reality* feature on the facing page.)

THE ACTION-REACTION SYNDROME The Internal Revenue Code consists of thousands of pages, thousands of sections, and thousands of subsections. In other words, our tax system is not simple. Part of the reason for this is that tax policy has always been plagued by the **action-reaction syndrome,** a term describing the following phenomenon: *for every government action, there will be a reaction by the public.* Eventually, the government will react with another action, and the public will follow with further reaction. The ongoing action-reaction cycle is clearly operative in

Table 15–1

Tax Rates for Single Persons and Married Couples (2010)

Single Persons		Married Filing Jointly	
Tax Bracket	Marginal Tax Rate	Tax Bracket	Marginal Tax Rate
$ 0–$ 8,350	10%	$ 0–$ 16,700	10%
$ 8,350–$ 33,950	15%	$ 16,700–$ 67,900	15%
$ 33,950–$ 82,250	25%	$ 67,900–$137,050	25%
$ 82,250–$171,550	28%	$137,050–$208,850	28%
$ 171,550–$372,950	33%	$208,850–$372,950	33%
$372,950 and higher	35%	$352,950 and higher	35%

Source: Internal Revenue Service.

Tax Rate Cuts Allow the Rich to Pay Lower Taxes

As the saying goes, only two things are certain—death and taxes. In recent years, though, different presidents have instituted a number of tax-rate cuts. The last one occurred in 2003 under the administration of George W. Bush.

The Perception

You often hear or read that the Bush tax-rate cuts favored the rich. After all, it's the rich who received the lion's share of the benefits from these tax-rate cuts.

The Reality

First, we must distinguish between tax rates and taxes paid. It is true that the Bush tax cuts dropped the top marginal tax rate from 39.6 percent to 35 percent and that the long-term capital gains tax rate dropped from 20 percent to 15 percent. Also, the rate applied to dividends fell. Therefore, the tax rates on the highest-income individuals did indeed fall after the tax cuts of 2003 were enacted.

At the same time, though, the percentage of taxes paid by the rich went up, not down. Indeed, the share of individual income tax liabilities paid by the top 1 percent of income earners rose steadily from about 1981 to 2000, dropped off a bit from 2000 to 2003, and has risen ever since. According to the nonpartisan Congressional Budget Office, the top 40 percent of income earners in the United States pay 99.1 percent of all income taxes. The top 10 percent pay over 70 percent of all income taxes. At the bottom end of the scale, about 40 percent of this nation's households pay no income taxes at all (though they do pay Social Security contributions). Finally, it is true that the rich have been getting richer in the United States. Nevertheless, their share of income has gone up more slowly than their share of individual tax liabilities.

These data give us some indication of what may happen if President Obama and the Democratic Congress succeed in "taxing the rich" more. During the presidential campaign, Obama recommended an increase in capital gains taxes from 15 percent to 20 percent. He argued for increasing the income tax rate for those making more than $250,000 per year from 35 percent to 39.6 percent. Finally, he proposed applying Social Security taxes without limit on these top earners. What we may see is an ironic reversal in the percentage of taxes (not the tax rate) paid by the rich—it will actually decrease when higher tax rates become reality.

Blog On *Scott Adams, creator of the* Dilbert *comic strip, makes hilarious and fresh observations about all sorts of things on his blog. Taxing the rich is just one of his topics—see* **dilbertblog.typepad.com/the_dilbert_blog/2007/07/how-to-tax-the-.html**. *The blog of Harvard economics professor Greg Mankiw has an interesting discussion at* **gregmankiw.blogspot.com/2006/04/are-rich-paying-enough.html**.

policymaking on taxes.

TAX LOOPHOLES Generally, the action-reaction syndrome means that the higher the tax rate—the action on the part of the government—the greater the public's reaction to that tax rate. Individuals and corporations facing high tax rates will react by making concerted attempts to get Congress to add various loopholes to the tax law that will allow them to reduce their taxable incomes.

Years ago, when Congress imposed very high tax rates on high incomes, it also provided for more loopholes. These loopholes enabled many wealthy individuals to decrease their tax bills significantly. For example, special tax provisions allowed investors in oil and gas wells to reduce their taxable income. Additional loopholes permitted individuals to shift income from one year to the next—which meant that they could postpone the payment of their taxes for one year. Still more loopholes let U.S. citizens form corporations outside the United States in order to avoid some taxes completely.

WILL WE EVER HAVE A TRULY SIMPLE TAX SYSTEM? The Tax Reform Act of 1986 was intended to lower taxes and simplify the tax code—and it did just that for most taxpayers. A few years later, however, large federal deficits forced Congress to choose between cutting spending and raising taxes, and Congress opted to do the latter. Tax increases occurred under the administrations of both George H. W. Bush (1989–1993) and Bill Clinton. In fact, the tax rate for the highest income bracket rose from 28 percent in 1986 to 39.6 percent in 1993. Thus, the effective highest marginal tax rate increased significantly.

Every year, millions of Americans go see their tax preparers to help them figure out the complicated forms that must be submitted to the Internal Revenue Service. The Tax Code consists of about 70,000 pages of less-than-easy-to-understand rules about taxes.

In response to this sharp increase in taxes, those who were affected lobbied Congress to legislate special exceptions and loopholes so that the full impact of the rate increase would not be felt by the wealthiest Americans. As a result, the tax code is more complicated than it was before the 1986 Tax Reform Act.

Some people see the complications of our tax code as a limitation on our economic freedom. For a look at the issue of economic freedom around the world, see this chapter's *The Rest of the World* feature.

While in principle everyone is for a simpler tax code, in practice Congress rarely is able to pass tax-reform legislation. Why? The reason is that those who now benefit from our complicated tax code will not give up their tax breaks without a fight. These groups include homeowners who deduct interest on their mortgages (and therefore the home-building industry as well), charities that receive tax-deductible contributions, and businesses that get tax breaks for research and development. Two other groups also benefit greatly from the current complicated tax code: tax accountants and tax lawyers.

public debt The total amount of money that the national government owes as a result of borrowing; also called the *national debt*.

The Public Debt

When the government spends more than it receives, it has to finance this shortfall. Typically, it borrows. The U.S. Treasury sells IOUs on behalf of the U.S. government. They are called U.S. Treasury bills or bonds. The sale of these bonds to corporations, private individuals, pension plans, foreign governments, foreign companies, and foreign individuals is big business. After all, except for a few years in the late 1990s and early 2000s, federal government expenditures have always exceeded federal government revenues.

Every time there is a federal government deficit, there is an increase in the total accumulated **public debt** (also called the *national debt*), which is defined as the total value of all outstanding federal government borrowing. If the existing public debt is $5 trillion and the government runs a deficit of $100 billion, then at the end of the year the public debt is $5.1 trillion. Table 15–2 shows what has happened to the *net* public debt over time. (The net public debt doesn't count sums that the government owes to itself.)

Table 15–2

The Public Debt

Year	Net Public Debt (Billions of Current Dollars)
1945	235.2
1950	219.0
1960	237.2
1970	284.9
1980	709.3
1990	2,410.1
1995	3,603.4
2000	3,448.6
2001	3,200.3
2002	3,528.7
2003	3,878.4
2004	4,420.8
2005	4,592.0
2006	4,829.0
2007	5,035.1
2008	5,802.7
2009	7,856.6*
2010	9,574.5*

*Estimate.
Source: U.S. Office of Management and Budget.

THE BURDEN OF THE PUBLIC DEBT

We often hear about the burden of the public debt. Some even maintain that the government will eventually go bankrupt. As long as the government can collect taxes to pay interest on its public debt, however, that will never happen. What happens instead is that when Treasury bonds come due, they are simply "rolled over," or refinanced. That is, if a $1 million Treasury bond comes due today and is cashed in, the U.S. Treasury

The Relationship between Economic Freedom and Prosperity

For decades, political scientists and economists, as well as sociologists, have examined the key differences between developing countries and developed countries. For decades, the consensus has been that developed countries must transfer more wealth to less developed countries if these poorer nations are to experience economic growth. International institutions such as the World Bank have argued for investments in infrastructure such as roads, sewers, and the like. Some specialists in development argue that impoverished people in developing countries will remain in permanent misery unless the richer countries transfer more wealth to them.

Freedom Enters the Picture

A small but growing band of development specialists see a different path out of misery for the world's poorest countries. They look at the degree of economic freedom and find some powerful correlations. As it turns out, freedom and prosperity are positively related. The freedom we are referring to here is economic freedom, not necessarily political freedom. (Note that in countries where citizens have obtained economic freedom, political freedom often follows after a number of years.)

The 2008 Index of Economic Freedom ranks countries from Hong Kong (number one) to North Korea (last on the list) in terms of how much economic freedom the citizens really have. It turns out that the freest 20 percent of the world's economies have average per-person incomes that are five times greater than those of the least free 20 percent.

Why Economic Freedom Matters

Development specialists who stress the positive relationship between economic freedom and prosperity offer several reasons why such freedom is so important. They believe that the degree of efficiency with which any society uses its scarce resources to produce goods and services is a key element in the speed of economic growth for all citizens. If there is little economic freedom in a society, entrepreneurs face huge barriers to innovation and to starting new businesses. The result is very little economic growth. This analysis holds true for such economically stagnant countries as Belarus, Burma (Myanmar), Cuba, Iran, North Korea, and Zimbabwe. Despite their oil wealth, Russia and Venezuela appear to be headed in this direction as well.

For Critical Analysis *Why do you think multinational agencies such as the World Bank are in favor of massive foreign aid programs for developing countries?*

These girls attend a rural school in Bangladesh, India. The Nike Foundation for Girls provided each of them with a microloan with which they bought livestock. They continued to go to school while building on their investments. Some went on to create beauty shops and vegetable farms.

Brent Stirton/Getty Images

pays it off with the money it gets from selling another $1 million bond.

The interest on these bonds is paid by federal taxes. Even though much of the interest is being paid to American citizens, the more the federal government borrows to meet these payments, the greater the percentage of its budget that is committed to making interest payments. This reduces the government's ability to supply funds for anything else, including transportation, education, housing programs, and the military.

PUBLIC DEBT EXPLOSION IN 2008 AND 2009 Due to the financial meltdown that began in 2008, Congress passed historic legislation that involved hundreds of billions of dollars in additional spending. Ultimately, the net public debt will rise by well over $1 trillion (that's not a typo). Some believe that it may rise by as much as $2 trillion. Just how much trouble is this explosion in public debt likely to cause? We consider that issue in this chapter's *Our Government's Response to the Economic Crisis* feature on the next page.

Our Government's Response to the Economic Crisis

Red Ink as Far as the Eye Can See

The major response of the federal government to the current economic crisis has been to spend more. Not since the buildup to World War II has the government increased its spending as fast as it did at the end of 2008 and during all of 2009. Because at the same time the economy was shrinking, tax revenues were shrinking, too. The combination of increased spending and lower revenues meant only one thing—a rising federal government deficit. The estimate for 2009 alone was $1.5 trillion. That is well above 10 percent of the entire economy. A similar deficit was predicted for 2010.

Deficit Spending to Fight the Great Recession

As you read in this chapter, in the aftermath of the Great Depression, the English economist John Maynard Keynes argued in favor of deficit spending during bad economic times in order to fill in the gaps in the economy left by reduced private investment. When Obama took office, his advisors recommended this Keynesian solution. Obama's $787 billion stimulus spending bill was meant to get us out of the Great Recession fast. Of course, everyone knew that the deficit would rise, but that was the idea.

As a policy tool, deficit spending did not work as well as planned. The unemployment rate reached about 10 percent in 2009, greater than it had been in decades. For the almost 14 million unemployed people in America at that time, Keynesian policy was not solving their problems.

What Does the Future Hold?

The Obama administration's future spending plans have been, in a word, colossal. It is pretty difficult to take on worldwide climate change, health-care reform, education reform, and infrastructure improvement—the list is long—and not spend a lot of taxpayers' money. The White House predicts a ten-year cumulative deficit of $9 trillion. That is more than all the debt accumulated from 1789 through 2008.

A Trillion Here, a Trillion There—What Does It Matter?

President Obama, members of Congress, and other proponents of deficit spending seem to forget one essential fact: eventually, someone has to pay for it. Men and women on Mars will not. Nor will citizens in other countries. Only Americans can pay for federal government outlays. The market value of the goods and services produced each year in the United States usually is measured by gross domestic product, or GDP. If our government spends, say, 40 percent of the GDP, that means that only 60 percent is left for the private sector to decide how to spend. Large and continuing government deficits are not just numbers. They represent additional resources taken out of the GDP by government.

Some people think that the burden of increased government spending will fall on the shoulders of future generations. But actually, those of us living in the United States today will be among those who are responsible for paying it.

For Critical Analysis *Why can't the government seem to live within its means?*

PERCENTAGE OF THE DEBT HELD BY FOREIGNERS An additional problem with a growing federal debt involves how much non-Americans own. Today, over 55 percent of the U.S. net public debt is owned by foreign individuals, foreign businesses, and foreign central banks. Some worry that these foreigners might not want to keep all of this U.S. debt. If that were ever to happen, their efforts to sell U.S. government bonds might lead to a collapse in the government bond market in this country. The result would be higher interest rates.

AMERICA AT ODDS Domestic Policy

The preamble to the U.S. Constitution stated that one of the goals of the new government was to "promote the general Welfare." Ever since, Americans have been at odds over what the general welfare is and how it should be promoted. Social-welfare policy is one way of contributing to the general welfare. Social-welfare policy consists of all government actions that are undertaken to give assistance to specific groups, such as the aged, the ill, and the poor. Social-welfare policy is often implemented through income redistribution—that is, income is taken from some people through taxation and given to others.

A major source of income redistribution in the United States is the Social Security system. This is essentially a program of compulsory saving financed from payroll taxes levied on both employers and employees. Workers pay for Social Security while working and receive the benefits later, usually after retirement. When the insured worker dies, benefits also accrue to the survivors, including the spouse and children. Special benefits provide for disabled workers.

Social Security is often thought of as a social-insurance program in which workers pay for their own benefits, which are determined by the size of their past contributions. In fact, Social Security is not an insurance program, because people are not guaranteed that the benefits they receive will be in line with the contributions they have made. The benefits are determined by Congress, and there is no guarantee that Congress will continue to legislate the same amount of benefits in the future as it does today. Congress could (and in the future may have to) push for lower levels of benefits instead of much higher ones.

ISSUES FOR DEBATE & DISCUSSION

1. **In essence, Social Security is an intergenerational income transfer that is only vaguely related to past earnings. It transfers income from Americans who work—younger and middle-aged individuals—to older, retired persons who do not work. Are transfers of this type fair? Would it be desirable for the federal government to get out of the business of providing pensions? Or should the redistributive character of Social Security be strengthened? Currently, the Social Security tax is not collected on incomes over a threshold of $106,800. (This cap changes from year to year.) Should it be? Some nations pay a benefit to the family of every young child—a sort of social security for the youngest citizens. Obviously, such a benefit is expensive, an important negative consideration. Could such a benefit yield any positive results? Why or why not?**
2. **A key problem with Social Security is the decline in the number of people who are working relative to the number of people who are retiring. This means that future workers will have to pay more of their income in Social Security taxes to fund the retirement benefits of older, retired workers. Today, Social Security collects about $805 billion each year and spends about $625 billion, yielding a surplus of $180 billion. The federal government can, in effect, spend the surplus on whatever it wants. By 2016, however, the Social Security Trust Fund is expected to be in balance, and the government will have to find the revenue it gained from Social Security somewhere else. After 2016, the trust fund is expected to go "into the red" by hundreds of billions of dollars each year. How would you fix this problem? Should benefits be cut? Should the retirement age be raised? Should taxes go up? All of the above? President George W. Bush proposed partially privatizing the system—investing some of a worker's taxes in the stock market, in the belief that this would increase returns. Given what happened to the stock market in late 2008 and early 2009, it is perhaps fortunate that such a plan was not implemented at the time. But what about today, now that Wall Street has taken its losses?**

TAKE ACTION

In 2007, John and Teresa Heinz Kerry published a book titled *This Moment on Earth: Today's New Environmentalists and Their Vision for the Future.*[2] The book details, in an eminently readable fashion, how numerous individuals and groups have successfully taken action over the years to help protect the health of the environment. If you want to take action to help protect the environment, read through the Kerrys' book. You, like many others, may find the stories of other people's successful actions inspiring. For a list of simple changes you can make in your day-to-day life to preserve energy—from buying energy-efficient appliances to turning off electric lights and electrical appliances when they're not in use—see Appendix B in their book, which is titled "What You Can Do." The appendix also includes a list of environmental groups, with contact information for each group.

POLITICS ON THE WEB

- The national debt is a hot topic at the end of each federal fiscal year (October), as well as when national elections come around. You can find out more about the size of the national debt at **www.treasurydirect.gov/govt/govt.htm**
- The U.S. Census Bureau provides "USA Statistics in Brief" at **www.census.gov/compendia/statab/brief.html**. If you can't find the data you're looking for here, start with the Census Bureau's home page at **www.census.gov**
- If you are interested in reading the *Economic Report of the President*, go to **www.gpoaccess.gov/eop**
- Information on federal departments and agencies can be obtained at **www.usa.gov**

Online resources for this chapter

This text's Companion Web site, at **www.4ltrpress.cengage.com/govt**, offers links to numerous resources that you can use to learn more about the topics covered in this chapter.

Moodboard/Corbis

Foreign Policy

GOVT 16

LEARNING OBJECTIVES

LO1 Discuss how foreign policy is made and identify the key players in this process.

LO2 Summarize the history of American foreign policy through the years.

LO3 Identify the foreign policy challenges presented by terrorism and the consequences of the "Bush doctrine" with respect to Iraq.

LO4 Describe the principal issues dividing the Israelis and the Palestinians and the solutions proposed by the international community.

LO5 Outline some of the actions taken by the United States to curb the threat of nuclear weapons.

LO6 Discuss China's emerging role as a world leader.

AMERICA AT ODDS

Do Russia's Ambitions Mean Trouble?

In August 2008, the Russian army invaded the small neighboring country of Georgia. The invasion was Russia's first use of troops outside of its own borders since the dissolution of the Soviet Union in 1991. Many people around the world drew the obvious conclusion: the "Russian bear" was back—and it posed a threat to world peace.

During the years of the Cold War, which lasted from the late 1940s until the end of the 1980s, the Russian-dominated Soviet Union clearly was a threat to peace. The Soviets had occupied Eastern Europe. By the 1960s, even the Chinese were worried that the Soviets might attack them. In 1985, the Soviets had more personnel in uniform than any other nation. Its nuclear weapons were at least equal to those of the United States. In 1985, the Soviet Union also had a population of 278 million, compared with 238 million in the United States.

The impact of the Soviet breakup on Russian power was almost beyond belief. With the loss of the fourteen other Soviet republics, Russia stood alone. Its population in 1995 was 150 million. Its economy was in a state of collapse. Its army had only 40 percent as many soldiers as the Soviet army had had, and its inventory of main battle tanks had fallen from 51,000 to 19,500.[1] Russia was unable to prevent its former "satellite states" in Eastern Europe from joining NATO, the American-led alliance originally established to defend the West against the Soviets.

Russia today is nowhere near as formidable as the Soviet Union was—but how much of a threat is it, really? Americans who take an interest in foreign affairs are at odds over this issue.

A Stronger Russia Is Bad News

Those who believe that Russia poses a substantial threat to world peace point to its attack on Georgia, threats made against Ukraine, and the cyberwar it recently launched against the tiny nation of Estonia. Furthermore, Russia is regaining the economic power needed to support a large military. Its economy experienced a substantial recovery during the presidency of Vladimir Putin (2000–2008). Naturally, Putin was popular, and his popularity was not damaged by the way he undermined Russia's democratic institutions.

Russia is the world's largest exporter of natural gas and the second-largest oil exporter. It is Europe's biggest supplier of oil and natural gas, currently providing 33 percent of Europe's oil imports and 38 percent of its natural gas. Ominously, Russia has repeatedly used its energy exports for political purposes. It has temporarily cut off gas supplies to Belarus, the Czech Republic, Georgia, Lithuania, and Ukraine.

Russia's Future as a Great Power Looks Grim

Those who are less worried about the return of the Russian bear point out several factors that may undermine its future as a world power. In many countries, oil wealth has led to gross corruption and inefficiency, and this may be happening in Russia. The greatest threat to Russia's future, however, is its collapsing population. Russia's population is now down to 140 million, and the United Nations estimates that it will fall to a mere 108 million by 2050. Many developed nations expect to lose people in forthcoming years. No nation, however, is experiencing losses that come close to what is predicted for Russia. If Russia is no longer one of the world's most populous countries, it will not be able to maintain its position as a great power. Russia not only has a low birth rate, but a very high death rate. The life expectancy of a Russian male is only about fifty-eight years. Experts attribute this in part to extremely high rates of alcoholism among men.

WHERE DO YOU STAND?

1. **What factors might cause Russia to take a belligerent stand toward neighboring countries?**
2. **In 2009, President Barack Obama and Secretary of State Clinton stated that they would "push the reset button" in relations with Russia, in an attempt to move beyond the negative feelings that had developed during the Bush administration. Later, Obama canceled a missile system scheduled to be built in Czechoslovakia and Poland. While the system was designed to protect Europe from Iranian missiles, the Russians were convinced it was directed at them. Are these steps likely to prove beneficial? Why or why not?**

EXPLORE THIS ISSUE ONLINE

- **You can find a vast amount of information on Russia, much of it written from a relatively sympathetic point of view, at www.russiaprofile.org.**
- **John Bolton is one of America's best known foreign-policy "hawks." For his criticism of Obama's missile decision, see www.aei.org/article/101060.**

Introduction

What we call **foreign policy** is a systematic and general plan that guides a country's attitudes and actions toward the rest of the world. Foreign policy includes all of the economic, military, commercial, and diplomatic positions and actions that a nation takes in its relationships with other countries. Although foreign policy may seem quite removed from the concerns of everyday life, it can and does have a significant impact on the day-to-day lives of Americans.

LO1 *Who Makes U.S. Foreign Policy?*

The framers of the Constitution envisioned that the president and Congress would cooperate in developing American foreign policy. The Constitution did not spell out exactly how this was to be done, though. As commander in chief, the president has assumed much of the decision-making power in the area of foreign policy. Nonetheless, members of Congress, a number of officials, and a vast national security bureaucracy help to shape the president's decisions and to limit the president's powers.

The President's Role

Article II, Section 2, of the Constitution names the president commander in chief of the armed forces. As commander in chief, the president oversees the military and guides defense policies. Presidents have interpreted this role broadly and have sent American troops, ships, and weapons to trouble spots at home and around the world. The Constitution also authorizes the president to make treaties, which must be approved by two-thirds of the Senate. In addition, the president is empowered to form executive agreements—pacts between the president and the heads of other nations. Executive agreements do not require Senate approval. Furthermore, the president's foreign policy responsibilities take on special significance because the president has ultimate control over the use of nuclear weapons.

As head of state, the president also influences foreign policymaking. As the symbolic head of our government, the president represents the United States to the rest of the world. When a serious foreign policy issue or international question arises, the nation expects the president to make a formal statement on the matter.

John Moore/Getty Images

Village elders speak with a U.S. Marine in the Korengal Valley of Kunar Province in eastern Afghanistan. The U.S. has had active troops in this country for almost a decade as part of its attempt to prevent the Taliban from regaining control.

The Cabinet

Many members of the president's cabinet concern themselves with international problems and recommend policies to deal with them. As U.S. power in the world has grown and as economic factors have become increasingly important, the departments of Commerce, Agriculture, Treasury, and Energy have become more involved in foreign policy decisions. The secretary of state and the secretary of defense, however, are the only cabinet members who concern themselves with foreign policy matters on a full-time basis.

THE DEPARTMENT OF STATE The Department of State is, in principle, the government agency most directly involved in foreign policy. The department is responsible for diplomatic relations with nearly two hundred independent nations around the globe, as well as with the United Nations and other multilateral organizations, such as the Organization of American States. Most U.S. relations with other countries are maintained through embassies, consulates, and other U.S. offices around the world.

foreign policy A systematic and general plan that guides a country's attitudes and actions toward the rest of the world. Foreign policy includes all of the economic, military, commercial, and diplomatic positions and actions that a nation takes in its relationships with other countries.

As the head of the State Department, the secretary of state has traditionally played a key role in foreign policymaking, and many presidents have relied heavily on the advice of their secretaries of state. Since the end of World War II, though, the preeminence of the State Department in foreign policy has declined dramatically.

> **"TO BE PREPARED FOR WAR** is one of the most effectual means of preserving peace."
>
> ~ GEORGE WASHINGTON ~ COMMANDER OF THE CONTINENTAL ARMY AND FIRST PRESIDENT OF THE UNITED STATES 1789–1797

THE DEPARTMENT OF DEFENSE The Department of Defense is the principal executive department that establishes and carries out defense policy and protects our national security. The secretary of defense advises the president on all aspects of U.S. military and defense policy, supervises all of the military activities of the U.S. government, and works to see that the decisions of the president as commander in chief are carried out. The secretary advises and informs the president on the nation's military forces, weapons, and bases and works closely with the U.S. military, especially the Joint Chiefs of Staff, in gathering and studying defense information.

The Joint Chiefs of Staff include the chief of staff of the Army, the chief of staff of the Air Force, the chief of naval operations, and the commandant of the Marine Corps. The chairperson of the Joint Chiefs of Staff is appointed by the president for a four-year term. The joint chiefs regularly serve as the key military advisers to the president, the secretary of defense, and the National Security Council (described below). They are responsible for handing down the president's orders to the nation's military units, preparing strategic plans, and recommending military actions. They also propose military budgets, new weapons systems, and military regulations.

Other Agencies

Several other government agencies are also involved in the foreign relations of the United States. Two key agencies in the area of foreign policy are the National Security Council and the Central Intelligence Agency.

THE NATIONAL SECURITY COUNCIL The National Security Council (NSC) was established by the National Security Act of 1947. The formal members of the NSC include the president, the vice president, the secretary of state, and the secretary of defense, but meetings are often attended by the chairperson of the Joint Chiefs of Staff, the director of the Central Intelligence Agency, and representatives from other departments. The national security adviser, who is a member of the president's White House staff, is the director of the NSC. The adviser informs the president, coordinates advice and information on foreign policy, and serves as a liaison with other officials.

The NSC and its members can be as important and powerful as the president wants them to be. Some presidents have made frequent use of the NSC, whereas others have convened it infrequently. Similarly, the importance of the role played by the national security adviser in shaping foreign policy can vary significantly, depending on the administration and the adviser's identity.

THE CENTRAL INTELLIGENCE AGENCY The Central Intelligence Agency (CIA) was created after World War II to coordinate American intelligence activities abroad. The CIA provides the president and his or her advisers with up-to-date information about the political, military, and economic activities of foreign governments. The CIA gathers much of its intelligence from overt sources, such as foreign radio broadcasts and newspapers, people who

The Pentagon is located across the Potomac River from Washington, D.C. This country's largest building, it is the headquarters for the Department of Defense. It was built in 1943.

AP Photo

travel abroad, the Internet, and satellite photographs. Other information is gathered from covert activities, such as the CIA's own secret investigations into the economic or political affairs of other nations. In addition to its intelligence-gathering functions, the CIA engages in covert operations. It may secretly supply weapons to a force rebelling against an unfriendly government or seize suspected terrorists in a clandestine operation and hold them for questioning.

The CIA has tended to operate autonomously, and the nature of its work, methods, and operating funds is kept secret. Intelligence reform passed by Congress in 2004, however, makes the CIA accountable to a national intelligence director. The CIA will likely cooperate more with other U.S. intelligence agencies in the future and lose a degree of the autonomy it once enjoyed.

Congress's Powers

Although the executive branch takes the lead in foreign policy matters, Congress also has some power over foreign policy. Remember that Congress alone has the power to declare war. It also has the power to appropriate funds to build new weapons systems, equip the U.S. armed forces, and provide for foreign aid. The Senate has the power to approve or reject the implementation of treaties and the appointment of ambassadors.

In 1973, Congress passed the War Powers Resolution, which limits the president's use of troops in military action without congressional approval. Presidents since then, however, have not interpreted the resolution to mean that Congress must be consulted before military action is taken. On several occasions, presidents have ordered military action and then informed Congress after the fact.

A few congressional committees are directly concerned with foreign affairs. The most important are the Armed Services Committee and the Committee on Foreign Affairs in the House, and the Armed Services Committee and the Foreign Relations Committee in the Senate. Other congressional committees deal with matters, such as oil, agriculture, and imports, that indirectly influence foreign policy.

James Monroe served as secretary of state before assuming the presidency (1817–1825). He opposed foreign intervention in the Western Hemisphere.

Library of Congress

LO2 *A Short History of American Foreign Policy*

Although many U.S. foreign policy initiatives have been rooted in moral idealism, a primary consideration in U.S. foreign policy has always been national security—the protection of the independence and political integrity of the nation. Over the years, the United States has attempted to preserve its national security in many ways. These ways have changed over time and are not always internally consistent. This is because foreign policymaking, like domestic policymaking, reflects the influence of various political groups in the United States. These groups—including the voting public, interest groups, Congress, and the president and relevant agencies of the executive branch—are often at odds over what the U.S. position should be on particular foreign policy issues.

Isolationism

The nation's founders and the early presidents believed that avoiding political involvement with other nations—**isolationism**—was the best way to protect American interests. The colonies were certainly not yet strong enough to directly influence European developments. As president of the new nation, George Washington did little in terms of foreign policy. Indeed, in his farewell address in 1797, he urged Americans to "steer clear of permanent alliances with any portion of the foreign world." During the 1700s and 1800s, the United States generally attempted to avoid conflicts and political engagements elsewhere.

In 1823, President James Monroe proclaimed what became known as the **Monroe Doctrine.** In his message to Congress in December 1823, Monroe stated that the United States would not tolerate foreign intervention in the Western Hemisphere. In return, promised Monroe, the United States would stay out of European

isolationism A political policy of noninvolvement in world affairs.

Monroe Doctrine A U.S. policy, announced in 1823 by President James Monroe, that the United States would not tolerate foreign intervention in the Western Hemisphere, and in return, the United States would stay out of European affairs.

Left Photo: The United States entered World War II after the surprise Japanese attack on Pearl Harbor, Hawaii, on December 7, 1941. Right Photo: World War II came to an end shortly after the United States dropped atomic bombs on Hiroshima and Nagasaki, Japan, in 1945.

affairs. The Monroe Doctrine buttressed the policy of isolationism toward Europe.

The Beginning of Interventionism

Isolationism gradually gave way to **interventionism** (direct involvement in foreign affairs). The first true step toward interventionism occurred with the Spanish-American War of 1898. The United States fought this war to free Cuba from Spanish rule. Spain lost and subsequently ceded control of several of its possessions, including Guam, Puerto Rico, and the Philippines, to the United States. The United States acquired a **colonial empire** and was acknowledged as a world power.

The growth of the United States as an industrial economy also confirmed the nation's position as a world power. For example, American textile manufacturers were particularly interested in China as a market for America's cheap cotton exports. The so-called open-door policy toward China, initiated by the United States in 1899, was a statement of the principle that Western nations should respect each other's equal trading privileges in China. Furthermore, in the early 1900s, President Theodore Roosevelt proposed that the United States could invade Latin American countries when it was necessary to guarantee political or economic stability.

interventionism Direct involvement by one country in another country's affairs.

colonial empire A group of dependent nations that are under the rule of a single imperial power.

neutrality A position of not being aligned with either side in a dispute or conflict, such as a war.

The World Wars

When World War I broke out in 1914, President Woodrow Wilson initially proclaimed a policy of **neutrality**—the United States would not take sides in the conflict. The United States did not enter the war until 1917, after U.S. ships in international waters were attacked by German submarines that were blockading Britain. After World War I ended in 1918, the United States returned to a policy of isolationism. We refused to join the League of Nations, an international body intended to resolve peacefully any future conflicts between nations.

The U.S. policy of isolationism lasted only until the Japanese attacked Pearl Harbor in 1941. The United States joined the Allies—Australia, Britain, Canada, China, France, and the Soviet Union—that fought the Axis nations of Germany, Italy, and Japan. One of the most significant foreign policy actions during World War II was the dropping of atomic bombs on the Japanese cities of Hiroshima and Nagasaki in August 1945.

The Cold War

After World War II ended in 1945, the wartime alliance between the United States and the Soviet Union began to deteriorate quickly. The Soviet Union opposed

America's political and economic systems. Many Americans considered Soviet attempts to spread Communist systems to other countries a major threat to democracy. After the war ended, countries in Eastern Europe—Bulgaria, Czechoslovakia, East Germany, Hungary, Poland, and Romania—fell under Soviet domination, forming what became known as the **Communist bloc.**

THE IRON CURTAIN Britain's wartime prime minister, Winston Churchill, established the tone for a new relationship between the Soviet Union and the Western allies in a famous speech in 1946:

> An iron curtain has descended across the Continent. Behind that line all are subject in one form or another, not only to Soviet influence but to a very high . . . measure of control from Moscow.

The reference to an **iron curtain** described the political boundaries between the democratic countries in Western Europe and the Soviet-controlled Communist countries in Eastern Europe.

THE MARSHALL PLAN AND THE POLICY OF CONTAINMENT In 1947, after Britain announced that it was withdrawing both economic and military aid from Greece and Turkey and it appeared that local Communists, backed by the Soviets, would take over those areas, President Harry Truman took action. He convinced Congress to appropriate $400 million in aid for those countries to prevent the spread of communism.[2] The Truman administration also instituted a policy of economic assistance to war-torn Europe, called the **Marshall Plan** after George Marshall, who was then the U.S. secretary of state. During the next five years, Congress appropriated $17 billion (about $160 billion in 2010 dollars) for aid to sixteen European countries. By 1952, the nations of Western Europe, with U.S. help, had recovered and were again prospering.

These actions marked the beginning of a policy of **containment**—a policy designed to contain the spread of communism by offering threatened nations U.S. military and economic aid.[3] To make the policy of containment effective, the United States initiated a program of collective security involving the formation of mutual defense alliances with other nations. In 1949, through the North Atlantic Treaty, the United States, Canada, and ten European nations formed a military alliance—the North Atlantic Treaty Organization (NATO)—and declared that an attack on any member of the alliance would be considered an attack against all members. President Truman stationed four American army divisions in Europe as the nucleus of the NATO armed forces. Truman also pledged military aid to any European nation threatened by Communist expansion.

Thus, by 1949, almost all illusions of friendship between the Soviet Union and the Western allies had disappeared. The United States became the leader of a bloc of democratic nations in Western Europe, the Pacific, and elsewhere. The tensions between the Soviet Union and the United States became known as the **Cold War**—a war of words, warnings, and ideologies that lasted from the late 1940s through the early 1990s. The term *iron curtain,* from Winston Churchill's speech in 1946, became even more appropriate in 1961, when Soviet-dominated East Germany constructed the Berlin Wall, which separated East Berlin from West Berlin.

Although the Cold War was mainly a war of words and belief systems, the wars in Korea (1950–1953) and Vietnam (1964–1975) grew out of the efforts to contain communism.

THE ARMS RACE AND DETERRENCE The tensions induced by the Cold War led both the Soviet Union and the United States to try to surpass each other militarily. They began competing for more and better weapons, particularly nuclear weapons, with greater destructive power. This phenomenon, known as the *arms race,* was supported by a policy of **deterrence**—of rendering ourselves and our allies so strong militarily that our very strength would deter (stop or discourage) any attack

Communist bloc The group of Eastern European nations that fell under the control of the Soviet Union following World War II.

iron curtain A phrase coined by Winston Churchill to describe the political boundaries between the democratic countries in Western Europe and the Soviet-controlled Communist countries in Eastern Europe.

Marshall Plan A plan providing for U.S. economic assistance to European nations following World War II to help those nations recover from the war; the plan was named after George C. Marshall, secretary of state from 1947 to 1949.

containment A U.S. policy designed to contain the spread of communism by offering military and economic aid to threatened nations.

Cold War The war of words, warnings, and ideologies between the Soviet Union and the United States that lasted from the late 1940s through the early 1990s.

deterrence A policy of building up military strength for the purpose of discouraging (deterring) military attacks by other nations; the policy of "building weapons for peace" that supported the arms race between the United States and the Soviet Union during the Cold War.

"SOVIET UNION FOREIGN POLICY IS
a puzzle inside a riddle wrapped in an enigma."

~ WINSTON CHURCHILL ~
BRITISH PRIME MINISTER DURING WORLD WAR II
1874–1965

on us. Out of deterrence came the theory of **mutually assured destruction (MAD),** which held that if the forces of both nations were equally capable of destroying each other, neither nation would take a chance on war.

THE CUBAN MISSILE CRISIS In 1962, the United States and the Soviet Union came close to a nuclear confrontation in what became known as the **Cuban missile crisis.** The United States learned that the Soviet Union had placed nuclear weapons on the island of Cuba, ninety miles from the coast of Florida. The crisis was defused diplomatically: a U.S. naval blockade of Cuba convinced the Soviet Union to agree to remove the missiles. The United States also agreed to remove some of its missiles near the Soviet border in Turkey. Both sides recognized that a direct nuclear confrontation between the two superpowers was unthinkable.

mutually assured destruction (MAD) A phrase referring to the assumption, on which the policy of deterrence was based, that if the forces of two nations are equally capable of destroying each other, neither nation will take a chance on war.

Cuban missile crisis A nuclear stand-off that occurred in 1962 when the United States learned that the Soviet Union had placed nuclear warheads in Cuba, ninety miles off the U.S. coast. The crisis was defused diplomatically, but it is generally considered the closest the two Cold War superpowers came to a nuclear confrontation.

détente French word meaning a "relaxation of tensions." Détente characterized the relationship between the United States and the Soviet Union in the 1970s, as the two Cold War rivals attempted to pursue cooperative dealings and arms control.

DÉTENTE AND ARMS CONTROL In 1969, the United States and the Soviet Union began negotiations on a treaty to limit the number of antiballistic missiles (ABMs) and offensive missiles that each country could develop and deploy. In 1972, both sides signed the Strategic Arms Limitation Treaty (SALT I). This event marked the beginning of a period of **détente,** a French word that means a "relaxation of tensions." The two nations also engaged in scientific and cultural exchanges.

Library of Congres

Prime Minister Winston Churchill led the United Kingdom during World War II.

In 1983, President Ronald Reagan (1981–1989) nearly reignited the arms race by proposing a missile defense system known as the strategic defense initiative (SDI, or "Star Wars"). Nonetheless, Reagan and Soviet leader Mikhail Gorbachev pursued arms control agreements, as did Reagan's successor, President George H. W. Bush (1989–1993).

THE DISSOLUTION OF THE SOVIET UNION In the late 1980s, the political situation inside the Soviet Union began to change rapidly. Mikhail Gorbachev had initiated an effort to democratize the Soviet political system and decentralize the economy. The reforms quickly spread to other countries behind the iron curtain. In 1989, the Berlin Wall, constructed nearly thirty years earlier, was torn down, and East Germany and West Germany were reunited.

In August 1991, a number of disgruntled Communist Party leaders who wanted to reverse the reforms briefly seized control of the Soviet central government. Russian citizens rose up in revolt and defied those leaders. The democratically elected president of the Russian republic (the largest republic in the Soviet Union), Boris Yeltsin, confronted troops in Moscow that were under the control of the conspirators. The attempted coup gained almost no support from the military as a whole, and it collapsed after three days. Over the next several weeks, the Communist Party in the Soviet Union lost virtually all of its power. The fifteen republics constituting

Collection/Corbis

After the Cuban missile crisis, President John F. Kennedy, surrounded by cabinet officials and senators, signed the Nuclear Test Ban Treaty with the Soviet Union in 1963.

the Soviet Union—including the Russian republic—declared their independence, and by the end of the year, the Union of Soviet Socialist Republics (USSR) no longer existed.

Post–Cold War Foreign Policy

The demise of the Soviet Union altered the framework and goals of U.S. foreign policy. During the Cold War, the moral underpinnings of American foreign policy were clear to all—the United States was the defender of the "free world" against the Soviet aggressor. When the Cold War ended, U.S. foreign policymakers were forced, for the first time in decades, to rethink the nation's foreign policy goals and adapt them to a world arena in which, at least for a time, the United States was the only superpower. Some have argued that the European Union, an economic and political organization of twenty-seven European states, could in time rival the United States. Others are skeptical, as you'll see in the *Perception versus Reality* feature on the following page.

U.S. foreign policymakers have struggled since the end of the Cold War to determine the degree of intervention that is appropriate and prudent for the U.S. military. Should we intervene in a humanitarian crisis, such as a famine? Should the U.S. military participate in peacekeeping missions, such as those instituted after civil or ethnic strife in other countries? Americans have faced these questions in Bosnia, Kosovo, Rwanda, Somalia, and Sudan. Yet no overriding framework emerged in U.S. foreign policy until September 11, 2001. Since that date, our goal has been to capture and punish the terrorists who planned and perpetrated the events of that day and to prevent future terrorist attacks against Americans—even if that means "regime change," which was one of the goals of the second Gulf War against Iraq in 2003.

LO3 *The War on Terrorism*

One of the most difficult challenges faced by governments around the world is how to control terrorism. Terrorism is defined as the use of staged violence, often against civilians, to achieve political goals. International terrorism has occurred in virtually every region of the world. The most devastating terrorist attack in U.S. history occurred on September 11, 2001, when radical Islamist terrorists used hijacked airliners as missiles to bring down the World Trade Center towers in New York City and to destroy part of the Pentagon building in Washington, D.C. A fourth airplane crashed in a Pennsylvania field after the hijackers were overtaken by the passengers. It was believed that the hijackers planned to crash this airliner into the White House or the Capitol building in Washington, D.C. In all, three thousand innocent civilians were killed as a result of these terrorist acts.

Terrorist attacks have occurred with increasing frequency during the past three decades. Other examples of terrorist acts include the Palestinian attacks on Israeli Olympic athletes in Munich in 1972; the Libyan

Somalia has been the battleground for fighting between rival Islamist factions. The United States has supported a United Nations–backed government, but that regime remains almost powerless. The Islamic Party combatants shown here rest after a fully armed conflict exercise.

AP Photo/Farah Abdi Warsameh

A United Europe?

Decades ago, European leaders had a dream of forging a common European union of nations so that world war would never occur again. As a result, the Common Market was created and then the European Union (EU), which now consists of twenty-seven nations, a third of which are former Communist countries.

The Perception

If you read the newspapers and listen to the TV talk shows in America, you get the impression that the EU represents a bloc of more than 400 million people that acts as a counterweight to America's 300 million citizens. The EU is portrayed as an economic and foreign policy powerhouse today.

The Reality

While the twenty-seven members of the EU have given up some of their sovereignty, particularly over manufacturing standards, food safety, and the like, they are still twenty-seven sovereign nations. This is most evident in the efforts of EU members to protect their own citizens' economic livelihood.

In Europe, as in the rest of the world, the authority of the individual nation-state is weakening because of the accelerating pace of globalization. Open and relatively unfettered worldwide capital markets and multinational production chains are making it impossible for any country to protect its domestic jobs and industries forever. Even within the EU, any nation that sets its taxes too high suffers because businesses and people leave.

Nevertheless, many members of the EU are struggling against these economic trends and, in the process, revealing that the EU is not the supranational political structure that it is often made out to be. As the insecurities wrought by globalization become increasingly evident, the citizens of each member country are looking to their own government for protection. The latest so-called minitreaty among the EU nations, conceived in 2007, is a case in point. France succeeded in removing from the treaty's preamble a statement to the effect that the EU was all about free competition in all countries. Instead, the French substituted the concept that each country must protect its "national champions" and preserve the jobs of its citizens.

In the United States, in contrast, no matter what the individual states would like to do, they cannot raise protectionist walls to prevent job losses due to competition from other states. The U.S. Constitution forbids that.

Blog On The Economist, *published in London, is one of the most highly regarded news magazines in the world. You can find its blog on Europe at* **www.economist.com/blogs.** *Politics in Europe generally is tilted further left than in the United States. Find out what left-of-center Europeans are thinking at* **www.blog.social-europe.eu.**

suitcase bombing of an American airliner over Lockerbie, Scotland, in 1988; the bombing of two U.S. embassies in Africa in 1998; the bombing of the navy ship USS *Cole* in a Yemeni port in 2000; and coordinated bomb attacks on London's transportation system in 2005.

Varieties of Terrorism

Terrorists are willing to destroy others' lives and property, and often sacrifice their own lives, for a variety of reasons. Terrorist acts generally fall into one of the three broad categories discussed next.

LOCAL OR REGIONAL TERRORISM Some terrorist acts have been committed by extremists who are motivated by the desire to obtain freedom from a nation or government that they regard as an oppressor. Terrorists have sometimes acted to disrupt peace talks. In Israel, for example, numerous suicide bombings by Palestinians against Israeli civilians have helped to stall efforts to forge a lasting peace between Israel and the Palestinians. The Irish Republican Army, which sought to unite British-governed Northern Ireland with the independent Republic of Ireland, conducted bombings and other terrorist acts in Northern Ireland and England over a period of many years. The attacks came to an end in 1997 as part of a peace process that lasted from 1995 until 2005. Basque separatists in Spain have engaged in terrorism for decades. The separatists were initially—and incorrectly—blamed for bombing a commuter train in Madrid, Spain, on March 11, 2004. That terrorist attack, actually perpetrated by Islamic radicals, killed 191 people and injured hundreds of others.

The United States has also been the victim of homegrown terrorists. The bombing of the Oklahoma City

AP Photo/William Kratzke

A hijacked airliner approaches New York's World Trade Center moments before striking the second tower, as seen from downtown Brooklyn on September 11, 2001. The 110-story towers collapsed in a shower of rubble and dust after two hijacked airliners slammed into them. Nearly three thousand people were killed on that day.

federal building in 1995 was the act of vengeful extremists in the United States who claimed to fear an oppressive federal government. Although Timothy McVeigh and Terry Nichols, who were convicted of the crime, were not directly connected to a particular political group, they expressed views characteristic of the extreme right-wing militia movement in the United States.

STATE-SPONSORED TERRORISM Some terrorist attacks have been planned and sponsored by governments. For example, the bombing of Pan Am Flight 103, which exploded over Lockerbie, Scotland, in 1988, killing all 259 people on board and 11 on the ground, was later proved to be the work of an intelligence officer working for Libya. The United Nations imposed economic sanctions against Libya in an effort to force Libyan dictator Muammar Qaddafi to extradite those who were suspected of being responsible for the bombing. More than a decade after the bombing, Libya agreed to hand the men over for trial, and one of them was found guilty and sentenced to twenty years in prison.

The case of Pan Am Flight 103 illustrates the difficulty in punishing the perpetrators of state-sponsored terrorism. The victim country must first prove who the terrorists were and for whom they were working. Then it must decide what type of retribution is warranted. Today, the U.S. State Department lists Cuba, Iran, North Korea, Sudan, and Syria as state sponsors of international terrorism.

FOREIGN TERRORIST NETWORKS A relatively new phenomenon in the late 1990s and early 2000s was the emergence of nonstate terrorist networks, such as al Qaeda. Al Qaeda is the nongovernmental terrorist organization that planned and carried out the terrorist attacks of September 11, 2001. Its leader is the Saudi dissident Osama bin Laden. It operates in "cells," so that often one cell of the organization does not know what the other cells are planning. Throughout the 1990s, al Qaeda conducted training camps in the mountains of Afghanistan, which was ruled by an ultraconservative Islamic faction known as the Taliban. After their training, al Qaeda operatives dispersed into small units across the globe, connected by e-mail and the Internet.

Before September 11, the U.S. government had monitored the activities and movements of al Qaeda operatives and had connected the terrorist attacks on two U.S. embassies in Africa and the bombing of the USS *Cole* to al Qaeda. In 1998, President Bill Clinton (1993–2001), ordered the bombing of terrorist camps in Afghanistan in retaliation for the embassy bombings, but with little effect. Al Qaeda cells continued to operate largely unimpeded until the terrorist attacks of September 11.

In 2004, terrorists detonated explosives in two packed commuter trains in Madrid, Spain. One hundred and ninety-one people were killed, and hundreds of others were injured.

Rafa Roa/Cover/Corbis

The U.S. Response to 9/11—The War in Afghanistan

Immediately after the 9/11 terrorist attacks, Congress passed a joint resolution authorizing President George W. Bush to use "all necessary and appropriate force" against nations, organizations, or individuals that the president determined had "planned, authorized, committed, or aided the terrorist attacks" or that "harbored such persons or organizations." In late 2001, supported by a **coalition** of international allies, the U.S. military launched an attack against al Qaeda camps in Afghanistan and the ruling Taliban regime that harbored these terrorists. Once the Taliban had been ousted, the United States helped to establish a government in Afghanistan that did not support terrorism. Instead of continuing the hunt for al Qaeda members in Afghanistan, however, the Bush administration increasingly looked to Iraq as a threat to U.S. security that needed to be addressed.

"FIGHTING TERRORISM IS LIKE BEING A GOALKEEPER. You can make a hundred brilliant saves but the only shot that people remember is the one that gets past you."

~ PAUL WILKINSON ~
BRITISH TERRORISM EXPERT
B. 1937

The Focus on Iraq

In January 2002, President Bush described Iraq as a regime that sponsored terrorism and sought to develop **weapons of mass destruction.** In October, Congress authorized Bush to use U.S. armed forces against Iraq on the grounds that Iraq had the "capability and willingness" to use weapons of mass destruction and was supporting al Qaeda. Both of these allegations later proved to be untrue.

In September, President Bush enunciated a doctrine under which the United States was prepared to strike "preemptively" at Iraq. A **preemptive war** occurs when a nation goes to war against another nation because it believes that an attack from that nation is imminent. When President Bush did go to war against Iraq, though, it was not a preemptive war but a **preventive war**—a war to prevent the possibility that Iraq could attack the United States in the future. International law offers no support for this type of war.

coalition An alliance of nations formed to undertake a foreign policy action, particularly a military action. A coalition is often a temporary alliance that dissolves after the action is concluded.

weapons of mass destruction Chemical, biological, or nuclear weapons that can inflict massive casualties.

preemptive war A war launched by a nation to prevent an imminent attack by another nation.

preventive war A war launched by a nation to prevent the possibility that another nation might attack at some point in the future; not supported by international law.

BACKGROUND TO INVASION—THE FIRST GULF WAR Back in 1990, Iraqi dictator Saddam Hussein had invaded neighboring Kuwait. Hussein's invasion was a spectacular violation of international law. The United Nations (UN) threatened Hussein with sanctions if he did not withdraw his troops. When he failed to do so, U.S.-led coalition forces attacked. Iraqi troops soon withdrew from Kuwait, and the first Gulf War ended. The coalition stopped short of sending troops to Baghdad to unseat Hussein.

The cease-fire that ended the conflict required Iraq to submit to inspections for chemical, biological, and nuclear weapons. In 1998, however, Hussein ceased to cooperate with the inspections. During 2002, the Bush administration sought a resolution from the UN on the use of military force in Iraq, but China, France, and Russia

Special Forces soldiers are on their way to conduct joint village searches with the Afghan National Army in southern Afghanistan. Such convoys are common as we continue to combat Taliban and al Qaeda forces in that country.

Darren McCollester/Getty Images

blocked the resolution. In March 2003, President Bush gave Saddam Hussein an ultimatum: leave Iraq or face war. Hussein was defiant.

THE SECOND GULF WAR BEGINS On March 20, 2003, U.S. and British forces entered Iraq. President Bush secured the support of several other nations, but most of the world opposed the attack. U.S. forces advanced rapidly and Iraqi military units crumbled. With the fall of the regime, massive looting and disorder broke out across the country, and coalition troops were unable to restore order immediately. Saddam Hussein was not captured until December 2003. He was convicted of crimes against humanity and executed in 2006.

THE INSURGENCY The Bush administration had hoped that the U.S. troops would be greeted as liberators, but that expectation soon faded. It became clear that many Iraqis opposed the occupation. Opposition was strongest among members of the Sunni branch of Islam, who had been Hussein's strongest supporters. Terrorists such as al Qaeda—which had not previously existed in Iraq—began to smuggle additional insurgents into Iraq to bolster the resistance. The rebels used terrorist tactics to kill occupation forces and Iraqis cooperating with the Americans. Between May 2003 and March 2004, casualty rates for American soldiers averaged more than fifty per month. The revelation that Americans had mistreated prisoners at Iraq's Abu Ghraib prison in 2003 and 2004 only served to stoke the opposition.

These Iraqi soldiers march during Army Day celebrations in Baghdad. The Multi-National Force (mainly U.S. troops) handed over control of several bases to the new Iraqi army during 2009.

AP Photo/Karim Kadim

In the midst of the growing chaos, elections were held to establish a new Iraqi government. In January 2005, Iraqis went to the polls in large numbers to vote in the first free elections in half a century. A political coalition of Shiite Muslims, Iraq's largest religious sect, won the most seats, while ethnic Kurds were the next largest group. The Shiites, who constituted over half of Iraq's population, had experienced severe repression under Saddam Hussein. The Kurds had suffered greatly as well. The Sunnis, who had dominated government posts under the previous regime, were largely shut out.

Sectarian strife between Shiites and Sunnis, plus terrorist bombings and attacks, placed the U.S. government in a difficult position. The majority of Americans wanted to begin withdrawing the troops and bring an end to the war. The voters made their sentiments clear in the 2006 elections by electing a majority of Democrats to Congress. Most Iraqis were also opposed to having the U.S. forces remain in their country, and a public opinion poll indicated that 51 percent of them believed that violence against U.S. forces was "acceptable."

Instead of withdrawing U.S. troops, however, the Bush administration increased troop levels in 2007 in a program known as the "surge." The hope was that given more time, Iraqis could work out their differences and establish a united government. The new U.S. strategy in Iraq involved more than the introduction of additional troops. Under General David Petraeus, American forces began for the first time to employ time-tested counterinsurgency tactics on a nationwide basis. The counterinsurgency effort sought to win the support of ordinary Iraqis by protecting their security.

WITHDRAWAL PLANS In mid-2008, Iraqi prime minister Nouri al-Maliki began to speak of a timetable for withdrawing U.S. forces. In October 2008, al-Maliki and President Bush set a withdrawal target for the end of 2011. (The agreement undercut Republican presidential candidate John McCain, who had denounced setting a withdrawal schedule.) In February 2009, President Barack Obama announced that U.S. combat forces would leave Iraq by the end of August 2010, and the rest of the troops would be out by the end of 2011.

Again, Afghanistan

The war in Iraq tended to draw the Bush administration's attention away from Afghanistan, which was never completely at peace even after the Taliban were ousted

President Obama looks on as Israeli Prime Minister Benjamin Netanyahu shakes hands with Mahmoud Abbas, president of the Palestinian Authority, in New York in the fall of 2009. The United States has been heavily involved in helping these two countries reach a mutually satisfactory "solution" to their ongoing conflict. Why would the United States choose to become involved in other countries' political problems?

from Kabul, the capital. In 2003, the North Atlantic Treaty Organization (NATO) took responsibility for coalition military operations in the relatively peaceful central and northern parts of Afghanistan. The hope was that with NATO in charge, European nations would be more willing to supply troops to assist the overstretched Americans. In 2004, Hamid Karzai became the first democratically elected president of Afghanistan, and in 2005 Afghans elected a parliament. By 2006, however, the Taliban had regrouped and were waging a war of insurgency against the new government. The United States remained responsible for the southern areas of the country, in which most of the fighting took place, although in 2006 NATO began to move some forces into the south.

A problem for the coalition forces was that the Taliban were able to take shelter on the far side of the Afghan-Pakistani border, in Pakistan's Federally Administered Tribal Areas. These districts are largely free from central government control. For several years, the United States complained that the government of Pakistan was not doing enough to keep the Taliban out of the Tribal Areas. In 2009, Taliban forces began to take complete control of districts in the Tribal Areas and in adjacent districts of the Northwest Frontier Province. Facing a direct challenge to its sovereignty, the Pakistani military began to engage the Taliban forces in what soon became a major struggle.

Barack Obama had opposed the war in Iraq when it was first launched, but he had always supported the U.S. entry into Afghanistan. In February 2009, Obama ordered 17,000 additional troops into the country. In September 2009, the public learned that the U.S. commander in Afghanistan, General Stanley A. McChrystal, was requesting 30,000 to 40,000 additional troops. In a report to Robert Gates, the U.S. secretary of defense, McChrystal warned that the war could be lost if more troops were not sent. In October, the Obama administration launched a major review of its Afghanistan policy.

LO4 *The Israeli–Palestinian Conflict*

The long-running conflict between Israel and its Arab neighbors has poisoned the atmosphere in the Middle East for more than half a century. Some experts have argued that resolving this conflict is key to solving additional problems, such as terrorism. Others doubt that a resolution would really have that effect. Regardless, the conflict has caused enough bloodshed and heartbreak over the years to deserve attention on its own merits. American presidents have attempted to persuade the parties to reach a settlement dating back at least to Richard Nixon (1969–1984). Barack Obama is only the latest American leader to address the problem.

The Arab-Israeli Wars

For many years after Israel was founded in 1948, the neighboring Arab states did not accept its legitimacy as a nation. The result was a series of wars between Israel and neighboring states, including Egypt, Jordan, and Syria, waged in 1948, 1956, 1967, and 1973. Following the 1948 Arab-Israeli War, a large number of Palestinians—Arab residents of the Holy Land, known as Palestine until 1948—were forced into exile, adding to Arab grievances. The failure of the Arab states in the 1967 war led to additional Palestinian refugees and the rise of the **Palestine Liberation Organization (PLO),** a nonstate body committed to armed struggle against Israel. In the late 1960s and early 1970s, Palestinian groups launched a wave of terrorist attacks against Israeli targets around the world.

In the 1973 Yom Kippur War, Egyptian armies acquitted themselves well, although Israel successfully repelled the attack. Egyptian president Anwar el Sadat was able to employ the resulting popular support to launch a major peace initiative. He traveled to Israel in 1977 and addressed the Israeli parliament, a major turning point. U.S. president Jimmy Carter (1977–2001) then sponsored intensive negotiations. Egypt and Israel signed a peace treaty in 1979 that marked the end to an era of major wars between Israel and other states. Lower-level conflicts continued, however. On several occasions, Israel launched attacks against nonstate militias in Lebanon in response to incursions across the Israeli-Lebanon border. Israel and Jordan eventually signed a peace treaty in 1994, but no peace treaty between Israel and Syria has yet been negotiated, and the conflict between Israel and the Palestinians has remained.

The Israeli-Palestinian Dispute

Resolving the Israeli-Palestinian dispute has always presented more difficulties than obtaining peace between Israel and neighbors such as Egypt. One problem is that the hostilities between the two parties run deeper. On the Palestinian side, not only had many families lost their homes after the 1948 war, but after the 1967 war, the West Bank of the Jordan River and the Gaza Strip fell under Israeli control. The Palestinians living in these areas became an occupied people.

On the Israeli side, the sheer viciousness of the Palestinian terrorist attacks—which frequently resulted in the deaths of civilians, including children—made negotiations with those responsible hard to imagine. A further complication was a series of Israeli settlements on the West Bank and the Gaza Strip, which the Palestinians considered their own. Settlers living on the West Bank had an obvious interest in opposing any peace deal that required them to move.

Despite the difficulties, the international community, including the United States, was in agreement on several principles for settling the conflict. Lands seized by Israel in the 1967 war should be granted to the Palestinians, who could organize their own independent nation-state there. In turn, the Palestinians would not only have to recognize Israel's right to exist, but take concrete steps to guarantee Israel's security. The international consensus did not address some important issues. These included what compensation, if any, should go to Palestinians who had lost homes in what was now Israel. A second issue is whether Israel could adjust its pre-1967 borders to incorporate some of the Israeli settlement areas, plus part or all of eastern Jerusalem, which had been under Arab control before 1967.

> "The purpose of foreign policy IS NOT TO PROVIDE AN OUTLET FOR OUR OWN SENTIMENTS OF HOPE OR INDIGNATION; it is to shape real events in a real world."
>
> ~ JOHN F. KENNEDY ~
> THIRTY-FIFTH PRESIDENT OF THE UNITED STATES
> 1961–1963

Negotiations Begin

A long-running uprising in the occupied territories, known as the *Intifada,* broke out in 1987 and helped ensure that the world would not forget the Palestinians. Under the leadership of U.S. president George H. W. Bush, plus Russia and Spain, talks between Israel, Arab nations, and non-PLO Palestinians commenced in Madrid in 1991. In 1993, Israel and the PLO met officially for the first time in Oslo, Norway. The resulting **Oslo Accords** were signed in Washington under the eye of President Bill Clinton. A major result was the establishment of a Palestinian Authority, under Israeli control, on the West Bank and Gaza Strip.

Negotiations Collapse

Further attempts to reach a settlement in 2000 at Camp David in Maryland collapsed in acrimony. After the failure of these talks, a second Intifada led to Israeli military incursions into the West Bank and the almost complete collapse of the Palestinian Authority's control over its people. Israeli prime minister Ariel Sharon, concluding that he had no credible peace partner, carried out a plan to unilaterally withdraw from the Gaza Strip in 2005 and also to build

Palestine Liberation Organization (PLO) An organization formed in 1964 to represent the Palestinian people. The PLO has a long history of terrorism but for some years has functioned primarily as a political party.

Oslo Accords The first agreement signed between Israel and the PLO; led to the establishment of the Palestinian Authority in the occupied territories.

an enormous security fence between Israel and the West Bank. The fence came under strong international criticism because it incorporated parts of the West Bank into Israel.

In 2007, Gaza was taken over by Hamas, a radical Islamist party that refuses to recognize Israel. After the imposition of an Israeli blockade, Hamas launched missile attacks on Israel, which in turn briefly occupied the strip in December 2008. The West Bank remained under the nominal control of the PLO-led Palestinian Authority, and so the Palestinians, now politically divided, were in an even worse bargaining position than before. Nevertheless, President Obama sought in 2009 to restart peace talks and appointed a special representative for the region.

LO5 *Weapons Proliferation in an Unstable World*

Although foreign policy in recent years has focused most visibly on Iraq, the U.S. government has also had to deal with other threats to U.S. and global security. The Cold War may be over, but the threat of nuclear warfare—which formed the backdrop of foreign policy during the Cold War—has by no means disappeared. The existence of nuclear weapons in Russia and in other countries around the world continues to challenge U.S. foreign policymakers. Concerns about nuclear proliferation mounted in 1998 when India and Pakistan detonated nuclear devices within a few weeks of each other—events that took U.S. intelligence agencies by surprise. Increasingly, American officials have focused on the threat of an attack by a rogue nation or a terrorist group that possesses weapons of mass destruction. Of most concern today are recent developments in North Korea and Iran.

> "The risk THAT THE LEADERS OF A ROGUE STATE WILL USE NUCLEAR, CHEMICAL, OR BIOLOGICAL WEAPONS AGAINST US OR OUR ALLIES **is the greatest security threat we face.**"
>
> ~ MADELEINE ALBRIGHT ~
> U.S. SECRETARY OF STATE
> 1997–2001

North Korea's Nuclear Program

North Korean scientists began to study nuclear technology in the 1950s and continued in the following years to pursue nuclear technology and development of nuclear energy facilities. Nevertheless, North Korea signed the Treaty on the Non-Proliferation of Nuclear Weapons in 1985 and submitted to weapons inspections by the International Atomic Energy Agency (IAEA) in 1992. Throughout the 1990s, however, there were discrepancies between North Korean declarations and IAEA inspection findings. In 2002, U.S. intelligence discovered that North Korea had been receiving equipment from Pakistan for a highly enriched uranium production facility. Later that year, North Korea openly lifted a freeze it had placed on its plutonium-based nuclear weapons program and expelled the IAEA inspectors.

OPENING NEGOTIATIONS For years, the Bush administration had been reluctant to engage in diplomatic relations with either North Korea or Iran, both of which President Bush had declared to be part of an "axis of evil." For its part, North Korea had long demanded direct talks exclusively with the United States, leaving out South Korea. This demand was based on the theory that South Korea was a complete U.S. puppet—a belief with no basis in reality. Bush, in contrast, insisted that any talks with North Korea must also include all of North Korea's neighbors—China, Japan, Russia, and South Korea. In 2003, North Korea finally agreed to such talks.

Since that time, it has proved quite difficult to keep North Korea at the bargaining table—its representatives

have stormed out of the talks repeatedly, for the most modest reasons. China is the one power with substantial economic leverage over North Korea, and typically, Chinese leaders have been the ones to lead the North Koreans back to the table.

Tensions between North Korea and the United States heightened in October 2006, when North Korea conducted its first nuclear test. Nevertheless, the Bush administration continued to participate with North Korea's neighbors (mentioned earlier) in multilateral negotiations. In the spring of 2007, North Korea agreed that it would begin to dismantle its nuclear facilities and would allow UN inspectors into the country. In return, the other nations agreed to provide $400 billion in various kinds of aid, and the United States would begin to discuss normalization of relations with North Korea. By mid-2007, North Korea had shut down one of its nuclear reactors and had admitted a permanent UN inspection team into the country, thus completing the first step toward nuclear disarmament.

NORTH KOREA GETS THE BOMB In April 2009, North Korea tested a long-range missile under the guise of attempting to launch a satellite. The UN Security Council unanimously condemned the test—which demonstrated that the Chinese, who have a permanent Security Council seat, were annoyed as well. North Korea then pulled out of the six-party talks and expelled all nuclear inspectors from the country. In May 2009, North Korea tested another nuclear device, to universal disapproval. In October, it indicated that it might be willing to resume negotiations.

Iran: An Emerging Nuclear Threat?

For some time, Western intelligence agencies have believed that Iran is attempting to join the ranks of nuclear powers. Investigators for the International Atomic Energy Agency have reported that Iran has initiated a uranium enrichment program while also attempting to separate plutonium for nuclear weapons. U.S. intelligence reports have also found evidence that Iran is working on a missile delivery system for nuclear warheads. Iran has made considerable progress in many aspects of its nuclear program, although Iranian leaders have publicly stated that they have no intention of using their nuclear program for destructive purposes and claim that they are seeking only to develop nuclear energy plants.

Like North Korea, Iran has been openly hostile to the United States. Iran has implemented an extensive terrorism campaign in hopes of undermining U.S. influence in the Middle East. Many analysts have also tied Iran to Iraqi insurgency efforts against American occupation forces. Dealing with a nuclear-equipped Iran would strain already tense relations. Considering Iran's ties to terrorist groups, U.S. national security at home and foreign policy efforts abroad could be significantly endangered.

EUROPE TAKES THE LEAD During the Bush administration, Britain, France, and Germany took the lead in diplomatic efforts to encourage Iran to abandon its nuclear program, and engaged in talks with that country. The UN has imposed sanctions on Iran in an attempt to curb its nuclear ambitions. The United States has threatened to impose its own sanctions to isolate Iran from the community of nations. Past attempts to strengthen UN sanctions, however, have been frustrated by the opposition of China and Russia.

In 2008, Iran's nuclear ambitions became a campaign issue in the presidential contest between Barack Obama and John McCain. During the Democratic primaries, Obama stated that he was willing to talk directly to Iran's president Mahmoud Ahmadinejad on the nuclear issue and other major U.S.-Iranian disagreements. McCain denounced the idea of meeting Ahmadinejad under any conditions, citing, among other reasons, statements that the Iranian leader has made that advocate the destruction of Israel.

AP Photo/Office of the Supreme Leader

Ayatollah Ali Khamenei is Iran's Supreme Leader—he is the spiritual head of that country. He refused to support those Iranians who contested the flawed reelection of that country's president, Mahmoud Ahmadinejad, in 2009. By the fall, many protesters remained in jail and several had been sentenced to death. Why does the U.S. continue to be concerned about events in Iran?

JOIN THE DEBATE

Can We Tolerate a Nuclear Iran?

On November 4, 1979, militant students in Tehran, Iran, seized the U.S. embassy and took fifty-two American citizens hostage. The crisis lasted 444 days. Ever since, Iran and the United States have been at odds with each other. In the years that followed, the rest of the world discovered that Iran was engaged in a covert nuclear program. It was enriching uranium that could be used in the fabrication of a nuclear bomb. In spite of numerous United Nations resolutions, Iran is still producing uranium, and at a faster speed. The existence of a second uranium enrichment plant was made public in the fall of 2009. Simultaneously, Iran has been developing missiles that eventually could be capable of carrying a nuclear payload.

We Must Prevent a Nuclear-Armed Iran at All Costs

Repeatedly, the president of Iran, Mahmoud Ahmadinejad, has called for the complete destruction of Israel. Presumably, if he is serious, when Iran has the bomb, it will be used on Israel. Thus, a nuclear Iran carries with it the possibility of a nuclear Holocaust. There would be retaliation, and the conflict could lead to massive destruction in the Middle East and elsewhere.

Currently, Iran is the largest state sponsor of terror. What if Iran does not use the bomb itself, but rather provides nuclear weapons to a terrorist group? There are many such groups that would have no scruples about killing millions of innocent civilians.

Finally, if Iran obtains a nuclear weapon, most oil-rich countries in the Middle East will feel obligated to do so, too. There will be a dangerous arms race on yet another part of this fragile planet. We must stop Iran's production of uranium now. If all else fails, that means bombing Iran's nuclear facilities.

Belligerent Talk Doesn't Mean We Should Go to War

The fact that Ahmadinejad says Israel should not exist does not necessarily mean much. Such crazy talk is mostly for domestic consumption—to strengthen the regime's political position at home by emphasizing Islamic grievances. Further, Ahmadinejad doesn't actually control Iran's military. Supreme Leader Ayatollah Ali Khamenei does.

The United States has two thousand nuclear weapons. We tolerate nuclear weapons in the hands of the Chinese, French, Indians, Israelis, North Koreans, Pakistanis, and Russians. North Korea is run by a megalomaniac dictator and is arguably a more dangerous supporter of terrorist groups than Iran. So why should Iran be singled out?

Rather than start a war with Iran, if we are worried about Israel's safety, we can do two things. First, we can extend our nuclear deterrence umbrella to that country. Iran will know that if it strikes Israel, the United States will retaliate. Second, we can help Israel build up its missile defenses. In that way, it can effectively defend against Iranian missiles as well as deter their use.

For Critical Analysis ***If the United States bombed Iran's uranium enrichment sites, what might be the consequences?***

AMERICA JOINS THE TALKS After a hiatus of over a year, talks with Iran concerning its nuclear program resumed in Geneva on October 1, 2009. Britain, China, France, Germany, Russia, and the United States were at the table. In early discussions, Iran agreed to allow international inspectors access to its facilities. Some observers are hopeful about the talks, but others see them as a way for the Iranians to play for time as they develop their nuclear capabilities. If the Iranians do develop nuclear weapons, what can the United States do about it? We examine that question in this chapter's *Join the Debate* feature above.

LO6 *China—The Next Superpower?*

Following former president Richard Nixon's historic visit to China in 1972, American diplomatic and economic relations with the Chinese gradually improved. Diplomacy with China focused on cultivating a more pro-Western disposition in the former isolationist nation. In 1989, however, when the Chinese government brutally crushed a pro-democracy student movement, killing many students and protesters while imprisoning others, Chinese-American relations experienced a distinct chill.

Chinese-American Trade Relations

During the Clinton administration, American relations with China began to improve once again. The rapid growth of the Chinese economy, and increasingly close trade ties between the United States and China, helped bring about a policy of diplomatic outreach. Many Americans protested, however, when the U.S. government extended **normal trade relations (NTR) status** to China on a year-to-year basis. Labor groups objected because they feared that American workers would lose jobs that could be performed at lower wages in Chinese factories. Human rights organizations denounced the Chinese government's well-documented mistreatment of its people. Despite this heavy opposition, Congress granted China permanent NTR status in 2000 and endorsed China's application to the World Trade Organization in 2001.

A Future Challenger to American Dominance

Many U.S. observers have warned that China is destined to challenge American global supremacy. With one of the fastest-growing economies in the world, along with a population of 1.3 billion, China's gross domestic product (GDP) could surpass that of the United States by 2039. China's GDP is nearly ten times greater than it was in 1978 when it implemented reforms to make the economy more market oriented. The United States already runs a multibillion-dollar trade deficit with China and could be vulnerable if Chinese economic growth continues at its present pace.

Diplomatic relations between China and the United States have been uneven. China offered its full support of the U.S. war on terrorism following the September 11 attacks, even providing intelligence about terrorist activities. The Chinese did not support the American invasion of Iraq in 2003, however. Although China has not shown ambitions to acquire more territory or become militarily aggressive, it has expressed a desire to take control of the island of Taiwan. China considers Taiwan, a former Chinese province, to be a legal part of China. In practice, however, the island has functioned as if it were an independent nation since 1949. The United States has historically supported a free and separate Taiwan and has reiterated that any reunion of China and Taiwan must come about by peaceful means. More recently, relations between China and several Western nations have become strained due to criticisms by these nations of Chinese behavior in Tibet. While supposedly autonomous, Tibet is under tight Chinese control.

Imaginechina via AP Images

This Chinese sailor stands guard in front of a new missile destroyer called a DDG-167. The Chinese navy is expanding rapidly. This ship participated in a multinational convoy fleet sent to Africa's Gulf of Aden in an attempt to reduce piracy.

normal trade relations (NTR) status A status granted through an international treaty by which each member nation must treat other members at least as well as it treats the country that receives its most favorable treatment. This status was formerly known as *most-favored-nation status.*

AMERICA AT ODDS *Foreign Policy*

Recall from Chapters 11 and 12 that one of the issues on which Congress and the president have disagreed is the extent of powers that a president, as opposed to Congress, is authorized to exercise during times of war. In 2007, after the Democrats took control of Congress, a conflict between these two branches again emerged over presidential war powers, this time concerning the war in Iraq. As a "wartime president," President George W. Bush expanded presidential powers to the point at which Congress seemed to have no say in the war or how it was to be executed. The president responded to attempts by Congress to end the war in Iraq or to change the course of the war policy by denying that Congress had the power to take such actions. If it came to a constitutional showdown between these two branches of government, which side would prevail?

The answer to that question, of course, would depend on the courts, and most likely the United States Supreme Court. In evaluating this issue, though, it is instructive to consider the founders' attitudes toward presidential power. One of the founders' major concerns when they created our republic was to prevent the possibility of tyranny or of a king eventually ruling the country. The founders, aware of how European kings often went to war for their own self-aggrandizement, were particularly reluctant to give the president power over war. When drafting the Constitution, the framers made the president the commander in chief and thus the highest-ranking official on the battlefield. Yet their view of the power attached to this position was much more limited than that claimed by President Bush. Alexander Hamilton, in *Federalist Paper* No. 69, stated that the president would be "nothing more" than "first general and admiral," and as such, the president would be responsible for the "command and direction" of military forces. Additionally, the founders specifically authorized Congress to appropriate funds for an army and prohibited appropriations for longer than two years. According to Hamilton, this limitation was intended to prevent Congress from vesting "in the executive department permanent funds for the support of an army."

ISSUES FOR DEBATE & DISCUSSION

1. **Some Americans believe that the United States should launch preventive wars against oppressive regimes that support terrorism and replace those regimes with democratic governments. They contend that applying a policy of preventive war and regime change will lead to a more democratic (and thus a more peaceful and secure) world. Others argue that democracy cannot be imposed externally by force but can only arise by consensus from within a society. Thus, claims this group, American foreign policy should focus more on cultivating democratic attitudes within the populations ruled by oppressive regimes and less on developing military strategies to oppose such regimes. What is your position on this issue?**
2. **According to John Robb, a former Air Force officer and author of the book *Brave New War: The Next Stage of Terrorism and the End of Globalization,*[4] the very nature of the terrorist threat is that it is random and cannot be anticipated. Therefore, democratic nations cannot fight terrorism in the way they have fought other wars with overwhelming military force. Rather, they should create their own decentralized counterinsurgency networks to respond to this threat. Others, including the Bush administration, believed that the war against terrorism required, at least as a last resort, military force to combat nations that harbor terrorists. What is your position on this issue?**

TAKE ACTION

Many Americans of all political persuasions are taking action to help "support the troops" now fighting in Afghanistan. For example, a number of groups are working to help improve the lives of soldiers who have returned from the war. For ideas on what you can do to help, you can contact a veterans' group in your area or visit the Web sites of veterans' groups. If you want to provide a long-distance calling card for a hospitalized veteran, for example, go to the Web site of Operation Uplink, a project of the Veterans of Foreign Wars, at **www.operationuplink.org**. Another organization, the Fisher House Foundation at **www.fisherhouse.org**, provides housing for family members of hospitalized soldiers.

POLITICS ON THE WEB

- You can find news about international events at an interesting Web site sponsored by the Peterson Institute for International Economics at **www.iie.com**. You can also get access to the group's working papers at this site.
- To learn more about national security policy and defense issues, you can go to the U.S. Department of Defense's DefenseLINK site at **www.defenselink.mil**. For information on the U.S. Department of State and its activities, go to **www.state.gov**
- One of the best resources on the Web for learning about foreign countries is the *World Factbook* of the CIA. You can find it at **www.cia.gov/library/publications/the-world-factbook**
- The Global Legal Information Network (GLIN) provides a database of national laws from countries around the world via the Web server of the U.S. Library of Congress. The site consists of more than 54,000 records of legislation enacted from 1976 to the present. To access this site, go to **glin.gov**
- The World Bank's home page offers a wealth of information on international development, research studies containing economic data on various countries, and the like. Go to **www.worldbank.org**
- The Washburn University School of Law offers, among other things, extensive information on international affairs, including United Nations materials. To access this site, go to **www.washlaw.edu**

Online resources for this chapter

This text's Companion Web site, at **www.4ltrpress.cengage.com/govt**, offers links to numerous resources that you can use to learn more about the topics covered in this chapter.

AP Photo/Microsoft, Tim Shaffer

Appendix A

THE DECLARATION OF INDEPENDENCE

IN CONGRESS, JULY 4, 1776

A Declaration by the Representatives of the United States of America, in General Congress assembled. When in the Course of human Events, it becomes necessary for one People to dissolve the Political Bands which have connected them with another, and to assume among the Powers of the Earth, the separate and equal Station to which the Laws of Nature and of Nature's God entitle them, a decent Respect to the Opinions of Mankind requires that they should declare the causes which impel them to the Separation.

We hold these Truths to be self-evident, that all Men are created equal, that they are endowed by their Creator with certain unalienable Rights, that among these are Life, Liberty, and the Pursuit of Happiness—That to secure these Rights, Governments are instituted among Men, deriving their just Powers from the Consent of the Governed, that whenever any Form of Government becomes destructive of these Ends, it is the Right of the People to alter or to abolish it, and to institute new Government, laying its Foundation on such Principles, and organizing its Powers in such Forms, as to them shall seem most likely to effect their Safety and Happiness. Prudence, indeed, will dictate that Governments long established should not be changed for light and transient Causes; and accordingly all Experience hath shewn, that Mankind are more disposed to suffer, while Evils are sufferable, than to right themselves by abolishing the Forms to which they are accustomed. But when a long Train of Abuses and Usurpations, pursuing invariably the same Object, evinces a Design to reduce them under absolute Despotism, it is their Right, it is their Duty, to throw off such Government, and to provide new Guards for their future Security. Such has been the patient Sufferance of these Colonies; and such is now the Necessity which constrains them to alter their former Systems of Government. The History of the present King of Great-Britain is a History of repeated Injuries and Usurpations, all having in direct Object the Establishment of an absolute Tyranny over these States. To prove this, let Facts be submitted to a candid World.

He has refused his Assent to Laws, the most wholesome and necessary for the public Good.

He has forbidden his Governors to pass Laws of immediate and pressing Importance, unless suspended in their Operation till his Assent should be obtained; and when so suspended, he has utterly neglected to attend to them.

He has refused to pass other Laws for the Accommodation of large Districts of People, unless those People would relinquish the Right of Representation in the Legislature, a Right inestimable to them, and formidable to Tyrants only.

He has called together Legislative Bodies at Places unusual, uncomfortable, and distant from the Depository of their Public Records, for the sole Purpose of fatiguing them into Compliance with his Measures.

He has dissolved Representative Houses repeatedly, for opposing with manly Firmness his Invasions on the Rights of the People.

He has refused for a long Time, after such Dissolutions, to cause others to be elected; whereby the Legislative Powers, incapable of Annihilation, have returned to the People at large for their exercise; the State remaining in the mean time exposed to all the Dangers of Invasion from without, and Convulsions within.

He has endeavoured to prevent the Population of these States; for that Purpose obstructing the Laws for Naturalization of Foreigners; refusing to pass others to encourage their Migrations hither, and raising the Conditions of new Appropriations of Lands.

He has obstructed the Administration of Justice, by refusing his Assent to Laws for establishing Judiciary Powers.

He has made Judges dependent on his Will alone, for the Tenure of their offices, and the Amount and payment of their Salaries.

He has erected a Multitude of new Offices, and sent hither Swarms of Officers to harrass our People, and eat out their Substance.

He has kept among us, in Times of Peace, Standing Armies, without the consent of our Legislatures.

He has affected to render the Military independent of, and superior to the Civil Power.

He has combined with others to subject us to a Jurisdiction foreign to our Constitution, and unacknowledged by our Laws; giving his Assent to their Acts of pretended Legislation:

For quartering large Bodies of Armed Troops among us:

For protecting them, by a mock Trial, from Punishment for any Murders which they should commit on the Inhabitants of these States:

For cutting off our Trade with all Parts of the World:

For imposing Taxes on us without our Consent:

For depriving us, in many cases, of the Benefits of Trial by Jury:

For transporting us beyond Seas to be tried for pretended Offences:

For abolishing the free System of English Laws in a neighbouring Province, establishing therein an arbitrary Government, and enlarging its Boundaries, so as to render it at once an Example and fit Instrument for introducing the same absolute Rule into these Colonies:

For taking away our Charters, abolishing our most valuable Laws, and altering fundamentally the Forms of our Governments:

For suspending our own Legislatures, and declaring themselves invested with Power to legislate for us in all Cases whatsoever.

He has abdicated Government here, by declaring us out of his Protection and waging War against us.

He has plundered our Seas, ravaged our Coasts, burnt our towns, and destroyed the Lives of our People.

He is, at this Time, transporting large Armies of foreign Mercenaries to compleat the works of Death, Desolation, and Tyranny, already begun with circumstances of Cruelty and Perfidy, scarcely paralleled in the most barbarous Ages, and totally unworthy the Head of a civilized Nation.

He has constrained our fellow Citizens taken Captive on the high Seas to bear Arms against their Country, to become the Executioners of their Friends and Brethren, or to fall themselves by their Hands.

He has excited domestic Insurrections amongst us, and has endeavoured to bring on the Inhabitants of our Frontiers, the merciless Indian Savages, whose known Rule of Warfare, is an undistinguished Destruction, of all Ages, Sexes and Conditions.

In every state of these Oppressions we have Petitioned for Redress in the most humble Terms: Our repeated Petitions have been answered only by repeated Injury. A Prince, whose Character is thus marked by every act which may define a Tyrant, is unfit to be the Ruler of a free People.

Nor have we been wanting in Attentions to our British Brethren. We have warned them from Time to Time of Attempts by their Legislature to extend an unwarrantable Jurisdiction over us. We have reminded them of the Circumstances of our Emigration and Settlement here. We have appealed to their native Justice and Magnanimity, and we have conjured them by the Ties of our common Kindred to disavow these Usurpations, which, would inevitably interrupt our Connections and Correspondence. They too have been deaf to the Voice of Justice and of Consanguinity. We must, therefore, acquiesce in the Necessity, which denounces our Separation, and hold them, as we hold the rest of Mankind, Enemies in War, in Peace, Friends.

We, therefore, the Representatives of the UNITED STATES OF AMERICA, in General Congress Assembled, appealing to the Supreme Judge of the World for the Rectitude of our Intentions, do, in the Name, and by the Authority of the good People of these Colonies, solemnly Publish and Declare, That these United Colonies are, and of Right ought to be, Free and Independent States; that they are absolved from all Allegiance to the British Crown, and that all political Connection between them and the State of Great-Britain, is and ought to be totally dissolved; and that as Free and Independent States, they have full Power to levy War, conclude Peace, contract Alliances, establish Commerce, and to do all other Acts and Things which Independent States may of right do. And for the support of this declaration, with a firm Reliance on the Protection of divine Providence, we mutually pledge to each other our lives, our Fortunes, and our sacred Honor.

Appendix B

THE CONSTITUTION OF THE UNITED STATES

PREAMBLE

We the People of the United States, in Order to form a more perfect Union, establish Justice, insure domestic Tranquility, provide for the common defence, promote the general Welfare, and secure the Blessings of Liberty to ourselves and our Posterity, do ordain and establish this Constitution for the United States of America.

ARTICLE I

SECTION 1. All legislative Powers herein granted shall be vested in a Congress of the United States, which shall consist of a Senate and House of Representatives.

SECTION 2. The House of Representatives shall be composed of Members chosen every second Year by the People of the several States, and the Electors in each State shall have the Qualifications requisite for Electors of the most numerous Branch of the State Legislature.

No Person shall be a Representative who shall not have attained to the Age of twenty five Years, and been seven Years a Citizen of the United States, and who shall not, when elected, be an Inhabitant of that State in which he shall be chosen.

Representatives and direct Taxes shall be apportioned among the several States which may be included within this Union, according to their respective Numbers, which shall be determined by adding to the whole Number of free Persons, including those bound to Service for a Term of Years, and excluding Indians not taxed, three fifths of all other Persons. The actual Enumeration shall be made within three Years after the first Meeting of the Congress of the United States, and within every subsequent Term of ten Years, in such Manner as they shall by Law direct. The Number of Representatives shall not exceed one for every thirty Thousand, but each State shall have at Least one Representative; and until such enumeration shall be made, the State of New Hampshire shall be entitled to chuse three, Massachusetts eight, Rhode Island and Providence Plantations one, Connecticut five, New York six, New Jersey four, Pennsylvania eight, Delaware one, Maryland six, Virginia ten, North Carolina five, South Carolina five, and Georgia three.

When vacancies happen in the Representation from any State, the Executive Authority thereof shall issue Writs of Election to fill such Vacancies.

The House of Representatives shall chuse their Speaker and other Officers; and shall have the sole Power of Impeachment.

SECTION 3. The Senate of the United States shall be composed of two Senators from each State, chosen by the Legislature thereof, for six Years; and each Senator shall have one Vote.

Immediately after they shall be assembled in Consequence of the first Election, they shall be divided as equally as may be into three Classes. The Seats of the Senators of the first Class shall be vacated at the Expiration of the second Year, of the second Class at the Expiration of the fourth Year, and of the third Class at the Expiration of the sixth Year, so that one third may be chosen every second Year; and if Vacancies happen by Resignation, or otherwise, during the Recess of the Legislature of any State, the Executive thereof may make temporary Appointments until the next Meeting of the Legislature, which shall then fill such Vacancies.

No Person shall be a Senator who shall not have attained to the Age of thirty Years, and been nine Years a Citizen of the United States, and who shall not, when elected, be an Inhabitant of that State for which he shall be chosen.

The Vice President of the United States shall be President of the Senate, but shall have no Vote, unless they be equally divided.

The Senate shall chuse their other Officers, and also a President pro tempore, in the Absence of the Vice President, or when he shall exercise the Office of President of the United States.

The Senate shall have the sole Power to try all Impeachments. When sitting for that Purpose, they shall be on Oath or Affirmation. When the President of the United States is tried, the Chief Justice shall preside: And no Person shall be convicted without the Concurrence of two thirds of the Members present.

Judgment in Cases of Impeachment shall not extend further than to removal from Office, and disqualification to hold and enjoy any Office of honor, Trust, or Profit under the United States: but the Party convicted shall nevertheless be liable and subject to Indictment, Trial, Judgment, and Punishment, according to Law.

SECTION 4. The Times, Places and Manner of holding Elections for Senators and Representatives, shall be prescribed in each State by the Legislature thereof; but the Congress may at any time by Law make or alter such Regulations, except as to the Places of chusing Senators.

The Congress shall assemble at least once in every Year, and such Meeting shall be on the first Monday in December, unless they shall by Law appoint a different Day.

SECTION 5. Each House shall be the Judge of the Elections, Returns, and Qualifications of its own Members, and a Majority of each shall constitute a Quorum to do Business; but a smaller Number may adjourn from day to day, and may be authorized to compel the Attendance of absent Members, in such Manner, and under such Penalties as each House may provide.

Each House may determine the Rules of its Proceedings, punish its Members for disorderly Behavior, and, with the Concurrence of two thirds, expel a Member.

Each House shall keep a Journal of its Proceedings, and from time to time publish the same, excepting such Parts as may in their Judgment require Secrecy; and the Yeas and Nays of the Members of either House on any question shall, at the Desire of one fifth of those Present, be entered on the Journal.

Neither House, during the Session of Congress, shall, without the Consent of the other, adjourn for more than three days, nor to any other Place than that in which the two Houses shall be sitting.

SECTION 6. The Senators and Representatives shall receive a Compensation for their Services, to be ascertained by Law, and paid out of the Treasury of the United States. They shall in all Cases, except Treason, Felony and Breach of the Peace, be privileged from Arrest during their Attendance at the Session of their respective Houses, and in going to and returning from the same; and for any Speech or Debate in either House, they shall not be questioned in any other Place.

No Senator or Representative shall, during the Time for which he was elected, be appointed to any civil Office under the Authority of the United States, which shall have been created, or the Emoluments whereof shall have been increased during such time; and no Person holding any Office under the United States, shall be a Member of either House during his Continuance in Office.

SECTION 7. All Bills for raising Revenue shall originate in the House of Representatives; but the Senate may propose or concur with Amendments as on other Bills.

Every Bill which shall have passed the House of Representatives and the Senate, shall, before it become a Law, be presented to the President of the United States; If he approve he shall sign it, but if not he shall return it, with his Objections to the House in which it shall have originated, who shall enter the Objections at large on their Journal, and proceed to reconsider it. If after such Reconsideration two thirds of that House shall agree to pass the Bill, it shall be sent together with the Objections, to the other House, by which it shall likewise be reconsidered, and if approved by two thirds of that House, it shall become a Law. But in all such Cases the Votes of both Houses shall be determined by Yeas and Nays, and the Names of the Persons voting for and against the Bill shall be entered on the Journal of each House respectively. If any Bill shall not be returned by the President within ten Days (Sundays excepted) after it shall have been presented to him, the Same shall be a Law, in like Manner as if he had signed it, unless the Congress by their Adjournment prevent its Return in which Case it shall not be a Law.

Every Order, Resolution, or Vote, to which the Concurrence of the Senate and House of Representatives may be necessary (except on a question of Adjournment) shall be presented to the President of the United States; and before the Same shall take Effect, shall be approved by him, or being disapproved by him, shall be repassed by two thirds of the Senate and House of Representatives, according to the Rules and Limitations prescribed in the Case of a Bill.

SECTION 8. The Congress shall have Power To lay and collect Taxes, Duties, Imposts and Excises, to pay the Debts and provide for the common Defence and general Welfare of the United States; but all Duties, Imposts and Excises shall be uniform throughout the United States;

To borrow Money on the credit of the United States;

To regulate Commerce with foreign Nations, and among the several States, and with the Indian Tribes;

To establish an uniform Rule of Naturalization, and uniform Laws on the subject of Bankruptcies throughout the United States;

To coin Money, regulate the Value thereof, and of foreign Coin, and fix the Standard of Weights and Measures;

To provide for the Punishment of counterfeiting the Securities and current Coin of the United States;

To establish Post Offices and post Roads;

To promote the Progress of Science and useful Arts, by securing for limited Times to Authors and Inventors the exclusive Right to their respective Writings and Discoveries;

To constitute Tribunals inferior to the supreme Court;

To define and punish Piracies and Felonies committed on the high Seas, and Offenses against the Law of Nations;

To declare War, grant Letters of Marque and Reprisal, and make Rules concerning Captures on Land and Water;

To raise and support Armies, but no Appropriation of Money to that Use shall be for a longer Term than two Years;

To provide and maintain a Navy;

To make Rules for the Government and Regulation of the land and naval Forces;

To provide for calling forth the Militia to execute the Laws of the Union, suppress Insurrections and repel Invasions;

To provide for organizing, arming, and disciplining, the Militia, and for governing such Part of them as may be employed in the Service of the United States, reserving to the States respectively, the Appointment of the Officers, and the Authority of training the Militia according to the discipline prescribed by Congress;

To exercise exclusive Legislation in all Cases whatsoever, over such District (not exceeding ten Miles square) as may, by Cession of particular States, and the Acceptance of Congress, become the Seat of the Government of the United States, and to exercise like Authority over all Places purchased by the Consent of the Legislature of the State in which the Same shall be, for the Erection of Forts, Magazines, Arsenals, dock-Yards, and other needful Buildings;—And

To make all Laws which shall be necessary and proper for carrying into Execution the foregoing Powers, and all other Powers vested by this Constitution in the Government of the United States, or in any Department or Officer thereof.

SECTION 9. The Migration or Importation of such Persons as any of the States now existing shall think proper to admit, shall not be prohibited by the Congress prior to the Year one thousand eight hundred and eight, but a Tax or duty may be imposed on such Importation, not exceeding ten dollars for each Person.

The privilege of the Writ of Habeas Corpus shall not be suspended, unless when in Cases of Rebellion or Invasion the public Safety may require it.

No Bill of Attainder or ex post facto Law shall be passed.

No Capitation, or other direct, Tax shall be laid, unless in Proportion to the Census or Enumeration herein before directed to be taken.

No Tax or Duty shall be laid on Articles exported from any State.

No Preference shall be given by any Regulation of Commerce or Revenue to the Ports of one State over those of another: nor shall Vessels bound to, or from, one State be obliged to enter, clear, or pay Duties in another.

No Money shall be drawn from the Treasury, but in Consequence of Appropriations made by Law; and a regular Statement and Account of the Receipts and Expenditures of all public Money shall be published from time to time.

No Title of Nobility shall be granted by the United States: And no Person holding any Office of Profit or Trust under them, shall, without the Consent of the Congress, accept of any present, Emolument, Office, or Title, of any kind whatever, from any King, Prince, or foreign State.

SECTION 10. No State shall enter into any Treaty, Alliance, or Confederation; grant Letters of Marque and Reprisal; coin Money; emit Bills of Credit; make any Thing but gold and silver Coin a Tender in Payment of Debts; pass any Bill of Attainder, ex post facto Law, or Law impairing the Obligation of Contracts, or grant any Title of Nobility.

No State shall, without the Consent of the Congress, lay any Imposts or Duties on Imports or Exports, except what may be absolutely necessary for executing its inspection Laws: and the net Produce of all Duties and Imposts, laid by any State on Imports or Exports, shall be for the Use of the Treasury of the United States; and all such Laws shall be subject to the Revision and Controul of the Congress.

No State shall, without the Consent of Congress, lay any Duty of Tonnage, keep Troops, or Ships of War in time of Peace, enter into any Agreement or Compact with another State, or with a foreign Power, or engage in War, unless actually invaded, or in such imminent Danger as will not admit of delay.

ARTICLE II

SECTION 1. The executive Power shall be vested in a President of the United States of America. He shall hold his Office during the Term of four Years, and, together with the Vice President, chosen for the same Term, be elected, as follows:

Each State shall appoint, in such Manner as the Legislature thereof may direct, a Number of Electors, equal to the whole Number of Senators and Representatives to which the State may be entitled in the Congress; but no Senator or Representative, or Person holding an Office of Trust or Profit under the United States, shall be appointed an Elector.

The Electors shall meet in their respective States, and vote by Ballot for two Persons, of whom one at least shall not be an Inhabitant of the same State with themselves. And they shall make a List of all the Persons voted for, and of the Number of Votes for each; which List they shall sign and certify, and transmit sealed to the Seat of the Government of the United States, directed to the President of the Senate. The President of the Senate shall, in the Presence of the Senate and House of Representatives, open all the Certificates, and the Votes shall then be counted. The Person having the greatest Number of Votes shall be the President, if such Number be a Majority of the whole Number of Electors appointed; and if there be more than one who have such Majority, and have an equal Number of Votes, then the House of Representatives shall immediately chuse by Ballot one of them for President; and if no Person have a Majority, then from the five highest on the List the said House shall in like Manner chuse the President. But in chusing the President, the Votes shall be taken by States, the Representation from each State having one Vote; A quorum for this Purpose shall consist of a Member or Members from two thirds of the States, and a Majority of all the States shall be necessary to a Choice. In every Case, after the Choice of the President, the Person having the greater Number of Votes of the Electors shall be the Vice President. But if there should remain two or more who have equal Votes, the Senate shall chuse from them by Ballot the Vice President.

The Congress may determine the Time of chusing the Electors, and the Day on which they shall give their Votes; which Day shall be the same throughout the United States.

No person except a natural born Citizen, or a Citizen of the United States, at the time of the Adoption of this Constitution, shall be eligible to the Office of President; neither shall any Person be eligible to that Office who shall not have attained to the Age of thirty five Years, and been fourteen Years a Resident within the United States.

In Case of the Removal of the President from Office, or of his Death, Resignation or Inability to discharge the Powers and Duties of the said Office, the same shall devolve on the Vice President, and the Congress may by Law provide for the Case of Removal, Death, Resignation or Inability, both of the President and Vice President, declaring what Officer shall then act as President, and such Officer shall act accordingly, until the Disability be removed, or a President shall be elected.

The President shall, at stated Times, receive for his Services, a Compensation, which shall neither be increased nor diminished during the Period for which he shall have been elected, and he shall not receive within that Period any other Emolument from the United States, or any of them.

Before he enter on the Execution of his Office, he shall take the following Oath or Affirmation: "I do solemnly swear (or affirm) that I will faithfully execute the Office of President of the United States, and will to the best of my Ability, preserve, protect and defend the Constitution of the United States."

SECTION 2. The President shall be Commander in Chief of the Army and Navy of the United States, and of the Militia of the several States, when called into the actual Service of the United States; he may require the Opinion, in writing, of the principal Officer in each of the executive Departments, upon any Subject relating to the Duties of their respective Offices, and he shall have Power to grant Reprieves and Pardons for Offenses against the United States, except in Cases of Impeachment.

He shall have Power, by and with the Advice and Consent of the Senate to make Treaties, provided two thirds of the Senators present concur; and he shall nominate, and by and with the Advice and Consent of the Senate, shall appoint Ambassadors, other public Ministers and Consuls, Judges of the supreme Court, and all other Officers of the United States, whose Appointments are not herein otherwise provided for, and which shall be established by Law; but the Congress may by Law vest the Appointment of such inferior Officers, as they think proper, in the President alone, in the Courts of Law, or in the Heads of Departments.

The President shall have Power to fill up all Vacancies that may happen during the Recess of the Senate, by granting Commissions which shall expire at the End of their next Session.

SECTION 3. He shall from time to time give to the Congress Information of the State of the Union, and recommend to their Consideration such Measures as he shall judge necessary and expedient; he may, on extraordinary Occasions, convene both Houses, or either of them, and in Case of Disagreement between them, with Respect to the Time of Adjournment, he may adjourn them to such Time as he shall think proper; he shall receive Ambassadors and other public Ministers; he shall take Care that the Laws be faithfully executed, and shall Commission all the Officers of the United States.

SECTION 4. The President, Vice President and all civil Officers of the United States, shall be removed from Office on Impeachment for, and Conviction of, Treason, Bribery, or other high Crimes and Misdemeanors.

ARTICLE III

SECTION 1. The judicial Power of the United States, shall be vested in one supreme Court, and in such inferior Courts as the Congress may from time to time ordain and establish. The Judges, both of the supreme and inferior Courts, shall hold their Offices during good Behaviour, and shall, at stated Times, receive for their Services a Compensation, which shall not be diminished during their Continuance in Office.

SECTION 2. The judicial Power shall extend to all Cases, in Law and Equity, arising under this Constitution, the Laws of the United States, and Treaties made, or which shall be made, under their Authority;—to all Cases affecting Ambassadors, other public Ministers and Consuls;—to all Cases of admiralty and maritime Jurisdiction;—to Controversies to which the United States shall be a Party;—to Controversies between two or more States;—between a State and Citizens of another State;—between Citizens of different States;—between Citizens of the same State claiming Lands under Grants of different States, and between a State, or the Citizens thereof, and foreign States, Citizens or Subjects.

In all Cases affecting Ambassadors, other public Ministers and Consuls, and those in which a State shall be a Party, the supreme Court shall have original Jurisdiction. In all the other Cases before mentioned, the supreme Court shall have appellate Jurisdiction, both as to Law and Fact, with such Exceptions, and under such Regulations as the Congress shall make.

The Trial of all Crimes, except in Cases of Impeachment, shall be by Jury; and such Trial shall be held in the State where the said Crimes shall have been committed; but when not committed within any State, the Trial shall be at such Place or Places as the Congress may by Law have directed.

SECTION 3. Treason against the United States, shall consist only in levying War against them, or, in adhering to their Enemies, giving them Aid and Comfort. No Person shall be convicted of Treason unless on the Testimony of two Witnesses to the same overt Act, or on Confession in open Court.

The Congress shall have Power to declare the Punishment of Treason, but no Attainder of Treason shall work Corruption of Blood, or Forfeiture except during the Life of the Person attainted.

ARTICLE IV

SECTION 1. Full Faith and Credit shall be given in each State to the public Acts, Records, and judicial Proceedings of every other State. And the Congress may by general Laws prescribe the Manner in which such Acts, Records and Proceedings shall be proved, and the Effect thereof.

SECTION 2. The Citizens of each State shall be entitled to all Privileges and Immunities of Citizens in the several States.

A Person charged in any State with Treason, Felony, or other Crime, who shall flee from Justice, and be found in another State, shall on Demand of the executive Authority of the State from which he fled, be delivered up, to be removed to the State having Jurisdiction of the Crime.

No Person held to Service or Labour in one State, under the Laws thereof, escaping into another, shall, in Consequence of any Law or Regulation therein, be discharged from such Service or Labour, but shall be delivered up on Claim of the Party to whom such Service or Labour may be due.

SECTION 3. New States may be admitted by the Congress into this Union; but no new State shall be formed or erected within the Jurisdiction of any other

State; nor any State be formed by the Junction of two or more States, or Parts of States, without the Consent of the Legislatures of the States concerned as well as of the Congress.

The Congress shall have Power to dispose of and make all needful Rules and Regulations respecting the Territory or other Property belonging to the United States; and nothing in this Constitution shall be so construed as to Prejudice any Claims of the United States, or of any particular State.

SECTION 4. The United States shall guarantee to every State in this Union a Republican Form of Government, and shall protect each of them against Invasion; and on Application of the Legislature, or of the Executive (when the Legislature cannot be convened) against domestic Violence.

ARTICLE V

The Congress, whenever two thirds of both Houses shall deem it necessary, shall propose Amendments to this Constitution, or, on the Application of the Legislatures of two thirds of the several States, shall call a Convention for proposing Amendments, which, in either Case, shall be valid to all Intents and Purposes, as part of this Constitution, when ratified by the Legislatures of three fourths of the several States, or by Conventions in three fourths thereof, as the one or the other Mode of Ratification may be proposed by the Congress; Provided that no Amendment which may be made prior to the Year One thousand eight hundred and eight shall in any Manner affect the first and fourth Clauses in the Ninth Section of the first Article; and that no State, without its Consent, shall be deprived of its equal Suffrage in the Senate.

ARTICLE VI

All Debts contracted and Engagements entered into, before the Adoption of this Constitution shall be as valid against the United States under this Constitution, as under the Confederation.

This Constitution, and the Laws of the United States which shall be made in Pursuance thereof; and all Treaties made, or which shall be made, under the Authority of the United States, shall be the supreme Law of the Land; and the Judges in every State shall be bound thereby, any Thing in the Constitution or Laws of any State to the Contrary notwithstanding.

The Senators and Representatives before mentioned, and the Members of the several State Legislatures, and all executive and judicial Officers, both of the United States and of the several States, shall be bound by Oath or Affirmation, to support this Constitution; but no religious Test shall ever be required as a Qualification to any Office or public Trust under the United States.

ARTICLE VII

The Ratification of the Conventions of nine States shall be sufficient for the Establishment of this Constitution between the States so ratifying the Same.

AMENDMENT I [1791]

Congress shall make no law respecting an establishment of religion, or prohibiting the free exercise thereof; or abridging the freedom of speech, or of the press; or the right of the people peaceably to assemble, and to petition the Government for a redress of grievances.

AMENDMENT II [1791]

A well regulated Militia, being necessary to the security of a free State, the right of the people to keep and bear Arms, shall not be infringed.

AMENDMENT III [1791]

No Soldier shall, in time of peace be quartered in any house, without the consent of the Owner, nor in time of war, but in a manner to be prescribed by law.

AMENDMENT IV [1791]

The right of the people to be secure in their persons, houses, papers, and effects, against unreasonable searches and seizures, shall not be violated, and no Warrants shall issue, but upon probable cause, supported by Oath or affirmation, and particularly describing the place to be searched, and the persons or things to be seized.

AMENDMENT V [1791]

No person shall be held to answer for a capital, or otherwise infamous crime, unless on a presentment or indictment of a Grand Jury, except in cases arising in the land or naval forces, or in the Militia, when in actual service in time of War or public danger; nor shall any person be subject for the same offense to be twice put in jeopardy of life or limb; nor shall be compelled in any criminal case to be a witness against himself, nor be deprived of life, liberty, or property, without due process of law; nor shall private property be taken for public use, without just compensation.

AMENDMENT VI [1791]

In all criminal prosecutions, the accused shall enjoy the right to a speedy and public trial, by an impartial jury of the State and district wherein the crime shall have been committed, which district shall have been previously ascertained by law, and to be informed of the nature and cause of the accusation; to be confronted with the witnesses against him; to have compulsory process for obtaining witnesses in his favor, and to have the Assistance of Counsel for his defence.

AMENDMENT VII [1791]

In Suits at common law, where the value in controversy shall exceed twenty dollars, the right of trial by jury shall be preserved, and no fact tried by a jury, shall be otherwise re-examined in any Court of the United States, than according to the rules of the common law.

AMENDMENT VIII [1791]

Excessive bail shall not be required, nor excessive fines imposed, nor cruel and unusual punishments inflicted.

AMENDMENT IX [1791]

The enumeration in the Constitution, of certain rights, shall not be construed to deny or disparage others retained by the people.

AMENDMENT X [1791]

The powers not delegated to the United States by the Constitution, nor prohibited by it to the States, are reserved to the States respectively, or to the people.

AMENDMENT XI [1798]

The Judicial power of the United States shall not be construed to extend to any suit in law or equity, commenced or prosecuted against one of the United States by Citizens of another State, or by Citizens or Subjects of any Foreign State.

AMENDMENT XII [1804]

The Electors shall meet in their respective states, and vote by ballot for President and Vice-President, one of whom, at least, shall not be an inhabitant of the same state with themselves; they shall name in their ballots the person voted for as President, and in distinct ballots the person voted for as Vice-President, and they shall make distinct lists of all persons voted for as President, and of all persons voted for as Vice-President, and of the number of votes for each, which lists they shall sign and certify, and transmit sealed to the seat of the government of the United States, directed to the President of the Senate;—The President of the Senate shall, in the presence of the Senate and House of Representatives, open all the certificates and the votes shall then be counted;—The person having the greatest number of votes for President, shall be the President, if such number be a majority of the whole number of Electors appointed; and if no person have such majority, then from the persons having the highest numbers not exceeding three on the list of those voted for as President, the House of Representatives shall choose immediately, by ballot, the President. But in choosing the President, the votes shall be taken by states, the representation from each state having one vote; a quorum for this purpose shall consist of a member or members from two-thirds of the states, and a majority of all states shall be necessary to a choice. And if the House of Representatives shall not choose a President whenever the right of choice shall devolve upon them, before the fourth day of March next following, then the Vice-President shall act as President, as in the case of the death or other constitutional disability of the President.—The person having the greatest number of votes as Vice-President, shall be the Vice-President, if such number be a majority of the whole number of Electors appointed, and if no person have a majority, then from the two highest numbers on the list, the Senate shall choose the Vice-President; a quorum for the purpose shall consist of two-thirds of the whole number of Senators, and a majority of the whole number shall be necessary to a choice. But no person constitutionally ineligible to the office of President shall be eligible to that of Vice-President of the United States.

AMENDMENT XIII [1865]

SECTION 1. Neither slavery nor involuntary servitude, except as a punishment for crime whereof the party shall have been duly convicted, shall exist within the United States, or any place subject to their jurisdiction.

SECTION 2. Congress shall have power to enforce this article by appropriate legislation.

AMENDMENT XIV [1868]

SECTION 1. All persons born or naturalized in the United States, and subject to the jurisdiction thereof, are citizens of the United States and of the State wherein they reside. No State shall make or enforce any law which shall abridge the privileges or immunities of citizens of the United States; nor shall any State deprive any person of life, liberty, or property, without due process of law; nor deny to any person within its jurisdiction the equal protection of the laws.

SECTION 2. Representatives shall be apportioned among the several States according to their respective numbers, counting the whole number of persons in each State, excluding Indians not taxed. But when the right to vote at any election for the choice of electors for President and Vice President of the United States, Representatives in Congress, the Executive and Judicial officers of a State, or the members of the Legislature thereof, is denied to any of the male inhabitants of such State, being twenty-one years of age, and citizens of the United States, or in any way abridged, except for participation in rebellion, or other crime, the basis of representation therein shall be reduced in the proportion which the number of such male citizens shall bear to the whole number of male citizens twenty-one years of age in such State.

SECTION 3. No person shall be a Senator or Representative in Congress, or elector of President and Vice President, or hold any office, civil or military, under the United States, or under any State, who having previously taken an oath, as a member of Congress, or as an officer of the United States, or as a member of any State legislature, or as an executive or judicial officer of any State, to support the Constitution of the United States, shall have engaged in insurrection or rebellion against the same, or given aid or comfort to the enemies thereof. But Congress may by a vote of two-thirds of each House, remove such disability.

SECTION 4. The validity of the public debt of the United States, authorized by law, including debts incurred for payment of pensions and bounties for services in suppressing insurrection or rebellion, shall not be questioned. But neither the United States nor any State shall assume or pay any debt or obligation incurred in aid of insurrection or rebellion against the United States, or any claim for the loss or emancipation of any slave; but all such debts, obligations and claims shall be held illegal and void.

SECTION 5. The Congress shall have power to enforce, by appropriate legislation, the provisions of this article.

AMENDMENT XV [1870]

SECTION 1. The right of citizens of the United States to vote shall not be denied or abridged by the United States or by any State on account of race, color, or previous condition of servitude.

SECTION 2. The Congress shall have power to enforce this article by appropriate legislation.

AMENDMENT XVI [1913]

The Congress shall have power to lay and collect taxes on incomes, from whatever source derived, without apportionment among the several States, and without regard to any census or enumeration.

AMENDMENT XVII [1913]

SECTION 1. The Senate of the United States shall be composed of two Senators from each State, elected by the people thereof, for six years; and each Senator shall have one vote. The electors in each State shall have the qualifications requisite for electors of the most numerous branch of the State legislatures.

SECTION 2. When vacancies happen in the representation of any State in the Senate, the executive authority of such State shall issue writs of election to fill such vacancies: Provided, That the legislature of any State may empower the executive thereof to make temporary appointments until the people fill the vacancies by election as the legislature may direct.

SECTION 3. This amendment shall not be so construed as to affect the election or term of any Senator chosen before it becomes valid as part of the Constitution.

AMENDMENT XVIII [1919]

SECTION 1. After one year from the ratification of this article the manufacture, sale, or transportation of intoxicating liquors within, the importation thereof into, or the exportation thereof from the United States and all territory subject to the jurisdiction thereof for beverage purposes is hereby prohibited.

SECTION 2. The Congress and the several States shall have concurrent power to enforce this article by appropriate legislation.

SECTION 3. This article shall be inoperative unless it shall have been ratified as an amendment to the Constitution by the legislatures of the several States, as provided in the Constitution, within seven years from the date of the submission hereof to the States by the Congress.

AMENDMENT XIX [1920]

SECTION 1. The right of citizens of the United States to vote shall not be denied or abridged by the United States or by any State on account of sex.

SECTION 2. Congress shall have power to enforce this article by appropriate legislation.

AMENDMENT XX [1933]

SECTION 1. The terms of the President and Vice President shall end at noon on the 20th day of January, and the terms of Senators and Representatives at noon on the 3d day of January, of the years in which such terms would have ended if this article had not been ratified; and the terms of their successors shall then begin.

SECTION 2. The Congress shall assemble at least once in every year, and such meeting shall begin at noon on the 3d day of January, unless they shall by law appoint a different day.

SECTION 3. If, at the time fixed for the beginning of the term of the President, the President elect shall have died, the Vice President elect shall become President. If the President shall not have been chosen before the time fixed for the beginning of his term, or if the President elect shall have failed to qualify, then the Vice President elect shall act as President until a President shall have qualified; and the Congress may by law provide for the case wherein neither a President elect nor a Vice President elect shall have qualified, declaring who shall then act as President, or the manner in which one who is to act shall be selected, and such person shall act accordingly until a President or Vice President shall have qualified.

SECTION 4. The Congress may by law provide for the case of the death of any of the persons from whom the House of Representatives may choose a President whenever the right of choice shall have devolved upon them, and for the case of the death of any of the persons from whom the Senate may choose a Vice President whenever the right of choice shall have devolved upon them.

SECTION 5. Sections 1 and 2 shall take effect on the 15th day of October following the ratification of this article.

SECTION 6. This article shall be inoperative unless it shall have been ratified as an amendment to the Constitution by the legislatures of three-fourths of the several States within seven years from the date of its submission.

AMENDMENT XXI [1933]

SECTION 1. The eighteenth article of amendment to the Constitution of the United States is hereby repealed.

SECTION 2. The transportation or importation into any State, Territory, or possession of the United States for delivery or use therein of intoxicating liquors, in violation of the laws thereof, is hereby prohibited.

SECTION 3. This article shall be inoperative unless it shall have been ratified as an amendment to the Constitution by conventions in the several States, as provided in the Constitution, within seven years from the date of the submission hereof to the States by the Congress.

AMENDMENT XXII [1951]

SECTION 1. No person shall be elected to the office of the President more than twice, and no person who has held the office of President, or acted as President, for more than two years of a term to which some other person was elected President shall be elected to the office of President more than once. But this Article shall not apply to any person holding the office of President when this Article was proposed by the Congress, and shall not prevent any person who may be holding the office of President, or acting as President, during the term within which this Article becomes operative from holding the office of President or acting as President during the remainder of such term.

SECTION 2. This article shall be inoperative unless it shall have been ratified as an amendment to the Constitution by the legislatures of three-fourths of the several States within seven years from the date of its submission to the States by the Congress.

AMENDMENT XXIII [1961]

SECTION 1. The District constituting the seat of Government of the United States shall appoint in such manner as the Congress may direct:

A number of electors of President and Vice President equal to the whole number of Senators and Representatives in Congress to which the District would be entitled if it were a State, but in no event more than the least populous state; they shall be in addition to those appointed by the states, but they shall be considered, for the purposes of the election of President and Vice President, to be electors appointed by a state; and they shall meet in the District and perform such duties as provided by the twelfth article of amendment.

SECTION 2. The Congress shall have power to enforce this article by appropriate legislation.

AMENDMENT XXIV [1964]

SECTION 1. The right of citizens of the United States to vote in any primary or other election for President or Vice President, for electors for President or Vice President, or for Senator or Representative in Congress, shall not be denied or abridged by the United States, or any State by reason of failure to pay any poll tax or other tax.

SECTION 2. The Congress shall have power to enforce this article by appropriate legislation.

AMENDMENT XXV [1967]

SECTION 1. In case of the removal of the President from office or of his death or resignation, the Vice President shall become President.

SECTION 2. Whenever there is a vacancy in the office of the Vice President, the President shall nominate a Vice President who shall take office upon confirmation by a majority vote of both Houses of Congress.

SECTION 3. Whenever the President transmits to the President pro tempore of the Senate and the Speaker of the House of Representatives his written declaration that he is unable to discharge the powers and duties of his office, and until he transmits to them a written declaration to the contrary, such powers and duties shall be discharged by the Vice President as Acting President.

SECTION 4. Whenever the Vice President and a majority of either the principal officers of the executive departments or of such other body as Congress may by law provide, transmit to the President pro tempore of the Senate and the Speaker of the House of Representatives their written declaration that the President is unable to discharge the powers and duties of his office, the Vice President shall immediately assume the powers and duties of the office as Acting President.

Thereafter, when the President transmits to the President pro tempore of the Senate and the Speaker of the House of Representatives his written declaration that no inability exists, he shall resume the powers and duties of his office unless the Vice President and a majority of either the principal officers of the executive department or of such other body as Congress may by law provide, transmit within four days to the President pro tempore of the Senate and the Speaker of the House of Representatives their written declaration that the President is unable to discharge the powers and duties of his office. Thereupon Congress shall decide the issue, assembling within forty-eight hours for that purpose if not in session. If the Congress, within twenty-one days after receipt of the latter written declaration, or, if Congress is not in session, within twenty-one days after Congress is required to assemble, determines by two-thirds vote of both Houses that the President is unable to discharge the powers and duties of his office, the Vice President shall continue to discharge the same as Acting President; otherwise, the President shall resume the powers and duties of his office.

AMENDMENT XXVI [1971]

SECTION 1. The right of citizens of the United States, who are eighteen years of age or older, to vote shall not be denied or abridged by the United States or by any State on account of age.

SECTION 2. The Congress shall have power to enforce this article by appropriate legislation.

AMENDMENT XXVII [1992]

No law, varying the compensation for the services of the Senators and Representatives, shall take effect, until an election of Representatives shall have intervened.

Appendix C

Supreme Court Justices since 1900

Chief Justices

Name	Years of Service	State App'd from	Appointing President	Age App'd	Political Affiliation	Educational Background*
Fuller, Melville Weston	1888–1910	Illinois	Cleveland	55	Democrat	Bowdoin College; studied at Harvard Law School
White, Edward Douglass	1910–1921	Louisiana	Taft	65	Democrat	Mount St. Mary's College; Georgetown College (now University)
Taft, William Howard	1921–1930	Connecticut	Harding	64	Republican	Yale; Cincinnati Law School
Hughes, Charles Evans	1930–1941	New York	Hoover	68	Republican	Colgate University; Brown; Columbia Law School
Stone, Harlan Fiske	1941–1946	New York	Roosevelt, F.	69	Republican	Amherst College; Columbia
Vinson, Frederick Moore	1946–1953	Kentucky	Truman	56	Democrat	Centre College
Warren, Earl	1953–1969	California	Eisenhower	62	Republican	University of California, Berkeley
Burger, Warren Earl	1969–1986	Virginia	Nixon	62	Republican	University of Minnesota; St. Paul College of Law (Mitchell College)
Rehnquist, William Hubbs	1986–2005	Virginia	Reagan	62	Republican	Stanford; Harvard; Stanford University Law School
Roberts, John G., Jr.	2005–present	District of Columbia	G. W. Bush	50	Republican	Harvard; Harvard Law School

*Source: Educational background information derived from Elder Witt, *Guide to the U.S. Supreme Court*, 2d ed. (Washington, D.C.: Congressional Quarterly Press, Inc., 1990). Reprinted with the permission of the publisher.

Associate Justices

Name	Years of Service	State App'd from	Appointing President	Age App'd	Political Affiliation	Educational Background*
Harlan, John Marshall	1877–1911	Kentucky	Hayes	61	Republican	Centre College; studied law at Transylvania University
Gray, Horace	1882–1902	Massachusetts	Arthur	54	Republican	Harvard College; Harvard Law School
Brewer, David Josiah	1890–1910	Kansas	Harrison	53	Republican	Wesleyan University; Yale; Albany Law School
Brown, Henry Billings	1891–1906	Michigan	Harrison	55	Republican	Yale; studied at Yale Law School and Harvard Law School
Shiras, George, Jr.	1892–1903	Pennsylvania	Harrison	61	Republican	Ohio University; Yale; studied law at Yale and privately
White, Edward Douglass	1894–1910	Louisiana	Cleveland	49	Democrat	Mount St. Mary's College; Georgetown College (now University)
Peckham, Rufus Wheeler	1896–1909	New York	Cleveland	58	Democrat	Read law in father's firm

Associate Justices (Continued)

Name	Years of Service	State App'd from	Appointing President	Age App'd	Political Affiliation	Educational Background*
McKenna, Joseph	1898–1925	California	McKinley	55	Republican	Benicia Collegiate Institute, Law Dept.
Holmes, Oliver Wendell, Jr.	1902–1932	Massachusetts	Roosevelt, T.	61	Republican	Harvard College; studied law at Harvard Law School
Day, William Rufus	1903–1922	Ohio	Roosevelt, T.	54	Republican	University of Michigan; University of Michigan Law School
Moody, William Henry	1906–1910	Massachusetts	Roosevelt, T.	53	Republican	Harvard; Harvard Law School
Lurton, Horace Harmon	1910–1914	Tennessee	Taft	66	Democrat	University of Chicago; Cumberland Law School
Hughes, Charles Evans	1910–1916	New York	Taft	48	Republican	Colgate University; Brown University; Columbia Law School
Van Devanter, Willis	1911–1937	Wyoming	Taft	52	Republican	Indiana Asbury University; University of Cincinnati Law School
Lamar, Joseph Rucker	1911–1916	Georgia	Taft	54	Democrat	University of Georgia; Bethany College; Washington and Lee University
Pitney, Mahlon	1912–1922	New Jersey	Taft	54	Republican	College of New Jersey (Princeton); read law under father
McReynolds, James Clark	1914–1941	Tennessee	Wilson	52	Democrat	Vanderbilt University; University of Virginia
Brandeis, Louis Dembitz	1916–1939	Massachusetts	Wilson	60	Democrat	Harvard Law School
Clarke, John Hessin	1916–1922	Ohio	Wilson	59	Democrat	Western Reserve University; read law under father
Sutherland, George	1922–1938	Utah	Harding	60	Republican	Brigham Young Academy; one year at University of Michigan Law School
Butler, Pierce	1923–1939	Minnesota	Harding	57	Democrat	Carleton College
Sanford, Edward Terry	1923–1930	Tennessee	Harding	58	Republican	University of Tennessee; Harvard; Harvard Law School
Stone, Harlan Fiske	1925–1941	New York	Coolidge	53	Republican	Amherst College; Columbia University Law School
Roberts, Owen Josephus	1930–1945	Pennsylvania	Hoover	55	Republican	University of Pennsylvania; University of Pennsylvania Law School
Cardozo, Benjamin Nathan	1932–1938	New York	Hoover	62	Democrat	Columbia University; two years at Columbia Law School
Black, Hugo Lafayette	1937–1971	Alabama	Roosevelt, F.	51	Democrat	Birmingham Medical College; University of Alabama Law School
Reed, Stanley Forman	1938–1957	Kentucky	Roosevelt, F.	54	Democrat	Kentucky Wesleyan University; Foreman Yale; Columbia University
Frankfurter, Felix	1939–1962	Massachusetts	Roosevelt, F.	57	Independent	College of the City of New York; Harvard Law School
Douglas, William Orville	1939–1975	Connecticut	Roosevelt, F.	41	Democrat	Whitman College; Columbia University Law School
Murphy, Frank	1940–1949	Michigan	Roosevelt, F.	50	Democrat	University of Michigan; Lincoln's Inn, London; Trinity College
Byrnes, James Francis	1941–1942	South Carolina	Roosevelt, F.	62	Democrat	Read law privately

Associate Justices (Continued)

Name	Years of Service	State App'd from	Appointing President	Age App'd	Political Affiliation	Educational Background*
Jackson, Robert Houghwout	1941–1954	New York	Roosevelt, F.	49	Democrat	Albany Law School
Rutledge, Wiley Blount	1943–1949	Iowa	Roosevelt, F.	49	Democrat	University of Wisconsin; University of Colorado
Burton, Harold Hitz	1945–1958	Ohio	Truman	57	Republican	Bowdoin College; Harvard University Law School
Clark, Thomas Campbell	1949–1967	Texas	Truman	50	Democrat	University of Texas
Minton, Sherman	1949–1956	Indiana	Truman	59	Democrat	Indiana University College of Law; Yale Law School
Harlan, John Marshall	1955–1971	New York	Eisenhower	56	Republican	Princeton; Oxford University; New York Law School
Brennan, William J., Jr.	1956–1990	New Jersey	Eisenhower	50	Democrat	University of Pennsylvania; Harvard Law School
Whittaker, Charles Evans	1957–1962	Missouri	Eisenhower	56	Republican	University of Kansas City Law School
Stewart, Potter	1958–1981	Ohio	Eisenhower	43	Republican	Yale; Yale Law School
White, Byron Raymond	1962–1993	Colorado	Kennedy	45	Democrat	University of Colorado; Oxford University; Yale Law School
Goldberg, Arthur Joseph	1962–1965	Illinois	Kennedy	54	Democrat	Northwestern University
Fortas, Abe	1965–1969	Tennessee	Johnson, L.	55	Democrat	Southwestern College; Yale Law School
Marshall, Thurgood	1967–1991	New York	Johnson, L.	59	Democrat	Lincoln University; Howard University Law School
Blackmun, Harry A.	1970–1994	Minnesota	Nixon	62	Republican	Harvard; Harvard Law School
Powell, Lewis F., Jr.	1972–1987	Virginia	Nixon	65	Democrat	Washington and Lee University; Washington and Lee University; Harvard Law School
Rehnquist, William H.	1972–1986	Arizona	Nixon	48	Republican	Stanford; Harvard; Stanford University Law School
Stevens, John Paul	1975–present	Illinois	Ford	55	Republican	University of Colorado; Northwestern University Law School
O'Connor, Sandra Day	1981–2006	Arizona	Reagan	51	Republican	Stanford; Stanford University Law School
Scalia, Antonin	1986–present	Virginia	Reagan	50	Republican	Georgetown University; Harvard Law School
Kennedy, Anthony M.	1988–present	California	Reagan	52	Republican	Stanford; London School of Economics; Harvard Law School
Souter, David Hackett	1990–present	New Hampshire	Bush, G. H. W.	51	Republican	Harvard; Oxford University
Thomas, Clarence	1991–present	District of Columbia	Bush, G. H. W.	43	Republican	Holy Cross College; Yale Law Columbia School
Ginsburg, Ruth Bader	1993–present	District of Columbia	Clinton	60	Democrat	Cornell University; Columbia Law School
Breyer, Stephen G.	1994–present	Massachusetts	Clinton	55	Democrat	Stanford; Oxford University; Harvard Law School
Alito, Samuel Anthony, Jr.	2006–present	New Jersey	G. W. Bush	55	Republican	Princeton University; Yale Law School
Sotomayor, Sonia	2009–present	New York	Obama	55	Democrat	Princeton University; Yale Law School

Appendix D

Party Control of Congress since 1900

Congress	Years	President	Majority Party in House	Majority Party in Senate
57th	1901–1903	T. Roosevelt	Republican	Republican
58th	1903–1905	T. Roosevelt	Republican	Republican
59th	1905–1907	T. Roosevelt	Republican	Republican
60th	1907–1909	T. Roosevelt	Republican	Republican
61st	1909–1911	Taft	Republican	Republican
62d	1911–1913	Taft	Democratic	Republican
63d	1913–1915	Wilson	Democratic	Democratic
64th	1915–1917	Wilson	Democratic	Democratic
65th	1917–1919	Wilson	Democratic	Democratic
66th	1919–1921	Wilson	Republican	Republican
67th	1921–1923	Harding	Republican	Republican
68th	1923–1925	Coolidge	Republican	Republican
69th	1925–1927	Coolidge	Republican	Republican
70th	1927–1929	Coolidge	Republican	Republican
71st	1929–1931	Hoover	Republican	Republican
72d	1931–1933	Hoover	Democratic	Republican
73d	1933–1935	F. Roosevelt	Democratic	Democratic
74th	1935–1937	F. Roosevelt	Democratic	Democratic
75th	1937–1939	F. Roosevelt	Democratic	Democratic
76th	1939–1941	F. Roosevelt	Democratic	Democratic
77th	1941–1943	F. Roosevelt	Democratic	Democratic
78th	1943–1945	F. Roosevelt	Democratic	Democratic
79th	1945–1947	Truman	Democratic	Democratic
80th	1947–1949	Truman	Republican	Democratic
81st	1949–1951	Truman	Democratic	Democratic
82d	1951–1953	Truman	Democratic	Democratic
83d	1953–1955	Eisenhower	Republican	Republican
84th	1955–1957	Eisenhower	Democratic	Democratic
85th	1957–1959	Eisenhower	Democratic	Democratic
86th	1959–1961	Eisenhower	Democratic	Democratic
87th	1961–1963	Kennedy	Democratic	Democratic
88th	1963–1965	Kennedy/Johnson	Democratic	Democratic
89th	1965–1967	Johnson	Democratic	Democratic
90th	1967–1969	Johnson	Democratic	Democratic
91st	1969–1971	Nixon	Democratic	Democratic
92d	1971–1973	Nixon	Democratic	Democratic
93d	1973–1975	Nixon/Ford	Democratic	Democratic
94th	1975–1977	Ford	Democratic	Democratic
95th	1977–1979	Carter	Democratic	Democratic
96th	1979–1981	Carter	Democratic	Democratic
97th	1981–1983	Reagan	Democratic	Republican
98th	1983–1985	Reagan	Democratic	Republican
99th	1985–1987	Reagan	Democratic	Republican
100th	1987–1989	Reagan	Democratic	Democratic
101st	1989–1991	G. H. W. Bush	Democratic	Democratic
102d	1991–1993	G. H. W. Bush	Democratic	Democratic
103d	1993–1995	Clinton	Democratic	Democratic
104th	1995–1997	Clinton	Republican	Republican
105th	1997–1999	Clinton	Republican	Republican
106th	1999–2001	Clinton	Republican	Republican
107th	2001–2003	G. W. Bush	Republican	Democratic
108th	2003–2005	G. W. Bush	Republican	Republican
109th	2005–2007	G. W. Bush	Republican	Republican
110th	2007–2009	G. W. Bush	Democratic	Democratic
111th	2009–2011	Obama	Democratic	Democratic

Appendix E

Information on U.S. Presidents

	Term of Service	Age at Inauguration	Party Affiliation	College or University	Occupation or Profession
1. George Washington	1789–1797	57	None		Planter
2. John Adams	1797–1801	61	Federalist	Harvard	Lawyer
3. Thomas Jefferson	1801–1809	57	Democratic-Republican	William and Mary	Planter, Lawyer
4. James Madison	1809–1817	57	Democratic-Republican	Princeton	Lawyer
5. James Monroe	1817–1825	58	Democratic-Republican	William and Mary	Lawyer
6. John Quincy Adams	1825–1829	57	Democratic-Republican	Harvard	Lawyer
7. Andrew Jackson	1829–1837	61	Democrat		Lawyer
8. Martin Van Buren	1837–1841	54	Democrat		Lawyer
9. William H. Harrison	1841	68	Whig	Hampden-Sydney	Soldier
10. John Tyler	1841–1845	51	Whig	William and Mary	Lawyer
11. James K. Polk	1845–1849	49	Democrat	U. of N. Carolina	Lawyer
12. Zachary Taylor	1849–1850	64	Whig		Soldier
13. Millard Fillmore	1850–1853	50	Whig		Lawyer
14. Franklin Pierce	1853–1857	48	Democrat	Bowdoin	Lawyer
15. James Buchanan	1857–1861	65	Democrat	Dickinson	Lawyer
16. Abraham Lincoln	1861–1865	52	Republican		Lawyer
17. Andrew Johnson	1865–1869	56	National Union†		Tailor
18. Ulysses S. Grant	1869–1877	46	Republican	U.S. Mil. Academy	Soldier
19. Rutherford B. Hayes	1877–1881	54	Republican	Kenyon	Lawyer
20. James A. Garfield	1881	49	Republican	Williams	Lawyer
21. Chester A. Arthur	1881–1885	51	Republican	Union	Lawyer
22. Grover Cleveland	1885–1889	47	Democrat		Lawyer
23. Benjamin Harrison	1889–1893	55	Republican	Miami	Lawyer
24. Grover Cleveland	1893–1897	55	Democrat		Lawyer
25. William McKinley	1897–1901	54	Republican	Allegheny College	Lawyer
26. Theodore Roosevelt	1901–1909	42	Republican	Harvard	Author
27. William H. Taft	1909–1913	51	Republican	Yale	Lawyer
28. Woodrow Wilson	1913–1921	56	Democrat	Princeton	Educator
29. Warren G. Harding	1921–1923	55	Republican		Editor
30. Calvin Coolidge	1923–1929	51	Republican	Amherst	Lawyer
31. Herbert C. Hoover	1929–1933	54	Republican	Stanford	Engineer
32. Franklin D. Roosevelt	1933–1945	51	Democrat	Harvard	Lawyer
33. Harry S Truman	1945–1953	60	Democrat		Businessman
34. Dwight D. Eisenhower	1953–1961	62	Republican	U.S. Mil. Academy	Soldier
35. John F. Kennedy	1961–1963	43	Democrat	Harvard	Author
36. Lyndon B. Johnson	1963–1969	55	Democrat	Southwest Texas State	Teacher
37. Richard M. Nixon	1969–1974	56	Republican	Whittier	Lawyer
38. Gerald R. Ford‡	1974–1977	61	Republican	Michigan	Lawyer
39. James E. Carter, Jr.	1977–1981	52	Democrat	U.S. Naval Academy	Businessman
40. Ronald W. Reagan	1981–1989	69	Republican	Eureka College	Actor
41. George H. W. Bush	1989–1993	64	Republican	Yale	Businessman
42. William J. Clinton	1993–2001	46	Democrat	Georgetown	Lawyer
43. George W. Bush	2001–2009	54	Republican	Yale	Businessman
44. Barack Obama	2009–	47	Democrat	Columbia	Lawyer

*Church preference; never joined any church.
†The National Union Party consisted of Republicans and War Democrats. Johnson was a Democrat.
**Inaugurated Dec. 6, 1973, to replace Agnew, who resigned Oct. 10, 1973.
‡Inaugurated Aug. 9, 1974, to replace Nixon, who resigned that same day.
§Inaugurated Dec. 19, 1974, to replace Ford, who became president Aug. 9, 1974.

Religion	Born	Died	Age at Death	Vice President	
1. Episcopalian	Feb. 22, 1732	Dec. 14, 1799	67	John Adams	(1789–1797)
2. Unitarian	Oct. 30, 1735	July 4, 1826	90	Thomas Jefferson	(1797–1801)
3. Unitarian*	Apr. 13, 1743	July 4, 1826	83	Aaron Burr	(1801–1805)
				George Clinton	(1805–1809)
4. Episcopalian	Mar. 16, 1751	June 28, 1836	85	George Clinton	(1809–1812)
				Elbridge Gerry	(1813–1814)
5. Episcopalian	Apr. 28, 1758	July 4, 1831	73	Daniel D. Tompkins	(1817–1825)
6. Unitarian	July 11, 1767	Feb. 23, 1848	80	John C. Calhoun	(1825–1829)
7. Presbyterian	Mar. 15, 1767	June 8, 1845	78	John C. Calhoun	(1829–1832)
				Martin Van Buren	(1833–1837)
8. Dutch Reformed	Dec. 5, 1782	July 24, 1862	79	Richard M. Johnson	(1837–1841)
9. Episcopalian	Feb. 9, 1773	Apr. 4, 1841	68	John Tyler	(1841)
10. Episcopalian	Mar. 29, 1790	Jan. 18, 1862	71		
11. Methodist	Nov. 2, 1795	June 15, 1849	53	George M. Dallas	(1845–1849)
12. Episcopalian	Nov. 24, 1784	July 9, 1850	65	Millard Fillmore	(1849–1850)
13. Unitarian	Jan. 7, 1800	Mar. 8, 1874	74		
14. Episcopalian	Nov. 23, 1804	Oct. 8, 1869	64	William R. King	(1853)
15. Presbyterian	Apr. 23, 1791	June 1, 1868	77	John C. Breckinridge	(1857–1861)
16. Presbyterian*	Feb. 12, 1809	Apr. 15, 1865	56	Hannibal Hamlin	(1861–1865)
				Andrew Johnson	(1865)
17. Methodist*	Dec. 29, 1808	July 31, 1875	66		
18. Methodist	Apr. 27, 1822	July 23, 1885	63	Schuyler Colfax	(1869–1873)
				Henry Wilson	(1873–1875)
19. Methodist*	Oct. 4, 1822	Jan. 17, 1893	70	William A. Wheeler	(1877–1881)
20. Disciples of Christ	Nov. 19, 1831	Sept. 19, 1881	49	Chester A. Arthur	(1881)
21. Episcopalian	Oct. 5, 1829	Nov. 18, 1886	57		
22. Presbyterian	Mar. 18, 1837	June 24, 1908	71	Thomas A. Hendricks	(1885)
23. Presbyterian	Aug. 20, 1833	Mar. 13, 1901	67	Levi P. Morton	(1889–1893)
24. Presbyterian	Mar. 18, 1837	June 24, 1908	71	Adlai E. Stevenson	(1893–1897)
25. Methodist	Jan. 29, 1843	Sept. 14, 1901	58	Garret A. Hobart	(1897–1899)
				Theodore Roosevelt	(1901)
26. Dutch Reformed	Oct. 27, 1858	Jan. 6, 1919	60	Charles W. Fairbanks	(1905–1909)
27. Unitarian	Sept. 15, 1857	Mar. 8, 1930	72	James S. Sherman	(1909–1912)
28. Presbyterian	Dec. 29, 1856	Feb. 3, 1924	67	Thomas R. Marshall	(1913–1921)
29. Baptist	Nov. 2, 1865	Aug. 2, 1923	57	Calvin Coolidge	(1921–1923)
30. Congregationalist	July 4, 1872	Jan. 5, 1933	60	Charles G. Dawes	(1925–1929)
31. Friend (Quaker)	Aug. 10, 1874	Oct. 20, 1964	90	Charles Curtis	(1929–1933)
32. Episcopalian	Jan. 30, 1882	Apr. 12, 1945	63	John N. Garner	(1933–1941)
				Henry A. Wallace	(1941–1945)
				Harry S Truman	(1945)
33. Baptist	May 8, 1884	Dec. 26, 1972	88	Alben W. Barkley	(1949–1953)
34. Presbyterian	Oct. 14, 1890	Mar. 28, 1969	78	Richard M. Nixon	(1953–1961)
35. Roman Catholic	May 29, 1917	Nov. 22, 1963	46	Lyndon B. Johnson	(1961–1963)
36. Disciples of Christ	Aug. 27, 1908	Jan. 22, 1973	64	Hubert H. Humphrey	(1965–1969)
37. Friend (Quaker)	Jan. 9, 1913	Apr. 22, 1994	81	Spiro T. Agnew	(1969–1973)
				Gerald R. Ford**	(1973–1974)
38. Episcopalian	July 14, 1913	Dec. 26, 2006	93	Nelson A. Rockefeller[§]	(1974–1977)
39. Baptist	Oct. 1, 1924			Walter F. Mondale	(1977–1981)
40. Disciples of Christ	Feb. 6, 1911	June 5, 2004	93	George H. W. Bush	(1981–1989)
41. Episcopalian	June 12, 1924			J. Danforth Quayle	(1989–1993)
42. Baptist	Aug. 19, 1946			Albert A. Gore	(1993–2001)
43. Methodist	July 6, 1946			Dick Cheney	(2001–2009)
44. United Church of Christ	August 4, 1961			Joe Biden	(2009–)

Appendix F

Federalist Papers No. 10 and No. 51

The founders completed drafting the U.S. Constitution in 1787. It was then submitted to the thirteen states for ratification, and a major debate ensued. As you read in Chapter 2, on the one side of this debate were the Federalists, who urged that the new Constitution be adopted. On the other side of the debate were the Anti-Federalists, who argued against ratification.

During the course of this debate, three men well known for their Federalist views—Alexander Hamilton, James Madison, and John Jay—wrote a series of essays in which they argued for immediate ratifcation of the Constitution. The essays appeared in the New York City Independent Journal *in October 1787, just a little over a month after the Constitutional Convention adjourned. Later, Hamilton arranged to have the essays collected and published in book form. The articles filled two volumes, both of which were published by May 1788. The essays are often referred to collectively as the* Federalist Papers.

Scholars disagree as to whether the Federalist Papers *had a significant impact on the decision of the states to ratify the Constitution. Nonetheless, many of the essays are masterpieces of political reasoning and have left a lasting imprint on American politics and government. Above all, the Federalist Papers shed an important light on what the founders intended when they drafted various constitutional provisions.*

Here we present just two of these essays, Federalist Paper No. 10 *and* Federalist Paper No. 51. *Each essay was written by James Madison, who referred to himself as "Publius." We have annotated each document to clarify the meaning of particular passages. The annotations are set in italics to distinguish them from the original text of the documents.*

#10

Federalist Paper No. 10 *is a classic document that is often referred to by teachers of American government. Authored by James Madison, it sets forth Madison's views on factions in politics. The essay was written, in large part, to counter the arguments put forth by the Anti-Federalists that small factions might take control of the government, thus destroying the representative nature of the republican form of government established by the Constitution. The essay opens with a discussion of the "dangerous vice" of factions and the importance of devising a form of government in which this vice will be controlled.*

Among the numerous advantages promised by a well-constructed Union, none deserves to be more accurately developed than its tendency to break and control the violence of faction. The friend of popular governments never finds himself so much alarmed for their character and fate as when he contemplates their propensity to this dangerous vice. He will not fail, therefore, to set a due value on any plan which, without violating the principles to which he is attached, provides a proper cure for it. The instability, injustice, and confusion introduced into the public councils have, in truth, been the mortal diseases under which popular governments have everywhere perished, as they continue to be the favorite and fruitful topics from which the adversaries to liberty derive their most specious declamations. The valuable improvements made by the American constitutions on the popular models, both ancient and modern, cannot certainly be too much admired; but it would be an unwarrantable partiality to contend that they have as effectually obviated the danger on this side, as was wished and expected. Complaints are everywhere heard from our most considerate and virtuous citizens, equally the friends of public and private faith and of public and personal liberty, that our governments are too unstable, that the public good is disregarded in the conflicts of rival parties, and that measures are too often decided, not according to the rules of justice and the rights of the minor party, but by the superior force of an interested and overbearing majority. However anxiously we may wish that these complaints had no foundation, the evidence of known facts will not permit us to deny that they are in some degree true. It will be found, indeed, on a candid review of our situation, that some of the distresses under which we labor have been erroneously charged on the operation of our governments; but it will be found, at the same time, that other causes will not alone account for many of our heaviest misfortunes; and, particularly, for that prevailing and increasing distrust of public engagements and alarm for private rights which are echoed from one end of the continent to the other. These must be chiefly, if not wholly, effects of the unsteadiness and injustice with which a factious spirit has tainted our public administration.

In the following paragraph, Madison clarifies for his readers his understanding of what the term faction *means.*

By a faction I understand a number of citizens, whether amounting to a majority or minority of the whole, who are united and actuated by some common impulse of passion, or of interest, adverse to the rights of other citizens, or the permanent and aggregate interests of the community.

In the following passages, Madison looks at the two methods of curing the "mischiefs of factions." One of these methods is removing the causes of faction. The other is to control the effects of factions.

There are two methods of curing the mischiefs of faction: the one, by removing its causes; the other, by controlling its effects.

There are again two methods of removing the causes of faction: the one, by destroying the liberty which is essential to its existence; the other, by giving to every citizen the same opinions, the same passions, and the same interests.

It could never be more truly said than of the first remedy that it was worse than the disease. Liberty is to faction what air is to fire, an aliment without which it instantly expires. But it could not be a less folly to abolish liberty, which is essential to political life, because it nourishes faction than it would be to wish the annihilation of air, which is essential to animal life, because it imparts to fire its destructive agency.

The second expedient is as impracticable as the first would be unwise. As long as the reason of man continues fallible, and his is at liberty to exercise it, different opinions will be formed. As long as the connection subsists between his reason and his self-love, his opinions and his passions will have a reciprocal influence on each other; and the former will be objects to which the latter will attach themselves. The diversity in the faculties of men, from which the rights of property originate, is not less an insuperable obstacle to a uniformity of interests. The protection of these faculties is the first object of government. From the protection of different and unequal faculties of acquiring property, the possession of different degrees and kinds of property immediately results; and from the influence of these on the sentiments and views of the respective proprietors ensues a division of the society into different interests and parties.

The latent causes of faction are thus sown in the nature of man; and we see them everywhere brought into different degrees of activity, according to the different circumstances of civil society. A zeal for different opinions concerning religion, concerning government, and many other points, as well of speculation as of practice; an attachment to different leaders ambitiously contending for pre-eminence and power; or to persons of other descriptions whose fortunes have been interesting to the human passions, have, in turn, divided mankind into parties, inflamed them with mutual animosity, and rendered them much more disposed to vex and oppress each other than to co-operate for their common good. So strong is this propensity of mankind to fall into mutual animosities that where no substantial occasion presents itself the most frivolous and fanciful distinctions have been sufficient to kindle their unfriendly passions and excite their most violent conflicts. But the most common and durable source of factions has been the various and unequal distribution of property. Those who hold and those who are without property have ever formed distinct interests in society. Those who are creditors, and those who are debtors, fall under a like discrimination. A landed interest, a manufacturing interest, a mercantile interest, a moneyed interest, with many lesser interests, grow up of necessity in civilized nations, and divide them into different classes, actuated by different sentiments and views. The regulation of these various and interfering interests forms the principal task of modern legislation and involves the spirit of party and faction in the necessary and ordinary operations of government.

No man is allowed to be a judge in his own cause, because his interest would certainly bias his judgment, and, not improbably, corrupt his integrity. With equal, nay with greater reason, a body of men are unfit to be both judges and parties at the same time; yet what are many of the most important acts of legislation but so many judicial determinations, not indeed concerning the rights of single persons, but concerning the rights of large bodies of citizens? And what are the different classes of legislators but advocates and parties to the causes which they determine? Is a law proposed concerning private debts? It is a question to which the creditors are parties on one side and the debtors on the other. Justice ought to hold the balance between them. Yet the parties are, and must be, themselves the judges; and the most numerous party, or in other words, the most powerful faction must be expected to prevail. Shall domestic manufacturers be encouraged, and in what degree, by restrictions on foreign manufacturers? Are questions which would be differently decided by the landed and the manufacturing classes, and probably by neither with a sole regard to justice and the public good. The apportionment of taxes on the various descriptions of property is an act which seems to require the most exact impartiality; yet there is, perhaps, no legislative act in which greater opportunity and temptation are given to a predominant party to trample on the rules of justice. Every shilling with which they overburden the inferior number is a shilling saved to their own pockets.

It is in vain to say that enlightened statesmen will be able to adjust these clashing interests and render them all subservient to the public good. Enlightened statesmen will not always be at the helm. Nor, in many cases, can such an adjustment be made at all without taking into view indirect and remote considerations, which will rarely prevail over the immediate interest which one party may find in disregarding the rights of another or the good of the whole.

The inference to which we are brought is that the causes of faction cannot be removed and that relief is only to be sought in the means of controlling its effects.

In the preceding passages, Madison has explored the causes of factions and has concluded that they cannot "be removed" without removing liberty itself, which is one of the causes, or altering human nature. He now turns to a discussion of how the effects of factions might be controlled.

If a faction consists of less than a majority, relief is supplied by the republican principle, which enables the majority to defeat its sinister views by regular vote. It may clog the administration, it may convulse the society; but it will be unable to execute and mask its violence under the forms of the Constitution. When a majority is included in a faction, the form of popular government, on the other hand, enables it to sacrifice to its ruling passion or interest both the public good and the rights of other citizens. To secure the public good and private rights against the danger of such a faction, and at the same time to preserve the spirit and the form of popular government, is then the great object to which our inquiries are directed. Let me add that it is the great desideratum by which alone this form of government can be rescued from the opprobrium under which it has so long labored and be recommended to the esteem and adoption of mankind.

According to Madison, one way of controlling the effects of factions is to make sure that the majority is not able to act in "concert," or jointly, to "carry into effect schemes of oppression."

By what means is this object attainable? Evidently by one of two only. Either the existence of the same passion or interest in a majority at the same time must be prevented, or the majority, having such coexistent passion or interest, must be rendered, by their number and local situation, unable to concert and carry into effect schemes of oppression. If the impulse and the opportunity be suffered to coincide, we well know that neither moral nor religious motives can be relied on as an adequate control. They are not found to be such on the injustice and violence of individuals, and lose their efficacy in proportion to the number combined together, that is, in proportion as their efficacy becomes needful.

From this view of the subject it may be concluded that a pure democracy, by which I mean a society consisting of a small number of citizens, who assemble and administer the government in person, can admit of no cure for the mischiefs of faction. A common passion or interest will, in almost every case, be felt by a majority of the whole; a communication and concert results from the form of government itself; and there is nothing to check the inducements to sacrifice the weaker party or an obnoxious individual. Hence it is that such democracies have ever been spectacles of turbulence and contention; have ever been found incompatible with personal security or the rights of property; and have in general been as short in their lives as they have been violent in their deaths. Theoretic politicians, who have patronized this species of government, have erroneously supposed that by reducing mankind to a perfect equality in their political rights, they would at the same time be perfectly equalized and assimilated in their possessions, their opinions, and their passions.

In the following six paragraphs, Madison sets forth some of the reasons why a republican form of government promises a "cure" for the mischiefs of factions. He begins by clarifying the difference between a republic and a democracy. He then describes how in a large republic, the elected representatives of the people will be large enough in number to guard against factions—the "cabals," or concerted actions, of "a few." On the one hand, representatives will not be so removed from their local districts as to be unacquainted with their constituents' needs. On the other hand, they will not be "unduly attached" to local interests and unfit to understand "great and national objects." Madison concludes that the Constitution "forms a happy combination in this respect."

A republic, by which I mean a government in which the scheme of representation takes place, opens a different prospect and promises the cure for which we are seeking. Let us examine the points in which it varies from pure democracy, and we shall comprehend both the nature of the cure and the efficacy which it must derive from the Union.

The two great points of difference between a democracy and a republic are: first, the delegation of the government, in the latter, to a small number of citizens elected by the rest; secondly, the greater number of citizens and greater sphere of country over which the latter may be extended.

The effect of the first difference is, on the one hand, to refine and enlarge the public views by passing them through the medium of a chosen body of citizens, whose wisdom may best discern the true interest of their country and whose patriotism and love of justice will be least likely to sacrifice it to temporary or partial considerations. Under such a regulation it may well happen that the public voice, pronounced by the representatives of the people, will be more consonant to the public good than if pronounced by the people themselves, convened for the purpose. On the other hand, the effect may be inverted. Men of factious tempers, of local prejudices, or of sinister designs, may, by intrigue, by corruption, or by other means, first obtain the suffrages, and then betray the interests of the people. The question resulting is, whether small or extensive republics are most favorable to the election of proper guardians of the public weal; and it is clearly decided in favor of the latter by two obvious considerations.

In the first place it is to be remarked that however small the republic may be the representatives must be raised to a certain number in order to guard against the cabals of a few; and that however large it may be they must be limited to a certain number in order to guard against the confusion of a multitude. Hence, the number of representatives in the two cases not being in proportion to that of the constituents, and being proportionally greatest in the small republic, it follows that if the proportion of fit characters be not less in the large than in the small republic, the former will present a greater option, and consequently a greater probability of a fit choice.

In the next place, as each representative will be chosen by a greater number of citizens in the large than in the small republic, it will be more difficult for unworthy candidates to practice with success the vicious arts by which elections are too often carried; and the suffrages of the people being more free, will be more likely to center on men who possess the most attractive merit and the most diffusive and established characters.

It must be confessed that in this, as in most other cases, there is a mean, on both sides of which inconveniencies will be found to lie. By enlarging too much the number of electors, you render the representative too little acquainted with all their local circumstances and lesser interests; as by reducing it too much, you render him unduly attached to these, and too little fit to comprehend and pursue great and national objects. The federal Constitution forms a happy combination in this respect; the great and aggregate interests being referred to the national, the local and particular to the State legislatures.

In the remaining passages of this essay, Madison looks at another "point of difference" between a republic and a democracy. Specifically, a republic can encompass a larger territory and a greater number of citizens than a democracy can. This fact, too, argues Madison, will help to control the influence of factions because the interests that draw people together to act in concert are typically at the local level and would be unlikely to affect or dominate the national government. As Madison states, "The influence of factious leaders may kindle a flame within their particular States but will be unable to spread a general conflagration through the other States." Generally, in a large republic, there will be numerous factions, and no particular faction will be able to "pervade the whole body of the Union."

The other point of difference is the greater number of citizens and extent of territory which may be brought within the compass of republican than of democratic government; and it is this circumstance principally which renders factious combinations less to be dreaded in the former than in the latter. The smaller the society, the fewer probably will be the distinct parties and interests composing it; the fewer the distinct parties and interests, the more frequently will a majority be found of the same party; and the smaller the number of individuals composing a majority, and the smaller the compass within which they are placed, the more easily will they concert and execute their plans of oppression. Extend the sphere and you take in a greater variety of parties and interests; you make it less probable that a majority of the whole will have a common motive to invade the rights of other citizens; or if such a common motive exists, it will be more difficult for all who feel it to discover their own strength and to act in unison with each other. Besides other impediments, it may be remarked that, where there is a consciousness of unjust or dishonorable purposes, communication is always checked by distrust in proportion to the number whose concurrence is necessary.

Hence, it clearly appears that the same advantage which a republic has over a democracy in controlling the effects of faction is enjoyed by a large over a small republic—is enjoyed by the Union over the States composing it. Does this advantage consist in the substitution of representatives whose enlightened views and virtuous sentiments render them superior to local prejudices and to schemes of injustice? It will not be denied that the representation of the Union will be most likely to possess these requisite endowments. Does it consist in the greater security afforded by a greater variety of parties, against the event of any one party being able to outnumber and oppress the rest? In an equal degree does the increased variety of parties comprised within the Union increase this security. Does it, in fine, consist in the greater obstacles opposed to the concert and accomplishment of the secret wishes of an unjust and interested majority? Here again the extent of the Union gives it the most palpable advantage.

The influence of factious leaders may kindle a flame within their particular States but will be unable to spread a general conflagration through the other States. A religious sect may degenerate into a political faction in a part of the Confederacy; but the variety of sects dispersed over the entire face of it must secure the national councils against any danger from that source. A rage for paper money, for an abolition of debts, for an equal division of property, or for any other improper or wicked project, will be less apt to pervade the whole body of the Union than a particular member of it, in the same proportion as such a malady is more likely to taint a particular county or district than an entire State.

In the extent and proper structure of the Union, therefore, we behold a republican remedy for the diseases most incident to republican government. And according to the degree of pleasure and pride we feel in being republicans ought to be our zeal in cherishing the spirit and supporting the character of federalists.

Publius
(James Madison)

#51

Federalist Paper No. 51, *which was also authored by James Madison, is one of the classics in American political theory. Recall from Chapter 2 that a major concern of the founders was to create a relatively strong national government but one that would not be capable of tyrannizing over the populace. In the following essay, Madison sets forth the theory of "checks and balances." He explains that the new Constitution, by dividing the national government into three branches (executive, legislative, and judicial), offers protection against tyranny.*

To what expedient, then, shall we finally resort, for maintaining in practice the necessary partition of power among the several departments as laid down in the Constitution? The only answer that can be given is that as all these exterior provisions are found to be inadequate the defect must be supplied, by so contriving the interior structure of the government as that its several constituent parts may, by their mutual relations, be the means of keeping each other in their proper places. Without presuming to undertake a full development of this important idea I will hazard a few general observations which may perhaps place it in a clearer light, and enable us to form a more correct judgment of the principles and structure of the government planned by the convention.

In the following two paragraphs, Madison explains that to ensure that the powers of government are genuinely separated, it is important that each of the three branches of government (executive, legislative, and judicial) should have a "will of its own." Among other things, this means that persons in one branch should not depend on persons in another branch for the "emoluments annexed to their offices" (pay, perks, and privileges). If they did, then the branches would not be truly independent of one another.

In order to lay a due foundation for that separate and distinct exercise of the different powers of government, which to a certain extent is admitted on all hands to be essential to the preservation of liberty, it is evident that each department should have a will of its own; and consequently should be so constituted that the members of each should have as little agency as possible in the appointment of the members of the others. Were this principle rigorously adhered to, it would require that all the appointments for the supreme executive, legislative, and judiciary magistracies should be drawn from the same fountain of authority, the people, through channels having no communication whatever with one another. Perhaps such a plan of constructing the several departments would be less difficult in practice than it may in contemplation appear. Some difficulties, however, and some additional expense would attend the execution of it. Some deviations, therefore, from the principle must be admitted. In the constitution of the judiciary department in particular, it might be inexpedient to insist rigorously on the principle: first, because peculiar qualifications being essential in the members, the primary consideration ought to be to select that mode of choice which best secures these qualifications; second, because the permanent tenure by which the appointments are held in that department must soon destroy all sense of dependence on the authority conferring them.

It is equally evident that the members of each department should be as little dependent as possible on those of the others for the emoluments annexed to their offices. Were the executive magistrate, or the judges, not independent of the legislature in this particular, their independence in every other would be merely nominal.

One of the striking qualities of the theory of checks and balances as posited by Madison is that it assumes that persons are not angels but driven by personal interests and motives. In the following two paragraphs, which are among the most widely quoted of Madison's writings, he stresses that the division of the government into three branches helps to check personal ambitions. Personal ambitions will naturally arise, but they will be linked to the constitutional powers of each branch. In effect, they will help to keep the three branches separate and thus serve the public interest.

But the great security against a gradual concentration of the several powers in the same department consists in giving to those who administer each department the necessary constitutional means and personal motives to resist encroachments of the others. The provision for defense must in this, as in all other cases, be made commensurate to the danger of attack. Ambition must be made to counteract ambition. The interest of the man must be connected with the constitutional rights of the place. It may be a reflection on human nature that such devices should be necessary to control the abuses of government. But what is government itself but the greatest of all reflections on human nature? If men were angels, no government would be necessary. If angels were to govern men, neither external nor internal controls on government would be necessary. In framing a government which is to be administered by men over men, the great difficulty lies in this: you must first enable the government to control the governed; and in the next place oblige it to control itself. A dependence on the people is, no doubt, the primary control on the government; but experience has taught mankind the necessity of auxiliary precautions.

This policy of supplying, by opposite and rival interests, the defect of better motives, might be traced through the whole system of human affairs, private as well as public. We see it particularly displayed in all the subordinate distributions of power, where the constant aim is to divide and arrange the several offices in such a manner as that each may be a check on the other—that the private interest of every individual may be a sentinel over the public rights. These inventions of prudence cannot be less requisite in the distribution of the supreme powers of the State.

In the next two paragraphs, Madison first points out that the "legislative authority necessarily predominates" in a republican form of government. The "remedy" for this lack of balance with the other branches of government is to divide the legislative branch into two chambers with "different modes of election and different principles of action."

But it is not possible to give to each department an equal power of self-defense. In republican government, the legislative authority necessarily predominates. The remedy for this inconveniency is to divide the legislature into different branches; and to render them, by different modes of election and different principles of action, as little connected with each other as the nature of their common functions and their common dependence on the society will admit. It may even be necessary to guard against dangerous encroachments by still further precautions. As the weight of the legislative authority requires that it should be thus divided, the weakness of the executive may require, on the other hand, that it should be fortified. An absolute negative on the legislature appears, at first view, to be the natural defense with which the executive magistrate should be armed. But perhaps it would be neither altogether safe nor alone sufficient. On ordinary occasions it might not be exerted with the requisite firmness, and on extraordinary occasions it might be perfidiously abused. May not this defect of an absolute negative be supplied by some qualified connection between this weaker department and the weaker branch of the stronger department, by which the latter may be led to support the constitutional rights of the former, without being too much detached from the rights of its own department?

If the principles on which these observations are founded be just, as I persuade myself they are, and they be applied as a criterion to the several State constitutions, and to the federal Constitution, it will be found that if the latter does not perfectly correspond with them, the former are infinitely less able to bear such a test.

In the remaining passages of this essay, Madison discusses the importance of the division of government powers between the states and the national government.

This division of powers, by providing additional checks and balances, offers a "double security" against tyranny.

There are, moreover, two considerations particularly applicable to the federal system of America, which place that system in a very interesting point of view.

First. In a single republic, all the power surrendered by the people is submitted to the administration of a single government; and the usurpations are guarded against by a division of the government into distinct and separate departments. In the compound republic of America, the power surrendered by the people is first divided between two distinct governments, and then the portion allotted to each subdivided among distinct and separate departments. Hence a double security arises to the rights of the people. The different governments will control each other, at the same time that each will be controlled by itself.

Second. It is of great importance in a republic not only to guard the society against the oppression of its rulers, but to guard one part of the society against the injustice of the other part. Different interests necessarily exist in different classes of citizens. If a majority be united by a common interest, the rights of the minority will be insecure. There are but two methods of providing against this evil: the one by creating a will in the community independent of the majority—that is, of the society itself; the other, by comprehending in the society so many separate descriptions of citizens as will render an unjust combination of a majority of the whole very improbable, if not impracticable. The first method prevails in all governments possessing an hereditary or self-appointed authority. This, at best, is but a precarious security; because a power independent of the society may as well espouse the unjust views of the major as the rightful interests of the minor party, and may possibly be turned against both parties. The second method will be exemplified in the federal republic of the United States. Whilst all authority in it will be derived from and dependent on the society, the society itself will be broken into so many parts, interests and classes of citizens, that the rights of individuals, or of the minority, will be in little danger from interested combinations of the majority. In a free government the security for civil rights must be the same as that for religious rights. It consists in the one case in the multiplicity of interests, and in the other in the multiplicity of sects. The degree of security in both cases will depend on the number of interests and sects; and this may be presumed to depend on the extent of country and number of people comprehended under the same government. This view of the subject must particularly recommend a proper federal system to all the sincere and considerate friends of republican government, since it shows that in exact proportion as the territory of the Union may be formed into more circumscribed Confederacies, or States, oppressive combinations of a majority will be facilitated; the best security, under the republican forms, for the rights of every class of citizen, will be diminished; and consequently the stability and independence of some member of the government, the only other security, must be proportionally increased. Justice is the end of government. It is the end of civil society. It ever has been and ever will be pursued until it be obtained, or until liberty be lost in the pursuit. In a society under the forms of which the stronger faction can readily unite and oppress the weaker, anarchy may as truly be said to reign as in a state of nature, where the weaker individual is not secured against the violence of the stronger; and as, in the latter state, even the stronger individuals are prompted, by the uncertainty of their condition, to submit to a government which may protect the weak as well as themselves; so, in the former state, will the more powerful factions or parties be gradually induced, by a like motive, to wish for a government which will protect all parties, the weaker as well as the more powerful. It can be little doubted that if the State of Rhode Island was separated from the Confederacy and left to itself, the insecurity of rights under the popular form of government within such narrow limits would be displayed by such reiterated oppressions of factious majorities that some power altogether independent of the people would soon be called for by the voice of the very factions whose misrule had proved the necessity of it. In the extended republic of the United States, and among the great variety of interests, parties, and sects which it embraces, a coalition of a majority of the whole society could seldom take place on any other principles than those of justice and the general good; whilst there being thus less danger to a minor from the will of a major party, there must be less pretext, also, to provide for the security of the former, by introducing into the government a will not dependent on the latter, or, in other words, a will independent of the society itself. It is no less certain than it is important, notwithstanding the contrary opinions which have been entertained, that the larger the society, provided it lie within a practicable sphere, the more duly capable it will be of self-government. And happily for the *republican cause*, the practicable sphere may be carried to a very great extent by a judicious modification and mixture of the *federal principle.*

Publius
(James Madison)

Appendix G

How to Read Case Citations and Find Court Decisions

Many important court cases are discussed in references in endnotes throughout this book. Court decisions are recorded and published. When a court case is mentioned, the notation that is used to refer to, or to cite, the case denotes where the published decision can be found.

State courts of appeals decisions are usually published in two places, the state reports of that particular state and the more widely used *National Reporter System* published by West Group. Some states no longer publish their own reports. The *National Reporter System* divides the states into the following geographic areas: Atlantic (A. or A.2d, where *2d* refers to *Second Series*), South Eastern (S.E. or S.E.2d), South Western (S.W., S.W.2d, or S.W.3d), North Western (N.W. or N.W.2d), North Eastern (N.E. or N.E.2d), Southern (So. or So.2d), and Pacific (P., P.2d, or P.3d).

Federal trial court decisions are published unofficially in West's *Federal Supplement* (F.Supp. or F.Supp.2d), and opinions from the circuit courts of appeals are reported unofficially in West's *Federal Reporter* (F., F.2d, or F.3d). Opinions from the United States Supreme Court are reported in the *United States Reports* (U.S.), the *Lawyers' Edition of the Supreme Court Reports* (L.Ed.), West's *Supreme Court Reporter* (S.Ct.), and other publications. The *United States Reports* is the official publication of United States Supreme Court decisions. It is published by the federal government. Many early decisions are missing from these volumes. The citations of the early volumes of the *U.S. Reports* include the names of the actual reporters, such as Dallas, Cranch, or Wheaton. *McCulloch v. Maryland,* for example, is cited as 17 U.S. (4 Wheat.) 316. Only after 1874 did the present citation system, in which cases are cited based solely on their volume and page numbers in the *United States Reports,* come into being. The *Lawyers' Edition of the Supreme Court Reports* is an unofficial and more complete edition of Supreme Court decisions. West's *Supreme Court Reporter* is an unofficial edition of decisions dating from October 1882. These volumes contain headnotes and numerous brief editorial statements of the law involved in the case.

State courts of appeals decisions are cited by giving the name of the case; the volume, name, and page number of the state's official report (if the state publishes its own reports); the volume, unit, and page number of the *National Reporter;* and the volume, name, and page number of any other selected reporter. Federal court citations are also listed by giving the name of the case and the volume, name, and page number of the reports. In addition to the citation, this textbook lists the year of the decision in parentheses. Consider, for example, the case *United States v. Curtiss-Wright Export Co.,* 299 U.S. 304 (1936). The Supreme Court's decision of this case may be found in volume 299 of the *United States Reports* on page 304. The case was decided in 1936.

Today, many courts, including the United States Supreme Court, publish their opinions online. This makes it much easier for students to find and read cases, or summaries of cases, that have significant consequences for American government and politics. To access cases via the Internet, use the URLs given in the *Politics on the Web* section at the end of Chapter 14.

Notes

Chapter 1

1. Harold Lasswell, *Politics: Who Gets What, When, and How* (New York: McGraw-Hill, 1936).
2. Charles Lewis, *The Buying of Congress* (New York: Avon Books, 1998), p. 346.
3. As quoted in Paul M. Angle and Earl Schenck Miers, *The Living Lincoln* (New York: Barnes & Noble, 1992), p. 155.
4. Martin J. Wade and William F. Russell, *The Short Constitution* (Iowa City: American Citizen Publishing, 1920), p. 38.
5. John W. Dean, *Conservatives without Conscience* (New York: Penguin, 2007), p. 11.
6. John Halpin and Karl Agne, *State of American Political Ideology, 2009: A National Study of Political Values and Beliefs* (Washington, D.C.: Center for American Progress, 2009).

Chapter 2

1. *District of Columbia v. Heller,* 128 S.Ct. 2783 (2008).
2. The first *European* settlement in today's United States was St. Augustine, Florida (a city that still exists), which was founded on September 8, 1565, by the Spaniard Pedro Menéndez de Ávilés.
3. Archaeologists recently discovered the remains of a colony at Popham Beach, on the southern coast of what is now Maine, that was established at the same time as the colony at Jamestown. The Popham colony disbanded after thirteen months, however, when the leader, after learning that he had inherited property back home, returned—with the other colonists—to England.
4. John Camp, *Out of the Wilderness: The Emergence of an American Identity in Colonial New England* (Middleton, Conn.: Wesleyan University Press, 1990).
5. Jon Butler, *Becoming America: The Revolution before 1776* (Cambridge, Mass.: Harvard University Press, 2000).
6. Ironically, the colonists were in fact protesting a tax reduction. The British government believed that if tea were cheaper, Americans would be more willing to drink it, even though it was still taxed. The Americans viewed the tax reduction as an attempt to trick them into accepting the principle of taxation. If the tea had been expensive, it would have been easy to organize a boycott. Because the tea was cheap, the protesters destroyed it so that no one would be tempted to buy it. (Also, many of the protesters were in the business of smuggling tea, and they would have been put out of business by the cheap competition.)
7. Paul S. Boyer *et al., The Enduring Vision: A History of the American People* (Lexington, Mass.: D. C. Heath, 1996).
8. Much of the colonists' fury over British policies was directed personally at King George III, who had ascended the British throne in 1760 at the age of twenty-two, rather than at Britain or British rule *per se.* If you look at the Declaration of Independence in Appendix A, you will note that much of that document focuses on what "He" (George III) has or has not done. George III's lack of political experience, his personality, and his temperament all combined to lend instability to the British government at this crucial point in history.
9. *The Political Writings of Thomas Paine,* Vol. 1 (Boston: J. P. Mendum Investigator Office, 1870), p. 46.
10. The equivalent in today's publishing world would be a book that sells between 9 million and 11 million copies in its first year of publication.
11. As quoted in Winthrop D. Jordan *et al., The United States,* 6th ed. (Englewood Cliffs, N.J.: Prentice Hall, 1987).
12. Some scholars feel that Locke's influence on the colonists, including Thomas Jefferson, has been exaggerated. For example, Jay Fliegelman states that Jefferson's fascination with the ideas of Homer, Ossian, and Patrick Henry "is of greater significance than his indebtedness to Locke." Jay Fliegelman, *Declaring Independence: Jefferson, Natural Language, and the Culture of Performance* (Stanford, Calif.: Stanford University Press, 1993).
13. Well before the Articles were ratified, many of them had, in fact, already been implemented. The Second Continental Congress and the thirteen states conducted American military, economic, and political affairs according to the standards and form specified later in the Articles of Confederation. See Robert W. Hoffert, *A Politics of Tensions: The Articles of Confederation and American Political Ideas* (Niwot, Colo.: University Press of Colorado, 1992).
14. Shays' Rebellion was not merely a small group of poor farmers. The participants and their supporters represented whole communities, including some of the wealthiest and most influential families of Massachusetts. Leonard L. Richards, *Shays' Rebellion: The American Revolution's Final Battle* (Philadelphia: University of Pennsylvania Press, 2003).
15. Madison was much more "republican" in his views—that is, less of a centralist—than Hamilton. See Lance Banning, *The Sacred Fire of Liberty: James Madison and the Founding of the Federal Republic* (Ithaca, N.Y.: Cornell University Press, 1995).
16. The State House was later named Independence Hall. The East Room was the same room in which the Declaration of Independence had been signed eleven years earlier.
17. Charles A. Beard, *An Economic Interpretation of the Constitution of the United States* (New York: Macmillan, 1913; New York: Free Press, 1986).
18. Morris was partly of French descent, which is why his first name may seem unusual. Note, however, that naming one's child *Gouverneur* was not common at the time in any language, including French.
19. Quoted in J. J. Spengler, "Malthusianism in Late Eighteenth-Century America," *American Economic Review* 25 (1935), p. 705.
20. For further detail on Wood's depiction of the founders' views, see Gordon S. Wood, *Revolutionary Characters: What Made the Founders Different* (New York: Penguin Press, 2006).
21. Some scholarship suggests that the *Federalist Papers* did not play a significant role in bringing about the ratification of the Constitution. Nonetheless, the papers have lasting value as an authoritative explanation of the Constitution.
22. The papers written by the Anti-Federalists are online (see the *Politics on the Web* section at the end of Chapter 2 for the Web URL). For essays on the positions, arranged in topical order, of both the Federalists and the Anti-Federalists in the ratification debate, see John P. Kaminski and Richard Leffler, *Federalists and Antifederalists: The Debate over the Ratification of the Constitution,* 2d ed. (Madison, Wis.: Madison House, 1998).
23. The concept of the separation of powers generally is credited to the French political philosopher Montesquieu (1689–1755), who included it in his monumental two-volume work entitled *The Spirit of the Laws,* published in 1748.
24. The Constitution does not explicitly mention the power of judicial review, but the delegates at the Constitutional Convention probably assumed that the courts would have this power. Indeed, Alexander Hamilton, in *Federalist Paper* No. 78, explicitly outlined the concept of judicial review. In any event, whether the founders intended for the courts to exercise this power is a moot point, because in an 1803 decision, *Marbury v. Madison,* the Supreme Court successfully claimed this power for the courts—see Chapter 14.
25. Eventually, Supreme Court decisions led to legislative reforms relating to apportionment. The amendment concerning compensation of members of Congress became the Twenty-seventh Amendment to the Constitution when it was ratified 203 years later, in 1992.
26. The Twenty-first Amendment repealed the Eighteenth Amendment, which had prohibited the manufacture or sale of alcoholic beverages nationwide (Prohibition). Special conventions were necessary because prohibitionist forces controlled too many state legislatures for the standard ratification method to work.

Chapter 3

1. The federal models used by the German and Canadian governments provide interesting comparisons with the U.S. system. See Arthur B. Gunlicks, *Laender and German Federalism* (Manchester, England: Manchester University Press, 2003); and Jennifer Smith, *Federalism* (Vancouver: University of British Columbia Press, 2004).
2. Text of an address by the president to the National Conference of State Legislatures, Atlanta, Georgia (Washington, D.C.: The White House, Office of the Press Secretary, July 30, 1981).
3. An excellent illustration of this principle was President Dwight Eisenhower's disciplining of Arkansas governor Orval Faubus when Faubus refused to allow a Little Rock high school to be desegregated in 1957. Eisenhower federalized the National Guard to enforce the court-ordered desegregation of the school.
4. 5 U.S. 137 (1803).
5. 17 U.S. 316 (1819).
6. 22 U.S. 1 (1824).
7. James L. Sellers, "The Economic Incidence of the Civil War in the South," *Mississippi Valley Historical Review* 14 (1927), pp. 179–191.
8. As quoted in Gavin Wright, *The Political Economy of the Cotton South: Households, Markets, and Wealth in the Nineteenth Century* (New York: W. W. Norton & Co., 1978), p. 147.
9. *Hammer v. Dagenhart,* 247 U.S. 251 (1918). This decision was overruled in *United States v. Darby,* 312 U.S. 100 (1941).
10. *Wickard v. Filburn,* 317 U.S. 111 (1942).
11. *McLain v. Real Estate Board of New Orleans, Inc.,* 444 U.S. 232 (1980).
12. 514 U.S. 549 (1995).
13. *Printz v. United States,* 521 U.S. 898 (1997).
14. *United States v. Morrison,* 529 U.S. 598 (2000).
15. 549 U.S. 497 (2007).
16. See George P. Fletcher, "The Indefinable Concept of Terrorism," *Journal of International Criminal Justice,* November 2006, pp. 894–911.

Chapter 4

1. 7 Peters 243 (1833).
2. 330 U.S. 1 (1947).
3. 370 U.S. 421 (1962).
4. 449 U.S. 39 (1980).
5. *Wallace v. Jaffree,* 472 U.S. 38 (1985).
6. See, for example, *Brown v. Gwinnett County School District,* 112 F.3d 1464 (1997).
7. *Santa Fe Independent School District v. Doe,* 530 U.S. 290 (2000).
8. 393 U.S. 97 (1968).
9. *Edwards v. Aguillard,* 482 U.S. 578 (1987).
10. 403 U.S. 602 (1971).
11. *Mitchell v. Helms,* 530 U.S. 793 (2000).
12. *Zelman v. Simmons-Harris,* 536 U.S. 639 (2002).
13. Holmes v. Bush (Fla.Cir.Ct. 2002). For details about this case, see David Royse, "Judge Rules School Voucher Law Violates Florida Constitution," *USA Today,* August 6, 2002, p. 7D.
14. 98 U.S. 145 (1878).
15. For more information on this case, see Bill Miller, "Firefighters Win Ruling in D.C. Grooming Dispute," *The Washington Post,* June 23, 2001, p. B01.
16. *Schenck v. United States,* 249 U.S. 47 (1919).
17. 341 U.S. 494 (1951).
18. *Brandenburg v. Ohio,* 395 U.S. 444 (1969).
19. *Liquormart v. Rhode Island,* 517 U.S. 484 (1996).
20. 413 U.S. 15 (1973).
21. *Reno v. American Civil Liberties Union,* 521 U.S. 844 (1997).
22. *Ashcroft v. American Civil Liberties Union,* 542 U.S. 656 (2004). The district court, located in Philadelphia, made its second ruling on the case in 2007. On July 22, 2008, the U.S. Court of Appeals for the Third Circuit upheld the decision in *American Civil Liberties Union v. Mukasey,* 534 F.3d 181 (3d Cir. 2008).
23. *United States v. American Library Association,* 539 U.S. 194 (2003).
24. *Ashcroft v. Free Speech Coalition,* 535 U.S. 234 (2002); *United States v. Williams,* 128 S.Ct. 1830 (2008).
25. *Morse v. Frederick,* 127 S.Ct. 2618 (2007).
26. See, for example, *Doe v. University of Michigan,* 721 F.Supp. 852 (1989).
27. "Meeting Minutes of the Wesleyan Student Assembly Meeting, 2002–2003," October 2, 2002, p. 10.
28. 249 U.S. 47 (1919).
29. 268 U.S. 652 (1925).
30. 484 U.S. 260 (1988).
31. *Smith v. Collin,* 439 U.S. 916 (1978).
32. *City of Chicago v. Morales,* 527 U.S. 41 (1999).
33. *Gallo v. Acuna,* 14 Cal.4th 1090 (1997).
34. Brandeis made this statement in a dissenting opinion in *Olmstead v. United States,* 277 U.S. 438 (1928).
35. 381 U.S. 479 (1965).
36. The state of South Carolina challenged the constitutionality of this act, claiming that the law violated states' rights under the Tenth Amendment. The Supreme Court, however, held that Congress had the authority, under its commerce power, to pass the act because drivers' personal information had become articles of interstate commerce. *Reno v. Condon,* 528 U.S. 141 (2000).
37. 410 U.S. 113 (1973). Jane Roe was not the real name of the woman in this case. It is a common legal pseudonym used to protect a party's privacy.
38. See, for example, the Supreme Court's decision in *Lambert v. Wicklund,* 520 U.S. 1169 (1997). The Court held that a Montana law requiring a minor to notify one of her parents before getting an abortion was constitutional.
39. *Schenck v. ProChoice Network,* 519 U.S. 357 (1997); and *Hill v. Colorado,* 530 U.S. 703 (2000).
40. *Stenberg v. Carhart,* 530 U.S. 914 (2000).
41. *Gonzales v. Carhart,* 127 S.Ct. 1610 (2007).
42. *Washington v. Glucksberg,* 521 U.S. 702 (1997).
43. *Gonzales v. Oregon,* 546 U.S. 243 (2006).
44. 372 U.S. 335 (1963).
45. *Mapp v. Ohio,* 367 U.S. 643 (1961).
46. 384 U.S. 436 (1966). In 1968, Congress passed legislation including a provision that reinstated the previous rule that statements made by defendants can be used against them as long as the statements were made voluntarily. This provision was never enforced, however, and only in 1999 did a court try to enforce it. The case ultimately came before the Supreme Court, which held that the *Miranda* rights were based on the Constitution and thus could not be overruled by legislative act. See Dickerson v. United States, 530 U.S. 428 (2000).
47. *Moran v. Burbine,* 475 U.S. 412 (1986).
48. *Arizona v. Fulminante,* 499 U.S. 279 (1991).
49. *Davis v. United States,* 512 U.S. 452 (1994).
50. Thomas P. Sullivan, *Police Experiences with Recording Custodial Interrogations* (Chicago: Northwestern University School of Law Center on Wrongful Convictions, Summer 2004), p. 4.
51. This example is drawn from Brenda Koehler, "Respond Locally to National Issues," in *50 Ways to Love Your Country* (Maui, Hawaii: Inner Ocean Publishing, 2004), pp. 110–111.

Chapter 5

1. *Michael M. v. Superior Court,* 450 U.S. 464 (1981).
2. See, for example, *Craig v. Boren,* 429 U.S. 190 (1976).
3. *Orr v. Orr,* 440 U.S. 268 (1979).
4. *Mississippi University for Women v. Hogan,* 458 U.S. 718 (1982).
5. 518 U.S. 515 (1996).
6. 163 U.S. 537 (1896).
7. 347 U.S. 483 (1954).
8. 349 U.S. 294 (1955).
9. *Swann v. Charlotte-Mecklenburg Board of Education,* 402 U.S. 1 (1971).
10. *Keyes v. School District No. 1,* 413 U.S. 189 (1973).
11. *Milliken v. Bradley,* 418 U.S. 717 (1974).
12. *Riddick v. School Board of City of Norfolk,* 627 F.Supp. 814 (E.D.Va. 1984).
13. Emily Bazelon, "The Next Kind of Integration," *The New York Times Magazine,* July 20, 2008.
14. See *Meritor Savings Bank, FSB v. Vinson,* 477 U.S. 57 (1986); and *Harris v. Forklift Systems, Inc.,* 510 U.S. 17 (1993).
15. *Oncale v. Sundowner Offshore Services,* 523 U.S. 75 (1998).
16. *Faragher v. City of Boca Raton,* 524 U.S. 775 (1998).
17. The Supreme Court upheld these actions in *Hirabayashi v. United States,* 320 U.S. 81 (1943); and *Korematsu v. United States,* 323 U.S. 214 (1944).
18. Historians in the early and mid-twentieth century gave much smaller figures for the pre-Columbian population—as low as 14 million people for the entire New World. Today, 40 million is considered a conservative estimate, and an estimate of 100 million has much support among demographers. If 100 million is correct, the epidemics that followed the arrival of the Europeans killed one out of every five people alive in the world at that time. See Charles C. Mann, *1491* (New York: Vintage, 2006).
19. The 1890 siege was the subject of Dee Brown's best-selling book *Bury My Heart at Wounded Knee* (New York: Holt, Rinehart & Winston, 1971).
20. *County of Oneida, New York v. Oneida Indian Nation,* 470 U.S. 226 (1985).
21. *Kimel v. Florida Board of Regents,* 528 U.S. 62 (2000).
22. *Board of Trustees of the University of Alabama v. Garrett,* 531 U.S. 356 (2001).
23. 539 U.S. 558 (2003).
24. 517 U.S. 620 (1996).
25. 438 U.S. 265 (1978).
26. 515 U.S. 200 (1995).
27. 84 F.3d 720 (5th Cir. 1996).
28. 539 U.S. 244 (2003).
29. 539 U.S. 306 (2003).
30. 127 S.Ct. 2738 (2007).

Chapter 6

1. *Democracy in America,* Vol. 1, ed. Phillip Bradley (New York: Knopf, 1980), p. 191.
2. Pronounced ah-*mee*-kus *kure*-ee-eye.
3. Fred McChesney, *Money for Nothing: Politicians, Rent Extraction and Political Extortion* (Cambridge, Mass.: Harvard University Press, 1997).
4. The Agricultural Adjustment Act of 1933 (declared unconstitutional) was replaced by the 1937 Agricultural Adjustment Act, which later was changed and amended several times.
5. 545 U.S. 913 (2005).
6. *United States v. Harriss,* 347 U.S. 612 (1954).

Chapter 7

1. Letter to Francis Hopkinson written from Paris while Jefferson was minister to France, as cited in John P. Foley, ed., *The Jeffersonian Cyclopedia* (New York: Russell & Russell, 1967), p. 677.
2. From Washington's Farewell Address. The U.S. Senate presents the text of the address at **www.access.gpo.gov/congress/senate/farewell/sd106-21.pdf.**
3. In most states, a person must declare a preference for a particular party before voting in that state's primary election (discussed in Chapter 9). This declaration is usually part of the voter-registration process.
4. For an interesting discussion of the pros and cons of patronage from a constitutional perspective, see the majority opinion versus the dissent in the Supreme Court case *Board of County Commissioners v. Umbehr,* 518 U.S. 668 (1996).
5. The term *third party,* although inaccurate (because sometimes there have been fourth parties, fifth parties, and even more), is commonly used to refer to a minor party.
6. Today, twelve states have multimember districts for their state houses, and a handful also have multimember districts for their state senates.

Chapter 8

1. Doris A. Graber, *Mass Media and American Politics,* 7th ed. (Washington, D.C.: CQ Press, 2005).
2. Jimmy Carter, *Palestine: Peace Not Apartheid* (New York: Simon & Schuster, 2007).
3. John M. Benson, "When Is an Opinion Really an Opinion?" *Public Perspective,* September/October 2001, pp. 40–41.
4. As quoted in Karl G. Feld, "When Push Comes to Shove: A Polling Industry Call to Arms," *Public Perspective,* September/October 2001, p. 38.
5. Pew Research Center for the People and the Press, survey conducted September 21–October 4, 2006, and reported in "Who Votes, Who Doesn't, and Why," released October 28, 2006.
6. *Guinn v. United States,* 238 U.S. 347 (1915).
7. *Smith v. Allwright,* 321 U.S. 649 (1944).

8. The argument about the vote-eligible population was first made by Michael P. McDonald and Samuel L. Popkin, "The Myth of the Vanishing Voter," *American Political Science Review,* Vol. 95, No. 4 (December 2001), p. 963.
9. As quoted in Owen Ullman, "Why Voter Apathy Will Make a Strong Showing," *BusinessWeek,* November 4, 1996.
10. Gordon S. Wood, *Revolutionary Characters: What Made the Founders Different* (New York: Penguin Press, 2006), p. 248.
11. *Ibid.,* p. 271.
12. Thomas E. Mann and Norman J. Ornstein, *The Broken Branch: How Congress Is Failing America and How to Get It Back on Track* (New York: Oxford University Press, 2006), p. 277.

Chapter 9

1. These states award one electoral vote to the candidate who wins the popular vote in a congressional district and an additional two electoral votes to the winner of the statewide popular vote. Other states have considered similar plans.
2. The word *caucus* apparently was first used in the name of a men's club, the Caucus Club of colonial Boston, sometime between 1755 and 1765. (Many early political and government meetings took place in pubs.) We have no certain knowledge of the origin of the word, but it may be from an Algonquin term meaning "elder" or from the Latin name of a drinking vessel.
3. Today, the Democratic and Republican caucuses in the House and Senate (the Republicans now use the term *conference* instead of caucus) choose each party's congressional leadership and sometimes discuss legislation and legislative strategy.
4. Due to the customs of the time, none of the candidates could admit that he had made a personal decision to run. All claimed to have entered the race in response to popular demand.
5. Parties cannot use their freedom-of-association rights to practice racial discrimination in state-sponsored elections: *Smith v. Allwright,* 321 U.S. 649 (1944). When racial discrimination is not involved, the parties have regularly won freedom-of-association suits against state governments. Examples are *Tashjian v. Republican Party of Connecticut,* 479 U.S. 208 (1986), and *California Democratic Party v. Jones,* 530 U.S. 567 (2000).
6. In Washington, the state government holds presidential primaries for both parties. The Democratic Party, however, ignores the Democratic primary and chooses its national convention delegates through a caucus/convention system. In 1984, following a dispute with the state of Michigan over primary rules, the state Democratic Party organized a presidential primary election that was run completely by party volunteers. In 2008, after a similar dispute with the state, the Virginia Republican Party chose its candidate for the U.S. Senate at its state party convention instead of through the Virginia primary elections.
7. The case was *California Democratic Party v. Jones,* cited in footnote 5.
8. Christopher Rhoads, "Candidates Try New Web Tactics in Battle to Tap Fresh Supporters," *Wall Street Journal,* October 30, 2008. p. 16.
9. This act is sometimes referred to as the Federal Election Campaign Act of 1972 because it became effective in that year. The official date of the act, however, is 1971.
10. 424 U.S. 1 (1976).
11. This figure is from the Center for Responsive Politics.
12. *Colorado Republican Federal Campaign Committee v. Federal Election Commission,* 518 U.S. 604 (1996).
13. Quoted in George Will, "The First Amendment on Trial," *The Washington Post,* December 1, 2002, p. B7.
14. 540 U.S. 93 (2003).
15. *Federal Election Commission v. Wisconsin Right to Life, Inc.,* 127 S.Ct. 2652 (2007).
16. *Bush v. Gore,* 531 U.S. 98 (2000).

Chapter 10

1. Bernard Cohen, *The Press and Foreign Policy* (Princeton, N.J.: Princeton University Press, 1963), p. 81.
2. Interestingly, in the 2000 campaigns, a Texas group supporting George W. Bush's candidacy paid for a remake of the "daisy" commercial, but the target in the new ad was Al Gore.
3. As quoted in Michael Grunwald, "The Year of Playing Dirtier," *The Washington Post,* October 27, 2006, p. A1.
4. John G. Geer, *In Defense of Negativity: Attack Ads in Presidential Campaigns* (Chicago: University of Chicago Press, 2006).
5. The commission's action was upheld by a federal court. See *Perot v. Federal Election Commission,* 97 F.3d 553 (D.C.Cir. 1996).
6. For more details on how political candidates manage news coverage, see Doris A. Graber, *Mass Media and American Politics,* 7th ed. (Washington, D.C.: CQ Press, 2005).
7. For suggestions on how to dissect spin and detect when language is steering one toward a conclusion, see Brooks Jackson and Kathleen Hall Jamieson, *unSpun: Finding Facts in a World of Disinformation* (New York: Random House, 2007).
8. *Red Lion Broadcasting Co. v. FCC,* 395 U.S. 367 (1969).
9. Kathleen Hall Jamieson, *Everything You Think You Know about Politics . . . and Why You're Wrong* (New York: Basic Books, 2000), pp. 187–195.
10. Debra Reddin van Tuyll and Hubert P. van Tuyll, "Political Partisanship," in William David Sloan and Jenn Burleson Mackay, eds., *Media Bias: Finding It, Fixing It* (Jefferson, N.C.: McFarland, 2007), pp. 35–49.
11. Jamieson, *Everything You Think You Know about Politics,* pp. xiii–xiv.
12. Pew Research Center for the People and the Press and the Project for Excellence in Journalism, *The State of the News Media 2007: An Annual Report on American Journalism.*
13. The term *podcasting* is used for this type of information delivery because initially podcasts were downloaded onto Apple's iPods.
14. Andrew Sullivan, "Video Power: The Potent New Political Force," *The Sunday Times,* February 4, 2007.

Chapter 11

1. These states are Alaska, Delaware, Montana, North Dakota, South Dakota, Vermont, and Wyoming.
2. 369 U.S. 186 (1962).
3. 376 U.S. 1 (1964).
4. See, for example, *Davis v. Bandemer,* 478 U.S. 109 (1986).
5. The plan was controversial because it was not implemented in response to the 2000 census. Rather, it was a "midterm" redistricting—held between censuses—that overturned what had been the postcensus redistricting plan in Texas.
6. *Amicus curiae* brief filed by the American Civil Liberties Union (ACLU) in support of the appellants in *Easley v. Cromartie,* 532 U.S. 234 (2001).
7. See, for example, *Shaw v. Reno,* 509 U.S. 630 (1993); *Miller v. Johnson,* 515 U.S. 900 (1995); *Shaw v. Hunt,* 517 U.S. 899 (1996); and *Bush v. Vera,* 517 U.S. 952 (1996).
8. *Easley v. Cromartie,* 532 U.S. 234 (2001).
9. *Powell v. McCormack,* 395 U.S. 486 (1969).
10. Some observers maintain that another reason Congress *can* stay in session longer is the invention of air-conditioning. Until the advent of air-conditioning, no member of Congress wanted to stay in session during the hot and sticky late spring, summer, and early fall months.
11. *U.S. Term Limits, Inc. v. Thornton,* 514 U.S. 779 (1995).
12. A term used by Woodrow Wilson in *Congressional Government* (New York: Meridian Books, 1956 [first published in 1885]).

Chapter 12

1. Lyndon B. Johnson, *The Vantage Point: Perspectives of the Presidency, 1963–1969* (New York: Henry Holt & Co., 1971).
2. Versailles, located about twenty miles from Paris, is the name of the palace built by King Louis XIV of France. It served as the royal palace until 1793 and was then converted into a national historical museum, which it remains today. The preliminary treaty ending the American Revolution was signed by the United States and Britain at Versailles in 1783.
3. *Ex parte Grossman,* 267 U.S. 87 (1925).
4. *Clinton v. City of New York,* 524 U.S. 417 (1998).
5. As cited in Lewis D. Eigen and Jonathan P. Siegel, *The Macmillan Dictionary of Political Quotations* (New York: Macmillan, 1993), p. 565.
6. The Constitution does not grant the president explicit power to remove from office officials who are not performing satisfactorily or who do not agree with the president. In 1926, however, the Supreme Court prevented Congress from interfering with the president's ability to fire those executive-branch officials whom he had appointed with Senate approval. See *Myers v. United States,* 272 U.S. 52 (1926).
7. Richard E. Neustadt, *Presidential Power: The Politics of Leadership* (New York: John Wiley, 1960), p. 10.
8. As quoted in Richard M. Pious, *The American Presidency* (New York: Basic Books, 1979), pp. 51–52.
9. A phrase coined by Samuel Kernell in *Going Public: New Strategies of Presidential Leadership,* 2d ed. (Washington, D.C.: Congressional Quarterly Press, 1992).
10. Congress used its power to declare war in the War of 1812, the Mexican War (1846–1848), the Spanish-American War (1898), and World War I (U.S. involvement lasted from 1916 until 1918) and on six different occasions during World War II (U.S. involvement lasted from 1941 until 1945).
11. As quoted in Thomas E. Cronin, *The State of the Presidency,* 2d ed. (Boston: Little, Brown, 1980), p. 11.

Chapter 13

1. This definition follows the classical model of bureaucracy put forth by German sociologist Max Weber. See Max Weber, *Theory of Social and Economic Organization,* ed. Talcott Parsons (New York: Oxford University Press, 1974).
2. It should be noted that although the president is technically the head of the bureaucracy, the president cannot always control the bureaucracy—as you will read later in this chapter.
3. For an insightful analysis of the policymaking process in Washington, D.C., and the role played by various groups in the process, see Morton H. Halperin and Priscilla A. Clapp, with Arnold Kanter, *Bureaucratic Politics and Foreign Policy,* 2d ed. (Washington, D.C.: The Brookings Institution, 2006). Although the focus of the book is on foreign policy, the analysis applies in many ways to the general policymaking process.
4. Colleen W. Cook, *CRS Report for Congress: Mexico's Drug Cartels* (Washington, D.C.: Congressional Research Service, 2008).

5. Agnes Gereben Schaefer, Benjamin Bahney, and K. Jack Riley, *Security in Mexico: Implications for U.S. Policy Options* (Santa Monica, Calif.: Rand Research, 2009).
6. *Garcetti v. Ceballos,* 126 S.Ct. 1951 (2006).
7. As quoted in George Melloan, "Bush's Toughest Struggle Is with His Own Bureaucracy," *The Wall Street Journal,* June 25, 2002, p. A13.
8. Gardiner Harris, "Surgeon General Sees Four-Year Term as Compromised," *The New York Times,* July 11, 2007.

Chapter 14

1. *Boumediene v. Bush,* 128 S.Ct. 2229 (2008).
2. Pronounced *ster*-ay dih-*si*-sis.
3. 347 U.S. 483 (1954).
4. See *Plessy v. Ferguson,* 163 U.S. 537 (1896).
5. 539 U.S. 558 (2003).
6. 478 U.S. 186 (1986).
7. Although a state's highest court is often referred to as the state supreme court, there are exceptions. In the New York court system, for example, the supreme court is a trial court, and the highest court is called the New York Court of Appeals.
8. Pronounced jus-*tish*-a-bul.
9. Pronounced sur-shee-uh-*rah*-ree.
10. Between 1790 and 1891, Congress allowed the Supreme Court almost no discretion over which cases to decide. After 1925, in almost 95 percent of appealed cases the Court could choose whether to hear arguments and issue an opinion. Beginning in October 1988, mandatory review was virtually eliminated.
11. *District of Columbia v. Heller,* 128 S.Ct. 2783 (2008).
12. *Baze and Bowling v. Rees,* 128 S.Ct. 1520 (2008).
13. *Boumediene v. Bush,* 128 S.Ct. 2229 (2008).
14. *Hopwood v. Texas,* 84 F.3d 720 (5th Cir., 1996).
15. *Gonzales v. Carhart,* 127 S.Ct. 1610 (2007).
16. *United States v. Williams,* 128 S.Ct. 1830 (2008).
17. *Northwest Austin Municipal Utility District No. 1 v. Holder,* 557 U.S. ___ (2009).
18. *Grutter v. Bollinger,* 539 U.S. 306 (2003); and *Gratz v. Bollinger,* 539 U.S. 244 (2003).
19. *Parents Involved in Community Schools v. Seattle School District No. 1,* 127 S.Ct. 2738 (2007).
20. 5 U.S. (1 Cranch) 137 (1803). The Supreme Court had considered the constitutionality of an act of Congress in *Hylton v. United States,* 3 U.S. 171 (1796), in which Congress's power to levy certain taxes was challenged. That particular act was ruled constitutional, rather than unconstitutional, however, so this first federal exercise of judicial review was not clearly recognized as such. Also, during the decade before the adoption of the federal Constitution, courts in at least eight states had exercised the power of judicial review.
21. Jeffrey A. Segal and Harold J. Spaeth, *The Supreme Court and the Attitudinal Model* (New York: Cambridge University Press, 1993), p. 65.
22. For an analysis of the Roberts Court's first term by a Georgetown University law professor, see Jonathan Turley, "The Roberts Court: Seeing Is Believing," *USA Today,* July 6, 2006, p. 11A.
23. For summaries of the major cases decided during the Roberts Court's second term (ending in June 2007) by a Pulitzer Prize winner and longtime Court watcher, see Linda Greenhouse, "In Steps Big and Small, Supreme Court Moved Right," *The New York Times,* July 1, 2007.
24. You can find an evaluation of the Roberts Court's third term in Jeffrey Rosen, "The Supreme Court's Group Hug," *Time,* July 3, 2008. National Public Radio's Nina Totenberg evaluates the Court's fourth term at **www.npr.org/templates/story/story.php?storyId=106185978**.
25. *U.S. Airways v. Barnett,* 535 U.S. 391 (2002).
26. As quoted in Linda Greenhouse, "The Competing Visions of the Role of the Court," *The New York Times,* July 7, 2002, p. 3.
27. Antonin Scalia, *A Matter of Interpretation* (Ewing, N.J.: Princeton University Press, 1997).
28. Letter by Thomas Jefferson to William C. Jarvis, 1820, in Andrew A. Lipscomb and Albert Ellery Bergh, *The Writings of Thomas Jefferson,* Memorial Edition (Washington, D.C.: Thomas Jefferson Memorial Association of the United States, 1904).
29. As quoted in Carl Hulse and David D. Kirkpatrick, "DeLay Says Federal Judiciary Has 'Run Amok,' Adding Congress Is Partly to Blame," *The New York Times,* April 8, 2005, p. 5.

Chapter 15

1. Stan Dorn, *Uninsured and Dying Because of It: Updating the Institute of Medicine Analysis on the Impact of Uninsurance on Mortality* (Washington, D.C.: Urban Institute, 2008).
2. John and Teresa Heinz Kerry, *This Moment on Earth: Today's New Environmentalists and Their Vision for the Future* (New York: PublicAffairs, 2007).

Chapter 16

1. David L. Rousseau, *Identifying Threats and Threatening Identities: The Social Construction of Realism and Liberalism* (Palo Alto, Calif.: Stanford University Press, 2006), p. 154.
2. *Public Papers of the Presidents of the United States: Harry S. Truman, 1947* (Washington, D.C.: U.S. Government Printing Office, 1963), pp. 176–180.
3. The containment policy was outlined by George F. Kennan, the chief of the policy-planning staff for the Department of State at that time, in an article that appeared in *Foreign Affairs,* July 1947, p. 575. The author's name was given as "X."
4. John Robb, *Brave New War: The Next Stage of Terrorism and the End of Globalization* (New York: Wiley, 2007).

Glossary

A

Action-reaction syndrome For every government action, there will be a reaction by the public. The government then takes a further action to counter the public's reaction—and the cycle begins again.

Adjudicate To render a judicial decision. In regard to administrative law, the process in which an administrative law judge hears and decides issues that arise when an agency charges a person or firm with violating a law or regulation enforced by the agency.

Administrative law The body of law created by administrative agencies (in the form of rules, regulations, orders, and decisions) in order to carry out their duties and responsibilities.

Affirmative action A policy calling for the establishment of programs that give special consideration, in jobs and college admissions, to members of groups that have been discriminated against in the past.

Agenda setting Getting an issue on the political agenda to be addressed by Congress; part of the first stage of the policymaking process.

Agents of political socialization People and institutions that influence the political views of others.

Anti-Federalists A political group that opposed the adoption of the Constitution because of the document's centralist tendencies and because it did not include a bill of rights.

Appellate court A court having appellate jurisdiction; an appellate court normally does not hear evidence or testimony but reviews the transcript of the trial court's proceedings, other records relating to the case, and the attorneys' arguments as to why the trial court's decision should or should not stand.

Apportionment The distribution of House seats among the states on the basis of their respective populations.

Appropriation A part of the congressional budgeting process that involves determining how many dollars will be spent in a given year on a particular set of government activities.

Articles of Confederation The nation's first national constitution, which established a national form of government following the American Revolution. The Articles provided for a confederal form of government in which the central government had few powers.

Australian ballot A secret ballot that is prepared, distributed, and counted by government officials at public expense; used by all states in the United States since 1888.

Authority The ability to exercise power, such as the power to make and enforce laws, legitimately.

Authorization A part of the congressional budgeting process that involves the creation of the legal basis for government programs.

Autocracy A form of government in which the power and authority of the government are in the hands of a single person.

B

Biased sample A poll sample that does not accurately represent the population.

Bicameral legislature A legislature made up of two chambers, or parts. The United States has a bicameral legislature, composed of the House of Representatives and the Senate.

Bill of attainder A legislative act that inflicts punishment on particular persons or groups without granting them the right to a trial.

Bill of Rights The first ten amendments to the U.S. Constitution. They list the freedoms—such as the freedoms of speech, press, and religion—that a citizen enjoys and that cannot be infringed on by the government.

Block grant A federal grant given to a state for a broad area, such as criminal justice or mental-health programs.

Blue Dog Coalition A caucus that unites most of the moderate-to-conservative Democrats in the House of Representatives.

Bureaucracy A large, complex, hierarchically structured administrative organization that carries out specific functions.

Bureaucrat An individual who works in a bureaucracy. As generally used, the term refers to a government employee.

Busing The transportation of public school students by bus to schools physically outside their neighborhoods to eliminate school segregation based on residential patterns.

C

Cabinet An advisory group selected by the president to assist with decision making. Traditionally, the cabinet has consisted of the heads of the executive departments and other officers whom the president may choose to appoint.

Campaign strategy The comprehensive plan for winning an election developed by a candidate and his or her advisers. The strategy includes the candidate's position on issues, slogan, advertising plan, press events, personal appearances, and other aspects of the campaign.

Cap-and-trade A method of restricting the production of a harmful substance. A cap is set on the volume of production, and permits to produce the substance that can then be traded on the market.

Capitalism An economic system based on the private ownership of wealth-producing property, free markets, and freedom of contract. The privately owned corporation is the preeminent capitalist institution.

Case law The rules of law announced in court decisions. Case law includes the aggregate of reported cases that interpret judicial precedents, statutes, regulations, and constitutional provisions.

Categorical grant A federal grant targeted for a specific purpose as defined by federal law.

Caucus A meeting held to choose political candidates or delegates.

Checks and balances A major principle of American government in which each of the three branches is given the means to check (to restrain or balance) the actions of the others.

Chief diplomat The role of the president in recognizing and interacting with foreign governments.

Chief executive The head of the executive branch of government. In the United States, the president.

Chief of staff The person who directs the operations of the White House Office and who advises the president on important matters.

Citizen journalism The collection, analysis, and dissemination of information online by independent journalists, scholars, politicians, and the general citizenry.

Civil disobedience The deliberate and public act of refusing to obey laws thought to be unjust.

Civil law The branch of law that spells out the duties that individuals in society owe to other persons or to their governments, excluding the duty not to commit crimes.

Civil liberties Individual rights protected by the Constitution against the powers of the government.

Civil rights The rights of all Americans to equal treatment under the law, as provided for by the Fourteenth Amendment to the Constitution.

Civil rights movement The movement in the 1950s and 1960s, by minorities and concerned whites, to end racial segregation.

Civil service Nonmilitary government employment.

Closed primary A primary in which only party members can vote to choose that party's candidates.

Cloture A method of ending debate in the Senate and bringing the matter under consideration to a vote by the entire chamber.

Coalition An alliance of individuals or groups with a variety of interests and opinions who join together to support all or part of a political party's platform.

Cold War The war of words, warnings, and ideologies between the Soviet Union and the United States that lasted from the late 1940s through the early 1990s.

Colonial empire A group of dependent nations that are under the rule of a single imperial power.

Commander in chief The supreme commander of a nation's military force.

Commerce clause The clause in Article I, Section 8, of the Constitution that gives Congress the power to regulate interstate commerce (commerce involving more than one state).

Commercial speech Advertising statements that describe products. Commercial speech receives less protection under the First Amendment than ordinary speech.

Common law The body of law developed from judicial decisions in English and U.S. courts, not attributable to a legislature.

Communist bloc The group of Eastern European nations that fell under the control of the Soviet Union following World War II.

Competitive federalism A model of federalism devised by Thomas R. Dye in which state and local governments compete for businesses and citizens, who in effect "vote with their feet" by moving to jurisdictions that offer a competitive advantage.

Concurrent powers Powers held by both the federal and the state governments in a federal system.

Concurring opinion A statement written by a judge or justice who agrees (concurs) with the court's decision, but for reasons different from those in the majority opinion.

Confederal system A league of independent sovereign states, joined together by a central government that has only limited powers over them.

Confederation A league of independent states that are united only for the purpose of achieving common goals.

Conference In regard to the Supreme Court, a private meeting of the justices in which they present their arguments concerning a case under consideration.

Conference committee A temporary committee that is formed when the two chambers of Congress pass separate versions of the same bill. The conference committee, which consists of members from both the House and the Senate, works out a compromise form of the bill.

Conference report A report submitted by a congressional conference committee after it has drafted a single version of a bill.

Congressional Budget Office (CBO) An agency established by Congress to evaluate the impact of proposed legislation on the federal budget.

Congressional district The geographic area that is served by one member in the House of Representatives.

Conservatism A set of beliefs that include a limited role for the national government in helping individuals and in the economic affairs of the nation, support for traditional values and lifestyles, and a cautious response to change.

Constitutional Convention The convention (meeting) of delegates from the states that was held in Philadelphia in 1787 for the purpose of amending the Articles of Confederation. In fact, the delegates wrote a new constitution (the U.S. Constitution) that established a federal form of government to replace the governmental system that had been created by the Articles of Confederation.

Constitutional law Law based on the U.S. Constitution and the constitutions of the various states.

Containment A U.S. policy designed to contain the spread of communism by offering military and economic aid to threatened nations.

Continuing resolution A temporary resolution passed by Congress when an appropriations bill has not been passed by the beginning of the new fiscal year.

Cooperative federalism The theory that the states and the federal government should cooperate in solving problems.

Corporate Average Fuel Economy (CAFE) standards A set of federal standards under which each manufacturer must meet a miles-per-gallon benchmark averaged across all cars or trucks that it sells.

Credentials Committee A committee of each national political party that evaluates the claims of national party convention delegates to be the legitimate representatives of their states.

Criminal law The branch of law that defines and governs actions that constitute crimes. Generally, criminal law has to do with wrongful actions committed against society for which society demands redress.

Cuban missile crisis A nuclear stand-off that occurred in 1962 when the United States learned that the Soviet Union had placed nuclear warheads in Cuba, ninety miles off the U.S. coast. The crisis was defused diplomatically, but it is generally considered the closest the two Cold War superpowers came to a nuclear confrontation.

D

***De facto* segregation** Racial segregation that occurs not as a result of deliberate intentions but because of past social and economic conditions and residential patterns.

***De jure* segregation** Racial segregation that occurs because of laws or decisions by government agencies.

Delegate A person selected to represent the people of one geographic area at a party convention.

Democracy A system of government in which the people have ultimate political authority. The word is derived from the Greek *demos* ("the people") and *kratia* ("rule").

Détente French word meaning a "relaxation of tensions." Détente characterized the relationship between the United States and the Soviet Union in the 1970s, as the two Cold War rivals attempted to pursue cooperative dealings and arms control.

Deterrence A policy of building up military strength for the purpose of discouraging (deterring) military attacks by other nations; the policy of "building weapons for peace" that supported the arms race between the United States and the Soviet Union during the Cold War.

Devolution The surrender or transfer of powers to local authorities by a central government.

Dictatorship A form of government in which absolute power is exercised by a single person who usually has obtained his or her power by the use of force.

Diplomat A person who represents one country in dealing with representatives of another country.

Direct democracy A system of government in which political decisions are made by the people themselves rather than by elected representatives. This form of government was practiced in some areas of ancient Greece.

Direct primary An election held within each of the two major parties—Democratic and Republican—to choose the party's candidates for the general election. Voters choose the candidate directly, rather than through delegates.

Direct technique Any method used by an interest group to interact with government officials directly to further the group's goals.

Dissenting opinion A statement written by a judge or justice who disagrees with the majority opinion.

Diversity of citizenship A basis for federal court jurisdiction over a lawsuit that arises (1) when the parties in the lawsuit live in different states or when one of the parties is a foreign government or a foreign citizen, and (2) the amount in controversy is more than $75,000.

Divine right theory The theory that a monarch's right to rule was derived directly from God rather than from the consent of the people.

Division of powers A basic principle of federalism established by the U.S. Constitution, by which powers are divided between the federal and state governments.

Domestic policy Public policy concerning issues within a national unit, such as national policy concerning welfare or crime.

Double jeopardy The prosecution of a person twice for the same criminal offense; prohibited by the Fifth Amendment in all but a few circumstances.

Dual federalism A system of government in which the federal and the state governments maintain diverse but sovereign powers.

Due process clause The constitutional guarantee, set out in the Fifth and Fourteenth Amendments, that the government will not illegally or arbitrarily deprive a person of life, liberty, or property.

Due process of law The requirement that the government use fair, reasonable, and standard procedures whenever it takes any legal action against an individual; required by the Fifth and Fourteenth Amendments.

E

Easy-money policy A monetary policy that involves stimulating the economy by expanding the rate of growth of the money supply. An easy-money policy supposedly will lead to lower interest rates and induce consumers to spend more and producers to invest more.

Economic policy All actions taken by the national government to smooth out the ups and downs in the nation's overall business activity.

Elector A member of the electoral college.

Electoral college The group of electors who are selected by the voters in each state to elect officially the president and vice president. The number of electors in each state is equal to the number of that state's representatives in both chambers of Congress.

Electorate All of the citizens eligible to vote in a given election.

Electronic media Communication channels that involve electronic transmissions, such as radio, television, and the Internet.

Enabling legislation A law enacted by a legislature to establish an administrative agency. Enabling legislation normally specifies the name, purpose, composition, and powers of the agency being created.

Entitlement program A government program (such as Social Security) that allows, or entitles, a certain class of people (such as elderly persons) to receive special benefits. Entitlement programs operate under open-ended budget authorizations that, in effect, place no limits on how much can be spent.

Equality A concept that holds, at a minimum, that all people are entitled to equal protection under the law.

Equal protection clause Section 1 of the Fourteenth Amendment, which states that no state shall "deny to any person within its jurisdiction the equal protection of the laws."

Establishment clause The section of the First Amendment that prohibits Congress from passing laws "respecting an establishment of religion." Issues concerning the establishment clause often center on prayer in public schools, the teaching of fundamentalist theories of creation, and government aid to parochial schools.

Exclusionary rule A criminal procedural rule requiring that any illegally obtained evidence not be admissible in court.

Executive agreement A binding international agreement, or pact, that is made between the president and another head of state and that does not require Senate approval.

Executive Office of the President (EOP) A group of staff agencies that assist the president in carrying out major duties. Franklin D. Roosevelt established the EOP in 1939 to cope with the increased responsibilities brought on by the Great Depression.

Executive order A presidential order to carry out a policy or policies described in a law passed by Congress.

Executive privilege An inherent executive power claimed by presidents to withhold information from, or to refuse to appear before, Congress or the courts. The president can also accord the privilege to other executive officials.

***Ex post facto* law** A criminal law that punishes individuals for committing an act that was legal when the act was committed.

Expressed powers Constitutional or statutory powers that are expressly provided for by the Constitution or by congressional laws.

F

Faction A group of persons forming a cohesive minority.

Federalism A system of shared sovereignty between two levels of government—one national and one subnational—occupying the same geographic region.

Federalists A political group, led by Alexander Hamilton and John Adams, that supported the adoption of the Constitution and the creation of a federal form of government.

Federal mandate A requirement in federal legislation that forces states and municipalities to comply with certain rules. If the federal government does not provide funds to the states to cover the costs of compliance, the mandate is referred to as an *unfunded* mandate.

Federal Open Market Committee (FOMC) The most important body within the Federal Reserve System. The FOMC decides how monetary policy should be carried out by the Federal Reserve.

Federal question A question that pertains to the U.S. Constitution, acts of Congress, or treaties. A federal question provides a basis for federal court jurisdiction.

Federal system A form of government that provides for a division of powers between a central government and several regional governments. In the United States, the division of powers between the national government and the states is established by the Constitution.

Filibustering The Senate tradition of unlimited debate undertaken for the purpose of preventing action on a bill.

First budget resolution A budget resolution, which is supposed to be passed in May, that sets overall revenue goals and spending targets for the next fiscal year, which begins on October 1.

First Continental Congress A gathering of delegates from twelve of the thirteen colonies, held in 1774 to protest the Coercive Acts.

Fiscal federalism The allocation of taxes collected by one level of government (typically the national government) to another level (typically state or local governments).

Fiscal policy The use of changes in government expenditures and taxes to alter national economic variables.

Fiscal year A twelve-month period that is established for bookkeeping or accounting purposes. The government's fiscal year runs from October 1 through September 30.

Foreign policy A systematic and general plan that guides a country's attitudes and actions toward the rest of the world. Foreign policy includes all of the economic, military, commercial, and diplomatic positions and actions that a nation takes in its relationships with other countries.

Free exercise clause The provision of the First Amendment stating that the government cannot pass laws "prohibiting the free exercise" of religion. Free exercise issues often concern religious practices that conflict with established laws.

Free rider problem The difficulty that exists when individuals can enjoy the outcome of an interest group's efforts without having to contribute, such as by becoming members of the group.

Fundamental right A basic right of all Americans, such as First Amendment rights. Any law or action that prevents some group of persons from exercising a fundamental right is subject to the "strict-scrutiny" standard, under which the law or action must be necessary to promote a compelling state interest and must be narrowly tailored to meet that interest.

G

Gender gap The difference between the percentage of votes cast for a particular candidate by women and the percentage of votes cast for the same candidate by men.

General election A regularly scheduled election to choose the U.S. president, vice president, and senators and representatives in Congress. General elections are held in even-numbered years on the Tuesday after the first Monday in November.

Gerrymandering The drawing of a legislative district's boundaries in such a way as to maximize the influence of a certain group or political party.

Glass ceiling An invisible but real discriminatory barrier that prevents women and minorities from rising to top positions of power or responsibility.

Global warming An increase in the average temperature of the Earth's surface over the last half-century and its projected continuation.

Government The individuals and institutions that make society's rules and that also possess the power and authority to enforce those rules.

Government corporation An agency of the government that is run as a business enterprise. Such agencies engage in primarily commercial activities, produce revenues, and require greater flexibility than that permitted in most government agencies.

Grandfather clause A clause in a state law that had the effect of restricting the franchise (voting rights) to those whose ancestors had voted before the 1860s; one of the techniques used in the South to prevent African Americans from exercising their right to vote.

Great Compromise A plan for a bicameral legislature in which one chamber would be based on population and the other chamber would represent each state equally. The plan, also known as the Connecticut Compromise, resolved the small-state/large-state controversy.

Greenhouse gas A gas that, when released into the atmosphere, traps the sun's heat and slows its release into outer space. Carbon dioxide (CO_2) is a major example.

H

Head of state The person who serves as the ceremonial head of a country's government and represents that country to the rest of the world.

I

Ideologue An individual who holds very strong political opinions.

Ideology Generally, a system of political ideas that are rooted in religious or philosophical beliefs concerning human nature, society, and government.

Implied powers The powers of the federal government that are implied by the expressed powers in the Constitution, particularly in Article I, Section 8.

Independent executive agency A federal agency that is not located within a cabinet department.

Independent expenditure An expenditure for activities that are independent from (not coordinated with) those of a political candidate or a political party.

Independent regulatory agency A federal organization that is responsible for creating and implementing rules that regulate private activity and protect the public interest in a particular sector of the economy.

Indirect technique Any method used by interest groups to influence government officials through third parties, such as voters.

Individual mandate In the context of health-care reform, a requirement that all persons obtain health-care insurance from one source or another. Those failing to do so would pay a penalty.

Inherent powers The powers of the national government that, although not always expressly granted by the Constitution, are necessary to ensure the nation's integrity and survival as a political unit. Inherent powers include the power to make treaties and the power to wage war or make peace.

Institution An ongoing organization that performs certain functions for society.

Instructed delegate A representative who mirrors the views of the majority of his or her constituents.

Interest group An organized group of individuals sharing common objectives who actively attempt to influence policymakers.

Interstate commerce Trade that involves more than one state.

Interventionism Direct involvement by one country in another country's affairs.

Iron curtain A phrase coined by Winston Churchill to describe the political boundaries between the democratic countries in Western Europe and the Soviet-controlled Communist countries in Eastern Europe.

Iron triangle A three-way alliance among legislators, bureaucrats, and interest groups to make or preserve policies that benefit their respective interests.

Isolationism A political policy of noninvolvement in world affairs.

Issue ad A political advertisement that focuses on a particular issue. Issue ads can be used to support or attack a candidate.

Issue networks Groups of individuals or organizations—which consist of legislators and legislative staff members, interest group leaders, bureaucrats, the media, scholars, and other experts—that support particular policy positions on a given issue.

J

Judicial review The power of the courts to decide on the constitutionality of legislative enactments and of actions taken by the executive branch.

Judiciary The courts; one of the three branches of the federal government in the United States.

Jurisdiction The authority of a court to hear and decide a particular case.

Justiciable controversy A controversy that is not hypothetical or academic but real and substantial; a requirement that must be satisfied before a court will hear a case.

K

Keynesian economics An economic theory proposed by British economist John Maynard Keynes that is typically associated with the use of fiscal policy to alter national economic variables.

Kitchen cabinet The name given to a president's unofficial advisers. The term was coined during Andrew Jackson's presidency.

L

Labor force All of the people over the age of sixteen who are working or actively looking for jobs.

Legislative rule An administrative agency rule that carries the same weight as a statute enacted by a legislature.

***Lemon* test** A three-part test enunciated by the Supreme Court in the 1971 case of *Lemon v. Kurtzman* to determine whether government aid to parochial schools is constitutional. To be constitutional, the aid must (1) be for a clearly secular purpose; (2) in its primary effect, neither advance nor inhibit religion; and (3) avoid an "excessive government entanglement with religion." The *Lemon* test has also been used in other types of cases involving the establishment clause.

Libel A published report of a falsehood that tends to injure a person's reputation or character.

Liberalism A set of political beliefs that include the advocacy of active government, including government intervention to improve the welfare of individuals and to protect civil rights.

Liberty The freedom of individuals to believe, act, and express themselves as they choose so long as doing so does not infringe on the rights of other individuals in the society.

Limited government A form of government based on the principle that the powers of government should be clearly limited either through a written document or through wide public understanding; characterized by institutional checks to ensure that government serves public rather than private interests.

Literacy test A test given to voters to ensure that they could read and write and thus evaluate political information; a technique used in many southern states to restrict African American participation in elections.

Lobbying All of the attempts by organizations or by individuals to influence the passage, defeat, or contents of legislation or to influence the administrative decisions of government.

Lobbyist An individual who handles a particular interest group's lobbying efforts.

Loophole A legitimate way of evading a certain legal requirement.

M

Madisonian Model The model of government devised by James Madison, in which the powers of the government are separated into three branches: executive, legislative, and judicial.

Majority leader The party leader elected by the majority party in the House or in the Senate.

Majority party The political party that has more members in the legislature than the opposing party.

Malapportionment A condition in which the voting power of citizens in one district is greater than the voting power of citizens in another district.

Managed news coverage News coverage that is manipulated (managed) by a campaign manager or political consultant to gain media exposure for a political candidate.

Markup session A meeting held by a congressional committee or subcommittee to approve, amend, or redraft a bill.

Marshall Plan A plan providing for U.S. economic assistance to European nations following World War II to help those nations recover from the war; the plan was named after George C. Marshall, secretary of state from 1947 to 1949.

Mass media Communication channels, such as newspapers and radio and television broadcasts, through which people can communicate to mass audiences.

Mayflower Compact A document drawn up by Pilgrim leaders in 1620 on the ship *Mayflower*. The document stated that laws were to be made for the general good of the people.

Media Newspapers, magazines, television, radio, the Internet, and any other printed or electronic means of communication.

Medicaid A joint federal-state program that pays for health-care services for low-income persons.

Medicare A federal government program that pays for health-care insurance for Americans aged sixty-five years or over.

Minority leader The party leader elected by the minority party in the House or in the Senate.

Minority-majority district A district whose boundaries are drawn so as to maximize the voting power of minority groups.

Minority party The political party that has fewer members in the legislature than the opposing party.

***Miranda* warnings** A series of statements informing criminal suspects, on their arrest, of their constitutional rights, such as the right to remain silent and the right to counsel; required by the Supreme Court's 1966 decision in *Miranda v. Arizona*.

Moderate A person whose views fall in the middle of the political spectrum.

Monarchy A form of autocracy in which a king, queen, emperor, empress, tsar, or tsarina is the highest authority in the government; monarchs usually obtain their power through inheritance.

Monetary policy Actions taken by the Federal Reserve Board to change the amount of money in circulation so as to affect interest rates, credit markets, the rate of inflation, the rate of economic growth, and the rate of unemployment.

Monroe Doctrine A U.S. policy, announced in 1823 by President James Monroe, that the United States would not tolerate foreign intervention in the Western Hemisphere, and in return, the United States would stay out of European affairs.

Mutually assured destruction (MAD) A phrase referring to the assumption, on which the policy of deterrence was based, that if the forces of two nations are equally capable of destroying each other, neither nation will take a chance on war.

N

National convention The meeting held by each major party every four years to select presidential and vice-presidential candidates, write a party platform, and conduct other party business.

National health insurance A program, found in many of the world's economically advanced nations, under which the central government provides basic health-care insurance coverage to everyone in the country. Some wealthy nations, such as the Netherlands and Switzerland, provide universal coverage through private insurance companies instead.

National party chairperson An individual who serves as a political party's administrative head at the national level and directs the work of the party's national committee.

National party committee The political party leaders who direct party business during the four years between the national party conventions, organize the next national convention, and plan how to obtain a party victory in the next presidential elections.

National Security Council (NSC) A council that advises the president on domestic and foreign matters concerning the safety and defense of the nation; established in 1947.

Natural rights Rights that are not bestowed by governments but are inherent within every man, woman, and child by virtue of the fact that he or she is a human being.

Necessary and proper clause Article I, Section 8, Clause 18, of the Constitution, which gives Congress the power to make all laws "necessary and proper" for the federal government to carry out its responsibilities; also called the *elastic clause*.

Negative political advertising Political advertising undertaken for the purpose of discrediting an opposing candidate in the eyes of the voters. Attack ads and issue ads are forms of negative political advertising.

Neutral competency The application of technical skills to jobs without regard to political issues.

Neutrality A position of not being aligned with either side in a dispute or conflict, such as a war.

New Deal A program ushered in by the Roosevelt administration in 1933 to bring the United States out of the Great Depression. The New Deal included many government-spending and public assistance programs, in addition to thousands of regulations governing economic activity.

New federalism A plan to limit the federal government's role in regulating state governments and to give the states increased power to decide how they should spend government revenues.

Nominating convention An official meeting of a political party to choose its candidates. Nominating conventions at the state and local levels also select delegates to represent the citizens of their geographic areas at a higher-level party convention.

Normal trade relations (NTR) status A status granted through an international treaty by which each member nation must treat other members at least as well as it treats the country that receives its most favorable treatment. This status was formerly known as *most-favored-nation status*.

O

Obscenity Indecency or offensiveness in speech, expression, behavior, or appearance. Whether specific expressions or acts constitute obscenity normally is determined by community standards.

Office-block ballot A ballot (also called the Massachusetts ballot) that lists together all of the candidates for each office.

Office of Management and Budget (OMB) An agency in the Executive Office of the President that assists the president in preparing and supervising the administration of the federal budget.

"One person, one vote" rule A rule, or principle, requiring that congressional districts have equal populations so that one person's vote counts as much as another's vote.

Open primary A primary in which voters can vote for a party's candidates regardless of whether they belong to the party.

Opinion A written statement by a court expressing the reasons for its decision in a case.

Oral argument A spoken argument presented to a judge in person by an attorney on behalf of her or his client.

Oslo Accords The first agreement signed between Israel and the PLO; led to the establishment of the Palestinian Authority in the occupied territories.

P

Palestine Liberation Organization (PLO) An organization formed in 1964 to represent the Palestinian people. The PLO has a long history of terrorism but for some years has functioned primarily as a political party.

Parliament The name of the national legislative body in countries governed by a parliamentary system, such as Britain and Canada.

Partisan politics Political actions or decisions that benefit a particular party.

Party activist A party member who helps to organize and oversee party functions and planning during and between campaigns.

Party-column ballot A ballot (also called the Indiana ballot) that lists all of a party's candidates under the party label. Voters can vote for all of a party's candidates for local, state, and national offices by making a single "X" or pulling a single lever.

Party identifier A person who identifies himself or herself as being a member of a particular political party.

Party platform The document drawn up by each party at its national convention that outlines the policies and positions of the party.

Party ticket A list of a political party's candidates for various offices. In national elections, the party ticket consists of the presidential and vice-presidential candidates.

Patron An individual or organization that provides financial backing to an interest group.

Patronage The practice of giving government jobs to individuals belonging to the winning political party.

Peer group Associates, often close in age to one another; may include friends, classmates, co-workers, club members, or religious group members. Peer group influence is a significant factor in the political socialization process.

Personal attack ad A negative political advertisement that attacks the character of an opposing candidate.

Picket-fence federalism A model of federalism in which specific policies and programs are administered by all levels of government—national, state, and local.

Pluralist theory A theory that views politics as a contest among various interest groups—at all levels of government—to gain benefits for their members.

Pocket veto A special type of veto power used by the chief executive after the legislature has adjourned. Bills that are not signed die after a specified period of time.

Podcasting The distribution of audio or video files to a personal computer or a mobile device, such as an iPod.

Police powers The powers of a government body that enable it to create laws for the protection of the health, morals, safety, and welfare of the people. In the United States, most police powers are reserved to the states.

Policymaking process The procedures involved in getting an issue on the political agenda; formulating, adopting, and implementing a policy with regard to the issue; and then evaluating the results of the policy.

Political action committee (PAC) A committee that is established by a corporation, labor union, or special interest group to raise funds and make contributions on the establishing organization's behalf.

Political advertising Advertising undertaken by or on behalf of a political candidate to familiarize voters with the candidate and his or her views on campaign issues; also advertising for or against policy issues.

Political consultant A professional political adviser who, for a fee, works on an area of a candidate's campaign. Political consultants include campaign managers, pollsters, media advisers, and "get out the vote" organizers.

Political culture The set of ideas, values, and attitudes about government and the political process held by a community or a nation.

Political party A group of individuals who organize to win elections, operate the government, and determine policy.

Political socialization The learning process through which most people acquire their political attitudes, opinions, beliefs, and knowledge.

Politics The process of resolving conflicts over how society should use its scarce resources and who should receive various benefits, such as public health care and public higher education. According to Harold Lasswell, politics is the process of determining "who gets what, when, and how" in a society.

Poll tax A fee of several dollars that had to be paid before a person could vote; a device used in some southern states to prevent African Americans from voting.

Poll watcher A representative from one of the political parties who is allowed to monitor a polling place to make sure that the election is run fairly and to avoid fraud.

Power The ability to influence the behavior of others, usually through the use of force, persuasion, or rewards.

Precedent A court decision that furnishes an example or authority for deciding subsequent cases involving identical or similar facts and legal issues.

Precinct A political district within a city, such as a block or a neighborhood, or a rural portion of a county; the smallest voting district at the local level.

Preemption A doctrine rooted in the supremacy clause of the Constitution that provides that national laws or regulations governing a certain area take precedence over conflicting state laws or regulations governing that same area.

Preemptive war A war launched by a nation to prevent an imminent attack by another nation.

Press secretary A member of the White House staff who holds news conferences for reporters and makes public statements for the president.

Preventive war A war launched by a nation to prevent the possibility that another nation might attack at some point in the future; not supported by international law.

Primary A preliminary election held for the purpose of choosing a party's final candidate.

Primary election An election in which voters choose the candidates of their party, who will then run in the general election.

Primary source of law A source of law that establishes the law. Primary sources of law include constitutions, statutes, administrative agency rules and regulations, and decisions rendered by the courts.

Print media Communication channels that consist of printed materials, such as newspapers and magazines.

Privatization The transfer of the task of providing services traditionally provided by government to the private sector.

Probable cause Cause for believing that there is a substantial likelihood that a person has committed or is about to commit a crime.

Progressivism An alternative, more popular term for the set of political beliefs also known as liberalism.

Public debt The total amount of money that the national government owes as a result of borrowing; also called the national debt.

Public-interest group An interest group formed for the purpose of working for the "public good." Examples of public-interest groups are the American Civil Liberties Union and Common Cause.

Public opinion The views of the citizenry about politics, public issues, and public policies; a complex collection of opinions held by many people on issues in the public arena.

Public opinion poll A numerical survey of the public's opinion on a particular topic at a particular moment.

Public option In the context of health-care reform, a government-sponsored health-care insurance program that would compete with private insurance companies.

Public services Essential services that individuals cannot provide for themselves, such as building and maintaining roads, providing welfare programs, operating public schools, and preserving national parks.

Push poll A campaign tactic used to feed false or misleading information to potential voters, under the guise of taking an opinion poll, with the intent to "push" voters away from one candidate and toward another.

Q

Quota system A policy under which a specific number of jobs, promotions, or other types of placements, such as university admissions, must be given to members of selected groups.

R

Radical left Persons on the extreme left side of the political spectrum, who would like to significantly change the political order, usually to promote egalitarianism (human equality).

Radical right Persons on the extreme right side of the political spectrum. The radical right includes reactionaries (who would like to return to the values and social systems of some previous era) and libertarians (who believe in no regulation of the economy or individual behavior).

Random sample In the context of opinion polling, a sample in which each person within the entire population being polled has an equal chance of being chosen.

Rating system A system by which a particular interest group evaluates (rates) the performance of legislators based on how often the legislators have voted with the group's position on particular issues.

Rational basis test A test (also known as the "ordinary-scrutiny" standard) used by the Supreme Court to decide whether a discriminatory law violates the equal protection clause of the Constitution. Few laws evaluated under this test are found invalid.

Realignment A process in which the popular support for and relative strength of the parties shift and the parties are reestablished with different coalitions of supporters.

Renewable energy Energy from technologies that do not rely on extracted resources, such as oil and coal, that can run out.

Representative democracy A form of democracy in which the will of the majority is expressed through smaller groups of individuals elected by the people to act as their representatives.

Republic Essentially, a representative democracy in which there is no king or queen and the people are sovereign.

Reverse discrimination Discrimination against those who have no minority status.

Rulemaking The process undertaken by an administrative agency when formally proposing, evaluating, and adopting a new regulation.

Rule of law A basic principle of government that requires those who govern to act in accordance with established law.

Rules Committee A standing committee in the House of Representatives that provides special rules governing how particular bills will be considered and debated by the House. The Rules Committee normally proposes time limits on debate for any bill.

S

Sample In the context of opinion polling, a group of people selected to represent the population being studied.

Sampling error In the context of opinion polling, the difference between what the sample results show and what the true results would have been had everybody in the relevant population been interviewed.

School voucher An educational certificate, provided by the government, that allows a student to use public funds to pay for a private or a public school chosen by the student or his or her parents.

Secession The act of formally withdrawing from membership in an alliance; the withdrawal of a state from the federal Union.

Second budget resolution A budget resolution, which is supposed to be passed in September, that sets "binding" limits on taxes and spending for the next fiscal year.

Second Continental Congress The congress of the colonies that met in 1775 to assume the powers of a central government and to establish an army.

Seditious speech Speech that urges resistance to lawful authority or that advocates the overthrowing of a government.

Self-incrimination Providing damaging information or testimony against oneself in court.

Senatorial courtesy A practice that allows a senator of the president's party to veto the president's nominee to a federal court judgeship within the senator's state.

Separate-but-equal doctrine A Supreme Court doctrine holding that the equal protection clause of the Fourteenth Amendment did not forbid racial segregation as long as the facilities for blacks were equal to those for whites. The doctrine was overturned in the *Brown v. Board of Education of Topeka* decision of 1954.

Separation of powers The principle of dividing governmental powers among the executive, the legislative, and the judicial branches of government.

Sexual harassment Unwanted physical contact, verbal conduct, or abuse of a sexual nature that interferes with a recipient's job performance, creates a hostile environment, or carries with it an implicit or explicit threat of adverse employment consequences.

Shays' Rebellion A rebellion of angry farmers in western Massachusetts in 1786, led by former Revolutionary War captain Daniel Shays. This rebellion and other similar uprisings in the New England states emphasized the need for a true national government.

Signing statement A written statement, appended to a bill at the time the president signs it into law, indicating how the president interprets that legislation.

Single-payer plan A system in which a single entity—usually the national government—has the sole responsibility for issuing health-care insurance policies.

Sit-in A tactic of nonviolent civil disobedience. Demonstrators enter a business, college building, or other public place and remain seated until they are forcibly removed or until their demands are met. The tactic was used successfully in the civil rights movement and in other protest movements in the United States.

Slander The public utterance (speaking) of a statement that holds a person up for contempt, ridicule, or hatred.

Social conflict Disagreements among people in a society over what the society's priorities should be when distributing scarce resources.

Social contract A voluntary agreement among individuals to create a government and to give that government adequate power to secure the mutual protection and welfare of all individuals.

Soft money Campaign contributions not regulated by federal law, such as some contributions that are made to political parties instead of to particular candidates.

Solidarity Mutual sympathy among the members of a particular group.

Solid South A term used to describe the tendency of the southern states to vote Democratic after the Civil War.

Sound bite In televised news reporting, a brief comment, lasting for only a few seconds, that captures a thought or a perspective and has an immediate impact on the viewers.

Speaker of the House The presiding officer in the House of Representatives. The Speaker has traditionally been a longtime member of the majority party and is often the most powerful and influential member of the House.

Special election An election that is held at the state or local level when the voters must decide an issue before the next general election or when vacancies occur by reason of death or resignation.

Spin A reporter's slant on, or interpretation of, a particular event or action.

Spin doctor A political candidate's press adviser, who tries to convince reporters to give a story or event concerning the candidate a particular "spin" (interpretation, or slant).

Standing committee A permanent committee in Congress that deals with legislation concerning a particular area, such as agriculture or foreign relations.

Standing to sue The requirement that an individual must have a sufficient stake in a controversy before he or she can bring a lawsuit. The party bringing the suit must demonstrate that he or she has either been harmed or been threatened with a harm.

Stare decisis A common law doctrine under which judges normally are obligated to follow the precedents established by prior court decisions.

State Children's Health Insurance Program (SCHIP) A joint federal-state program that provides health-care insurance for low-income children.

Statutory law The body of law enacted by legislatures (as opposed to constitutional law, administrative law, or case law).

Straw poll A nonscientific poll; a poll in which there is no way to ensure that the opinions expressed are representative of the larger population.

Subcommittee A division of a larger committee that deals with a particular part of the committee's policy area. Most standing committees have several subcommittees.

Suffrage The right to vote; the franchise.

Supremacy clause Article VI, Clause 2, of the Constitution, which makes the Constitution and federal laws superior to all conflicting state and local laws.

Suspect classification A classification, such as race, that provides the basis for a discriminatory law. Any law based on a suspect classification is subject to strict scrutiny by the courts—meaning that the law must be justified by a compelling state interest.

Symbolic speech The expression of beliefs, opinions, or ideas through forms other than speech or print; speech involving actions and other nonverbal expressions.

T

Third party In the United States, any party other than one of the two major parties (Republican and Democratic).

Three-fifths compromise A compromise reached during the Constitutional Convention by which three-fifths of all slaves were to be counted for purposes of representation in the House of Representatives.

Trade organization An association formed by members of a particular industry, such as the oil industry or the trucking industry, to develop common standards and goals for the industry. Trade organizations, as interest groups, lobby government for legislation or regulations that specifically benefit their groups.

Treaty A formal agreement between the governments of two or more countries.

Trial court A court in which trials are held and testimony taken.

Trustee A representative who serves the broad interests of the entire society, and not just the narrow interests of his or her constituents.

Two-party system A political system in which two strong and established parties compete for political offices.

Tyranny The arbitrary or unrestrained exercise of power by an oppressive individual or government.

U

Unicameral legislature A legislature with only one chamber.

Unitary system A centralized governmental system in which local or subdivisional governments exercise only those powers given to them by the central government.

V

Veto A Latin word meaning "I forbid"; the refusal by an official, such as the president of the United States or a state governor, to sign a bill into law.

Veto power A constitutional power that enables the chief executive (president or governor) to reject legislation and return it to the legislature with reasons for the rejection. This prevents or at least delays the bill from becoming law.

Vital center The center of the political spectrum; those who hold moderate political views. The center is vital because without it, it may be difficult, if not impossible, to reach the compromises that are necessary to a political system's continuity.

Vote-eligible population The number of people who are actually eligible to vote in an American election.

Voting-age population The number of people residing in the United States who are at least eighteen years old.

W

Ward A local unit of a political party's organization, consisting of a division or district within a city.

Watergate scandal A scandal involving an illegal break-in at the Democratic National Committee offices in 1972 by members of President Nixon's reelection campaign staff. Before Congress could vote to impeach Nixon for his participation in covering up the break-in, Nixon resigned from the presidency.

Weapons of mass destruction Chemical, biological, or nuclear weapons that can inflict massive casualties.

Whip A member of Congress who assists the majority or minority leader in the House or in the Senate in managing the party's legislative preferences.

Whistleblower In the context of government employment, someone who "blows the whistle" (reports to authorities) on gross governmental inefficiency, illegal action, or other wrongdoing.

White House Office The personal office of the president. White House Office personnel handle the president's political needs and manage the media.

White primary A primary election in which African Americans were prohibited from voting. The practice was banned by the Supreme Court in 1944.

Winner-take-all system A system in which the candidate who receives the most votes wins. In contrast, proportional systems allocate votes to multiple winners.

Writ of *certiorari* An order from a higher court asking a lower court for the record of a case.

Writ of *habeas corpus* An order that requires an official to bring a specified prisoner into court and explain to the judge why the person is being held in prison.

Index

A

C

D

F

G

H

I

J

M

N

O

P

Q

R

S

T

U

V

W

X

Y

CHAPTER IN REVIEW 1 The Contours of American Democracy

To help you succeed, we have designed a review card for each chapter.

KEY TERMS

authority The ability to exercise power, such as the power to make and enforce laws, legitimately. *4*

autoc... A form of government in which the power and aut... of a single ...

Key terms and definitions listed in alphabetical order with page references.

bicameral leg... two chamb... bicameral l... Representa...

capitalism An economic system based on the private ownership of wealth-producing property, free markets, and freedom of contract. The privately owned corporation is the preeminent capitalist institution. *13*

conservatism A set of beliefs that includes a limited role for the national government in helping individuals and in the economic affairs of the nation, support for traditional values and lifestyles, and a cautious response to change. *16*

democracy A system of government in which the people have ultimate political authority. The word ... ple) and

Review cards are perfed so you can tear them out and study wherever you need to.

... hich ... person who ... by the use

... nent in which political decisions are made by the people themselves rather than by elected representatives. This form of government was practiced in some areas of ancient Greece. *8*

divine right theory A theory that the right to rule by a king or queen was derived directly from God rather than from the consent of the people. *7*

equality A conce... all people are ... the law. *13*

government Th... make society's... power and aut...

ideologue An in... political opinio...

ideology Genera... that are rooted... beliefs concer... government.

institution An o... certain functio...

liberalism A set ... the advocacy ... government i... individuals an...

liberty The freed... and express th... doing so does... individuals in t...

limited governm... on the princip...

How to Use This Card

1. Look over the card to preview the new concepts you'll be introduced to in the chapter.
2. Read your chapter to fully understand the material.
3. Go to class (and pay attention!)
4. Review the cards one more time to make sure you've registered the key concepts.
5. Don't forget to go online for many more learning tools to help you succeed in your course. 4ltrpress.cengage.com/govt

OUTLINE

Chapter Outline lists all major headings with page numbers for easy reference.

AP Photo/Paul Sakumap

SUMMARY & OBJECTIVES

LO1 Explain what is meant by the terms politics and government. ***1*** **Politics** can be defined as the process of resolving **social conflict**—disagreements over how the society should use its scarce resourc... nd who should receive various benefits. ***2*** **Government** can be defined as the individuals and ... possess the **power** and **authority** to enforce th... tial purposes: (a) it resolves conflicts; (b) it provide... nd its culture against attacks by other nations.

Summary points are linked to Learning Objectives to help you review important concepts.

...he various typ... racy, the ... of the government are in the hands of a single person. Monarchies and ... uding totalitarian dictatorships, are all forms of autocracy. In a constitutional ...r, the monarch shares governmental power with elected lawmakers. ...system of government in which the people have ultimate political authority. ...only by the consent of the people and reflects the will of the majority. **Direct** ... when the people participate directly in government decision making. In a ...**mocracy,** the will of the majority is expressed through groups of individuals ...le to act as their representatives. A **republic** is essentially a representative ... there is no king or queen; the people are sovereign. Forms of representative ... presidential democracy and **parliamentary** democracy. ***5*** An aristocracy is ...ich a small privileged class rules. Other forms of government characterized by ...lude plutocracy (the wealthy exercise ruling power) and meritocracy (rulers ...nt to govern because of their special skills or talents). Theocracy is a form of ...h there is no separation of church and state. The government rules according ...s.

LO3 **Summarize some of the basic principles of American democracy and the basic American political values.** ***6*** In writing the U.S. Constitution, the framers incorporated two basic principles of government that had evolved in England: **limited government** and representative government. Our democracy resulted from a type of **social contract** among early Americans to create and abide by a set of governing rules. Social-contract theory was developed in the seventeenth and eighteenth centuries by such philosophers as John Locke, Thomas Hobbes, and Jean-Jacques Rousseau. ***7*** The fundamental principles of American democracy are (a) equality in voting, (b) individual freedom, (c) equal protection of the law, (d) majority rule and minority rights, and (e) voluntary consent to be governed. ***8*** From its beginnings as a nation, America has been defined less by the culture shared by its diverse population than by a patterned set of ideas, values, and ways of thinking about government and politics—its **political culture.** Fundamental values shared by most Americans include the rights to **liberty, equality,** and property. Some Americans fear that rising numbers of immigrants will threaten traditional American political values and culture. ***9*** Generally, assumptions as to what the government's role should be in promoting basic values, such as liberty and equality, are important determinants of political **ideology.** When it comes to political ideology, Americans tend to fall into two broad camps: **liberals** and **conservatives.** Liberals, or **progressives,** often identify with the Democratic Party, and conservatives tend to identify politically as Republicans. People whose views fall in the middle of the traditional political spectrum are generally called **moderates.** On both ends of the spectrum are those who espouse radical views. ***10*** Many Americans do not adhere firmly to a particular political ideology. They may not be interested in all political issues and may have a mixed set of opinions that do not fit neatly under a liberal or conservative label.

LO4 **Describe how the various topics discussed in this text relate to the "big picture" of American politics and government.** ***11*** The U.S. Constitution is the supreme law of the land. It sets forth basic governing rules by which Americans agreed to abide. Some of the most significant political controversies today have to do with how various provisions in this founding document should be applied to modern-day events and issues. ***12*** Generally, those who acquire the power and authority to govern in our political system are the successful candidates in elections. The electoral process is influenced by interest groups, political parties, public opinion, voting behavior, campaign costs, and the media. ***13*** Those persons who have been selected for public office become part of one of the institutions of government. They make laws and policies to decide "who gets what, when, and how" in our society. Interest groups, public opinion, and the media not only affect election outcomes but also influence the policymaking process.

should be clearly limited either through a written document or through wide public understanding; characterized by institutional checks to ensure that government serves public rather than private interests. ***9***

moderate A person whose views fall in the middle of the political spectrum. ***17***

monarchy A form of autocracy in which a king, queen, emperor, empress, tsar, or tsarina is the highest authority in the government; monarchs usually obtain their power through inheritance. ***7***

natural rights Rights that are not bestowed by governments but are inherent within every man, woman, and child by virtue of the fact that he or she is a human being. ***10***

parliament The name of the national legislative body in countries governed by a parliamentary system, such as Britain and Canada. ***10***

political culture The set of ideas, values, and attitudes about government and the political process held by a community or a nation. ***11***

politics The process of resolving conflicts over how society should use its scarce resources and who should receive various benefits, such as public health care and public higher education. According to Harold Lasswell, politics is the process of determining "who gets what, when, and how" in a society. ***4***

power The ability to influence the behavior of others, usually through the use of force, persuasion, or rewards. ***4***

progressivism An alternative, more popular term for the set of political beliefs also known as liberalism. ***17***

public services Essential services that individuals cannot provide for themselves, such as building and maintaining roads, providing welfare programs, operating public schools, and preserving national parks. ***4***

radical left Persons on the extreme left side of the political spectrum who would like to significantly change the political order, usually to promote egalitarianism (human equality). ***17***

radical right Persons on the extreme right side of the political spectrum. The radical right includes reactionaries (who would like to return to the values and social systems of some previous era) and libertarians (who believe in no regulation of the economy and individual behavior, except for defense and law enforcement). ***17***

representative democracy A form of democracy in which the will of the majority is expressed through smaller groups of individuals elected by the people to act as their representatives. ***8***

republic Essentially, a term referring to a representative democracy—in which there is no king or queen and the people are sovereign. The people elect smaller groups of individuals to act as the people's representatives. ***8***

social conflict Disagreements among people in a society over what the society's priorities should be with respect to the use of scarce resources. ***3***

social contract A voluntary agreement among individuals to create a government and to give that government adequate power to secure the mutual protection and welfare of all individuals. ***10***

CHAPTER IN REVIEW 1 The Contours of American Democracy

KEY TERMS

authority The ability to exercise power, such as the power to make and enforce laws, legitimately. *4*

autocracy A form of government in which the power and authority of the government are in the hands of a single person. *7*

bicameral legislature A legislature made up of two chambers, or parts. The United States has a bicameral legislature, composed of the House of Representatives and the Senate. *10*

capitalism An economic system based on the private ownership of wealth-producing property, free markets, and freedom of contract. The privately owned corporation is the preeminent capitalist institution. *13*

conservatism A set of beliefs that includes a limited role for the national government in helping individuals and in the economic affairs of the nation, support for traditional values and lifestyles, and a cautious response to change. *16*

democracy A system of government in which the people have ultimate political authority. The word is derived from the Greek demos (people) and kratia (rule). *7*

dictatorship A form of government in which absolute power is exercised by a single person who has usually obtained his or her power by the use of force. *7*

direct democracy A system of government in which political decisions are made by the people themselves rather than by elected representatives. This form of government was practiced in some areas of ancient Greece. *8*

divine right theory A theory that the right to rule by a king or queen was derived directly from God rather than from the consent of the people. *7*

equality A concept that holds, at a minimum, that all people are entitled to equal protection under the law. *13*

government The individuals and institutions that make society's rules and that also possess the power and authority to enforce those rules. *4*

ideologue An individual who holds very strong political opinions. *17*

ideology Generally, a system of political ideas that are rooted in religious or philosophical beliefs concerning human nature, society, and government. *14*

institution An ongoing organization that performs certain functions for society. *3*

liberalism A set of political beliefs that includes the advocacy of active government, including government intervention to improve the welfare of individuals and to protect civil rights. *16*

liberty The freedom of individuals to believe, act, and express themselves as they choose so long as doing so does not infringe on the rights of other individuals in the society. *11*

limited government A form of government based on the principle that the powers of government

OUTLINE

AP Photo/Paul Sakumap

SUMMARY & OBJECTIVES

LO1 Explain what is meant by the terms politics and government. ***1*** **Politics** can be defined as the process of resolving **social conflict**—disagreements over how the society should use its scarce resources and who should receive various benefits. ***2*** **Government** can be defined as the individuals and **institutions** that make society's rules and that also possess the **power** and **authority** to enforce those rules. Government serves at least three essential purposes: (a) it resolves conflicts; (b) it provides **public services;** and (c) it defends the nation and its culture against attacks by other nations.

LO2 Identify the various types of government systems. ***3*** In an **autocracy,** the power and authority of the government are in the hands of a single person. Monarchies and **dictatorships,** including totalitarian dictatorships, are all forms of autocracy. In a constitutional **monarchy,** however, the monarch shares governmental power with elected lawmakers. ***4*** **Democracy** is a system of government in which the people have ultimate political authority. Government exists only by the consent of the people and reflects the will of the majority. **Direct democracy** exists when the people participate directly in government decision making. In a **representative democracy,** the will of the majority is expressed through groups of individuals elected by the people to act as their representatives. A **republic** is essentially a representative democracy in which there is no king or queen; the people are sovereign. Forms of representative democracy include presidential democracy and **parliamentary** democracy. ***5*** An aristocracy is a government in which a small privileged class rules. Other forms of government characterized by "rule by the few" include plutocracy (the wealthy exercise ruling power) and meritocracy (rulers have earned the right to govern because of their special skills or talents). Theocracy is a form of government in which there is no separation of church and state. The government rules according to religious precepts.

LO3 Summarize some of the basic principles of American democracy and the basic American political values. ***6*** In writing the U.S. Constitution, the framers incorporated two basic principles of government that had evolved in England: **limited government** and representative government. Our democracy resulted from a type of **social contract** among early Americans to create and abide by a set of governing rules. Social-contract theory was developed in the seventeenth and eighteenth centuries by such philosophers as John Locke, Thomas Hobbes, and Jean-Jacques Rousseau. ***7*** The fundamental principles of American democracy are (a) equality in voting, (b) individual freedom, (c) equal protection of the law, (d) majority rule and minority rights, and (e) voluntary consent to be governed. ***8*** From its beginnings as a nation, America has been defined less by the culture shared by its diverse population than by a patterned set of ideas, values, and ways of thinking about government and politics—its **political culture.** Fundamental values shared by most Americans include the rights to **liberty, equality,** and property. Some Americans fear that rising numbers of immigrants will threaten traditional American political values and culture. ***9*** Generally, assumptions as to what the government's role should be in promoting basic values, such as liberty and equality, are important determinants of political **ideology.** When it comes to political ideology, Americans tend to fall into two broad camps: **liberals** and **conservatives.** Liberals, or **progressives,** often identify with the Democratic Party, and conservatives tend to identify politically as Republicans. People whose views fall in the middle of the traditional political spectrum are generally called **moderates.** On both ends of the spectrum are those who espouse radical views. ***10*** Many Americans do not adhere firmly to a particular political ideology. They may not be interested in all political issues and may have a mixed set of opinions that do not fit neatly under a liberal or conservative label.

LO4 Describe how the various topics discussed in this text relate to the "big picture" of American politics and government. ***11*** The U.S. Constitution is the supreme law of the land. It sets forth basic governing rules by which Americans agreed to abide. Some of the most significant political controversies today have to do with how various provisions in this founding document should be applied to modern-day events and issues. ***12*** Generally, those who acquire the power and authority to govern in our political system are the successful candidates in elections. The electoral process is influenced by interest groups, political parties, public opinion, voting behavior, campaign costs, and the media. ***13*** Those persons who have been selected for public office become part of one of the institutions of government. They make laws and policies to decide "who gets what, when, and how" in our society. Interest groups, public opinion, and the media not only affect election outcomes but also influence the policymaking process.

should be clearly limited either through a written document or through wide public understanding; characterized by institutional checks to ensure that government serves public rather than private interests. ***9***

moderate A person whose views fall in the middle of the political spectrum. ***17***

monarchy A form of autocracy in which a king, queen, emperor, empress, tsar, or tsarina is the highest authority in the government; monarchs usually obtain their power through inheritance. ***7***

natural rights Rights that are not bestowed by governments but are inherent within every man, woman, and child by virtue of the fact that he or she is a human being. ***10***

parliament The name of the national legislative body in countries governed by a parliamentary system, such as Britain and Canada. ***10***

political culture The set of ideas, values, and attitudes about government and the political process held by a community or a nation. ***11***

politics The process of resolving conflicts over how society should use its scarce resources and who should receive various benefits, such as public health care and public higher education. According to Harold Lasswell, politics is the process of determining "who gets what, when, and how" in a society. ***4***

power The ability to influence the behavior of others, usually through the use of force, persuasion, or rewards. ***4***

progressivism An alternative, more popular term for the set of political beliefs also known as liberalism. ***17***

public services Essential services that individuals cannot provide for themselves, such as building and maintaining roads, providing welfare programs, operating public schools, and preserving national parks. ***4***

radical left Persons on the extreme left side of the political spectrum who would like to significantly change the political order, usually to promote egalitarianism (human equality). ***17***

radical right Persons on the extreme right side of the political spectrum. The radical right includes reactionaries (who would like to return to the values and social systems of some previous era) and libertarians (who believe in no regulation of the economy and individual behavior, except for defense and law enforcement). ***17***

representative democracy A form of democracy in which the will of the majority is expressed through smaller groups of individuals elected by the people to act as their representatives. ***8***

republic Essentially, a term referring to a representative democracy—in which there is no king or queen and the people are sovereign. The people elect smaller groups of individuals to act as the people's representatives. ***8***

social conflict Disagreements among people in a society over what the society's priorities should be with respect to the use of scarce resources. ***3***

social contract A voluntary agreement among individuals to create a government and to give that government adequate power to secure the mutual protection and welfare of all individuals. ***10***

The Constitution

KEY TERMS

Anti-Federalists A political group that opposed the adoption of the Constitution because of the document's centralist tendencies and because it did not include a bill of rights. *37*

Articles of Confederation The nation's first national constitution, which established a national form of government following the American Revolution. The Articles provided for a confederal form of government in which the central government had few powers. *31*

Bill of Rights The first ten amendments to the U.S. Constitution. They list the freedoms—such as the freedoms of speech, press, and religion—that a citizen enjoys and that cannot be infringed on by the government. *25*

checks and balances A major principle of American government in which each of the three branches is given the means to check (to restrain or balance) the actions of the others. *40*

commerce clause The clause in Article I, Section 8, of the Constitution that gives Congress the power to regulate interstate commerce (commerce involving more than one state). *39*

confederation A league of independent states that are united only for the purpose of achieving common goals. *30*

Constitutional Convention The convention (meeting) of delegates from the states that was held in Philadelphia in 1787 for the purpose of amending the Articles of Confederation. In fact, the delegates wrote a new constitution (the U.S. Constitution) that established a federal form of government to replace the governmental system that had been created by the Articles of Confederation. *33*

faction A group of persons forming a cohesive minority. *38*

federal system A form of government that provides for a division of powers between a central government and several regional governments. In the United States, the division of powers between the national government and the states is established by the Constitution. *39*

Federalists A political group, led by Alexander Hamilton and John Adams, that supported the adoption of the Constitution and the creation of a federal form of government. *37*

First Continental Congress A gathering of delegates from twelve of the thirteen colonies, held in 1774 to protest the Coercive Acts. *27*

Great Compromise A plan for a bicameral legislature in which one chamber would be based on population and the other chamber would represent each state equally. The plan, also known as the Connecticut Compromise, resolved the small-state/large-state controversy. *35*

interstate commerce Trade that involves more than one state. *36*

Madisonian Model The model of government devised by James Madison, in which the powers

OUTLINE

Shutterstock

SUMMARY & OBJECTIVES

LO1 Point out some of the influences on the American political tradition in the colonial years. ***1*** American politics owes much to England, but the colonists derived most of their understanding from their own experiences. The Pilgrims founded the first New England colony at Plymouth in 1620. Before going ashore, they drew up the **Mayflower Compact,** in which they set up a government and promised to obey its laws. Connecticut colonists developed America's first written constitution, the Fundamental Orders of Connecticut. Under it, an elected assembly made laws, and the governor and judges were popularly elected. The Pennsylvania Charter of Privileges of 1701 established principles later expressed in the Constitution and the **Bill of Rights.** ***2*** By participating in colonial governments, the colonists became familiar with the practical problems of governing. They learned how to build coalitions and make compromises.

LO2 Explain why the American colonies rebelled against Britain. ***3*** Initially, most colonists were strongly loyal to Britain. After the British victory in the Seven Years' War (1756–1763), however, the British Parliament sought to pay its war debts and to finance the defense of North America by imposing taxes on the colonists and controlling colonial trade. ***4*** In response, the colonists set up the **First Continental Congress** and petitioned the king, explaining their grievances. Americans boycotted British goods and established colonial armies. Britain responded with repression. ***5*** In 1775, British soldiers fought colonial citizens in the first battles of the American Revolution. Delegates gathered for the **Second Continental Congress,** which assumed the powers of a central government. ***6*** The Second Continental Congress adopted the Declaration of Independence on July 4, 1776.

LO3 Describe the structure of government established by the Articles of Confederation and some of the strengths and weaknesses of the Articles. ***7*** The **Articles of Confederation,** the nation's first constitution, established a Congress as a governing body. Congress was a **unicameral** body in which each state had only one vote. A president presided over meetings but had no executive authority. Congress could declare war, enter into treaties, and settle certain disputes among the states. ***8*** In spite of several accomplishments, the central government created by the Articles was weak. Congress could not raise revenues for the militia or to force the states to meet military quotas. It could not regulate commerce between the states or with other nations. It had no power to enforce its laws. There was no national judicial system and no executive branch.

LO4 List some of the major compromises made by the delegates at the Constitutional Convention, and discuss the Federalist and Anti-Federalist positions with respect to ratifying the Constitution. ***9*** Dissatisfaction with the Articles and disruptions such as **Shays' Rebellion** persuaded American leaders that a true national government was necessary. Congress called for delegates to a meeting in Philadelphia in 1787 that became the **Constitutional Convention.** ***10*** Delegates resolved the small/large-state controversy with the **Great Compromise**—a plan for a bicameral legislature. In one chamber, the number of people in each state would determine the number of representatives. The other chamber would have two members per state. The **three-fifths** compromise settled a deadlock on how slaves would be counted to determine representation in the House of Representatives and the delegates also agreed that Congress could prohibit the importation of slaves into the country beginning in 1808. The South agreed to give Congress the power to regulate both **interstate commerce** and commerce with other nations in exchange for a ban on export taxes. ***11*** **Federalists** favored the new Constitution. The *Federalist Papers* attempted to allay the fears of the Constitution's critics. **Anti-Federalists** argued that the Constitution would lead to aristocratic **tyranny** or an overly powerful central government that would limit personal freedom. To gain support for ratification, the Federalists promised to add a bill of rights to the Constitution. By 1790, all of the states had ratified.

LO5 Summarize the Constitution's major principles of government, and describe how the Constitution can be amended. ***12*** The Constitution incorporates the principle of limited government: government can do only what the people allow it to do. Limited government rests on the concept of popular sovereignty—the people create the government. Under the principle of federalism, the national government shares power with the states. By separating the powers of the national government and establishing a system of **checks and balances,** the framers ensured that no one branch—legislative, executive, judicial—could dominate the others. ***13*** An amendment to the Constitution can be proposed either by a two-thirds vote in each chamber of Congress or by a national convention called at the request of two-thirds of the state legislatures. Ratification of an amendment requires either approval by three-fourths of the state legislatures or by three-fourths of special conventions called in each state.

of the government are separated into three branches: executive, legislative, and judicial. ***40***

Mayflower Compact A document drawn up by Pilgrim leaders in 1620 on the ship *Mayflower.* The document stated that laws were to be made for the general good of the people. ***25***

rule of law A basic principle of government that requires those who govern to act in accordance with established law. ***39***

Second Continental Congress The congress of the colonies that met in 1775 to assume the powers of a central government and to establish an army. ***40***

separation of powers The principle of dividing governmental powers among the executive, the legislative, and the judicial branches of government. ***41***

Shays' Rebellion A rebellion of angry farmers in western Massachusetts in 1786, led by former Revolutionary War captain Daniel Shays. This rebellion and other similar uprisings in the New England states emphasized the need for a true national government. ***32***

three-fifths compromise A compromise reached during the Constitutional Convention by which three-fifths of all slaves were to be counted for purposes of representation in the House of Representatives. ***35***

tyranny The arbitrary or unrestrained exercise of power by an oppressive individual or government. ***38***

unicameral legislature A legislature with only one chamber. ***30***

veto power A constitutional power that enables the chief executive (president or governor) to reject legislation and return it to the legislature with reasons for the rejection. This prevents or at least delays the bill from becoming law. ***42***

KEY TERMS

block grant A federal grant given to a state for a broad area, such as criminal justice or mental-health programs. ***68***

categorical grant A federal grant targeted for a specific purpose as defined by federal law. ***68***

competitive federalism A model of federalism devised by Thomas R. Dye in which state and local governments compete for businesses and citizens, who in effect "vote with their feet" by moving to jurisdictions that offer a competitive advantage. ***69***

confederal system A league of independent sovereign states, joined together by a central government that has only limited powers over them. ***52***

concurrent powers Powers held by both the federal and the state governments in a federal system. ***57***

cooperative federalism The theory that the states and the federal government should cooperate in solving problems. ***62***

devolution The surrender or transfer of powers to local authorities by a central government. ***64***

division of powers A basic principle of federalism established by the U.S. Constitution, by which powers are divided between the federal and state governments. ***55***

dual federalism A system of government in which the federal and the state governments maintain diverse but sovereign powers. ***60***

expressed powers Constitutional or statutory powers that are expressly provided for by the Constitution or by congressional laws. ***55***

federal mandate A requirement in federal legislation that forces states and municipalities to comply with certain rules. If the federal government does not provide funds to the states to cover the costs of compliance, the mandate is referred to as an *unfunded* mandate. ***64***

federalism A system of shared sovereignty between two levels of government—one

OUTLINE

SUMMARY & OBJECTIVES

LO1 Explain what federalism means, how federalism differs from other systems of government, and why it exists in the United States. ***1*** The United States has a federal form of government, in which governmental powers are shared by the national government and the states. For a system to be truly federal, the powers of both the national units and the subnational units must be specified and limited. Alternatives to **federalism** include a **unitary system** and a **confederal system.** In a unitary system any subnational government is a "creature of the national government." Subnational governments exercise only those powers given to them by the national (central) government. In a confederal system, the central government exists and operates only at the direction of the subnational governments. ***2*** The Articles of Confederation failed because they did not allow for a sufficiently strong central government. The framers of the Constitution, however, were fearful of tyranny and a too-powerful central government. The appeal of federalism was that it retained state powers and local traditions while establishing a strong national government capable of handling common problems. Federalism has been viewed as well suited to the United States for several reasons, but it also has some drawbacks.

LO2 Indicate how the Constitution divides governing powers in our federal system. ***3*** The Constitution delegates certain powers to the national government and also prohibits the national government from exercising certain powers. The national government possesses three types of powers: **expressed, implied,** and **inherent.** The Constitution expressly enumerates twenty-seven powers that Congress may exercise, such as the power to coin money and the power to regulate interstate commerce. The Constitution's **"necessary and proper" clause** is the basis for implied powers. Thus, Congress has the power to make all laws "necessary and proper" for the federal (national) government to carry out its responsibilities. The national government also enjoys certain inherent powers—powers that governments must have simply to ensure the nation's integrity and survival. ***4*** The Tenth Amendment to the Constitution states that powers that are not delegated to the national government by the Constitution, nor prohibited to the states, are "reserved" to the states or to the people. In principle, each state has the ability to regulate its internal affairs and to enact whatever laws are necessary to protect the health, safety, morals, and welfare of its people. These powers of the states are called **police powers.** Some powers, called **concurrent powers,** can be exercised at either the state or the national level. ***5*** The Constitution also contains provisions relating to interstate relations. The full faith and credit clause, for example, requires each state to honor every other state's public acts, records, and judicial proceedings. The Constitution's **supremacy clause** provides that national laws are supreme. National government power always takes precedence over any conflicting state action.

LO3 Summarize the evolution of federal-state relationships in the United States over time. ***6*** Two early Supreme Court cases, *McCulloch v. Maryland* (1819) and *Gibbons v. Ogden* (1824), played a key role in establishing the constitutional foundations for the supremacy of the national government. The nation's great struggle over slavery also took the form of a dispute over states' rights versus national supremacy. ***7*** The relationship between the states and the national government has evolved through several stages since the Civil War. The model of **dual federalism,** which prevailed until the 1930s, assumes that the states and the national government are more or less equals, with each level of government having separate and distinct functions and responsibilities. The model of **cooperative federalism,** which views the national and state governments as complementary parts of a single governmental mechanism, grew out of the need to solve the pressing national problems caused by the Great Depression. The 1960s and 1970s saw an even greater expansion of the national government's role in domestic policy, but the massive social programs undertaken during this period also precipitated greater involvement by state and local governments. The model in which every level of government is involved in implementing a policy is sometimes referred to as **picket-fence federalism.**

LO4 Describe developments in federalism in recent years. ***8*** Starting in the 1970s, several administrations favored a shift from nation-centered federalism to state-centered federalism. One of the goals of the **"new federalism"** was to return to the states certain powers that had been exercised by the national government since the 1930s. During and since the 1990s, many Supreme Court decisions have had the effect of enhancing the power of the states. ***9*** The federal government and the states now seem to be in a constant tug-of-war over federal regulation, federal programs, and federal demands on the states. Recently, decisions made about welfare reform, educational funding, same-sex marriages, homeland security, and the economic crisis have involved the politics of federalism and have not always reflected clear-cut partisan divisions.

LO5 Explain what is meant by the term *fiscal federalism.* ***10*** To help the states pay for the costs associated with implementing policies mandated by the national government, the national government gives back some of the tax dollars it collects to the states—in the form of **categorical** and **block grants.** The states have come to depend on grants as an important source of revenue. Through the awarding of grants, the federal government has been able to exercise control over matters that traditionally have been under the control of state governments.

national and one subnational—occupying the same geographic region. ***51***

fiscal federalism The allocation of taxes collected by one level of government (typically the national government) to another level (typically state or local governments). ***68***

implied powers The powers of the federal government that are implied by the expressed powers in the Constitution, particularly in Article I, Section 8. ***55***

inherent powers The powers of the national government that, although not always expressly granted by the Constitution, are necessary to ensure the nation's integrity and survival as a political unit. Inherent powers include the power to make treaties and the power to wage war or make peace. ***55***

necessary and proper clause Article I, Section 8, Clause 18, of the Constitution, which gives Congress the power to make all laws "necessary and proper" for the federal government to carry out its responsibilities; also called the *elastic clause.* ***55***

New Deal A program ushered in by the Roosevelt administration in 1933 to bring the United States out of the Great Depression. The New Deal included many government-spending and public-assistance programs, in addition to thousands of regulations governing economic activity. ***62***

new federalism A plan to limit the federal government's role in regulating state governments and to give the states increased power to decide how they should spend government revenues. ***64***

picket-fence federalism A model of federalism in which specific policies and programs are administered by all levels of government—national, state, and local. ***63***

police powers The powers of a government body that enable it to create laws for the protection of the health, morals, safety, and welfare of the people. In the United States, most police powers are reserved to the states. ***56***

preemption A doctrine rooted in the supremacy clause of the Constitution that provides that national laws or regulations governing a certain area take precedence over conflicting state laws or regulations governing that same area. ***63***

secession The act of formally withdrawing from membership in an alliance; the withdrawal of a state from the federal Union. ***60***

supremacy clause Article VI, Clause 2, of the Constitution, which makes the Constitution and federal laws superior to all conflicting state and local laws. ***57***

unitary system A centralized governmental system in which local or subdivisional governments exercise only those powers given to them by the central government. ***52***

CHAPTER IN REVIEW 4 Civil Liberties

KEY TERMS

bill of attainder A legislative act that inflicts punishment on particular persons or groups without granting them the right to a trial. *76*

civil liberties Individual rights protected by the Constitution against the powers of the government. *76*

commercial speech Advertising statements that describe products. Commercial speech receives less protection under the First Amendment than ordinary speech. *86*

double jeopardy The prosecution of a person twice for the same criminal offense; prohibited by the Fifth Amendment in all but a few circumstances. *97*

due process clause The constitutional guarantee, set out in the Fifth and Fourteenth Amendments, that the government will not illegally or arbitrarily deprive a person of life, liberty, or property. *77*

due process of law The requirement that the government use fair, reasonable, and standard procedures whenever it takes any legal action against an individual; required by the Fifth and Fourteenth Amendments. *77*

establishment clause The section of the First Amendment that prohibits Congress from passing laws "respecting an establishment of religion." Issues concerning the establishment clause often center on prayer in public schools, the teaching of fundamentalist theories of creation, and government aid to parochial schools. *80*

exclusionary rule A criminal procedural rule requiring that any illegally obtained evidence not be admissible in court. *97*

***ex post facto* law** A criminal law that punishes individuals for committing an act that was legal when the act was committed. *76*

free exercise clause The provision of the First Amendment stating that the government cannot pass laws "prohibiting the free

OUTLINE

© Peter Maiden/Sygma/Corbis

SUMMARY & OBJECTIVES

LO1 Define the term *civil liberties,* explain how civil liberties differ from civil rights, and state the constitutional basis for our civil liberties. ***1*** **Civil liberties** are legal and constitutional rights that protect citizens from government actions. While civil rights specify what the government *must* do, civil liberties are limitations on government action, setting forth what the government *cannot* do. ***2*** The Bill of Rights (the first ten amendments to the Constitution) sets forth most of our civil liberties. Other safeguards to protect citizens against an overly powerful government, such as the writ of ***habeas corpus,*** are specified in the original Constitution. For many years, the courts assumed that the Bill of Rights limited only the actions of the national government, not those of the states. Over time, however, the United States Supreme Court has used the **due process clause** of the Fourteenth Amendment to say that the states could not abridge a civil liberty that the national government could not abridge. In other words, the Court has incorporated most of the protections guaranteed by the Bill of Rights into the liberties protected under the Fourteenth Amendment.

LO2 List and describe the freedoms guaranteed by the First Amendment and explain how the courts have interpreted and applied these freedoms. ***3*** The First Amendment prohibits government from passing laws "respecting an establishment of religion, or prohibiting the free exercise thereof." The first part of this statement is referred to as the **establishment clause;** the second part is known as the **free exercise clause.** Issues involving the establishment clause include prayer in the public schools, the teaching of evolution versus creationism, and government aid to parochial schools. The Supreme Court has ruled that the public schools cannot sponsor religious activities, and has held unconstitutional state laws forbidding the teaching of evolution in the schools. Some aid to parochial schools has been held to violate the establishment clause, while other forms of aid have been held permissible.

4 The free exercise clause does not necessarily mean that individuals can act in any way they want on the basis of their religious beliefs. The Supreme Court has ruled consistently that the right to hold any religious belief is absolute. The right to practice one's beliefs, however, may have some limits. The free exercise of religion in the workplace was bolstered by Title VII of the Civil Rights Act of 1964, which requires employers to accommodate their employees' religious practices unless such accommodation causes an employer to suffer an "undue hardship." **5** Although the Supreme Court has zealously safeguarded the right to free speech under the First Amendment, at times it has imposed limits on speech in the interests of protecting other rights. These rights include security against harm to one's person or reputation, the need for public order, and the need to preserve the government. **6** The First Amendment freedom of the press generally protects the right to publish a wide range of opinions and information. Over the years, the Supreme Court has developed various guidelines and doctrines to use in deciding whether freedom of speech and the press can be restrained. **7** The First Amendment protects the right of the people "peaceably to assemble" and communicate their ideas on public issues to government officials, as well as to other individuals. It also guarantees the right of the people to "petition the government for a redress of grievances." This right allows citizens to lobby members of Congress and other government officials.

LO3 Discuss why Americans are increasingly concerned about privacy rights. **8** The Supreme Court has held that a right to privacy is implied by other constitutional rights guaranteed in the Bill of Rights. The government has also passed laws ensuring the privacy rights of individuals. The nature and scope of this right, however, are not always clear. **9** In 1973, the Supreme Court held that the right to privacy is broad enough to encompass a woman's decision to terminate a pregnancy, though the right is not absolute throughout pregnancy. Since that decision, the Court has upheld restrictive state laws requiring counseling, parental notification, and other actions prior to abortions. The issue of "partial-birth" abortion has been particularly controversial. **10** The Supreme Court upheld the states' rights to ban physician-assisted suicide in situations involving terminally ill persons, but it did not hold that state laws permitting physician-assisted suicide were unconstitutional. Americans continue to be at odds over this issue. **11** Since the terrorist attacks of September 11, 2001, Americans have debated how the United States can address the need to strengthen national security while still protecting civil liberties, particularly the right to privacy. Various programs have been proposed or attempted, and some have already been dismantled after public outcry. Many civil libertarians point out that trading off even a few civil liberties, including our privacy rights, for national security is senseless. These liberties are at the heart of what this country stands for. Other Americans believe that we have little to worry about. Those who have nothing to hide should not be concerned about government surveillance or other privacy intrusions undertaken by the government to make our nation more secure against terrorist attacks.

LO4 Summarize how the Constitution and the Bill of Rights protect the rights of accused persons. **12** Constitutional safeguards provided for criminal defendants include the Fourth Amendment protection from unreasonable searches and seizures and the requirement that no warrant for a search or an arrest be issued without **probable cause;** the Fifth Amendment prohibition against **double jeopardy** and the protection against **self-incrimination;** the Sixth Amendment guarantees of a speedy trial, a trial by jury, a public trial, the right to confront witnesses, and the right to counsel at various stages in some criminal proceedings; and the Eighth Amendment prohibitions against excessive bail and fines and against cruel and unusual punishments. The Constitution also provides for the writ of *habeas corpus*—an order requiring that an official bring a specified prisoner into court and show the judge why the prisoner is being kept in jail.

exercise" of religion. Free exercise issues often concern religious practices that conflict with established laws. ***80***

Lemon* test** A three-part test enunciated by the Supreme Court in the 1971 case of *Lemon v. Kurtzman* to determine whether government aid to parochial schools is constitutional. To be constitutional, the aid must (1) be for a clearly secular purpose; (2) in its primary effect, neither advance nor inhibit religion; and (3) avoid an "excessive government entanglement with religion." The Lemon test has also been used in other types of cases involving the establishment clause. ***83

libel A published report of a falsehood that tends to injure a person's reputation or character. ***86***

Miranda* warnings** A series of statements informing criminal suspects, on their arrest, of their constitutional rights, such as the right to remain silent and the right to counsel; required by the Supreme Court's 1966 decision in *Miranda v. Arizona.* ***97

obscenity Indecency or offensiveness in speech, expression, behavior, or appearance. Whether specific expressions or acts constitute obscenity normally is determined by community standards. ***87***

probable cause Cause for believing that there is a substantial likelihood that a person has committed or is about to commit a crime. ***97***

school voucher An educational certificate, provided by the government, that allows a student to use public funds to pay for a private or a public school chosen by the student or his or her parents. ***83***

seditious speech Speech that urges resistance to lawful authority or that advocates the overthrowing of a government. ***85***

self-incrimination Providing damaging information or testimony against oneself in court. ***97***

slander The public utterance (speaking) of a statement that holds a person up for contempt, ridicule, or hatred. ***86***

symbolic speech The expression of beliefs, opinions, or ideas through forms other than speech or print; speech involving actions and other nonverbal expressions. ***85***

writ of *habeas corpus* In order that requires an official to bring a specified prisoner into court and explain to the judge why the person is being held in prison. ***76***

CHAPTER IN REVIEW 5 Civil Rights

KEY TERMS

affirmative action A policy calling for the establishment of programs that give special consideration, in jobs and college admissions, to members of groups that have been discriminated against in the past. *122*

busing The transportation of public school students by bus to schools physically outside their neighborhoods to eliminate school segregation based on residential patterns. *106*

civil disobedience The deliberate and public act of refusing to obey laws thought to be unjust. *107*

civil rights The rights of all Americans to equal treatment under the law, as provided for by the Fourteenth Amendment to the Constitution. *103*

civil rights movement The movement in the 1950s and 1960s, by minorities and concerned whites, to end racial segregation. *107*

***de facto* segregation** Racial segregation that occurs not as a result of deliberate intentions but because of past social and economic conditions and residential patterns. *106*

***de jure* segregation** Racial segregation that occurs because of laws or decisions by government agencies. *106*

equal protection clause Section 1 of the Fourteenth Amendment, which states that no state shall "deny to any person within its jurisdiction the equal protection of the laws." *103*

fundamental right A basic right of all Americans, such as First Amendment rights. Any law or action that prevents some group of persons from exercising a fundamental right is subject to the "strict-scrutiny" standard, under which the law or action must be necessary to promote a compelling state interest and must be narrowly tailored to meet that interest. *104*

OUTLINE

AP Photo/Charles Tasnadi

SUMMARY & OBJECTIVES

LO1 Explain the constitutional basis for our civil rights and for laws prohibiting discrimination. ***1*** Civil rights specify what the government must do to ensure equal treatment under the law. The **equal protection clause** of the Fourteenth Amendment has been interpreted by the courts to mean that states must treat all persons in an equal manner and may not discriminate unreasonably against a particular class of individuals unless there is a sufficient reason to do so. The United States Supreme Court has developed various standards for determining whether the equal protection clause has been violated. In addition, Section 5 of the Fourteenth Amendment provides a legal basis for **civil rights** legislation.

LO2 Discuss the reasons for the civil rights movement and the changes it effected in American politics and government. ***2*** The equal protection clause was originally intended to protect the newly freed slaves from discrimination after the Civil War. By the late 1880s, however, southern states had begun to pass a series of segregation ("Jim Crow") laws. In 1896, the Supreme Court held that a law did not violate the equal protection clause if separate facilities for blacks equaled those for whites. The **separate-but-equal doctrine** justified segregation for nearly sixty years. ***3*** In the landmark case of *Brown v. Board of Education of Topeka* (1954), the Supreme Court held that segregation by race in public education violated the equal protection clause. One year later, the arrest of Rosa Parks for violating local segregation laws spurred a boycott of the bus system in Montgomery, Alabama. The protest was led by the Reverend Dr. Martin Luther King, Jr. In 1956, a federal court prohibited the segregation of buses in Montgomery, marking the beginning of the **civil rights movement.** ***4*** Civil rights protesters in the 1960s applied the tactic of nonviolent **civil disobedience** in actions throughout the

South. In response, Congress passed a series of civil rights laws, including the Civil Rights Act of 1964 (which forbade discrimination on the basis of race, color, religion, gender, and national origin), the Voting Rights Act of 1965, and the Civil Rights Act of 1968. **5** Today, the percentages of voting-age blacks and whites registered to vote are nearly equal. Political participation by African Americans has increased, as has the number of African American elected officials. African Americans have achieved high government office, including secretary of state. In 2008, Barack Obama became the first African American elected president of the United States.

LO3 **Describe the political and economic achievements of women in this country over time and identify some obstacles to equality that they continue to face.** **6** The struggle of women for equal treatment initially focused on gaining the franchise—voting rights. In 1920, the Nineteenth Amendment, which granted voting rights to women, was ratified. Although they remain underrepresented, increasingly women have gained power as public officials. Following the 2006 elections, a woman was chosen as Speaker of the House of Representatives for the first time. Women have mounted serious campaigns for president or vice president, and several women have held cabinet posts. Three women have been appointed to the Supreme Court. **7** In spite of federal legislation to promote equal treatment of women in the workplace, they continue to face various forms of discrimination. The wage gap has narrowed significantly since 1963, when the Equal Pay Act was passed, but it still remains. Additionally, a **glass ceiling** often prevents women from rising to top positions of responsibility in the workplace. **8** The prohibition of gender discrimination has been extended to **sexual harassment.** Court decisions and legislation have expanded the remedies available to its victims.

LO4 **Summarize the struggles for equality faced by other groups in America.**
9 Hispanics, or Latinos, constitute the largest ethnic minority in the United States. Each year, the Hispanic population grows by nearly 1 million. A disproportionate number of Hispanic families live below the poverty line. Hispanic leaders tend to attribute the low income levels to language problems, lack of job training, and continuing immigration. **10** Asian Americans have also suffered from discriminatory treatment. Immigration was restricted by the Chinese Exclusion Act of 1882. During World War II, most of the West Coast Japanese American population was evacuated to internment camps. **11** The Europeans arriving in the New World brought with them diseases that caused a severe collapse in the Native American population. In 1789, Congress designated the Native American tribes as foreign nations so that the government could sign land and boundary treaties with them. In the early 1830s, boundaries were established between lands occupied by Native Americans and those occupied by white settlers. In the 1880s, the U.S. government changed its policy to one of assimilation. Reservations were reduced dramatically, and schools were established to teach American Indian children to speak English and to practice Christianity. Native Americans had no civil rights under U.S. law until 1924. In the 1960s, some Native Americans formed organizations to strike back at the U.S. government and to reclaim their heritage, including their lands. New legislation passed in the 1980s and the 1990s allowed gambling on reservation lands and promoted Native American languages. **12** To protect the rights of older Americans, Congress passed the Age Discrimination in Employment Act in 1967. This act prohibits employers from discriminating against individuals over the age of forty. **13** The Americans with Disabilities Act of 1990 is the most significant legislation protecting the rights of these Americans. It includes a requirement that all public buildings and services be accessible to persons with disabilities. **14** Until the late 1960s and early 1970s, gay men and lesbians tended to keep quiet about their sexual preferences because exposure usually meant facing harsh consequences. In the decades following the launch of the gay power movement, sodomy laws were repealed or invalidated. Many states have laws prohibiting discrimination against gay men and lesbians, in housing, education, banking, employment, or public accommodations. Same-sex marriage is legal in several states, and public support for gay rights continues to rise.

LO5 **Explain what affirmative action is and why it has been so controversial.**
15 Affirmative action gives special consideration, in jobs or college admissions, to members of groups that have been discriminated against in the past. It has been tested in court cases involving claims of **reverse discrimination,** and the United States Supreme Court has held that any government **affirmative action** program that uses racial classifications to make decisions is subject to "strict scrutiny." A discriminatory law or action must be narrowly tailored to meet a compelling government interest. Some states have banned affirmative action or replaced it with alternative policies. Also, some programs have been deemed unconstitutional by the courts.

glass ceiling An invisible but real discriminatory barrier that prevents women and minorities from rising to top positions of power or responsibility. *113*

quota system A policy under which a specific number of jobs, promotions, or other types of placements, such as university admissions, must be given to members of selected groups. *122*

rational basis test A test (also known as the "ordinary-scrutiny" standard) used by the Supreme Court to decide whether a discriminatory law violates the equal protection clause of the Constitution. Few laws evaluated under this test are found invalid. *104*

reverse discrimination Discrimination against those who have no minority status. *122*

separate-but-equal doctrine A Supreme Court doctrine holding that the equal protection clause of the Fourteenth Amendment did not forbid racial segregation as long as the facilities for blacks were equal to those for whites. The doctrine was overturned in the *Brown v. Board of Education of Topeka* decision of 1954. *105*

sexual harassment Unwanted physical contact, verbal conduct, or abuse of a sexual nature that interferes with a recipient's job performance, creates a hostile environment, or carries with it an implicit or explicit threat of adverse employment consequences. *113*

sit-in A tactic of nonviolent civil disobedience. Demonstrators enter a business, college building, or other public place and remain seated until they are forcibly removed or until their demands are met. The tactic was used successfully in the civil rights movement and in other protest movements in the United States. *108*

suffrage The right to vote; the franchise. *110*

suspect classification A classification, such as race, that provides the basis for a discriminatory law. Any law based on a suspect classification is subject to strict scrutiny by the courts—meaning that the law must be justified by a compelling state interest. *104*

CHAPTER IN REVIEW 6 Interest Groups

KEY TERMS

direct technique Any method used by an interest group to interact with government officials directly to further the group's goals. *142*

free rider problem The difficulty that exists when individuals can enjoy the outcome of an interest group's efforts without having to contribute, such as by becoming members of the group. *134*

indirect technique Any method used by interest groups to influence government officials through third parties, such as voters. *143*

interest group An organized group of individuals sharing common objectives who actively attempt to influence policymakers. *131*

labor force All of the people over the age of sixteen who are working or actively looking for jobs. *139*

lobbying All of the attempts by organizations or by individuals to influence the passage, defeat, or contents of legislation or to influence the administrative decisions of government. *142*

lobbyist An individual who handles a particular interest group's lobbying efforts. *142*

patron An individual or organization that provides financial backing to an interest group. *132*

pluralist theory A theory that views politics as a contest among various interest groups—at all levels of government—to gain benefits for their members. *135*

political action committee (PAC) A committee that is established by a corporation, labor union, or special interest group to raise funds and make contributions on the establishing organization's behalf. *143*

public-interest group An interest group formed for the purpose of working for the "public good." Examples of public-interest groups are the American Civil Liberties Union and Common Cause. *136*

OUTLINE

Mark Lyons/Getty Images

SUMMARY & OBJECTIVES

LO1 Explain what an interest group is, how interest groups form, and how interest groups function in American politics. ***1*** An **interest group** is an organization of people sharing common objectives who actively attempt to influence government policymakers through direct and indirect methods. Interest groups may form in response to change: a political or economic change, a dramatic shift in population or technology that affects how people live or work, or a change in social values or cultural norms. Some groups form to support the change or even speed it along, while others form to fight change. ***2*** Interest groups (a) help bridge the gap between citizens and government; (b) help raise public awareness and inspire action on various issues; (c) often provide public officials with specialized and detailed information, which may be useful in making policy choices; and (d) serve as another check on public officials to make sure that they are carrying out their duties responsibly. The **pluralist theory** of American democracy focuses on the participation of groups in a decentralized government structure that offers many points of access to policymakers. According to the pluralist theory, politics is a contest among various interest groups that compete at all levels of government to gain benefits for their members.

LO2 Indicate how interest groups differ from political parties. ***3*** Although interest groups and political parties are both groups of people joined together for political purposes, they differ in several ways. Interest groups focus on a handful of key policies; political parties are broad-based organizations that must attract the support of many opposing groups and consider a large number of issues. Interest groups are usually more tightly organized than political parties, and they are often financed through contributions or dues-paying memberships. Interest groups try to influence policy and may try to influence the outcome of elections, but unlike parties, they do not compete for public office.

LO3 Identify the various types of interest groups. ***4*** The most common interest groups are those that promote private interests. These groups seek government policies that benefit the economic interests of their members. Other groups, sometimes called **public-interest groups,** are formed with the broader goal of working for the "public good," though there is no such thing as a clear public interest in a nation of more than 300 million diverse people. In reality, all lobbying groups represent special interests. Many major interest groups are concerned with issues affecting the following areas or groups of persons: business, labor, agriculture, consumers, senior citizens, the environment, and professionals. ***5*** Business has long been well organized for effective action. There are umbrella organizations that include small and large corporations and businesses, and **trade organizations** that support policies that benefit specific industries. Interest groups representing labor have been some of the most influential groups in the nation's history, though the strength and political power of labor unions have waned in the last several decades. Many groups work for general agricultural interests at all levels of government, and producers of various specific farm commodities have formed their own organizations. ***6*** Groups organized for the protection of consumer rights were very active in the 1960s and 1970s, and some are still active today. Groups formed to promote the interests of elderly persons have been very outspoken and persuasive. With the current concern for the environment, the membership of established environmental groups has blossomed, and many new groups have formed. ***7*** Most professions that require advanced education or specialized training have organizations to protect and promote their interests. These groups are concerned mainly with the standards of their professions, but they also work to influence government policy. ***8*** Numerous interest groups focus on a single issue. Efforts by state and local governments to lobby the federal government have escalated in recent years.

LO4 Discuss how the activities of interest groups help to shape government policymaking. ***9*** Interest groups operate at all levels of government and use a variety of strategies to steer policies in ways beneficial to their interests. Sometimes interest groups attempt to influence policymakers directly, but at other times they try to exert indirect influence on policymakers by shaping public opinion. Lobbying and providing election support are two important **direct techniques** used by interest groups to influence government policy. ***10*** **Lobbying** refers to all of the attempts by organizations or individuals to influence the passage, defeat, or contents of legislation or to influence the administrative decisions of government. Interest groups often become directly involved in the election process, particularly by raising funds and making campaign contributions through **political action committees (PACs).** Interest groups also provide campaign support for legislators who favor their policies and urge their members to vote for candidates who support the views of the group. ***11*** Interest groups also try to influence public policy through third parties or the general public. Indirect techniques include advertising and other promotional efforts, **rating systems,** issue advocacy, mobilizing constituents, going to court, and organizing demonstrations and protests.

LO5 Describe how interest groups are regulated by government. ***12*** The Federal Regulation of Lobbying Act of 1946 was very limited and contained many loopholes. In 1995, Congress passed the Lobbying Disclosure Act. This legislation reformed the 1946 act in several ways, particularly by creating stricter definitions of who is a lobbyist. The number of registered lobbyists nearly doubled in the first few years of the new legislation. In the wake of lobbying scandals in the early 2000s, additional lobbying reform efforts were undertaken. The Honest Leadership and Open Government Act of 2007 increased lobbying disclosure and placed further restrictions on the receipt of gifts and travel by members of Congress paid for by lobbyists and the organizations they represent.

rating system A system by which a particular interest group evaluates (rates) the performance of legislators based on how often the legislators have voted with the group's position on particular issues. ***144***

trade organization An association formed by members of a particular industry, such as the oil industry or the trucking industry, to develop common standards and goals for the industry. Trade organizations, as interest groups, lobby government for legislation or regulations that specifically benefit their groups. ***136***

CHAPTER IN REVIEW 7 Political Parties

KEY TERMS

coalition An alliance of individuals or groups with a variety of interests and opinions who join together to support all or part of a political party's platform. *160*

electorate All of the citizens eligible to vote in a given election. *160*

majority party The political party that has more members in the legislature than the opposing party. *159*

minority party The political party that has fewer members in the legislature than the opposing party. *159*

national convention The meeting held by each major party every four years to select presidential and vice-presidential candidates, write a party platform, and conduct other party business. *163*

national party chairperson An individual who serves as a political party's administrative head at the national level and directs the work of the party's national committee. *165*

national party committee The political party leaders who direct party business during the four years between the national party conventions, organize the next national convention, and plan how to obtain a party victory in the next presidential elections. *165*

party activist A party member who helps to organize and oversee party functions and planning during and between campaigns. *161*

party identifier A person who identifies himself or herself as being a member of a particular political party. *161*

party platform The document drawn up by each party at its national convention that outlines the policies and positions of the party. *163*

party ticket A list of a political party's candidates for various offices. In national elections, the party ticket consists of the presidential and vice-presidential candidates. *163*

OUTLINE

Damon Winter/The New York Times/Redux

SUMMARY & OBJECTIVES

LO1 Summarize the origins and development of the two-party system in the United States. ***1*** Two major political factions—the Federalists and Anti-Federalists—were formed even before the Constitution was ratified. After ratification, the Federalist Party supported a strong central government that would encourage the development of commerce and manufacturing. Opponents of the Federalists referred to themselves as Republicans. Today, they are often referred to as Jeffersonian Republicans, or Democratic Republicans, to distinguish this group from the later Republican Party. The Jeffersonian Republicans, who favored a more limited role for government, dominated American politics during the early nineteenth century. In the mid-1820s, however, the Republicans split into two groups. Supporters of Andrew Jackson called themselves Democrats. They appealed to small farmers and the growing class of urbanized workers. The other group, the National Republicans (later the Whig Party), had the support of bankers, business owners, and many southern planters. As the Democrats and the Whigs competed for the presidency during the 1840s and 1850s, the **two-party system** as we know it today emerged. ***2*** By the mid-1850s, the Whig **coalition** had fallen apart, and most northern Whigs were absorbed into the new Republican Party, which opposed the extension of slavery. Abraham Lincoln was elected as the first Republican president in 1860. When the former Confederate states rejoined the Union after the Civil War, the Republicans and Democrats were roughly even in strength, although the Republicans were more successful in presidential contests. In the 1890s, however, the Democrats allied themselves with the Populist movement, which advocated inflation as a way of lessening the debts of farmers in the West and South. Urban workers in the Midwest and East strongly opposed this program, which would erode the value of their paychecks. After the election of 1896, the Republicans established themselves in the minds of many Americans as the party that knew how to manage the nation's economy, and they remained dominant in national politics until the onset of the Great Depression. **3** The realigning election of 1932 brought Franklin D. Roosevelt to the presidency and the Democrats back to power at the national level. (The elections of 1860 and 1896 are also considered to represent **realignments.** The popular support for and relative strength of the parties shifted.) From the 1960s on, however, conservative Democrats left the party in increasing numbers. The result of this "rolling realignment" was that the two major parties were now fairly evenly matched.

LO2 Describe the current status of the two major parties. **4** Individuals with similar characteristics tend to align themselves more often with one or the other major party. Such factors as race, income, education, marital status, and geography all influence party identification. In recent years, polls on party identification showed a rough parity in the support for the two major political parties. Since 2006, though, pollsters have noted a shift in party identification. More people are now identifying with or leaning toward the Democratic Party, and surveys have also found that public attitudes are drifting toward Democratic values. The changing political landscape made 2008 a promising year for the Democrats. With almost 53 percent of the popular vote, Barack Obama won the strongest personal mandate of any Democratic president in a generation.

LO3 Explain how political parties function in our democratic system. **5** Political parties link the people's policy preferences to actual government policies. They also recruit and nominate candidates for political office, which simplifies voting choices. Parties help educate the public about important current political issues, and they coordinate policy among the various branches and levels of government. The "out party" does what it can to influence the "in party" and its policies, and to check the actions of the party in power. Political parties also balance competing interests and effect compromises among different groups. Parties coordinate campaigns and take care of a large number of tasks that are essential to the smooth functioning of the electoral process.

LO4 Discuss the structure of American political parties. **6** Each of the two major political parties consists of three components. The party in the **electorate** is the largest component, consisting of **party identifiers** (those who identify themselves as being members of a **political party**) and **party activists** (party members who help to organize and oversee party functions and planning). Generally, people belong to a political party because they agree with many of its main ideas and support some of its candidates. **7** Each major party has a national organization with national, state, and local offices. Neither party is a closely knit or highly organized structure. State party organizations are all very different and are only loosely tied to the party's national structure. Local party organizations are often quite independent from the state organization. Most of the public attention that the party receives comes at the **national convention,** which is held every four years during the summer before the presidential elections. Delegates to the convention nominate the party's presidential and vice-presidential candidates, and they adopt the **party platform.** **8** The third component of the two major parties is the party in government, which consists of all of the party's candidates who have won elections and now hold public office. The party in government helps to organize the government's agenda by convincing its own party members to vote for its policies.

LO5 Describe the different types of third parties and how they function in the American political system. **9** The United States has a two-party system in which two major parties, the Democrats and the Republicans, dominate national politics. The two-party system has become entrenched in the United States for several reasons. The first major political division between the Federalists and the Anti-Federalists established a precedent for a two-party system, and there are several reasons for the perpetuation of the two-party system. **10** Third parties have traditionally found it extremely difficult to compete with the major parties for votes. American election laws tend to favor the major parties, and the rules governing campaign financing also favor the major parties. There are also institutional barriers that prevent third parties from enjoying electoral success, such as the single-member district and the winner-take-all feature of the electoral college system for electing the president. Finally, because third parties normally do not win elections, Americans tend not to vote for them. **11** Despite difficulties, throughout American history, third parties have competed for influence in the nation's two-party system. There are many different kinds of third parties. An issue-oriented party is formed to promote a particular cause or timely issue. An ideological party supports a particular political doctrine or a set of beliefs. A splinter party develops out of a split within a major party. This split may be part of an attempt to elect a specific person. **12** Third parties have brought many political issues to the public's attention. They can influence not only voter turnout but also election outcomes. Third parties also provide a voice for voters who are frustrated with and alienated from the Republican and Democratic parties.

patronage A system of rewarding the party faithful and workers with government jobs or contracts. ***161***

political party A group of individuals who organize to win elections, operate the government, and determine policy. ***153***

precinct A political district within a city, such as a block or a neighborhood, or a rural portion of a county; the smallest voting district at the local level. ***163***

primary A preliminary election held for the purpose of choosing a party's final candidate. ***159***

realignment A process in which the popular support for and relative strength of the parties shift and the parties are reestablished with different coalitions of supporters. ***156***

solidarity Mutual sympathy among the members of a particular group. ***161***

third party In the United States, any party other than one of the two major parties (Republican and Democratic). ***167***

two-party system A political system in which two strong and established parties compete for political offices. ***167***

ward A local unit of a political party's organization, consisting of a division or district within a city. ***163***

CHAPTER IN REVIEW 8 Public Opinion and Voting

KEY TERMS

agents of political socialization People and institutions that influence the political views of others. *177*

biased sample A poll sample that does not accurately represent the population. *181*

gender gap The difference between the percentage of votes cast for a particular candidate by women and the percentage of votes cast for the same candidate by men. *194*

grandfather clause A clause in a state law that had the effect of restricting the franchise (voting rights) to those whose ancestors had voted before the 1860s; one of the techniques used in the South to prevent African Americans from exercising their right to vote. *187*

literacy test A test given to voters to ensure that they could read and write and thus evaluate political information; a technique used in many southern states to restrict African American participation in elections. *187*

media Newspapers, magazines, television, radio, the Internet, and any other printed or electronic means of communication. *178*

peer group Associates, often close in age to one another; may include friends, classmates, co-workers, club members, or religious group members. Peer group influence is a significant factor in the political socialization process. *179*

political socialization The learning process through which most people acquire their political attitudes, opinions, beliefs, and knowledge. *177*

poll tax A fee of several dollars that had to be paid before a person could vote; a device used in some southern states to prevent African Americans from voting. *187*

public opinion The views of the citizenry about politics, public issues, and public policies; a complex collection of opinions held by many people on issues in the public arena. *176*

public opinion poll A numerical survey of the public's opinion on a particular topic at a particular moment. *181*

push poll A campaign tactic used to feed false or misleading information to potential voters, under the guise of taking an opinion poll, with the intent to "push" voters away from one candidate and toward another. *185*

random sample In the context of opinion polling, a sample in which each person within the entire population being polled has an equal chance of being chosen. *182*

sample In the context of opinion polling, a group of people selected to represent the population being studied. *181*

sampling error In the context of opinion polling, the difference between what the sample results show and what the true results would have been had everybody in the relevant population been interviewed. *182*

OUTLINE

Don Emmert/AFP/Getty Images

SUMMARY & OBJECTIVES

LO1 Explain what public opinion is and how it is measured. ***1*** **Public opinion** is the sum total of a complex collection of opinions held by many people on issues in the public arena. Public officials learn about public opinion through election results, personal contacts, interest groups, and **media** reports. Other than elections, however, the only relatively precise way to measure public opinion is through the use of **public opinion polls.**

LO2 Describe the political socialization process. ***2*** Most people acquire their political attitudes, opinions, beliefs, and knowledge through a complex learning process called **political socialization,** which begins early in childhood and continues throughout life. Most political socialization is informal. The strong early influence of the family later gives way to the multiple influences of school, peers, television, co-workers, and other groups. People and institutions that influence the political views of others are called **agents of political socialization.** ***3*** The family's influence is strongest when children clearly perceive their parents' attitudes. Education also strongly influences an individual's political attitudes. From their earliest days in school, children learn about the American political system. They also learn citizenship skills through school rules and regulations. Generally, those with more education have more knowledge about politics and policy than those with less education. The media also have an impact on political socialization. Television continues to be a leading source of political and public affairs information for most people. Opinion leaders, major life events, **peer groups,** economic status, and occupation may also influence a person's political views.

LO3 Summarize the history of polling in the United States, and explain how polls are conducted and how they are used in the political process. ***4*** A public opinion poll is a numerical survey of the public's opinion on a particular topic at a particular moment. Early polling efforts often relied on **straw polls.** The opinions expressed in straw polls, however, usually represent an atypical subgroup of the population, or a **biased sample.** Over time, more scientific polling techniques were developed. To achieve the most accurate results possible, pollsters use **random samples,** in which each person within the entire population being polled has an equal chance of being chosen. If the **sample** is properly selected, the opinions of those in the sample will be representative of the opinions held by the population as a whole. Nevertheless, how a question is phrased can significantly affect how people answer it, and any opinion poll contains a **sampling error.** ***5*** Polling is used extensively by political candidates and policymakers to learn which issues are of current concern to Americans. Many journalists base their political coverage during campaigns almost exclusively on poll findings, though the media sometimes misuse polls. News organizations also use exit polls to give an early indication of the outcome of elections, though there have been problems with the reliability of exit polls in some recent elections. One tactic in political campaigns is to use **push polls,** which ask "fake" polling questions that are actually designed to "push" voters toward one candidate or another.

LO4 Indicate some of the factors that affect voter turnout and discuss what has been done to improve voter turnout and voting procedures.

6 Some historical restrictions on voting, including religion, property ownership, and tax-payment requirements, disappeared early on in the history of the republic. Restrictions based on race and gender continued, however. The Fifteenth Amendment to the Constitution (1870) guaranteed suffrage to African American males. Yet, for many decades, African Americans were effectively denied the ability to exercise their voting rights. Today, devices used to restrict voting rights, such as the **poll tax** and **literacy tests,** are explicitly outlawed by constitutional amendments and by the Voting Rights Act of 1965. Furthermore, the Nineteenth Amendment (1920) gave women the right to vote, and the Twenty-sixth Amendment (1971) reduced the minimum voting age to eighteen. ***7*** Some restrictions on voting rights, such as registration, residency, and citizenship requirements, still exist. Attempts to improve voter turnout and voting procedures include simplifying the voter-registration process, allowing voting by mail, and updating voting equipment. ***8*** Just because an individual is eligible to vote does not necessarily mean that the person will actually go to the polls on Election Day. Voter turnout is affected by several factors, including educational attainment, income level, age, and minority status.

LO5 Discuss the different factors that affect voter choices. ***9*** Several factors influence voters' choices. For established voters, party identification is one of the most important and lasting predictors of how a person will vote. Voters' choices often depend on the perceived character of the candidates rather than on their qualifications or policy positions. When people vote for candidates who share their positions on particular issues, they are engaging in policy voting. Historically, economic issues have had the strongest influence on voters' choices. ***10*** Socioeconomic factors also influence how people vote. These factors include educational attainment, occupation and income level, age, gender, religion and ethnic background, and geographic region. A person's political ideology is another indicator of voting behavior.

Solid South A term used to describe the tendency of the southern states to vote Democratic after the Civil War. ***195***

straw poll A nonscientific poll; a poll in which there is no way to ensure that the opinions expressed are representative of the larger population. ***181***

vital center The center of the political spectrum; those who hold moderate political views. The center is vital because without it, it may be difficult, if not impossible, to reach the compromises that are necessary to a political system's continuity. ***195***

vote-eligible population The number of people who are actually eligible to vote in an American election. ***191***

voting-age population The number of people residing in the United States who are at least eighteen years old. ***191***

white primary A primary election in which African Americans were prohibited from voting. The practice was banned by the Supreme Court in 1944. ***187***

CHAPTER IN REVIEW 9 Campaigns and Elections

KEY TERMS

Australian ballot A secret ballot that is prepared, distributed, and counted by government officials at public expense; used by all states in the United States since 1888. ***201***

campaign strategy The comprehensive plan for winning an election developed by a candidate and his or her advisers. The strategy includes the candidate's position on issues, slogan, advertising plan, press events, personal appearances, and other aspects of the campaign. ***211***

caucus A meeting held to choose political candidates or delegates. ***204***

closed primary A primary in which only party members can vote to choose that party's candidates. ***207***

Credentials Committee A committee of each national political party that evaluates the claims of national party convention delegates to be the legitimate representatives of their states. ***210***

delegate An official meeting of a political party to choose its candidates. Nominating conventions at the state and local levels also select delegates to represent the citizens of their geographic areas at a higher-level party convention. ***206***

direct primary An election held within each of the two major parties—Democratic and Republican—to choose the party's candidates for the general election. Voters choose the candidate directly, rather than through delegates. ***206***

elector A member of the electoral college. ***202***

electoral college The group of electors who are selected by the voters in each state to elect officially the president and vice president. The number of electors in each state is equal to the number of that state's representatives in both chambers of Congress. ***202***

general election A regularly scheduled election to choose the U.S. president, vice president, and senators and representatives in Congress. General elections are held in even-numbered years on the Tuesday after the first Monday in November. ***201***

independent expenditure An expenditure for activities that are independent from (not coordinated with) those of a political candidate or a political party. ***216***

loophole A legitimate way of evading a certain legal requirement. ***216***

nominating convention An official meeting of a political party to choose its candidates. Nominating conventions at the state and local levels also select delegates to represent the citizens of their geographic areas at a higher-level party convention. ***206***

office-block ballot A ballot (also called the Massachusetts ballot) that lists together all of the candidates for each office. ***201***

open primary A primary in which voters can vote for a party's candidates regardless of whether they belong to the party. ***207***

OUTLINE

AP Photo/Alex Brandon

SUMMARY & OBJECTIVES

LO1 Explain how elections are held and how the electoral college functions in presidential elections. ***1*** **General elections** are regularly scheduled elections held in even-numbered years in November. During general elections, the voters decide who will be the U.S. president, vice president, and senators and representatives in Congress. General elections are also held to choose state and local government officials. Since 1888, all states have used the **Australian ballot**—a secret ballot that is prepared, distributed, and counted by government officials. ***2*** Elections are held in voting precincts (districts within each local government unit). An election board supervises the polling place and the voting process. Poll watchers from each of the two major parties typically monitor the polling place as well. ***3*** In the presidential elections, citizens do not vote directly for the president and vice president; instead, they vote for electors who will cast their ballots in the electoral college. Each state has as many electoral votes as it has U.S. senators and representatives; there are also three electors from the District of Columbia. ***4*** The **electoral college** is a **winner-take-all system** because, in nearly all states, the candidate who receives the most popular votes in the state wins all of that state's electoral votes. To be elected through this system, a candidate must win at least 270 electoral votes, a majority of the 538 electoral votes available.

LO2 Discuss how candidates are nominated. ***5*** The methods used by political parties to nominate candidates have changed over time. Today, the elections that nominate candidates for Congress and for state or local offices are almost always direct primaries, in which voters cast their ballots directly for candidates. **6** Most of the states hold presidential primaries, beginning early in the election year. These indirect primaries are used to elect delegates to the national nominating conventions. In some states, delegates are chosen through a caucus/convention system instead of through primaries. In late summer, each political party holds a national convention. Convention delegates adopt the official party platform and declare their support for the party's presidential and vice-presidential candidates.

LO3 Indicate what is involved in launching a political campaign today, and describe the structure and functions of a campaign organization.

7 To run a successful campaign, the candidate's campaign staff must be able to raise funds, get media coverage, produce and pay for political ads, schedule the candidate's time effectively with constituent groups and political supporters, convey the candidate's position on the issues, conduct research on the opposing candidate, and get the voters to go to the polls. Because political party labels are no longer as important as they once were, campaigns have become more candidate-centered. Professional political consultants now manage nearly all aspects of a presidential candidate's campaign.

LO4 Describe how the Internet has transformed political campaigns.

8 Today, the ability to make effective use of the Internet is essential to a candidate. Barack Obama took Internet fund-raising to a new level during his 2008 presidential bid. The Obama campaign attempted to recruit as many supporters as possible to act as fund-raisers who would solicit contributions from their friends and neighbors. As a result, Obama was spared much of the personal fund-raising effort that consumes the time of most national politicians. **9** Microtargeting, a technique that involves collecting as much information as possible about voters in a database and then filtering out various groups for special attention, was pioneered by the George W. Bush campaign in 2004. In 2008, microtargeting was supplemented with behavioral targeting. This technique uses information about people's online behavior to tailor the advertisements that they see. **10** In 2008, Barack Obama took Web-based organizing to a new level. His campaign used existing sites, such as Facebook and MySpace. Obama's videos were on YouTube and his own Web site racked up more than a million members. The Obama campaign was also able to create local support groups in towns and counties across the country.

LO5 Summarize the laws that regulate campaign financing and the role of money in modern political campaigns.

11 In the 2007–2008 election cycle, presidential campaign expenditures reached about $2.4 billion. Campaign-financing laws enacted in the 1970s provide public funding for presidential primaries and general elections, limit presidential campaign spending if candidates accept federal support, require candidates to file periodic reports with the Federal Election Commission, and limit individual and group contributions. **12** Two major loopholes in the campaign-financing laws involved **soft money** and **independent expenditures.** The Bipartisan Campaign Reform Act (BCRA) of 2002 addressed these concerns to a certain extent. Issue advocacy groups soon attempted to exploit loopholes in BCRA by establishing 527 committees and 501(c)4 organizations.

LO6 Describe what took place during recent presidential elections and what these events tell us about the American electoral system.

13 The presidential elections of 2000 and 2004 were very close. In 2000, Democrat Al Gore won the popular vote but lost in the electoral college after the disputed vote in Florida was resolved. In 2004, President George W. Bush edged out the Democratic challenger by a mere thirty-five electoral votes and a 2.5 percentage vote margin of popular votes. In 2008, however, Democrat Barack Obama's popular-vote margin over John McCain was about 7.2 percentage points. Obama won approximately 52.9 percent of the popular vote and 365 electoral votes.

party-column ballot A ballot (also called the Indiana ballot) that lists all of a party's candidates under the party label. Voters can vote for all of a party's candidates for local, state, and national offices by making a single "X" or pulling a single lever. ***201***

political consultant A professional political adviser who, for a fee, works on an area of a candidate's campaign. Political consultants include campaign managers, pollsters, media advisers, and "get out the vote" organizers. ***211***

poll watcher A representative from one of the political parties who is allowed to monitor a polling place to make sure that the election is run fairly and to avoid fraud. ***202***

primary election An election in which voters choose the candidates of their party, who will then run in the general election. ***206***

soft money Campaign contributions not regulated by federal law, such as some contributions that are made to political parties instead of to particular candidates. ***216***

special election An election that is held at the state or local level when the voters must decide an issue before the next general election or when vacancies occur by reason of death or resignation. ***201***

winner-take-all system A system in which the candidate who receives the most votes wins. In contrast, proportional systems allocate votes to multiple winners. ***202***

CHAPTER IN REVIEW 10 Federalism

KEY TERMS

citizen journalism The collection, analysis, and dissemination of information online by independent journalists, scholars, politicians, and the general citizenry. *238*

electronic media Communication channels that involve electronic transmissions, such as radio, television, and the Internet. *225*

issue ad A political advertisement that focuses on a particular issue. Issue ads can be used to support or attack a candidate. *230*

managed news coverage News coverage that is manipulated (managed) by a campaign manager or political consultant to gain media exposure for a political candidate. *232*

mass media Communication channels, such as newspapers and radio and television broadcasts, through which people can communicate to mass audiences. *225*

negative political advertising Political advertising undertaken for the purpose of discrediting an opposing candidate in the eyes of the voters. Attack ads and issue ads are forms of negative political advertising. *230*

personal attack ad A negative political advertisement that attacks the character of an opposing candidate. *230*

podcasting The distribution of audio or video files to a personal computer or a mobile device, such as an iPod. *238*

political advertising Advertising undertaken by or on behalf of a political candidate to familiarize voters with the candidate and his or her views on campaign issues; also advertising for or against policy issues. *229*

print media Communication channels that consist of printed materials, such as newspapers and magazines. *225*

sound bite In televised news reporting, a brief comment, lasting for only a few seconds, that captures a thought or a perspective and has an immediate impact on the viewers. *229*

OUTLINE

Chip Somodevilla/Getty Images

SUMMARY & OBJECTIVES

LO1 Explain the role of a free press in a democracy. ***1*** The **mass media** include the **print media** (newspapers and magazines) and the **electronic media** (radio, television, and the Internet). The media play a vital role in our political lives, and a free press is essential to the democratic process. If people are to cast informed votes, they must have access to a forum in which they can discuss public affairs fully and assess the conduct and competency of their officials. ***2*** What the media say and do has an impact on what Americans think about political issues, but the media also reflect what Americans think about politics. By helping to determine what people talk and think about, the media help set the political agenda. Of all the media, television has the greatest impact. Television is the primary news source for most Americans, but the limitations of the TV medium significantly affect the scope and depth of news coverage.

LO2 Summarize how television influences the conduct of political campaigns. ***3*** Candidates for political office spend a great deal of time and money obtaining a TV presence through political ads, debates, and general news coverage. Televised **political advertising** consumes at least half of the total budget for a major political campaign. Candidates often use **negative political advertising,** including **personal attack ads** (which attack the character of an opposing candidate) and **issue ads** (which focus on flaws in an opponent's position on issues). Televised debates are now a routine feature of presidential campaigns and may have influenced the outcome of several elections. ***4*** Candidates and their political consultants have become increasingly sophisticated in creating newsworthy events for the media to cover. Each candidate's press advisers also try to convince reporters to give a story or event a **spin** that is favorable to the candidate.

LO3 Explain why talk radio has been described as the "Wild West" of the media. ***5*** Modern talk radio took off in the United States during the 1990s. Talk-show hosts do not attempt to hide their political biases; if anything, they exaggerate them for effect. No journalistic conventions are observed. ***6*** Those who think that talk radio is good for the country argue that talk shows, taken together, provide a great populist forum. Others are uneasy because they fear that talk shows empower fringe groups, perhaps magnifying their rage. Prominent hosts have had great fun organizing potentially disruptive activities. Those who think talk-show hosts go too far ultimately have to deal with the constitutional issue of free speech.

LO4 Describe types of media bias and explain how such bias affects the political process. ***7*** The media are frequently accused of having a liberal bias. A number of media scholars suggest that even if many reporters hold liberal views, these views are not reflected in their reporting. Media bias against losers, however, may be playing a role in shaping presidential campaigns and elections. The media use the winner-loser framework to describe events throughout the campaigns. ***8*** The expansion of the media universe to include cable channels and the Internet has increased the competition among news sources. News directors select programming they believe will attract the largest audiences and garner the highest advertising revenues. Competition for viewers and readers has become even more challenging in the wake of a declining news audience. Many journalists believe that economic pressure is making significant inroads on independent editorial decision making. Today's news culture is in the midst of change as news organizations are redefining their purpose and increasingly looking for special niches in which to build their audiences.

LO5 Indicate the extent to which the Internet is reshaping news and political campaigns. ***9*** The Internet is now a major source of information for many people. All major newspapers are online, as are transcripts of major television news programs. In addition, there has been a virtual explosion of blogs in recent years. Many blogs are political in nature, both reporting political developments and discussing politics. Another nontraditional form of news distribution is **podcasting.** Still another new Internet technology is Twitter, a method for sending short messages to large numbers of people. ***10*** The use of the Internet is an inexpensive way for candidates to contact, recruit, and mobilize supporters, as well as disseminate information on their positions. Having an Internet strategy has become an integral part of political campaigning. Candidates typically hire Web managers to create a well-designed Web site, to track credit-card contributions, to hire bloggers to promote the candidate's views, to arrange for podcasting of campaign information, to monitor the Web for news about the candidate, and to track online publications of netroots groups—online activists who support the candidate but are not controlled by the candidate's organization. ***11*** Citizen videos have also changed the traditional campaign. A candidate can never know when a comment that he or she makes may be caught on camera by someone with a cell phone or digital camera and published on the Internet for all to see.

spin A reporter's slant on, or interpretation of, a particular event or action. ***233***

spin doctor A political candidate's press adviser, who tries to convince reporters to give a story or event concerning the candidate a particular "spin" (interpretation, or slant). ***233***

CHAPTER IN REVIEW 11 Congress

KEY TERMS

apportionment The distribution of House seats among the states on the basis of their respective populations. ***247***

appropriation A part of the congressional budgeting process that involves determining how many dollars will be spent in a given year on a particular set of government activities. ***264***

authorization A part of the congressional budgeting process that involves the creation of the legal basis for government programs. ***264***

cloture A method of ending debate in the Senate and bringing the matter under consideration to a vote by the entire chamber. ***257***

conference committee A temporary committee that is formed when the two chambers of Congress pass separate versions of the same bill. The conference committee, which consists of members from both the House and the Senate, works out a compromise form of the bill. ***261***

conference report A report submitted by a congressional conference committee after it has drafted a single version of a bill. ***261***

congressional district The geographic area that is served by one member in the House of Representatives. ***248***

continuing resolution A temporary resolution passed by Congress when an appropriations bill has not been passed by the beginning of the new fiscal year. ***266***

entitlement program A government program (such as Social Security) that allows, or entitles, a certain class of people (such as elderly persons) to receive special benefits. Entitlement programs operate under open-ended budget authorizations that, in effect, place no limits on how much can be spent. ***264***

filibustering The Senate tradition of unlimited debate undertaken for the purpose of preventing action on a bill. ***256***

first budget resolution A budget resolution, which is supposed to be passed in May, that sets overall revenue goals and spending targets for the next fiscal year, which begins on October 1. ***266***

OUTLINE

Doug Mills/The New York Times/Redux

SUMMARY & OBJECTIVES

LO1 Explain how seats in the House of Representatives are apportioned among the states. ***1*** The Constitution provides for the **apportionment** of House seats among the states on the basis of their respective populations, though each state is guaranteed at least one seat. Every ten years, the 435 House seats are reapportioned based on the outcome of the census. ***2*** Each representative to the House is elected by voters in a **congressional district.** Districts must contain, as nearly as possible, equal numbers of people. **Gerrymandering** occurs when a district's boundaries are drawn to maximize the influence of a certain group or political party.

LO2 Describe the power of incumbency. ***3*** If a member of Congress wants to run for reelection in the next congressional elections (representatives are elected every second year and senators are elected every six years), that person's chances are greatly enhanced by the power that incumbency brings to a reelection campaign. ***4*** Incumbent legislators enjoy several advantages over their opponents. They benefit from name recognition, access to the media, congressional franking privileges, and lawmaking power. They also have professional staffs both in Washington, D.C., and in their home districts. A key advantage is their fund-raising ability. Most incumbents in Congress are reelected.

LO3 Identify the key leadership positions in Congress, describe the committee system, and indicate some important differences between the House of Representatives and the Senate. ***5*** The Constitution provides for the presiding officers of both the House and the Senate, and each chamber has added other leadership positions as it has seen fit. The majority party in each chamber chooses the major officers of that chamber, controls debate on the floor, selects committee chairpersons, and has a majority on all committees. ***6*** Chief among the leaders in the House of Representatives is the **Speaker of the House,** who has a great deal of power. Other leaders include the **majority and minority leaders,** and the **whips.** ***7*** The vice president of the United States is the president of the Senate, and senators elect another presiding officer, the president pro tempore (pro tem), who is ordinarily the member of the majority party with the longest continuous service in the Senate. The real power in the Senate is held by the majority leader, the minority leader, and their respective whips. ***8*** Most of the actual work of legislating is performed by the committees and **subcommittees** in the House and in the Senate. The permanent and most powerful committees are the **standing committees.** Before any bill can be considered by the entire House or Senate, it must be approved by a majority vote in a standing committee. ***9*** Because of its large size, the House requires more rules and formality than the Senate. The House **Rules Committee** proposes time limits on debate for most bills. The Senate allows extended debate. The use of unlimited debate to obstruct legislation is called **filibustering,** which can be ended with a vote of **cloture.** The House originates bills for raising revenues and may impeach federal officials. The Senate has the power of advice and consent on presidential appointments and treaties and may convict federal officials of impeachable offenses. Senators typically enjoy more prestige and access to the media than do members of the House, and they have more opportunities to engage in national leadership.

LO4 Summarize the specific steps in the lawmaking process. ***10*** After a bill is introduced by a member of Congress, it is sent to a standing committee. A committee chairperson usually sends the bill to a subcommittee, where public hearings might be held. After a **markup session,** in which changes may be made to the bill, the bill goes to the full committee for further action. The bill may be reported to the full chamber, or, if it lacks sufficient support, it may not make it out of the committee. ***11*** After a bill is reported, it is scheduled for floor debate, and votes are taken on the legislation. When the House and Senate pass separate versions of the same bill, a **conference committee,** which includes members from both chambers, is formed to work out the differences. The **conference report** is sent to each chamber for a vote. If the bill is approved by both chambers, it is sent to the president. The president has ten days to sign the bill or veto it (with a two-thirds majority vote in both chambers, Congress can override the president's veto). If the president does nothing, the bill becomes law unless Congress has adjourned before the ten-day period expires. In that case, the bill dies in what is called a **pocket veto.**

LO5 Identify Congress's oversight functions and explain how Congress fulfills them. ***12*** One of the most important functions of Congress is its oversight of the executive branch and its many departments and agencies. Congress can rein in the power of the executive bureaucracy by choosing not to provide the money necessary for the bureaucracy to function or by refusing to fund government programs. ***13*** Congress also has the authority to investigate the actions of the executive branch, the need for certain legislation, and even the actions of its own members. It has the power to impeach and remove from office federal officials. ***14*** The Senate confirms the president's nominees for the Supreme Court, other federal judgeships, and members of the cabinet.

LO6 Indicate what is involved in the congressional budgeting process. ***15*** The congressional budgeting process involves **authorization** (creating the legal basis for government programs) and **appropriation** (determining how many dollars will be spent in a given year on a particular set of government activities). ***16*** The budgeting process begins when the president submits a proposed federal budget for the next **fiscal year.** In the **first budget resolution,** Congress sets overall revenue goals and spending targets. The **second budget resolution** sets "binding" limits on taxes and spending. Whenever Congress is unable to pass a complete budget by the beginning of the fiscal year, it passes **continuing resolutions,** which enable the executive agencies to keep doing whatever they were doing the previous year with the same amount of funding.

fiscal year A twelve-month period that is established for bookkeeping or accounting purposes. The government's fiscal year runs from October 1 through September 30. ***265***

gerrymandering The drawing of a legislative district's boundaries in such a way as to maximize the influence of a certain group or political party. ***249***

instructed delegate A representative who mirrors the views of the majority of his or her constituents. ***250***

majority leader The party leader elected by the majority party in the House or in the Senate. ***254***

malapportionment A condition in which the voting power of citizens in one district is greater than the voting power of citizens in another district. ***248***

markup session A meeting held by a congressional committee or subcommittee to approve, amend, or redraft a bill. ***260***

minority leader The party leader elected by the minority party in the House or in the Senate. ***254***

minority-majority district A district whose boundaries are drawn so as to maximize the voting power of minority groups. ***249***

"one person, one vote" rule A rule, or principle, requiring that congressional districts have equal populations so that one person's vote counts as much as another's vote. ***249***

pocket veto A special type of veto power used by the chief executive after the legislature has adjourned. Bills that are not signed die after a specified period of time. ***261***

Rules Committee A standing committee in the House of Representatives that provides special rules governing how particular bills will be considered and debated by the House. The Rules Committee normally proposes time limits on debate for any bill. ***256***

second budget resolution A budget resolution, which is supposed to be passed in September, that sets "binding" limits on taxes and spending for the next fiscal year. ***266***

Speaker of the House The presiding officer in the House of Representatives. The Speaker has traditionally been a longtime member of the majority party and is often the most powerful and influential member of the House. ***253***

standing committee A permanent committee in Congress that deals with legislation concerning a particular area, such as agriculture or foreign relations. ***255***

subcommittee A division of a larger committee that deals with a particular part of the committee's policy area. Most standing committees have several subcommittees. ***255***

trustee A representative who serves the broad interests of the entire society, and not just the narrow interests of his or her constituents. ***250***

whip A member of Congress who assists the majority or minority leader in the House or in the Senate in managing the party's legislative preferences. ***254***

CHAPTER IN REVIEW 12 The Presidency

KEY TERMS

cabinet An advisory group selected by the president to assist with decision making. Traditionally, the cabinet has consisted of the heads of the executive departments and other officers whom the president may choose to appoint. *288*

chief diplomat The role of the president in recognizing and interacting with foreign governments. *276*

chief executive The head of the executive branch of government. In the United States, the president. *273*

chief of staff The person who directs the operations of the White House Office and who advises the president on important matters. *290*

commander in chief The supreme commander of a nation's military force. *273*

diplomat A person who represents one country in dealing with representatives of another country. *276*

executive agreement A binding international agreement, or pact, that is made between the president and another head of state and that does not require Senate approval. *284*

Executive Office of the President (EOP) A group of staff agencies that assist the president in carrying out major duties. Franklin D. Roosevelt established the EOP in 1939 to cope with the increased responsibilities brought on by the Great Depression. *289*

executive order A presidential order to carry out a policy or policies described in a law passed by Congress. *282*

executive privilege An inherent executive power claimed by presidents to withhold information from, or to refuse to appear before, Congress or the courts. The president can also accord the privilege to other executive officials. *287*

OUTLINE

Stephen Crowley/The New York Times/Redux

SUMMARY & OBJECTIVES

LO1 List the constitutional requirements for becoming president. ***1*** Article II of the Constitution sets forth relatively few requirements for becoming president. A person must be a natural-born citizen, at least thirty-five years of age, and a resident within the United States for at least fourteen years.

LO2 Explain the roles that a president performs while in office. ***2*** The president has the authority to exercise a variety of powers. Some of these are explicitly outlined in the Constitution, and some are simply required by the office. In the course of exercising these powers, the president performs a variety of roles. The president is the nation's **chief executive**—the head of the executive branch—and enforces laws and federal court decisions. The president leads the nation's armed forces as **commander in chief.** As **head of state,** the president performs ceremonial functions as a personal symbol of the nation. As **chief diplomat,** the president directs U.S. foreign policy and is the nation's most important representative to foreign governments. The president has become the chief legislator, informing Congress about the condition of the country and recommending legislative measures. As political party leader, the president chooses the chairperson of his or her party's national committee and exerts political power within the party by using presidential appointment and removal powers.

LO3 Indicate the scope of presidential powers. ***3*** The Constitution gives the president specific powers, such as the power to negotiate treaties, to grant reprieves and pardons, and to veto bills passed by Congress. The president also has inherent powers—powers that are necessary to carry out the specific responsibilities of the president as set forth in the Constitution. ***4*** Several presidents have greatly expanded the powers of the president. Congress has come to expect the president to develop a legislative program. The president's political skills, the ability to persuade others, and the strategy of "going public" play a large role in determining the administration's success. Since the 1930s, the president has been expected to be actively involved in economic matters and social programs. ***5*** The president's executive authority has been enhanced by the use of **executive orders** and **signing statements,** and the ability to make **executive agreements** has enhanced presidential power in foreign affairs. As commander in chief, the president can respond quickly to a military threat without waiting for congressional action, and since 1945, the president has been responsible for deciding if and when to use nuclear weapons.

LO4 Describe key areas of advantage for Congress and for the president in their institutional relationship. ***6*** The relationship between the president and Congress is arguably one of the most important institutional relationships in American government. Congress traditionally has had the advantage in this relationship in the areas of legislative authorization, the regulation of foreign and interstate commerce, and some budgetary matters. The president has the advantage over Congress in dealing with a national crisis, in setting foreign policy, and in influencing public opinion. ***7*** The relationship between Congress and the president is affected by their different constituencies, their different election cycles, and the fact that the president is limited to two terms in office. The relationship between Congress and the president is also affected when government is divided, with at least one house of Congress controlled by a different party than the White House.

LO5 Discuss the organization of the executive branch and the role of cabinet members in presidential administrations. ***8*** The fifteen executive departments are an important component of the executive branch. The heads of the departments are members of the president's **cabinet.** The president may appoint other officials to the cabinet as well. Some presidents have relied on the advice of their cabinets, while other presidents have preferred to rely on the counsel of close friends and associates (sometimes called a **kitchen cabinet**). To a certain extent, the growth of other components of the executive branch has rendered the formal cabinet less significant as a presidential advisory board. ***9*** Since 1939, presidents have had top advisers and assistants in the **Executive Office of the President (EOP)** who help carry out major duties. The EOP is subject to frequent reorganizations at the discretion of the president. Some of the most important agencies in the EOP are the **White House Office,** the **Office of Management and Budget,** and the **National Security Council.** In recent years, the responsibilities of the vice president have grown immensely, and the vice president has become one of the most important of the president's advisers.

head of state The person who serves as the ceremonial head of a country's government and represents that country to the rest of the world. ***274***

kitchen cabinet The name given to a president's unofficial advisers. The term was coined during Andrew Jackson's presidency. ***289***

National Security Council (NSC) A council that advises the president on domestic and foreign matters concerning the safety and defense of the nation; established in 1947. ***291***

Office of Management and Budget (OMB) An agency in the Executive Office of the President that assists the president in preparing and supervising the administration of the federal budget. ***290***

patronage The practice of giving government jobs to individuals belonging to the winning political party. ***276***

press secretary A member of the White House staff who holds news conferences for reporters and makes public statements for the president. ***290***

signing statement A written statement, appended to a bill at the time the president signs it into law, indicating how the president interprets that legislation. ***283***

treaty A formal agreement between the governments of two or more countries. ***277***

veto A Latin word meaning "I forbid"; the refusal by an official, such as the president of the United States or a state governor, to sign a bill into law. ***278***

Watergate scandal A scandal involving an illegal break-in at the Democratic National Committee offices in 1972 by members of President Nixon's reelection campaign staff. Before Congress could vote to impeach Nixon for his participation in covering up the break-in, Nixon resigned from the presidency. ***287***

White House Office The personal office of the president. White House Office personnel handle the president's political needs and manage the media. ***290***

CHAPTER IN REVIEW 13 *The Bureaucracy*

KEY TERMS

adjudicate To render a judicial decision. In regard to administrative law, the process in which an administrative law judge hears and decides issues that arise when an agency charges a person or firm with violating a law or regulation enforced by the agency. ***310***

bureaucracy A large, complex, hierarchically structured administrative organization that carries out specific functions. ***297***

bureaucrat An individual who works in a bureaucracy. As generally used, the term refers to a government employee. ***297***

civil service Nonmilitary government employment. ***308***

enabling legislation A law enacted by a legislature to establish an administrative agency. Enabling legislation normally specifies the name, purpose, composition, and powers of the agency being created. ***309***

government corporation An agency of the government that is run as a business enterprise. Such agencies engage in primarily commercial activities, produce revenues, and require greater flexibility than that permitted in most government agencies. ***306***

independent executive agency A federal agency that is not located within a cabinet department. ***304***

independent regulatory agency A federal organization that is responsible for creating and implementing rules that regulate private activity and protect the public interest in a particular sector of the economy. ***305***

iron triangle A three-way alliance among legislators, bureaucrats, and interest groups to make or preserve policies that benefit their respective interests. ***311***

issue networks Groups of individuals or organizations—which consist of legislators and legislative staff members, interest group leaders, bureaucrats, the media,

OUTLINE

Paul J. Richards/AFP/Getty Images

SUMMARY & OBJECTIVES

LO1 Describe the size and functions of the U.S. bureaucracy. ***1*** The **bureaucracy** is a large, complex administrative organization. Government **bureaucrats** carry out the policies of elected government officials. In the federal government, the head of the bureaucracy is the president of the United States, and the bureaucracy is part of the executive branch. The reason the federal bureaucracy exists is that Congress, over time, has delegated certain tasks to specialists. ***2*** The federal government that existed In 1789 had only three departments and about fifty employees. Today, the federal government has about 2.9 million employees. Together, the local, state, and federal levels of government employ more than 15 percent of the civilian labor force.

LO2 Discuss the structure and basic components of the federal bureaucracy. ***3*** The executive branch of the federal government includes four major types of bureaucratic structures: executive departments, independent executive agencies, independent regulatory agencies, and government corporations. ***4*** The fifteen executive departments are the major service organizations of the federal government. Each department manages a specific policy area. **Independent executive agencies** are federal bureaucratic organizations that have a single function. Sometimes agencies are kept independent because of the sensitive nature of their functions; at other times, Congress created independent agencies to protect them from **partisan politics. Independent regulatory agencies** create and implement rules that regulate private activity and protect the public interest in a particular sector of the economy. **Government corporations** are businesses that are owned by the government. They provide a service that could be handled by the private sector, and they charge for their services.

LO3 **Indicate when the federal civil service was established and explain how bureaucrats get their jobs.** ***5*** Federal bureaucrats holding top-level positions are appointed by the president and confirmed by the Senate. Rank-and-file bureaucratic employees are part of the **civil service** and obtain their jobs through the Office of Personnel Management (OPM), which was created by the Civil Service Reform Act of 1978. The OPM recruits, interviews, and tests potential government workers and makes recommendations to agencies as to which persons meet relevant standards. The 1978 act also created the Merit Systems Protection Board to oversee promotions and employees' rights. The idea that the civil service should be based on a merit system dates back more than a century, when the Civil Service Reform Act of 1883 established the principle of government employment on the basis of merit through open, competitive examinations.

LO4 **Explain how regulatory agencies make rules and how "iron triangles" affect policymaking in government.** ***6*** Regulatory agencies are sometimes regarded as the fourth branch of government because of the powers they wield. They can make **legislative rules** that are as legally binding as laws passed by Congress. When they are engaging in **rulemaking,** agencies must follow certain procedural requirements, and they must make sure that their rules are not "arbitrary and capricious." ***7*** One way to understand the bureaucracy's role in policymaking is to examine **iron triangles**—alliances among legislators, bureaucrats, and interest groups working together to create mutually beneficial legislation in specific policy areas.

LO5 **Identify some of the ways in which the government has attempted to curb waste and improve efficiency in the bureaucracy.** ***8*** The government has made several attempts to reduce waste, inefficiency, and wrongdoing. Both the federal government and state governments have passed laws requiring more openness in government. Further attempts at bureaucratic reform have included encouraging government employees to report to appropriate government officials any waste and wrongdoing that they observe. Congress has passed laws to protect **whistleblowers** and the federal government has been experimenting with pay-for-performance systems. Another idea for reforming the bureaucracy is **privatization,** which means turning over certain types of government work to the private sector. "Performance-based budgeting" was initiated by President George W. Bush, and President Barack Obama has created the position of a chief performance officer who works with other economic officials in an attempt to increase efficiency and eliminate waste in government. The need to reform the bureaucracy is widely recognized, but some claim that it may be impossible to do so effectively.

scholars, and other experts—that support particular policy positions on a given issue. ***311***

legislative rule An administrative agency rule that carries the same weight as a statute enacted by a legislature. ***308***

neutral competency The application of technical skills to jobs without regard to political issues. ***310***

partisan politics Political actions or decisions that benefit a particular party. ***305***

privatization The transfer of the task of providing services traditionally provided by government to the private sector. ***315***

rulemaking The process undertaken by an administrative agency when formally proposing, evaluating, and adopting a new regulation. ***310***

whistleblower In the context of government employment, someone who "blows the whistle" (reports to authorities) on gross governmental inefficiency, illegal action, or other wrongdoing. ***312***

CHAPTER IN REVIEW 14 The Judiciary

KEY TERMS

administrative law The body of law created by administrative agencies (in the form of rules, regulations, orders, and decisions) in order to carry out their duties and responsibilities. *324*

appellate court A court having appellate jurisdiction. An appellate court normally does not hear evidence or testimony but reviews the transcript of the trial court's proceedings, other records relating to the case, and attorneys' arguments as to why the trial court's decision should or should not stand. *327*

case law The rules of law announced in court decisions. Case law includes the aggregate of reported cases that interpret judicial precedents, statutes, regulations, and constitutional provisions. *324*

civil law The branch of law that spells out the duties that individuals in society owe to other persons or to their governments, excluding the duty not to commit crimes. *324*

common law The body of law developed from judicial decisions in English and U.S. courts, not attributable to a legislature. *321*

concurring opinion A statement written by a judge or justice who agrees (concurs) with the court's decision, but for reasons different from those in the majority opinion. *329*

conference In regard to the Supreme Court, a private meeting of the justices in which they present their arguments concerning a case under consideration. *329*

constitutional law Law based on the U.S. Constitution and the constitutions of the various states. *323*

criminal law The branch of law that defines and governs actions that constitute crimes. Generally, criminal law has to do with wrongful actions committed against society for which society demands redress. *324*

dissenting opinion A statement written by

OUTLINE

AP Photo/Ross William Hamilton, Pool

SUMMARY & OBJECTIVES

LO1 Summarize the origins of the American legal system and the basic sources of American law. ***1*** The American legal system evolved from the **common law** tradition that developed in England over hundreds of years. A cornerstone of the English and American judicial systems is the practice of deciding new cases with reference to previous decisions, or **precedents.** This practice forms a doctrine called ***stare decisis,*** which theoretically obligates judges to follow the precedents established in their jurisdictions. ***2*** Primary sources of American law include constitutions (**constitutional law**); laws enacted by legislatures (**statutory law**); rules, regulations, orders, and decisions of administrative agencies (**administrative law**); and the rules of law announced in court decisions (**case law**). ***3*** **Civil law** spells out the duties that individuals in society owe to other persons or to their governments. **Criminal law** has to do with wrongs committed against the public as a whole. ***4*** Before any court can hear a case, it must have **jurisdiction** (the authority to hear and decide a particular case). To bring a lawsuit before a court, a person must have **standing to sue** (the person must have a sufficient stake in the case), and the issue must be a **justiciable controversy** (it must be real and substantial, not hypothetical). In addition to these basic judicial requirements, both the federal and the state courts have established procedural rules that apply in all cases.

LO2 Delineate the structure of the federal court system. ***5*** The federal court system includes the U.S. district courts, the U.S. courts of appeals, and the United States Supreme Court. ***6*** The district courts are **trial courts;** they have jurisdiction over cases arising under federal law and over cases involving **diversity of citizenship.** There is at least one federal district court in every state, and there is one in the District of Columbia. Currently, there are ninety-four judicial districts. The U.S. courts of appeals are **appellate courts** that hear cases on review from the U.S. district courts located within their respective judicial circuits, as well as appeals from decisions made by federal administrative agencies. There are thirteen federal courts of appeal, one of which has national jurisdiction over certain types of cases (the Court of Appeals for the Federal Circuit). The United States Supreme Court has some original jurisdiction, but most of the Court's work is as an appellate court. The Supreme Court may take appeals of decisions made by the U.S. courts of appeals as well as appeals of cases decided in the state courts when federal questions are at issue. To bring a case before the Supreme Court, a party may request that the Court issue a **writ of *certiorari*.** The Court will not issue a writ unless at least four of the nine justices approve.

LO3 **Indicate how federal judges are appointed.** ***7*** Federal judges are appointed by the president and confirmed by the Senate. The Senate Judiciary Committee holds hearings on judicial nominees and makes its recommendation to the Senate, where it takes a majority vote to confirm a nomination. **Senatorial courtesy** is a practice that gives home-state senators of the president's party some influence over the choice of nominees for district courts (and, to a lesser extent, the U.S. courts of appeals). Presidents have attempted to strengthen their legacies by appointing federal judges with similar political and philosophical views.

LO4 **Explain how the federal courts make policy.** ***8*** In the United States, judges play an important policymaking role. Federal judges can decide on the constitutionality of laws or actions undertaken by the other branches of government through the power of **judicial review.** Moreover, when a court interprets a law or a constitutional provision and applies that interpretation to a specific set of circumstances, the court is essentially "making the law" on that issue. ***9*** One issue that is often debated is how the federal courts should wield their policymaking power. Activist judges or justices believe that the courts should actively check the actions of the other two branches of government to ensure that they do not exceed their authority. Restraintist judges or justices generally assumes that the courts should defer to the decisions of the other branches, because members of Congress and the president are elected by the people, whereas federal judges are not.

LO5 **Describe the role of ideology and judicial philosophies in judicial decision making.** ***10*** There are numerous examples of ideology or policy preferences affecting Supreme Court decisions. However, judicial decision making, particularly at the Supreme Court level, can be very complex. At times, the Court may take demographic data, public opinion, and foreign laws into account, though how much weight is given to each of these factors will vary from justice to justice. The approaches justices take toward the interpretation of law (strict versus broad construction) or toward constitutional interpretation (original intent versus modernism) are also important in determining why justices decide as they do. How justices view the role of the Supreme Court in the federal judiciary affects their decision making as well.

LO6 **Identify some of the criticisms of the federal courts and some of the checks on the power of the courts.** ***11*** Policymaking by unelected judges in the federal courts has important implications in a democracy. Critics, especially on the political right, frequently accuse the judiciary of "legislating from the bench." ***12*** There are several checks on the courts, however. Supreme Court justices have traditionally exercised a great deal of self-restraint, due, in part, to various judicially established traditions and doctrines, including the doctrine of *stare decisis*. The judiciary is also constrained by its lack of enforcement powers and by potential congressional actions in response to court decisions. The American public continues to have a high regard for the Supreme Court and the federal courts generally.

a judge or justice who disagrees with the majority opinion. ***329***

diversity of citizenship A basis for federal court jurisdiction over a lawsuit that arises when (1) the parties in the lawsuit live in different states or when one of the parties is a foreign government or a foreign citizen, and (2) the amount in controversy is more than $75,000. ***325***

federal question A question that pertains to the U.S. Constitution, acts of Congress, or treaties. A federal question provides a basis for federal court jurisdiction. ***325***

judicial review The power of the courts to decide on the constitutionality of legislative enactments and of actions taken by the executive branch. ***334***

judiciary The courts; one of the three branches of the federal government in the United States. ***321***

jurisdiction The authority of a court to hear and decide a particular case. ***325***

justiciable controversy A controversy that is not hypothetical or academic but real and substantial; a requirement that must be satisfied before a court will hear a case. ***326***

opinion A written statement by a court expressing the reasons for its decision in a case. ***329***

oral argument A spoken argument presented to a judge in person by an attorney on behalf of her or his client. ***329***

precedent A court decision that furnishes an example or authority for deciding subsequent cases involving identical or similar facts and legal issues. ***322***

primary source of law A source of law that establishes the law. Primary sources of law include constitutions, statutes, administrative agency rules and regulations, and decisions rendered by the courts. ***323***

senatorial courtesy A practice that allows a senator of the president's party to veto the president's nominee to a federal court judgeship within the senator's state. ***330***

standing to sue The requirement that an individual must have a sufficient stake in a controversy before he or she can bring a lawsuit. The party bringing the suit must demonstrate that he or she has either been harmed or been threatened with a harm. ***325***

stare decisis A common law doctrine under which judges normally are obligated to follow the precedents established by prior court decisions. ***323***

statutory law The body of law enacted by legislatures (as opposed to constitutional law, administrative law, or case law). ***324***

trial court A court in which trials are held and testimony taken. ***325***

writ of *certiorari* An order from a higher court asking a lower court for the record of a case. ***328***

CHAPTER IN REVIEW 15 Domestic Policy

KEY TERMS

action-reaction syndrome For every government action, there will be a reaction by the public. The government then takes a further action to counter the public's reaction—and the cycle begins again. ***356***

agenda setting Getting an issue on the political agenda to be addressed by Congress; part of the first stage of the policymaking process. ***346***

Blue Dog Coalition A caucus that unites most of the moderate-to-conservative Democrats in the House of Representatives. ***351***

cap-and-trade A method of restricting the production of a harmful substance. A cap is set on the volume of production, and permits to produce the substance can then be traded on the open market. ***354***

Congressional Budget Office (CBO) An agency established by Congress to evaluate the impact of proposed legislation on the federal budget. ***350***

Corporate Average Fuel Economy (CAFE) standards A set of federal standards under which each manufacturer must meet a miles-per-gallon benchmark averaged across all cars or trucks that it sells. ***352***

domestic policy Public policy concerning issues within a national unit, such as national policy concerning health care or the economy. ***345***

easy-money policy A monetary policy that involves stimulating the economy by expanding the rate of growth of the money supply. An easy-money policy supposedly will lead to lower interest rates and induce consumers to spend more and producers to invest more. ***355***

economic policy All actions taken by the national government to smooth out the ups and downs in the nation's overall business activity. ***354***

Federal Open Market Committee (FOMC) The most important body within the Federal Reserve System. The FOMC decides how monetary policy should be carried out by the Federal Reserve. ***355***

OUTLINE

Luke Sharrett/*The New York Times*/Redux

SUMMARY & OBJECTIVES

LO1 Explain what domestic policy is and summarize the steps in the policymaking process. ***1*** Public policy can be defined as a plan or course of action taken by the government to respond to a political issue or to enhance the social or political well-being of society. **Domestic policy** consists of public policy concerning issues within a national unit. ***2*** Public policies are formed through a **policymaking process** involving several phases. First, a problem in society must be identified as an issue that can be solved politically, and then the issue must be included on the political agenda. The next stage in the policymaking process involves the formulation and adoption of specific plans for achieving a particular goal. The final stages of the process focus on the implementation of the policy and evaluating its success. Each phase of the policymaking process involves interactions among various individuals and groups.

LO2 Discuss the issue of health-care funding and recent proposals for universal health insurance. ***3*** Our system for funding health care suffers from two major problems. One is that health care is expensive; about 16 percent of national spending in the United States goes to health care. Also, more than 47 million Americans—about 16 percent of the population—have no health-care insurance. ***4*** The federal government pays for health care in a variety of ways. It buys health insurance for its employees, and members of the armed forces, veterans, and Native Americans receive medical services provided directly by the government. Most federal spending on health care is accounted for by **Medicare** and **Medicaid.** Medicaid is a joint federal-state program that provides health care subsidies to low-income persons. Another program, the **State Children's Health Insurance Program (SCHIP),** covers children in families with incomes that are modest but too high to qualify for Medicaid. Medicare is the federal government's health-care program for persons over the age of sixty-five. Medicare is now the government's second-largest domestic spending program, after Social Security. Medicare costs are expected to soar as millions of "baby boomers" retire over the next two decades. ***5*** Health-care funding was an important issue during the 2008 presidential campaigns, and in 2009, Congress considered several proposals for reforming the way we pay for health care. Some of the proposals called for a new Health Insurance Exchange, which would allow individuals and small employers to shop for plans, including a government-sponsored insurance plan, known as the **public option.** Other ideas that were the subject of debate included requirements that health insurance companies not be allowed to deny anyone coverage; subsidies for those with low-to-middle incomes to help pay insurance premiums; and an **individual mandate,** which would require that all adults buy insurance. ***6*** The public option was strongly opposed by Republicans and by moderate-to-conservative Democrats in the House of Representatives (the **Blue Dog Coalition**) as well. One of the major arguments against the public option was that it could eventually lead to a nearly complete federal takeover—a **single-payer plan,** or **national health insurance.** Indeed, conservative hostility to the various Democratic proposals to reform health-care funding was fueled by anger over what many saw, in the wake of bank bailouts and dramatic increases in spending to combat the recession, as the growing power of the government in general.

LO3 Summarize the issues of energy independence, global warming, and cap-and-trade legislation. ***7*** A priority for the Obama administration, energy policy is important because of two problems. One problem is our reliance on imported oil from nations that are not particularly friendly to the United States, including Iran, Libya, and Venezuela. When the price of oil was low, the U.S. government was under little pressure to address our dependence on imports. With steep rises in oil prices, the issue of reducing U.S. fuel consumption is back on the political agenda. In 2009, President Obama issued higher fuel efficiency standards for cars and trucks. ***8*** A second reason energy policy is important has to do with the problem of global warming. Most climatologists believe that **global warming** is the result of human activities, especially the release of **greenhouse gases** into the atmosphere. A rise in global temperatures could cause seawater to expand and polar ice to melt, causing sea levels to rise. Rainfall patterns are expected to change, and increases in extreme weather are likely. ***9*** Efforts to combat global warming include turning away from energy that depends on burning carbon, which releases greenhouse gases into the environment, and turning to sources of **renewable energy,** including solar power, hydropower, and wind energy. The chief proposal to respond to global warming is **cap-and-trade** legislation. Under this Democratic plan, the government would establish a "cap" for carbon dioxide emissions. Major emitters would need permits, which they could buy and sell, or trade, on the open market. Over time, the cap would decline, resulting in a reduction in emissions.

LO4 Describe the two major areas of economic policymaking. ***10*** **Monetary policy** involves changing the amount of money in circulation to affect interest rates, credit markets, the rate of inflation, the rate of economic growth, and the rate of unemployment. Monetary policy is under the control of the Federal Reserve System (the Fed), an independent regulatory agency. The Fed and its **Federal Open Market Committee** make decisions about monetary policy several times each year. ***11*** **Fiscal policy** is the use of changes in government expenditures and taxes to alter national economic variables, including the rate of unemployment, the level of interest rates, the rate of inflation, and the rate of economic growth. One of the problems with fiscal policy (and with monetary policy as well) is that typically a lag exists between the government's decision to institute fiscal policy and the actual implementation of that policy. The government raises revenues to pay its expenses by levying taxes on business and personal income or through borrowing. When the federal government spends more than it receives, it has to finance this shortfall. Typically, it borrows. Every time there is a federal government deficit, there is an increase in the total accumulated **public debt.**

fiscal policy The use of changes in government expenditures and taxes to alter national economic variables. ***354***

global warming An increase in the average temperature of the Earth's surface over the last half century and its projected continuation. ***353***

greenhouse gas A gas that, when released into the atmosphere, traps the sun's heat and slows its release into outer space. Carbon dioxide (CO_2) is a major example. ***353***

individual mandate In the context of health-care reform, a requirement that all persons obtain health-care insurance from one source or another. Those failing to do so would pay a penalty. ***350***

Keynesian economics An economic theory proposed by British economist John Maynard Keynes that is typically associated with the use of fiscal policy to alter national economic variables. ***356***

Medicaid A joint federal-state program that provides health-care services to low-income persons. ***348***

Medicare A federal government program that pays for health-care insurance for Americans aged sixty-five years or over. ***348***

monetary policy Actions taken by the Federal Reserve Board to change the amount of money in circulation so as to affect interest rates, credit markets, the rate of inflation, the rate of economic growth, and the rate of unemployment. ***354***

national health insurance A program, found in many of the world's economically advanced nations, under which the central government provides basic health-care insurance coverage to everyone in the country. Some wealthy nations, such as the Netherlands and Switzerland, provide universal coverage through private insurance companies instead. ***351***

policymaking process The procedures involved in getting an issue on the political agenda; formulating, adopting, and implementing a policy with regard to the issue; and then evaluating the results of the policy. ***345***

public debt The total amount of money that the national government owes as a result of borrowing; also called the *national debt.* ***358***

public option In the context of health-care reform, a government-sponsored health-care insurance program that would compete with private insurance companies. ***350***

renewable energy Energy from technologies that do not rely on extracted resources, such as oil and coal, that can run out. ***353***

single-payer plan A system in which a single entity—usually the national government—has the sole responsibility for issuing health-care insurance policies. ***351***

State Children's Health Insurance Program (SCHIP) A joint federal-state program that provides health-care insurance for low-income children. ***348***

CHAPTER IN REVIEW 16 Foreign Policy

KEY TERMS

coalition An alliance of nations formed to undertake a foreign policy action, particularly a military action. A coalition is often a temporary alliance that dissolves after the action is concluded. ***374***

Cold War The war of words, warnings, and ideologies between the Soviet Union and the United States that lasted from the late 1940s through the early 1990s. ***369***

colonial empire A group of dependent nations that are under the rule of a single imperial power. ***368***

Communist bloc The group of Eastern European nations that fell under the control of the Soviet Union following World War II. ***369***

containment A U.S. policy designed to contain the spread of communism by offering military and economic aid to threatened nations. ***369***

Cuban missile crisis A nuclear stand-off that occurred in 1962 when the United States learned that the Soviet Union had placed nuclear warheads in Cuba, ninety miles off the U.S. coast. The crisis was defused diplomatically, but it is generally considered the closest the two Cold War superpowers came to a nuclear confrontation. ***370***

détente French word meaning a "relaxation of tensions." Détente characterized the relationship between the United States and the Soviet Union in the 1970s, as the two Cold War rivals attempted to pursue cooperative dealings and arms control. ***370***

deterrence A policy of building up military strength for the purpose of discouraging (deterring) military attacks by other nations; the policy of "building weapons for peace" that supported the arms race between the United States and the Soviet Union during the Cold War. ***369***

foreign policy A systematic and general plan that guides a country's attitudes and

OUTLINE

AP Photo/Farah Abdi Warsameh

SUMMARY & OBJECTIVES

LO1 Discuss how foreign policy is made and identify the key players in this process. ***1*** **Foreign policy** includes all of the economic, military, commercial, and diplomatic positions and actions that a nation takes in its relationships with other countries. ***2*** The president oversees the military, guides defense policies, and represents the United States to the rest of the world. The Department of State is responsible for diplomatic relations with other nations and with multinational organizations. The Department of Defense establishes and carries out defense policy and protects our national security. Several other agencies, including the National Security Council and the Central Intelligence Agency, are also involved in U.S. foreign relations. Congress has the power to declare war and the power to appropriate funds to equip the armed forces and provide for foreign aid. The Senate has the power to ratify treaties. A few congressional committees are directly concerned with foreign affairs.

LO2 Summarize the history of American foreign policy through the years. ***3*** Early U.S. leaders sought to protect American interests through **isolationism.** After the Spanish-American War of 1898, which marked the first step toward **interventionism,** the United States acquired a **colonial empire** and was acknowledged as a world power. ***4*** After World War I, the U.S. returned to a policy of isolationism until the attack on Pearl Harbor in 1941. After World War II ended in 1945, the wartime alliance between the U.S. and the Soviet Union began to deteriorate. Many Americans considered Soviet attempts to spread Communist systems to other countries a major threat to democracy. The **Marshall Plan** for economic aid to Europe marked the beginning of a policy of **containment.** ***5*** During the **Cold War,** the U.S. and the Soviet Union engaged in an arms race that was supported by a policy of **deterrence,** and out of that policy emerged the theory of **mutually assured destruction (MAD).** The collapse of the Soviet Union in 1991 brought about the end of the Cold War and altered the framework and goals of U.S. foreign policy.

LO3 Identify the foreign policy challenges presented by terrorism and the consequences of the "Bush doctrine" with respect to Iraq. ***6*** Terrorist attacks have occurred with increasing frequency during the past three decades, and the attacks on September 11, 2001, by al Qaeda put the United States on the offensive against terrorists and rogue nations. ***7*** In 2002, President George W. Bush described Iraq as a regime that sponsored terrorism and sought to develop **weapons of mass destruction,** and he enunciated a doctrine under which the United States was prepared to strike "preemptively" at Iraq. ***8*** The invasion of Iraq in 2003, in what was a **preventive war** rather than a **preemptive war,** succeeded in deposing the Iraqi dictator, Saddam Hussein, but it also led to ongoing sectarian violence and terrorist insurgency. ***9*** In the midst of growing chaos, elections were held in 2005 to establish a new Iraqi government. A "surge" of U.S. troops in early 2007 and better counterinsurgency tactics helped to improve the situation in Iraq. In 2009, President Barack Obama announced that U.S. combat forces would leave Iraq in 2010 and the remaining troops would be out by the end of 2011.

LO4 Describe the principal issues dividing the Israelis and the Palestinians and the solutions proposed by the international community. ***10*** Following the 1948 Arab-Israeli war, a large number of Palestinians—Arab residents of the Holy Land—were forced into exile. The aftermath of another war in 1967 gave rise to the **Palestine Liberation Organization (PLO),** a nonstate body committed to armed struggle against Israel. The West Bank of the Jordan River and the Gaza Strip fell under Israeli control, and the Palestinians living in these areas became an occupied people. ***11*** The international community was in agreement on several principles for settling the conflict. Lands seized in the 1967 war should be granted to the Palestinians, who could organize their own independent nation-state there. In turn, the Palestinians would have to recognize Israel's right to exist and take concrete steps to guarantee Israel's security. Palestinian terrorist attacks and Israeli settlements in the occupied territories have impeded the peace effort. In 1993, Israel and the PLO met officially for the first time in Oslo, Norway. A major result of the **Oslo Accords** was the establishment of a Palestinian Authority, under Israeli control, on the West Bank and Gaza Strip. ***12*** Further attempts to reach a settlement collapsed in acrimony. In 2007, Gaza was taken over by Hamas, a radical Islamist party that refuses to recognize Israel. President Obama sought to restart peace talks in 2009.

LO5 Outline some of the actions taken by the United States to curb the threat of nuclear weapons. ***13*** The pursuit of nuclear technology in North Korea and Iran is of major concern to the United States. North Korea tested nuclear devices in 2006 and 2009, and long-range missiles as well. Six-nation talks that include China and the United States have not resolved the issue. ***14*** Iran has made considerable progress in many aspects of its nuclear program, which many fear will result in a bomb. In 2009, the United States joined talks with Iran that had been initiated earlier by European nations.

LO6 Discuss China's emerging role as a world leader. ***15*** China may be destined to challenge American global supremacy. China has one of the fastest-growing economies in the world and a population of 1.3 billion. Although China has not shown ambitions to acquire more territory or become militarily aggressive, it has expressed a desire to take control of the island of Taiwan, a former Chinese province that has functioned as if it were an independent nation since 1949.

actions toward the rest of the world. Foreign policy includes all of the economic, military, commercial, and diplomatic positions and actions that a nation takes in its relationships with other countries. ***365***

interventionism Direct involvement by one country in another country's affairs. ***368***

iron curtain A phrase coined by Winston Churchill to describe the political boundaries between the democratic countries in Western Europe and the Soviet-controlled Communist countries in Eastern Europe. ***369***

isolationism A political policy of noninvolvement in world affairs. ***367***

Marshall Plan A plan providing for U.S. economic assistance to European nations following World War II to help those nations recover from the war; the plan was named after George C. Marshall, secretary of state from 1947 to 1949. ***369***

Monroe Doctrine A U.S. policy, announced in 1823 by President James Monroe, that the United States would not tolerate foreign intervention in the Western Hemisphere, and in return, the United States would stay out of European affairs. ***367***

mutually assured destruction (MAD) A phrase referring to the assumption, on which the policy of deterrence was based, that if the forces of two nations are equally capable of destroying each other, neither nation will take a chance on war. ***370***

neutrality A position of not being aligned with either side in a dispute or conflict, such as a war. ***368***

normal trade relations (NTR) status A status granted through an international treaty by which each member nation must treat other members at least as well as it treats the country that receives its most favorable treatment. This status was formerly known as *most-favored-nation status.* ***381***

Oslo Accords The first agreement signed between Israel and the PLO; led to the establishment of the Palestinian Authority in the occupied territories. ***377***

Palestine Liberation Organization (PLO) An organization formed in 1964 to represent the Palestinian people. The PLO has a long history of terrorism but for some years has functioned primarily as a political party. ***377***

preemptive war A war launched by a nation to prevent an imminent attack by another nation. ***374***

preventive war A war launched by a nation to prevent the possibility that another nation might attack at some point in the future; not supported by international law. ***374***

weapons of mass destruction Chemical, biological, or nuclear weapons that can inflict massive casualties. ***374***